C000052681

Tribute to Anthony Sutton; killed in Northern Ireland in 1977

Share not this common earth with me, not yet;
But live to tell, of we who laughed and loved, then fell.
Remember me, in years of plenty
As a friend and comrade left behind
A random name and serial number
Bullet and shrapnel, torn asunder;
A home left wanting, dreams undreamt,
A choir of millions at history's door,
Not heroes all, but silent souls left cold
By the memory of an unwanted war.
So speak truly of me, and carry me well
For generations who will never know me
Tell them all that I am no statue
Raised to honour long distant dead.
No faded photograph can hold me
In the same regard we shared this day;
And when they ask you if you knew me
Smile, and laugh the past away.

Steve Hale

I did my duty
I did my best
I hid behind my bullet-proof vest

I walked the streets with gun in hand
I held the peace in a foreign land
People didn't want me there
They would often stand and stare
But my duty was to keep the peace
I tried to save a life, at least.

I saw men die
I saw men suffer
Life couldn't get too much tougher

Bombs and bullets played their tune
And forced me deep in to the gloom

My duty there was never done
I worked until the passing sun.

Then one day the years have passed
But memories would last and last.

No corner of my mind is safe
I am haunted by that foreign place.

I try to run
I try to hide
My demons always by my side.

Did I serve my country true?
Would I really die for you?

Did I do my very best?
Did I need my bomb-proof vest?

Did I see my colleagues die
Or is it just a wicked lie?

All I know is this you see
I can never be set free.

The Troubles they have left their mark
They keep me trembling in the dark.

So enjoy your freedom that I won,
For this soldier's work is done.

Stephen Carr

NORTHERN IRELAND: AN AGONY CONTINUED

The British Army and the Troubles 1980–83

Ken M. Wharton

HELION & COMPANY

Helion & Company Limited
26 Willow Road
Solihull
West Midlands
B91 1UE
England
Tel. 0121 705 3393
Fax 0121 711 4075
Email: info@helion.co.uk
Website: www.helion.co.uk
Twitter: @helionbooks
Visit our blog http://blog.helion.co.uk/

Published by Helion & Company 2015

Designed and typeset by Bookcraft Ltd, Stroud, Gloucestershire
Cover designed by Paul Hewitt, Battlefield Design (www.battlefield-design.co.uk)
Printed by Lightning Source Limited, Milton Keynes, Buckinghamshire

Front cover: Belfast mural, early 1980s.
Rear cover: Footsies: Lenadoon, Belfast. Both photographs from author's collection.

The opinions expressed in this book are those of the individuals quoted and do not necessarily accord with views held by the author or publisher.

The author would be delighted to receive comments about his writing or for future publications at ken_wharton@hotmail.co.uk

ISBN 978-1-910294-39-0

British Library Cataloguing-in-Publication Data.
A catalogue record for this book is available from the British Library.

For details of other military history titles published by Helion & Company Limited contact the above address, or visit our website: http://www.helion.co.uk.

We always welcome receiving book proposals from prospective authors.

For my parents
Mark and Irene Wharton
I didn't appreciate you at the time but now that you are gone, I wish that I had

To the eternal memory of Sue Judge
1953–2013
Taken too early from this life
Wife of my comrade Dave Judge

To the loving memory of Royal Artillery Soldier, Sergeant John Haughey
murdered by the IRA in 1974. To his lovely little girl Anita Bailkoski
who became my very dear friend.

To the eternal memory of UDR soldier, Alfie Johnston, murdered
by the IRA in 1972

DEDICATIONS

To every man and woman who served in Northern Ireland, irrespective of your Corps or Regiment, irrespective of your roles; you are my comrades and the honour of knowing you is all mine

To the innocent civilians on both sides of the sectarian divide who only wanted to lead a peaceful life, my empathy and my respect

To the late Ken 'B' and Colour Sergeant Ken Ambrose, your passing has left a void in all our lives

To the 1,300 and more who never returned to their loved ones

To Steven McLaughlin, Darren Ware, Dave Hallam, Ken Pettengale, Gren Wilson, Dave Judge, Dave Pomfret, John Corr, Len Chappell and Tim Marsh; to the Royal Green Jackets, *Celer et Audax*

To Mike Sangster, John and Bernie Swaine, Mick Potter, Royal Artillery, *Ubique*

To Mike Day; for your inspiration and tireless help

To Mick 'Benny' Hill, Steve 'Foxy' Norman, Andy Thomas, Royal Anglians

To Mark 'C', James Henderson, BR, Haydn Williams, Glen Espie and the men and greenfinches of the Ulster Defence Regiment

To Mark and Allison Overson who started me on a long road

To Dave Parkinson, RTR

To JB, ATO

To Kenneth Anderson, Kev Wright, Tommy Clarke, Royal Corps of Transport

To Dave 'Slops' Langston, Army Catering Corps

To Eddie Atkinson and Mick Brooks, Green Howards

To Tam Hutton and the Royal Highland Fusiliers

My cousin John Leighton, a Royal Artillery TA soldier

To the children and loved ones of our fallen: Anita Bailkoski, Scott Haughey, Tammy Card, Tracey Abraham, Stevie Rumble, Carol Richards, Mark Olphert

To my children: Anne-Marie, Anna-Martina, Jonathan, Jenny, Robbie, Alex and Nathan; love you all and always will

To my grandchildren: Sherriden, Kelsy, William, Sammy, Layla-Mae, Megan, Clara and Lydia; also to Morgan Addy

To Jeanne Griffin for your friendship and support

My dear friends Rachel Barnard and Sophie Sheldon on the Gold Coast

Finally to Adam Griffiths, Zoe Forrest, Andy Thomas, Fiona Addy and Dean Holmes, ever patient, ever persevering partners of my children

To my Aunt Ada who nagged me for years to put her name in my books

Bob Bankier, Dave Walker, Davie Card
I see your names and my tears fall, uncontrollably

Contents

List of Maps & Illustrations   ix
Foreword by Steven McLaughlin   xi
Preface by Dave Judge   xiii
Quotations   xiv
The Author's Personal Thoughts   xv
Note by Michael Sangster, Royal Artillery   xvi
Abbreviations   xvii
Maps   xx
Introduction   xxv

Part One: 1983   27
1   January   29
2   February   45
3   March   53
4   April   69
5   May   79
6   June   91
7   July   100
8   August   106
9   September   112
10   October   118
11   November   125
12   December   130

Part Two: 1981   145
13   January   147
14   February   152
15   March   157
16   April   162
17   May   173
18   June   195
19   July   200
20   August   209
21   September   216
22   October   224
23   November   242
24   December   251

Part Three: 1982   255
25   January   257
26   February   263
27   March   266
28   April   274
29   May   284
30   June   288
31   July   293
32   August   308
33   September   312
34   October   317
35   November   322
36   December   329

Part Four: 1983   345
37   January   347
38   February   352
39   March   358
40   April   363
41   May   369
42   June   375
43   July   380
44   August   387
45   September   393
46   October   399
47   November   406
48   December   419

Appendices
I   Northern Ireland Roll of Honour, 1969–1998   435
II   RUC Roll of Honour, 1969–1998   469

Select Bibliography   484
Index   486

List of Maps and Illustrations

Northern Ireland   xx

Londonderry   xxi

Belfast   xxii

South Armagh ('bandit country')   xxiv

Photographs taken during the early 1980s in various parts of Belfast, both
Loyalist and Republican, in the days before the muralists became 'professional
painters'. (Sourced by the author)   61-68

PIRA car bomb in Belfast City Centre.   134

Grand Central Hotel Army Base, Belfast.   134

Helicopter inserting troops: South Armagh.   135

Footsies, West Belfast.   135

ADU and dog land at Crossmaglen.   136

'B' Coy, 2 RGJ: Beruki Sangar, Crossmaglen.   136

Unity Flats, Belfast.   137

Footsies: Lenadoon, Belfast.   137

Royal Artillery on patrol Belfast City Centre.   138

Scene of Command Wire Improvised Explosive Device attack near Newr
July 1981, injuring two RUC.   138

Damage to Royal Ulster Constabulary vehicle following attack July 1981.   139

Scene following Radio Controlled Improvised Explosive Device attack in
Crossmaglen Square November 1981 injuring 3 soldiers.   139

Royal Army Ordnance Corps Ammunition Technical Officer clearing scene
of explosion in Crossmaglen Square, Novemeber 1981   140

Royal Army Ordnance Corps Ammunition Technical Officer neutralises a
150kg Radio Controlled device near Newry in 19893.   140

Heavy Goods Vehicle clearance near Meigh 1982, vehicle contained a 15kg
booby trap.   141

200kg Vehicle borne time bomb attack against Belfast – Dublin railway 1982.   141

Scene showing collapsed bridge on Belfast – Dublin railway line from vehicle
bomb attack 1982.   142

Scene of 100kg car bomb attack against Morrows Garage in Bessbrook 1982.   142

Another view of the car bomb attack against Morrows Garage in 1982.   143

Scene of car bomb attack showing civilian vehicle blasted through wall of local
house, Morrow's Garage, Bessbrook 1982.   143

Scene following a failed Command Wire Improvised Explosive Device attack
against an Royal Ulster Constabulary patrol in 1983.   144

Ammunition Technical Officer neutralising 160kg Radio Controlled Improvised
Explosive Device South Armagh 1982.   144

Looking towards the junction between Antrim Road and Cavehill Road where
their expected SF targets would stop at traffic lights.   339
369/371, Antrim Road: Scene of May, 1980 killing of SAS Captain Herbert
Westmacott.   339
Red Hand Commando mural: Shankill Road, Belfast.   339
Plaque at site of 1976 Kingsmill Massacre where a PIRA murder gang shot
down 11 Protestant workmen, 10 of whom died.   340
Site of the former RUC station, Andersonstown, Belfast; exact spot where
Blues & Royals' soldiers Thornett and Dykes were killed by PIRA M60
gang in August, 1979.   340
Crumlin Road Courthouse, scene of many dozens of terror trials.   340
Bogside mural depicting the then Bernadette Devlin, the 'MP in blue jeans'   340
Lower Bogside in Londonderry; close to the PIRA haunt of the 'Bogside Inn.' 341
Loyalist heartland: Rathcoole, North Belfast.   341
UFF Mural, Rathcoole.   341
The rebuilt La Mon House restaurant. PIRA napalm-bombed the crowded
restaurant in February, 1978, killing 12 people.   342
Lenny Murphy.   342
'Boundary Bar' Shore Road, North Belfast; interface between sectarian areas;
scene of several killings, including sectarian murders.   342
Lenny Murphy's headstone.   343
Warrenpoint: Parachute Regiment memorial to the 18 dead soldiers; destroyed
by Republican thugs.   343

Foreword

Steven McLaughlin

When Ken Wharton asked me to write the foreword to this, his eighth and latest book on 'The Troubles', I was profoundly honoured and puzzled. Honoured, because no one writes of Northern Ireland like Ken and merely to have one's name alongside his is a privilege; puzzled, because my six-month tour of Crossmaglen in 2004, during the dying days of Op Banner, hardly qualifies me as a troubles authority. And whilst it's fair to say that South Armagh was still a scary place a decade ago, I would never dream to compare it with the hellhole it was during the period depicted in this book. Nonetheless it still felt strange and foreboding though. The grim history resonated through the fortress walls of our security bases and ubiquitous watchtowers, as if the troubles were merely yesterday –and the whole time I was there I never let myself forget or disrespect that fact.

During 2004 I was based in the XMG security/police station and the 'Golf-One-Zero' watchtower, overlooking a glorious green countryside that seemed ludicrously lush and verdant, given the bloody historical context of the times and troubles they represented. Before we deployed we were given long lectures from various old hands who'd soldiered through the worst of the troubles and advised us to 'read-up and study' on all that we could about Northern Ireland and Sough Armagh in particular. A dog-eared copy of Toby Harden's classic Bandit Country was doing the rounds of the battalion, but rather than wait my turn I impatiently bought a new one and devoured every word. Bandit Country was recommended reading because it brought us bang upto date with South Armagh as things stood then, from the late '90s post ceasefire 'peace' to the early 21st century stalemate. The book gave us an uncomfortable pre-tour familiarisation with the then king of the hill, Slab Murphy, and his band of merry followers, many of whom I'm sure are known in a more visceral sense to readers of Ken's works. The closest I ever got to him and 'them' was peering into their backyards scattered along the border or being glared at by them as they strode past our town-square patrols contemptuously ignoring us, so I tip my hat to Ken's many readers who suffered an altogether closer experience, 'back in the day'.

Northern Ireland in 2004 was a strange place for a soldier to patrol. The IRA, although on an agreed ceasefire, still hadn't disarmed and we were told by our commanders that if the ceasefire broke down, then the first we would know of it would probably be a successful attack on one of our patrols. So bizarrely – but quite rightly – we still had to patrol as if it was 1984, and every bush, car, 'easy crossing', or farmyard gate could conceal a bomb or a sniper. We spent long hours trekking across glorious

Armagh countryside and through at-first-glance picturesque villages – picturesque until you spied the numerous IRA murals and granite statues, often more impressive than our mainland cenotaph stones. It was strange and surreal to patrol professionally and 'assertively' when you knew there was probably no real threat – but nonetheless you couldn't take that chance. Because we were in the IRA controlled Crossmaglen area we were – ironically – relatively safe from attack, unless a particularly brave and foolish Real IRA or Continuity IRA member would have the gall to attempt something in Slab Murphy's backyard.

To think that the IRA was 'protecting us' from rival factions was a little unsettling to say the least. But again – strangely and bizarrely – it was a comfort, for both the RIRA and CIRA were struggling, but growing forces; in 2009 they finally killed two Royal Engineers at Massereene Barracks and have since launched several successful attacks on the PSNI that have left serving policemen limbless and crippled. So the threat – although vastly reduced – was very much real and we had to patrol as such. We still did VCPs, carried out arrests, cordoned off suspect sites and confiscated weapons and potential bomb making equipment; yes, the IRA was stood down, but they were still very much around and only a fool would have dared forget it.

In the end we had nothing but minor aggro and a few scuffles from the local 'Brits out' brigade to deal with, which after a 2003 tour of Iraq came as a welcome respite, in all honesty. There were cuts and bruises but nothing remotely like what our illustrious, overworked predecessors had to deal with, thirty years ago and more. From my perspective the final days of Op Banner were reduced to a tolerable 'police-action' type tour, but what earlier generations had to go though was intense, sustained urban warfare against a determined guerrilla foe, and I don't kid myself that the two are remotely comparable.

But the one thing I took from my own stint in Northern Ireland – and from Ken's superb books – is how utterly gruelling and incredibly hard it must have been to have soldiered through the worst of the troubles. Whenever I crossed a hill or traipsed through a field in 2004 I quite deliberately forced my mind back to a darker time before my own. And I asked myself this question repeatedly: How unbelievably hard must this tour have been twenty years ago, when at any moment a shot could ring out or a blast erupt, and leave you there – eviscerated in a puddle – waiting for a clattering, too-slow Lynx chopper to arrive, while your trembling mate attempts to give you first-aid and bring you back from the dead? How hard and how immensely stressful must that have been?

Well dear reader I don't know the answer to that question and I'm glad I never had to find out. But thanks to Ken's incredible books, detailing your arduous and honourable services, I now have at least some idea. Northern Ireland was a very hard and unforgiving conflict – that is what I have learnt from Ken's books and your services. So please take my words on Northern Ireland not as a qualified essay from a fellow soldier, but merely as the musings and admiration of a student of military history – as one who knows a little bit about it, but at the same time knows absolutely nothing when set against what you fellows had to endure, long before my time.

And as for Ken, my fellow Rifleman – well done again my friend.

Celer et Audax

Steven McLaughlin, Former Royal Green Jackets
Author of *Squaddie: A Soldier's Story*
July 2014

Preface

Dave Judge

I was a little surprised that Ken Wharton asked me to write the preface to this book. I have never met Ken; I have however read his work. He has filled me with pride, and he has humbled me with his tributes to those who walked the streets of Northern Ireland during those dark and frightening days gone by. His attention to detail and his quest to get the TRUTH out there! To those who may only ever have been fed propaganda from both sides of the fence read this. The stories you will read in all of Ken's books are written by the very men who patrolled, shivered and froze, during the long dark winter months and who sweated pints of water during the heat of the summer. We were wearing our heavy combat clothing, and flak jackets, while carrying helmets, weapons, ammunition, batons, and shields. Running; hiding; skulking; lurking; searching. Doing this for a full tour (four months) in Northern Ireland certainly took it out of us. Even as young men we were worn out after just a few hours patrolling on the streets. All of that was before you encountered any incident that could cloud your thoughts forever. I hope you, the reader, can absorb the depth of feeling in each and every event covered in this book. Remember these are real and most were life changing events for some, if not for all of those involved.

Dave Judge was a soldier in the 2nd Battalion Royal Green Jackets

35 years since my first tour to the New Lodge in Belfast and I still look at the top windows when I drive up to a junction, still watch all alleyways and doorways; I can't walk in a straight line as I hard-target, disappear into doorways when I hear a car back-fire, and I still turn around every few paces when I'm walking.

Doug Hook, Royal Artillery

'The bullets that killed James didn't just travel in distance, they travelled in time. Some of those bullets never stopped travelling.'

James Kennedy Snr, whose son aged 15, was killed by UFF terrorists at the Sean Graham Bookmakers' massacre

I always avoided groups of young children; they always used to stop me near gaps in buildings. I learned later that the IRA used to get them to do this so as to set up a through shoot.

Marcus Townley, Welsh Guards

I remember as a child, the anger I felt about not knowing how dangerous it was for my Father out there. Naturally we were protected from that worry, but I felt I had been cheated of the truth.

Anita Bailkoski, Daughter of Royal Artillery Sergeant John Haughey, murdered by the IRA

For all the demonising of the security forces, and the re-writing of history, there is still a vast section of the community that remembers what really happened after 1969. Their memories of those dark days should be transmitted, in a non-bitter way, to those people who were not alive at the time. If young folk know what preceded the current peace, they will cherish the present more, and be less likely to repeat the past.

Belfast Newsletter

I get so angry about NORAID and the way that the Irish-Americans collected money to fund Irish terrorism. What would the Yanks do if, say, the Mormons were killing policemen and soldiers and blowing up buildings, and we collected money for them in Britain?

Soldier, Royal Green Jackets

The Author's Personal Thoughts

I start this, my eighth book on the Northern Ireland Troubles, on a wet stormy night in Queensland. Much the same as many nights I spent in the back streets of Belfast all those many years ago. I grieve for the loss of over 1,300 of my comrades and I am forced to continue grieving as people continue to die in order to pay for an unrealistic, impossible dream. Though I feel contempt for their methods and their tactics, I do accept that Republicans had a vision, a hope that one day, the island of Ireland would be reunited. The premise of their argument was, however, naïve in the extreme in that they saw the situation in Ulster as being them versus the Protestant ruling classes, and that the working class Protestants would come to accept that their aims were mutually inclusive, and 'rise' against their leaders. The premise was that it would be a political 'struggle' and not a sectarian one.

With over two-thirds of the population of the North being Protestant and expressing a desire to remain in the United Kingdom and therefore, British, the coming together has not happened and nor is it likely to do so. Thus, the Republican dream is unachievable and unrealistic. Between 1969 and 1997, over 4,000 people died, a nation was torn apart, communities were 'Berlinised' along sectarian lines and the economy was very nearly destroyed. In the end, the British people, the British Army and the British Government remained unmoved and resolute, and both sides were eventually happy to see the signing of the Good Friday Agreement (GFA) and, seemingly, the end of violence.

If the three decades of what can only be described as a civil war didn't alter the political make-up of the island of Ireland, and the Protestant working classes didn't stand on the same barricades as the Republicans, why do the dissidents think that by re-opening the old wounds and divisions, the dream is any more realistic?

Ken Wharton, Queensland February 2013

Michael Sangster,
Royal Artillery

Most of us veterans did, and probably still do, bear a great hatred towards the population of Northern Ireland because it was those people we confronted day after day. It is only now that the truth has come out, that the majority of those same people were either coerced or forced by fear into acting the way they did. You either ran with the herd or suffered the consequences. It took 40 years, but I think that those people, and the terrorist cannon fodder, have finally realised that they were mugged. The majority of them are still jobless, they live in the same council estates, albeit no longer slums, while their erstwhile 'heroes' and 'defenders' are living it up in big houses in fancy areas, drive about in expensive cars and take holidays abroad several times a year. Another example of the 'Paddy factor', I suppose.

Abbreviations

2IC	Second in Command
3LI	Third Battalion Light Infantry
AAC	Army Air Corps
ADU	Army Dog Handling Unit
APC	Armoured Personnel Carrier
APNI	Alliance Party of Northern Ireland
ASU	Active Service Unit
ATO	Ammunition Technical Officer
AWOL	Absent Without Leave
BFBS	British Forces Broadcasting Service
Bn HQ	Battalion Headquarters
BOI	Board of Inquiry
CESA	Catholic Ex-serviceman's Association
CO	Commanding Officer
CS	Tear Gas
CVO	Casualty Visiting Officers
DC	Detective Constable
DERR	Duke of Edinburgh's Royal Regiment
DOE	Department of the Environment
DoW	Died of Wounds
DOWR	Duke of Wellington's Regiment
DUP	Democratic Unionist Party
DWR	Duke of Wellington's Regiment
EOD	Explosive Ordnance Disposal
ETA	*Euskadi Ta Askatasuna* (Basque Separatist Terrorist group)
FOI	Freedom of Information
FRG	Federal Riot Guns
GAA	Gaelic Athletic Association (Irish: *Cumann Lzithchleas Gael*)
GC	George Cross
GHQ	General Head Quarters
GPMG	General Purpose Machine Gun
GPO	General Post Office
HET	Historical Enquiries Team
HQNI	Head Quarters Northern Ireland
IJLB	Infantry Junior Leaders Battalion
INLA	Irish National Liberation Army
Int	Intelligence
IRA	Irish Republican Army
IRSP	Irish Republican Socialist Party

KIA	Killed in Action
KOSB	King's Own Scottish Borderers
LSL	Landing Ship Logistics
MO	Medical Officer
MoD	Ministry of Defence
NAAFI	Navy, Army and Air Force Institute
NCND	neither confirm nor deny
NCO	Non-Commissioned Officer
NG	Negligent Discharge
NI	Northern Ireland
NIVA	Northern Ireland Veteran's Association
NMA	National Memorial Arboretum
NORAID	Northern Aid Committee
NTH	Newtownhamilton
ODC	Ordinary decent criminals
OP	Observation Post
OTR	On the Run
Pig	Armoured Vehicle (named as such due to its pig-like appearance)
PIRA	Provisional Irish Republican Army
PLA	People's Liberation Army
POA	Prison Officers' Association
POW	Prisoner of War
PRO	Public Relations Officer
PSNI	Police Service Northern Ireland
QLR	Queen's Lancashire Regiment
QOH	Queen's Own Highlander's
QRF	Quick Reaction Force
RAF	Royal Air Force
RSF	Republican Sinn Féin
RCT	Royal Corps of Transport
RE	Royal Engineers
REHQ	Royal Engineers Headquarters
REME	Royal Electrical and Mechanical Engineers
RGJ	Royal Green Jackets
RIRA	Real Irish Republican Army
RMP	Royal Military Police
RAOC	Royal Army Ordnance Corps
ROE	Rules of Engagement
RPG-7	Rocket Propelled Grenade
RRF	Royal Regiment of Fusiliers
RRW	Royal Regiment of Wales
RSM	Regimental Sergeant Major
RTA	Road Traffic Accident
RUC	Royal Ulster Constabulary
RUCR	Royal Ulster Constabulary Reserve
RVH	Royal Victoria Hospital

SB	Special Branch
SDLP	Social Democratic and Labour Party
SF	Security Forces
SIB	Special Investigation Branch
SLR	Self Loading Rifle
SOP	Standard Operating Procedure
SUIT	Sight Unit Infantry Trilux
TA	Territorial Army
TD	*Teachta Dála* (Member of the Irish Parliament)
TAOR	Tactical Area of Responsibility
UDA	Ulster Defence Association
UDR	Ulster Defence Regiment
UFF	Ulster Freedom Fighters
USC	Ulster Special Constabulary
UTV	Ulster Television
UUP	Ulster Unionist Party
UVBT	Under vehicle booby trap
UWC	Ulster Worker's Council
VCP	Vehicle Check Point
WOII	Warrant Officer Second Class
WRAC	Women's Royal Army Corps

Maps

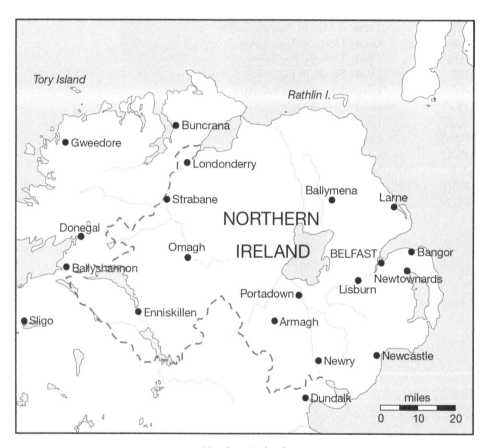

Northern Ireland

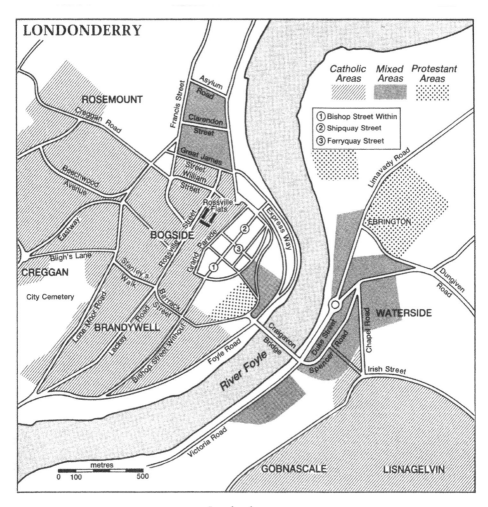

Londonderry

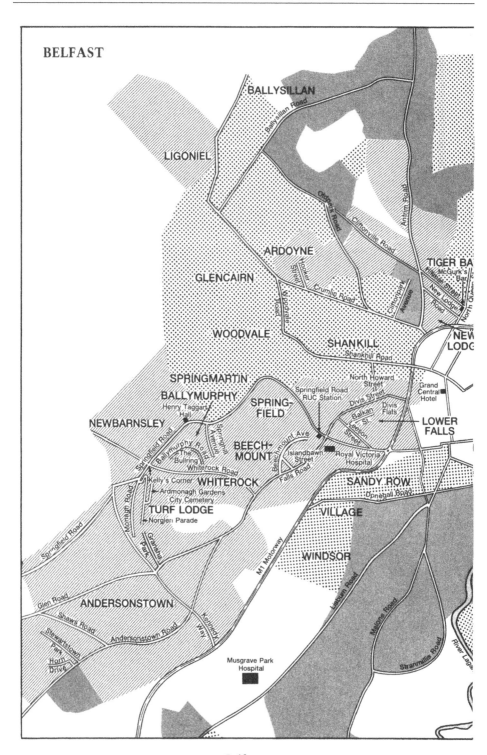

Belfast

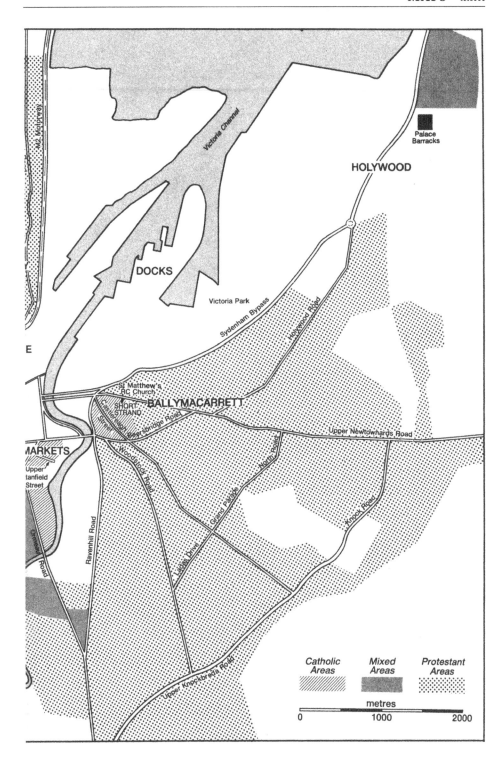

HOLYWOOD

Palace
Barracks

Victoria Channel

DOCKS

Victoria Park

Sydenham Bypass

Holywood Road

St Matthew's
RC Church

SHORT
STRAND

BALLYMACARRETT

Upper Newtownards Road

MARKETS

Upper
tanfield
Street

Beersbridge Road

Woodstock Road

North Road

Knock Road

Ravenhill Road

Grand Parade

Ladas Drive

Upper Knockbreda Road

M2 Motorway

| Catholic Areas | Mixed Areas | Protestant Areas |

metres

0   1000   2000

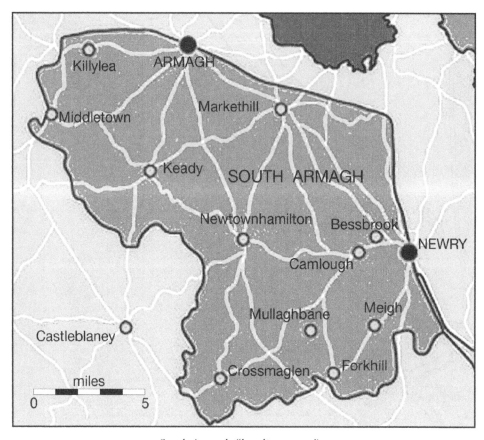

South Armagh ('bandit country')

Introduction

I thought long and hard before coming up with a title for this book and what better than *An Agony Continued,* because it was simply that: an agony. It was an agony which commenced at the end of the 1960s and, as the new decade of the 80s arrived, so the pain, the grief, the loss and the economic destruction of Northern Ireland continued. Little did any of us know at the time, but it was to do so for almost a further two decades.

Between January 1980 and December 1989, around 1,000 people would die; some were soldiers and policemen; some were prison officers; some were paramilitaries and some were innocent civilians. The Provisional IRA (PIRA) and their slightly more psychopathic cousins in the Irish National Liberation Army (INLA) would continue to kill innocent civilians by the score during this decade. Across the sectarian divide the Ulster freedom Fighters (UFF) and the equally vicious Ulster Volunteer Force (UVF) would continue to slaughter Catholics in streets and in pubs and in restaurants.

This book will look at the period which encompassed the 48 months of 1980 to 1983. It was a near half-decade which saw the Hyde Park and Regent's Park massacre of soldiers and horses from the Blues and Royals and the cowardly bombing of the Royal Green Jackets' band. It further witnessed the murder of 18 people by the INLA at a disco held in the Droppin' Well in Ballykelly and also the death – unmourned by this author – of the leader of the Shankill Butchers, Lenny Murphy. The years under study include the 1981-deaths of 10 Republican paramilitaries who starved themselves to death in protest against the loss of their status as 'political prisoners'.

The four years under review demonstrate just how apt the title of this book is: Northern Ireland; *An Agony Continued.*

Part One

1980

Whereas the total number of deaths fell in this year, there were, nevertheless 46 soldiers or former soldiers killed, with the UDR paying an unacceptably high toll. A further nine Police officers were killed as well as 45 civilians. It was a year which witnessed the sickening spectacle of the murder of an off-duty Green Jacket by the Provisionals, as he visited his grieving wife in hospital following the stillbirth of their baby. This author will not hold his breath awaiting an apology from either Mr Adams or Mr McGuinness – or, for that matter, their PIRA comrades. The New Year commenced with the tragedy of a 'blue on blue' as two soldiers from the Parachute Regiment were killed.

1

January

uring the Troubles, every New Year's Eve with the promise of a new dawn to follow, came the fresh hope that this particular one might be the one which brought peace. There were 29 such New Years' Eves over the long and tortuous course of the Troubles and, as the final minutes of 1979 ticked away, so there was fresh hope in the hearts of those who wanted an end to the violence. 1 January, 1980 arrived – and by the end of the day three people would be dead and two would be badly injured. Two soldiers would be among those whose lives had been ended prematurely and two more CVOs were being dispatched to Hampshire and Dorset with the news that soldiers' loved ones did not wish to hear. It would also see the death of Anne Maguire, mother of the three children killed in Andersonstown in 1976. Their tragic deaths were the catalyst behind the Peace People's Movement.

In the very early hours of the 1st, an eight-man patrol group from the Parachute Regiment had set up an ambush position in wooded country at Tullydonnell, South Armagh, close to the Irish border. Lieutenant Simon Bates (25) and his Signaller, Private Gerald Hardy (18) had located themselves a short distance away from the others. Standard Operating Procedure (SOP) is that once an ambush position is set, no further movement should be made unless ordered. For reasons which will remain known only to the two men, they moved and approached the others. In the pitch black – it was 0130 hours – and 'cammed up', their comrades thought that they were IRA gunmen and after a quick challenge, opened fire on the two men and both were killed. A member of the patrol told the later inquest: "Two blokes walked into the ambush. We positively identified weapons and we had to open fire." Why SOP was broken by the two dead Paras will never be known as both died fairly instantly. Lieutenant Bates was from Christchurch, Dorset and Private Hardy was from Southampton.

TRAGIC START TO THE NEW YEAR
Marcus Townley, Welsh Guards

On December 31st, I found myself on QRF (Quick Reaction Force) at Bessbrook Mill and all ready for the New Year of 1980. After patrolling around the 'cuds' (rural ops), we rotated on to Mill security (i.e. sangar protection) as well as QRF.

Anyway, as midnight approached we were allowed our two cans of beer to celebrate the New Year and new decade. The church bells chimed and we all shook hands, but because I was on stag (guard duty) at 0100 on the PVCP (permanent vehicle checkpoint), I decided to get my head down. At about 0015 the helicopters started to warm up and I thought: "Fuck me; something has kicked off." We made our way to the ready room, and sure enough we were to be crashed out, as there had been a shooting on the border.

We boarded the helicopters just as we were about to lift off. 'Kestrel' (code name for the helicopter ops team) came out of his ops room and told us that the flight had been scrubbed. We very soon learned that it had been a 'blue on blue'[1] involving two members of 2 Para. By all accounts the Platoon Commander had decided to have a chat to his platoon, and approached from the front, which was designated as the killing zone. Sadly, he had got himself shot and killed along with a young private. Believe you me, it put a real dampener on the festive period.

A couple of hours later a brick returning back to the Mill asked why we were so glum on New Year's Day; on being told they too were pissed off. The effect of that one incident is that for the last 33 years now, I never celebrate New Year's Day. Come midnight I always walk away from the celebrations; yes, I toast those two Paras, perhaps shed a tear. But celebrate – no.

The scene then shifted further north, this time to Belfast. As this author has commented in his books, *passim*, 'joyriding' during the Troubles was a lethal pastime. As 1980 began, so ended the life of Doreen McGuinness (16) after the car in which she was a passenger ran through a VCP manned by soldiers from the Parachute Regiment and was fired upon. The VCP was placed on the Whiterock Road between the Ballymurphy ('Murph) and Turf Lodge Estates in order to deter the transfer of arms and explosives. The car approached the VCP and accelerated through, forcing the soldiers to leap out of the way. Under the in place Rules of Engagement (ROE) they were entitled to open fire and did so, striking the car several times. The bullet-riddled car was abandoned at the Royal Victoria Hospital (RVH) on the Falls Road and the driver ran off. Ms McGuinness was already dead and a fellow passenger had had most of his foot shot away. The practice was always dangerous, but the price of failing to stop at a VCP when ordered to do so by armed – and sometimes nervous – soldiers could be fatal and was often so.[2]

VCPS
Rifleman 'L' Royal Green Jackets
I did a fair few of these on my two tours of NI, both times in West Belfast and I was always on edge. The truth is that you didn't always know what to expect. It could be a couple of hours – sometimes less – of sheer mind-numbing boredom, but it could also be a time when you were pissing yourself and worried about the next car to come along. Most times we would flag a driver down and ask for his docs and then 'P' check him and then wave him on the way; true you would often get the usual comments of "Fuckin' Brits; youse got nothing better to do?" or "Fuck off back ter England!" Other times, we would get a cheery "What about yez, lads?" or "God bless yez, lads; youse take care, now." We stopped one guy and his Mrs and we knew straight away we were in for trouble. He was just sullen, but

---

1   The term 'blue on blue' is thought to originate in the US military. Basically, as friendly forces' positions are marked in blue on field commanders' battle maps, the term arose from there.

2   See Chapter 3, which describes the death of another joyrider – Paul Moan – at a VCP.

she was what the Belfast people would call a "gob-shite!" It was "Brit-this, fucking Brit that" for a minute or two while we 'P' checked them. She then informed me that she knew my name and my mother was going to be shot by the boyos when she shopped at Tesco! I thought: "Fuck me; how does she know where my Mum shops?" Then she said: "You are fuckin' dead you English fuck-pig!" At that, I'd had enough and shouted to a mate: "Fuck it, Yorkie: shoot the bitch!" I only did it for effect, but the other lad cocked his SLR (self-loading rifle) and pointed it straight at her head. Fortunately, he knew what I was up to and shouted: "In her head or chest?" She went white and clamped her obscene lips together and we didn't hear a peep from her after that. We waved them away and I called into the car: "The Royal Green Jackets thank you for your co-operation and patience." I bet the husband was happy with it, because at least he wouldn't have to listen to her bitching!

The worst times were when a car would approach us at speed and the arse muscles would tighten up and then they would screech to a halt; always testing us, pushing us. Mind, as soon as one of the lads stuck the business end of his SLR into the driver's face, he would turn white and hopefully soil his underpants! Other times you would see a car stop a hundred yards away as he saw us and do a 'U' turn or pull out of a queue of traffic and roar away. Was it someone impatient who was late for somewhere or something, or was it a player with arms in the boot trying to get away? After I came out of the Army, I saw on the news that several joyriders had been killed for trying to crash through VCPs and I can honestly say that although I feel for the people killed, I can understand the actions of the soldiers who felt that their lives were threatened. That's why I never condemned Private Clegg for what happened in September 1990;[3] been there and done that as they say.

Far too frequently, the Provisionals – as well as the Loyalist paramilitaries – set up illegal VCPs in their areas of influence. It was a show of bravado, a show of strength to send a message to their supporters and to snub the SF. On the news of the approach by an Army patrol, the signs, the guns and the masks all disappeared and the IRA men would melt into the background. The following is an account of what one soldier thought was an IVCP and led to a hilarious, although nearly tragic, incident.

---

3   Private Lee Clegg was convicted of murder for his involvement in the shooting dead of two teenage joyriders in West Belfast. The shooting took place in West Belfast on 30 September 1990. Clegg, from Bradford, West Yorkshire, and his fellow soldiers while they were manning a VCP on the Upper Glen Road, fired 19 rounds into a stolen Vauxhall Astra which passed through the checkpoint travelling at high speed. Clegg fired four of the bullets, the last of which killed 18-year-old passenger Karen Reilly. The driver, 17-year-old Martin Peake, also died at the scene, and the third passenger, Markiewicz Gorman, escaped with minor injuries. His conviction was later overturned.

IVCP OR WAS IT?
Ken Pettengale, Royal Green Jackets

I married a WRAC driver who was based in Aldergrove. After a whirlwind romance, we got married in Hexham. As I had been refused permission to marry, I did anyway as I always did when I was told I couldn't. To keep us apart, she was posted to Londonderry, so one night I borrowed my mate's car (a covert bright orange 2.0 Capri), 'persuaded' two pistols from the armourer and set off for a night of passion. I got completely lost once I got to Londonderry, and didn't fancy stopping for directions. I did know however, that I was on the wrong side of the river and the wrong side of town! After driving around for ages, I finally got pulled over by the RUC and after a bit of finger wagging and chest beating, they escorted me to my destination, only to find I had no fucking ID card and they wouldn't let me in! My new wife came to the gates, we had a kiss and I set off back to Belfast.

Schlepping down the M1 motorway in the pitch black, up ahead I could see torches going on and off in the middle of the road. However, it seemed amateurish and not the way we were taught to flag vehicles at night! I had an instant 'arse twitch' because I thought that I was heading straight into an IRA VCP!

I put both pistols on the passenger seat and – fucking dangerously – cocked one and jammed it between my knees! I decided to slow down and get to the check and then put my toe down and crash through. By this time I was truly in a panic; on my own and wondering if I would get out alive. As I got closer, the car in front caught figures in his headlights before he turned them off; they were in uniform! As I slowed down and stopped, I was relieved to find they were UDR, until one of them shone his/her torch through the passenger window and saw the 9-mls! Fucking hell! Then I knew how close you can come to being an own goal! After being checked out (no ID remember?) I was told to report to the duty room at Aldergrove. That is when the trouble really started! I am sure Martin Brookes who was one of the Mortar Platoon Serjeants[4] who will remember this incident. My knob has led me into many a problem in my life; he's a good mate, but boy, does he drop me in it at times!

There was clearly a touch of black humour about the above incident, but one has to remember, that when a minibus driver stopped at what appeared to be a legitimate VCP but what turned into an IRA ambush in Kingsmills in January, 1976, the men doing the stopping were wearing stolen British Army uniforms; the result was 10 dead. When the driver of the Miami Showband's minibus was stopped near Newry in July of the previous year, the UVF killers were also wearing stolen British Army uniforms; three band members were killed. Both incidents are dealt with in detail in *Wasted Years, Wasted Lives* by the same author[5]. The Provisionals also used stolen uniforms to 'smoke out' a suspected tout (informer) in South Armagh. In this one particular incident, a PIRA member had been suspected of touting for some time and a fake VCP was set up. When his car was stopped at the fake VCP, he was told that the 'soldiers' were SAS and

---

4   Royal Green Jackets spell 'Sergeant' as 'Serjeant'.
5   Wharton, Ken M., *Wasted Years, Wasted Lives* (Solihull: Helion, 2014).

were going to kill him. In a panic, he identified himself as an informer for the RUC and that sealed his death warrant. He was taken away by the 'nutting squad' and during torture was likely to have been asked 'which road do you want to close?' This was a sickening reference to the fact that the SF would close a road off after the discovery of a body for fear it may be booby-trapped. That particular man was later hooded and then shot twice in the back of the head while a 'tame' Catholic priest added 'dignity' to the murder by reading him the last rites.

This sickening act of making 'respectable' the sordid and brutal interrogation, torture and finally shooting of a 'tout' or 'suspected tout' by inviting or intimidating a Catholic priest into giving the condemned man the action of contrition or final rites was a favourite of the Provisionals. Often after the 'nutting squad' had carried out the above, a priest was summoned to hear the beaten suspect make his final confession. In his excellent *God and the Gun,* Martin Dillon perfectly illustrates one such event where the squad had all but finished their dirty business and the bleeding and bruised man wished to make his peace. Dillon interviewed a priest known only as 'Father Pat' who had been summoned to a PIRA safe house and led upstairs to the bathroom which had clearly been employed as a torture room:

> I froze when the bathroom door closed. I was suddenly dealing with evil and not just talking about it. The man in the chair was one of my parishioners. I remember looking at the bath filled with water wondering what they had done with him. He was stripped to a pair of wet underpants. His hair and body were wet so they'd obviously been holding him under the water … He was badly bruised and his eyes were so swollen he could hardly see me … The victim was incapable of walking. I put my arm around him … it seemed the only loving thing I could do. His lips were swollen and I heard him murmur: 'Please help me, Father'. I felt so helpless. Leaving that room was a nightmare I have to live with.[6]

These torture rooms according to the priests which Martin Dillon interviewed, along with accounts from some of the informers and agents, as well as other contemporary accounts, were places of almost mediaeval barbarity. Some of the methods employed by the 'nutting squad' might well have been taken from the handbook of the Middle Ages torturer or the despicable 'Spanish Inquisition'. Witnesses speak of stained and soiled clothes where the tortured suspect had lost control of their bodily functions; vomit-ridden areas; blood-stained clothes and bedding, pools of blood and broken teeth and blood-covered saws, chisels and screwdrivers. This was hardly the image with which to impress their Irish-American backers, and those 'romantic' priests in the Catholic faith who saw them as freedom-fighters.

On the 2nd of the month, Gerry Adams, later President of Sinn Féin, who was apparently never a Company Commander of the Ballymurphy IRA and later was apparently not Belfast Brigade Commander, was arrested by soldiers and RUC officers in the Andersonstown area. He and another Sinn Féin member were found in a house which the SF was attempting to search. Several knocks had been made at the door of the house

6   Dillon, Martin, *God and the Gun: The Church and Irish Terrorism* (London: Routledge, 1999), pp. 99–100.

and Police identified themselves. Neither man in the house made an effort to respond and when officers broke in, the two men were arrested although later released. Adams – or 'Teflon man' as he is known in some quarters – might well have been squirming with embarrassment on 2 October 2013, during the writing of this book. His younger brother Liam, himself a former PIRA commander, was convicted on that day of sexually abusing his own daughter – Áine – and it emerged during the court case that 'Saint Gerry' was cognisant of the paedophile activity which was going on underneath his own nose. Under a headline of 'Unfit for Office' the *Belfast Telegraph* wrote:

> In the witness box Liam Adams strongly denied all the charges he faced. He initially denied having been confronted by his brother and other family members about abuse, but later changed his story. He explained in court that his father had always warned him to not to speak about his brother, adding: "You don't talk about Gerry in the barracks, to the soldiers at the time, to the Police, even in social gatherings as you got older. You didn't talk about Gerry Adams full stop."

The newspaper's Leader on the same day proclaimed:

> There will be some who will argue that no blame should be attached to Gerry Adams because he took risks for peace and he helped to bring former enemies to the negotiating table resulting in today's power-sharing administration. They will also point out that people who were guilty of terrorist activities, up to and including murder, have been rehabilitated into society and are now among the political classes. But we cannot forever continue to excuse the activities of people in prominent positions who do not use their influence well. In this case, Gerry Adams fails the test of what would be expected of a man in his position and armed with his knowledge. And it should throw into grave doubt his fitness to be leader of one of the major political parties on this island and – although it is not in this jurisdiction – his fitness to continue to represent County Louth in the Dáil. If he was a politician anywhere else in these islands he would be out of office and party leadership very swiftly, and that is the standard by which we should judge him here.[7]

Indeed, in the same edition of the *Belfast Telegraph,* political commentator Alex Kane wrote this of Mr Adams:

> He reminds me of the leader of a cult rather than of a political party: a bit like one of those beardy end-of-days gurus who convinces himself, and a band of tunnel-vision followers, that the long-awaited prophecy of Irish unity is imminent. When he says he was never in the IRA I don't believe him. He's been at the very core of Sinn Féin for most of his life and his public profile was built on the assumption that when he spoke he did so with the authority of the IRA Army Council. In 1972 he was one of the people chosen to represent the IRA at negotiations with the British Government – a role he retained, even as others came and went. He was the

---

7   *Belfast Telegraph*, 2 October 2013.

wordsmith who provided the language to justify terror; the man who carried the coffins of terrorists. The man entrusted to produce the strategy which determined the rate at which violence would be turned on and off.

Earlier on that day, the Provisionals had murdered a former UDR soldier – Samuel Lundy (62) – at Kingsmills, County Armagh. Mr Lundy was a lorry driver and had resigned from the UDR the previous year; he was shot by waiting gunmen as he returned home from work to his house in Drumnahuncheon Road, close to the scene of the massacre of 10 Protestant workmen four years earlier; almost exactly to the day. As he jumped from the cab of the lorry, he was hit several times by automatic fire and he died almost instantly. The Nationalist newspaper *The Irish News* incredibly appeared to apportion the blame for his murder on the former UDR man himself, stating that he should have informed the IRA that he had resigned and requesting that he be removed from the target list.

On 3 January, the fifth death of the New Year occurred when a Catholic man was beaten to death with bricks in what was clearly a senseless sectarian killing. In the perverted logic of the Loyalists who killed him, it was 'just' desserts for the killing of Mr Lundy. The deadly game of 'tit for tat' had recommenced in earnest. Alexander Reid (20) and a fellow Catholic had been drinking in Belfast City Centre and had hailed a taxi to take them to the Ardoyne. However, the driver deliberately drove them onto the Shankill Road and stopped outside a Loyalist drinking den. Several UFF members dragged the two Catholic men into the club where they were beaten. Later they were taken to Berlin Street between the Shankill Road and Riga Street. One of the men managed to escape, but Mr Reid was taken inside a derelict building and beaten to death with bricks. Retaliation was a mere nine days away and the weapon of choice would remain the same – a brick.

In South Armagh, on the same day, an Army patrol found several milk churns stuffed with explosives just outside of Crossmaglen. Three milk churns were found which between them contained 600 lbs (273 kg) of explosives. Earlier in the week, several other milk churns containing 700 lbs (320 kg) had also been found and defused in the same area. It is clear that had these devices been detonated, loss of life amongst the frequent Army patrols would have been immense. The first bomb, had it exploded, would have likely demolished nearby farm buildings – this was only prevented by the sterling work of ATO, for hours in the snow and ice, in order to render the bombs safe.

Later that same day, the Provisionals murdered an off-duty policeman as he worked in his garage in Main Street, Newtownbutler in County Fermanagh. Robert Crilly (60) was a member of the Royal Ulster Constabulary Reserve (RUCR) and ran a repair garage in the town. Dickers had already observed his working patterns when he was not in police uniform and carrying out routine patrols. At lunchtime on the 3rd, a car containing two IRA men pulled up close to where he was working on a car and without warning opened fire from close range, mortally wounding him. A young boy aged 12, who had been helping him with the repairs, could only stand in shocked silence, as the cowardly assassins cut him down. They raced off in the car to the border with the Republic, crossing into County Cavan which was a short five-minute journey. The part-time policeman was dead before medical assistance arrived.

Seán MacBride was an Irish Government Minister, and a former Chief of Staff of the IRA. On the 5th, he sensationally revealed that secret cross-border talks between representatives of both the Irish and British Governments had been taking place for over 30 years. The negotiations had been carried out since 1949; clearly little had been achieved of any note, but it at least destroyed the myth that the two sides never talked.

On the 6th, the death toll for 1980 reached nine, when three full-time UDR soldiers were killed in an IRA bomb blast at Castlewellan, County Down. That day was a Sunday and a seven-man patrol from 3UDR set off on mobile patrol in several vehicles. As it passed close to Loughislandreavy Reservoir and Burren Bridge, en-route for Ballykinlar, one of the vehicles passed over a culvert. The culvert was only the size of a pipe, but a PIRA unit of the 'South Down Command' had packed in 600 lbs (273 kg) of explosives, and concealed a command wire which led to a firing point in a deserted cottage some 250 yards away. As the first vehicle passed over the culvert, it was detonated and the massive blast shattered the Land Rover, hurling it high into the air and back into the massive crater, which was some 30 feet deep. The following vehicle, unable to stop, crashed into the same crater, injuring four soldiers.

All of the three soldiers in the first vehicle were killed; one man was possibly still alive, but trapped in the twisted wreckage, may have drowned as the hole filled instantly with water. The two other men died instantly from blast injuries. The three soldiers were: Private Richard 'Rickie' Wilson (21) from Newcastle; Private Jim Cochrane (21) from Downpatrick and Private Robert Smyth (18) of Comber; all three men were full-time members of the UDR. A trusted source within the UDR told the author: "I knew one of the injured very well; he has severe back problems, eventually he moved to Spain for the heat but last reports was that he killed himself there, but can't confirm that at this time."

The deaths of these soldiers carried the number of deaths from the beginning of the Troubles in 1969 to well over 2,100. A follow-up patrol found that the terrorists had covered the command wire with earth, and then passed it inside the hollow interior of a drystone wall in order to hide it from passing soldiers. They had hidden in an unused outhouse from where they had a perfect view of the ambush point. The road between Castlewellan and Newry was closed for over a day with traffic diversions set up as workmen filled in the 40-foot crater.

At the funeral of Private Cochrane, Priest Joseph Maguire condemned the thugs of the IRA and asked: "How long will it be before the perpetrators of these outrages listen to the voices of reason?" Father Rory MacDonald said: "the town is repulsed by these deaths!" At another of the funerals, Bishop of Down, Dr George Quin said: "the utter callousness of these murders does not seem to reach the people who commit such acts of violence, and far from attaining any end of furthering some ideology they may have in mind, they only serve to strengthen the resolve and determination of people not to submit to such acts of terror." In the wake of the deaths, Robert Bradford, MP called for the immediate shooting of captured IRA men who should be treated as: "wartime saboteurs, war criminals or spies." The men of PIRA's Army Council remembered those words and showed that they had long memories. The MP was assassinated by PIRA gunmen on 14 November 1981.[8]

Ken Johnson from *The Newsletter* interviewed two of the injured UDR soldiers after the funeral. Both chose to remain anonymous; one said:

---

8   See Chapter 23 of this book.

We were travelling along the Dublin Road when, just about 500 yards from the bridge, the next thing we saw was a blinding flash. It was yellow and blue, the colours were mixed. Then we heard a terrific explosion. We were just 50 yards behind the first Land Rover. [Shortly afterwards] Civilians began arriving and we tried to get the injured soldiers out. Ambulances came after this along with Police and the Fire Brigade. I was taken to the hospital in Downpatrick.

His injured comrade also told of how he tried to brake as soon as he saw the flash. He continued:

But we were lifted up into the air and we couldn't stop. We went over the edge into the crater and bang into the first Land Rover. I was very dazed and I can remember crawling out … with the radio. I crawled up a ditch at the side of the road and took up a firing position. I thought that the people who had attacked us were going to start shooting. I tried to contact base, but the Land Rover had been flooded with water and the radio was broken … I could see that the first Rover was buried deep in the rubble of the crater.

He went on to tell the reporter of stabbing pains in his shoulder and head and that he had realised that he was bleeding. "Ahead of me, I could see that the front of the other vehicle had caved in and trapped the men inside."

Later on, families of the dead soldiers placed a discreet and unobtrusive memorial near the scene. Within days, the scum of the area had smashed it up. The hatred of these people is almost unimaginable. No terrorist was ever brought to justice for the murder of these men and weapons and funds continued to pour in from the Irish-Americans and the mad Colonel Muammar Muhammad Abu Minyar al-Gaddafi of Libya.

On the 7th, constitutional talks called by Northern Ireland Secretary Humphrey Atkins got under way at Stormont. As part of the wider Atkins talks, a constitutional conference was arranged at Stormont involving the Democratic Unionist Party (DUP), the Social Democratic and Labour Party (SDLP), and the Alliance Party (APNI). The Ulster Unionist Party (UUP) refused to take part in the conference. Atkins conceded a parallel conference which would allow the SDLP to raise issues, in particular an 'Irish dimension', which were not covered by the original terms of reference. The DUP refused to get involved with the parallel conference. These talks continued until 24 March but sadly did not succeed in achieving consensus amongst the parties.

On 9 January, a Coroner's Inquest in County Sligo in the Irish Republic met for the final time in order for the Coroner to give his, not unexpected verdict into the Mountbatten killings.[9] The Coroner ruled that all members of the party had been killed unlawfully. It revealed that Lord Mountbatten had died from drowning after he had been terribly injured and hurled into the water. Lady Brabourne who died the day after the explosion, had appalling injuries to her lungs; Nicholas Knatchbull, her grandson, drowned and an Irish boy, Paul Maxwell, died from multiple injuries. In what was a

---

9   See Wharton, Ken M., *Wasted Years, Wasted Lives*, Vol 2 (Solihull: Helion, 2014), Part Five.

cruel twist of irony, it was later revealed by the media that Mountbatten had spoken privately about his wish for the eventual reunification of Ireland.

Two days later, in swoops by Gardaí Siochana in Dublin, several INLA suspects wanted in connection with the murder of Airey Neave MP were arrested. The arrests followed the kidnapping of the family of a leading Irish banker. Mr Thomas Scully's wife and teenage daughters were held hostage by INLA kidnappers and were released only after Mr Scully left £30,000 in a telephone kiosk near Dublin, but not before informing the Police. All the arrested men were suspected of being involved in both the kidnapping and the murder of Mr Neave at the House of Commons car park in March, 1979.

On 12 January, another RUCR officer was killed by Republican terrorists. David Purse (43), father of three, was on duty at a football match on Shore Road, Belfast. As the game between Crusaders and Portadown at Seaview football ground neared its end, a PIRA gunman walked up behind the part-time policeman and shot him five times in the head, killing him instantly. The crowd dived for cover but the match continued, stopping only when it was pointed out to the referee that the policeman was dead.

A few hours after the football match murder, in what was described as the work of "… mindless morons…" the deadly game of tit for tat continued. Thomas Montgomery (46), a taxi driver from the Ballysillan area, was driving along Crumlin Road close to the sectarian interface with the Nationalist Ardoyne in the 'wee hors' of 12 January. The morning was cold and foggy and, as he drove slowly through the murk, several Catholic youths hurled pieces of brick and concrete at the windscreen. One of the missiles hit Mr Montgomery in the head, fracturing his skull and forcing him to crash into a wall. He died very shortly afterwards with witnesses stating that the murderous pack of youths called out in triumph: "We've got the bastard!" Three of the gang later appeared in court and were convicted of manslaughter, with the trial Judge declaring: "You attacked and killed this unfortunate man for no other reason than he was Protestant … your actions have caused great pain and grief to your families but it will not last as long as the pain and grief suffered by the Montgomery family." The court was told was that the gang had plotted revenge for the murder of Alexander Reid on the 3rd of the month.

On the following day John Brown (49), who had been injured in an INLA attack at a post office in County Armagh, died from his injuries.[10] His killer was later sentenced to 30 years for this murder as well as the murders of UDR man Robert McNally and former policeman Jim Wright.[11]

On the same day that Mr Brown died from his wounds, raids by Gardaí officers on a farm close to Dundalk uncovered ready-prepared explosive devices weighing in excess of one ton. It was a major blow to the Provisionals and curtailed attacks over the border for several weeks. It saved lives, or as the cynic might say, it merely extended the lives of many innocents for a few more weeks or months.

A NICE FIND
Dougie Durrant

It was a normal day in the New Lodge area of Belfast; the smell of burning vehicles and people going about their normal stone-throwing etc. I was to meet up

---

10   See Wharton, *Wasted Years, Wasted Lives*, Vol 2, Part Five, Chapter 51.
11   Ibid., Chapter 55.

with the Devon and Dorsets' Unit Search Team Advisor, a Pioneer Sergeant called Rodger. He was a man who knew his stuff and planned his searches down to the last finest details. He wanted to search around the area of the RUC station itself, as he knew that the best place to hide anything was right under the Police and Army's noses.

Henry Place in the New Lodge district was located just to the rear of the station itself, and seemed to have at least one occupied house still standing, so that was his random search target for the day; I walked Bluce (a specially trained 'searcher' dog) and got him ready for the task ahead. Due to the short distance, we decided to walk with all the search kit, and when we reached the aforementioned house, an RUC officer knocked at the door and entry was gained to the residence with no trouble all. A man in his mid-50s was the only occupant of the house; he seemed nervous and whatever questions were asked, he simply replied "No!" to all of them. With that, I put the harness on Bluce and off we went, starting from the top of the house; it was a real mess and I don't think he owned a brush.

We went into a small room which was full of boxes and the dog showed an indication on one of them, so I pulled him back and praised him up. My minder looked into it and saw that it was full of transmitting equipment. Rodger was informed and he came up to have a look and informed us that it would need a communications team to have a look at it. The owner was brought in and shown the equipment, and he replied: "Don't know how that got there", informing us that it was just junk which he had collected over time.

About an hour later a signals team arrived from Lisburn and collected all the bits and a few more items we had found in the same room. When they put it all together, it turned that it was a sophisticated transmitter and receiver and the man – clearly a dicker – had been monitoring the Police and Army frequencies. Quite a good find at the end of the day.

On the 14th, Lieutenant-General Sir Richard Lawson took over as GOC, Northern Ireland. He was quick to announce to all service personnel in the Province his support for them. He said:

> I am honoured to take command of the Armed Forces in Northern Ireland where they are engaged in operations alongside the other forces of law and order trying to achieve the return to normality of life enjoyed in the rest of Great Britain. We all look forward to the days when construction and not destruction is once again the pattern in Ulster.

The Provisionals responded within 24 hours and bombs were exploded in all but one of the six Northern Counties. In Forkhill, County Armagh, a routine RUC mobile patrol was ambushed by a PIRA bombing team. As their vehicle was passing over a culvert, a massive landmine was detonated, wrecking their vehicle and seriously injuring all three officers. A civilian in a passing car was also badly injured as once again Republican terrorists were unprepared to discriminate between the lives of their own community and those of the SF.

On the morning of the 16th, armed PIRA members hijacked a car on the Nationalist Drumrallugh Estate in Strabane. Strabane was affected by countless incidents between 1970 and the late 1990s. These incidents included: gun battles, car bombings, incendiary devices exploding in commercial premises, sustained rioting, hoax bomb alerts and pipe bomb attacks. Particularly in the early to mid-1970s, such incidents occurred on a daily basis and mostly in the Ballycolman and Head of the Town areas. Strabane was a stronghold of PIRA and, to a lesser extent, the INLA. The car was used to transport two bombs; one of which was left at the front of Stewarts' Supermarket in Railway Street in the town. The Provisionals had telephoned a warning through to the RUC but had failed to specify a place, and more importantly, a time. The device exploded without warning and a 74-year-old male shopper was badly injured in the blast. The area was immediately cordoned by Police and soldiers from the Staffordshire Regiment, and the second bomb was found nearby and defused. Ten days later, a dawn raid on the Drumrallugh netted a substantial find of explosives and weapons.

On the 17th, in a repeat of the attack on the Dublin–Belfast train in October 1978, the Provisionals bombed the Ballymena–Belfast train. It was carrying passengers between Ballymena railway station and Belfast Central station. The train had stopped at Dunmurry, having disembarked the bulk of its passengers and set off for Belfast. It had just entered the outskirts of Belfast, crossing under the M1 motorway on its way to Finaghy just before 1700 hours. Without warning, a massive explosion in the rear carriage sent a huge fireball throughout its length. Two members of a PIRA bombing team had been priming incendiary devices when one of the bombs exploded prematurely. Three men were killed instantly and a fourth dived from the train, on fire and other passengers desperately tried to beat out the flames.

The train was brought to an immediate standstill and shocked passengers leapt for their lives onto the tracks. Smoke and flames quickly spread through the remaining carriages. The survivors then moved down the track to safety while fast-arriving emergency services fought the blaze. After several hours and combined efforts from fire, Police and soldiers, the blaze was contained.

When the bomb exploded, there were only four passengers in the carriage, three of whom were killed instantly, with the other passenger previously mentioned being terribly injured. The three dead men were burned so badly that identification was impossible using conventional means. A senior Rail Executive described the bodies as 'three heaps of ashes'. Two of the dead were innocent civilians and the third was the IRA bomber himself; his fellow-terrorist was the man injured.

The dead civilians were Mark Cochrane (17), a keen and talented rugby player who was still at school in Lisburn, and Abayonni Max Olorenda (35), father of three children, from Nigeria but who had lived for 10 years in Finaghy, Belfast. The third dead man was one of the PIRA bombers – Kevin Delaney (26). The surviving bomber was Patrick Joseph Flynn who suffered very serious burns to his face, torso and legs, and was reported to be close to death upon arrival at the hospital. Five people were injured, including a fireman, two teenagers who were treated for minor injuries, and an older man who suffered much more serious burns.

After the blast, the Provisionals were forced to issue a grovelling apology and acknowledge responsibility. They apologised to those who were harmed and stated that it was 'grave and distressing' but an 'accident, caused by the war situation'.

The statement in full read:

The explosion occurred prematurely and the intended target was not the civilians travelling on the train. We always take the most stringent precautions to ensure the safety of all civilians in the vicinity of a military or commercial bombing operation. The bombing mission on Thursday night was not an exception to this principle. Unfortunately the unexpected is not something we can predict or prevent in the war situation this country is in, the consequences of the unexpected are often grave and distressing, as Thursday night's accident shows.

On the mainland, Conservative MP Winston Churchill called for the death penalty to be reinstated for terrorists as a result of this incident. The RUC responded to the IRA's announcement with a short statement stating:

The fact is that innocent people are dead and the Provisional IRA are responsible, as they have been on hundreds of other occasions. Once again they stand condemned in the eyes of the civilised world.

There was a postscript to the death of the bomber when his local Catholic church refused to allow his funeral to take place in West Belfast. Nevertheless, shots were later fired over his coffin and Sinn Féin attacked the Catholic Church for its 'duplicity and stark hypocrisy'. The Republicans would surely recognise those 'qualities' as they had themselves practised the same over the preceding 11 years. Soldiers made several arrests after shots were fired at the funeral which was eventually held at the terrorist's home near Springhill.

The day after the bombing, two further trains were bombed and on one of them, a passenger bravely picked up a suspicious package and hurled it through a window where it exploded harmlessly. The Provisionals in their obsessive quest to 'drive the British into the sea' displayed their usual tact and sensitivity. While one or more PIRA ASUs were bombing trains, another was in the process of a fatal attack on a Prison Officer (PO). Graham Cox (35), father of two, was attached to Magilligan Prison in County Londonderry. Like all other safety-aware officers, he tried to vary his route to and from the jail, but as in all cases, there were only a finite number of routes. He left work and headed for his home in Kilfennan in the late afternoon and, after dropping a colleague off, drove towards his house. However, somewhere near Stradreagh, as he negotiated a bend, armed men leapt from bushes and opened fire on his car with automatic weapons. He received multiple gunshot wounds and was probably dead before his car careered off the road and down a small hill. His body was not found until the following morning after an extensive search by the RUC and soldiers.

On the 18th, it was announced that part of the Divis complex was to be demolished and the families who lived there rehoused. The odd-shaped blocks which lay to the right of the main Divis Tower were known to soldiers as the 'Zanussi'. This was due to the white goods such as refrigerators, washing machines and the like which were hurled from the upper floors with the intention of killing or maiming soldiers and RUC officers. On the morning after a riot, the wrecked goods often resembled a 'Zanussi showroom'.

On Monday 21st, Mrs Anne Maguire was found dead in what was believed to be a case of suicide. She was the mother of the three children who had been killed in an incident on 10 August 1976 which led to the formation of the Peace People.[12] Having endured the type of pain which only a bereaved parent would understand and lived an empty life without her children, she could take no more. She slashed her wrists with an electric carving knife and bled to death. As *Lost Lives*[13] points out, her death is not recorded as Troubles-related. I do not agree with that assertion and have sadly included her name.

At the same time, one of the men accused of the La Mon Restaurant atrocity in February 1978[14] began a jail sentence in Northern Ireland. Edward Manning Brophy was found guilty of the murders and sentenced to life imprisonment. However, in a later appeal, the trial Judge at Belfast Crown Court, Mr Justice Basil Kelly, not believing the evidence of the police interrogators, held the Crown had not proved beyond reasonable doubt that the confessions were not induced by 'torture, or inhuman or degrading treatment' and accordingly the confessions were ruled inadmissible. Brophy was however sentenced to an additional 10 years in jail for membership of the IRA.

In the first court case, Brophy had refused to name the driver who had driven the bombing team to the La Mon because: "it would put life in danger." He declined to specify, however, to whose life he was referring. He allegedly told the Police that he had carried the La Mon bomb from its hiding place in a coal shed and instructed a young boy sitting in the back seat of the car stolen for the mission. He was also charged with 11 other bombings in various parts of Belfast on behalf of the IRA, as well as possession of an Armalite rifle, ammunition and explosives; one can see why he thought himself blameless! He also claimed during the initial court case that the IRA "were like the British Army, only better." He agreed that he had joined the IRA in 1971 and then, following a period of imprisonment, he had left; he further claimed that he was merely a Republican sympathiser!

In relation to his allegations of beatings at Castlereagh RUC Centre, the Crown Prosecutor Ronald Appleton, QC referring to Brophy's admitted inconsistencies during evidence, said: "These inconsistencies are there, I suggest, because the beatings just didn't happen." A doctor who examined the New Lodge man said that he was also unable to attach any substance to the defendant's claims of beatings.

THE MAN IN THE BATH
Dougie Durrant, Army Dog Handlers Unit

In 1979/80, the Duke of Wellington's Regiment was located in West Belfast. It was my turn to spend two weeks at Macrory Park just off the junction with the Whiterock and Falls Road. It was a typical Belfast Summer's day; the birds were singing and the smell of smoke was in the air. Just at that point, a large burst of gunfire was heard from the direction of the Falls/Whiterock Road junction no further than 100

---

12   See Wharton, *Wasted Years, Wasted Lives*, Vol 1.

13   McKitterick, David *et al.*, *Lost Lives: The stories of the men, women and children who died as a result of the Northern Ireland Troubles* (Edinburgh: Mainstream, 2000).

14   See Wharton, *Wasted Years, Wasted Lives*, Vol 2, Chapter 38.

metres from the camp gates. The QRF ran out the gate towards the incident. We knew then there was a man down; I had seen the patrol just leave the base.

I ran to the ops room, kit in hand with my search dog, Bluce, having heard the contact report asking for 'Groundhog' and 'Wagtail'. "I am ready to go, Sir," I said to the ops officer who at this point was very calm. The tracker dog team was located at Flax Street Mill comprising Lance Bombardier 'Moby' Dick and his black Labrador. A request was sent to 39 Brigade to get the dog on the ground, and, in the meantime I made my way with the QRF to the location on foot. They were just removing the casualty who I believed was fatally wounded. The firing point had been located across the road in a dental surgery, and the follow up action was ongoing. However, I knew that no one had been in the house due to the fear of booby traps. I made my way across the road and searched the front entrance of the building but found nothing. I then made my way around the back; Bluce went mad on a bin that was located near the rear of the premises. It was a large explosive device, and by now Moby had turned up and was being briefed by the commander, at the incident control point.

Moby got his dog ready and found a point of interest from where to start the track, and tracked from the back door to the main road just a short distance away. It seemed as if the gunman had had a getaway car ready. He then asked the commander if a vehicle had been taken from here during the incident. He replied in the affirmative and said that they had taken the owner's Volvo estate. Moby then informed the commander that if the car was found under no circumstances was he to let anyone near it; the commander alerted the ops room to the request.

A short time later we received information that the car had been found in the Turf Lodge area. We were on our way and, within 10 minutes we had located the vehicle. Moby then got his dog onto the track across the Turf Lodge back across the City Cemetery, across the Whiterock Road and into the Ballymurphy Estate. I said to him: "The fucker has done a 360." "I hope so," said Moby, and we began running at full pelt to find the shooter. The commander asked if we were sure that we had the right man, and Moby replied: "We will soon find out!"

We stopped at a front door, certain that the track had entered this house he told the commander, and we were ordered in. With this, the door was kicked in and we went straight up the stairs, and there in the bath was a man fully clothed and washing himself and his clothes, desperately trying to get rid of the forensics. Laid on the sink was a loaded AK47: "Ah, fuck," came the reply. He was taken away by the RUC and his house was ripped apart, looking for more evidence. It was an outstanding operation from start to finish with the commander on the ground putting his training into gear; that got the result. Moby was awarded 'Mentioned in Dispatches', which he deserved, but I felt very sad for the family for the loss of their son and a good soldier.

The soldier was Private Errol Lynford Pryce (21) from Sheffield, shot by an IRA sniper at St James Road, near the junction with the Falls Road. The killing, on 26 January 1980, took place after IRA members took a family hostage and opened fire from an upstairs window. He is buried at City Road Cemetery, Sheffield. His gravestone reads:

"Born Jamaica 10–6–1958. Killed in action Northern Ireland 26–1–1980. Gone from our home, but not from our hearts."

Two civilians were also injured as a result of the indiscriminate firing of an M60 machine gun by the terrorists. Afterwards, an unrepentant spokesman/apologist for Sinn Féin tried to blame soldiers for the wounding. I will not dignify their claims by commenting.

Also on the 26th, an armed PIRA gang hijacked a lorry in the Irish Republic belonging to Shamrock Foods of Dublin. It was packed with explosives and driven into the North. The crew abandoned the vehicle on the Newry–Dundalk Road, leaving a potentially lethal headache for the SF. The bombing team had packed six milk churns with around 600 lbs (273 kg) of explosives. The driver of the lorry was brought in and he immediately noticed that a new aerial had been fitted. Closer inspection showed that there was wiring leading from the new aerial to the driver's cab. ATO, supported by elements of the Welsh Guards sealed off the lorry and began what turned out to be a seven-hour operation to make the bombs – hidden behind cases of cereal – safe enough to remove. The ATO officer, Lieutenant-Colonel Peter Foreshaw said: "To have found and neutralised a bomb of this type and size was a major triumph for all concerned."

On the 29th, Giuseppe Conlon, father of Gerry Conlon who had been wrongly convicted of the Guildford pub bombings in 1975, died in prison. Giuseppe, like his son, was innocent and it was a major miscarriage of British justice. In December 1979, Mr Conlon's health (he had a chronic chest condition) became so poor that he had to be moved from Wormwood Scrubs prison in London to the nearby Hammersmith Hospital. Just over a week later he was returned to prison where he died, shortly after his return. I believe that his death was very much Troubles-related and consequently, he is included in the sad toll of lost lives.

The first month of the new decade – the third of the Troubles – came to an end and a total of 19 people had died in or as a consequence of the madness which was gripping the Province. Seven soldiers – including one former soldier – were killed; five at the hands of the IRA. Two RUC officers and one PO were killed, all by the Provisionals. This month, eight civilians lost their lives, two of these in overtly sectarian killings, and one Republican paramilitary was killed in an 'own goal' explosion.

2

February

This was a month in which 13 people would die – six of them soldiers and two policemen – but it would witness the first murder of a British soldier in mainland Europe by the IRA. The UVF (Ulster Volunteer Force) would also emerge from the shadows after months of inactivity and commit several sectarian murders.

On the 2nd, in what was some sort of tragic cross between a sectarian murder and a case of mistaken identity, a man was murdered by the UVF and in the process five children were left fatherless. William McAteer (50) was walking with a friend in the Lower Ormeau area of South Belfast. As the two men walked towards Rugby Avenue, they were confronted by several armed masked men and, realising that their lives were in danger, ran off. However, the gunmen – from the UVF – fired several shots at Mr McAteer and mortally wounded him. As he fell to the ground, the gunmen escaped in a waiting car. A spokesman for 'Captain Black' of the UVF announced blandly that they had shot the wrong man and claimed that the one who escaped was a Republican and the actual target; no apologies were made to the grieving family of the dead man.

On the same day as the Lower Ormeau killing, the Provisionals targeted an off-duty UDR soldier at his home in Lisnaskea, County Fermanagh. He was shot and very seriously wounded close to his home outside the town. The ambush took place as he drove home from work and the shock caused his wife who was eight months pregnant to lose their baby. This author understands that he later recovered after months of pain. The next day, the Royal Engineers lost the first of three of their soldiers who would die in February. Sapper Fraser Jones (21) from Weald in Kent died in 'circumstances unknown' while serving at HM Prison, Maze. Sources close to the RE say that he was killed in an 'accident'. The author is aware of the nature of this soldier's death, but there is nothing official other than his date of birth, service number and the location of his funeral; Church of St Georges, Weald, Kent.

On the 5th, masked PIRA terrorists struck in a remote area of Kinawley, County Fermanagh, killing a part-time UDR soldier. The assassins chose their target because of the remoteness of the farmland on which he worked and it is not certain at what time of day he was killed. Corporal Aubrey Abercrombie (44), father of five, was a farmer when he wasn't wearing the uniform of the UDR. When he failed to return home from the fields, worried family members called in the Security Forces who went searching for him. His lifeless body was found slumped over the steering wheel of his tractor; he had been shot several times in the head. The murder took place at Florencecourt and with the Irish border just a few miles away, it had been easy for his murderers to make good their escape. Although the body was discovered in the late evening, it could not be removed until dawn as there was a real fear the terrorists might have planted booby traps.

AUBREY ABERCROMBIE
Mark Shaw, ADU

I can remember getting crashed out from Omagh to this incident and on arrival I was given a rundown from the troops on the ground. I set my dog off to pick up the track, if any existed. I was so close to this body slumped over the tractor and I can remember thinking what sort of people can do this to a man going about his work? There was a track, but alas only a short one as the PIRA ASU got away by car. Not long after this, my time in Ulster was up along with my time in the Army, but it has remained with me all these years the waste of life and to what end?

At the Corporal's funeral, the Reverend George Good spoke the words which many people around the world – other than Irish-Americans – must have thought about on many occasions:

> I am an Irishman and I love my country and I used to be very proud to be an Irishman. But I spent nearly half of the 1970s in Sri Lanka and as I listened to people in that far-away country talking about the wickedness of the deeds of violence which they read about taking place in Ireland, I had to hang my head in shame.

He condemned them for their awful acts of meaningless violence and said that he was disgusted that they claimed to carry out the murder of Corporal Abercrombie in the name of Ireland. He continued: "Men made in the image of God could not behave in that sort of way and get away with it, even from their own consciences." But much more certain was the fact they would have to face God, and his prayer for them was that they would realise the wickedness of their ways. The soldier was buried with full military honours at Druminiskill.

At approximately the same time that the killing of the UDR soldier was taking place, the Londonderry IRA made several bomb attacks in the city. Three incendiary devices were planted at a post office in Water Street on the west bank of the Foyle. The devices were hung from security grills over the post office window and were noticed by soldiers from the Staffordshire Regiment. The area was being policed by the Royal Regiment of Fusiliers and together with ATO (Army Technician Officers, Bomb Disposal) and the Fire Brigade ensured that damage from the explosions was kept to a minimum.

On the 7th, masked UVF gunmen, driving around the New Lodge area of Belfast, clearly seeking 'targets of opportunity' chanced upon two Catholic teenagers who were attempting to repair a car on waste ground. In what was a blatantly sectarian attack as neither boy was connected with paramilitary forces, they opened fire. On this occasion the shots missed, and the car sped away to a nearby Loyalist area.

On the 9th, a wealthy Jewish businessman was kidnapped from his home in Thornhill, just off the Malone Road, South Belfast, and taken to a staunchly Republican area. The kidnappers of Leonard Kaitcer (50) demanded a ransom of one million pounds and gave his family details of where to take the money. His two adult sons were ordered to take the money to a pub in Newry. However, the kidnappers failed to keep the rendez-vous and the following day, Mr Kaitcer's body was found in Glen Road, Andersonstown; he had been shot dead. It is thought that his kidnappers were either PIRA or INLA, and they had panicked and killed him. His killers were never found. The RUC issued a warning to all wealthy businessmen to be extra-vigilant in view of the re-emergence of this tactic. After a post-mortem, the bullets taken from Mr Kaitcer's body showed that the gun used to kill him had been used in two previous murders by the Provisionals.

The following day, a young child was killed due to the irresponsibility of rioters, intent on attacking the Army. The loss of the child – Hugh Maguire (9) – was tragic and it is morally wrong that his life was cut short, but Republicans attempted to make political capital from the tragedy. Clearly nothing was sacred to these people as the Godfathers of the IRA tried to exploit the death. The young boy was standing close to a Saracen armoured vehicle when a metal bar thrown by a rioter hit him on the head, fracturing his skull, and mortally injuring him. At an inquest some time later, the IRA wheeled out witnesses who swore blind that the Saracen deliberately mounted the pavement and mowed young Hugh down. Following a post-mortem by State pathologists, the Coroner showed how the injuries were consistent with being hit by a metal bar and the 'eye witnesses' were denounced as liars.

At the same time, there was a lucky escape for a female UDR soldier – a 'Greenfinch' – when PIRA gunmen set up an ambush outside her parents' home in rural County Tyrone. The unnamed woman had joined the UDR in 1978 following the murder of her boyfriend Private Alan Ferguson by the Provisionals at Scribbagh on 25 June, 1978[1]. PIRA INT had determined that her UDR father lived at the house and accordingly laid a trap for him. Three men drove up to the house and opened up the bonnet in order to give the impression that it had broken down. Two others stood next to the car as though watching the 'repairs' as the third man fiddled about with the engine. The Greenfinch and her mother walked out of their house to see if they could help, whereupon, the men produced weapons and opened fire. The female soldier was hit in the leg and barely managed to retreat inside the house. At this stage, after closing the bonnet, the gunmen raced away to the safety of the Irish border.

On the 11th, two more policemen and an innocent bystander were killed, this time on a rural road in County Fermanagh, again by a PIRA culvert bomb. For the uninitiated, a culvert is a drain or pipe that allows water to flow under a road, or similar obstruction. Culverts differ from bridges mainly in size and construction, and are generally concrete in construction. A two-vehicle RUC patrol was driving along the Roslea to Lisnaskea Road close to the Irish border when it passed over a culvert overlooked by high ground inside the Republic. A device estimated at 800 lbs (364 kgs) exploded and the police Land Rover was destroyed by the blast; two officers inside were killed instantly. The men were Constable Winston Howe (35), father of two, and Constable Joseph Rose (21). According to reports in the following day's edition of the *Belfast Telegraph*, Constable Rose had only just been transferred to the village from Enniskillen. In a report titled 'Transfer to Death for RUC Victim' it described how the deaths were the third in a week following the murder of UDR soldier, Corporal Abercrombie and another explosion at nearby Florencourt which injured a UDR soldier. A local Church of Ireland official, Edwin Kille told afterwards how he "heard a dull thud" and "felt the house shake." He continued to say that he "felt sick as it was only too obvious that evil had been done."

---

1   See Wharton, Ken M., *Wasted Years, Wasted Lives* (Solihull: Helion, 2014), Chapter 42.

In that same explosion RUCR officer Ernest Johnston was injured; he would be killed by the Provisionals in September of this year.[2] Mrs Sylvia Crowe (32) – a Protestant – a missionary on holiday from Belfast was killed instantly as she stood at a bus stop very close to the explosion. She was in a group which included her mother as well as a local brother and sister; all three were badly injured. Local Councillor Bert Johnston called for the resignation of the Northern Ireland Secretary, stating:

Does your position as Secretary of State, your political expediency, the interests of your respective political party and the Government mean more to you than the apprehension of murders of innocent men, women and children in Northern Ireland? If this is the case … I call upon you to resign immediately so that you may be no longer party to a lamentable and hypocritical Government security policy which has brought heartache and untold misery to thousands of law-abiding Ulster citizens.

Ian Paisley also demanded immediate action from both the Secretary of State and from Margaret Thatcher.

The morally bankrupt 'policy' of tit for tat was bound to raise its ugly head again following the murder of the two Protestant officers and a Protestant woman and it would be less than 72 hours before retribution killings began. In the process, it would leave seven children without a father. John Morrow (37), father of seven, had been drinking in a Catholic pub in Lower Ormeau in South Belfast. He made the fatal mistake of cutting through an alleyway between Hatfield Street and Farnham Street. As he did so, a UFF gunman stepped from the shadows and shot him three times in the head from close range. The killing was probably random, and the gunman – or gunmen – would have known that anyone who approached them in that part of Belfast would have almost certainly been a Catholic. Mr Morrow had no Republican or paramilitary connections and his senseless murder by a depraved Loyalist murder gang deprived seven children of their father.

On the 15th, there was an incredibly lucky escape for a soldier working on an outside project within the Fort Whiterock base. The soldier – thought to have been a Sapper from the Royal Engineers – was working on the giant radio mast and, as he had been up the 70-foot high structure for some time, he had been dicked and a PIRA ASU had been summoned in order to carry out a 'shoot'. A gang of up to four armed men took over a house at Divismore Crescent in the north-western sector of the Ballymurphy Estate. The family, consisting of a man and wife and their nine-year-old daughter, were kept hostage in one room at gunpoint while the actual sniper prepared to fire into the camp. Although held at gunpoint, it is somewhat of a moot point as no-one at that time on that estate would have dared to confront or resist the 'RA' for fear of instant and bloody retribution. At least four shots were fired from the family's bedroom window, before the weapon was disassembled and the gang melted into the labyrinthine hotbed of Republicanism.

The soldier was hit once – in the abdomen – but managed to remain conscious and slithered down the mast to the safety of the ground from where he was rushed to hospital. He recovered after medical treatment; a very lucky escape from what was a well-executed though nonetheless spontaneous operation by the local Provisionals. Within hours of the shooting in an unrelated incident, Loyalist gunmen tricked an unsuspecting Catholic

---

2   See Chapter 9 of this book.

man into giving them a lift. They claimed to be Catholics and lived in the Catholic Andersonstown area. However, as the driver stopped at Tullymore Drive, the pair shot the 'good Samaritan' several times before running off; he later recovered in hospital.

The British Army of the Rhine (BAOR) was stationed in camps throughout the British sector of West Germany and was regarded as a 'plum' posting for many of its soldiers. It was certainly considered a bit of a haven for those returning from tours of Northern Ireland. The 2nd British Army on the Rhine was formed on 25 August 1945 from 21st Army Group. Its original function was to control the corps districts which were running the military government of the British zone of occupied Germany. After the assumption of government by civilians, it became the command formation for the British troops only, rather than being responsible for administration as well. On the night of the 16th, the Provisionals made a move which meant that West Germany was no longer a haven of any sort for British soldiers and would lead ultimately to the deaths of 12 British and Commonwealth citizens. Their 'European ASU' killed in West Germany, Holland and Belgium; four soldiers, four RAF personnel and two Army family members, including a small baby were murdered by PIRA. Included in this sad total were the deaths of two Australian civilians on holiday who were mistaken for off-duty British soldiers. Additionally, the British Ambassador to The Hague and his Dutch chauffeur were also murdered in 1979.

Bielefeld is a city in the Ostwestfalen-Lippe Region in the north-east of North-Rhine Westphalia, Germany, with a population of 323,000. It was of strategic importance in NATO defence plans, lying as it did on one of the proposed main axis of the Soviet 3rd Shock Army. Over the years of the Soviet threat, it has housed 1st, 7th ('Desert Rats') and 20th Armoured Brigades as well as Logistical units. In February 1980, one of the units based there was the Royal Engineers. Colonel Mark Coe (44), father of six children, was one of the most senior officers in the Bielefeld area. On that fateful night – February 16th – he had just returned to his Married Soldiers' Quarters (MSQ) and was about to garage his car when he was approached by a man and a woman. The Provisionals had links with the *Rote Armee Fraktion* (Red Army Faction), also known as the Baader-Meinhof Gang, a West German terrorist group. The terrorist organisation described itself as a "communist and anti-imperialist urban guerrilla group engaged in armed resistance against a fascist state." It is highly likely that it had sympathisers working inside the vast army of West German civvies who helped operate the BAOR barracks and as such, had a ready source of information about who lived where. The fact that they went directly to a senior officer's MSQ bears this out.

The man and the woman drew pistols and shot the Colonel down in cold blood; he died shortly afterwards. His murderers – part of PIRA's European ASU – made good their escape. The ASU moved onto the town of Munster and just two weeks later shot and critically wounded an RMP soldier. This will be dealt with in the next chapter.

THE THREAT IN GERMANY
Mark 'C', UDR and Royal Artillery

When I was first posted to what was then West Germany in 1977, a lot of the camps were practically open to the public, with little visible security, no armed guards and very few checks. However, this was to change by the late 70s, as around 1979 and well into the 1980s the Provos started attacking service personnel in and around Army bases in Germany; this would leave around eight people dead including women and children of servicemen.

I noticed a big change in security when we returned to Paderborn in January 1980 after a four-month tour of Belfast. There had been shootings at Bielefeld and Dortmund and soon after it was our turn. On one particular day, a car drove up to the front of the camp and gunmen fired several bursts of automatic fire at our Guardroom. Luckily no one was killed or injured, but it was a bit of wake up call. Security was immediately stepped up; sand bags placed around the windows of the Guardroom, gates kept shut, IDs checked and arms issued. Initially they were unloaded but as the alert status went up – Bikini Black was the highest – then we were issued with live rounds. We also set up VCPs on the road leading to the camp and did foot patrols around the perimeter, again with unloaded weapons; I think it was to show what we could do instead of a proper deterrent.

At this time I and a few others were given, what on reflection was a very foolhardy task, to check on the security of the Tank Regiment which shared our camp. Only the respective Cos and a selected few knew what was going on. We had to make up dummy bombs using candles, wire, batteries etc., and then stage a mock raid which involved climbing over the fence at some point. I choose a section near the back gate where new pads houses were being built as it had more cover. We planted these devices at the Officers' Mess and I even went right to the top floor of RHQ and put one there. We did it all successfully and climbed back over the fence and a waiting car supplied by own of the boys drove us back into the camp.

Thinking about it now, though it may have been an exercise, given the security climate that prevailed at that time, it was maybe a stupid thing to be ordered to do. God knows what would have happened if we had been spotted; the least we would have got would have been a good kicking; at worst, we might have been shot! Anyway I thought life in Germany changed a bit in those days, never the big security threat of NI or anything but you did have to watch who you talked to in bars (the author has covered this slightly in previous books) and when you travelled about, but the threat was real and the families of the dead can confirm that sadly.

CHATTING TO NORAID?

MARCUS TOWNLEY, WELSH GUARDS

This tale begins while stationed in Germany; at the time I was posted away from my Battalion, in Bavaria, the US sector of West Germany at the time. I was taking part in the NATO Small Arms trial testing the SA80 – which would eventually replace the SLR – as well as other weapons from several NATO Armies. One Friday night, myself and three others were enjoying a beer in one of the local bars, and being squaddies our behaviour was a tad shocking. We noticed a group of three on the next table: two male one female, and we started to make crude remarks thinking they did not understand English. The young woman in the group asked in an Irish accent "What part of Wales do you four come from?" Shocked, we apologised for our behaviour, and continued the conversation, with the girl doing most of the talking. Something clicked in my mind enough to sober me up a little, and be on my guard. She asked us what we were doing in the American zone of Germany. We replied we were on an exchange trip.

After a minute or two, I asked the trio what they were doing so far from home; reply came back that they were selling stainless steel cutlery. We then left to carry on with our task of drinking beer and chasing German Frauleins. The following day we went to Schweinfurt PX to do our dhobi and hang out; lo and behold we bumped into the Irish trio. After a brief hello we went on our way but strangely, they scarpered rather sharpish, never to be seen again.

I mentioned this to the OC commanding the Brits and he asked me if I could remember much about them, but all I could remember was the blonde Irish woman. To be honest it escaped my mind, until I started to read your books, and the name NORAID (Northern Irish Aid) popped up. I am now mortified that at the time I did not say anything, because I am sure they were NORAID who were trawling American Bases in Germany to raise funds for the 'cause'.

A mere two days later, two more soldiers were killed in Northern Ireland in what was a tragic accident close to the HQNI town of Lisburn. An Aérospatiale SA 341B Gazelle AH1 on a routine flight and carrying several soldiers crashed into high tension electricity cables at White Hill Mountain in Co Antrim. Two soldiers were killed instantly; they were Lance Corporal Robin Lister (22) from Colchester, the Royal Corps of Signals and Acting Sergeant Kenneth Robson (27), Royal Engineers. Several other soldiers were injured in the accident. Sergeant Robson was the third Royal Engineer to die this month.

The day after the accident, the Provisionals admitted that they had murdered Colonel Coe and their pathetic attempt at justifying the cold-blooded murder of an off-duty and unarmed soldier, away from Northern Ireland was that he had served in the Province in 1972! They admitted the murder of the British Ambassador Sykes in Holland in 1979. A spokesman said: "Colonel Coe was executed for being a British soldier and senior administrator of an Army which is engaged in oppressing the Nationalist people in the occupied Six Counties." Such romantic rhetoric was employed by the terror group when it felt necessary to justify their cowardly actions as well as impress their bank-rollers on the eastern seaboard of the USA. They further warned that the Colonel's murder would not be the last and, as we shall see in the following chapter, they made every effort to back up that threat with another attack, this time in Munster.

In Londonderry, the Army finally moved out of Creggan Camp on the notorious Republican Creggan housing estate. Immediately they pulled out, a Royal Engineers demolition squad – under the protective eye of other soldiers – demolished the site. The camp was built on the high ground which dominates the south-eastern section of the city; the same high ground was an excellent vantage point to watch over the volatile estate where some 20 members of the SF were killed over the years.

On the 28th, UDR Woman Private Mary Elizabeth Karen Cochrane (19) was killed in a tragic RTA in the Province. The author understands that the young Greenfinch was on duty at the time.

On the 29th of the month – February 1980 was a Leap Year – the deadly game of tit for tat continued and the UVF murdered another Catholic. Brendan McLaughlin (35), father of three, worked for the Housing Executive in Belfast. It is thought likely that someone from his own office revealed the fact that he was a Catholic to the Loyalist paramilitaries from something as prosaic as a job application form and this sealed his murder. In the early evening, as he stood talking to other men – including a Sinn Féin representative whom it was thought might have been the target – in Clonard Gardens, a stolen van pulled up. Two masked men got out of the van and opened fire at the men and Mr McLaughlin fell dying from several wounds. The gunmen escaped, although one of them was later caught and jailed for life.

February ended with 13 deaths; six of these were soldiers and two were policemen. Additionally, five civilians died, of whom four were Catholics and three of these were overtly sectarian murders. The Provisionals killed five, and Loyalist paramilitaries killed three.

3

March

This month saw the deaths of another six soldiers (including an Airman), or former soldiers – three at the hands of the Provisionals – and two civilians. Deaths due to terrorist activity were 'only' four during this period. March also witnessed the death of another joyrider following the killing of Doreen McGuinness in January.

On the 2nd, the IRA's European ASU struck again, this time at Munster some 30 miles away from where Colonel Coe had been murdered. It is in the northern part of the state and is considered to be the cultural centre of the Westphalia region. It is also the capital of the local government region Munsterland. A 22-year-old Corporal in the Royal Military Police (RMP) was driving through the outskirts of the German city, in the company of another RMP NCO on a routine patrol. It was a Saturday evening and the men were trawling the soldiers' popular drinking haunts on the lookout for fights between units and fights with the local West German youth. As they neared a corner, two armed men – belonging to the IRA – opened fire and both soldiers were wounded. The would-be killers ran off, leaving 22-year-old Corporal Stewart Leach fighting for his life; fortunately, he later made a full recovery.

Both the British and the West German authorities were reluctant to admit that the Provisional IRA was operating in mainland Europe, but an announcement from PIRA made it clear that a new and deadly campaign was under way. It also became clear that German sympathisers – as stated in the previous chapter – were providing the ASU not only with information on camp layouts and soldiers' off-duty habits but also with 'safe houses'. Earlier that day, a Sinn Féin-organised demonstration in West Belfast had degenerated into severe rioting and five members of the RUC and four soldiers were all badly injured. Among the civilians injured was a local 9-year-old boy who was caught up in the crush. There were scores of arrests made.

Tomás Ó Fiaich, then Catholic Primate of Ireland, and Edward Daly, then Bishop of Londonderry, held a meeting with Humphrey Atkins, Secretary of State for Northern Ireland, to express their concerns about conditions within the Maze Prison. A former chairman of the Peace People, Peter McLachlan, resigned from the organisation. Twenty days later, the British Government made an announcement following on from this meeting which would have fatal consequences for many people.

On 6 March, the IRA targeted a former UDR soldier Henry Livingstone (38) who had left the Regiment three months earlier in order to concentrate on his farm, which was located at Cortynan, County Armagh. He lived with his widowed mother in the tiny hamlet of Tynan and farmed the land very close by, approximately half a mile from the border with the Republic. On the night in question, he had gone to the farm to meet his cattle, but PIRA gunmen, knowing of his habits were lying in wait. As he approached a shed, at least two gunmen fired at him and he slumped to the ground, wounded. As he lay helpless, they stood over him and fired a burst of automatic fire into his body; he died instantly. He was the second UDR or former UDR soldier to be murdered in the immediate neighbourhood, as Thomas Armstrong was killed nearby by the IRA in April, 1979.[1]

The King's Own Royal Border Regiment (KORBR) was only formed in 1959 as an amalgamation between two regiments of the line, including the Border Regiment who fought with such distinction at Arnhem in 1944. However, their earliest forebears were the 4th, or Kings Own Regiment of Foot, formed in 1680 as the 2nd Tangier Regiment; the fourth Foot regiment in seniority in the British Army. Its motto is *'Nec Aspera Terrent'*(Difficulties be damned). During the Troubles, it lost 10 of its soldiers; in March 1980, it lost three men in just 10 days on its Crossmaglen tour.

On the 7th, a KORBR foot patrol was passing through Crossmaglen, en-route for the RUC base and had just entered North Street. The patrol was passing several parked cars when, without warning, a Ford Cortina exploded. Private Seán Walker (18), a Morecambe lad, took the full brunt and was mortally wounded. There were some other injuries, but Private Walker was in a terrible state and required immediate 'casualty evacuation'. There were too many telephone wires in the vicinity, so the Royal Engineers hacked them down in order to allow the Army helicopter to land. He was rushed to Belfast where his injuries were found too serious to treat and consequently was flown to England in order to be treated at the Woolwich Military Hospital in London. Surrounded by family, he succumbed to his terrible injuries on the 21st, some two weeks after the explosion. Seán George Walker had only just turned 18 on 16 February, less than three weeks before he was fatally injured. He had been in Northern Ireland for only nine days before the explosion.

Also on the 7th, the INLA ventured back onto the English mainland for the first time since the murder of Airey Neave, MP, in the House of Commons car park in March of the previous year. Several devices were smuggled into the School of Infantry Weapons Support Wing at Warminster, Salisbury Plain. The explosions caused some damage, but there were no injuries. The attack prompted PIRA to warn that they too, were likely to attack on English soil very soon.

NEGLIGENT DISCHARGES

This author was once told by his lecturer at the University of Warwick that using a dictionary definition was an unsafe method of beginning an essay. However unsafe this may be, this section will commence with such a definition as it illustrates clearly the literal meaning of the term 'negligent discharge'.

> A negligent discharge (ND) is a discharge of a firearm involving culpable carelessness. In judicial and military technical terms, a negligent discharge is a chargeable offence. A number of armed forces automatically consider any accidental discharge

---

1   See Wharton, Ken M., *Wasted Years, Wasted Lives* (Solihull: Helion, 2014), Chapter 52.

to be negligent discharge, under the assumption that a trained soldier has control of his firearm at all times; this is the case in the British Army.

In cold, calculated English the term implies carelessness or involuntary action and yet in human terms it can and does mean so much more. Take the case of the deaths of Tommy Stoker, Light Infantry (19/9/1972) Herbert Shingleston, King's Own Scottish Borderers (25/11/1976), David Forman, Parachute Regiment (14/4/1973) or Owen Pavey, King's Own Border Regiment (11/3/1980). These were just four of the unacceptably high toll of ND deaths which occurred in Northern Ireland during the Troubles. We shall deal with the tragic ND death of Private Pavey (19) a Barnsley boy in due course, but the following anonymous piece makes for grim reading. The contributor is no longer a serving officer but wishes neither his name nor his regiment to be mentioned; I will not only respect and honour his wishes, but further, nothing would ever compel me to reveal the name of this very trusted source.

On the 11th, as a foot patrol of the KORBR prepared to leave its base in Crossmaglen, one of those aforementioned negligent discharges occurred and it led to the death of Private Owen Christopher Pavey (19). From an impeccable source, the author understands that there was a little good-natured horseplay in the exit to the base as the soldiers prepared to go out on duty. At this stage, although terribly wounded, Private Walker was still alive, although it was only four days since the explosion. There was naturally some tension in the air and possibly it was this that led to some horseplay in order to reduce it. The soldier immediately behind Private Pavey was tasked with carrying the LMG (Light Machine Gun) of which each four-man brick had one, and Private Pavey playfully pulled the LMG towards himself. It would then appear that the LMG carrier accidentally discharged a single round into Pavey's face, entering just below his eye and he slumped to the ground, mortally wounded. It may be said that it was a sort of miracle that only one round was discharged, because had the weapon been set on automatic fire, a burst of rounds being fired in the narrow confines of the exit might have killed or injured more soldiers.

Private Pavey was a Barnsley boy and his funeral was held at a cemetery in the centre of the town close to the General Hospital. There was a very sad postscript to the death, when it was revealed that the soldier and his father were estranged and Mr Pavey did not attend his son's funeral.

On the same day as the accidental but avoidable death of Private Pavey, another chapter in the tragic history of the Troubles was closed with the discovery of one of its earlier victims. The following is reprinted from an earlier book by the same author:

Thomas Niedermayer was a German industrialist who ran the Grundig plant at Dunmurry, in the western part of Belfast. He was a man not only prepared to try and bring economic prosperity to war-torn Belfast but also served as the honorary consul to Northern Ireland. Niedermayer was abducted on 27 December 1973 at around 11.00 pm, by two men who lured him outside his house on the pretext that they had crashed into his car. The incident was witnessed by his 15-year-old daughter Renate who had answered the door to the kidnappers and by a neighbour who worked at the Grundig factory. Niedermayer was never seen alive again and it would be over six years before a breakthrough in the investigation of his disappearance led to the recovery of his body. The investigation revealed that he had been pistol-whipped and then buried face down in a shallow grave under a rubbish dump at Colin Glen.[2]

Niedermayer's remains were found when an excavator was tasked by Belfast City Council to clean up an unauthorised dump.

On the 12 March, the Royal Air Force (RAF) lost one of its Airmen when SAC Stephen Henseler (23) was killed in an RTA close to Ballykelly, Co Londonderry; he was from Kent. His was the first RAF death in the Province for nine years. In all, the RAF – whose motto is '*Per Ardua ad Astra*' [through difficulty to the stars] – and the RAF Regiment lost 13 men during the Troubles.

There was more sorrow for the KORBR on the 15th when it suffered its second fatality in four days and a third member of the Regiment would die just six days later. Around 1430 hours a foot patrol was on Newry Road, Crossmaglen close to Fairy Glen when an IRA sniper concealed in the walls of St Patrick's Catholic Cemetery opened fire and killed Private John Birkbeck Bateman (18). The sniper waited until Private Bateman's back was towards him and fired a single shot which mortally wounded him. He died shortly afterwards before he could be 'casualty evacuated'. He was a Cumbria boy from the village of Upperby and he is buried in the village cemetery there.

CROSSMAGLEN, 1980
Major Andrew Macdonald, 1 King's Own Border

XMG is the soldiers' abbreviation for Crossmaglen – arguably this was the most dangerous part of Northern Ireland in which to serve. XMG is a small town situated in so called 'Bandit Country' of South Armagh. During the 70s and through to the 90s, it featured in the many very serious incidents involving death and wounding of soldiers and members of the Security Forces. It had a fearsome reputation and a four-month tour there was a time you'd remember. It has to be said that the current tours in Afghanistan and Baghdad (longer and in worse conditions) are considerably harder, I believe.

My job as a young 28-year-old Company Commander (rank of Major) was to run the base and all the attendant operations for the four-month tour. We had 120 men under or command and a 25 km border with the Irish Republic into where we were not allowed to pursue fleeing terrorists. The base was heavily fortified, including from the threat of mortars. There was no vehicle movement – everything went in and out by helicopter – and patrolling in the town of XMG was highly dangerous especially as it had six exit roads, three leading directly to the border less than three to five miles away.

Every unit that occupied XMG for a tour knew that it faced a major challenge. While the task was technically 'to support the civil power', there was no civil power activity – so much of the job was about staying alive and taking the fight to the enemy who were, in the main, smugglers and gangsters taking advantage of the lawless nature of the area to benefit from scams that took advantage

---

2   Wharton, Ken M., *Sir, They're Taking the Kids Indoors,* (Solihull: Helion, 2011), Chapter 52.

of EU regulations (cross border agricultural carousel crime, fuel scams etc.) Police and customs activity was sporadic and had to be supported by large numbers of Army in support.

In a four-month tour there is not enough time to put in place a strategy but long enough to get hit badly by the enemy as soon as they recognise your weaknesses. And if they don't get you, they get the next lot. You had to be both defensive and offensive. But without intelligence, going onto the offensive is pointless work and the British have been good at Counter-insurgency because they've paid careful attention to his aspect. The problem as always was shortage of real intelligence.

We had an intelligence section that was not hugely effective; the Special Branch and SAS operations were based on specific high-level intelligence that was their preserve. In the middle there was nothing. However, on the morning of 15 March, we took our second fatal casualty and I decided to act decisively – I had all the intelligence I needed now. The shooting was from a churchyard and the escape was straight across the border – they'd have been drinking and laughing in a pub in Dundalk within 30 minutes. So, we went onto the offensive.

The Concession Road ran across our territory. This was a road that cut across the bottom end of the County of South Armagh thus providing a short cut for motorists travelling from Monaghan to Dundalk (this, a staunchly Republican town where the Mountbatten murderers planned their operation). Control of the Concession Road's two unmanned crossing points (designated H29 and H31) was something of a right that the local PIRA organisation felt that they had; they seemed to be free to mount illegal check points whenever they liked and then melt way across the border. To deny this 'short cut' would have been hugely inconvenient and would also demonstrate that PIRA were not in charge. This we did, but it gets better.

They became angry that we controlled 'their area' and began to attack our check points which were well dug in with machine gun support (yes, this was technically the UK). After skirmishes, they gave up trying. We then moved up a gear by putting 'weak' forces on the ground to draw them out. Behind these weak positions were concealed reinforcements and reaction forces. On one particular occasion, a large party of gunmen attacked a disused farm which we'd occupied but unknown to them we'd concealed a heavy machine gun post (GPMG SF) on the hill overlooking the farm under cover of darkness the night before. The fire-fight lasted for 30 minutes and I had to re-supply the position at dusk with additional ammunition by helicopter (scary but fun). We don't know how many we killed as you cannot pursue over the border for fear of creating an international incident through the incursion. There were several incidents like this when we were establishing control of the Concession Road and they were all one-sided affairs. After the big one, but they never attacked us again.

When it was time to handover to the next company coming in – traditionally the most dangerous part of a tour – we secured reinforcements and created a ring of fortifications around XMG effectively controlling every road in and out of the town. We called this 'Strongpoint'. For the first time in years, we were able to patrol in the town in safety and allow the police to arrest car tax dodgers, collect unpaid fines and go about the normal duties of the civil power. We left with no further incidents.

We felt that we settled some of the outstanding imbalance on the account for the two young soldiers we'd lost even if we didn't actually collect the skulls of those who had been shooting and bombing us. Knowing we'd taken it to the enemy was the most important bit for the soldiers who'd worked hard to do their duty unquestioningly. I established for future commanders in XMG several important operating lessons and tactics. We were able to feed back into the pre-tour training organisation additional experience and realistic lessons not previously taught to incoming units. Several of my soldiers were decorated for their courage – and most of them went there as boys but came back as men.

I learnt that it's easy when it's going well – the important bit about leadership and management is what you do when the shit hits the fan and people look at you to stand up and deliver. None of this mentions the role the soldiers, NCOs and young officers played in helping me as commander to recover from the early setbacks on that tour. I include in this the CO who was 100 per cent supportive throughout. They were outstanding.

On the 18th, a UVF murder squad attacked a Catholic business premises in St Peter's Hill and shot the manager seven times; the gang escaped towards the nearby Shankill Road. He fortunately recovered, however, his friend Elsie Claire (56) collapsed and died from a heart attack upon hearing the news. The following day Lance Corporal Andrew Snell (18) of the Royal Army Pay Corps died of his injuries after being accidentally shot. He was attached to the McRory Park base in West Belfast and died shortly afterwards in the Military Wing of the Musgrave Park Hospital. The author was informed of the nature of his shooting and has decided not to make public any of the tragic details. He was buried in Aldershot Military Cemetery; he was 12 days short of his 19th birthday.

On the 21st, the same day as the mortally wounded Private Walker of the KORBR died of his terrible injuries, the SF closed several rural roads which criss-crossed the border with the Irish Republic in Co Fermanagh. The actual border is extremely porous and, in only a handful of cases were HM Customs points manned. In the County Londonderry, County Fermanagh, County Tyrone and County Armagh areas, scores of terrorists had carried out hit-and-run murders before scuttling across these rural rat-runs into the sanctuary of the Republic. In a five-day operation over 100 soldiers and RUC officers had blocked some of these roads with four-foot high steel containers filled with concrete. In the past, Royal Engineers' demolition squads had blown craters in the roads only for farmers sympathetic to PIRA to come along and bulldoze rubble into the craters and make them passable again.

Two days later at one of the manned crossing points at Newry, Co Down on the main Dublin Road another PIRA 'own goal' explosion occurred. In this instance, the hapless bomber – Robert Carr – succeeded in fatally injuring himself as his bomb exploded en-route to the customs point. The badly injured PIRA was smuggled back across the border by his cronies and he was taken to hospital in County Louth. He died just over a week later.

On the 26th, in what is widely regarded as the most significant precursor of the 1980–1981 hunger strikes, the British Government of Margaret Thatcher announced that jailed terrorists in Northern Ireland would no longer be afforded the special category 'Political' status. However, at the same time, some minor concessions were granted to prisoners in the Maze who were undergoing a 'dirty protest'. These concessions included additional visiting rights, additional letter writing privileges, and they would be allowed normal exercising clothes instead of exercising in uniform, underwear or even being naked. The 'dirty protest' was part of a five-year campaign by PIRA and INLA prisoners held in the Maze Prison and also at Armagh Women's Prison.

At the start of the protest, the prisoners began refusing to leave their cells, and as a result the prison officers were unable to clear them. This resulted in in the 'dirty protest' as the prisoners were unable to 'slop out' so resorted to smearing excrement on the walls of their cells. The prison authorities attempted to keep the cells clean by spraying disinfectant, then temporarily removing the prisoners and sending in rubber-suited prison officers with steam hoses to clean the walls. However, as soon as the prisoners were returned to their cells they resumed their protest.

SINN FÉIN GET THEIR WAY
Mark C, UDR and Royal Artillery

I have spoken before about the incidents in which I was involved. In my opinion, there was blatant political interference which caused the Army to fight the NI war with one hand tied behind our backs. There are two incidents of note which reinforced my opinion about that. I called them 'International Incidents' as was the furore they caused, and they occurred around the Divis Street/Castle Street areas in Belfast.

At some point, the UDR took over the guard/QRF duties at Hasting Street RUC Station. This station, sitting very close to the notorious Divis Flats Complex was attacked many times throughout the conflict, so it was a step up and an increase of responsibility which was handed to the UDR. As a force, it was becoming very professional in its internal security role, especially the full time Companies.

Hasting Street had two main sangars; one on Divis Street itself, from which you could observe Divis Tower and report on any players coming into the City Centre, the other was at the gate, from which you could observe the complex blocks to the right of the main Tower or 'Zanussi City' as the author called it. Again we could watch the main players coming and going from a shop owned by one of the top players 'BG'. It seemed when he was seen standing at the shop door, an attack was imminent. As well as defence and intelligence gathering, we had to supply a QRF which had to deploy onto Divis Street if there had been an incident in the area or if the OP (observation point) in Divis Tower had spotted a player. If they wanted him/her stopped and searched, we would basically stop all the traffic.

One day there was an incident on the nearby Falls Road and Divis Tower OP called out the QRF to 'rat trap' Divis Street.[3] We rushed out of the side gate and onto the then bridge over the old railway line, which would later become the Westlink and we stopped the traffic coming out of West Belfast. However, we had only been there about five minutes, when I heard comments about the

---

3   This contributor reports on a further similar incident in a later chapter in this book.

UDR being in West Belfast from a crowd that had started to gather. Just then my radio crackled into life, telling me to return to base immediately and lift the 'rat trap'. Apparently the sight of UDR Berets on their sacred Republican soil was too much for Sinn Féin/PIRA, who by some means unknown to us had communicated with higher authority to get us returned to base. Here lies the dilemma: were we the QRF for Divis Tower OP or not? It turned out we were but, in future, we were ordered to put on 'skid lids' (riot helmets) before we set foot on Divis Street; some would call it petty by Sinn Féin/PIRA, but I call it political cowardice on behalf of my Government.

This author has spoken about the dangers inherent in joy-riding, especially in such a highly-charged and violent period such as the Troubles. I have written about the deaths of John Collins (7 May 1978), Karen Reilly and Martin Peake (30 September 1990) and in Chapter 1 of this book of Doreen McGuinness at VCPs in Northern Ireland. I understand that there were 10 such deaths during the Troubles and on the last day of March, a fresh name was added, when Paul Moan (16) was shot dead by the Army.

The teenager was a passenger in a stolen red Ford Escort which was driving around Glen Road between the Lenadoon and Andersonstown Estates. Soldiers had set up a VCP where Glen Road meets Suffolk Road on the evening of the 31st. The stolen car, containing six youths approached the VCP at 2117 and, instead of stopping as ordered, the driver drove straight through, forcing the soldiers to scatter. The soldiers opened fire on at the car as it passed through the checkpoint, shattering the back window of the vehicle. The car then went out of control and crashed a short distance away. Five of the youths scrambled out of the wrecked car and ran away in all directions. However, one youth was critically injured, and Paul Moan, who was sitting in the back seat, was killed instantly; he had received head and neck wounds.

This author, as a former British soldier, will not glorify this death nor overly condone it, but there had been enough well-publicised joy-riding deaths at VCPs by this stage of the Troubles for people to be aware of the significant dangers of ignoring orders to stop. Doreen McGuinness had been killed in the same area barely three months earlier and the driver of the stolen car on this occasion should have stopped. He would have received only a warning and a juvenile record; instead he had the death of Paul Moan on his conscience. The youths who were in the car with him were later all arrested and convicted with offences connected with stealing and driving a stolen car. They all pleaded guilty and received conditional discharges.

March ended with eight deaths; of these six were military personnel, including an Airman and a former soldier; two civilians died, both of whom were Catholics. The Provisional IRA was responsible for three of the deaths.

Photographs taken during the early 1980s in various parts of Belfast, both Loyalist and Republican, in the days before the muralists became 'professional painters'. (Sourced by the author)

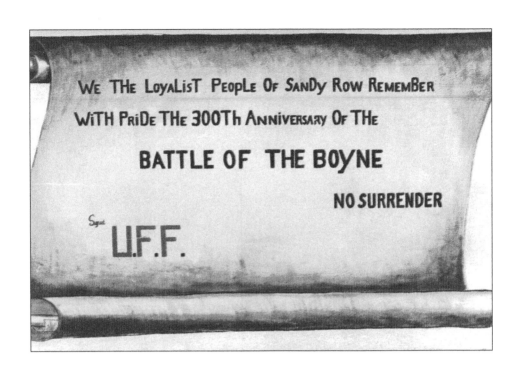

4

April

The month of April saw the deaths of 12 people, including a former soldier and three more police officers; it also witnessed the ND [negligent discharge] death of an innocent civilian when a soldier accidentally discharged a weapon and killed a retired nurse. The Kincora Boys' Home scandal hit the headlines once again.

All Fools' Day began with the death of PIRA would-be bomber, Robert Carr (21) who had badly wounded himself in a classic 'own goal' explosion close to the Irish border on the 22nd of the previous month. After the explosion, en-route to the Customs' Post at Newry, he was smuggled across the border and taken to a Louth hospital. Just 24 hours later, the UVF which had been quiet for a month or so targeted a man in the Clonard area of the Lower Falls whom they suspected of PIRA membership. Carl McParland (21) had no paramilitary links whatsoever and the Loyalists in targeting him, based their justification on flawed evidence. Five years previously, he had been charged and acquitted of handling weapons for the Provisionals. On the night of the 2nd, a UVF murder gang walked into his house in Leoville Street, having found the front door open. Leoville Street once ran parallel with the Springfield Road and stood between Kashmir Road and Oranmore Street and, as such, was close to the Peace line; today it is no more. Mr McParland was talking to his sister when the gunmen walked in and shot him several times at close range; he died almost immediately but his killers ignored his sister. The car used to convey the gunmen was later found abandoned in a Loyalist area.

On the 3rd, the name of the Kincora Boys' Home came prominently to the world's attention when the first arrests were made into charges of systematic sexual abuse of the children in care there. The scandal first came to public attention in January 1980 after a news report in the *Irish Independent*. On 3 April, three members of staff at the home, William McGrath, Raymond Semple and Joseph Mains, were charged with a number of offences relating to the systematic sexual abuse of children in their care over a number of years. All three were later convicted and jailed on charges of paedophilia. Mains, the former warden, received a term of six years, Semple, a former assistant warden, five years and McGrath was jailed in December 1981 for four years. Allegations were later made that the Royal Ulster Constabulary had been informed of the abuse at the home for years previously, but had not moved to prevent it. In his superb book *The Dirty War*[1] (Arrow Books, 1990) Martin Dillon claims that McGrath, who was also the leader of an obscure Loyalist paramilitary group called Tara, was being blackmailed into providing

---

1   Dillon, Martin, *The Dirty War* (London: Arrow Books, 1990).

intelligence on other Loyalist groups. The sensationalist tabloid press then linked the home with a whole series of establishment figures without any evidence being provided.

Ian Paisley, leader of the Democratic Unionist Party and moderator of the Free Presbyterian Church which he founded in 1951, was accused of failing to report the fact of McGrath's homosexuality to the relevant authorities although he initially denied ever being advised by his informant, a church member, Valerie Shaw, that McGrath worked in a boys' home. The name 'Kincora' has now become synonymous with the sexual abuse of young boys.

The 4th of April was a Friday, and it started a seven-day period of murder with the Provisionals killing three more policemen. Bernard Montgomery (34) was born in 1946, some four years after his namesake Field Marshal Bernard Law Montgomery led the British 8th Army to victory at El Alamein; whether he was named after the famous Field Marshal is unknown. Bernard was a part-time member of the RUCR and had applied to become full-time. Prior to joining, he was employed at his brother's company in Ligoniel, north of Belfast. He had been dicked by PIRA INT; two masked gunmen walked into the office and Mr Montgomery walked over to them to see if he could help. The two men opened fire immediately and hit the RUCR man and a colleague. Mr Montgomery was killed and his colleague badly wounded.

SILLY STUFF
Dave Judge, Royal Green Jackets

We had been in Londonderry for about a year when one of our pals who had a car was due to join us. He was travelling under his own steam to Northern Ireland in his car. His name was Terry 'A' and the car was a nice sky blue Ford Capri. Within a day or so of his arrival he asked what all the fuss was about, specifically why certain areas were out of bounds when off duty! So as a bunch of young dick-heads, we went out on the town – four of us – me, Alan, Terry and Chalky. We first went to Limavady for a few pints, and it was here that Terry pushed us into taking him to some of the hot spots: Bogside, Creggan and out into the countryside too. We ended up in an illegal Prod drinking hole, where exactly I don't remember, but it was outside of Londonderry.

The main door to this place had one of those drop-down flaps that you could thrust your shot gun through if you wanted. We eventually were allowed in and began mingling. All night long some middle-aged bloke was trying to sell me a small pistol; don't know what make/type. We had been gone for a long time now, and had been reported missing by our Battalion. They had told the police to be on the lookout for four men in a light blue Capri with such and such registration number. So when a routine police patrol found the car in the car park, they didn't know we were squaddies. I was in the club when the bloke with the pistol told me that my mates were in trouble outside. I went out to the front door which was now open and bright lights were shining in through it! I stepped out into the light and a pistol was pushed immediately into my head and a copper told me to do as I was told. I didn't know it was a copper initially and I must admit I thought: 'Oh, fuck!' They arrested us and took us to a police station, again I can't remember but it could have been Kilrea or similar. It was a small station and we were put into, and locked into, the TV room with the TV removed.

Early in the morning a Rover came and we were taken back to Shackleton barracks guard room. We later had an interview – without cakes or coffee – with the CO and were given heavy fines. We were lucky that Terry was a substantive full screw[2] because to bust him would have required the Brigadier's say so! The CO didn't want to bring his unit to the attention of the higher-ups, so none of us were reduced in rank. Moral of this story: If you're going to fuck up, do it with a substantive full screw or higher!!

In another part of the Province on that same day, the Chief of the General Staff (CGS) Northern Ireland paid tribute to the men and the women of the severely under pressure UDR. He said: When exactly 10 years ago, the Ulster Defence Regiment became operational and joined the British Army's Order of Battle, it took its place uniquely in the annals of military history, not so much because of its youth but because of the circumstances under which it was raised and that place is no less unique today.' He went on to praise it for the service and distinction and spoke of its baptism in violence and disorder. He praised its remarkable record and spoke of the dangers the men faced both on and off duty. Over the course of the Troubles, the Regiment lost over 300 members to a variety of causes in and related to the near-30-year campaign against terror. In addition, 65 former members, including seven who went on to join the RUCR, were killed by Republican terrorists for their former connections.

On the 5th, REME Corporal Peter Lyle Bailey (26) from Featherstone in Yorkshire was killed in an RTA [road traffic accident] in the Province. His funeral took place in the small Yorkshire town, a former mining community. Just four days later another RTA claimed the life of Colour Sergeant Edwin James Murrison (27) of the Scots Guards. The author has learned that the Colour Sergeant may have been working undercover and was killed in a car chase.

On the 6th and 7th of the month, Army ATO officers were put under severe pressure in South Armagh by PIRA bomb-makers. Over the course of 48 dangerous hours, bomb-disposal experts worked almost non-stop to defuse 650 lbs (295 kgs) of explosives which had been packed into seven milk churns and hidden in a culvert under the Armagh-Middletown Road. The PIRA bombing team had laid a command wire which led some 150 yards to an aiming position in hills overlooking the culvert. Experts estimate that the resulting massive explosion would have devastated nearby houses and endangered the lives of innocent motorists using the road at the same time as the intended military targets.

LONDONDERRY BOMBS
Dave Young, Ammunition Technical Officer
I went back for a second tour in 1980, and though things had calmed down a bit there were still many dangers to catch us out. We had better equipment and were better at our job, but so were the bombers; it was still a dangerous 'cat and mouse' game. Blast incendiaries were becoming much more common as the ingredients were readily available and the security forces were getting better at

---

2   A 'full screw' is a corporal. 'Substantive' means 'acting' or 'temporary'.

controlling the supply of explosives. All they needed for a blast incendiary was some petrol and a very small explosive charge; just enough to vaporise the fuel and mix it with air before setting it off. The Provisionals 'trialled' a new type of incendiary bomb at about this time, and had used two one-gallon blast incendiaries the year before in the La Mon Restaurant bombing, which had killed 12 people[3].

I was tasked to an incident at the Derry Working Persons' Cub just inside the walled city of Londonderry, and as I arrived, I spoke to a witness who said three bombs had been taken into the three storey club. I discovered there was a restaurant on the top floor, a billiard hall on the first and a gym on the ground floor. Just then ... BANG! There was a loud explosion from the top floor restaurant, and flames shot out of all the windows followed by BANG; another on the first floor billiard hall and shortly after that: BOOM a third. The Fire Brigade were about to enter the building, but I said that the last blast didn't sound like a bomb to me. As the road by the Londonderry wall was narrow they insisted we return to our base as the building was well alight and they wanted to get water onto the fires.

They were pouring water onto the roof as we set off back to base, only to receive an urgent call on the radio with the Fire Brigade screaming at us to come back! To their horror they had discovered another bomb under a billiard table in the now burning first floor billiard hall. When we got back, smoke and flames poured out of the windows. The rather shocked fireman described a large metal container jammed under the billiard table. I thought it was either going to be about 50 lbs of explosive, or more likely a five gallon blast incendiary! I knew if it was a blast incendiary of that size, it would be capable of causing a 50 to 70 feet fireball in the open and inside; it would instantly cremate anything in the same room.

I knew I was supposed to use a remote method of dealing with this type of incident, but at that time our wheelbarrows were still not up to climbing stairs, so I suited up in the bomb suit – over 75 lbs of 16 layers of Kevlar cloth and Kevlar armoured plates – and went in with a disruptor and a hook and rope line reel. As I entered the billiard room, I saw it was well alight and rapidly filling with smoke from the earlier explosion at a fire escape door, at the end of the room; I knew I had to get a move on. I located the bomb, jammed under a billiard table; it was a yellow, five-gallon metal can; a plywood box that usually contained the arming, timer and power unit. This was wired to two home-made detonators, each usually contain the small amount of explosive needed to cause mayhem!

I removed my very bulky helmet and crawled in under the table to place a line around the can, so I could drag it out to where I could reach the timer box with the disruptor. As I stretched my arms around the can: CRASH! There was an almighty crash: what the fuck? A very soggy six by four foot gypsum ceiling panel had fallen down on the back of my legs. By then, due to the time since the bombs had been placed, I knew that this was a failed IED; maybe a lapsed or failed timer. There are many things that could have been causing the mechanical

---

3   Wharton, Ken M., *Wasted Years, Wasted Lives* (Solihull: Helion, 2014).

Parkway timer in the box to stick: a bit of dirt, a loose wire or poor connection and the slightest movement could easily cause it to re-start, complete the circuit with fatal results for me. Incidentally I have never seen the time left on an IED timer or clock; pure TV 'Spooks' or Hollywood!

I was well aware of the dangers and the fact that I had just banged my head on the timer box. I waited and tried to listen for the sound of a clock; my ear was right up against it, but my heart was thumping so fast it was impossible to hear anything else. I moved back out the door and tugged the line, pulling the can over and it didn't go off. I then went back and aimed the disruptor, retried and fired it. After just a few seconds I returned, bagged up the forensics and left. As I did so I picked up the black from the table, as a souvenir trophy. As I approached the incident control point my team and the Fire Brigade were all laughing and said I looked like 'Mr Snowman.' I threw the billiard ball at my number two, who immediately started juggling it, because I hadn't noticed it was as hot as a baked potato off the barbecue.

The next day the top of a copper hot water tank was found in the next street. There had been three bombs and three explosions, but the third explosion had been the water tank bursting in the loft. It had nearly caused the death of several brave fire fighters! That was the very first of that type and size of blast incendiary bomb ever neutralised in NI and photos of it went on exhibition around the United States to try and discourage Irish Catholics from supporting IRA terrorists and their causes.

On the 9th, another policeman was killed – the second in five days – when a PIRA team manning an M60 machine gun killed Constable William Magill (24) on the mainly Nationalist Suffolk Estate. Following a contrived break-in at Suffolk Library on Stewartstown Road in West Belfast, an RUC team was dispatched to investigate. One of their colleagues had been killed the previous year by another such contrived library break-in and the officers were extra vigilant. However, on the night before the murder, armed PIRA men had taken over a house in Doon Road, close to where Stewartstown Road and Andersonstown Road meet, south of Lenadoon Park. While they held the family hostage, the gun crew had set up the deadly M60 machine gun and waited for the police to arrive at the nearby library. As the RUC car arrived, the first officer to alight was Constable Magill; as he did so, the PIRA men opened fire and several bursts containing around 100 rounds of 7.62 mm hit in and around the car. The young policeman was hit several times and died very quickly. Three of his colleagues were also hit and wounded, one of them female. In fact, despite being wounded, the female officer managed to radio for reinforcements. The gun crew melted away into the Lenadoon area. It is true that a policeman wasn't killed every day, but it is nonetheless true that every time an officer got out of a vehicle, pausing only to check his weapon and ensure his peaked cap was on straight, his or her life was at risk. The author drove past the scene on one of his return trips to Belfast and noted that the library is still there, next door to Funeral Directors O'Neill's and in close proximity to the cheap and cheerful supermarket, Lidl.

On the same day, despite the recent VCP killings of joyriders, in two separate incidents, two more cars tried to run Army VCPs in West Belfast. Soldiers opened fire on both vehicles and six civilians were shot and wounded.

Just two days later, another RUC officer was killed, making it three fatalities for the police in the space of just one week. Constable Frederick Wilson (43), father of two was a part-time policeman and through the day, he was employed by Belfast Housing Executive. He had clearly been dicked by the Provisionals who were aware that he walked to his office in the city centre through the Nationalist Markets area. As he walked along Franklin Street, a stolen motorcycle with two men on board drove up to where he had stopped to chat to colleagues and the pillion passenger produced a pistol. The gunman shot the RUCR man several times and drove off in the direction of the Falls Road area.

On the 14th, the British Government announced that more links between the 'freedom fighters' of the IRA and organised crime in the USA had been discovered. An investigation by the FBI had shown that top Mafia bosses in the USA were helping fuel the violence in Northern Ireland by assisting Irish-American supporters to smuggle weapons into Ireland for the Provisionals. The FBI stated that crime families with links to Ireland had masterminded the theft of top grade weapons from the US Army in raids on Army camps and military convoys and overseen their shipment to the IRA.

In February 1983, the *Belfast Telegraph* ran a story heavily critical of the Americans under the banner headline of: 'IRA kept alive by Dollars of Death.' The article read:

> Seventy Five per cent of the cash needed by the IRA to sustain its campaign in Ulster comes from the USA according to a memo drawn up by the American Justice Department. The confidential document alleges that … NORAID is the main source of funds. It is estimated that takes about 1.5m Dollars a year to keep the IRA operating in the Province. The memo which was written up during a 12-year nationwide investigation in America was obtained by Reuters the international news agency. And in it, the Justice Department describes the situation as having become a major embarrassment to the United States.

The article continues to disclose that 75 per cent of the terror campaign is financed from the funds received from NORAID. Extremely naïve, British-hating Irish-Americans, many of whom had never even been to Ireland ploughed their hard-earned wages into supporting a campaign of terror which cost the lives of over 4,000 people. Yet many of those questioned who admitted a hatred of the British and England's Empire – many Americans, like many Australians, have difficulty distinguishing between 'English' and 'British' – would be pushed to explain this hatred; they just knew that it was something that they had to do!

DIVIS STREET
Ken Pettengale, Royal Green Jackets
During our Belfast tour in '81–2, I was based in NHSM; my section, 33C had been boosted by a guy from the Pioneer Corps and a lad from the LI. The remainder were all my own lads from previously. I did have some misgivings about having blokes we didn't know in such an environment, but I had no choice; we were understrength. Even worse for me was the fact that the Pioneer, a gangly Jock lad, had next to no idea about being an infantryman, and equally poor weapon handling skills. I did complain about it to my CSM Don Duncan (RIP) but, in his usual way, he had me feeling good about the whole thing; how did he do that?

We decided, whether as a Company or at Battalion level I don't know, that the notorious Divis Flats Complex was to be patrolled and 'taken' back from being virtually a no go area, to one that was regularly patrolled. We were under no illusions that we were never going to win 'hearts and minds' but we would show them we didn't fear them. For those that don't know what the Divis was like, it was sort of a hexagonal shaped grouping of linked flats, each block having its own name (St Peter's, St Jude's, Cullingtree etc.) Each of these blocks had three levels: Path, Walk and Row – so someone could live at 3 Cullingtree Path, while his mate could live at 3 Cullingtree Row; you get the idea?[4]

In the centre of this mass of concrete and hatred was a 'play' area, part of which was used as a PROVO pipe range! This was also where hijacked vehicles were regularly taken and burned out. Overlooking all of this was the Divis Tower; a multi-storey block of flats, on the roof of which the Army maintained a permanent OP. The only problem with this, was the fact that the OP was blind to most of the activity within the complex. When our foot patrols were tasked to do a routine within the flats, the 'O' group was very complex: entry, exit and movement was precisely planned to give mutual support for the three brick multiple when moving between each level and in and out. Every junction had a code word, every level did too, so we knew precisely where and when everybody was at any given moment.

One of these patrols took me and my two bricks into the flats; one commanded by Lance Corporal Si Coe, the other by me; the third brick was commanded by our Platoon Commander. Everything went great; entry was clean, movement was good, for a lot of the time we could see each other moving around, 'P' checking those we saw. As we were at the top level of one of the blocks – I think it must have been Cullingtree, Pound or Whitehall, definitely along that side – we started to notice we were being crowded. Lots of kids and women began appearing from everywhere, pushing, grabbing at my kit, shouting; all sorts. I got on my radio and asked for a '*loc stat*' for the rest of them, and was shocked to hear they were crossing the Falls just about to go into North Howard Street, some several hundred yards away! The OP came on the net, and said they could see the crowds but couldn't make us out! Si came back on, panting, saying they were running back to get us! I was, I will admit, very scared. We had all heard stories and knew full well what could happen. I shouted above them all to the lads to make ready! That, believe it or not, had very little effect, and their reaction made me the more nervous.

We moved back to the nearest stairwell in a block, and I decided that unless I intended to open fire, leapfrogging wasn't going to work; it would leave us split and vulnerable. As we crowded into the stairwell to go down the six flights to get to the ground, they were dropping all sorts onto us. A couple of lads and kids I'm afraid, were dropped on their arses when they got in the way! As we got further down, the way below us became clear. This was NOT looking good. I thought we were being set up for something, when Si came on and said he was firm.

4   Located close to the notorious 'bad arse' tower block which was 16 stories high, this hexagonal shape was known as the 'Zanussi' to some soldiers.

As we got to the bottom, there was no-one barring our way; we had stopped being bombarded, and I could see Si's brick. I got all the lads together and told them we would keep running, straight out together, move through Si, and go firm beyond.

As we were running down, Ian 'Boggy' Whittle fell. At first I thought he had been shot, but he got back up and carried on; as we ran out and across the road, he went again. By this time we were all taking up defensive positions and Boggy staggered up. We all pissed ourselves at him – you know the laughter: that release of tension when you laugh at anything. We got ourselves together and the two bricks, my section, moved back tactically to NHSM. Boggy went to see the MO as he said he had hurt himself: poof; I had taken a harder whack a couple of weeks previously! That was it; tour carried on, and Boggy was limping about for the rest of the tour.

In 2011, I saw some pictures of a Regimental reunion and noticed Boggy was in a wheelchair. When I asked what had happened, I was told that he had done it in Belfast, falling over leaving the Divis. I cried; I never knew.

On the 15th, at the same time that Secretary of State for Northern Ireland Humphrey Atkins was meeting members of the Irish Government in Dublin, the IRA planted bombs at three major hotels in the Province clearly to send a message to the leaders of both countries. Using a mixture of both high-explosive and incendiary devices, they attacked hotels in Strabane, Lisburn and Armagh. Several people were cut by flying glass and over one million pounds worth of damage was caused.

On the same day of the Irish-British conference, a Loyalist bomb-maker – William Livingstone (38) – succeeded in removing himself from the gene pool when he was killed in a UFF 'own goal' explosion. He had been handling a gas cylinder bomb at a petrol station in Connsbrook Avenue, between Holywood Road and the Sydenham bypass, when it exploded as he handled it, killing him instantly. He received a full UDA 'military' funeral as the Loyalist paramilitaries – motto *'Quis separabit'* [who shall separate us] buried one of their own. He was one of two UDA men to die this year in such a way.[5]

Forty-eight hours later, PIRA murdered another former member of the UDR close to his home in Mulladuff, Newtownbutler near the Co Fermanagh–Irish Republic border. Victor Morrow (61) had been a founder member of the UDR, but had resigned over 12 months previously. His regular habits had been observed by PIRA dickers and he was known to walk into Mulladuff in order to get a lift to the factory in Lisnaskea where he worked. He left home to walk down the Newtownbutler–Clones Road but was ambushed by IRA gunmen who had hidden behind a hedge and waited until he passed, and then shot him nine times in the back of the head. His cowardly killers then scuttled across the nearby border and into the terrorist haven of Ireland.

On the 19th there came one of those deaths, impossible to justify and almost as impossible to explain; it was the inexcusable and inexplicable killing of a retired nurse by a British soldier. Mary Doherty (53), her husband and several friends were returning home in the evening after celebrating their Silver Wedding anniversary. While driving

---

5   See Chapter 6.

home, they approached an Army VCP at Camels Hump, close to the Irish border over which they had just crossed. A young soldier, aged 21 and a member of the Argyll and Sunderland Highlanders accidentally discharged one round from his GPMG. That round hit Mrs Doherty in her face and she died almost immediately. A later investigation showed that he had squeezed the trigger, thinking that it was not cocked. By some miracle, the weapon jammed, having been set on 'Sustained Fire' which meant it should have fired off a burst. Had that happened, there would have been possibly five dead innocent civilians. The soldier concerned was charged with unlawful killing, but this was reduced to manslaughter and he was sentenced to 12 months in a young offenders centre, suspended for two years. The author would like to extend his genuine but necessarily belated condolences and regret to the Doherty family.

At the same time that the Doherty family would begin a lifetime's grieving, a UVF gang attempted to kill a 19-year-old Catholic boy who was visiting from Londonderry. The boy was standing in the doorway to a Catholic church when armed men in a stolen car leapt out and shot and beat him. He was left very badly wounded. The stolen car then raced off towards the Shankill Road.

On the 22nd, there was the unexplained spectacle of an unidentified Loyalist paramilitary group murdering a fellow Protestant. There was no obvious reason why George Kerr (44) was killed. He was a pub singer, well known in the Loyalist Newtownards Road area of East Belfast, with no known Paramilitary links. He lived on Chadolly Street in sight of the iconic yellow Harland & Wolff cranes where the keel of the ill-fated RMS *Titanic* was laid over 100 years ago. He was disturbed by men bursting into his bedroom shouting 'Police' before shooting him with a machine gun as he lay in bed; he died instantly. Quite why a Loyalist murder gang should target him remains unknown.

Early that month – on the 9th – an RUC Officer, Stephen Magill had been killed in an M60 attack, outside Suffolk Library. The police had questioned a number of people in the Suffolk / Andersonstown / Lenadoon area, both suspects and anyone who might be willing to give them any scraps of information. One of those questioned was Michael Madden (68) a Catholic old-age pensioner from Lenadoon Avenue, some 3–400 yards away from the murder scene. It is highly unlikely that Mr Madden gave any information about the murder gang or the American-manufactured killing machine as the M60 was known. However, dickers or jealous neighbours may have seen him being questioned by the RUC and put two and two together and come up with 84! On the night of the 25th, two hooded PIRA gunmen burst into his house and forced him into the back garden where, without mercy or questioning, they shot him in the head and chest six times and left his lifeless body lying in the dirt. Perhaps this was the Provisional IRA which raged against the SF's supposed 'shoot-to-kill' policy while at the same time exercising a more vicious version of their own.

On the 29th–30th, ATO men fought a 48-hour battle to contain a whole series of bombs at Cappagh, Co Tyrone, as the Provisionals attempted to devastate the small town. Almost 1,000 lbs (455 kgs) of explosives had been packed into several milk churns by a PIRA bomb team and linked to a command wire. A routine mobile patrol from 8 UDR discovered the explosives and immediately called in ATO. A Company of soldiers from 2 Queens immediately cordoned off the area, having evacuated all civilians from nearby houses before the bomb-disposal experts began their perilous jobs. With Royal

Engineers also in attendance, the near-1,000 lb bomb was the largest ever defused up to that point of the Troubles.

On the last day of the month, Marion Price, who had been serving a sentence along with her sister Dolours for a car bombing in London on 8 March 1973, was released from Armagh Women's Prison on humanitarian grounds. She had been suffering from anorexia. As one of the Price sisters, she was jailed for her part in the IRA London bombing campaign of 1973. She was part of a PIRA ASU which placed four car bombs in London. The Old Bailey and army recruitment centre in Whitehall were damaged and over 200 injured, with one man dying from a heart attack. The two sisters were apprehended along with Hugh Feeney and seven others as they were boarding a flight to Ireland. They were tried and convicted at the Great Hall in Winchester Castle on 14 November after two days of deliberation by the jury; Marian Price was sentenced to two life terms. She and her sister Dolours Price, along with Gerry Kelly and Hugh Feeney, immediately went on hunger strike in a campaign to be repatriated to a prison in Northern Ireland. Dolours passed away in 2013 and the surviving sister is, at the time of publication serving a prison sentence for dissident activities.

April ended and the toll continued. Twelve people died during the month, three of whom were soldiers or former soldiers and three RUC officers were murdered by the IRA. Four civilians – three Catholics and one Protestant – were killed, of whom, one was an overtly sectarian death. One Republican and one Loyalist paramilitary died, at their own hands following own goal explosions. Republicans killed six and Loyalists killed three.

5

May

During this month, only four people died in or as a consequence of the Troubles; it was the lowest in the almost 11 years for which they had raged to date. Only one soldier was killed in May, but the aftermath and consequences of the murder of SAS Captain Herbert Westmacott, MC were still being felt almost 10 years after he had been laid to rest. The deaths of all four people this month can be laid at the door of, if not solely the Provisionals, then at least of the Republicans.

The following contribution from an ADU soldier actually occurred the previous year, but I have chosen to use in in this chapter as it leads in to the tragedy of SAS officer, Herbert Westmacott.

MILLTOWN CEMETERY: M60 SHOOTING
Dougie Durrant, ADU

Milltown Cemetery was a considerable piece of real estate. It was generally known that, if an audit took place, there would be more bodies than the records would show. It was searched on numerous occasions as the IRA would make papier mâchié bricks and stash their weapons and ammunition in there for a long-term or short-term hide. It was also the place where the IRA would bury their dead and build shrines to them, so searching it would sometimes cause a bit of a nightmare. I was attached to the King's Own Scottish Borderers (KOSB) at this time and I wanted to conduct a number of rummage searches in the graveyard. Shortly after I was attached, a cordon was put in place and off we went, dog in hand. As we arrived at the cemetery, the cordon was firmly in place so we were relatively safe to carry on searching.

I put Bluce's harness on and off he went, tail wagging as he searched between the headstones. Suddenly out of nowhere, a hail of high-velocity rounds were heard flying overhead, so we all hit the deck. It was the M60 crew at it again! I tried digging myself a hole to get into, as I'd seen what a 7.62 did to a headstone in an earlier incident. The Jocks were also trying to do the same; we knew that the contact was just down the road and just as soon as it stopped, the QRF tuned up and told me to jump on board.

They had already picked up Moby the tracker dog handler and he gave me a quick brief of what was going on. He explained that an RUC patrol had come under attack just up the road from Woodbourne base, with one injured: a female officer. We arrived there a short time later, and on jumping out of the PIG, it became apparent that the firing point was from the flats across the road from the shops. In fact, what gave it away was that there were down feathers everywhere as they must have used a mattress to hide the report of the weapon. Moby tried to get as much detail as possible before he started to try and locate a track.

I gave the area a quick search just to check if they had left any booby traps for us, but nothing was found. The police officer was getting medical attention while Moby and I with escort went around the back of the flats. I told him that there was a door to the rear and that it was possibly the escape route they took. As usual we were getting a lot of abuse from the locals. Moby harnessed his dog up and tried to pick up a trail but unfortunately they had used a vehicle to make their escape; from evidence later obtained it seems as if they had made their getaway on a motorbike. The M60 crew would later be caught but only after killing a Captain in the SAS.

On 2 May, the Army put into effect an operation designed to take out the so-called M60 gang, which consisted of Joe Doherty, Paul 'Dingle' Magee, Angelo Fusco and Robert Campbell, all known 'players' and from North and West Belfast. It was alleged by Seán O'Callaghan that the gang came under the control of Frankie 'Lucas' Quigley whom he described as 'particularly dangerous'[1]. An RUC informer – a 'tout' in the parlance of the Provisional IRA – had informed his handlers that the deadly M60 machine gun was to be used again, against a 'target of opportunity' in the Antrim Road area of North Belfast on 2 May. There were several of these rapid fire 7.62 mm weapons inside the Province, smuggled in from Irish-American supporters. They had already been used to kill members of the SF, including Constable William Magill the previous month. The M60 is an American general-purpose machine gun which fires 7.62×51 mm NATO cartridges from a disintegrating belt of M13 links. There are several types of live ammunition approved for use in the M60, including ball, tracer, and armour-piercing rounds. It has a muzzle velocity of 2,800 feet (853 metres) per second and is capable of firing around 10 rounds per second.

The plan was to take over a house in the Antrim Road which would overlook the main A6 directly across from the traffic lights. This was the point where the Antrim Road crossed over Cavehill Road and Limestone Road and carried SF traffic to and from Girdwood barracks which was only a little over half a mile away to the south. There was also police traffic from the nearby RUC station on Antrim Road. The house chosen by the terrorists had a bird's-eye view of the cross-section with an unobstructed line of sight to all traffic approaching the junction, making it easy for shooters to clearly identify vehicles that had to stop when the traffic signals at any of the four points of the cross section turned red. In particular, they were anticipating military vehicles approaching from the city centre direction. They reckoned an armoured personnel carrier or Jeep stopped at the lights would be a sitting duck for them. When a military or RUC vehicle stopped on red or at least crossed with caution – for many SF vehicles realised the dangers of coming to a complete halt – it would be raked with several bursts of 7.62 mm fire.

Today number 369 is still standing – it is a full storey lower than 371 – and is now an optometrists; its bigger neighbour, by all accounts, is unchanged since that fateful

1   O'Callaghan, Seàn, *The Informer* (London: Corgi Books, 1999), pp. 358–9.

day. The ASU finally decided upon number 371 and, having secured the services of a stolen car, which was forcibly taken from Spamount Street in the Nationalist New Lodge, PIRA gunmen drove to the specified house. The PIRA men were all members of the aforementioned M60 gang: Doherty, Magee, Fusco and Campbell. Once there, one IRA man – Magee – would keep the hostage family under control; two would mount and then man the M60 while Magee went around the back to wait with the stolen van for a quick getaway once the killing was complete.

Their plan was already compromised by the time the ASU was positioned inside 371 Antrim Road, as the informer had passed on the details to the RUC and an SAS team was already en-route to the address. Captain Herbert Richard Westmacott (28) was a soldier in the Grenadier Guards – motto: *'Honi soit qui mal y pense'* [Evil be to him who evil thinks] – but who had passed 'selection' and was on attachment to the Special Air Service (SAS). He was in command of an eight-man patrol in plain clothes which had been briefed about the proposed shooting and the hostage-taking situation. A car carrying three SAS men went to the rear of the house, and another car carrying five SAS men went to the front of the house. However, due to some confusion in the numbering of the houses in that part of Antrim Road, the front section went to number 369 instead! A couple of the team smashed in the door with a sledgehammer and raced in to 'take out' the terrorists and free the hostages. It was the wrong house and, alerted by the crashing sounds from next door, Doherty and the other members went to the front in order to investigate and saw armed 'civilians'.

As Westmacott and two troopers took cover behind the car, facing the wrong house, the ASU had a perfect line of sight to the side and rear of the crouching soldiers. Having seen the SAS-style high-velocity weapons and the tell-tale sign of men in plain clothes, they knew that they were likely to be SAS. They also knew it likely that troops such as these were not interested in taking prisoners. It is perhaps a moot point that undercover soldiers had no intention of capturing POWs but then if the Provisionals wished to play by big boys' games they equally could not complain at being subject to big boys' rules! Whether in self-preservation or whether to simply add an SAS 'scalp' to their CV, the gun crew opened fire from an upstairs window. The first burst hit the SAS officer, hitting him in the head and in the neck; he was killed instantly and fell to the street, very close to the vehicle. My understanding from an extremely reliable source is that the other personnel in the car had urged him not to get out of the car.

Several of the four SAS men, including RUC SB officer Ian Phoenix – later killed in the 1994 Mull of Kintyre disaster – who were at the front with Westmacott, returned fire but, being in the dark as to the location of the hostages, were compelled to withdraw. Magee, who was guarding the hostages, realised that the firing was not as he had expected, nor at the time he had anticipated and dashed out of the back, with the intention of readying the stolen van for a faster than envisaged getaway. He was seen by the soldiers almost at the same time that further shots were fired at them – this time from a back window. He was immediately arrested and told to lie down whilst they restrained him. He was possibly only saved from death by the uncertainty amongst the soldiers as to his identity. It is mere speculation but likely nevertheless, that he would have been summarily killed. The other three IRA men were still in the house and knew that if they came out, they would be shot down; this author has no hesitation in reiterating 'big boys' rules'.

There then followed a tense stand-off which involved firstly a senior RUC officer – Superintendent Charles Morrison – who offered to negotiate and stood bravely in full view of the terrorists, attempting to talk them out; at the time he was unarmed. Doherty who emerged as some kind of 'spokesman' for the ASU refused to come out, knowing that there were only military witnesses to what might happen. In the end he insisted on surrendering only to a Catholic priest and one was duly sent for. A local man, Father Hutton, arrived and after the IRA weapons were thrown out of the window, he led them out to be arrested by soldiers and driven away to join Magee who had already been taken to the RUC Interrogation Centre at Castlereagh.

By this time, it had been confirmed that Westmacott was dead and his body had been covered up. The father of two young children, he is commemorated at the SAS memorial in Hereford. His death left him as the highest ranking SAS officer to be killed in Northern Ireland. He was posthumously awarded the Military Cross later on. The story does not stop there and a brief résumé is necessary in order to complete it.

In June 1981, during the trial of the ASU for the killing of the Captain and other associated crimes, Joe Doherty escaped from Crumlin Road Gaol, aided by handguns which had been smuggled inside the prison. He escaped in the company of the following PIRA men: Paul Patrick Magee, Robert Joseph Campbell, Michael Anthony McKee, Angelo Fusco, Anthony Gerard Sloan, Michael Thomas Ryan and Gerard Sloan (no relation). A short fire fight ensued at a car park on the opposite side of Crumlin Road to the Gaol before several stolen cars sped away and the men melted in to the Nationalist estates of West Belfast. Doherty was found guilty *in absentia* and sentenced to a minimum of 30 years in prison.

All the men were eventually recaptured; some almost immediately, others took a little while to re-apprehend, but Doherty was smuggled across the Irish border into Dundalk and joined other Provisionals who were also OTR (on the run). Once all of the 'celebrity' escapees had begun to filter back to Gaol, the Army Council, aware of the downturn in morale caused by the recaptures, decided to send Doherty to that other terrorist haven, the USA. However, this was not before he started an affair with a local woman while living in a safe house in Tralee, County Kerry. He bragged to this woman about being one of the escapers from the 'Crum' and because of these and other indiscretions, the IRA knew that he had to be moved – for his own safety if nothing else. Seán O'Callaghan alleges that Doherty then started an affair with the wife of Mick Brassil, a PIRA member from Gortatlea, thus ensuring further local tensions. He began his new life in the USA doing a variety of jobs, provided by wealthy Irish-American supporters. He was later arrested in the United States – in 1983 – and became a rallying cause for the Irish-Americans and the other 'armchair terrorists'.

Doherty fought a nine-year legal battle against extradition and deportation and it is said, that no less a personage than Prime Minister Margaret Thatcher, threw her considerable and personal weight behind the efforts to persuade the US Government to send him back. Over the years of the extradition wrangle, Thatcher heaped much pressure on successive US Presidents –Reagan and Bush – because she felt that she was 'owed' by the USA. During the US bombing of Libya, she had personally approved raids being launched from USAAF bases in Cambridgeshire and to the use of British airspace for planes en-route for Libya. Much of her pressure was applied in secret, because although she felt that she was 'owed', the knowledge that a British PM was putting pressure on *'the good old US of A'* to release a 'freedom fighter' would have caused political uproar. The American mindset is still firmly fixed in the years of rebellion against 'England's Empire'[2] and many see the IRA as an extension of the 'Minutemen' and citizen militia; in short as a sort of spiritual version of their own patriots.

Over the course of the nine years, all the major Irish-Americans – Edward Kennedy, New York Governor Carey, Tip O'Neill, Senator Daniel Patrick Moynihan and the considerable offices of NORAID positively queued up to offer Doherty support, solace and a safe haven. This unedifying spectacle was completed when PIRA apologists fought to have a street corner in New York City named after him. Throughout the time of Doherty's fight to remain in the USA, Thatcher's pressure was relentless as she was determined not only to get her man, but to see that the USA ceased to continue as the terrorist bolt-hole which the Irish Republic had become.

In August 1991, he was transferred to a Federal prison in Pennsylvania, and on 16 January 1992 the Supreme Court of the United States finally paved the way for his deportation. In February 1992, the PIRA OTR man was deported back to Northern Ireland. Even at the bitter end, more Irish-Americans crawled out of the woodwork, and notable citizens of the like of New York City Mayor David Dinkins, and the Cardinal Archbishop of New York, John Joseph O'Connor and several members of Congress attempted 'a stay of execution'. Doherty was returned to Crumlin Road Gaol before being transferred to HM Prison Maze to serve his sentence. He was eventually released from prison on 6 November 1998 under the terms of the Good Friday Agreement.

Further information as to the nine-year struggle to extradite Doherty can be found Martin Dillon's excellent book, *Killer in Clowntown*.[3] The book is a fascinating insight into both the public and the private scenes of the extradition of the killer of a soldier. There are those likeminded people who will be nauseated at the very prospect of a killer having a New York street named after him; it is somewhat of an affront to Westmacott's comrades and loved ones. However, look no further than Sinn Féin-dominated councils in Northern Ireland who have done the self-same thing. In late 2012, in County Down, Sinn Féin and SDLP councillors voted to retain the title of a Newry playground which was named after an IRA gunman, who was caught with a weapon used in the Kingsmills massacre. The council voted to name the Patrick Street playground after IRA man Raymond McCreesh in 2001, despite his links with the Provisional IRA murder gang who killed 10 Protestant workers in January 1976 (16 per cent of residents opposed the change in a survey). In 1977, McCreesh was convicted of attempted murder, conspiracy to murder, possession of firearms with intent to endanger life and PIRA membership. He died on hunger strike in 1981. In 2014, the PSNI Historical Enquiries Team linked him, along with two others, to a string of IRA murders committed with the Armalite he was caught with, including the Kingsmills massacre in 1976.

In that attack, 11 Protestant workmen were stopped on their way home from work and gunned down; 10 men died.[4] Further, there is a Republican Club in Dungiven

2   Americans, for a similar reason to Australians, have a difficulty in recognising the subtle difference between 'England' and 'Britain'.

3   Dillon, Martin. *Killer in Clowntown: Joe Doherty, The IRA and The Special Relationship.* (London: Arrow Books, 1992).

4   See Wharton, Ken M., *Wasted Years, Wasted Lives* (Solihull: Helion, 2014), Vol 1.

named after INLA gunman Kevin Lynch, who was tried, convicted and sentenced to 10 years for stealing shotguns, taking part in a punishment shooting and conspiring to take arms from the security forces and was sent to the Maze Prison in December 1977. One can only guess at the opprobrium among Nationalists if Belfast City Council were to name a street in the Shankill 'Lenny Butcher Boulevard' or 'Basher Bates Kiddies' Playground' after another of the psychopathic 'Shankill Butchers' Gang. There is still, as a consequence of the Good Friday Agreement, much that is being done to salve the feelings of the Nationalists whilst at the same time ignoring the feelings of other.

There is an interesting postscript to Doherty's final return to Crumlin Road Prison. The author, Martin Dillon told me that Doherty was being led under heavy guard into Crumlin Road Prison; a prison warder stepped forward with a copy of the recently completed book on Doherty's case and asked him to sign it. Martin Dillon was quite sure that he would have disapproved of what was in it.

One of the other escapees from the 'Crum' was Paul Dingus Magee; after recapture, he served a prison sentence in the Republic. On release, he resumed his terrorist activities and was sent to join up with the IRA's England team. He was sent on a bombing mission, it is thought, to Queen Elizabeth Barracks at Strensall in York. On 7 June 1992 Magee and another IRA member, Michael O'Brien, were travelling in a car on the A64 road between York and Tadcaster, in West Yorkshire when they were stopped by local police. They were questioned by the officers, who became suspicious and called for back-up. Magee shot Special Constable Glenn Goodman, who died later in hospital, and then shot the other officer, PC Kelly, four times. PC Kelly escaped death when a fifth bullet ricocheted off the radio he was holding to his ear, and the IRA members drove away. Another police car began to follow the pair, and came under fire near Burton Salmon, close to where the author was living in the village of South Milford. The two PIRA men fled the scene after a member of the public arrived, and a manhunt was launched, involving hundreds of police officers. Armed officers searched woods and farmland in the Brotherton, Byram, Knottingley, Castleford and Pontefract area. They evaded capture for four days by hiding in a culvert, before they were both arrested in separate police operations in the town of Pontefract.[5]

Under the terms of the Good Friday Agreement, Paul Dingus Magee was repatriated to the Republic of Ireland before being released from prison in 1999, and subsequently avoided extradition back to Northern Ireland to serve his sentence for killing Captain Westmacott.

PLASTIC PADDIES
Jeanne Griffin

My sympathies go out to the three killed people killed on 15 April 2013 by the terrorist bombing in Boston, Mass., especially the Richard family who lost their precious son Martin, aged eight. Boston 'plastic paddies', some six generations in the US and many mixed with other ethnicities, financed and morally supported the IRA killing machine. This, as I told the author in an earlier interview, amounts to treason seeing as the US and UK are allies. Yet shockingly, a group of Americans

---

5   The murder of PC Goodman will be covered in a future volume by this author.

were giving succour to the IRA; this was even more treasonable as the IRA had close links to Libya and the PLO, both of whom were America's enemies. These countries had ruthlessly murdered US servicemen and civilians alike. The fact that the IRA was not just aided by red-faced patrons of 'Shamrock bars' but also prominent Irish-American politicians such as Hugh Carey, Tip O'Neill, Peter King, NORAID founder Tom Enfield and the 'swimming champ himself,' baby brother Teddy boy makes the entire affair a shameful chapter in recent US history. This connection needs to be fully exposed in the wake of the horrific Boston bombings which unfortunately inflicted gruesome death, mutilations and pain on the innocent just as the IRA did throughout the British Isles, an archipelago which has myriad visitors and residents who are in point of fact, American. However the dollar-lobbing cretins were never perturbed by any of the deaths their cousins from Holy Mother 'Eye-er-land' caused; and still are not, as is evidenced by the Friends of Irish Freedom Facebook page!

What happened in Boston, Mass., was of course, a terrible tragedy and this author can find no justification for it whatsoever. However let us recall the reaction in this same US city after the IRA bombing in Warrington on 23 February 1993, where there was cheering in the Irish bars and over one million dollars was raised for the IRA after two young British boys were killed.

On the 5th, the IRA carried out a bomb attack on the North-South electricity link at Crossmaglen in South Armagh. The attack again severed the link and caused widespread disruption to power supplies in the area. The British and Irish Governments had been attempting to re-establish the link following an earlier explosion. The following piece explains one such incident in the life of an ATO. While it did not occur in 1980, but earlier, it illustrates the dangers inherent in the 'longest walk'.

THE 'MURPH
Carl Ball, Royal Welch Fusiliers
1980–81 is a time that will always be etched in my memory as this was the year I did my first tour of Northern Ireland; that year will be synonymous in Irish history as the year of the hunger strikes. The Battalion TAOR was to be Belfast, and my Company was to spend six months at Whiterock Camp situated opposite the Turf Lodge. Our other areas of responsibility were the Ballymurphy, New Barnsley and Springhill Estates.

The tour got off to a good start when our search team in a joint operation with the RRF discovered an M60, which was believed to have been brought in to welcome our main party that was arriving a couple of days later. Once the company had settled in and took full responsibility for our area we experienced a quiet couple of months with nothing of note happening in our area of responsibility! This was certainly about to change.

During the evening of 4 May, we were tasked to control the interface on the Springfield Road which separated the Ballymurphy Estate (Catholic) and Springhill Estate (Protestant). The reason we were tasked is that one of the hunger strikers Bobby Sands was close to death! In the early hours of the 5th, we were waiting for our relief when the night with the sound of dustbin lids being banged into the ground; we all looked at each other and knew straight away that Sands had gone to pastures greener. This was confirmed by our ops room which tasked us to move further up the Springfield Road to New Barnsley Police Station. On our arrival, we were met by two RUC teams and, while in the courtyard of the police station, we were alerted to a crowd gathering on the Springfield Road opposite the 'Murph. RUC and us set up a position just outside the station. We placed the PIG in the road but, on looking up the road noticed there must have been at least 4–500 people walking towards us; we had a total of 16 and two RUC patrols.

There was a standoff for about 20 minutes then all hell broke loose with both petrol and acid bombs – the latter painted black to make them impossible to see – coming towards us plus anything else they could get their hands on being thrown at us. This went on for a further couple of hours; during which we fired over 200 baton rounds. Then came the sound of a whistle and the parting of the crowd, this usually meant that there was going to be a someone firing at us, so we took up firing positions but thankfully, this did not happen. As it kicked off again, Patrol Commander Wally decided to set up a snatch squad and I was tasked to cover them. A baton round was fired at one of the main rioters and he went down; forward went the snatch squad and got close to the rioter when all of a sudden a petrol bomb exploded on top of Wally's head, covering him in flames. We grabbed him and pulled him back, where, eventually we got him behind a PIG and extinguished the flames. There was no screams of pain just: 'Is my moustache singed?'

We were there till about 0700 in the morning when the crowd started to disperse; we came very close to being overrun and were down to our very last baton rounds which were keeping them at bay. We returned to Whiterock Camp, a very relieved group of squaddies just glad we had no serious injuries.

On Tuesday 13th, John Hume, then leader of the Social Democratic and Labour Party (SDLP), travelled to Downing Street, London, to hold a meeting with Prime Minister Margaret Thatcher. Whatever the private outcome of that meeting, a mere five days later, she was in a belligerent frame of mind when she entertained another Irish visitor. On the 20th, she stated in the House of Commons: "The future of the constitutional affairs of Northern Ireland is a matter for the people of Northern Ireland, this Government and this Parliament and no one else." This statement was made the day before Irish Taoiseach Charles Haughey was due to arrive in London with talks with Thatcher. However a communiqué released after the meeting promised greater political co-operation between the two governments on the issue of Northern Ireland and referred to the 'unique relationship' between the two countries. It certainly was that, alright!

Over the space of the seven days between the 8th and 14th of May, PIRA gunmen killed two men; both as a result of flawed INT. On the 8th, having watched the working and leisure habits of RUC employee, John Harman, PIRA gunmen lay in wait for him near his home in Carrickfergus, Co Antrim. Mr Harman – age unknown – worked as an RUC driver/mechanic and he was shot dead by the Provisionals because he dared to work for 'Crown Forces'. In a pious and incredible statement, they justified his cold-blooded murder by stating that he had been involved in torturing Republican prisoners.

On the 13th, PIRA's South Armagh 'nutting squad' was back in operation and doing what it did best: abducting, 'interrogating' and murdering those with the misfortune to fall into their evil grasp. Anthony Shields (57) lived in Crossmaglen and worked for a local company. Following a few setbacks for the local PIRA unit, the finger of suspicion fell on him. As with all 'touts' – real or imaginary – there could have been a number of reasons why the 'internal security' department might have become involved. It might be that an individual was an informer and he had been caught red-handed; it might have been petty jealousies within an area or unit; it might have even been score-settling by another individual who used the 'nutting squad' to redress his grievances. Or, more significantly, it may well have been, as author-activists such as Fulton, McGartland and Gilmour[6] and 'tell-all' former PIRA men such as Eamon Collins have maintained, that it was an informant within the PIRA ASU who was trying to shift attention from himself and quite prepared to sacrifice an innocent.

Whatever the reason, Mr Shields was warned to leave Crossmaglen but didn't heed the threats. On the night of the 13th, he was returning from a drinking session over the border with friends when a PIRA IVCP stopped their car. Masked gunmen fired shots into the air and then dragged Mr Shields out of the car and ordered the other men to drive on and forget what they had seen. The local Provisional leadership assured the man's family that he was perfectly safe and they were only questioning him and they expected him to be released shortly. Presumably this was the IRA's sickening mocking of the oft-used Police phrase; 'helping with enquires'. He was taken to Mounthill, close to the village of Crossmaglen, and roughly questioned and beaten, over the course of two days before being shot twice in the back of the head and his body dumped. Although his body was discovered on the 13th, the SF were not able to examine and recover it for almost four days because of the fear that the IRA had booby-trapped it. It was a common tactic of the Republican terror groups as it was always hoped that they could kill or maim a soldier or policeman when they investigated. Eamon Collins talks of how the 'nutting squad' would taunt a condemned man with the words *Which road do you want to close?* This was a reference to the fact that the SF were often forced to close off stretches of roads where bodies had been dumped for fear of hidden explosives.

The fears were not groundless, and the SF suspicions proved accurate, as over 300 lbs (137 kgs) of explosives were discovered at three separate points around the body. The grieving family had been assured by the IRA that the body was safe to move and it could be taken away to be prepared for a Christian burial. It was sickening enough that the family had been told that Mr Shields was still alive but this latest depraved move was adding insult to injury. A cordon of men from the King's Own Royal Border Regiment were in place to safeguard ATO personnel and they came under fire on several occasions from PIRA gunmen over the border. Three separate gas cylinders packed with explosives were placed between 40 and 100 yards of the body of Mr Shields.

The body was eventually recovered after the devices were made safe on the evening of the 16th. The SF were indebted to Gardaí officers who discovered the command wires on the southern side of the border which led to the finding of the explosive devices. Several months later, another employee from the same company that Mr Shields worked for was also killed by the IRA.[7]

6   See the Select Bibliography at the back of this book.
7   See Chapter 11.

BEING TURNED INTO A PINK MIST!
Dave Young, Ammunition Technical Officer

One very hot and long day, I was tasked to a suspect bomb in a Land Rover parked in the centre of a large village of Garvagh at about midnight. The mostly Protestant population of about 1,200 people had been evacuated and several hundred were in their night clothes at the cordon 400 yards down the street. It was good job for them it was a heat wave! This was a Proxy bomb, where the terrorists forced someone else to deliver the bomb. It was parked alongside security barriers in the centre of Garvagh and the driver got out shouting: "There's a bomb in here."

I was told there was a metal oil drum of possibly explosives in the back. I took far too long trying remotely to place a special explosive charge against the Land Rover to gain access, but I failed as it fell over. Then my remote Wheelbarrow failed too. They weren't as reliable as they are today and the batteries didn't last long in those early days of their development. I got suited up in the bomb suit and made the long walk with a hook and line, a disruptor – my favourite weapon – and a little pocket tool kit that I still have today. As I approached I had a plan in mind: find the arming, power and timing unit, usually in a little plywood box and zap it with the disruptor – job done!

When I got up to the bomb, I could see there were two 45-gallon oil drums. This wasn't a 300 lb bomb, but a 6–700 pounder; nearly three quarters of a ton of explosives. My team were 75 yards away and, if it went off, were sure to be killed or severely injured. I yelled to them to "move back" and searched for the plywood box. It was just inside the lid of the lower drum, just behind the centre of the bench seat and well out of reach of my disruptor. I looked back at the team and they had retired down the road.

I made an assessment that this was now a failed device. It was now time for Plan 'B'. I carefully reached in and took hold of the box and eased it gently out towards me, listening for the tell-tale sound of the parkway timer elapsing, which would have been the end for me. I laid it just outside the nearside window where I aimed my disruptor. I set off back to my team and was thinking this wasn't going to be simple at all! The drums were jammed in with a very large heavy tyre on top of them; we were all in for a long night! I fired the disruptor with a crack that echoed down the empty street and a cheer went up from the crowd, but it wasn't over yet!

I made another long walk carrying a tow rope. I bagged up the remains of the timer unit and put them safely to one side. I climbed into the Land Rover and with great difficulty pushed a large tyre out the back door. I somehow managed to get a rope around the top drum, but had to get both feet on it to roll it in to the centre of the door and yelled to the team to heave. After much grinding of gears and smoking of tyres, the whole Land Rover moved down the street towards my team, complete with me in the back jammed on top of the bomb, almost comical now but not at the time. After a few more extra hard kicks from me the drum was eventually ejected and some of the contents spilled in the road.

Delicate examination of the contents revealed a detonator inside a large booster charge of powerful commercial explosives, and several hundred pounds of homemade explosives. I cut out the detonator, bagged the forensics and repeated the operations on the identical second drum – all the time looking and checking for any booby traps, secondary circuits and any other detonators that were always a frightening possibility.

By the time I finished the job, it had taken over eight hours and it was daylight. As the cordon came down, just in time for breakfast, the crowd cheered and clapped, as they passed us clearing up our kit. I must have lost almost a stone in sweat and certainly one more of my nine lives, but I had saved their houses and businesses from destruction. I can honestly say at no time was I in any way worried about what might have been. It was exactly what I had been trained to do. If it had gone off I wouldn't have known a thing about it, I would have just been pink mist! The flash I might have seen, but I wouldn't hear the bang. Anyone caught in an explosion of a huge IED like this would be instantly reduced to small body parts, scattered widely.

On the 14th, the dangers of working close to the Irish border were made very apparent, when three PIRA gunmen crossed over between County Donegal and County Londonderry. They had targeted an off-duty UDR soldier who was possibly working on a building site at Ballymagroarty, approximately one mile on the northern side. Roy Hamilton (22) a Protestant building worker was employed at the site, but he was neither a part-time soldier nor had any connections with Loyalist paramilitaries. He saw the men approach with guns drawn and immediately turned to run but he was shot in the back and in the back of his head by at least two of the IRA murder gang. One of the killers is named by Eamon Collins only as 'Seán from Belfast.' He was rushed to Altnagelvin Hospital in Londonderry, but he was already dead. Mr Hamilton was from Douglas Bridge, Co Tyrone and was working on a freelance basis with a mobile work squad for Londonderry Housing Executive. To this day, the Provisionals have neither explained nor apologised for his murder.

As the month ended, the KORBR were again in action and a busy and exacting tour continued. On one day in the Crossmaglen area, the battalion was involved in two shooting incidents. In the first, a foot patrol was examining possible terrorist firing points right on the border when shots were fired at them. The shots missed and two men were observed running back over the border; no shots were fired in return. The soldiers had just taken cover, when two further shots came in from a different direction, but again both missed. Earlier in the day, the unit observed two men carrying rifles in the same immediate area and opened fire; hitting at least one of the suspected PIRA men. Men from the Parachute Regiment were then involved in an incident at Kilnasaggart Bridge near Jonesborough. The spot was only 1.5 miles from the scene of the Warrenpoint massacre which had occurred the previous August.[8] As troops came upon the bridge, they observed two men behaving suspiciously and they were challenged. The men dashed for the lorry and Paras immediately opened fire, hitting at least one of the men. The injured man and his accomplice then drove off in the lorry in the direction of Jonesborough. As the troops moved towards the bridge, another man

---

8   See *Wasted Years, Wasted Lives*, Vol 2, Chapter 56.

opened fire with a shotgun and fire was returned. As the soldiers lit up the underneath of the bridge with their torches, two men were observed running away and when they refused to stop, one of them was hit by a shot from one of the Paras. The two escaped men ran over a nearby railway line and escaped over the border. A blood trail ran right over the border which suggested a very bad wound, but the soldiers were forbidden from crossing over after them.

Once over the border, the IRA suspects would have been able to melt into Drumad Wood or Ravensdale Park, the hamlet of Mountpleasant or surrounding area, where they would have found a friendly cottage willing to give them shelter from either Gardaí or pursuing British soldiers who may have ignored the one-sided border crossing regulations. From there, a friendly doctor with IRA sympathies could have been sent for to tend their wounds, or they would have been smuggled into a 'no-questions asked' cottage hospital.

May ended with the lowest number of deaths for some considerable time; four deaths which included one soldier and three civilians. The Provisionals were responsible for all four deaths this month.

6

June

uring this month, eight people would lose their lives, five of whom were soldiers or former soldiers; the UFF would murder a Protestant whom they regarded as a 'traitor' and a leading INLA member – Miriam Daly – would be assassinated by the Loyalists. There would also be the mystery of two unexplained deaths of two members of the Royal Regiment of Fusiliers, possibly cousins, just 48 hours apart.

John Turnley (44) was a former British soldier and he was a Protestant, and as such, seemed a more likely candidate to be marked for execution by either PIRA or INLA. On the 4th of this month, however he was shot dead by the Loyalist UFF. He was, in their perverted eyes, a traitor, not only because he had been a member of the SDLP, a mainly Nationalist party, but also because he had campaigned for the 'National H Blocks Committee' an organisation with Republican links and sympathy. The Committee had several major aims: The right to wear their own clothes; the right to refrain from compulsory prison work; the right to free association with other political prisoners; to receive one letter, one parcel and one visit per week, and the restoration of remission of sentence lost through the protest. That a Protestant had allied himself to a Republican pressure group and that he should also ostensibly ally himself to the cause of Republicanism effectively sealed his death warrant.

UFF members were aware of his regular habits and it was known that he would be addressing a public meeting in the seaside town of Carnlough, on the North Co Antrim coast, some 40 miles or so north of Belfast. He had lived there for some time and his movements were known to his murderous stalkers. In June 1980, Turnley, together with his Japanese wife and two young children drove to the designated meeting place in Carnlough to discuss development in the area with other councillors. When his car stopped, he got out and was immediately confronted by three masked gunmen from the UFF. They fired several shots, hitting him in the chest and body. He was placed in an ambulance but died en-route to Larne's Moyle Hospital. The killing was later referred to as "a carefully planned murder, carried out with a horrifying and frightening brutality." The area of Larne was known as a hotbed of Loyalist paramilitaries and John Potter in his *A Testimony to Co*refers to the fact that two known UVF men actually served with the Larne unit of the UDR. However, less than three hours after the murder, a VCP near Ballymena from 5 UDR stopped and arrested the murderers, and were instrumental in seeing that they were brought to trial for the killing of Mr Turnley. A year later, Eric McConnell received a life sentence, and his brother Robert and three other members of the UFF received jail sentences for their part in the murder. Two of the men convicted were William McClelland and William McFetteridge. The McConnells and McClelland also received life sentences for the murder of Rodney McCormick in August

1980. Matthew Martin, who was a former UDR soldier, and David Hastings received prison sentences for their peripheral part in the murder and in other UFF attacks.

On the same day, the Glosters lost one of their men in a terrible road traffic accident (RTA) at Limavady, Co Londonderry. Lance Corporal Anthony Peter Bennett (29) lost his life while his famous Regiment was based at RAF Limavady.

Three days later, it was the turn of the Provisionals to display a cold-blooded ruthlessness as they ended the life of a part-time UDR soldier. Like many other brave young men in Northern Ireland, Richard Latimer (39) lived a double life; through the day he ran a hardware store in Main Street, Newtownbutler, County Fermanagh; on a night time and at weekends he was a Private in 4 UDR. In 1976, his life was disrupted when the Provisionals attacked his remote house close to the border with the Republic and he had moved his wife and young son into the centre of Newtownbutler. On the morning of Saturday 7 June, he was working in his shop, in the company of his son aged 11, when several PIRA gunmen in a stolen Cortina parked up nearby. As Private Latimer served a customer, one man wearing a mask burst into the shop and shot him several times in full view of his son and other customers; he died almost immediately. His killer ran outside and jumped into the car which raced off in the direction of the Irish border, which was less than three miles away.

The KORBR were again involved in action in the Crossmaglen area, following their several fire fights in May. A patrol was providing cover to an Army helicopter at Cullaville as it collected a heavy load. As the underslung load was being raised, PIRA gunmen from positions across the border opened fire with rifles from about 100 yards. At least 20 rounds were fired before the soldiers returned fire and the helicopter managed to lift off. One of the IRA gunmen was hit by a KORBR marksman and seen to fall before being dragged off by his comrade. Immediately the soldiers came under fire from another position inside the Irish Republic and naturally fired back. A second gunman was hit – this author has no evidence that it was the same British marksman who fired – and he too fell to the ground wounded. All of the terrorists, wounded and unwounded then escaped in a vehicle. A later follow-up by Gardaí officers discovered 17 spent Armalite casings.

MAJOR ANDREW MACDONALD, 1 KING'S OWN BORDER
Incident Report Concession Road, Crossmaglen 7 June

I had placed call-sign 13 Sierra (4 x 4 man bricks) in a dug in position to act as a lure with which to entice the enemy into an attack which we would then ambush. I had concealed a team of men in a covert OP equipped with GPMGs on SF. The position was established on the Sunday and then on the Wednesday (4 June) a replacement team was put in. The 'lure' position had been 'dicked' during the 6th and 7th June by three known players – whom I described in my report as 'well known hoods'. (The author was advised not to print the names of the three IRA members.) The day before the changeover, an IRA gunman had fired a round at the 'lure' position. I decided to extract both positions by Wessex helicopter and although I had also removed the covert OP their positions had not been dismantled. However, as the Wessex was lifting an underslung load, seven rounds were fired at it at the pick-up point. It returned safely to base, but we had identified the FP.

On the 7th, I moved both 13 Sierra and 13 Alpha forward to O'Neill's garage (identified as a firing point) and to the Watter's house. At this moment, 13 Sierra was engaged by a gunman who fired at them through a gap in the hedge; we returned fire and hit one man and the enemy firing ceased immediately. But, as they moved towards the garage, enemy fire restarted and continued from another FP. Meanwhile, 13 Alpha had moved forward to engage the enemy – who then also opened fire at them. There was a lull of three to four minutes when the firing stopped and the commander, whose Storno (radio) was unserviceable, moved back towards the hedge to get a replacement radio. As he neared the hedge, two of the soldiers informed him that two of the enemy were dragging something (presumably their wounded comrade) down the hedgerow. The team opened fire but did not hit either target and then a few moments later a vehicle was observed moving off from the nearby farm.

Another lull followed and 13 Sierra moved towards the garage and made a 'contact' report to base. They were immediately ordered to do a 'weapons tight' (make safe) as Irish Republic SF were on the scene; just as he acknowledged this, a round was fired at him. Then, 13 Alpha shot at a gunman and further enemy rounds came in. The commander ran with one man to the cover of a wall – covered by his team – and further enemy small-arms fire came in. We engaged them with an MG and their firing ceased and then we spotted two of the enemy break cover and run south-east. One soldier opened fire at them and with his first shot hit one of them who then disappeared from view; concentrated fire was put on the position but the other man escaped. We followed up towards the area where the enemy had been firing from. The firing had ceased and we spotted that the Gardaí were in the area. I went forward to meet the Gardaí Inspector and we discussed exactly where we were; I thought that in our hot pursuit of the enemy, we had followed up across the border (this could have caused a diplomatic incident). He thought that we were actually on the border and so we settled on the latter. We discovered 15 x 5.56 mm spent shells nearby.

The incident closed at 2300 and I moved back with the patrol on foot into Crossmaglen.

On the 8th of the month, the Provisionals planted a series of devices in Custom House Street in Londonderry, at around 0700 on the Sunday morning. Extensive damage was caused and an ATO had a narrow escape while attempting to defuse them. The following day's *Derry Journal* reported the incident under the banner: 'Derry Car Bomb Causes Extensive Damage'. It went on to say:

A British Army bomb disposal expert had a narrow escape and extensive damage was caused when a car bomb partially exploded … shortly after seven o'clock on Sunday morning. The car had been stolen earlier in the Glenbrook Terrace area of the city and the bomb packed into milk churns and placed in the car. It was parked around 1:30 AM in Custom House Street outside the Northern Counties Building which houses the local BBC station Radio Foyle and the Steak House Restaurant. A 35-minute warning was telephoned to the local branch of the Samaritans and the area was cleared. However two members of the Steak House staff were sleeping in an upstairs part of the flats, unknown to the police. The men had decided to remain in the building after rioting in the Waterloo Place area earlier in the morning.

When the bomb went off, one of them was blown out of bed but was uninjured and the other one slept through the explosion.

Army experts had been working at the car bomb for about three hours and had carried out two controlled explosions. The bomb went off shortly after an Army bomb disposal expert had walked away from the vehicle.

On the 13th, one of the UDA/UFF's most senior bomb-makers killed himself while assembling an explosive device at the Highfield Community Centre, in Highfield Drive, a Protestant area close to both the Ballygomartin Road and the West Circular Road. Michael Wright (25) was in the final stages of putting together a bomb, when it exploded prematurely, killing him instantly and causing extensive damage. Like the equally callous Provisionals, they had no qualms about using areas in close proximity to innocent civilians.

On the 9th, Irish Taoiseach Charles Haughey argued on the BBC programme 'Panorama' that it was in the best interests of both Britain and Ireland for Britain to withdraw from Northern Ireland. He indicated that some form of federation could be possible in the event of a British withdrawal. Successive Irish leaders had been trotting out the same tedious diatribe since the days of the Irish-American President Eamon De Valera. It rarely changed and what it achieved, in that it laid institutional and Constitutional claims to the ownership of the North, was to 'legitimise' the violent activities and objectives of the IRA. Edgar Graham, Legal Spokesman for the Official Ulster Unionist Party (OUUP) summed up the situation in a statement made that year: "The Constitution of the Republic is an encouragement to the IRA. The Dublin Government claims jurisdiction over Northern Ireland and the IRA say that they are trying to fulfil that claim." Mr Graham was shot in the back of the head by PIRA gunmen on 7 December, 1983 outside Queen's University in Belfast.

On Wednesday 11 June 1980, the IRA – through their mouthpiece Sinn Féin – issued a statement that threatened to renew attacks on prison officers. At that stage of the Troubles, 16 POs had already been killed and the latter part of 1979 had witnessed no less than seven murders among PO staff. More were to die as a consequence of this latest Provisional statement. However, as the next piece will show, it was not only Republican terrorists who killed POs.

WEAPONS SEARCH IN A LOYALIST AREA
Dougie Durrant, Army Dog Handlers' Unit

It was a wet and windy morning in 1979; it was my day off and I was having a nice lie-in for once. Then came a knock on the door; it was Steve the duty handler and he said succinctly: "Doug you're wanted for a quick task in East Belfast, so grab your kit, it was between you and another lad, and unfortunately you got the short straw." With a little complaining I reluctantly took the task, grabbed my kit and then made my way up to the office. I asked what the task was but the reply which came back intrigued me: "Don't know yet, mate; it's Special Branch led and they have called in three of us to search a number of houses."

Twenty minutes later a van arrived and we all pilled in for the short drive to Ladas Drive, Belfast the home of SB and other intelligence units. We all walked into the briefing room and it soon transpired that they wanted to search a long row of houses as they had received good intelligence that there was a weapon in one or more of the residences. My mate Frank was going to search the target address and we were just along for the 'cover story.' We all jumped on board the Police hotspurs and headed to the east of the City. Twenty minutes later we were at the subject's address, I looked up the street and all I could see was RUC Police teams ready to go in. In a well-coordinated operation, entry was gained all at once with the RUC constable entering first, followed by Bluce and myself; and then the rest of the Police search team including the SB boys. A male came to the door on the first knock. "Fuck me!" I said to myself as he was shirtless and only had his trousers on, together with a pair of boots, and his face was covered in cam cream. Bluce went straight in and walked immediately to a large built in cupboard and started to give a good indication that something was in there.

Due to operational procedures, I could not tell anyone at this point as there was a few legal questions to go through first, which the Police search team did while trying not to show their joy as to what greeted them at the front door. With the questions out the way and the male not saying anything, we started searching. Unfortunately the room we were in and the same room that Bluce had shown a positive indication, had to be searched last. So I went through the rest of the house trying to find more but I could see it was hard for the dog as I called him off an indication and not rewarded him, so I thought to myself: "Fuck it I'll take him back there now".

I took him back to the room and off he went, straight back to the cupboard and he gave a positive indication as did the male with the cam cream on his face; by his expression I knew we were onto something. I pulled Bluce back and put my hand under the cupboard door and there was a black bag with something large inside it. I called in a member of SB who pulled the bag out and looked in: "Jackpot!" he shouted and with that the rest of the team came in. He had found a homemade SMG with a number of rounds in two magazines. By this time the male had succumbed to his fate and slumped down in an armchair, crying. This was a Loyalist weapons find, however we later learned that the weapon had been used in a number of killings including that of a prison officer.

Markethill is a village in County Armagh, with a population of around 1300 people. It sits at the southern side of Gosford Forest Park. Among its few claims to fame is a livestock market which is held there three times a week. On the 12th, an IRA ASU parked a car packed with explosives in the centre of this sleepy village and the resulting explosions caused extensive damage throughout.

Between the 16th and 19th, one of those enduring mysteries which tax historians until their last breath occurred in Northern Ireland. Two soldiers from the Royal Regiment of Fusiliers (RRF), who apparently were not related, died while based at Palace Barracks, Belfast, within three days of each other. On the 16th Fusilier George Wilfred Foxall (17), whose service number was 24548113, died from 'violent or unnatural causes'. A mere 72 hours later, in the same barracks, Fusilier Thomas Foxall (18) also died and the cause of his death is noted as an RTA. His service number was 24523676. Thomas had reached his 18th birthday on 14 June, some two days before George died. George was born only four months after Thomas which precludes the possibility that they were brothers. Even if he had been allowed out on foot patrol, Thomas would have been only 'on the streets' a matter of five days, as soldiers were not permitted to serve under active service conditions until they reached 18. This was a Government ruling put into effect after the murder of the young Scottish soldier John McCaig of the Royal Highland Fusiliers on 9 March, 1971, when he was only 17. Therefore, George Foxall would have been confined to base duties for several more months. Generally speaking, under-aged soldiers were not kept with their units in the Province, but more usually with their rear parties until they reached the age at which they could be deployed. Both men were from the Birmingham area.

The author was given the following information:

There were two Foxalls – it is not certain if they were related – who died within three days of each other; one was killed in an RTA (Thomas) and the other (George) on the Magillian training camp ranges in a Very pistol accident. A round, accidentally or negligently discharged hit him in the side of the neck causing fatal injuries. When the first one died they sent the casualty visiting officer to the wrong Foxall family; the same CVO then had to go back and tell them it was not their son. Three days later, the lad was killed in this accident. I know the visiting officer in this case and he said that he reported that he should not go back to the family a third time and RHQ agreed and sent a more senior officer in the end.

THE UNDER-18S
Mick 'Benny' Hill, Royal Anglians
We had under-18s with us in Palace Barracks when we were there. They weren't allowed out on ops, so they did Camp Security duties instead until their 18th Birthday; after that they could be posted to Rifle Platoons. All of them would much rather have been with the battalion, than stuck in the depot waiting for their birthday!

Also on the 19th, the European Commission on Human Rights rejected a case brought on behalf of Republican prisoners taking part in the 'blanket protest' at the Maze Prison. The Commission found that the conditions were self-inflicted but the Commission also criticised the British Government for being inflexible. That day was still not over, as the IRA hijacked a Tipper lorry near Dungannon, packed it with over 1,000 lb (455 kgs) of explosives, and abandoned it in Lurgaboy Lane. Army ATO was called out and an Army Dog Handler (ADU) with his 'wagtail' (dogs specially trained to sniff out explosives) examined the suspect lorry. The local Army unit – 2 Queen's Regiment – were also called out to cordon off the area during the clearance operation. Concealed under the lorry's legitimate load were 10 milk churns each containing 100 lb (45 kgs) of explosives, command wires and other detonation materiel. It is thought that the devices were to be placed inside a culvert close to a military route. Thanks to the bravery of the ADU man and his 'wagtail' and the ATO team, what could have been a catastrophic explosion was averted.

At a policy conference on the 25th, the Democratic Party in the USA adopted as Party policy a proposal put forward by Senator Edward Kennedy. The 'new policy' called for an end to the divisions of the Irish people and a solution based on the consent of all of the parties. This author has discussed *passim* the US interference in the affairs of the United Kingdom, especially in relation to Northern Ireland. Precisely how genuine Kennedy, Carey, O'Neill, Senator Daniel Patrick Moynihan *et al.* were will probably never be known, but there is inevitably the suspicion that they were 'playing to the gallery.' In this instance, the 'gallery' was the Irish-American vote and it was vital for this 'gang of four' that they stayed in with their electorate. Pressure group politics in the USA are all powerful and other than the National Rifle Association and the Jewish-American lobbies, there is no more influential a group than the Irish-American lobby. This group influenced decisions on the legitimate supply of arms to the RUC, the extradition of convicted terrorists back to the UK – in some cases, such as Joe Doherty, treating them as celebrities – and ensured that on many occasions, a blind eye was turned to the illegal supply of arms to the IRA. Britain's discomfort was a source for merriment and enjoyment by the Irish-Americans and while news that a British soldier had killed an Irish 'patriot' was greeted with disdain and disgust, the reverse or some PIRA atrocity was a cause to celebrate.

Respected journalist Ruth Dudley Edwards wrote in 2009: "Sometimes it is right to speak ill of the dead. The truth matters, even when it is deeply unsavoury. The truth about Ted Kennedy is certainly unsavoury." One finds it impossible to argue with her profound words. Edward Kennedy of Chappaquiddick and the abandoning of Mary Jo Kappechnie fame was no friend of Britain. Like his obnoxious father, Joe Kennedy Snr – incredibly for a committed Anglophobe, appointed as Ambassador to the Court of King James during the Second World War – he despised the English. As Miss Edwards wrote at the time of his death: "Ted did his father proud. As a politician dependent on Irish-American votes, this master of empty rhetoric had no scruples about spreading the bitter message of Irish Republicanism, especially if there was an election at stake." This was the man who put pressure on his own government to deny the legitimate sale of arms to the RUC while turning a blind eye to the shipment of weapons and the raising of funds for PIRA. This was also the man who famously demanded that 'Scottish Protestants' should be given every assistance to repatriate themselves to Scotland! There was also the infamous moment when he humiliated himself on a 'fact-finding' trip to Northern Ireland by telling a UDR soldier to "get back to his own country!" The curse that was Irish-American support for the Provisional IRA will be covered further in this book.

IRISH-AMERICANS
William Young, Royal Artillery
When I first moved to the States I stayed in New Jersey and I met many Irish-Americans with some of the most ridiculous and distorted views of Northern Ireland. I had an article published in the *Washington Post* and I referred to them as 'second generation, pseudo-homesick Irish-Americans.' Having an Irish surname doesn't make you Irish. I did get a lot of hate mail and some weird phone calls. A national reporter (Mary McGrory) had one of her people call me at home and I hung up on them. She was a hard-line Irish Nationalist who wrote sympathetically about the Irish struggle and 'The Boys' (Meaning the IRA of course). Her only link to Ireland was her last name of course and she was born in Boston and a friend of the Kennedy family.

Irish benevolent organisations, such as NORAID, did raise a lot of money from homesick fake Irish who, for the most part, couldn't find Ireland on a map. Fortunately very little of this money got further than off-shore bank accounts and laundered into private accounts. The IRA propaganda was more effective with the help of Boston politicians such as the former Speaker of the House, Tip O'Neil.

It is very easy to provide money, arms and propaganda when you don't have to live with the consequences and are safely tucked away in the States 3,000 miles away. A friend of mine a while ago referred to them as 'plastic paddies' and I tend to cringe when Americans tell me they are Irish. Of course they are not, their ancestors were. I still have a Scottish accent and it bugs me when Americans ask me if I am Irish.

Miriam Daly (45) was a member of the INLA and also a militant member of the Prisoners' Relatives Action Committee, and the national Hunger Strike Committee. In that campaign, she worked with Seamus Costello, and soon joined him in the Irish Republican Socialist Party and the Irish National Liberation Army. Costello was a former member of the OIRA and led a militant breakaway from them in 1973–4 and founded the IRSP and its political wing, the INLA. He was an intellectual and argued for a combination of socialist politics on economic issues in tandem with Republican terrorist activity. He had, allegedly masterminded the OIRA attack on the Officers' Mess of the Parachute Regiment in Aldershot on 22 February, 1972. On the 5th, having survived a previous attempt on his life and knowing that he was a marked man, he was shot dead in Dublin. After Costello's death Miriam Daly became chairperson, leading the party for two years. On the 26th, she was shot dead at home in the Andersonstown area of West Belfast.

Both Miriam and her husband Jim were being targeted by the UFF and their murder gang would have already 'staked' out the Daly home. In the late morning they drove into the Nationalist Andersonstown area, and burst into their house on Andersonstown Road with the intention of killing both. However, Jim Daly was at a German language course in Dublin and the Loyalist murder gang contented themselves with tying up Miriam Daly. After approximately three hours, they realised that he would not be returning and they shot her dead before making good their escape. One of the killers placed a pillow over her head in order to reduce the noise and shot her twice in the head. The Daly children discovered their murdered mother when they returned from school. As her funeral cortège passed the family home four masked INLA gunmen fired a volley of shots over the passing coffin. There were the usual accusations of collusion from the Republicans who saw a conspiracy under every bush; the truth was more prosaic. Just as the Provisionals and INLA killed anyone whom they saw as an enemy, so too did the Loyalist paramilitaries.

The hazards of having once belonged to the UDR and then omitting to 'request' that one's name be removed from PIRA's death list were ever more evident on the 28th. William Elliott (47), father of five, had once belonged to the Ulster Defence Regiment but had resigned and was instead concentrating on being a farmer. He was also an execu- tive member of the Official Ulster Unionists and as such was, in the perverted and insular view of the IRA, 'double' the enemy. On a sunny Saturday morning in Ballybay, County Monaghan inside the Irish Republic, he had gone into the small market town to buy cattle and was inspecting his purchases when a gunman walked up behind him. In the manner which has become traditional for the IRA, the gunman fired four shots into the back of Mr Elliott's head, killing him instantly. He then disappeared, knowing that he would be safe inside the terrorist haven which the Irish Republic, through its indifference to the suffering which the IRA had caused, stood for.

June was over and half of 1980 was already gone; eight people were dead, including five soldiers or former soldiers and a Protestant civilian. One Republican had been murdered by Loyalists, and one Loyalist had died in an 'own goal' explosion.

7

July

uring this month, seven more people would lose their lives, although deaths stayed mercifully in single figures again; three of whom would be soldiers and two would be police officers, this time from Gardaí Siochana. Two others, one of whom was a PIRA member would die in the tired old cliché '*disputed circumstances*'. One has the greatest respect for 'Lost Lives', but it is an overworked and overused expression. When we deal with the death of a Christopher Watson, an off-duty soldier, who was grieving the loss of his baby, we will note that the same publication omits to use the same words to describe the disgraceful actions of the Provisionals.[1]

IRA punishment squads which kept 'order' on the Nationalist housing estates ruled with a rod of iron, with a merciless ruthlessness and a cold-hearted approach to anyone who transgressed their 'laws'. Unlike the 'nutting squads' these PIRA personnel's task was to stop before the victim died; favoured methods of punishment included tarring and feathering, beating with Hurley sticks and knee-capping. Kneecapping is a form of malicious wounding, in which the victim is injured in the knee, using either a firearm or power drill to damage the knee joint. Contrary to popular belief, the patella (knee cap) is usually not injured in these incidents; rather damage to soft tissues that include nerves and arteries is the primary objective. Some victims can walk with a limp afterwards, others are crippled for life and there have been instances of a bungled job which has severed the femoral artery and caused the victim to bleed to death.

One such punishment squad was in operation in the Ballymurphy Estate on the night of 1 July 1980. An unnamed teenager was knee-capped by a two-man squad, alleged to include Terence 'Teddy' O'Neill (26) a volunteer in the PIRA's 2nd battalion. He and another man had just shot aforementioned teenager and were observed running away, still armed, from the Ballymurphy Tenants' Association building close to Glenalina Crescent, by an RUC patrol. The officers opened fire and hit both men, fatally wounding O'Neill and, judging by the blood stains found in a car which his companion had used to escape, badly wounding the second man. He was rushed to the RVH but he was found to be dead on arrival. There were of course allegations of 'cold-blooded murder' from Republican apologists, but after a near thousand deaths as a result of PIRA actions, no-one but the most sycophantic supporter was even listening.

On US Independence Day, the Newry Brigade of the IRA also decided to have a firework display and set in motion a plan to devastate the centre of Banbridge in Co

---

1   Thornton, David, Seamus Kelters, Brian Feeney and David McKittrick. *Lost Lives: The Stories of the Men, Women and Children who Died as a Result of the Northern Ireland Troubles.* (Edinburgh: Mainstream, 1999, revised ed. 2007).

Down. The town's main street is very unusual, and rises to a steep hill before levelling out. In 1834 an underpass was made, apparently because horses with heavy loads would faint before reaching the top of the hill. It was built by William Dargan and is officially named 'Downshire Bridge', though it is often called 'The Cut'. Around mid-morning, a caller claiming to represent the Provisionals telephoned a warning through to a hospital in nearby Newry, stating that the town centre would be blasted in exactly eight minutes. A warning was flashed to the RUC and the Army but it clearly was not enough time and desperate efforts were made to clear the shopping area around Newry Road and The Cut. The bomb – inside a stolen Ford Granada – was located and UDR soldiers were in the process of evacuating Saturday morning shoppers when the bomb's detonator fired. A car containing a woman and a young child were passing the car-bomb at that precise moment.

Had the normal sequence of events occurred, this author would be discussing how the young lady and her child had been killed instantly in a terrorist blast. However, happily to say, the expected explosion did not follow and all that the woman and nearby soldiers heard was a 'fizzing' sound as the bomb misfired. ATO officers could not be certain that the planned detonation would still not happen and the car had to be examined for a booby-trap and to ensure the device was truly a dud. When the car was finally made safe, five beer kegs packed with around 400 lb (182 kgs) of explosives were removed.

On the following day, Corporal Raymond Joseph Jackson (32) of the Army Air Corps was killed in a tragic RTA in Co Londonderry. On the 7th, the MOD announced that an Irish Regiment – the 5th Royal Inniskilling Dragoon Guards – was to be deployed in Northern Ireland. It was not considered politically correct to use Irish troops inside the Province for fear of the turmoil such a move might cause. However, as Mark 'C' of the UDR so succinctly put it: "No Irish troops in Northern Ireland? What the fuck do they think that the UDR was?" The famous 'Skins' whose Latin motto was: *'Vestigia nulla retrorsum'* (We do not retreat) was made up of 30 per cent Northern Irish as well as soldiers from the Irish Republic. Their battle honours stretch from Blenheim through the Boer War, to Mons, Ypres, the Somme and on to the Dunkirk Evacuation and to the Hook, Korea in 1952. Their actual physical presence on the streets was to depend on requirements, but a spokesman for the 'Skins' stated that the Regiment was enthusiastic to play its part in the peace-keeping. Their CO said: "We believe the Unit's tour in Northern Ireland will be to the advantage of the Security Forces as a whole." David Barzilay in his excellent book wrote: "Even in the early '70 when the proportion of Irish troops was lower, it would have been unreasonable to expect Irish soldiers to carry out operations, such as controlling riots in areas where they had perhaps been born and brought up."[2]

On the same day, two Irish police officers were killed by INLA members during a bank robbery in the Irish Republic. Constable Henry Byrne (29), father of two and Detective John Morley (38), father of three were killed in the pursuit of INLA men who had just carried out a robbery at Loughglynn, Co Roscommon. Three armed and masked men raided the Bank of Ireland in Ballaghaderreen, where they held staff and customers at gunpoint before leaving with IR£35,000. Gardaí arrived on the scene but

2   Barzilay, David, *The British Army at War in Ulster,* Vol 1. (London: Century, 1973).

were unarmed and unable to stop the armed men from escaping in a stolen Ford Cortina. However, as the robbers drove away, they were intercepted by a Gardaí patrol car from Castlerea containing four officers, and the two cars collided. One of the raiders jumped out of the Cortina and sprayed the patrol car with bullets, killing Gardaí Officer Henry Byrne instantly.

Detective John Morley, who was armed with an Israeli Uzi machine gun, wounded one of the men, but he himself was fatally wounded. One man left the Cortina and ran off while his two accomplices ran in the opposite direction. Both of these men were later arrested, while a third man was apprehended in the city of Galway almost two weeks later. The officers' deaths provoked a national outrage. Three men were tried, convicted and sentenced to death for their murders. Two of the sentences were later reduced to 40 years imprisonment while the third was overturned. Morley and Byrne were posthumously awarded the Scott Medal for their actions; the medals were presented to their families at a special ceremony in 1982.

On the 19th, the Provisional IRA plumbed new depths; they sank even lower into the sewer than it was considered possible. No longer could they claim to be the 'brave urban guerrillas' which they liked to portray themselves to a gullible Irish-American audience; no longer could they claim to have assumed the mantle of freedom fighters fighting the *'perfidy of Albion'*. Christopher John Watson (20) from Beaconsfield, Herts was a Rifleman in the Royal Green Jackets. On a tour of Northern Ireland, he had fallen in love with a Catholic girl from the Rosemount area of Londonderry and they had moved to England and had obtained Married Soldiers' Quarters (MSQ) in Cambridgeshire. However, when the battalion was posted to Cyprus, she returned to Londonderry where sadly, her baby was stillborn.

Naturally Rifleman Watson sought permission to return to the UK to comfort her, and he was granted compassionate leave with the strict proviso that he did not enter Londonderry. However, he chose to ignore this and met up with his wife and her family in the Village Inn in Rosemount Avenue on the edge of the Creggan. That he was dicked is absolutely unquestioned; by whom and whether or not there was any relationship between the dickers and his wife's family is open to question. As he sat with his in-laws, several men from the Creggan IRA walked into the pub and made a beeline for the unarmed young soldier. Without hesitation, one of the men shot Rifleman Watson twice in the head from point-blank range; he died instantly. William Ross, a Loyalist MP said of the IRA: "They showed the compassion that one would expect – from snakes." A pitiful specimen of a human being, in his role as apologist for the murderers stated afterwards: "As a guerrilla army confronted with a highly sophisticated and technologically advanced army, we cannot allow ourselves the luxury of fighting a war on our opponents' terms." There has never been an apology for the cowardly and shameful murder of the young Green Jacket. One does not always agree with the words of my contributors but on this occasion, one can only heartily endorse the bulk of the words of Lance Corporal 'A' whose memories follow.

David McAlinden, RUC

Words do not come easy to me at the best of times. On that night I was on duty with N1 Mobile Support Unit in the Creggan Estate. Our vehicles were at the scene fairly quickly. I then had the task of travelling in the ambulance with Rifleman

Watson to the Hospital. I can only say that he was not in pain and he had a fellow member of the Security Forces with him.

I'm sorry. RIP Chris.

LECTURES FROM THE PROVOS?
Lance Corporal 'A' Royal Green Jackets

I was getting towards the end of my time in the Army and after another bad tour of Ulster we were over in Cyprus on UN peace-keeping duties. Some bright spark said that Cyprus would be just like Belfast and Derry because the Turks hated the Greeks every bit as much as the Prods hated the Catholics. Was it bollocks the same; it was nothing like it! The Greek Cypriots had it in for the Turkish Cypriots and wouldn't have done each other any favours, but it was nothing remotely like the deadly loathing the two sides had in Ireland. I thought that they were animals the lot of them. The Catholics would throw shit and bricks at you and the Prods would offer us cups of tea but most likely spit in the cups and laugh about it behind your backs. Anyway, what happened to Chris Watson was the lowest thing a human being could do to another. To lure a kid into that trap, to shoot him down while he was unarmed and trying to get over the loss of a little one shows to me that the IRA were just filth; scum the lot of them and every time we killed one of the bastards, I cheered; I really did.

When I was a civvie, I had a job with a Printing Company in Watford and it was after the two undercover scaleybacks (Royal Signals) were lynched by the Catholic mob in Andersonstown after the Gibraltar funeral. This twat at work on the Monday morning was giving it large about how they got what they deserved! You know they say 'the red mist just descended' – well for me it did. I lamped him one, put him on his backside and loosened a few of his teeth. The bottom line was that he said that if I apologised, he wouldn't push it and the personnel department called me in and they also said that if I said sorry, it would just be a written warning for me. I thought of the two lads torn to pieces by them heathens and I thought of Chris Watson and I just went: "Fuck that for a game of soldiers!" and walked out. I got a letter dismissing me a couple of days later.

I heard that big daft Chris had gone back to see his Mrs and he was dicked and the cowardly animals shot him in the head in a pub. Fucking scumbags; we didn't shoot enough of them and I felt like throwing things at the telly every time one of them smarmy Sinn Féin came on bleating about 'shoot-to-kill' and collusion this and collusion that! Well, you might not want to print what I say, but we were always hearing about the morality of the IRA and that we were fighting Army bully boys! Well you can print this; I will not take any fucking lessons in morality from those twats!

Poignantly enough, all sections of the community and from both sides of the sectarian divide were quick to condemn the Provisionals for their despicable actions. There was almost a feeling of *déjà vous* in relation to the murder of another off-duty soldier in virtually the same area in 1972 and the local outrage was very similar. The incident refers to the murder of a young soldier home on leave from West Germany. Ranger William Best was promised a safe passage in and around the Creggan when he came home. However, on his first night home, he was abducted; beaten and shot dead by the OIRA after the Provisionals had goaded them into doing so.

On Sunday 20th a PIRA team planted a car bomb in Lisnaskea, Co Fermanagh, causing extensive damage to the centre of the town. Warnings were given and the Army/ RUC was able to evacuate the town; damage included a destroyed branch of Barclay's Bank and several pubs. A spokesman for Sinn Féin warned that further attacks would be made until the British announced their plans for a phased withdrawal from the island of Ireland. On occasions such as this one, when a pub could be safely evacuated before an explosion – often the bombs were no-warning and instant detonations – a common sight would be to witness drinkers being led outside, still jealously clutching their pint glasses. They would cling on to them for dear life and then retire a safe distance to the police cordons and watch as young men from ATO went inside to attempt to defuse the deadly devices. The author has witnessed this phenomenon of Northern Ireland, because make no mistake, it was a phenomenon. Where else in the world for example would evacuated civilians hold so much hatred for the very men who were trying to save their lives at the mortal risk to their own? These callous-minded and insular people held so much contempt for young men from England, Scotland, Wales or even their own Northern Ireland and yet the actions of these young men was designed to preserve their worthless lives as they looked on, beer glasses in hand, willing the bomb to explode in the faces of their rescuers.

The work of the British Army in Northern Ireland could take on many aspects and it wasn't simply all foot patrols, mobile patrols or fire fights or riots; there was the mundane and the prosaic. In a 48-hour operation, units of the Royal Engineers' 29th Field Squadron and the newly arrived Royal Artillery's 19th Field Regiment plugged some major holes in their section of the Irish border. Having previously cratered one of the routes known to be used by PIRA cross-border teams, Royal Engineers returned to the crossing in a remote area of Co Fermanagh for routine inspection. It was found that IRA sympathisers had driven an old mini-bus into the crater, placing steel and wood on top and had effectively improvised a bridge over which they could drive vehicles. As part of the operation, just over 100 soldiers had dug in around the site and, living off their rations of food and water, had maintained a 24-hour vigil as a 20 man strong team worked on making the border crossing impassable once more. Using explosives and lifting gear, the 'obstruction' was lifted clear. Once done, using more explosives and excavating equipment, they constructed a 35 metre-long trench on the Ulster side of the border. Thus, the Army had again sealed off an important crossing point for the Provisionals.

On the 23rd, a 16 year-old Catholic youth was shot near the Lower Ormeau Road in South Belfast by the RUC. It was a dreadful accident as an RUC officer had glimpsed Michael McCartan (16) carrying a paintbrush but had mistaken it for a handgun and had fired at him. The boy who lived in Artana Street had gone to Dromara Street, some 30–40 yards away, in order to paint PIRA graffiti on a gable-end wall. He was challenged by an RUC patrol and in a panic he turned to run away when the officer shot. One has to remember, that this was 1980, it was the 11th year of the Troubles; approaching 2,400 had already been killed and a substantial number of those were policeman. In this context, the officer had to make a split second, life-or-death decision. He chose wrongly and an innocent young boy died. That is to the regret of this author, but significantly *Lost Lives* describes the shooting as '*disputed*' – now almost their standard cliché – when it was clearly a mistaken killing with no premeditation.

It is also important to note that although PIRA stated that they were not active in the area, bombs had been thrown locally, and the reason that the RUC patrol was in the area was because reports of a gunman in the locality had been received; tension was bound to be high. The Provisional IRA chose to turn these residential areas into battlefields and they must shoulder a high measure of responsibility for all that happened. The death came just four days after the callous murder of Rifleman Watson and yet the words '*disputed*' or '*controversial*' appear nowhere in this august tome's description of the killing. The officer concerned was later charged with murder but acquitted after a trial lasting five days. The McCartan family was no stranger to violence and tragedy and a family member was shot by Loyalists and another had been injured in the Loyalist bomb attack on the 'Rose and Crown' pub in 1974.

Aughnacloy (Irish: *Achadh na Cloiche*, meaning 'field of the stone') is a village in Co Tyrone, close to the border with the Republic and Co Monaghan; the village is about 12 miles southwest of Dungannon. Because of its strategic importance, there were very often VCPs at the crossing on Moy Bridge; however, there was no permanent VCP and the IRA often used the area to smuggle arms and explosives over from the Irish Republic. On Monday 27th, the RUC were warned that a bomb had been planted on Moy Bridge. A patrol went out but found nothing and declared it a hoax call. However, the local Army unit – 2nd Queen's, including an advance squad from the Royal Highland Fusiliers (RHF) – was called out to set up a temporary VCP.

During its stay on Moy Bridge, Corporal Robert 'Bob' McNamee Thompson (26), father of a young child and another comrade from the Queen's Regiment approached a car parked near the bridge which had aroused their suspicions. The RHF had not been long in-Province and like all units coming out for either a two-year Residential Battalion tour or the four-month emergency tours, had sent an advance squad whose job was to familiarise themselves with the ground, study local INT and get to know the faces of the players. The young NCO who lived in Hamilton in Scotland and his Queens comrade walked around the vehicle and looked inside; as he did so, he said: "It's all right; it's just a dumped car." At that precise moment, the vehicle exploded and he was killed absolutely instantly and his comrade – Private William Ellis – badly injured. Private Ellis was casualty evacuated to Musgrave Park Hospital (MPH) before flown to a military hospital on the mainland. Corporal Thompson was buried at Bent Cemetery near Hamilton. His death left a 5-year-old girl without a father; she will be now 33.

The last day of July witnessed a PIRA attempt to kill or maim soldiers from the Royal Marines in the Crossmaglen area. A 50 lb (23 kg) device had been left in a field close to the RUC base where soldiers were known to patrol and where, in the past, VCPs had been set up. The site was on the edge of the Ardross Estate near Castleblaney Street. The device was a remote-controlled bomb. It was spotted under some rubbish with a radio antennae protruding and ATO were immediately called in. However, during the disarming process, it exploded; the blast damaged houses up to 70 yards away and killed five cows in an adjoining field. The bomb had been fired remotely by a watching PIRA bomber with little regard for anyone on the nearby Nationalist Ardross.

July ended with seven more deaths; three soldiers and two policemen – Gardaí Siochana officers – and one civilian died. The Republicans lost one of their members, shot by the RUC. There were no sectarian deaths this month.

8

August

The death toll was slightly higher this month, with nine deaths including four soldiers and another policeman. Two 'ordinary decent criminals' were killed in this month and the Provisionals perpetrated a sickening hoax to make the wife of a policeman believe that her husband was still alive.

A major investigation was launched on both sides of the Irish border to look at suggestions of either collusion – on the part of Gardaí – or incompetence into how a stolen car, containing 100 1b (46 kg) of explosives could be left abandoned on the border crossing. Corporal Thompson of the RHF[1] [see previous chapter] was killed and his comrade Private Ellis badly injured. Upon investigation by ATO personnel, it would appear that the car was intended to be left elsewhere, but was either abandoned on seeing troops, or had simply broken down. The bomb had being primed and set on a timer as the bombers left the car and it was just ghastly bad luck that it exploded just as the two soldiers were standing next to it. No doubt PIRA members were complimenting themselves on a 'precision bombing.'

Dave Young, Ammunition Technical Officer
Several years later I was called to give expert witness evidence against two terrorist bombers in Belfast Crown Court. They were pleading not guilty. During the trial, the forensic evidence I had recovered was discussed, including some PVC tape. The court heard there were two perfect fingerprints imbedded in the adhesive near the roughly torn ends of the tape. It matched some found in the terrorist's home – the Bomb Factory, with fingerprints and ragged torn ends. They changed their plea to guilty and were put away for 14 years! Without the forensic evidence I had recovered they would have been free to make and place more bombs, cause untold destruction and maybe deaths.

On the 3rd, a PIRA murder gang having received intelligence that a serving part-time UDR soldier would cross into the Republic set up an ambush for him. William 'Willie' Clarke (59), father of four was known to cross into Ireland and visit family members in Pettigo, County Donegal. Private Clarke lived at Castlederg, County Tyrone and often drove the 12 or so miles to the border town of Pettigo, north of Lough Derg. Private Clarke had only crossed over the border a matter of seconds before masked men carrying automatic weapons opened fire on his car. He was killed almost instantly and his car

---

1   See previous chapter.

crashed at the side of the country lane. Gardaí officers were called and very quickly, his lifeless body was found dead in his Austin car which was riddled with bullet-holes.

Gardaí officers set up a VCP on the road with the border to the North and it quickly paid dividends and a stolen car approached the snap check point. The car containing three PIRA men stopped on seeing the police and reversed away, crashing into the side of the lane, close to where they had – in all likelihood – murdered the UDR man. A chase continued on foot across fields but the Gardaí had to stop the pursuit when the IRA men pulled out weapons. A helicopter was called in to no avail and the murderers of Private Clarke escaped. At his funeral, his local Church leader said this of him:

> When the bullets of the assassin strike in the heart of the peaceful countryside there arise feelings of disgust and anger, but such murders in no way help the terrorist's cause. Rather they strengthen the determination of all right-thinking people never to allow these callous and evil men to win the day.

On Saturday 9 August, the ninth anniversary of Internment, major riots broke out all over Northern Ireland, with special flashpoints in major Republican areas of Belfast, Londonderry and Newry. By the end of the following day, after 48-hours of mindless violence, four people, including two soldiers were dead and scores had been injured. First to die was Gunner Peter Arthur Clark (22) who was helping to remove burning barricades at Ligoniel north of Belfast. The barricade comprising a burning car was blocking the main road and Gunner Clark was caught between an RE bulldozer and a PIG and was crushed to death.

Nat Campbell, Royal Engineers
Ken I'm not too good at writing, with all the commas and dots etc., but will tell you what actually happened. On the night in question, we were called from our squat at Girdwood Barracks and taken up through the Shankill to the top of the hill near the 'Seven Mile Straight' and then told to start a descent toward Ligoniel Road. It must have been a 1-in-4 descent and we should never have attempted it in the bulldozer, aka the 'Scooby'. It did not fare well, once we started downhill. I was in the Land Rover with Corporal Chris Moore and Pete Lord was driving the Barford dump truck. When we got into position above the barricade a PIG pulled on front of the 'Scooby', and the lads started to de-bus. At that point, the 'Scooby' started to roll forward and the operator – a Sapper called Pete Legg tried to drop the bucket, but in seconds it had collided with the PIG. Sadly, this crushed Gunner Clark who was closing the back doors; he was killed instantly. We radioed for an ambulance and one came up from the city, on the wrong side of the barricade, so the locals tried to stop it, as they knew something was wrong. After that, the order was given to let the 'Scooby' move the barricade as well as the local idiots off the road.

Sadly, it was all far too late to save Gunner Clark, whom we all called 'Ginge', but it was a most tragic death which need never have happened, as the barricade was not blocking a major route. That is the whole story of this incident; it's good to finally get it all out.

Claire Piwinski, Civilian

I remember that tour of Ireland so vividly; I was only 18 when I married and went first to Germany. I was young, stupid and very green. I remember 'Ginge' coming to my Army quarter one night when he was on duty. I think my hubby was the duty Sergeant. Bless him; he was just a boy, around my age. All us wives saw it on the news that a soldier from 5 Regiment was dead, and we all waited for the call which we dreaded to tell us it was our husband. Young 'Ginge' Clark was just a boy; he was so unlucky that day. It could have been anyone of them, with what was going on at that time. Belfast was not a good place to be then.

Bill Parsons, Royal Artillery

Pete was in the lead PIG with the 'Scooby' following them. When they arrived they turned off down a side road, to avoid being silhouetted by the burning road block. When they stopped, Pete was one of the first to get out of the back, as the heavy doors were trying to close; they were facing downhill. He returned to help open the back door, just as the 'Scooby' got there. Its brakes had failed at the top of the hill, and as Pete was opening the doors on the PIG, he was hit in his midsection by the large bucket and pinned to the back of the PIG. I remember 'Ginge' as an argumentative – in a funny way – gobber! But he was our gobber. RIP mate.

The next to die on this anniversary of Internment was a 19-year-old civilian who had no connections with the Troubles nor with that day's rioting. James McCarron, a young Catholic boy was on the way to his home in Ramoan Drive, close to Glen Road on the Andersonstown Estate. He had stopped to chat to friends on Shaw's Road, some 400 yards or five minutes brisk walk from where he lived. Sadly for him, sporadic rioting which had begun earlier in the day and soldiers were close by trying to extricate a PIG which had caught fast on a barricade. An INLA sniper was trying to hit soldiers but one of his shots missed and hit Mr McCarron, killing him instantly. *An Phoblacht* (Republican News) was quick to blame the Army for shooting the young man, but an INLA member was later jailed for life for his and another man's murder.

Very shortly afterwards, another innocent civilian was killed – this time, regrettably by the Army – when a Catholic social worker was hit by a baton round; a plastic bullet in common parlance. Michael Donnelly (21) had just finished supervising a group of handicapped children in the Leeson Street area off the Falls Road. He was confronted by several soldiers and for reasons not explained, a baton round was fired and hit Mr Donnelly in the chest. He managed to stagger off but very shortly afterwards, he collapsed and died. This author regrets this man's death and can offer no explanation as to why an innocent man died in such tragic circumstances.

The madness of the anniversary 48-hours came to an end the following day when a PIRA bomb, estimated at 200 lb (91 kg) was detonated electronically in the Forkhill area of South Armagh. At around 1400 hours, a Parachute Regiment foot patrol passed the hidden device placed at the side of the Carrive Road. As it exploded, Sergeant Brian Michael Brown (29), father of three was hit directly and killed instantly. Another soldier and a passing motorist were very badly injured. The bomber had to have an excellent line of sight view and clearly saw the passing motorist and fired anyway, irrespective of the possibility of an innocent death. Sergeant Brown of 2 Para was from Portsmouth and his funeral was held at Porchester in Hampshire.

Even during the Troubles, amidst the terror, 'routine' crimes of murder, abuse, common assault and, naturally theft still occurred. The criminals who perpetrated these crimes often ended up in places like Crumlin Road Jail, alongside gunmen and bombers, but liked to consider themselves as 'ordinary decent criminals' or ODCs. Two of these ODCs found themselves facing armed soldiers when they robbed the Greenvale Restaurant at Cookstown, County Tyrone. On the night of the 14th, they emerged from the premises carrying stolen items and were confronted by an Army foot patrol; they were ordered to stop. Now, at this juncture, one has to take into consideration the IRA's penchant for bombing pubs and restaurants as part of their 'economic warfare' and the patrol had to take this into the equation. When the men ran, the soldiers fired and although one man escaped, James Bell (24), father of three and an ODC fell dying. The man who escaped – the dead man's brother – was later recaptured and taken to Court.

The following evening there was a shocking and gruesome murder, which even by the shocking and gruesome standards of the Troubles showed that Northern Ireland's decent people still had the capacity to be horrified. An elderly father and his middle-aged daughter were found slaughtered in a house in Wolfhill Avenue in the Ligoniel area, north of Belfast. Not very far from where Gunner Clark had been accidentally killed, William Younger (87) and his daughter Letitia (50), both Protestants living in a Catholic area, were found murdered. Mr Younger was stabbed and shot in his bed and his daughter was stabbed through the neck with a pitchfork, pinned to the ground and as she lay dying in agony and totally helpless, she had been shot twice. When neighbours investigated, she was still alive, though barely, but died in the Mater Hospital on Crumlin Road. No organisation claimed responsibility, but informed speculation states that the type of crazed killing which was more reminiscent of extreme Loyalist paramilitaries could well have been the UVF.

The Ardoyne – from the Irish: *Ard Eoin* meaning Eoin's height – is a fiercely nationalist, working class area in north Belfast. It is also a large rundown area comprised of some post war semi-detached but mainly terraced housing. During the Troubles, 13 serving soldiers, two former soldiers and one RUC officer were killed in the Ardoyne; additionally, Loyalist murder gangs killed at least eighr innocent Catholics. On the 17th, in what was clearly a 'come on', the RUC were called onto the estate in order to investigate a burglary in Alliance Avenue. Unknown to the officers, armed PIRA had taken over a house in Etna Drive, which forms a 'T' junction with Alliance Avenue. As officers got out of their vehicle, the gunmen opened fire and a salvo of at least 30 rounds was fired at the officers from a distance of well over 100 yards. Colette Meek (47), mother of four, was standing with a group of neighbours watching the incident with the police when the firing started. Before the group of mainly women had chance to react, Mrs Meek was hit and mortally wounded. She was rushed to hospital where she died shortly afterwards. Two members of Fianna Éireann, the youth wing of the Provisionals, were later jailed for manslaughter. It was foolhardy for the IRA or '*Pinnies*' as they are sometimes known to have allowed this shot to take place from such a long distance and criminally irresponsible to allow the area to be turned into a battlefield, especially with so many civilians gathered around the policemen. The death of Mrs Meek rests firmly and squarely upon their shoulders.

On the 22nd, a member of the Royal Pioneer Corps was killed in an RTA 'somewhere in the Province.' Lance Corporal Graham Lee (23) was a member of an unsung, yet vital cog in the machine which was the British Army. Raised as the Auxiliary Military Pioneer Corps on 17 October 1939, it was renamed the Pioneer Corps on 22 November 1940. The late Stanley Whitehouse, author of *Fear is the Foe* which dealt with his personal slog from the beaches of Normandy in June 1944 to the battle of the Reichswald in February 1945, told the author that he and his comrades referred to them as 'grave-diggers.' He once told the author: "Right before an advance, we'd all be having a nervous pee and then, just to cheer up us, the Pioneer chappies arrived with dozens of wooden crosses to mark the lads who were to be killed. You looked at those brilliant white crosses and realised that one could be for you!" The Corps gained many awards for gallantry and in addition received American, French, Dutch, Greek, Belgian and Italian awards. Some 2,800 men of the Corps laid down their lives overseas. The Corps' motto is *Labor omnia vincit*, which translates as 'work conquers all.' The author is aware of this soldier's date of birth, service number and rank but has no further information surrounding the circumstances of his premature death.

On the same day, the Provisionals planted a car bomb containing 500 lb (227 kg) of explosives in Cathedral Road, Armagh, north of the town centre, on the route of a UDR mobile patrol. Although there are houses and commercial premises along this road, there are many open fields. The bombers had a clear line of sight, and they cannot have failed to notice that as the UDR patrol in two vehicles passed the parked car, two civilian cars were in exactly the same spot on the opposite side of the road. Despite this, they fired the bomb – from a safe distance, of course, with the border just 9–10 miles away – as all the vehicles crossed. There was a massive explosion and all the cars were wrecked. Miraculously, no-one died, but in addition to three UDR men who were hurt, four civilians including a tiny 6-week-old baby were seriously injured. One wonders whether these bombers who clearly had no hearts or compassion also had no brains.

On the 24th, there was another, what can only be described as sectarian, murder as the UFF killed a Catholic and then tried to pass it off as the assassination of a member of the IRSP/INLA. Rodney McCormick (22) from Larne in Co Antrim had been tried and convicted of a robbery which he had committed in 1975 when he was only 17. Somewhat naively, he had allied himself to INLA prisoners while in prison, for what can only be described as reasons of bravado; perhaps a sense of 'safety in numbers'. However, on release from prison, he had worked in several factories and had not continued any Republican associations. On the night in question, he returned home with his wife after a night out at a local pub and as they reached their front door, masked gunmen from the UFF confronted them. One man shouted to Mrs McCormick: "It's your husband we want!" and pulled her away before shooting Rodney 10 times from very close range. He died almost immediately.

On the 29th, a top INLA bomb-maker who himself was killed some 11 years later, prepared a bomb which killed another innocent civilian. An INLA unit had left a booby-trapped magazine on the side of the road, knowing that a passing Army unit would pick it up and see if it was loaded. They then called in a hoax warning of a dead body and sat back and waited for the Army/RUC to appear. However, before any SF could arrive, Frank McGrory (52) an unemployed farmworker cycled past the magazine and stopped to pick it up; it exploded as he touched it and he was killed instantly. An apologist for the

Republican terror group; later tried to blame the Army for not sealing off the area. One thing which the INLA shared with their Provisional brothers-in-arms was hypocrisy twice the size of Belfast's Black Mountain.

On the final day of August, the Provisionals killed another policeman, close to Newtownhamilton in South Armagh. Wallace Allen (49) was a Reserve Constable in the RUCR and also worked as a Government Inspector as well as assisting with a part-time milk delivery round. At around 0800, he was attacked by PIRA gunmen and although it would appear that he was shot in the head and died immediately, his body was not found for 12 days. Although the police found bloodstains inside the cab of the lorry he was driving, the IRA's silence led to a false hope that he was still alive and being held captive somewhere close to the border. When his vehicle was discovered, on the Northern side of the border, officers had a narrow escape when a booby-trapped milk churn exploded. It was almost as though the Republican terror group was taunting his loved ones and colleagues as they maintained their silence. It led to searches of the area, appeals for his safe return by churchmen and senior politicians. Indeed, Seamus Mallon of the SDLP even offered to meet his 'kidnappers' anywhere and offered also guarantees for their safety. Allen's dead body was finally found at Trainor's Bridge in Co Armagh just yards north of the Irish border on 12 September. On 4 September, in a very belated statement, delayed so as to stretch the agony of waiting for his family, a PIRA apologist admitted that he had been shot while 'resisting arrest.'

August ended and deaths had risen after the several months of falling figures, and 13 people had died. Soldiers made up four of the deaths with a policeman also dying. During this month, eight civilians – six Catholics and two Protestants – had been killed; just one of the deaths could be said to be overtly sectarian. Three of the deaths were at the hands of the Republicans and certainly one; possibly three of the others were down to Loyalists. Almost half of the murders in August can be laid at the door of the Republicans.

9

September

Deaths in this autumnal month were amongst the lowest of the Troubles, with only four deaths, including a UDR 'Greenfinch' and the continuing agony for the Hearst family. An ambulance man was also murdered because he had once served in the RUCR.

On 8 October, 1977 part-time UDR soldier Margaret Hearst was murdered by PIRA gunman Dessie '*The Border Fox*' O'Hare at her caravan home in Middletown, Co Armagh. She was a part-time soldier – a Greenfinch – and also a single mother of a 3-year-old girl. As she relaxed in the caravan, masked gunmen threw an empty milk churn through the window, shattering it and waking up Miss Hearst as they burst into the caravan. They shot her 10 times and a round went through a partition wall and just missed her sleeping toddler, hitting her *Kermit the Frog* toy as it lay on the pillow next to her head. As the third anniversary of her cowardly murder approached, her loved ones and, by now 6-year-old little girl, thought that they were over the worst of their grief, but fate thought otherwise. The sickness inherent in the leaders of the Provisional IRA ensured that their grief would continue. On the night of the 4th of September, her father – Ross Hearst (55) – whose only 'crime' was to be a member of the local Orange Lodge was abducted by PIRA gunmen as he drove over the Irish border to attend a religious service. He had stopped at a bar before crossing over en-route to Tullylush, County Monaghan. They drove him away in his own car and stopped at Middletown on the County Armagh side of the border. They shot him four times in the head and then set his car on fire. An Irish citizen was later caught and tried inside the Irish Republic; he was convicted and sentenced to life in an Irish jail.

The murder of Margaret Hearst who was unarmed at the time was cowardly beyond belief and really illustrates the pathological nature of the Provisional IRA. What purpose – other than pure terrorism – her murder served can never be explained to this author. To perpetuate the agony of the Hearst family by another needless and cowardly murder leaves one in utter despair. A most notable author advised me not to become emotionally involved in the crimes of the terrorists, but simply and calmly and dispassionately report them. I have failed that test but will not resist my instincts to condemn the nature and behaviour of these people who shamed Ireland; they did not re-unite her, they simply made the divisions ever wider.

O'Hare is still alive and whether or not he has any kind of guilt feeling about his life of terror is known only to him. One would like to know if he feels that the murder of Margaret Ann Hearst in 1977 advanced the cause of Republicanism in Ireland; this author would like an answer to that question. In 1987 O'Hare told a journalist he was only interested in the bomb and the bullet and did not believe in politics. He also allegedly confessed to murdering 26 people. This man was once described as a "psychotic killer who (could) be charming and manipulative." Further to this, I would like to know who sanctioned the murder of Mr Hearst and why this was thought necessary to the Provisionals' long-term strategy of reuniting Ireland.

Earlier that day, the Provisionals had bombed the centre of Cookstown, County Tyrone as they continued to destroy the heart of the country's economy. A stolen car was parked outside a shop in William Street, with a beer keg in the boot, packed with 100 lb (45 kgs) of explosives, timed to go off once the bombers had driven off in a second stolen car. ATO attended and soldiers from the Royal Highland Fusiliers searched the town for more devices. The bomb caused widespread damage, several injuries and terrified scores of people into spending their money elsewhere rather than risk being maimed by the IRA. Injuries were caused to people by flying glass and shops up to 50 yards away were also damaged. An ATO spokesman said afterwards: "The device was obviously designed to cause maximum destruction to shops in a busy town centre. It is extremely fortunate that warning time was given to enable shop owners and families doing their shopping to evacuate the area. Had that not been possible, the injuries to people in the street would have been horrific."

William Street is part of the busy A29 which runs into the centre of the town. Today, there is a busy Boots the Chemists, a branch of 'Cardland', McGlaughlin's Bakery, Brevery Grill Bar, several High Street banks and even a Falls Pharmacy. The memories of the Troubles are still fresh and when the author drove through Cookstown in 2008 and noticed all the parked cars there, one was forced to recognise how easy it would be to leave a car, packed with explosives there amongt all the other innocently parked vehicles. It may well be a truism to state: "the bomber will always get through."

Further south, the South Armagh PIRA was carrying out a similar operation this time in Newtownhamilton. Several gunmen had hijacked a milk tanker and placed a large amount of explosives inside. It appears that an attempt was made to transport the bomb into the town, but it had been abandoned on the outskirts. As ATO officers were carrying out disposal procedures, it exploded, utterly destroying the tanker. No soldiers were hurt and a unit of the Royal Marines assisted in ensuring that there were no further devices.

On the 7th, in an excellent example of the cross-border co-operation which only rarely existed between the Irish SF and their Northern counterparts, 3 tonnes (3,000 kgs) were intercepted and seized as the IRA attempted to drive it into the North. The seizures came in two separate incidents on the County Donegal/County Londonderry section of the border. At the same time in Dungannon, County Tyrone, a British Army foot patrol was covering a rural area just outside the Nationalist Ponderosa Estate. The soldiers from the Royal Highland Fusiliers (RHF) had gone firm by the side of a country road where, unknown to them a large roadside explosive device with a command wire had been left. A watching bomber waited until the patrol was virtually on top of the device and then fired from his vantage point. The RHS men were somewhat bemused to hear a fizzing device as the detonator fired but failed to explode the primary charge. ATO discovered the actual device which was 10 lb (4.5 kgs) of explosives inside a plastic bag, next to a shoe-box packed with metal bolts. Had it exploded, injuries would have been severe if not fatal. That day ended with another explosion at Silverbridge, close to Crossmaglen when a 100 lb (45 kgs) device exploded close to where Royal Engineers were resupplying an Army unit. A bus had just passed by only seconds before the blast and a young girl had to be treated for shock afterwards.

On the 16th, there was another attempt to kill and maim soldiers when a PIRA bombing unit packed 700 lb (319 kgs) in milk churns and loaded them inside a water-filled culvert underneath the Lisnaskea-Newtownbutler Road, a route used by the SF. At around midday, a border patrol from 19 Field Regiment Royal Artillery, aided by Royal Engineers and Army Dog Units (ADU) discovered the devices as well as a command wire leading to an elevated hedgerow some 250 yards away. As there were several families in the immediate vicinity, some less than 50 yards away from what would have been a massive explosion, the soldiers were forced to evacuate the area.

SUICIDES IN THE UDR
Mark 'C', UDR and Royal Artillery
Nearly every Regiment which served during Op Banner suffered suicides or 'death by violent or unnatural causes' as the MOD like to call it, but for some reason it became a bigger problem for the UDR and Royal Irish Regiment. I can only think it was because of the constant threat that we were under 24/7, 365 days a year that finally wore them down.

10 UDR had a particular bad time in the early 80s when we lost three full-time and one part-time soldier in just over a three-and-a-half year period; two of them in a terrible three day period in November 1984. Then, to make matters worse, another full-time soldier cracked up and fired a full mag of 7.62 up the corridor next the Armoury at Girdwood the same week; how he didn't hit anyone is a miracle, as there was one platoon coming off duty and another going on. Also at the same time, civvie workmen were building a new fence, and in places it was only a roll of barbed wire, separating the camp and houses, so we all thought the camp was under attack, I have never seen so many soldiers taking up fire positions with a wide range of army issue and personal protection weapons! Again it was a miracle that none of the civilians who appeared at their house windows overlooking the fence, were not shot.

After the incidents I described and the two funerals which followed, a lot of the boys were very unhappy and there was even talk of mass resignations as part of a protest. Owing to the dangers the Regiment was under, soldiers were allowed to leave giving two weeks' notice at that time. However, it came to nothing as we all knew we had to soldier on and get on with the job of trying to defeat terrorism.

Another unfortunate victim of all this tragedy was my own brother-in-law and I imagine his story is not unique. In 1982 he was Guard Commander in Girdwood when one of the lads shot himself with his own .38 PPW in front of him. He tried to save him by putting his fist into the head wound but the lad died at the scene. Vic was haunted by this and started drinking heavily; slowly over the years his body succumbed to the alcohol and he eventually died of organ failure. I don't know of the full extent of suicides during or after Operation Banner, but I know it was a terrible toll and the unmention-able part of the whole conflict.

On the 23rd, Constable Ernest Johnston (34) of the RUCR was murdered by PIRA gunmen at his home in Lisrace, County Fermanagh. He had just returned home after finishing duty at Rosslea and was about to open the garage door before going inside to his wife and two children. As he did so, masked gunmen who had been hiding in his garden opened fire with automatic weapons and he was shot in the head and back and mortally wounded. Neighbours stated that the gunmen, in a frenzy of shooting fired at least 15 rounds at the part-time policeman. His neighbours drove him to the nearby Erne Hospital but he was dead on arrival. He had already been injured on 11 February this year, in the explosion which killed his two colleagues, Winston Howe and Joseph Rose.

Johnston had recently put his border farm up for sale with the intention of moving out of the area. In 1982, known PIRA gunman Séamus McElwaine was convicted of his murder. The previous year, a 20-year-old County Monaghan woman was found guilty of conspiracy to murder and sentenced to six years for her part in the policeman's death. Séamus Turlough McElwaine was a member of PIRA's South Fermanagh Brigade and received a life sentence for the cowardly murder of Constable Johnston. However, in 1986, he escaped from the Maze Prison during a mass break out of 38 convicted terrorists. He was at liberty for three years and allegedly killed at least 10 people.

His murderous past caught up with him on 26 April 1986, when he and McElwaine and Seán Lynch, were preparing to ambush an army patrol near Roslea in County Fermanagh. Unknown to them, an undercover SAS unit were also in the area and it was the IRA men who instead were ambushed. Both men were wounded – McElwaine mortally – but Lynch managed to crawl away to safety. In April 2006 approximately 1,000 people in Roslea paid tribute to McElwaine during the traditional commemoration to mark the Easter Rising. It is utterly astounding that these people could pay homage to such an evil and cold-blooded killer.

The author visited the village in 2014 and found it astounding that that such a Republican stronghold, anti-British, certainly anti-English hatred spilling over was actually a part of the United Kingdom. Dominated by McCague's Bar, the village boast at least four PIRA memorials as well as a homage to the 1981 hunger-strikers. The daughter of a slain UDR soldier told me:

> They can spout that they are anti-English and don't want to be part of the UK, but they still accept our dole and social security payments and other British Government handouts. They are two-faced hypocrites and should be made to go live in the bankrupt Republic!

The day after the murder of the RUCR man, there was another attempt in the Silverbridge area, in South Armagh; in 'bandit country'. The attempt took place at Ford's Cross, approximately three miles from the Irish border and involved a large amount of explosives linked to a booby trap and designed to be sprung if and when patrolling soldiers examined derelict farm buildings. The devices had been packed inside several empty gas cylinders and buried inside a barn and another building, both of which, as stated previously were derelict. However, the troops in the area – from 41 Royal Marine Commando – were already in a state of high alert as in the preceding days, several bombs had exploded in the district; empty farm buildings on a known patrol route was just too obvious a target. Using ADU and Royal Engineers, a path to the site was cleared before ATO officers were able to make all of the devices safe.

On the 25th, a UDR 'Greenfinch' – Women Private Constance Evelyn Beattie (42) – died on duty. Sadly, the author has no further details other than her date of birth and

Service number. Although the circumstances of her demise are unknown, she was the only soldier to die this month. In the early days of the UDR, female members of the RMP accompanied patrols when available to enable female suspects to be searched. There were never enough of these RMP searchers, so it was deemed necessary to supplement their numbers. In 1973 an act enabled the recruitment of women into the UDR. On 16 August 1973, a regular army officer from the Women's Royal Army Corps (WRAC) Major Eileen Tye took up the post of Commander Women at the Regiment's HQ. By September, over 350 had been enrolled and the first enlistments were carried out at 2 UDR's HQ in Armagh on the 16th of that month. Uniforms were initially a problem as the only available clothing was mostly Auxiliary Territorial Services (ATS) surplus from the last war. This was resolved in time although many women were unhappy with the semi-formal skirts and knee length boots which they were forced to wear in all weathers; they also wore a silk cravat in their battalion colour.

On the same day, the Belfast-Dublin rail line was again closed following another bomb alert. An anonymous caller warned that a device had been placed at Altnaveigh Bridge near to Newry and all services were immediately halted. Shortly after the warning, an explosion caused the tracks to buckle. Within minutes and without any warning, a second bomb exploded, this time at Batleagh Bridge on the Lurgan–Portadown stretch of the line. The Provisionals were not known to do things by half, and a search of the track was then launched, with troops from 11 UDR and the Royal Engineers examining every inch of the track. A short distance from the explosion, another viable device was found, and defused by ATO.

On the last day of the month, a former policeman who served in the RUCR was shot dead at his place of work as an ambulance man at Belfast's RVH. The Royal Victoria Hospital, commonly known as 'the Royal', the RVH or the Royal Belfast is located at the corner of the Falls Road and Grosvenor Road in the heart of Nationalist territory. Work on the hospital began in 1888 and was completed in 1906 at a time when the island of Ireland was one country and before the Easter uprising of 1916. Since the onset of the Troubles in 1969, the bulk of the consequent injuries – bombings, shootings, stabbings etc. – which have occurred in the immediate area, have been treated there. Indeed the surgeons and nursing staff have developed the RVH into the foremost centre for the treatment of gunshot wounds in the world. The hospital has also been the site of many murders, of soldiers, policemen and of staff.

One such murder was that of Robin Shields (44), father of four who worked in the Ambulance Dispatch office in the RVH. On the morning of the 30th, PIRA men hijacked a car – a Ford Cortina – on the Broadway in West Belfast. The Broadway which links the Falls Road, via the new Westlink with Donegal Avenue and the southern part of the City Centre, cuts through the heart of nationalist country. As such, any resident with a sense of self-preservation will not resist the demands of the 'RA' if they demanded their car. The car containing at least three men, two of them armed and wearing stolen hospital uniforms parked close to the hospital entrance. Two of the gunmen, looking for all the world as though they 'belonged' walked into the Ambulance office and singled out Mr Shields. He had been targeted because he had once served as a Reserve Constable in the RUCR. The two men approached him and immediately opened fire, shooting him from close range in the head. He died almost immediately as the gunmen calmly walked away to their waiting stolen car. It was later found abandoned in the Beechmounts; no doubt the relieved owner would have sworn to God when questioned by the RUC that he didn't recognise the men who had forcibly taken his car.

September was over and autumn was upon Northern Ireland. Four people had died in the month including a soldier, a policeman, an innocent civilian and a former member of the RUCR. All three of the intentional deaths had been carried out by the Provisionals.

10

October

On the 26th of this month, the first 'hunger strike' began but this one would be called off in December; the next one would end with 10 deaths in 1981. It would be a month when a scaling down by the Army would take place, but in many respects it was 16 years too early. A top INLA man was killed and inevitably, the Republicans rolled out their well-worn phrases of 'collusion' and 'Security Force-Loyalist cooperation'.

On the 2nd of the month, Lance Corporal Nicolas Paul Bushwell (21) of the Royal Tank Regiment was killed in an RTA in the Province. He was from Dunstable in Bedfordshire and his funeral was held at West Street, Dunstable; other than that, nothing further is known about the circumstances.

On the 3rd of the month, a plan by the British Government in conjunction with the Army was set in motion as the policy of 'Ulsterisation' and 'Police Primacy' continued apace. In recognition of the apparent drift towards a less violent state, one full battalion – the Royal Scots Dragoon Guards who were deployed in Belfast City Centre and the Ardoyne – were pulled out of the Province. This troop reduction which included two other battalions were on the 18 week 'emergency' tours was in line with their stated intentions. Their places were taken by the UDR and by an increased RUC presence on the streets and lanes of the country. The Army base at Glassmullan on the nationalist Lenadoon estate in Belfast was evacuated and torn down in less than 72 hours by the Royal Engineers under the watchful rifles of two Scots Guards.

A week later, troops handed back ownership of Flax Street Mill, their main base in the Ardoyne, to the original owners. However, it was announced that there was to be a small military presence there. PIRA and INLA units in Lenadoon and the Ardoyne must have rubbed their hands with glee at the reduction in the Army's presence. Although patrolling and VCPs would continue, there was no substitution for troops permanently on the ground at instance readiness. Finally, it was announced that the Grand Central Hotel (GCH) was also to close its doors to the Army and would eventually be pulled down.

The following is reprinted from *Wasted Years, Wasted Lives*:

The Grand Central Hotel, was located on Royal Avenue in Belfast, and was opened in 1893. The building existed as a hotel until 1972, when it was taken over by the Army as a military base with a TAOR of the city centre. The hotel contained around 200 guest bedrooms and was, over its lifetime able to boast guests such as the Beatles and the Rolling Stones in the 1960s. In 1972, the Army acquired the building, converting it to a military barracks which was in place until the early 1980s. Soldiers based there were protected by anti-rocket screens constructed around the front of the building on the main street to repel everything from bricks and bottles to paint and blast bombs. It was one of the most bombarded hotels in the world; it was attacked more than 150 times by PIRA/INLA. As the Troubles eased, the hotel was no longer required as a military base and was acquired by developers and partly demolished to make way for the Castle Court shopping centre which was completed in 1990.[1]

However, the Government stated that should there be a serious deterioration in Northern Ireland, the 'Spearhead' battalions on the mainland were ready for immediate deployment when and if required. This meant that troop levels were down to 10 major units of regular troops or around 12,000 men plus 11 battalions from the UDR. A spokesman in HQNI said: "This is not a case of the Army pulling out of Ulster. Northern Ireland is a part of the United Kingdom and we shall continue to garrison troops here in the normal way."

On the 10th, the Provisionals killed a part-time UDR soldier who was also a well-known farmer in the Portadown area of County Armagh. Private Marcus James Hewitt (48) was a part-time soldier but he also had a thriving cattle business to run and on the morning of Friday 10 October, he and his adult sons drove into Portadown and parked up outside the Automart Livestock market in Tandragee Road. The three men walked into the market in order to conduct some business. During the time that Private Hewitt was away from his car, a stolen car driven by a PIRA member which had in all likelihood been tailing the Hewitt's car, pulled up close by and one, possibly two men planted an explosive device underneath; the author is uncertain, but it is possible that it was a mercury tilt device, similar to one used to murder Airey Neave, MP in 1979. Several hours later, the part-time soldier returned to his car alone and started the engine. There was a massive explosion and he was mortally injured. He was rushed to hospital at Craigavon but his injuries were so severe, he was dead on arrival. He was laid to rest at Kilmre Parish Church; approaching 2,500 people had now lost their lives in a country of 1.5 million in a little over 11 years.

Between the 12th and the 20th, the same unit – the Scots Guards – lost two men serving in Northern Ireland, both in unclear circumstances. Rather like the RRF's Foxalls who died three days apart in Palace Barracks,[2] these were two soldiers from the same unit who died in circumstances which have never been made public. On the 12th, Guardsman Gary Connell (20) died and under Cemetery details, he is listed as 'Lost at Sea'. Just eight days later, Lance Sergeant (Corporal) Iain Hanna (23) died from 'violent or unnatural causes'. He was a member of the unit's Close Observation Platoon (COP) and was based at Aldergrove barracks. His body was returned to his native Edinburgh and he is buried at Mount Vernon Cemetery.

On the 13th, a member of the Gardaí Siochana was killed in a shoot-out inside the Irish Republic with a Provisional IRA gunman. The man, Peter Rogers had already staked his claim in Republican folklore, by being one of the 'Magnificent Seven' who escaped from HM Prison Ship 'Maidstone' in 1972. The PIRA men escaped from the prison

---

1   Wharton, Ken M. *Wasted Years, Wasted Lives* (Solihull: Helion, 2013), Vol 1, p.55.
2   See Chapter 6.

ship which was moored in Belfast Lough, by darkening their bodies, sawing through a ship port hole and swimming to shore.[3] Rogers had not kept his head down and was still involved in Republican activities. Earlier that day, five masked gunmen had participated in a robbery in Callan, County Kilkenny and Rogers was one of the first men whom the Gardaí suspected. Two officers – Detective Seamus Quaid and Donal Lyttleton – were dispatched to monitor his movements. When they spotted Rogers, he was driving his van on a road outside of the town of Wexford. What the two Garda didn't know was that he was transporting arms and explosives in his van and was desperate to avoid it being searched. Siochana officers are not routinely armed, but on this occasion, both men had pistols. However, as both men were familiar with Rogers, Lyttleton left his gun in the police car and Quaid's was in his pocket. But, while they were searching the van with their backs towards the IRA man, Rogers pulled his gun on the pair and forced them to walk towards a nearby quarry.

There was a scuffle as the men were forced towards what they must have thought was their place of execution, and Lyttleton managed to escape, in the hope of reaching the patrol car and retrieving his weapon. Rogers shot Quaid several times and mortally wounded him, but the dying Gardaí managed also to fire at least 20 shots at the PIRA man and succeeded in wounding him. He drove off and Quaid was left lying badly injured on the ground; he was dead within 15 minutes. Rogers was unable to get treatment for his wound and surrendered himself the following morning at Wexford Gardaí Station. His van was examined and the following was found: an Armalite Rifle, two pistols, ammunition, explosives, detonators and wigs which it was believed had been used in the previous day's robbery in Callan.

Rogers was tried and convicted of the murder of the Gardaí officer – a Capital Crime in the Republic – and he was sentenced to death. In the end, he was sentenced to 40 years in 1981, but was released in 1998 under the terms of the Good Friday Agreement. He served only 17 years. Michael Quinn writing in the *Irish News* of 22 December, 1998, said:

> The early Christmas release of the man who murdered Wexford detective Seamus Quaid has deeply angered and devastated his family, the dead garda's son said last night. Eamonn Quaid (32), who was 14 when his father was gunned down by IRA man Peter Rogers, said the shock of the imminent release was like another bereavement in the family. "We were handling the situation when we thought his killer was serving 40 years in prison," he said. "Now he is getting out after serving less than half the sentence and we feel let down by the Government. It will be a dark day for justice in this country when terrorists are rewarded for their crimes by being released. Christmas is a particularly difficult time for us and this just makes it worse," he said.[4]

Also on the 13th of the month, more military cut backs were announced and it was made clear that the Army would be pulled out of the border town of Newry, County Down and the RUC barracks there would be reinforced and extended. It had long been

---

3   See Wharton, Ken M. *The Bloodiest Year* (Stroud: The History Press, 2011), Chapter 1.

4   Source: www.independent.ie/irish-news/victims-family-let-down-by-freedom-for-garda-killer-26166136.html

a hotbed of Nationalism and the Nationalist Derrybeg estate was a source of constant danger to the SF:

What was unique about the Derrybeg estate in Newry was that, for the first time, young families were up-rooted from closely-knit communities, and transplanted to a green field site, housed among complete strangers. This move was seen as a bold and imaginative initiative by Newry Urban Council, to provide badly-needed homes for the growing population of newly-weds, forced to live with parents or in-laws. But, at Derrybeg, the new tenants found themselves crammed into 360 houses, devoid of social or recreational facilities, far from shops, pubs or cinemas. A bus-service was non-existence, few owned cars, and there was a dearth of taxis.[5]

However, the Derrybeg soon became synonymous with deprivation, unemployment and violence. Derrybeg made world headlines in January 1972, being the setting for a major and very angry Civil Rights March after 'Bloody Sunday'. Over 60,000 people marched from the estate in a powerful, display of opposition to the Stormont regime. It soon became a victim of the Troubles, being used as a battleground between the Army and the Provisional IRA. When Internment came in 1971, as a result of out-dated intelligence lists, a large number of Derrybeg men were imprisoned; some mistakenly. That was followed by the death of IRA bomber Patrick Hughes in an explosion at the Customs Clearance Station on 22 August, 1972; his son later shot dead by soldiers on the Camlough Road. Then the death of schoolboy, Kevin Heatley; shot by a soldier on 28 February, 1973 during a fire fight on the estate. The 12 year-old was tragically caught in the crossfire. A foot patrol came under attack from a mob in the notorious run down estate when a soldier of the Royal Hampshire Regiment claimed that he had witnessed someone with a gun. He fired one shot from his SLR and the boy was hit and died at the scene. The soldier was later arrested and charged with unlawful killing and was sentenced to three years after some unacceptable behaviour in court from both sides. He was later released on appeal, but the death of young Heatley merely served to deepen the already deep hatred the residents of the Derrybeg held for the soldier. Finally, another IRA bomber Eddie Grant was killed in an 'own goal' bomb-blast at a pub, on Christmas Eve, 1973.

By the mid-seventies, over 100 houses were derelict and boarded up; no points were required by the Housing Executive to secure any dwelling; people applying for a house were told to simply find an empty one and move in. The estate was regarded as a 'no-go area'; anyone applying for a job would give the address of a relative in another part of town. Newry was also synonymous with two major attacks on the RUC. On 28 February 1985, a PIRA mortar attack killed nine police officers at Corry Square, Newry. Then on 26 July the following year, in the 'Bloody poke'[6] murders, three RUC officers were shot dead by PIRA gunmen in Market Street, Newry, as they enjoyed an ice-cream on a blisteringly hot day.

---

5   Taken from Newrymemories.com
6   'Poke' is Northern Irish slang for ice-cream cornet.

On the 18th, Banbridge in County Down was attacked by the Provisionals again following their failed attempt at 'The Cut' on 4 July.[7] On this occasion, a stolen car was packed with 400 lb (182 kgs) of explosives and left close to commercial buildings. There was a massive explosion which caused injuries and extensive structural damage but fortunately, like the July bomb, there were no deaths.

A day later, there was some excitement – albeit of the deadly kind – for schoolchildren in West Belfast. An IED had been planted on a metal fence surrounding a Catholic school in the Whiterock area by a PIRA unit in order to catch an Army foot patrol. This was in spite of the fact that there was a Kindergarten class at the St Peter's Secondary School and Westrock Community Centre at the time. The device was spotted by troops from the Royal Regiment of Fusiliers who were in the process of evacuating the young children when the bomb exploded. Fortunately, the nearby playground was deserted at the time of the blast and no children were injured. Windows in the school however were shattered and the blast was heard by thousands of people in the area. Shrapnel was hurled over 50 yards as PIRA again demonstrated their absolute irresponsibility. Quite what the mothers of these thought is not recorded, but how many of them would have dared to speak out against these Republican bullies who were turning what should have been places of safety for their young ones into a battlefield is also not known.

Ronnie Bunting was a member of INLA and he was unique in several ways. First of all, he was a Protestant and secondly, he was the son of one of the main Loyalist leaders – who was a staunch ally of the Reverend Ian Paisley and had been brought up in a Loyalist household and on various British Army barracks around the world. Bunting briefly became a teacher of history in Belfast, but from the early 70s, he became a full time political and paramilitary activist. Unlike most Protestants in Northern Ireland – his father was Major Ronald Bunting – he became an Irish Republican and joined the OIRA. His father, was as stated, a staunch Loyalist, who organised armed stewards to protect Ian Paisley as well as intimidate those opposed to him. Major Bunting was infamously involved with the Loyalist ambush of Civil Rights marchers at Burntollet, on 4 January 1969.

In 1974, Bunting followed the lead set by Seamus Costello and other OIRA members who disagreed with the organisation's ceasefire which occurred after the anger caused by the murder of Ranger William Best on the Creggan in 1972. The breakaway group formed the INLA and a major internecine feud broke out between both organisations. During the feud, INLA leader Seamus Costello was killed by OIRA gunman Jim Flynn in October 1977.[8] Two years before the killing of Costello, a former comrade fired several shots at Bunting as he drove along the Monagh Road in West Belfast and shots were fired into the Bunting home shortly afterwards. He took his family to Wales and lived a low-key existence there before returning to Northern Ireland in 1978.

He then became the INLA's military leader and worked closely with the political wing of the terror group, the Irish Republican Socialist Party (IRSP). The organisation regularly attacked the SF and was also responsible for the assassination of Margaret Thatcher's main political supporter, Airey Neave MP, at the House of Commons car

---

7 See Chapter 7.
8 See *Wasted Years, Wasted Lives*, Vol 1.

park in March 1979. Bunting called in claims of responsibility to the media using the code name 'Captain Green'.

In the early hours of the 15th, Bunting (32) and IRSP member Noel Little (45) were at the house which he shared with Mrs Suzanne Bunting and their three children in Downfine Gardens, between Norglen Gardens and Gortnamona Way in the Andersonstown area. At around 0300 hours, masked UFF gunmen smashed down the front door of the house and the first person to confront them as the men barged their way into the master bedroom was Suzanne Bunting. She was shot four times; in the shoulder and in her side. They then stormed into the room and shot Ronnie Bunting at least six times; he died very quickly afterwards. Other UFF gunmen then went into the children's bedroom where Noel Little was sleeping and shot him several times, with one of the rounds narrowly missing a sleeping child. Mrs Bunting was shot in the mouth when she attempted to grab one of her husband's murderers. The men then escaped and drove off in a waiting car which was later abandoned in a Loyalist area.

IRSP members were quick to allege collusion and claimed that it had simply been too easy for the gunmen to have driven into the heart of Nationalist Andersonstown, execute two murders in a 'professional' manner and then escape without interference from either the Army or RUC. The truth was far more prosaic and didn't produce the 'propaganda' angle which the IRSP so desperately wanted. The Loyalist UDA/UFF contained a fair number of Protestants who had once served in the British Army – and other Armies for that matter – and were trained to exacting professional standards. Furthermore, a glance at the topography of the Bunting family home reveals that Downfine Gardens leads directly into Norglen Gardens, which is then a short burst to the Monagh Link and then straight on to the A55, Monagh Bypass. This is then a fast drive to either the Upper Springfield Road and escape into the countryside, or the Springfield Road proper and over to Woodvale or Ballygomartin and safe Loyalist territory. This author does not believe that it was the SAS, although this was where the IRSP and INLA leadership were quick to point the finger of suspicion. No doubt the words 'SAS' were quickly on the lips of all their supporters at the IRSP's base in the Divis Street flats, also known as the *'Planet of the Irps'*.

Major Bunting was finally reunited in grief with his politically estranged son at the family funeral a few days later. He steadfastly refused to let his son be buried with other dead INLA men and instead buried him in a family plot. Henry McDonald and Jack Holland's superb book carries a photograph of Major Bunting at his son's funeral; it shows an elderly man, weeping at his murdered son's graveside.[9]

On the 23rd, an IRA bombing team planted a no-warning car bomb near to an RUC Training College close to the centre of Enniskillen. It exploded causing serious damage and injured 16 people including five RUC recruits, some very badly. Almost seven years to the day later, it created absolute outrage all over the world – except in Irish-American bars in the Eastern USA it would appear – when another no-warning bomb exploded in the town. This explosion occurred on 8 November 1987 at the Cenotaph during a Remembrance Day service. This day is a most sacred day throughout the British Commonwealth and to perpetrate such an outrage caused revulsion against the

9   McDonald, Henry and Jack Holland. *INLA: Deadly Divisions* (Dublin: Poolbeg Books, 1996).

Republican cause. Eleven civilians were killed and a twelfth died 13 years later, having being sent into a coma by the blast.

The day after the first Enniskillen blast, the Provisionals attempted to assassinate a UDR 'Greenfinch' near Strabane. The 28 year-old part-time soldier was driving to work when masked gunmen opened fire on her car. The car was raked by fire and she was hit several times. She survived her injuries and was quickly taken to hospital.

Finally, on the 26th October, a chain of events was set in motion which would ultimately lead to the deaths of 10 convicted terrorists, a dozen or more soldiers and policemen and further sectarian mayhem and violence. It would also lead to the strengthening of the hand of Prime Minister Margaret Thatcher who would be despised in Republican circles and revered in Loyalist ones because of her resolution in the face of the Provisional IRA and INLA. On that day, the first hunger strike began and it would only be called off 53 days later on 18 December. Seven Republican prisoners began a hunger-strike to protest at the ending of special category status. One of their key demands was that they should be allowed to wear their own clothes rather than prison uniforms. The Republican prisoners viewed themselves as 'prisoners of war' and were refusing to be treated, as they saw it, as ordinary criminals. The tactic of the hunger strike has a special place in Republican history and they had developed it into an art form. The second one, when it came, would lead to desperate consequences for all in Northern Ireland and sometimes beyond.

Seven people died in October; four soldiers and one policeman (a Gardaí) and two members of the INLA/IRSP. There were no sectarian deaths this month and the Republicans and Loyalist paramilitaries were responsible for two deaths each.

11

November

A total of eight people died this month, and it included another cowardly hospital-related murder by the Provisionals. Quite how they imagined that shooting unarmed men, visiting hospital would further their cause and their efforts to drive the British into the sea is beyond the limited comprehension of this soldier-scribe. Flawed INT by INLA led to the death of an innocent as did a PIRA landmine. Between them, the Republican terrorists would leave 28 children fatherless through their actions during this month.

On the 3rd of the month, the Royal Corps of Signals or '*Scaleybacks*' as they are known to other units in the British Army lost one of their men in circumstances unknown. Lance Corporal Paul James Holt (23) was from the Nottingham area and is buried at Wilford Cemetery in the city.

All decent thinking people, especially those who had an acute sense of right and wrong would have been horrified by the ruthless and underhanded tactics of the Provisional IRA when they murdered Green Jacket Christopher Watson on 19 July this year. Their actions in killing another off-duty soldier at a Maternity Hospital on 11 November were equally despicable. Owen McQuade (31), father of two was a soldier in the famous Scottish regiment, the Argyle and Sutherland Highlanders. This Regiment, now part of the Royal Regiment of Scotland was formed in 1881 by the amalgamation of the 91st and 93rd Regiments of Foot. Its motto is '*Sans Peur, Ne Obliviscaris*' (without fear, do not forget) and the 'ladies from hell' as the Germans saw them fought with distinction through both World Wars, including Sidi Barani in the Western Desert, Crete, Sicily and in the Far East in Burma and Malaya where they earned the sobriquet the 'jungle beasts'. In modern times they are known for their actions under their CO 'Mad Mitch' who at the head of his Battalion, flanked by a Piper marched into the Crater district of Aden and routed the Arab rebels who had killed 23 British soldiers.

Corporal McQuade was living with his wife and two children in MSQ at Ballykelly, County Londonderry. On the evening of the 11th, he took a fellow soldier whose pregnant wife was in the maternity section of Altnagelvin Hospital in Londonderry to the hospital. As he sat outside, unarmed and in civilian clothes in an unmarked minibus, several IRA gunmen pulled up close by in a stolen taxi which had been hijacked from the Nationalist Gobnascale Estate. The men approached the soldier and opened fire hitting him from close range several times; he died at the scene. Owen McQuade was from Glasgow and was the 10th of his regiment to die during the Troubles. 1972 had been the Regiment's worst year, when they lost eight soldiers.

On the very next day, there was an attempt to kill two soldiers in South Armagh, but instead an innocent civilian was blown to pieces by the Provisionals and six children were left fatherless. Oliver Walsh (39) an employee of Newcell Paper Converter Ltd., the same company which employed Anthony Shields, himself killed by the IRA in May this year, was killed near Lislea, County Armagh.[1] He was driving along the Newry-Crossmaglen Road en-route for a business appointment. Ahead of him on the same road was an unmarked 'Q' car containing two Royal Engineers officers. The senior officer noticed Mr Walsh's car coming up behind him and chose to slow down and let it pass so that they could check that they were not under surveillance or threat. Unfortunately for the civilian – a Catholic – a PIRA bombing team had planted a 500 lb culvert bomb on the road and it was detonated by command wire from a firing position 500 yards away. The device exploded as Mr Walsh passed over the culvert and his car was absolutely destroyed, being thrown high into the air, crashing into a field. He was killed instantly.

Two days later, the West Belfast 'nutting squad' was called into action again and collected a man from the Unity Flats in Belfast and took him away for interrogation. Peter Valente (33), father of four was taken to a safe house – probably in West Belfast – where he would have been questioned by a 'kangaroo court' and then possibly tortured in order to extract a confession from him. Sometimes a 'tame' Catholic priest would have been sent for and shamefully heard his final confession in order to add an air of respect-ability to this sordid affair; I am assured however, that on this occasion, that was not the case. Afterwards, he was taken to a quiet alleyway on the Protestant Highfield Estate where was then shot twice in the back of the head; the location of his body was to divert attention onto the UVF or UFF. Afterwards, a Sinn Féin apologist did indeed try to place the blame on the UDA/UFF. According to Martin Dillon, Valente was a low level 'tout.'[2] He may well have been unmasked by a PIRA sympathiser inside the RUC. The officer concerned was angry at failing to achieve his ambitions and tried to prove – in a most perverse manner – his value to his employers. He contacted Martin Meehan of the IRA's Ardoyne Brigade, and may have revealed the nature of Valente's duplicity which was, of course, the Unity Flats' man's death warrant.

The 'old' Irish Republican Army had been linked almost inextricably with the Roman Catholic Church and it is no secret that many priests openly aided and abetted IRA gunmen. If it was not the hiding of arms, the looking away when a gunman committed an act of violence, the strategic locking and unlocking of doors to assist their murderous efforts, then it was the spiritual act of blessing their sins and hearing their confessions. If a gunman admitted to the murder of a soldier or a policeman during the act of confession, then a priest could claim to be constrained under the laws of sacrilege and privilege and refuse to reveal this information to the Security Forces. This author knows of at least two acts of murder – Rifleman David Walker (Royal Green Jackets) in 1971 and Gunner Edmund Muncastle (Royal Artillery) in 1972 – where Catholic priests aided in the set-up of the PIRA shoot and assisted in the getaway. There is also the brutally infamous incident in Claudy in July 1972 when Father Chesney actually planted one of the three fatal car bombs in that sleepy little Londonderry town. The Provisional IRA were less set on the religious path and, unlike the IRA of old, did not feel that they had to have a spiritual link with the Roman Catholic faith.

---

1   See Chapter 5.
2   Dillon, Martin, *The Dirty War* (London: Arrow Books, 1990).

UDR soldiers, both full and part-time, in the vast majority of cases carried out a magnificent job; it was dangerous and often unsung, but without their back-up and courage the full-time soldiers would have had a more difficult task. For the soldiers of the regular Army, there were 18 weeks of intensity and then escape to the mainland or out to West Germany, Malta, Gibraltar, Cyprus and the like, before they would be called back to Ulster. After patrol duties were done for the day or the night, they could relax in bases as diverse as Springfield Road RUC Station, North Howard Street Mill, Albert Street Mill and Flax Street Mill in Belfast, and scores of places throughout the Province. However, they were with friends, comrades, soldiers in a support role; in short, they were with the emotional and physical back-up which they needed. For the UDR soldier it was different. During a few hours of patrol, they might see people from their own communities, man VCPs where they may stop cars belonging to the 'other side' containing people who might recognise them, even 'P' check known players who would have an idea of where they lived. After that it was back to their wives and families, knowing that the next knock on the door might herald the arrival of a PIRA or INLA murder gang.

The Republican paramilitaries, committed to killing members of the Security Forces whether they were on or off duty, saw the part-time UDR soldiers and policemen of the RUCR – male as well as female – as soft targets. They had various ways of targeting them. Dickers would often follow an individual soldier home; in many cases, they would already know that 'Joe Bloggs' lived at a quiet house in rural Lisnaskea or at a house on the periphery of a Nationalist area, and that egress was easy and the proximity of a safe house made the 'job' safer. PIRA INT was exemplary – on occasions – and dickers/sympathisers inside some of the companies where the part-time soldiers worked, might see a snippet of information in personnel files which would lead to the discovery that 'Fred' in the warehouse was a member of Britain's 'war machine'. Everywhere that the part-time UDR soldier or RUCR officer went when off-duty was dangerous. At his home, leaving home or arriving home; at work, leaving work, or – as in the following case – arriving at work.

LONDONDERRY CAR BOMB
Dave Young, Ammunition Technical Officer

Later on during my tour in 1980, I was called out in the early hours of the morning to a suspect car in a narrow street close to the Guildhall in Londonderry. This beautiful old building had been seriously damaged a couple of years earlier by the so-called 'bin men bomb' and was now almost fully repaired, including restoring the beautiful stained glass windows. I set up my ICP just around a corner and sent the remote-controlled Wheelbarrow forward. I could see the car was heavily weighted down at the rear end.

Within a few minutes of arriving I had carried out the first small controlled explosion. The idea was to gain access to see what I was dealing with. The boot had been blown open, so I suited up and made the long walk. As I stood up against the car I looked into the boot and there were two milk churns jammed in and a timer mechanism, wiring to a detonator and detonating cord linking the two churns. Each could easily contain up to 130 lbs of explosive. It was all still intact and the timer clock would still have been ticking as it was just 20 minutes after the car had been parked. I set up a disruptor aimed at the timer, retired and fired it with the aim of destroying the timer and stopping the clock.

After a prudent short wait I made my second long walk and saw my actions had severed the detonating cord links to the churns, and the arming, timing and power box was in pieces. Job almost done, I could take my time finishing off. I considered heaving the churns out of the boot, but something didn't seem right … the hairs on the back of my neck were standing up even more than normal, my sixth sense was telling me something! I thought I would play safe because it might be booby-trapped. I walked away and said the churns were well stuck in there. I would use a larger remote vehicle we had just got called the Eager Beaver.

Just about two minutes later the Eager Beaver reached in to haul the churn out and as soon as it moved the first churn: bang! There was an almighty explosion, the ground shook and a split second later pieces of metal rained down all around us, but by then we were all scrabbling for space under our armoured vehicles. When the smoke and dust had cleared I went forward and examined the scene. There was a large crater where the car had been, but it had vanished. The largest piece was about grapefruit size. The two churns had been blown out and were intact, but there were small fragments of a third churn scattered around. I found out later that had been under the rear seat and most probably booby trapped set up to go off as the two churns in the boot were moved. It was about a 400 lb bomb, but only about 130 lbs had exploded.

I dealt with the two churns, cutting them in half with one of our new-fangled bits of kit – Broadsword. The newly replaced stained glass windows of the Guildhall had been blown in, but there was no real structural damage; there certainly would have been had the two churns in the boot gone up too. It was very sobering to think I had been standing beside the bomb just a few minutes before. Something had made me walk away and I can't say 'til this day what, but I knew I had been very, very lucky. I call it sixth sense!

I went back there last year during the making of a documentary called 'The Long Walk' and it was very emotional to see where I could have so easily died. At that very moment I thought about all the very good operators, who had been much better at their job than I had, but were just unlucky and had tragically died. We lost 18 of our operators, killed in Northern Ireland. I knew them all. Not just them, but their families because we were a very small group of about 250 strong and just 70 or so trained as ATO operators. They were all very good people, well trained and exceptionally good at what they did, but mostly just unlucky.

On the morning of the 19th, Thomas Orr (39), father of two arrived at a branch of the Ulster Bank where he worked in Boucher Road, South Belfast. The road itself connects the Broadway with Stockman's Lane and is close to Milltown Cemetery and the Andersonstown Estate. INLA gunmen were lying in wait for a part-time RUCR officer who worked at the bank and they knew the colour and make of the car he drove. By an utterly tragic coincidence, the RUCR man had sold the car to his work colleague Mr Orr but the INLA intelligence was, not for the first time, seriously flawed. As Mr Orr arrived, he was shot immediately by the gunmen who then raced off in a stolen car; the innocent man was hit seven times and died almost immediately. He left a wife and two children aged six and three. This author is unaware of any apology made by INLA or their apologists in the IRSP to the family of Mr Orr.

On the following day, Thursday 20 November, Margaret Thatcher, stated in the House of Commons:

> Let me make one thing clear about the hunger strike in the Maze Prison. I want this to be utterly clear. There can be no political justification for murder or any other crime. The government will never concede political status to the hunger strikers, or to any others convicted of criminal offences in the province.

The present hunger strike which included Bobby Sands – or *'Marcella'* as he was known in PIRA prison code – was now in its 24th day. It would continue for another 29 days before a short respite until the second one started.

On the 25th, PIRA gunmen attacked the RUC station at Derrygonnelly in County Fermanagh. Derrygonnelly is a small town, just south of Lough Erne and approximately 12 miles from the border with the Irish Republic. It is unclear if they were simply making a hit and run raid on the station, or if they were specifically targeting a full-time UDR soldier who was known to be visiting the station. Private Norman Henry Donaldson (59), father of eight, had gone to the station in order to collect charity donations for a local hospital from officers there. He was ambushed by gunmen who fired on him from behind bushes about 30 yards from the station; he died almost immediately. It was thought that officers who routinely closed the station at 1900 hours were possibly the real targets. Within minutes, a very close friend – John Dundas (65), father of six – drove by to investigate. The shock of the murder of his friend gave him a fatal heart attack and he too died at the scene. His death can be laid very firmly at the door of the Provisionals. His funeral was held at Inishmacsaint, County Fermanagh.

On the 29th, an RCT soldier was killed in an RTA while on duty. The starting rank in the RCT is not Private; like the Engineers (Sapper), REME (Craftsman), Royal Green Jackets (Rifleman), Kings Regiment (Kingsman) for example, it is different. Their starting rank is Driver; one of their men, Driver Steven Nicholas Atkins (20) was killed in the Province; the author has no further details.

A further eight people had died during the month of November; four were soldiers and three were civilians; a Catholic and two Protestants. One Republican paramilitary had died at the hands of the 'nutting squad'. Republican paramilitaries were responsible for five of the deaths this month.

12

December

Five people died during this month, including two soldiers and a prison officer (PO). The INLA were involved in two of the deaths. For the first time, Loyalist paramilitaries were responsible for killing a PO. Additionally, three women Republican prisoners in Armagh Prison joined the hunger strike; it was however, short-lived. The major IRA hunger strike continued until the 18th when it was called off.

On the 8th, in what was the first visit to Dublin by a British PM since partition in 1921, a British Government team comprised of Prime Minister Margaret Thatcher, Foreign Secretary Lord Carrington, Chancellor of the Exchequer Geoffrey Howe, and Humphrey Atkins, Secretary of State for Northern Ireland, went to Dublin for talks with Taoiseach Charles Haughey, and other senior members of his Cabinet. It was agreed at the meeting to conduct joint studies on a wide range of subjects. The phrase 'totality of relationships' was first used at this meeting. It was understood to mean that the future political relationship between the two islands would be looked at more often and more deeply. However it was later revealed that the constitutional position of Northern Ireland had not been discussed at the meeting. It also set up an Anglo-Irish intergovernmental council – comprised in the main of Civil Servants – which later became the foundations for the 1985 Anglo-Irish agreement. The 'accord' was sold at every opportunity by Haughey as an historic breakthrough, but one rather suspects that the British were just 'buying time'. Thatcher later had a meeting with Loyalist leader Ian Paisley in order to allay his suggestions that continued talks between the Governments in London and Dublin were a prelude to a 'British sell-out'.

On the 9th, Heather Pollock (53) was fatally wounded by IRA gunmen during a shoot-out on the Ballycolman Estate in Strabane. In what was a classic IRA 'come on', a 999 call to the police claimed that a house had been broken into and the police had to investigate, even during that period of violent lawlessness known as the Troubles. Several gunmen had taken a family hostage in the same street as Mrs Pollock – Saint Colman's drive – and set up a firing position before settling in to await the arrival of the police. As the three officers cautiously got out of their vehicle, the gang opened up from just across the street and all three policemen were hit and fell to the ground. However, the hail of bullets as with most PIRA shootings was uncoordinated. Mrs Pollock was hit in the back and her spine was badly damaged. She remained conscious and was rushed to hospital at the same time as the wounded RUC men. The three recovered later but, despite several emergency operations, Heather Pollock died in Altnagelvin Hospital just two days after Christmas.

Two days after the wounding of the innocent Ballycolman woman, the first Troubles-related fatality of the month occurred when a part-time soldier in the UDR was shot as he left work for the day. Private Hartley Colin Quinn (20) was a printer and worked for a company close to Durham Street which is located between Divis Street and the Grosvenor Road. His brother and another work colleague were close by when a car pulled up alongside the young part-time soldier. Two INLA gunmen – Gerard 'Dr Death' Steenson and Gerard 'Sparky' Barkley – began shooting, and around 10 shots were fired at very close range. Private Quinn died almost immediately. Private Quinn's funeral was held at Rose Lawn Cemetery, Crossmacreery in Belfast. Dr Ronald Craig said: "Some murderer may think that he has done an heroic thing, but we would tell him that this foul deed will strengthen the resolve of the citizens of this Province never to yield to the thugs or murderers."

Barkley was later killed in October 1983 by INLA Chief of Staff Dominic McGlinchey on the alleged grounds that he had informed. Steenson later joined the IPLO and was himself killed by his former comrades in the INLA on 14 March, 1987. He is still regarded as a 'soldier' amongst his supporters and also by many who eventually turned on him when he left *Arm Saoirse Náisiúnta na hÉireann* to join the Irish People's Liberation Organisation.

COLIN QUINN
Anonymous UDR Soldier
I knew Colin Quinn, the UDR Soldier shot in Durham Street, very well. We were in same class, from the First to Fifth Form. He was the guy that accidentally broke my nose which is still bent to this day during a football match where he headed my nose instead of the ball. Good guy. I didn't know he was in the UDR until I got a letter from my mum in Germany to tell me he had been shot. It happened at a garage where Grosvenor Road PSNI Station now is. Also I didn't know his proper first name was Hartley; could have taken the piss with that during school.

On the 12th, six members of the UDA/UFF in the Maze prison started a hunger strike in support of their demand for segregation from Republican prisoners. This Loyalist attempt to either parody or mock the Republican hunger strike was called off on the 17th. Of the original seven IRA hunger strikers, Seán McKenna's medical condition had begun to deteriorate and he was moved to Musgrave Park Hospital in Belfast.

On the 16th, there was a sensational escape from Brixton Prison in London when a convicted terrorist – Gerard Tuite and two non-IRA prisoners got away from the maximum security jail. In 1978, he wormed his way into a young English nurse's affections and was living in her London flat in Trafalgar Road, Greenwich. Before the end of the year he was found guilty of possession of explosives with intent to endanger life and a search of the flat revealed a sawn-off shotgun and an Armalite rifle. These and other items, including car keys and voice recordings, linked him to other bombings as well as the targeting of senior British politicians and members of the Royalty. He had also been involved in no less than 18 bombing attacks in five British cities with the man who later bombed the Grand Hotel at Brighton in 1984. He escaped with two English criminals, including one Jimmy Moody who later made fame for himself as a member of PIRA's 'nutting squad' after he crossed over to Northern Ireland with Tuite.

On the 18th, believing that they had gained partial agreement from the British Government to their demands, the Republican hunger strike at the Maze Prison and other prisons in Northern Ireland, was called off. Tomás Ó Fiaich, Catholic Primate of Ireland, had appealed to the men on the 17th and it was ended the next day – the 53rd day of the strike – as there had been suggestions that there would be a move towards conceding aspects of special status. He also appealed to Margaret Thatcher to intervene personally in the protest. Sinn Féin claimed to have a document setting out proposals which would have met many of their demands. *The Irish Times* proclaimed: 'Hunger Strike Over!' It followed with: "In a dramatic, unexpected move, the seven Republican hunger strikers in Long Kesh [sic] Prison last night ended their 53 day protest – without, it is understood, winning any concessions from the British Government." In the North, OUP leader James Molyneaux said, somewhat prematurely, that the Prime Minister had: "demoralised terrorists generally by making clear that she would not surrender." One thing that many hunters know, is that a wounded animal will turn and react even more viciously for that pain; the Provisional IRA was such a wounded animal and it would turn. Bobby Sands, a convicted terrorist and OC of the Provisionals in the Maze is reported to have said: "We haven't won, but we're not beat yet!" His words were soon to be prophetic.

The prisoners had made five demands. These involved the right to wear their own clothes, freedom from doing prison work, free association with other prisoners, freedom to organise recreational activity and the restoration of lost remission as a consequence of their 'dirty protest'. The first, unsuccessful hunger strike had involved the following Republican paramilitaries: IRA members: Brendan Hughes, Tommy McKearney, Raymond McCartney, Tom McFeeley, Seán McKenna, Leo Green, and INLA member John Nixon. The next hunger strike, which will be dealt with in Part Two of this book, began on 1 March, 1981, and ended on 3 October the same year. In all, 23 Republicans took part, 10 of whom died.

Christmas Eve arrived and the season of goodwill to all men; all that is except the Protestant and Catholic residents of the interface area of Newtownards Road and Seaforde Street. Gangs of Nationalist and Loyalist youths had been involved in a fracas and property was damaged and in several instances, bricks were thrown at both windows and also at human beings. William Stevenson (50) and a Protestant went outside his home on the Newtownards Road and was hit in the head by a brick thrown from the direct of the Nationalist Seaforde Street. He was fatally injured, dying seven days later.

The day after Heather Pollock succumbed to her wound, the INLA targeted a 'weekend warrior' as members of the Territorial Army are sometimes known. My own cousin, John Leighton, was a Corporal in the Royal Artillery (TA) and I can attest to the magnificent job which he and the other 'Terriers' carry out. Hugh McGinn (40), father of six, was a Warrant Officer in the Royal Irish Regiment (Volunteers) and had served in a purely voluntary capacity for over 20 years. He was a Catholic but chose to live outside, though in close proximity to, the Drumargh Housing Estate in Armagh City. Late on the evening of the 29th, there was a knock at the door which he unwisely answered. The man who had knocked was Gerard 'Dr Death' Steenson and another INLA man. Steenson who had already killed that month, some 19 days earlier when he shot UDR soldier Colin Quinn, opened fire and Sergeant Major McGinn fell dying. Sadly the INLA psychopath remained at liberty to kill and maim for seven more years.

At this stage of the conflict, some 18 prison officers had been killed by the IRA, but they had been left alone by the Loyalist paramilitaries. That changed, however, as

New Year's Eve approached. On the 30th, which fell on a Tuesday, masked gunmen shot dead an off-duty PO from Crumlin Road Gaol. William Burns (45), father of four was leaving for work from his home in Knocknagoney Park on the eastern side of Belfast at around 0700. He was approached by two men who opened fire without warning and ran off leaving the PO dying outside his own front door. Minutes later, two more gunmen shot another PO in Castlereagh Street which is just one mile away, but he survived his wounds. Very shortly afterwards, a caller to a local radio station claimed that the two shootings were carried out by the Loyalist Prisoners' Action Force in retaliation for the mistreatment of Loyalist prisoners. It was roundly condemned by the UDA/UFF and it is a widely held belief that the LPAF was a cover name for the UVF.

1980 ended and the 13th year of Troubles got under way with what can only be described as a sectarian death when William Stevenson died from the injuries he received on Christmas Eve. The year ended as it started 366 days earlier – with death; it was after all, the Troubles.

Five people had died during December, including two soldiers both killed by the INLA, a PO and two civilians; one Catholic and one Protestant. The latter death might reasonably be categorised as sectarian.

1980 had ended and although fatalities were down from the previous year, it was nevertheless another year of violence.

The figures were as follows:

Total	110
Army	46
Police	13
Prison officers	2
Civilians	40[1]
Catholics	25
Protestants	13
Republicans	7
Loyalists	2

Deaths were down by 41 on the previous year, and 32 fewer soldiers or former soldiers had been killed. Both RUC and PO deaths were down but civilian deaths had risen, particularly among Catholics.

---

1   Of these, six could be said to be sectarian murders.

PIRA car bomb in Belfast City Centre.

Grand Central Hotel Army Base, Belfast.

Helicopter inserting troops: South Armagh.

Footsies, West Belfast.

ADU and dog land at Crossmaglen.

'B' Coy, 2 RGJ: Beruki Sangar, Crossmaglen.

Unity Flats, Belfast.

Footsies: Lenadoon, Belfast.

Royal Artillery on patrol Belfast City Centre.

Scene of Command Wire Improvised Explosive Device attack near Newry July 1981, injuring two RUC.

Damage to Royal Ulster Constabulary vehicle following attack July 1981.

Scene following Radio Controlled Improvised Explosive Device attack in Crossmaglen Square
November 1981 injuring 3 soldiers.

Royal Army Ordnance Corps Ammunition Technical Officer clearing scene of explosion in Crossmaglen Square, Novemeber 1981.

Royal Army Ordnance Corps Ammunition Technical Officer neutralises a 150kg Radio Controlled device near Newry in 1983.

Heavy Goods Vehicle clearance near Meigh 1982, vehicle contained a 15kg booby trap.

200kg Vehicle borne time bomb attack against Belfast – Dublin railway 1982.

Scene showing collapsed bridge on Belfast – Dublin railway line from vehicle bomb attack 1982.

Scene of 100kg car bomb attack against Morrows Garage in Bessbrook 1982.

Another view of the car bomb attack against Morrows Garage in 1982.

Scene of car bomb attack showing civilian vehicle blasted through wall of local house, Morrow's Garage, Bessbrook 1982.

Scene following a failed Command Wire Improvised Explosive Device attack against an Royal Ulster Constabulary patrol in 1983.

Ammunition Technical Officer neutralising 160kg Radio Controlled Improvised Explosive Device South Armagh 1982.

Part Two

1981

This year would see 49 soldiers killed, with the Royal Green Jackets suffering the loss of five of their number. However, the Regiment which – as always – suffered more grievously than any other was the Ulster Defence Regiment. The UDR lost 17 of their soldiers, and a further five former members killed by association. This was the year of Altnaveigh, it was the year of 'honey trap' killings, and it was the year that 10 Republicans died on hunger strike.

13

January

The first month of the new year would see the deaths of seven people – three soldiers and two RUC men – and the Provisionals exacted 'revenge' for the shooting of three of their men.

On the 9th, Gerard Steenson was again in action, doing what he was best at; killing people in cold blood. A plan was hatched by several INLA men who included Steenson, Harry Kirkpatrick and Jimmy Brown. The plan was to drive to the Botanic area of Belfast, near Queen's University where an RUC foot patrol was known to operate. The three drove around but were unable to find any suitable targets and instead drove to Great Victoria Street and parked up. One RUC officer and his RUCR colleague went to check out the car; as they did so, Steenson waited until the RUCR man – Lindsay McDougal (36), father of three – had turned his back and then shot him with a handgun. As he fell dying, Brown also opened fire but the magazine was accidentally ejected and the officer was able to reach cover. The car roared off and Constable McDougall died in the street.

Henry 'Harry' Kirkpatrick turned informer against other members of the INLA, having been arrested, in February 1983 on charges including the murder of two RUC officers, two UDR soldiers, and Hugh McGinn, a member of the Territorial Army.[1] As evidence emerged that he was going to turn 'supergrass' he was segregated from other INLA prisoners at the Maze. However, the INLA kidnapped his wife Elizabeth, in order to put pressure on him to change his mind. They then kidnapped his sister and his stepfather also, but were later released unharmed. INLA Chief of Staff Dominic McGlinchey carried out the execution of Kirkpatrick's lifelong friend Gerard 'Sparky' Barkley because it was believed that he may have passed on information to the police.[2] In December 1985, 27 people were convicted based on Kirkpatrick's statements, but by December 1986, 24 would have their convictions overturned. Kirkpatrick was convicted of the murder of Constable McDougal and sentenced to life imprisonment. He was released early and now lives under a secret identity, and his whereabouts are unknown.[3]

UDR: LIVING UNDER THREAT
Mark 'C', UDR and Royal Artillery

I transferred into the full-time UDR in Belfast in 1981 after five years' service with the Royal Artillery and completing one tour of duty in Belfast. It was a bit of a culture shock to be living at home with my parents instead of in barracks, but therein lay

---

1   See Chapter 12.
2   As reported in Chapters 12 and 13.
3   See Chapters 41 and 46 for more details.

the danger and vulnerability of UDR Soldiers: full-time as well as part-time, men, women and their families. I was maybe better prepared for the constant security at home as both my father and one of my brothers were RUC officers and indeed our house had been targeted on several occasions, with my parents finally forced out in 1985 after attacks by the UDA.

As I say, at first living with my parents it was just getting into a routine, watching who came to the door, checking under the car, taking different routes to work. But when I got married, and had my own wife, kids and house that all gets stepped up a notch. It was then necessary to stop the kids going to the door first; you had to check the car before they got in it, even had to watch for any unfamiliar faces standing out when you picked them up from school.

But for me personally, the most dangerous and scariest time was going and coming off duty from Girdwood Park Barracks on the Antrim Road; there is no need to tell people reading this book, how dangerous an area it was and still is. The worst times were when we were on the early guard, and we had to take over from the part-time units at 3AM so they could get home and prepare for their civvie jobs. A few of the lads who lived close would liaise, and take turns giving lifts etc. – sort of get a routine going. It would go something like this: get up around 1:30am; get ready to leave and, if one of the others had a house phone, I would phone saying that I was preparing to move. I would then stand at the side of the window, lights out and scan the street, personal protection weapon (PPW) in hand, for about 5mins, then slowly and quietly open the front door, always scanning, weapon ready, slowly move to the car and put down my kitbag beside car. I could have a quick 'Jeff Duke' (look) under it. All this time I knew several guys would be doing the same routine. Satisfied, I would finally get into the car, PPW ready under my thigh; drive and watch for my approaching comrades emerging from the shadows. We would then make our way to Girdwood, not stopping at traffic lights as we got nearer the Crumlin or Antrim Roads depending on what gate we choose to drive into that night and finally breathe a sigh of relief when finally into camp.

Remember this routine was non-stop but had to be done, as many paid the price for letting their guard slip; almost 80% of UDR Soldiers who were killed in the Troubles were murdered off duty. Being aware of this, I always felt very scared for my wife and kids when I was on duty, especially when we were away on Border Ops two weeks at a time in Newtownhamilton or Fermanagh. On those occasions, she always got her sister to stay with her and for that I was grateful. One of her other sisters was married to one of my comrades, so they helped each other through, but this was the life for all UDR Families living through the 1980s, always under threat.

On the 16th, Bernadette McAliskey (formally Devlin) and her husband were shot and seriously injured in a gun attack in their home near Coalisland, Co Tyrone. Several gunmen from the UFF broke into the house, unaware that an undercover unit of the Army were actually dug in around the grounds keeping surveillance on the firebrand former MP. She had lost her seat in Parliament some years earlier after an election in 1974, largely as a consequence of her 'immoral' behaviour. The 'MP in blue jeans' as she was once known to journalists, had had a child out of wedlock and this had caused a raised eyebrow or two. It might have been morally acceptable to Republican supporters to blow up soldiers and shoot policemen in front of their children, but morally repugnant for a good Catholic girl to bear a child without a wedding ring on her finger. In 1971, while still unmarried, she gave birth to a daughter Róisín, which cost her much support in Roman Catholic areas.

The gunmen, who drove up to the house in a stolen car, smashed down the front door with sledgehammers and fired on Mrs McAliskey with hand guns, hitting her in the chest, arm, and thigh. They shot her husband in the kitchen, but fortunately, their three small children were not harmed. She was hit seven times and critically injured. A unit of 3 Para, which was in the area, heard the shots and hurried to the house. The first soldier on the scene rushed to give the badly wounded former MP emergency treatment. Despite her pain, she was unable to forget her hatred of the British and is reported to have spat out: "What! You come to finish me off?" The attackers had torn out the McAliskeys' telephone and, while the wounded couple were being given first aid by the troops, a soldier ran to a neighbour's house, commandeered a car, and drove to the home of a councillor to telephone for help. The injured pair were flown by helicopter to hospital in the nearby town of Dungannon for emergency treatment and then to the Musgrave Park Hospital in Belfast, where intensive care facilities were required. Earlier, the gunmen had run outside, virtually into the arms of the soldiers, and surrendered without a fight.

One of the UDA's leading men at that time was Ray Smallwoods and he was arrested outside the McAliskey's house with the other UFF men. Smallwoods had not personally fired any shots but had been the driver of the getaway car. He was sentenced to 15 years in prison for his involvement. The other men involved in the assassination attempt, the author understands from very reliable Loyalist sources were Aidy Bird and a Loyalist paramilitary called Andrew James Watson. The UFF leadership had drawn up a shopping list of leading targets to eliminate. Amongst the names on the list were John Turnley and INLA/IRSP activists, Miriam Daly, Ronnie Bunting and Noel Lyttle.

Earlier that day, Major Ivan Toombs (45), a part-time soldier in the UDR was killed by a gunman from the Newry Brigade of the Provisionals. He was a father of five and was set up for murder by Eamon Collins, a PIRA member and a work colleague of Major Toombs. Collins, who later revealed all in his book *Killing Rage*,[4] worked with the murdered man at HM Customs Post, Warrenpoint in Co Down. Collins had made all of the arrangements and had timed it to the precise minute when it would be possible to kill him. A masked PIRA gunman – reputed to be a cousin of Collins – walked into the office and shot him dead. Years later, Collins was on a train and a pretty girl smiled at him. He casually enquired of a friend who she was, to be told that she was the daughter of Major Ivan Toombs. Sickened by the senseless brutality of the IRA and by his own part in it, he turned 'supergrass' and informed on his former fellow-terrorists. Eamon Collins was murdered by the Provisionals on 27 January 1999 while walking his dogs near Barcroft Park, Newry. He was stabbed and beaten so badly that police initially thought he had been hit by a car.

---

4   Collins, E. *Killing Rage* (London: Granta Books, 1997).

One of the units which fought with such courage and tenacity against overwhelming German forces at Arnhem in 1944 was the 2nd South Staffordshire Regiment. Two of their number were awarded the highest honour available to a British or Commonwealth soldier – the coveted Victoria Cross. Major Robert Henry Cain who survived the battle was one and Lance-Sergeant John Daniel Baskeyfield the other, for outstanding gallantry on the corner of Benedendorpsweg and Acacialaan in Oosterbeck. He Baskeyfield was killed while engaging German armour. On 20 January, 1981, one of their successors was killed at Castle Gate, Londonderry. Private Christopher Shenton (21) was helping comrades close up the security gates on a cold winter's night. Gunmen from the Creggan IRA had set up a firing point at Waterloo Street and fired around a dozen shots at the soldiers. Private Shenton was hit in the back and died shortly afterwards; another soldier was badly wounded but later recovered. The murder gang sneaked back into the rat-hole which was the Creggan estate.

On June 21, 1978 in an incident which this author deals with elsewhere,[5] three PIRA gunmen who had been compromised by an informer in the Ardoyne IRA walked into a trap at Ballysillan Postal Depot. Their intention was to bomb the depot and, given that Girdwood Barracks was close and a quick response almost guaranteed, they had arrived heavily armed. Undercover soldiers were waiting and challenged the three men who opened fire, prompting the soldiers to fire back. Denis Brown, Jackie Mailey and James Mulvenna were all shot and killed as was, tragically, Mr William Hanna, an innocent passer-by who was caught in the crossfire. On 14 November,[6] the IRA's 'nutting squad' killed Peter Valente on the grounds that he was an informer. It is not certain, but there is a possibility that, under torture, he may have implicated Maurice Gilvarry (24) as being a fellow informer. On the same day as the murder of Private Shenton, the South Armagh 'nutting squad', having questioned Gilvarry for several days, took his beaten body to a quiet road close to the border and shot him twice in the head. He was left at the side of the road.

Collins, in his previously quoted *Killing Rage,* writes about the squad, also known as the ISU – Internal Security Unit – and its rule of terror and its utter ruthlessness. It had five main functions: security and character vetting of new recruits to the IRA; collecting and collating material on failed and compromised IRA operations; collecting and collating material on suspect or compromised individuals (informers); interrogation and debriefing of suspects and compromised individuals; and carrying out killings of those judged guilty by IRA courts martial. In less than two months, they had been busy and had executed two alleged 'touts.' Four weeks after the murder of Gilvarry, the ISU killed another alleged 'tout.'[7]

On the 21st, a PIRA ASU struck a major blow for *freedom* and for the cause of Irish *unity* by killing an 86-year-old man as he was a *'symbol of hated Unionism'* [author's italics]. They burst into Tynan Abbey in Co Armagh, home of the Stronge family. It was a large neo-gothic-romantic country house built c. 1750 and situated outside the village of Tynan. It was their family home until 1981, when It was bombed; it was finally demolished in 1998, having stood for 249 years. Tynan is close to Middletown and only

---

5   See Wharton, Ken M., *Wasted Years, Wasted Lives* (Solihull: Helion, 2013), Vol. 1.
6   See Chapter 11.
7   See Chapter 14.

a shade over one mile from the Irish border. Gunmen burst in and having singled out Sir Norman Stronge (86) and his son James (48), who was a part-time policeman, shot them both dead. Not content with the double murder, they left explosives and incendiary devices, and set the building alight. In the time that it took the local Fire Brigade to arrive, the mansion was gutted. Coming just five days after the attempted murders of Bernadette McAliskey and her husband by a Loyalist murder gang, the double killings can only be seen as a direct retaliatory strike. Indeed, the former 'MP in blue jeans' said: "My own reaction to the killing of the Stronges was the same as it has been to all that kind of incident; that it is politically counter-productive and confuses the issue, and that it is totally non-progressive." James Stronge was not only RUCR, he was also a former British soldier having served as a Captain in the Grenadier Guards.

Just three days later, a soldier from the Royal Regiment of Fusiliers (RRF) was fatally wounded while manning a security gate in Belfast City Centre. The gate was located near Berry Street and Chapel Lane, in the vicinity of St Mary's Church. Today the huge and modern Castle Court Shopping Centre stands close by; the author shopped there on a recent trip to Belfast, sadly aware that a young life had been lost, almost on the very spot that he stood. On that day back in January 1981, gunmen with their weapons concealed had walked almost right up to where Corporal Phillip Barker (25) father of two young children was manning the gate. It is entirely possible that he may have glanced at his would-be assassins, possibly even smiled at them. As they stood almost toe-to-toe with him, they produced those weapons and fired point-blank into the young soldier's head. He slumped to the ground as the two IRA men dashed into a crowd of Saturday afternoon shoppers. A comrade from the RRF, accompanied only by two unarmed WRACs, attempted to return fire but was unable to shoot for fear of hitting the packed shoppers. Corporal Barker died the next day in the RVH. He was from Oldham and his funeral was held at Hollinwood Crematorium in his home town.

January had seen the deaths of seven people; these included three soldiers and two police officers. One civilian – a Protestant – had died in what can only be described as a sectarian killing and one Republican paramilitary had been killed by PIRA's ISU.

14

February

This month, seven more people died, including an off-duty UDR soldier and two policemen. A top IRA man was assassinated by Loyalists and the 'nutting squad' was in action again. The countdown started to the next Republican hunger strike but this one would see not just hunger strikers dead but kill scores of people in the backlash.

On the 2nd of the month, Colour Sergeant Norman Redpath (34) of the Royal Scots collapsed and died of a heart attack while on duty. His was not a battle fatality, but he is included on the ROH for Northern Ireland not only by this author and the people of NIVA, but also by the National Memorial Arboretum. One cannot say if his death was a combination of Troubles-related stress, but he nonetheless gave his life serving his country in Northern Ireland.

On the 5th, there was an ominous announcement from Sinn Fèin/IRA that the Republican prisoners in the Maze were unhappy that they had had caved in after the last strike and received barely any concessions. In a statement they warned that there could be further hunger strikes if they were not granted special category status. That time was only 24 days away.

On the following day, in what was imaginatively known as the 'Firearm Certificates Protest' Ian Paisley, leader of the Democratic Unionist Party (DUP), led a group of 500 men up a hillside in Co Antrim at night. Those taking part in the gathering were photographed holding firearms certificates above their head. Firearm certificates are issued by the RUC to those people who possess legally held firearms. The implication of the demonstration was that those taking part could as easily have been holding their weapons above their head.

The British commercial Coaster 'Nellie M' had departed from Liverpool with a cargo valued at £1 million and on the 6th was at anchor in the Lough Foyle inlet, barely 300 yards from the Republic's shoreline. A PIRA ASU consisting of 12 IRA men hijacked a pilot boat at a pier on Moville, on the northwest bank of the inlet. Five of the group remained watching on shore, while another seven members of the ASU, carrying two high-explosive charges, forced the skipper to take them to the British coal ship. Once on board, the cell informed the Nellie M's captain about their intentions and ordered him to gather the crew and to get his men into the lifeboat. At the same time, three others planted the charges in the engine room. The hijacked motor launch then took in tow the lifeboat, leaving her adrift close to the eastern shore, and headed back for Moville. As the lifeboat reached the beach, the first explosion shook the British Coaster and gigantic flames, visible from several miles away, engulfed the bridge. A second blast, some hours later, blew up the bulkheads and the ship began to sink. PIRA claimed that the boat was a 'legitimate' commercial target and promised more attacks on British shipping.

On the same day, the Provisionals killed an RUCR man as he stopped at a shop in South Belfast en-route for work in the Malone Road area. Dickers had regularly monitored the movements of Constable Charles Lewis (38) and another colleague and reported that they stopped at virtually the same time every day at a newspaper shop in Balmoral Avenue, close to the Lisburn Road. The two officers went inside the shop as normal and failed to notice a car parked nearby. The car was a stolen car, and in it were a driver and two gunmen all waiting for the RUCR men to arrive. The two officers came out of the shop – Constable Lewis in the lead – and the gunmen opened fire. Lewis was hit several times and slumped to the ground, mortally wounded; he died minutes later. His comrade was unhurt and the men jumped back into the waiting car which disappeared up Balmoral Avenue and Stockman's Lane. It was later found abandoned on the Nationalist Lenadoon Estate. The RUCR man left two young children.

Two days later, on the 8th, another RUCR officer was killed, this time by INLA gunmen, including the psychopathic *'Doctor Death'* Gerard Steenson. Alexander Scott (37) was a part-time Constable who also ran a shop with his wife in the Ravenhill Road area of East Belfast. He had just locked up the shop and was about to get into his car with his daughter when gunmen, including as mentioned, Steenson opened fire and Constable Scott was hit several times and died at the scene. One of the other gunmen was James Power and he was to die in an 'own goal' explosion in May.[1]

On the 9th, Ian Paisley was in the news yet again. He and other senior members of the DUP held a rally at Belfast City Hall were they signed a covenant, the 'Ulster Declaration', based on the Ulster Covenant of 1912. Paisley also announced that there was to be a series of protest rallies against the continuing dialogue between Margaret Thatcher and Charles Haughey. There was to be no stopping this man who referred to the Pope as the *'Whore of Rome,'* and he was suspended from the House of Commons when he repeatedly called Humphrey Atkins, then Secretary of State for Northern Ireland, a liar.

The slaughter of off-duty Security Forces continued on the 10th, with the third murder in less than 96 hours, this time of a part-time UDR soldier. Lance-Corporal Samuel David Montgomery (27) doubled his Security Force duties with work at a timber yard in Bay Road, Londonderry on the western side of the River Foyle. At around 1600 hours, two PIRA gunmen from the Creggan Estate parked up outside the yard in a stolen car. They calmly walked up to the UDR man who had his back to them – just as the Provisionals liked it – and shot him several times in the back of his head, mortally wounding him. They were racing off back to the Creggan while an ambulance was rushing the dying man to Altnagelvin Hospital which is the other side of the Foyle, some two to three miles away from where he was shot. He died before he could receive emergency treatment.

The Reverend Ian Paisley, leader of the Democratic Unionist Party (DUP) who was rarely out of the news with his anti-Catholic rhetoric and somewhat bigoted views, then dropped a bombshell with a claim that he was target for assassination. This in itself was not the bombshell; what did shock observers was not that someone one wanted to kill him – suspects ran to around half a million – but it was the Ulster Unionist Party (UUP).

---

1   See Chapter 17.

The leader of the UUP, Mr James Molyneaux, dismissed Mr Paisley's claims as 'ludicrous'. It is perhaps apocryphal that the various paramilitary factions had an unwritten but acknowledged rule that they would not try and assassinate each other's leaders. With the exception of the assassination attempt on Gerry Adams' life on 14 March, 1984 one is not aware of any on the lives of people such as Paisley or McGuinness.

On the 16th, the Royal Electrical and Mechanical Engineers (REME) lost one of their men in an RTA in the Province. Craftsman Alan Coombe (20) from Aldershot, Hants was killed just a month before his 21st birthday. He was cremated at Park Crematorium in Aldershot, the spiritual home of the British Army.

On the 21st and on the busiest day of the shopping week – Saturday – the Provisionals carried out two mini-bombing blitzes in Belfast and Londonderry the Republican terror group firebombed eight shops in Belfast and three in Londonderry which resulted in extensive damage to all 11 stores. The bombing teams had been quieter for a few months, largely as a consequence of tighter security in the shopping areas and the use of security gates in most of the major towns and cities in the North.

That weekend was also to be the last on this Earth for Patrick Trainor (28), a Catholic who was on the fringe of the Provisional IRA. He lived with his wife and three young children in the Andersonstown area and was suspected – it is thought as a consequence of allegations by Peter Valente, made under torture – of 'touting' for either the RUC or the Army. He was picked up by the ISU or 'nutting squad', interrogated and probably tortured himself before being shot twice in the back of the head. Patrick Trainor's body dumped at Upton Cottages close to Glen Road in West Belfast. An apologist for the Provisionals claimed that he been informing since 1976 and stated: "He was recruited as an informer after a robbery and for the last five years has been passing on information concerning weapons, the movement of volunteers and Republican sympathisers." Both the RUC and the Army vehemently denied that he was one of their informers. His heartbroken widow said:

> They say that he got money but if he did I certainly didn't see any of it! He was not in any organisations and hardly ever went out so I don't even see how he could have got any information to pass on. My husband had no love for the Army because he was shot by soldiers on Grosvenor Road about 10 years ago. He just lived for the kids....'[2]

With the passage of time, we can now see that the Provisionals were quite right to be as paranoid about informers as they apparently were for, if not exactly riddled with 'touts', a high number of British and RUC Intelligence penetrations at every level certainly existed. People such as Marty McGartland, Raymond Gilmour, Kevin Fulton, Sean O'Callaghan, Dennis Donaldson (among others) were possibly just the tip of the iceberg. It is estimated that between 63 and 100 informers – real and imaginary – were executed by the IRA's nutting squad over the course of the Troubles. Indeed Donaldson, a former 'pre-sixty niner' Provisional recruited by British Intelligence in 1983, was only revealed as an informer as recently as 2006. He was murdered by shotgun blast at a

---

2   Thornton, David, Seamus Kelters, Brian Feeney and David McKittrick. *Lost Lives: The Stories of the Men, Women and Children who Died as a Result of the Northern Ireland Troubles.* (Edinburgh: Mainstream, 1999, revised ed. 2007), p. 851.

remote cottage in Co Donegal by the 'Real IRA'. As this author has previously stated, the informer, once found guilty by a 'Kangaroo Court' would, often after torture, be taken to a lonely country location with his hands bound and a black hood over his head. Once there, he would be forced to kneel and many times a 'tame' priest would be called in to attempt to dignify what was nothing more than a sordid murder by intoning the last rites. Once that 'absolution' was out of the way, he would be dispatched with two rounds to the back of his head and a brand new £20.00 note would be stuffed into his lifeless hands to mark him as a 'Judas'. That was not the end of the man's indignity as on many occasions the body would be booby-trapped and rather than risk more bloodshed, the Security Forces would carefully tie a rope around the corpse's ankles, attach to a PIG and drag it along like the carcass of an animal to ensure that no explosive devices had been planted underneath the body.

It is alleged by some writers that a leading member of the West Belfast ISU was Freddie Scappaticci (sometimes referred to as '*Steak knife*' or '*Stake knife*'). It is further thought that he may well have been in the ISU when Gilvarry[3] as well as Valente and Trainor were 'executed'. Scappaticci was fined for rioting in 1970 after being caught up in trouble in West Belfast and one year later was interned without trial at the age of 25 as part of 'Operation Demetrius'. Among contemporaries interned with him were men later to become prominent in the Provisional IRA: Ivor Bell, Gerry Adams, and Alex Maskey. He was released from detention in 1974 and allegedly by this time was a member of PIRA, and by 1980, is said to have been a lead member in the IRA's ISU for their Northern Command.

On the 23rd, Loyalists involved themselves in the killing with the assassination of a leading Provisional, when a UVF gunman made his way into the Republican heartland and murdered James 'Skipper' Burns (33) alleged to be the Northern IRA's Quartermaster. Robert 'Squeak' Seymour of the UVF cycled across Belfast to the home of Burns in Rodney Parade, Donegall Road, in the Falls area. He broke into the house while Burns and his partner were out, and then concealed himself until the couple returned and went to bed. He then went up to their bedroom and shot Burns dead as he lay sleeping, using a pistol with a silencer. Burns' partner didn't wake when the shots were fired, and Seymour escaped undetected. However, as it had started to snow, Seymour, fearing that his bicycle would leave tracks which would ultimately lead the Army or RUC to him, carried the bicycle on his back along the Donegall Road, over the M1 motorway and on to the loyalist Village area. This feat, along with the shooting of such a high-ranking IRA member in the heartland of the 'enemy' made him a local 'legend' and Loyalist folk hero. So much so, that a song was written about him (like the Republicans, the Loyalists too eulogised their murderers). Part of it went: "Some come listen to my story now of a brave young Ulster man whose life was cruelly taken by a rebel's murdering hand. He's a man that we will remember and a friend for evermore." The Republicans eventually caught up with him however, when in June 1988, two masked PIRA gunmen entered the video shop he owned in Woodstock Road, South East Belfast. Seymour tried to escape by running out the back door, but he was cornered by the gunmen in an alley behind his shop and shot dead.

---

3   See Chapter 13.

On the 28th, a large van bomb exploded in the centre of Limavady, Co Londonderry, causing damage to 40 shops and commercial premises. An IRA bombing team had hijacked the van in Londonderry City, packed it with explosives and driven into the centre of the small town where it was left to devastate the commercial heart. Adequate warnings were given and, other than shock and cuts and bruises, there were no significant injuries.

February had ended with seven people dead; three soldiers and two policemen were killed as were one civilian and one Republican paramilitary. Republicans were responsible for four of the deaths this month.

15

March

Five people died this month, including three soldiers, and another joy-rider died at a VCP. More ominously, the second hunger strike began but this one was to the death; literally.

On Sunday 1 March, following discussions amongst Republican prisoners in the Maze, confirmed by PIRA's Army Council and the leadership of the INLA, the second hunger strike of the Troubles got under way. This time, it was decided, the individual commencements would be staggered for maximum impact. Bobby Sands, one of leaders of PIRA prisoners in the Maze, refused food and so began a new hunger strike. The choice of the start date was significant because it marked the 5th anniversary of the ending of special category status. The main aim of the new strike was to achieve the reintroduction of political status for Republican prisoners. Edward Daly, then Catholic Bishop of Derry, criticised the decision to begin another hunger strike.

Bobby Sands was to lead the strike but it was decided that Brendan McFarlane would take over his role as leader of the PIRA prisoners in the Maze. It was not immediately clear whether or not the IRA leadership outside the prison was in favour of a new hunger strike, following the outcome of the 1980 strike. The main impetus came from the prisoners themselves. The strike was to last until 3 October 1981 and was to see 10 Republican prisoners starve themselves to death in support of their protest. The strike led to a heightening of political tensions in the region.

Forty-eight hours later, the British Government made its intentions clear, when Humphrey Atkins, Secretary of State for Northern Ireland, made a statement in the House of Commons in which he said that there would be no political status for prisoners regardless of the hunger strike.

The first hunger striker to die was Bobby Sands on 5 May, and on the 66th day of his refusal to eat. The last to die was Michael Devine on 20th August and on the 60th day of his refusal to eat. Over the course of the following chapters, I will write a small 'pen picture' of each of the 10 men.

In 1972, Sands joined the Provisional IRA and in the October of that year, he was arrested and charged with possession of four handguns found in the house where he was staying. He was convicted in April 1973 and sentenced to five years' imprisonment and released in April 1976. Upon his release from prison in 1976, he resumed his active role within the IRA. In the October of 1976, he was charged with the bombing of the Balmoral Furniture Company in Dunmurry, South Belfast.[1] Although he was

---

1   See Wharton, Ken M., *Wasted Years, Wasted Lives* (Solihull: Helion, 2013).

never convicted of this charge there was sufficient evidence to convince the judge that he was guilty. Sands and five others were alleged to have been involved in a gun battle with the RUC and he was convicted on the evidence of a pistol left in the car in which he was travelling. Following the shoot-out, he was forced to leave behind two wounded fellow-terrorists: Seamus Martin and Gabriel Corbett. Sands, Joe McDonnell, Seamus Finucane, and Sean Lavery tried to escape in a car, but were arrested. In 1977, Sands was charged with possession of the revolver from which bullets were fired at the RUC after the bombing. After his trial and conviction, He was sentenced to 14 years' imprisonment in HM Prison Maze.

On the 5th, Frank Maguire, then Independent MP for Fermanagh / South Tyrone, died. In the aftermath of his death there was some debate amongst Nationalists as to the possibility of an agreed candidate for the forthcoming by-election. Initially Noel Maguire, Frank's brother, Austin Curry, a member of the SDLP, and Bernadette McAliskey – still recovering from an earlier assassination attempt – all expressed an interest in standing for the vacant seat. However McAliskey later stated that she would be willing to step down in favour of a candidate chosen by the prisoners in the H-Blocks. Eventually the leadership of Sinn Féin decided to put forward a candidate, and on 26 March 1981 Bobby Sands was nominated. After an embarrassing victory, the government attempted to put in place legislation to prevent serving criminals from standing in elections. The argument quite naturally was that if a prisoner hadn't the right to vote, it was ludicrous to then give him the right to stand as an MP.

On the same day as the MP's death, Margaret Thatcher paid a visit to Northern Ireland and denied claims that the constitutional position of Northern Ireland would be threatened by the on-going talks between the British and Irish Governments. Loyalists, however, remained sceptical about her intentions and there was, and still is, a suspicion that Britain would gladly ditch that part of the Union if it were expedient to do so. Their fears were exacerbated a few weeks later, when Brian Lenihan, then Irish Foreign Minister, said that the on-going talks between the British and Irish Governments could lead to a United Ireland in 10 years.

On the 8th, a soldier from the RCT was killed in circumstances unknown. Driver Ian Michael MacDonald (20) was from the Birkenhead area. His funeral was held at Landican Cemetery on the Wirrall Peninsula. On Sunday 15th, Francis Hughes, a PIRA member serving time in the Maze became the second man to join the hunger strike. By this stage, Bobby Sands was into his 15th day of refusing food and was only taking water.

Back on 8 April 1977, Hughes, Dominic McGlinchey and another PIRA member Ian Milne were travelling in a car near the town of Moneymore, Co Londonderry when an RUC patrol car carrying four officers signalled them to stop. The IRA members attempted to escape but lost control of the car which ended up in a ditch. They abandoned the car and opened fire on the RUC car killing two officers and wounding another, before escaping. The two officers killed by Hughes and co. that day were Constable John McCracken and Constable Kenneth Sheehan. Hughes was also said to have been behind the murder of UDR Corporal William Hughes and his 10-year-old daughter who were killed by a bomb placed under the family car on 8 February, 1978. He was eventually arrested on 16 March, in the same year after a shoot-out with the SAS at Glenshane Pass, Co Londonderry during which he killed Lance Corporal David Jones. He was described by the Security Forces as "an absolute fanatic and a ruthless killer." At one stage, he was the most wanted man in Northern Ireland.

On the same day that IRA prisoner Francis Hughes began his hunger strike a soldier from the Royal Scots was killed in what was very likely an ND, or negligent discharge. Private Patrick Joseph McKenna (20) was accidentally shot somewhere in the Province; beyond that, the author has no further details.

On the 19th, the Provisionals killed an innocent civilian. A Catholic man, Gerry Roland (45), father of six, was driving with a friend who had once been a member of the UDR. A lorry, owned by his friend had been hijacked en-route from the Irish Republic and Mr Roland had volunteered to help search for it, as he was more familiar with the area. The lorry was found in a remote area, but as they drove towards it, IRA gunmen opened fire and Mr Roland was hit and mortally wounded. His friend drove the vehicle to the nearest hospital which was across the border in Co Louth, but he was dead on arrival. A Sinn Féin spokesman said that they apologised but the men had failed to stop at an IRA (illegal) checkpoint and they were "forced to open fire."

The very next day, joy-riders drove through an Army VCP on Ross Road in the Divis area of Belfast and were chased by UDR soldiers. The Army stated that the soldiers opened fire when they thought that they saw a pistol pointed at them. Six shots were fired at the stolen car and Patrick McNally (20) was hit and died at the scene. He was the third joy-rider to be killed in Belfast alone in a very short period of time. The Belfast Coroner warned how dangerous the practice of driving around in stolen cars was especially in times of high tension such as the Troubles. Sinn Féin/IRA were quick to condemn the soldiers for killing Patrick McNally but, 24 hours earlier, they had done exactly the same thing at their IVCP/vehicle hijack in South Armagh.

LUCKY MAN
Carl Ball, Royal Welch Fusiliers

An incident that occurred directly outside Fort Whiterock; a car had been abandoned and set on fire, my brick was tasked to provide covering support to the engineers to clear away the car. The Engineers proceeded to leave camp in their Scooby (bulldozer) and we followed in the PIG, as the Scooby was clearing the car about four to five shots rang out we de-bussed from the PIG and took up firing points, but could not locate the area the shots came from which was somewhere from the Turf Lodge, we quickly secured the area and covered the Scooby as it speedily made its way back to the camp. We then followed the Engineers back into camp, once inside we spoke to the Engineer and observed the Scooby which had a perfect grouping of about three rounds in the armoured glass right where the Engineer's head was, I always wonder to this day if he kept the glass as a good luck charm as it certainly saved his life that day.

On the 21st, Tomás Ó Fiaich, Catholic Primate of Ireland issued a statement calling on the IRA to end its use of violence. He was to prove a tireless negotiator on behalf of the hunger strikers, and was known by the British media as 'Chaplain to the IRA'. Martin Dillon writes of a meeting that Ó Fiaich had with Margaret Thatcher: "When he met with Margaret Thatcher ... he was appalled at her demand to know if the IRA hunger strikers were 'dying to prove their virility'."[2]

On the 22nd, PIRA prisoner Raymond McCreesh, and fellow prisoner Patsy O'Hara, INLA became the third and fourth prisoners in the Maze, to join the hunger strike. McCreesh was from the Newry area and first joined na Fianna Éireann, the IRA's youth wing, in 1973, and later that year he progressed to join PIRA's South Armagh Brigade. On 25 June 1976, at the age of 19, McCreesh, along with two other PIRA men – Danny McGuinness and Paddy Quinn – had been captured by soldiers from 3 Para, and all were sentenced to 14 years. Later enquiries linked McCreesh, along with two others, to a string of IRA attacks committed with the Armalite he was caught with; these included the Kingsmill massacre in 1976 as well as many other murders of soldiers and policemen.

Patsy O'Hara was interned in Long Kesh, and on his release in April 1975 he joined the IRSP/INLA. He was arrested and released several times between 1975 and 1978 and finally was arrested in Londonderry in 1979. He was convicted of possessing a hand grenade and sentenced to eight years in prison in January 1980.

Bobby Sands was nominated as a candidate in the by-election in Fermanagh / South Tyrone to be held on 9 April 1981. Three days afterwards the SDLP decided to withdraw the nomination of Austin Currie from the by-election in order not to impede the election chances of Sands. Within 24 hours, Noel Maguire decided to withdraw his nomination also which meant that voters were faced with a straight choice between the leading hunger striker and Harry West, the Unionist candidate.

On the 25th, Sammy Millar a local Councillor for the Shankill area, with strong UDA connections was shot and seriously wounded by INLA gunmen. He stood for the NUPRG grouping, or New Ulster Political Research Group, set up by the UDA leadership in 1978. He was sitting in his house in the Shankill Road, working on some papers when gunmen burst into his house and shot him. A bullet severed his spine and he was left for dead by the INLA murder gang. He was rushed to the nearby Mater Hospital and later to the MPH where staff saved his life. He lost a brother-in-law who was a full time member of the UDR in 1972 and a cousin, Robin Shields, who was an ambulance controller in the Royal Victoria Hospital in 1980.[3]

Retaliation was swift and beyond the control of Councillor Millar. On the 27th, UFF gunmen crammed into a 'borrowed' car and began cruising around the Nationalist Ardoyne looking for a Catholic victim. As they drove onto Berwick Road, they saw Peter Blake (26) walking by. At least two of the gunmen opened fire on Mr Blake and he fell, mortally wounded; he died at the scene. There is absolutely no evidence to link him with Republican paramilitaries and he was simply an innocent Catholic on his way home. Two years later, some of the murder gang were convicted and one told the court that UDA leader Jim Craig had paid him £2.00 for the murder and congratulated him on the killing; another of the gang said that he was paid the princely sum of £7.00 and given a glass of whisky to steady his nerves. Craig himself was killed by his own organisation when, having been lured to the Castle Inn pub in Beersbridge Road, East Belfast, he was shot by UFF gunmen on 15 October, 1988.

2   Dillon, Martin, *God and the Gun* (London: Routledge, 1999), p.216.
3   See Chapter 9.

On the same day as this sectarian murder, the IRA targeted an off-duty UDR soldier as he walked to work. Private John David Smith (25) lived in the Cregagh district of East Belfast and was known by PIRA dickers to walk from there, through the Nationalist Markets' area to the City Centre where he worked. He had covered most of the two miles or so and was on Cromac Street when two men, in white overalls and carrying tins of paint followed him along the street and shot him from point blank range in the back of the head. As he fell, mortally wounded, his killers raced off in a stolen car. Nearby office workers rushed into the street and tried to save him but he died shortly afterwards.

So this momentous and ultimately seminal month ended with six deaths. Three of the dead were soldiers and three were civilians. Three Catholics died this month, the killing of one of whom was overtly sectarian.

16

April

This month was marked by the deaths of 11 people, including five soldiers or former soldiers and two policemen. It also included the death of a defenceless census worker, shot dead by cowardly terrorists.

Appropriately enough, on All Fools' Day, the DUP organised three late-night rallies on top of hills near Armagh, Gortin and Newry. At the rally near Gortin, County Tyrone, two RUC vehicles were overturned by the crowd. The rallies were similar to one held on 6 February 1981 when firearm certificates were displayed by those taking part.

On the 2nd, a young police Constable was killed by a UVBT planted by IRA bombers outside Bessbrook RUC station. Constable Kenneth Acheson (23), father of an 11-month-old baby had parked up close to the RUC station at around lunchtime. Between then and the end of his shift that evening, an IRA bombing team had planted a deadly device under his car. Whether or not he checked at the day's end is a moot point; he may have been fatigued, he may have been careless, but he had only driven a short distance, en-route for his home in Ballynahone and was on the Derrywilliam Road when the device exploded. The car was destroyed in a flash of flame and noise; he was killed instantly.

This author has read much about the life and death of hunger striker, Bobby Sands; one has some slight sympathy for his plight in that he didn't kill anyone and was never actually convicted of the Balmoral Warehouse bombing in Dunmurry. The 14 years he received for being in the same car as a pistol which could have been used by others, appears savage. That is, until one considers that people could have been killed or injured – with his knowledge – either in the Balmoral Warehouse bombing or by the pistol. There was a place in my heart for the despair which this young man's family was suffering, but this was wiped out on 7 April, when his fellow terrorists killed an unarmed census collector, shamefully in cold blood. Any lingering sympathy was further wiped out by the deaths of an RUC officer in Belfast and five soldiers killed at Altnaveigh the following month.

On 7 April, Mrs Joanne Mathers (29), mother of a young child was collecting census forms on the Nationalist Gobnascale in Londonderry. Mrs Mathers was the mother of a toddler son, Shane, and was trying to earn some 'pin' money by collecting census forms. She was at a house in Anderson Crescent when a gunman ran up to her and snatched her clipboard and census forms and then shot her in the head at point blank range. She died almost immediately. The Provisionals have always denied responsibility but the gun used to kill Mrs Mathers had been previously used by them in punishment shootings. Someone in the Londonderry IRA knew who carried out the cowardly and despicable murder of a helpless young woman. At this point in history, any sympathy this author had for Bobby Sands or any of the other nine hunger strikers died in an instant.

The following is reprinted from a newspaper interview with Mrs Mathers' husband:

Joanne Mathers' son Shane was under two years of age when a police officer arrived at the family home in Bready to tell Mr Mathers his wife had been gunned down in broad daylight as she went door-to-door collecting completed census forms. Shane has no memory of his mother, other than what his father has told him. Mr Mathers says it is this more than anything else that means he will never be able to forgive the IRA members who murdered his wife.

Speaking from the same home he and Joanne shared as a newly married couple, Mr Mathers said he often wonders how the killers live with themselves. "Over the years I have wondered if they went on to have children of their own, and did they ever look at them and think about my son who was a year and 10 months when he was left with no mother? The simplest things have been the hardest for me, like watching other children running to their mothers at the school gate, but Shane missed out on that and so much more. Shane has no memories of Joanne except for what I have told him. I know she would have been so proud of him, but they took that away from her and from him, and for that I will never, ever forgive them. I want the HET to reinvestigate her death for Shane, more than anything else. Joanne deserves justice, even if it is 30 years later."[1]

The author was told by a reliable source, that after she was killed, her little boy would still run to the front door every time he heard it open thinking it was his mother returning.

Deputy First Minister Martin McGuinness — a former IRA leader in Londonderry — was challenged to help with a new investigation. UUP leader Tom Elliott is quoted as saying: "It is long past time he came clean about what he knows about the crimes committed by the IRA in Londonderry while he was in command." A book by Raymond Gilmour, to be published in 2014, will allege that McGuinness was responsible for the woman's death, and that everything in Londonderry went through him; the book will allege that he gave the order for the death of this innocent census-taker.

During the census, Sinn Féin/IRA campaigned for non-completion of the census forms as a demonstration of support for the hunger strike. As a result, the census enumerators in many Republican areas were unable to collect completed forms. This, as a consequence, led to a large under representation of Catholics in the published figures. The population of Northern Ireland was recorded as 1,481,959 with 28 per cent giving their religion as Catholic; 18.5 per cent of the population had refused to state their religion. Later estimates of the true Catholic population put the figure at 38.5 per cent.

THE MURDER OF MRS MATHERS
Soldier, Royal Artillery

As we know, the murder of Joanne was a disgusting act of revenge because the terrorists didn't want the census carried out and when their wishes were ignored they replied in their usual fashion. If you have a copy of Raymond Gilmour's

---

1   *Belfast Telegraph* (18 March, 2011).

book *Dead Ground*[2] the incident is mentioned. There appeared to be a bit of anger amongst the grass roots boyos about the murder, but the Londonderry Brigade commander dismissed it with a wave of his hand. That person is called 'Shorty McNally' by Gilmour to hide his real identity. I recognised who it was by his description and he was McGuiness's sidekick when he ran the Bogside, and later the whole west battalion PIRA. His real name is (censored) normally known as 'Drew.' Pity you can't name and shame the bastard. It's him in the photo that was taken of the gunman firing a handgun during Bloody Sunday. Much as it goes against the grain saying anything good about them, as you know, the PIRA were not an out of control bunch of freelance murderers. They were quite disciplined and no operation was carried out without the say so of their director of operations who was usually the second in command of the brigade. So it is plain as the nose on your face that Joanne's murder was carried out on the orders from the top. Whether she was the intended target, or was just unfortunate enough to have been the one doing the collecting in that area that day is open to comment.

Prior to the publication of this book, the author was approached by representatives of Raymond Gilmour, former PIRA/INLA member who turned 'supergrass'. My advice was requested and given in association with a new publication –*What Price Truth* – by Mr Gilmour[3]. It is alleged that Martin McGuinness gave the order to kill a census worker in Londonderry. The order was conveyed by Creggan PIRA member Brendan Docherty who, together with another person, delivered a .357 Magnum to the Waterside to a local Volunteer called Gary Flynn. He was the Explosives Officer in the unit which operated in the mainly Protestant Waterside area and he was said by Gilmour to be: 'a ruthless bastard.'

As this book was going to print, Gilmour made another revelation about the murder, stating that the weapon used in the cowardly murder was couriered by a woman. Writing in *The Belfast Daily,* he said:

> This woman, who was a good looking girl in her day, came over from the Shantallow area and walked to the Waterside in the east to provide the gun. The murder weapon was .357 Magnum revolver which had been stolen from the home of a part-time RUC officer. This girl was a courier for the IRA in the city. She never came to the attention of the police which allowed her to move easily from the west bank to the east bank of Derry.[4]

STIRRING UP THE NATIVES
Mark 'C', UDR and Royal Artillery
In 1981, when the hunger strikes were in full swing, we had what could be called an interesting incident at the Kinnaird Street sangar at Girdwood Camp Belfast. This sangar was manned 24/7 by the part-time and full time UDR companies

---

2   Gilmour, Raymond, *Dead Ground: Infiltrating the IRA* (Bosston: Little, Brown & Co).

3   Gilmour, Raymond, *What Price Truth* (Create Space Independent Publishing Platform, 2015)

4   22 September, 2014.

stationed there. As you all know this was a very dangerous time with daily rioting on the nearby Antrim Road/New Lodge areas and Republican crowds often attacked the sangar.

On one particular night a crowd starting stoning the camp and in particular, the front sangar, so our Sergeant Major decided to set up the fire hose and we soaked them over the secured gate and fence. The UDR was not allowed to get involved in riot situations and held no baton rounds or any such riot gear, except helmets. Of course this for some reason upset them slightly and the attack continued to the extent that a riot squad was sent for from what we called the 'middle camp' where the Regular Battalion were based. I think it may have been the Scots Guards.

They came down and deployed into a base line on the other side of the gate on Kinnaird Street with the intent of pushing them down towards the Antrim Road away from the camp. However, the officer in charge could not understand why the crowd was getting even madder and then trying to get closer to the gate, intensifying their attack. He got his answer when he came back in through the gate to use his radio, only to see a near whole platoon of UDR soldiers in red PT vests, denims and boots throwing back the stones at the rioters over the heads of the other soldiers!

Of course he went mad and ordered us all back into the accommodation, where we received a very big bollocking but with a sort of "that will teach the Republicans not to attack a UDR sangar." I'm not sure what the officer made of it all though.

The by-election was held on Thursday, 9th of April and the results were revealed on the following Saturday. There was a shock for the Government and a slap in the face not only for the loved ones of the innocent Joanne Mathers but also for the loved ones of the thousand or more people who had been murdered by the Provisional IRA. Bobby Sands, then on hunger strike in the Maze Prison, was elected as Member of Parliament for the constituency. The turnout for the contest was 86.9 per cent; Sands obtained 30,492 votes while Harry West, the Unionist candidate, obtained 29,046 votes. That people could vote for a man unlikely to be able to represent them was a bad enough blow, but the thought that over 30,000 people could be blinkered enough, to vote for a party that wanted to kill its way into government, was simply too much. Following the announcement that Bobby Sands had won there were celebration parades in many Republican areas across Northern Ireland. In Belfast, Cookstown and in Lurgan these celebrations ended in rioting.

Thatcher moved quickly to ensure that this was unlikely to happen again, because later, on 12 June, the Government published proposals to change the Representation of the People Act making it impossible for prisoners to stand as candidates for election to Parliament.

On the 15th, during severe rioting in support of the hunger strikers in Londonderry, a gang of youths, some of whom were masked, attempted to hijack a lorry from a Bakery in William Street, close to the Little Diamond and Rossville Flats. The police were called and in an effort to stop the mob, a baton round was fired by one of the officers. Paul Whitters (15) was said to have been wearing a balaclava in order to mask his features and was hit and fatally injured by the round. He was rushed to Altnagelvin Hospital and later to the RVH in Belfast but he sadly died 10 days later on 25 April.

The first 'celebration' of Sands' victory, and a portent of the violence to come, occurred five days after the election result. Jack Donnelly (56) was a part-time Private in the UDR and lived at Gorestown, Co Tyrone. He was a creature of habit and was known to regularly stop for a drink at a pub in Moy. On the night of the 16th, he arrived at the pub and if he noticed two men in a parked nearby, it probably didn't register. As he was served, those two men – from the INLA – burst in and shot him several times in the head from very close range; he died at the scene. As local UUP MP Harold McCusker was quick to point out, the dicker who had set him up to be murdered was probably a workmate or a neighbour. Ian Paisley said of the killing: "The 30,000 votes had made the IRA feel they have a mandate to go ahead with a campaign of Protestant genocide."

On Sunday 19th, there were two more tragic deaths, but it was a question of who do you believe – the soldiers or the Nationalists? Troops were called out to rioting taking place on the fiercely Nationalist Creggan Estate in West Londonderry, and came under attack from rocks and petrol bombs on Creggan Road. An Army Land Rover containing two soldiers allegedly drove into a crowd of rioters and two teenagers were hit and killed. Hostile witnesses claimed that the vehicle was deliberately driven at the rioters with the intention of hitting them; the soldiers maintained that they were trying to disperse them. The bottom line was two of the rioters died at the scene; James Brown (18) and James English (19). They were both from the Creggan. The soldiers were charged with reckless driving but were later acquitted to angry scenes in the courtroom. The brother of James English, who was 16 at the time, later joined the IRA and was himself killed in an 'own goal' explosion in August, 1985, just minutes away from where his older brother was killed.

APRIL 19, 1981: INCIDENT AT CREGGAN CROSS
Soldier 'B'

I was based at Rosemount, near to the Creggan Estate. We had experienced a number of days rioting as the hunger strikers were starting to die. Days were spent clearing barricades and moving burnt out vehicles, which were dumped near to the river Foyle. An annoying fact was that the Military JCBs could not pick up paving slabs so we had to hand-ball them into the JCB bucket. Later in the evenings the local youth would come out and rioting would start again, which usually commenced with vehicles being hi-jacked.

At approximately 1830 hours on that day, rioting was taking place around the William Street area and a base line was established in Infirmary Road. The CO was deployed near the base line, and it was decided to launch an arrest operation, with the base line withdrawing towards the city; hopefully drawing the rioters with them. Then the Creggan Cross junction could be blocked, trapping the rioters between the base line and our vehicles, which were tasked to block the junction. Snatch squads would then be deployed to effect arrests.

About 15 minutes later, my commander received orders over the radio to mount an arrest operation. He was in the lead Land Rover with me as his driver and to the rear would be a half-ton Rover. These orders were received while we were mounted in vehicles, with engines running in Rosemount Base. Doors had been removed from both Land Rovers, and for my own protection I had bungeed a six-foot shield onto my side. We then deployed from Rosemount and headed downhill to the Creggan Cross junction. As we got about 30 metres from the junction, the stragglers at the rear of the rioters warned off the hard core rioters at the front. At this point my vehicle came under attack from a number of petrol bombers. Later I asked a colleague, who was on duty in the Rossville Flats Observation Post, how many petrol bombs had hit my vehicle. He replied that it was difficult to keep count after a dozen or so, as they were coming over in volleys. As I reached the junction, a mass of rioters ran across my front. I struck the rioters on the junction. Brakes had been applied prior to this stage and the vehicle was slowing down. A mass of bodies raced across my front.

The intention was to stop and then make arrests, which is what happened. However due to the accident the situation changed and the priority became one where we needed to withdraw. Two of the locals – Gary English and James Brown – were unfortunately killed in this incident. The rear vehicle picked up English, but the crowd took the injured Brown away. We had to reverse all the way back to Rosemount as all roads were blocked by barricades.

At about 1900 hours, we got back into Rosemount and the other injured lad, English, was removed to the Altnagelvin Hospital by Military ambulance. Three hours later, I gave a statement to the RUC in the presence of a lawyer who had been tasked from Belfast. Not sure about the dates, but myself and my Commander were charged with two counts of reckless driving, causing death. The charges were read out at Londonderry Magistrates Court, opposite Masonic Base. I replied 'not guilty' and was released to the military on bail £250.

I was concerned as to how my parents would react once they heard the news of this incident so I warned my mother that she would see my name in the news. She phoned the Battalion 2/IC and he reassured her saying: "Don't worry Mrs B. If I think he is in danger, I'll have him in Germany in six hours." It put my mother's mind at rest.

Patrolling got difficult after the incident and I was recognised by English's mother twice whilst out on patrol in the Creggan estate. I thought they lived in Cable Street in the Bogside, but they had moved up to the Creggan. On this occasion, I was ordered out of the area as intelligence had been tipped off that a shoot was being set up for me. From then on I restricted myself to night patrols only, for security reasons.[5]

The next day, three Irish MPs (or TDs: *Teachta Dáil*) met with Bobby Sands' election agent, Owen Carron, and travelled to the Maze Prison. Afterwards, they called for urgent talks with the British Government, but their hopes of a meeting and a possible settlement were dashed by Margaret Thatcher's refusal to meet with them. In fact, she was in Saudi Arabia and told assembled journalists that the British Government would not meet with the TDs to discuss the hunger strike. She said: "We are not prepared to

---

5   This contributor tells the story of the subsequent court case later in this book.

consider special category status for certain groups of people serving sentences for crime. Crime is crime is crime, it is not political."

Dolours Price, who had been a part of the IRA's first 'England Team in 1973, was in the news again when she was released from Armagh Women's Gaol after serving less than eight years of a life sentence. On the 22nd, she received a medical release on the grounds of her anorexia, the same condition as her sister Marian, who was released the previous year. After their conviction for the Old Bailey bombing in March 1973, the sisters had gone on hunger strike and had been transferred to a Northern Ireland gaol on 'compassionate grounds'. Dolours was part of a unit that placed four car bombs in London on 8 March 1973; the Old Bailey and Whitehall army recruitment centre were damaged, with over 200 injured and one man dead. In 2009 she was one of two people arrested in connection with an attack on the Massereene Barracks in March of that year, in which two British soldiers were shot dead. Two years later, she was charged with providing property for the purposes of terrorism and, in 2011, she was charged with encouraging support for an illegal organisation. This related to her involvement in a statement given at an Easter rising rally in Londonderry. On the same day, the Secretary of State for Northern Ireland Owen Paterson revoked her release from prison on licence. Paterson said the decision was made because the threat posed by Price had significantly increased. The charges against her were later dismissed at Londonderry Magistrate's Court in May 2012.

Following Dolours' release in 1980, she married Irish actor Stephen Rea, who was farcically hired to speak the words of Gerry Adams when Sinn Féin was under a broadcasting ban. She later admitted to driving Jean McConville, accused by the IRA of being an informer, to the place where she was killed in 1972.[6] She claimed the killing of Mrs McConville, a mother of 10, was ordered by Sinn Féin President, Gerry Adams, who denied her story. On 24 January 2013, she was found dead at her home. Dolours Price was buried in Milltown Cemetery in West Belfast on 28 January.

On the 22nd, an Army nurse from the Queen Alexandra's Royal Army Nursing Corps (QARANC) died in circumstances unknown. Captain Lynda Maureen Smith (29) was cremated at Porchester Crematorium in Hampshire; the author has no further details. Earlier that day, two more Republican prisoners in the Maze joined Bobby Sands and Francis Hughes on the hunger strike; it was part of PIRA's strategy to keep attention focused on the strike by ensuring almost daily 'developments' in order keep both the media and the public's attention.

THE CROSS
Martin Wells, Royal Green Jackets

Crossmaglen, or the 'Cross' as we called it, was a notoriously dangerous place to serve. The number of soldiers killed or wounded in and around there in the 12 years since the Army was called in in late 1969, was out of all proportion to both its size and its importance in the overall picture of Northern Ireland. The word 'Crossmaglen' had taken on a notoriety of its own and, amongst Army units, had become synonymous with danger. As if all that wasn't bad enough, we started

---

6   See Wharton, Ken, *The Bloodiest Year: Northern Ireland 1972* (Stroud: The History Press, 2011).

our tour against the backdrop of the start of the Provisional IRA Maze prisoners hunger strike. And as the condition of the dozen or so on the strike worsened, so feelings amongst the Republican community in general became more and more angry; and the 'Cross' was 100 per cent Republican!

By the time early May arrived, the condition of one prisoner in particular, Bobby Sands, was reaching a critical point. Sands had bizarrely been put forward for election to Parliament whilst being both a convicted terrorist and a Maze prisoner on hunger strike. He narrowly won that election on 9 April, just as his condition was starting to become very serious. This only served to further worsen a bad situation, and the atmosphere of hostility towards us in Crossmaglen began to rise even further. Regardless of what was going on with the hunger strike, we simply got on with the job of patrolling the village and the countryside around it, out to about five or six miles in all directions. Rural patrols, or 'cuds' patrols as we called them, were concentrated on the area around the border. Of the five roads leading out of the 'Cross,' three went directly over the border within a matter of about a one or two minute drive from the centre of Crossmaglen.

Even though Crossmaglen had recent 'history' as a dangerous place to patrol, it did not mean we were completely powerless to influence the situation, and would simply walk around till we were shot at. The Company Commander, Major 'B', and his Operations Officer Major 'S', put in place a policy and strategy of patrolling that would try and take the initiative away from the PIRA gunmen and bombers that would do us harm. In short, we would try to stop PIRA freely coming into the centre of the village, where they seemed to have had most of their major success in the past, both with the gun and bomb. To do this, we had to maintain a high intensity of patrolling on the ground, 24 hours a day, and be unpredictable in that patrolling, particularly in the village.

Within the confines of the village boundary, we constantly had three patrols walking around in different areas of what was essentially, a very small village, with the Saracen acting as a protective mobile bunker and transport. It would drive at walking pace within a few metres of the patrol, alternating from being behind or in front of it, and covering the patrol with the Browning as they crossed open spaces or street junctions. At random times during the four-hour patrol, all 12 soldiers would jump into their Saracens and drive to a different part of the village, before de-bussing and carrying on with their foot patrol.

In addition to the total of 18 men of these patrols, we would flood the village at various times during the day with every available man in the company not patrolling or sleeping. It was not unusual to have as many as 40 or 50-plus men on the ground in the village at various times of the day, with perhaps five or six Saracens whizzing around. The idea was to put the village in lockdown for an hour and check the IDs of as many people as possible. All of this village patrolling was done to try and keep gunmen and bombers on the back foot as to exactly where a patrol might pop up next, and show them that coming into the centre of the village was a much more risky business than it perhaps used to be.

We also had a 12-man 'satellite patrol' out 24 hours a day. This patrol moved together, in three groups of four, and they prowled around the fields and gardens on the outskirts of the village. They were in contact and support of the patrols inside it. Each four-man group carried either a GPMG machine gun, or the ever popular Bren gun, along with the M79 grenade launcher. At times they would use stealth and concealment and perhaps 'lie-up' and observe; and at others, they would be highly visible, like when crossing a road into the village where they might set up a vehicle check point for a few minutes. Again their route was random and they had the task of trying to cut of the nearest road to them in the event of an incident and to deter the opposition from venturing into the village.

A further group of twelve men, armed and equipped exactly as the satellite patrol, would be involved in Rural Patrols. These patrols were independent of the town and satellite patrols and ventured out much further from the village, sometimes dropped off or picked up by helicopter, and normally with a specific task to carry out, usually involving the border area. These patrols were carried out either day or night and would normally last a minimum of eight hours.

We also had a stand-by section of twelve men held at a moment's notice to move in support of any of the patrols out on the ground, should an emergency arise. They were held back in Crossmaglen Police Station, where we all lived. This section would take part in the 'flooding' of the village I have described. And lastly, we had about 25 men involved in guarding our base. The drain on manpower was extremely high and the men were worked hard. For almost all soldiers in The Cross, life was a never-ending round of non-stop patrolling and guarding, throwing food down your throat when you could, and trying to catch up on lost sleep.

On the 23rd, Marcella Sands, the sister of the hunger-striking MP, made an application to the European Commission on Human Rights claiming that the British Government had broken three articles of the European Convention on Human Rights in their treatment of Republican prisoners. Two Commissioners tried to visit him in the Maze on the 25th, but were unable to gain access because he demanded the presence of representatives of Sinn Féin. Early the next month, the European Commission on Human Rights announced that it had no power to proceed with the Sands' case. He was now on the 54th day of his hunger strike.

The following day, another former UDR soldier was murdered by the Provisionals simply because he was 'tainted' by his former association. As a terror group, they had shown their 'humane' face with their pathetic bleatings about the men in the Maze who were on hunger strike and their desperate efforts to get the rest of the world on their side. Their arch-apologist in the USA, Edward Kennedy, was spreading the word about the plight of the 'political prisoners' in Northern Ireland refusing food for their cause and yet, there is no record of him expressing his emotions to the loved ones of John Robinson (36) who was cold-bloodedly shot down by his Republican 'heroes'. This may be somewhat rhetorical, but while Kennedy, Carey, Moynihan and O'Neill were busy trying to pressurise Thatcher over the hunger strike, their silence over the murders of Mrs Mathers and the aforementioned John Robinson was of the thunderous kind.

Mr Robinson drove his company's minibus which transported workers to and from their building sites. At around 1700 hours on the evening of the 23rd, as he drove towards the Nationalist Mullacreevie Estate near Armagh City, gunmen in a stolen car pulled up alongside him. Without warning, five shots were fired into the driver's window and he was hit in the head and chest; he died almost immediately. Mr Robinson had left the UDR in 1973 but this was sufficient 'grounds' for the Provisionals who, instead of keeping their heads down and milking the outpourings of sympathy for the Maze hunger strikers, continued to murder indiscriminately and without justification. Sadly, the only people unable to see through them were, naturally, the Irish-Americans and, judging by the sight of the Irish Martyrs Memorial at Waverley in Sydney, NSW, the Irish-Australians also. Harold McCusker of the UUP said angrily: "I am sick to my stomach of hearing this unrelenting, nauseous hypocrisy about this IRA man Sands, about him only having a couple of days to live, about the efforts to save him. John Robinson hasn't a few days to live and no one tried to save him."

On that same day, another soldier's life was claimed by the scourge of the UDR, an RTA. This author has previously explained the phenomena that cut a swathe through so many young UDR lives and the one which killed Lieutenant David Trevor Patterson (33) in Co Tyrone was no different. He is buried in St Johns Parish Church Cemetery at Moy, near Dungannon. On the 27th, another policeman was killed, this time in the Andersonstown area of West Belfast. The RUC had been called out to inspect a stolen lorry which had been taken from in the Lenadoon and then abandoned in Shaw's Road. Several officers had inspected the cab and the rear of the lorry and had looked underneath but found nothing. Gary Martin (28), father of two, then volunteered to drive the vehicle away from the residential area so as to not risk innocent lives. However, unknown to himself or his colleague, the driver's seat had been booby-trapped by the INLA and a mercury tilt device attached to explosives placed under the seat. As he placed his hand on the seat, in order to pull himself inside the cab, the device detonated and he was blown to pieces, dying instantly. Two of his colleagues were very seriously injured in the blast. Constable Martin left two toddler children and a young widow.

On the 28th, a former soldier from the 'Skins' (Inniskilling Dragoon Guards) who had joined the UDR was killed in an ambush by the IRA near Castlewellan, Co Down. Three UDR soldiers were travelling towards Castlewellan when gunmen opened fire with automatic weapons from a position in the hills at Burren Bridge. The driver was hit twice, but Lance Corporal Richard William James McKee (27) was hit in the head and killed instantly. The driver struggled to keep control and in the end managed to crash the vehicle into a ditch to obtain cover. The gunmen ran away before reinforcements could arrive, no doubt to congratulate themselves in some pub over the Irish border on a job well done. The UDR man had celebrated his 27th birthday on the 13th day of Bobby Sands' hunger strike. The inquest into the murder was not held for over a year, but in Court, the soldier who survived described the scene as the military vehicle drove along the Rathfriland-Castlewellan Road. He said that his comrade ducked down and yelled: "They're shooting at us!" The survivor, who was driving, tried to accelerate. He told the Court:

> The shots were still coming and I felt myself hit on the right hand, and then I was hit in the stomach. I started to lose control and decided to ditch the van. I drove towards the right-hand ditch to find cover and hit a large boulder which threw the van over onto its side. Lance Corporal McKee fell into the back of the van. I managed to get out of the back with my other colleague – a Sergeant. The sergeant

stopped a Cortina and asked the driver to go for help. I then stopped a cattle lorry and the driver took me to a police station.[7]

That same day, Pope John Paul II's private secretary paid a visit to Bobby Sands in the Maze Prison but was unable to persuade him to end his hunger strike. Humphrey Atkins, Secretary of State for Northern Ireland, stated that: "If Mr Sands persisted in his wish to commit suicide that was his choice. The government would not force medical treatment upon him." He then had a meeting with Mr Atkins, before paying a further visit to Bobby Sands in the Maze Prison. US President Ronald Reagan, said that America would not intervene in the situation in Northern Ireland, but he was 'deeply concerned' at events there. Those 'events' were about to take a significant turn for the worse.

April was over, and the last two weeks had seen nine deaths. May was to be far bloodier and would be the worst month for almost two years. In all, 11 died during April. Five were soldiers or former soldiers, and two policemen were dead. Four civilians were killed – three Catholics and one Protestant. Republican paramilitaries were responsible for over half of the deaths.

---

7   The Sergeant also gave evidence to the Court, describing the gunfire as heavy and had lasted for at least two minutes.

17

May

Without intending to sound over melodramatic, May was a month in which the Province went insane, with 27 deaths or almost as many as had been killed in the previous five months. It was also the month in which four of the Republican hunger strikers died. Repercussions from the IRA came almost as fast as nauseatingly pious comments from the Americans or statements of pure ignorance from other countries in the world.

CROSSMAGLEN: FRIDAY 4 MAY
Martin Wells, Royal Green Jackets

By now the condition of Bobby Sands had reached a critical point and he was expected to die at any moment. In the two or three days leading up to that Friday, feelings among the local population were running very high in the Cross, particularly from the younger element of 14 and 15-year-olds who clearly saw the opportunity, or were orchestrated, to indulge in the abuse and occasional stoning of village patrols.

This was a very unusual phenomenon for Crossmaglen, and made for a dangerous situation for the young kids involved in throwing stones. Quite simply, we were not equipped to deal with 'riotous' situations that were more common-place in Belfast or Londonderry. We had no riot shields, helmets, baton guns or other types of riot equipment. Crossmaglen was, and always had been, a place where we operated more or less as we would in a war zone. Unlike in Belfast, we carried machine guns and grenade launchers and moved around the country-side using conventional Infantry tactics. There were no riots in Crossmaglen, so we had no need of that type of equipment. To come up against that type of situation now, was not only a surprise and maybe a minor danger to us, it spelt great danger for the yobs doing it. Because we simply had no other means to defend ourselves other than lethal force. And just one day before, on the Thursday, that danger manifested itself when a Saracen Vehicle Commander had to fire a burst of his Browning machine gun over the heads of a large group of kids who were stoning a four-man village patrol. Luckily he exercised a large degree of control and the kids eventually backed off and nobody was injured. But it could have been a very different outcome. On the plus side, we experienced no further stoning in The Cross for the rest of our tour!

During the course of that Friday evening, the Corporal Commander of one of our village patrols, Corporal 'H' noticed the arrangement of curtains in the windows of the St Patrick's Primary School, in the Ardross Estate, as he passed.

There was no particular reason to pay any attention to the curtains or even remember the way they were arranged. It was the smallest of details in what was a quite long and difficult patrol, and for most people, it might not have been something to register or remember. But he did. And it was to play a significant part in what was to follow almost 48 hours later.

On 5 May, at 0117 hours, after 66 days on hunger strike Bobby Sands (26), convicted PIRA terrorist and newly elected MP, died in the Maze Prison. The Northern Ireland Officer (NIO) announced: *"He took his own life by refusing food and medical intervention for 66 days."* Much greater detail can be found in David Beresford's excellent – if somewhat coloured – account of the hunger strike, *Ten Men Dead*.[1] The announcement of Sands' death sparked riots in many areas of Northern Ireland but also in the Republic of Ireland. The IRA announced that it was stepping up its attacks on members of the security services. Following the death of Sands, the British Government faced extensive international condemnation for the way in which it had handled the hunger strike. The relationship between the British and Irish Governments continued to be most strained. The day after, a 'spearhead battalion' of 600 troops was deployed to Northern Ireland to help cope with the increasing tension in the wake of Sands' death. He had this to say of the Maze: "H-Block is the rock That British monsters shall perish upon. For we in H-Block stand upon the unconquerable rock of the Irish Socialist Republic."

Reaction around the world was swift and in most cases, entirely predictable. In France, ignorant and uninformed French students protested in the streets under banners proclaiming: "The IRA will conquer." In Italy, 5,000 students – blessed with the same ignorance as their French counterparts – burned several Union flags. In Norway, demonstrators threw a tomato at the Queen who was on a State visit, but missed. Incredibly, in the Portuguese parliament, the opposition benches rose for a minute's silence for the dead terrorist. In the USSR, the State newspaper, *'Pravda'* described it as: "another tragic page in the grim chronicle of [British] oppression, discrimination, terror, and violence in Ireland." In New York, the International Longshoremen's Association announced a 24-hour boycott of British ships. Over 1,000 people gathered in New York's St Patrick's Cathedral to hear Cardinal Terence Cooke offer a mass of reconciliation for Northern Ireland. Irish bars in the city were closed for two hours in mourning, and in Hartford, Connecticut, a memorial was dedicated to Bobby Sands and the other hunger strikers in 1997, the only one of its kind in the United States and set up by NORAID and local Irish-Americans. In New Jersey the General Assembly, the lower house of the New Jersey Legislature, voted 34–29 for a resolution honouring Sands' "courage and commitment."

A year later, as 100,000 Irish-Americans and their equally gullible supporters gathered for the 220th St Paddy's Day celebrations, the mood was decidedly anti-British. The St Patrick's Day committee in New York City named the dead PIRA terrorist as 'Honorary Marshal' and dedicated its theme as 'England get out of Ireland.' No doubt, Irish-Americans from several generations back, tanked up on green-dyed Guinness, the pulses on their sloping foreheads throbbing with a mixture of pride, hatred and a little too much cheap Irish beer, would have roared their approval at each anti-British speech

---

1 Beresford, David, *Ten Men Dead* (London: Harper Collins, 1994).

or placard. The Unionist MP, Harold McCusker, later told politicians in the US Congress that he appreciated that some members not only deprecated the efforts of NORAID to prolong the terror on the other side of the Atlantic but that he appreciated those in the US Legislature who condemned the organisation. He told them that in his constituency alone, the IRA had murdered over 20 Roman Catholics, some of them young boys. "Some Americans might think that they are helping to alleviate distress in Catholic areas. The reality is that American Dollars sustain and fortify the IRA murder machine."

Refreshingly, and most surprisingly, *The San Francisco Chronicle* argued that political belief should not exempt activists from criminal law: "Terrorism goes far beyond the expression of political belief. And dealing with it does not allow for compromise as many countries of Western Europe and United States have learned. The bombing of bars, hotels, restaurants, robbing of banks, abductions, and killings of prominent figures are all criminal acts and must be dealt with by criminal law."[2] The New York Times, more mindful of its large Irish-American leadership than its West Coast counterpart wrote: "Britain's prime minister Thatcher is right in refusing to yield political status to Bobby Sands, the Irish Republican Army hunger striker, (but that) in appearing unfeeling and unresponsive, the British Government was giving Sands the crown of martyrdom."[3]

The Irish-American 'gang of four' – Kennedy, Moynihan, Carey and O'Neill – or the '*Four Horsemen*' as they apparently liked to be known were quick off the mark. These apologists for the Provisional IRA and Brit-haters extraordinaire sent a telegram condemning Thatcher for her intransigence and inflexibility. She was quick to respond, outlining what the British Government had done and the co-operation given to all of the mediating parties. She finished with: "None of these actions has had any effect on the prisoners whose sole purpose is to establish a political justification for their appalling record of murder and violence."

John Lambert, 1 Royal Scots

My first tour was in West Belfast in 1980; my Battalion was then posted to Ballykinlar for two years, between 1981–1983, where we were involved in the aftermath of the hunger strikes and also Ian Paisley's 'third force' stuff.

The night Bobby Sands died I had to be at the Royal Victoria Hospital on the Falls Road as my wife was there after undergoing treatment. The noise outside was terrific! There were riots and gun battles all over the Falls/Springfield/Andersonstown area. Being a squaddie in civvie clothes, I was seriously shitting myself when it was time to go back to camp. The duty battalion – Coldstream Guards if I remember correctly – sent an armoured vehicle to get me and my driver out. We jumped into their Saracen which was promptly surrounded by the rioters. I swear they nearly toppled the bloody thing over. All respect to the RCT driver for getting us out, because looking back now, I think we would have suffered the same fate as those two Royal Signal guys in 1988 who got caught up in the PIRA funeral.

I remember the Warrenpoint tragedy so well, although I wasn't there; I was a young soldier in 1 Royal Scots at the time. About two years after the massacre,

---

2   "The death of Bobby Sands," *The San Francisco Chronicle*, 6 May, 1981.
3   "Britain's gift to Bobby Sands," New York Times, 29 April, 1981.

we were based in Ballykinlar where the Paras had been at the time. One evening I was on guard and a member of 3UDR drove up to the camp and asked who the guys were who were manning a VCP on THAT road. His car had been stopped by guys wearing cam cream; he said there were loads of them 'milling around looking hard' all had British accents! He said what made the hairs on the back of his neck stand up, was that there was an incredible smell of burning oil and hay! The guy was obviously in distress so we sent out a patrol and found nothing. We had no call signs in that area, nor had the UDR and I doubt whether PIRA had set up an IVCP because they wouldn't speak to people with English and Scots accents. We reckoned that they (the Paras) still had work to do and were still doing their duty.

CROSSMAGLEN: SATURDAY 5 MAY
Martin Wells, Royal Green Jackets

During the course of the day, three events of significance happened. The first was the news that Bobby Sands MP, had succeeded in committing suicide by starvation. In my view, he was no great loss to mankind. He was after all, a convicted terrorist. But to Republicans, it served to heighten the tensions between them, and the Army and RUC. The second event was much closer to home and it involved the village foot-patrols. All of them were reporting that they were being heavily 'dicked' by the young teenagers in the village, most of which were probably already involved with Sinn Féin Fianna. There is very little you can do about being 'dicked'. We were told to be 'aware' of what was going on, but walking round a village we jokingly referred to as, the 'shooting gallery', we didn't need to have our awareness raised! The only other thing you gain is to get a good look at the faces of the local would-be terrorists of the future, who are stalking you!

The third event, and perhaps the most crucial, was a late Saturday afternoon patrol by Corporal 'H' who again noted the position of the curtains at St Patrick's school. Only this time, their arrangement had changed significantly. I have no idea if he lingered in front of the school windows to ponder the position of the curtains in relation to the previous evening. He would have been about 30 metres away and plainly visible in a large gap of 15 metres or so between a row of houses with the school behind it. If he did, he could not possibly know that behind the upper school room windows he was looking at were three PIRA gunmen waiting for the opportunity open fire. It is worth noting at this point, that all Army patrols had recently been barred from entering the grounds of both the primary and secondary school grounds in Crossmaglen, and the church grounds and cemetery. At the beginning of our tour we simply went into them whenever we wanted and moved around quite freely. However, the locals, never slow to pick up on any perceived wrong doing by us, had complained very loudly to their MP, HQNI, and just about everyone else, causing a huge row. The upshot was, we were banned from routinely entering them and had been ordered to keep out. No doubt the locals were just waiting to catch us breaking that ban and we had no option but to obey the order.

Having noted a change to the curtains arrangement, 'H' continued on his patrol. On return to Crossmaglen Police Station, sometime around 6 or 7PM, he and his patrol were debriefed by an NCO from the intelligence cell and the subject of the curtains was mentioned verbally. 'H' had also made mention of the curtains in his written patrol report and that he was suspicious about them. It was after that debrief that I was made aware of the concerns. I read the report through and my initial reaction was that it was a little on the flimsy side. I thought that it would not be unreasonable for a caretaker or some cleaners to be in the classroom over the Saturday daytime, carrying out work, and had maybe moved the curtains to a different position. Despite my reservations, I took the report into the operations room where the operations officer Major 'S' was, and showed it to him. I informed him of the concerns but, like me, he took the view that it was a little on the light side to warrant action, other than to note it and bring it to the attention of outgoing patrols. 'H' had currently been in and out patrolling for three days almost non-stop. He had just come back in and no doubt was looking forward to a hot meal and some sleep before his next patrol, which was scheduled for about 3AM Sunday morning, less than seven hours away.

On speaking to him, I discovered he remained convinced that all was not right down at the school. Even when I raised the subject of cleaners or a caretaker moving them, he accepted it was a possibility, but remained convinced 'something was not right'. I offered to come out with him to view the spot.   I reckoned that if he was exaggerating the case a bit, he would decline to back up his suspicions with lost sleep time. He in fact leapt at the chance to show me for myself. I was a little surprised but left him, after arranging to meet him at the camp gate at 0100 hours, convinced in my own mind that he was not exaggerating and genuinely thought he was onto something. I discussed this again with Major 'S' but he warned me: "under no circumstances, Colour, are you to enter the school grounds." In effect, he was giving me a direct order.

At 0100 hours, with two other guys from my intelligence section, the four of us duly crept out of camp and after a short five-minute walk, arrived at the point from where we could get a good look at the school windows. We stood in full view, in front of the first floor classroom concerned, and pretended to be referring to our map. After two or three minutes and with no other obvious signs to alert us to a major problem, we left to return to camp. The trick now was to convince the Major that we should perhaps be doing something about it. And I knew that would not be easy. However, he was adamant that the 'evidence' was too flimsy and asked me if I really thought that the PIRA would mount an attack on us from a primary school and piss off the locals? I understood all that, and tried to put the case that in the light of no hard intelligence or proof, we had nothing better to do than act on hunches, and it would be better than taking no action at all. But it was clear no action would be taken and that was the end of the conversation.

It did cross my mind to ignore my orders, but what I could not possibly know, was that by tea time that very day, it would all come back to bite me on the arse, big time! And worse, two guys would nearly lose their lives.

On the day after Sands' death, with sectarian tensions mounting, the RUC were called to control rioting and clashes between Catholic and Protestant youths in the interface of the New Lodge and Tiger's Bay in North Belfast. RUC officers were manning the 'peace line' at Duncairn Gardens. An IRA sniper had set up a firing point in a house at Edlingham Street and when Constable Philip Ellis (33) came into his sights, despite the proximity of a young child, he fired several times and the policeman was hit in the head and died almost immediately; a female colleague and a nine-year-old boy were both wounded. Constable Ellis left a pregnant widow. A church spokesman described the PIRA sniper team as "the tools of Satan." The spokesman – the Reverend Henry Heatley – told *The Belfast Telegraph*: "No cause can justify their evil deeds. I wish to condemn the murder. It happened just about 10 yards from my church and this is an atrocious happening. I also condemn all those church leaders and political leaders who are giving support to the IRA thugs."

CROSSMAGLEN: SUNDAY 6 MAY
Martin Wells, Royal Green Jackets

After a few hours' sleep, I received news that patrols around the village were still reporting being 'dicked' even at this early hour. Again, no great change and of course the full effect of Sands' death the previous day was starting to sink in. We all fully expected that even moderate Republicans might want to show some form of anger, let alone the hot-headed young teenagers. Or, it could point to something much worse about to happen. As the morning wore on reports of 'dicking' increased and some patrols were saying up to a dozen youths were following them around. I made the decision that I needed to see what was going on myself and sought out Serjeant Bob 'M'. He was due to go out into the village about 1300 hours and I asked if he would drop off one of his four-man team and let me come out with him. He was happy to do that and after lunch I met up with his patrol at our main gate. Usually when I went out, I carried my own small Pye radio to enable me to speak directly with the intelligence cell. I could also switch to the company ops room frequency and monitor all the patrols out on the ground. But on this occasion, due to the large amount of company radios being broken or unusable, I did not have it on me. It was a bit inconvenient and meant I could not listen in to what the rest of the village patrols were reporting, but it wasn't anything vital. So I thought! In the event, it almost turned out to be critical, and I think that if I had been carrying it, I might well have been able to direct our accompanying Saracen support a little better.

The second thing that was different about my personal equipment that day, was the magazine I had on my rifle. When going out of camp, I normally always put a magazine on my rifle that contained twenty armour-piercing rounds. In the village, or out on a rural patrol, I always put that magazine on. There had been a number of occasions when the PIRA had parked a van on the side of a road leading out of Crossmaglen and used it as a mobile firing point. That van would have armoured plates welded to the inside of the back doors, with one or two small firing slits cut out, giving anyone inside a large degree of protection from our normal type of ammunition, when returning fire. But on this particular occasion for a reason unknown to me, I did not put that magazine on my rifle. I certainly could have done with it!

Almost as soon as we stepped outside of our base we 'picked up' half a dozen kids who followed us for a few minutes. As we moved from one area of the village to another, we picked up yet more kids. The whole thing was almost carried out in complete silence and the atmosphere was tense to say the least. We knew and could feel that and as I walked level with Serjeant 'M', each other on opposite sides of the small roads, we constantly chatted and pointed out areas to watch. Even though we both thought this had all the makings of a bad situation, and however apprehensive or frightened we were, we had no choice but to carry on doing what we were tasked with. There would be no hiding; no saying, "Fuck this! I'm going back in!" We just had to get on with it for the next four hours and deal with whatever might happen. During the course of the first three-and-a-half hours we walked around the village, we slipped into the usual pattern of walking, riding to another area, walking, riding etc. At times we would pass the other two four-man patrols and at others, our Saracens would pass in the huge village square. During this period of time we entered the Ardross Estate twice from the Carron Road end without any sign of anyone in the school windows with the moved curtains. And there was a very good reason for that. On entering the estate on both occasions, our Saracen Commander had positioned his vehicle exactly in the gap facing those windows, where I had stood just over 12 hours ago. And his Browning machine gun was pointing up at the windows.

As we drew close to the end of our patrol time we found ourselves at the southern end of the village. We decided we had time for one more complete circuit of the whole village before going in. We walked into the large village square and headed for the Rathview Estate opposite our base, all the time being 'dicked' by kids. A few minutes later, we came out of the Rathview and went down and crossed over, the Blaney Road, with the intention of going into the back garden of a house situated at the top end of the Ardross Estate. We were going to make entry into that estate via someone's back and front gardens, instead of using the road. As Serjeant 'M' climbed over the low garden wall, a woman came out of the back door of the house and started to shout and scream obscenities at us for using her garden. She was extremely angry and was on the verge of attacking him. Ordinarily we would not have expected anyone to be like this. While they may not have liked it, we entered back and front gardens whenever we wanted and nobody ever really objected because it was pointless. It would have made no difference. But feelings were running high about Sands dying and things were not as they normally were. He rightly decided it was more bother to get involved with her, just as we are going in, than to walk round the road way. Without saying a word to the woman, he climbed back over the wall and nodded his head in direction of the road.

We entered the Ardross estate from Blaney Road and started walking down the double dog leg road that forms the estate, towards the primary school. After the second dog leg in the road, there is a very slight half bend at the bottom of the road facing the school. Walking quite slowly we negotiated the slight bend, with Serjeant 'M' and Rifleman 'C' walking on the right of the road, and me and another rifleman on the left. At this point we were about 100 metres from the school, with our Saracen further back up the road covering behind us, but out of sight of the school. All of the kids 'dicking' us were around the Saracen. It was the moment that the three PIRA gunmen in the school had been waiting for. In the space of just a couple of seconds, 30 or 40 shots were fired at Serjeant 'M' and Rifleman 'C' from the Primary School first floor classroom. Both of them were struck on the ceramic and titanium plate in their flak jacket, which was worn under their combat jacket, by a first and obviously well aimed bullet. This plate was contained in a pouch on the front and back of Flak Jackets and covered the heart and lung area of the body.

The impact of the bullet on the ceramic plate knocked both men down and they were struck by second bullet as they fell, this time in an unprotected part of the body. Serjeant 'M' was hit in the back of his upper thigh and Rifleman 'C' was shot through the front of his upper shoulder, with the bullet exiting out of his shoulder blade.

My initial reaction was to drop down on one knee to try and present a smaller target should I also come under fire. But from where I was, the gunmen would have been unable to see me. I jumped up and ran across the road to where Serjeant 'M' was lying and stood over him, firing back at the school. As I stood there firing about a dozen rounds or so, I was aware of two things: he was talking and a woman came out of the front door of the house on the left side of the gap through to the school. He was saying 'I saw them Sandy! I saw them!' And the woman was shouting at me hysterically, as I was firing! It was almost surreal. I have no idea what she shouted and she quickly went back inside. Life had turned real shitty, real quick, and a whole lot of things needed to happen all at once. I had my work cut out. As the Serjeant started to send a contact report from where he was lying, I tried to drag him behind a car. I was very conscious that a further exchange of gunfire might finish us all off, and that I had one man wounded who might be bleeding badly. At this point I was unaware of Rifleman 'C' being wounded, or even where he was!

I looked over to the young rifleman who had been behind me and told him to take up a position and cover the school windows. He had managed to take cover in a gateway as the first shots were fired. At this point the Saracen screamed around the corner at speed and, still trying to move Serjeant 'M', I shouted to the commander above the high pitched engine whine, and waved my arm toward the school, 'Get behind the school!' I wanted him to crash through the locked school gates and get into the playground area, as I reasoned the gunmen would be fleeing out the back. Unfortunately, with his radio earphones on and the noise from the engine, he was unable to hear or understand my instructions properly and went and stopped the Saracen in the gap between the houses, some 30 metres from us, covering the school with his Browning. Conscious that the gunmen might not be finished with us, I examined my wounded comrade who was talking on his radio. At this time he had no idea as to the seriousness of his wound or if he was dying or bleeding to death. Only that he had been shot. A matter of seconds had passed since the shooting started and you have to take your hat off to him for managing to send a contact report and let every other patrol know where we were etc.

As I tried to move him to some sort of protective cover behind a car, he told me he had been hit in the back of his leg. I rolled him over and I could see a bullet hole in his green lightweight trousers and a small bloodstain just below his buttocks. I put my finger into the hole in his trousers and ripped them wide open. The wound seemed like a bullet had caught him a glancing type of hit and reminded me of the type of gouging wound a chisel might make. The good news was it did not appear to be life-threatening and there was very little bleeding. I gave him the good news he wasn't dying and told him his bollocks appeared to be OK as well! I then shouted and asked if anyone else had been hit and it was then I became aware of Rifleman 'C' as I heard a very faint voice a few yards away say, 'I have'. He had managed to crawl down a short garden path into the doorway of a house, and was sitting in an upright position, holding his shoulder. Picking up my rifle and leaving Serjeant 'M' behind the car, I went over to him. It was very clear to me he was going into shock. He was pale and appeared to be in a great deal of pain.

I quickly took off his combat jacket and then his flak jacket and shirt, as gently as I could. There was a neat hole in the front of his shoulder in the area just below his collar bone, with a small amount of blood round it. When I looked at his back, I could see a larger exit wound where the bullet appeared to have come out of his shoulder blade. Again, I was surprised at how little blood there was coming from both wounds and grateful that I was not dealing with someone in danger of bleeding to death. I took his First field dressing from his flak jacket and I placed it gently over the entry wound and secured it. All the time I was helping him I was talking to him and telling him what I was doing and that his wound did not look too serious, and we would all be OK etc. But he never said another word and I was fearful that the shock he was going into might yet prove fatal.

By now three or four minutes had passed and as I was in the process of trying to apply my field dressing to the rifleman's exit wound, the cavalry started to arrive. First the Saracens with the rest of the village patrol and then all the Company HQ elements along with every available man in camp, including our resident medic, Serjeant 'S', who then took over the treatment of our two wounded men. As the large follow-up operation started to swing into action, I did very little else except to explain what happened.

As part of the follow-up, entry was made into the school and it was found that the three gunmen had indeed been in there since the early hours of Saturday morning and had moved the curtains to conceal themselves as they peered out of the windows, which Corporal 'H' had correctly spotted that during the Saturday daytime. The gunmen had broken a small window in the downstairs cloakroom to the rear of the school in order to make entry, and had kicked in the door of the upstairs classroom. They had even sat playing chess at one of the desks as they waited for the right moment! Three separate firing points were identified, along with three different types of weapons, A Garrand, an M1 Carbine and an FN rifle. A large amount of empty cases were recovered.

Sniffer dogs brought in tracked the gunmen's getaway route across the fields to the farm of a known PIRA member on the Blaney Road, just on the outskirts of Crossmaglen, and no doubt, a waiting car to drive them across the border into Southern Ireland. It almost goes without saying that they made good their escape and nobody was arrested in connection with this shooting.

The contributor of these excellent pieces on a three-day period in Crossmaglen – Martin 'Sandy' Wells – wrote to me and revealed the outcome of the two injuries; Serjeant 'M' returned to the Battalion in the fullness of time; none the worse for his wound. He went on to complete and finished his career as a Warrant Officer. He received a Mention in Dispatches (MID) award for his actions that day. Sadly, however, Rifleman 'C' needed treatment to his wound for several months and eventually returned to duty at the Regimental Depot in Winchester. He never fully recovered and left the Army two years later. Martin received a GOC's commendation for his part in the actions of that near fatal day.

On 7 May the funeral of Bobby Sands was held, with over 100,000 people lining the route from his home to St Luke's Church and then on to the Republican plot at Milltown Cemetery at the top of the Falls Road close to Andersonstown RUC Station which is now no longer there.

The same day, as the Sands' funeral circus was taking place and close to the killing of the policeman in Duncairn Gardens, rioters caused the deaths of two innocent Protestants. It was the May Day holiday and the teenagers of the New Lodge were out in force stoning and petrol-bombing. Most of the thugs hadn't enough brain cells between them to realise what they were rioting about and were just swept along by the usual ringleaders. Many of these riots were spontaneous and possibly even genuine but others were initiated and orchestrated by local IRA commanders or even the leading lights of *an Fianna* Éireann, the IRA's youth wing. Eric Guiney (45), father of four, was a milkman who delivered on both sides of the sectarian divide. He was delivering milk along the New Lodge Road, along with his son Desmond (14) when his vehicle came under heavy attack with dozens of missiles thrown by rioters. Dozens smashed through the front of the vehicle and Desmond was hit in the head and mortally wounded; the milk van went out of control and smashed into a lamp post, fatally injuring Mr Guiney, who died six days later having been in a coma since the attack. The Republican thugs continued to hurl rocks and other objects even as the dreadfully injured pair were placed into the ambulance. Father and son were later buried in the same grave. They were laid to rest in Carnmoney Cemetery in North Belfast; it seems such a travesty that fallen UDR soldiers such as Alex Gore and slain innocents such as the Guineys should share a cemetery with monsters such as Lenny Murphy. The anger over the death of Bobby Sands was to take even more people into the grave. Young Desmond had celebrated his 14th birthday a scant few days earlier. He was dangerously ill in hospital and fighting for his life when his Uncle – David Guiney – issued this statement: "I feel nothing only bitterness and anger – a milkman and his son going to do his job – trying to help people who have now tried to endanger his life." *The Belfast Telegraph* also quoted his embittered comments about the death of the hunger striker, Bobby Sands: "What happened to my brother and nephew – that's more important than Sands is. Sands has created the likes of this." Shortly after the death of her son, and while en-route to visit her desperately ill husband, Mrs Roberta Guiney told *The Belfast Telegraph* when speaking of the thugs who had devastated her family: "Their mothers should not have let them out on the streets. I would never have let any child of mine out on the streets doing something like that – the kids are being used by the perpetrators of violence." The boy's funeral was attended by almost one thousand people; family members, school friends and well-wishers. Janet Devlin, a Belfast journalist wrote: "Two children on horseback led the funeral cortege of the 14-year-old boy who was told he would not grow up much so he may as well become a jockey. And dozens of wreaths covered the lawn of the Rathcoole home of Desmond Guiney."

A relative of the family in a clearly aimed attack at Irish-Americans and the gullible naïve Governments of the world who were demonstrating their support for Sands and the other hunger-strikers said:

[They] sympathise without any real understanding of our problems. They are as guilty of his death as surely as if they threw the stones themselves. I hope that the death of an innocent 14-year-old boy will satisfy them. He was given neither a choice nor a chance. He was not allowed to die with dignity, but he will never be forgotten.

That day was not yet over, and before the night closed on an eventful 24 days, an INLA 'own goal' had taken place in the Nationalist Markets area. INLA bomber James Power (21) had planted a bomb designed to kill a passing Army foot patrol, but it had either failed to explode or the soldiers had taken another route. Power had retrieved the bomb and took it to his home with the intention of making it safe, but it exploded and he was removed from the gene pool instantly. It was later alleged that he murdered RUCR officer Alexander Scott in February.[4]

THE DEATH OF BOBBY SANDS
Mark 'C', UDR and Royal Artillery
Some of the most challenging times I faced in NI came during the 1981 Republican hunger strikes. I had transferred into the UDR, full-time, in early April after five years as a Gunner, which included one tour in Belfast in 1979. Less than a month later, Bobby Sands became 'Slimmer of the year' and the country descended in to violent chaos; the worst seen since the early 1970s; talk about a baptism of fire.

For me it all started in the early hours of the 5th May; we were on guard at the BBC TV mast complex above Ligoniel/Glencairn in North Belfast, when word came through the net that Sands had died. Almost immediately the nearby Republican Wolfshill area erupted; from our position in the elevated sangar at the front gate, we could see the burning, hear the noise and hear the gunshots. Several times the Clarabell system in the sangar went off, indicating that shots had been fired at our location. I don't think this was a serious attempt at an attack, more of PIRA loosing of at a convenient target. We did think about shooting back but thought better of it; in hindsight, this was a good idea. The trouble continued all night and the same was getting replicated all over Republican areas of Belfast and the whole of Northern Ireland.

For the next two days or so we were deployed to the Areema Drive sectarian interface in Dunmurry/Twinbrook, to cover the regular battalions dealing with riots there and to protect the Protestant houses which had been coming under attack including gunfire. I have already covered an incident there in detail which is still

4   See Chapter 14.

resounding with me to this day, in the author's second book.[5] I won't dwell on that, other than to say, I witnessed the 100,000 plus crowd in Twinbrook for Sands' funeral and thought to myself, if they turn on us, this will have to end up with live rounds being fired; gladly they didn't.

Other times we were deployed to guard the various bus stations throughout the City as they had been coming under attack from rioters; burning many and hijacking others for barricades. If you were at the Grosvenor Road, close to the Falls or Oxford Street near the markets, you always knew that another hunger striker had died! The sounds of dustbin lid banging and whistles started, calling the rioters back onto the streets before we heard even on the radio net.

On the 7th, Republican rioters attacked a milk float at the top of the New Lodge Road and the Antrim Road close to our base at Girdwood; on board was Eric Guiney and his 14-year-old son Desmond. Desmond died at the scene and Eric never regained consciousness and died six days later.

The irony of all this was that the Guiney's came from the Loyalist Rathcoole Estate in Newtownabbey, once the biggest Housing Estate in Europe in the 1970s and the exact same place that a young Bobby Sands grew up and went to school nearby. Rathcoole had once been mixed but as the Troubles unfolded, Catholics were evicted or burnt out. In other of mixed areas, such as parts of West Belfast like Ballymurphy and Twinbrook the same happened to Protestant families. It was the same for RC families in Estates like Rathcoole or Monkstown in Newtownabbey; basically there was a whole shift of population, with each respective religious group taking over the vacant houses left in the exodus. The Sands family was one of these, moving to Twinbrook. My wife is from Rathcoole and I remember my now late brother-in-law telling me that the Sands lived in the same street and he often played football etc. with Bobby in the 1960s.

The violence continued on and off each time another striker died up to the end of August when the families put pressure on Sinn Féin to call it off. I do believe the strikers were sacrificed by the leadership of Sinn Féin/PIRA (and we all know who they are) to rejuvenate a failing terrorist campaign and it indeed that did happen in my view. So to sum it all up, it was four months of excitement, fear, mayhem but probably the hardest four months of my 12-year Army career.

On the 8th, PIRA prisoner Joe McDonnell joined the hunger strike to take the place of Bobby Sands. He was born in Slate Street, in the Falls Road district of Belfast. He was arrested in *Operation Demetrius* and interned on the prison ship HMS Maidstone along with Gerry Adams and others. He was later moved to HMP Maze for several months. Upon release he joined the PIRA's Belfast Brigade. McDonnell met Bobby Sands in the run-up to an IRA firebomb attack on the Balmoral Furnishing Company. During the ensuing shoot-out between the IRA and soldiers both men, along with Séamas Finucane and Seán Lavery, were arrested. McDonnell and the others were sentenced to 14 years in prison for possession of a firearm.

---

5   Wharton, Ken, *Bullets, Bombs and Cups of Tea* (Solihull: Helion, 2009).

On Saturday 9th, a PIRA bombing team exploded a bomb at an oil terminal in the Shetland Islands. A quarter of a mile away at that time, the Queen was attending a function to mark the official opening of the terminal; it was a timely reminder that they could strike at any time. She was on her way back to Britain after a State visit to Norway. At around the same time, John Hume, then leader of the SDLP, travelled to London to meet Margaret Thatcher, to demand that she conceded to two of the points on which the hunger strike impasse might be ended. He asked Thatcher to concede to the hunger strikers demand for free association and the right to wear civilian clothes. The 'Iron Lady' was not for turning and she refused.

On Tuesday 12 May, a second hunger striker died when, after 59 days without food, Francis Hughes (25), passed away in the Maze hospital wing. He was known to have killed at least one British soldier – Lance Corporal David Jones in March 1978 at Glenshane Pass – and at least two RUC officers. In fact, he reportedly killed at least nine other members of the Security Forces and few British soldiers would have mourned the loss of this man who seemed to excel at killing. In Dublin a group of 2,000 people tried to break into the British Embassy, which had not long been rebuilt – at the Irish Government's expense following the post-Bloody Sunday riots – but hundreds of Gardaí and Irish troops had kept them at bay.

During the evening of Hughes' death, soldiers came under fire in the Divis Street Complex and a burst of five rounds was fired as they were seeking to control rioting in the area. A man was seen with a rifle running away and naturally they returned fire, hitting the man who was observed to fall. By the time that troops reached where he was seen to fall, both he and weapon had been moved and there were bloodstains. Shortly afterwards, the body of INLA gunman Emmanuel 'Matt' McClarnon (21) was found at the nearby RVH; he had died from the wound inflicted on him at Divis Street. Somewhat incredulously, the *An Camchéachta* (Starry Plough) described the scenes at his funeral when "crowds gathered to pay their last respects to an outstanding soldier."

On the same evening, The Royal Regiment of Wales (RRW) was called into the area around Stewartstown Road in order to quell disturbances arising from the death of the latest hunger striker. The RRW deployed in armoured vehicles and petrol bombers were warned to disperse. An NCO fired a baton round at a petrol bomber, but a young Catholic girl was fatally injured when she was struck in the head as she walked along the Stewartstown Road. It is entirely possible that the round ricocheted and hit Julie Livingstone (14) as it is unlikely either that the round was fired at her, or that she was involved in the rioting. It is with extreme regret that this author must report that she died the following night. Even with the passage of time – 22 years at the time of writing – the family will feel no less grief. This author extends his deepest sympathies to the Livingston family. The author also knows the soldier who fired that fateful baton round that night and understands the agonies which have gone through his mind.

FRANCIS HUGHES AND ALL THAT
William Clive Hawkins, Royal Regiment of Wales

A day or two later, we were deployed on a mobile patrol to circulate around Stewartstown and Twinbrook and deal with any disturbances and generally pass information back; again mainly to show a presence and gather intelligence. The reason we were deployed initially was to deal with the disturbances and aid the brigade troops in dealing with issues arising from the hunger strikers, Sands et al. We then received a message via radio that Francis Hughes had died, and that it was known that Thatcher had refused him an eleventh hour agreement.

We were told a large crowd was gathering on Stewartstown Road and our two Saracens were to go in and see what was happening. Almost immediately on turning into Stewartstown Road, we were ambushed by about 2,000 Sands supporters with petrol bombs, house bricks and acid bombs. We came to an immediate stop as they had set fire to cars in the road ahead of us. Straight away we were engulfed in flames, they kept throwing unlit petrol bombs onto the roofs and the petrol was seeping through the hatches and seals. Both commanders in the turrets were splashed by the acid and we had to pull them down several times to put out the flames and dilute the acid.

Both drivers were on fire and we had to deal with them as well. We then heard small arms fire – probably Armalite M16 – hitting the side of our vehicle. I was carrying my SLR and an FRG and was told to monitor the back door to watch out for IRA men planting bombs on the back door or step.

About two minutes later, I noticed what appeared to be two men, step up waist high above the crowd, one on either side of the road and wearing balaclavas. Generally the only ones who dressed like that were PIRA; they knew that if we saw them and recognised them as players, we could photo them or, better, shoot them! At about the same time a little old man with white hair emerged and sat down facing me with his back to a lit traffic bollard in the middle of the road. He was clearly orchestrating what was going on; waving his arms and pointing and shouting. I thought that the other two were going to open fire once they were passed weapons, which was the practice then. The tempo picked up and things started to get worrying; they were trying to get beer kegs under the front of both vehicles as they clearly planned on keeping us there. All of a sudden due to the intensity of the riot and the volume of petrol bombs, I was told Brigade had authorised an upgrade from 25–grain baton rounds to 45 grain, which were much more lethal.

I focussed on the two men in balaclavas and gave them one shot each, without following through which is watching to see the rounds strike, so I don't know whether or not I hit anyone. The crowd surged, so I stepped out of the vehicle with the intention of holding them back as I still had both weapons; almost immediately I realised my stupidity and began to shit myself. I realised that the door was two-inch thick steel, and if I knocked to get back in, with all the noise, they might not hear me. I could get left behind here and torn to pieces. I turned to bang on the door, it was only two metres away, but it may as well have been 200 metres; my legs had gone to jelly; I didn't know if I was going to be able to stand up let alone move.

I made the three strides to the door and banged like hell but was terrified that I wasn't being heard; the hair on the back of my neck was standing up; I was waiting for a house brick, or a bullet. I was even anticipating the breath of some big bastard on my neck as he tried to rip my rifle from my shoulders grip me by the neck and throw me backwards, but none of these things happened. Like a prayer, the door opened; I could have converted to Christianity and shit my trousers out of sheer relief all at the same time, I scrambled in and sat down, the door was locked and I felt like crying my eyes out, I felt so relieved, so safe with my mates.

As I got in, the Sergeant shouted down from the hatch: 'Someone has taken a girl out!' We drove back to camp but I was totally dysfunctional, and when we got there he told me that the RUC had fired so many rounds, that they were claiming the hit. I wasn't really interested; I couldn't really give a shit, I was just grateful that I got back in. Out of the blue an NCO strolled up and said to me: "Thanks very fuckin' much!" I asked him what he was on about and he shouted back: "You killed that girl; now we can look out!" Obviously gossiping had started and an unwanted 'claim to fame' had changed to one of apportioning blame. I walked off and left him standing there, I knew he was married to an Irish Catholic and put it down to looking after his own. Nothing more was said about the incident, and we eventually returned to Aldershot.

Life went on as normal, then one day the Sergeant informed me that I was wanted in the Guardroom. Half way there I was met by two fat guys in suits who produced warrant cards and identified themselves as Northern Ireland Special Branch. They asked me to verify who I was, which I did, they then cautioned me and told me that I was charged with murder of Julie Livingstone, the girl who had been hit by a baton round. They took me inside the Guardroom and showed me a grainy video of a Saracen Armoured Car driving about a hundred yards down a typical Belfast Street. They said: "This is our evidence!" I told them that there was no visible number plate; there is no date signature on the tape, and that there were no rioters in the clip. I said to them: "It could be any vehicle on any tour, anywhere in Belfast." They were unimpressed and said coldly: "You can go now; you will receive a letter informing you of the hearing at Belfast Crown Court and how to get there; you are on bail!"[6]

Early on the 14th, Brendan McLaughlin, PIRA joined the hunger strike to replace Francis Hughes; he was only able to last 13 days and was taken off the strike on the 26th, when he suffered a perforated ulcer and internal bleeding. He was serving 12 years for possession of firearms. Sinn Féin subsequently admitted that it would have achieved little propaganda value from his early death of a stomach ulcer. He suffered a stroke in 1999 and when he was interviewed in the *Sunday Tribune* in 2006, he had still not recovered. Patrick Bolger wrote:

Photographs and Republican paraphernalia wainscot the walls of his council bungalow; photographs of volunteer graves, pictures of famous IRA men, a bodhran made in Portlaoise gaol. But it's a pencil sketch of the 10 men who carried their protest right to the end that draws his eye. 'You see them boys up there?' he says. 'They died for nothing.' He's angry about a lot of things. Gerry Adams and Martin McGuinness ('scum bastards'), the peace process ('a sell-out') and the Brits ('no business being here; never had, never will.') 'They're all getting ready to sit in

---

6   The account of the court case and other incidents will be described later in this book.

Stormont,' he says, 'when there's still a war to fight.' Paralysed down one side, he's no longer capable of prosecuting that war, but it goes on in the theatre of his head.[7]

Two days after Hughes' death, the PIRA blood orgy of revenge commenced and it robbed a family of a dream move to Canada, a pregnant woman of her husband and the soon-to-be-born child of a father and a 16-month-old toddler of a father she would not remember. On the night of the 14th, two RUC Land Rovers were responding to a riot at Kelly's Corner, at the top end of the Ballymurphy Estate and close to their base at New Barnsley police station. A newly acquired RPG-7 (rocket-propelled grenade) fired from the garden of a PIRA sympathiser was launched at the cars. With an effective range of 200 yards and a speed of c. 445' per second, it tore through the rear of one the vehicles and exploded, killing Constable Samuel Vallely (23) instantly. The following contribution is from a soldier who was there at the time.

KELLY'S CORNER: DEATH OF A POLICEMAN
Carl Ball, Royal Welch Fusiliers

There is one incident that I find hard to talk about, but here goes I will try to relive the moment concerned. I remember the day well as it was the evening of the FA cup replay between Man City and Spurs. As we settled down to watch the game, one of our QRF teams was 'crashed out.' We would the next! About 20 minutes later we were, indeed 'crashed out' to Kelly's Corner – a notorious part of the Ballymurphy Estate – as youths were throwing stones at passing vehicles. The spot was about 200 yards away from the camp on the Springfield Road. As we got close, the youths ran away, which we thought was unusual as they usually stood and had a go before we reacted with baton rounds. On seeing them run we carried straight on to New Barnsley Police Station to see what was happening. We were met by a few RUC officers having a kick about; we joined in for about 10–15 minutes when they were sent back to Kelly's Corner as the group of youths had congregated there again!

They then boarded their Hotspur and left, but two or three minutes later there was:

... an almighty noise which sounded like a 'whoosh', and then a loud explosion which turned out to be an RPG-7 being fired at the RUC. We ran to the sangar overlooking the Springfield Road and saw the most horrendous site of the RUC Hotspur coming down the road at speed, severely damaged and several of the RUC officers sprawled in the road. We found out later that the driver was in shock and headed back to the station. We went straight to Kelly's Corner and secured the area but the IRA scum had made good their escape. This episode was placed at the back of my mind and I rarely thought about it. I never knew the name of the RUC officer who died until I read one of the author's books and it gave a brief explanation into the death of the RUC officer; this brought a tear to my eye as it personalised it more.

---

7   'The hunger strikers 25 Years Later.' (*Sunday Tribune,* 30 April, 2006).

I remember this tragic day and always will, still angry that we just missed the killers. To this day I still think about those RUC men doing their duty and often think it could have been us after passing the firing point five minutes earlier. RIP my friend and comrade.

It took the UFF just 48 hours to retaliate and find a suitable Catholic victim. The mood was 'Let's show those Fenian bastards. Let's kill a Taig!' as a murder gang targeted Ardoyne butcher Patrick Martin (38) at his home in Abbeydale Parade, close to the Crumlin Road. Mr Martin was a butcher by profession but also worked part-time at the Star Social Club in the Ardoyne. He had returned home late and went to sleep in his spare room so as not to disturb his wife. Masked gunmen broke into his house and found him asleep in the early hours of the morning. They had taken the precaution of cutting the telephone wires to the house before sneaking inside. Mr Martin was shot four times in the head and died instantly. Apparently Loyalist dickers had seen him amongst the thousands attending the Sands' funeral and had marked him for death. His sleeping family had not heard the shots which killed him, but his daughter had found his body and screamed: "Daddy's lying in a pool of blood!" Another senseless sectarian slaying had occurred, in order to keep up the bloody game of tit for tat.

The Royal Green Jackets (motto: *'Celer et Audax'*, 'swift and bold') had one of the highest casualty rates of any of the regiments which served in Northern Ireland and suffered greatly outside of the Province also. They lost 49 soldiers to all causes – equal with the losses of the Parachute Regiment – and only the UDR and the Royal Artillery suffered more fatalities. On 20 July 1982 seven members of the Regimental band were killed by an IRA bomb planted underneath the bandstand at Regent's Park.[8] On 19 May, they suffered their second worst day of the Troubles on a country road near to Altnaveigh, Co Armagh. Five soldiers, including four Jackets and their RCT driver were driving towards Camlough along Chancellor's Road in a Saracen armoured vehicle, as part of a two-vehicle patrol. A 1,000 lb (455 kgs) landmine, allegedly planted by PIRA bomber Brendan Burns, exploded in a culvert underneath the road hitting the leading Saracen. The blast totally wrecked the vehicle with a massive engine part being blown over 200 yards away. A farmer on a tractor in a nearby field – the Belfast-Dublin A1 now sits to the right, south bound of the scene – heard the explosion and a few seconds later was showered by body parts and tiny pieces of the vehicle and the soldiers' equipment.

All five men in the vehicle were obliterated and died in a millisecond without, mercifully even being aware of what had happened to them. The soldiers were Lance Corporal Grenville Winston (27); Rifleman Andrew Gavin (19); Rifleman Michael Bagshaw (24); Rifleman John King (20) and Driver Paul Bulman (19) from the Royal Corps of Transport. Paul Kendon Bulman was from the North East and his funeral took place at Preston Cemetery in North Shields; John William King had just turned 20; Michael Edward Bagshaw was from Abingdon, Oxon and was buried at Abingdon New Cemetery; Andrew Gavin was a London boy and Grenville Winston was from Bedford and was buried at Fosterhill Road in his hometown.

---

8   See Chapter 31.

Brendan Burns, the IRA man suspected of being behind the Altnaveigh landmine, was killed in 1988 when a bomb he was transporting exploded prematurely. He was also questioned about the bombs at Warrenpoint in August 1979 when 18 soldiers were killed in two explosions close to Warrenpoint.

In 2012, the author visited the spot three miles from Altnaveigh where four members of his regiment were killed alongside their RCT comrade. It was a chilly summer's day and the road is now closed; a heavy metal and padlocked gate prevents vehicular traffic. Together with my four comrades, we walked up a slight incline until we reached the spot where five young lives were snuffed out in a second. All around the land is rural, broken only by a modern and very busy road which speeds traffic to and from Belfast and Dublin; two capital cities on the same island of Ireland. To one side, the verdant green stretches to the beautiful Mourne Mountains and on the other, the gently rolling hills of South Armagh. It is hard to believe that this is what the late Merlyn Rees MP dubbed 'bandit country'. I bowed my head as did we all, and thought about the Jackets and their driver and paid silent homage to their memories. Reality came when we returned to the car and went down on our knees to scan anxiously underneath. These are still frightening days in this part of Northern Ireland.

In his *'Ten Men Dead'* David Beresford quotes from a smuggled letter or 'comm' from the Maze between the hunger strike leader, Brendon 'Bic' McFarlane:

> Have you heard about that cunning little operation in South Armagh. Oh, you wonderful people!! Far from home they perish, yet they do not know the reason why! Tis truly a great shame. They kill and die and never think to question. Such is the penalty for blind folly. God bless. Bik[9]

Just a few hundred yards away from where this mass murder took place, another atrocity involving Republicans had occurred. A little under half a century earlier a bloody event took place just outside of Newry, involving the slaughter of nine people which became deeply embedded on the psyche of local people – the 'Altnaveigh Massacre'. The murders were coordinated by Republican leader Frank Aiken, who went on to become External Affairs and Deputy Prime Minister in the Republic during the 1950s under De Valera. During the early hours of the morning of June 17, 1922, Aiken's men claimed the lives of six Protestants at Altnaveigh and a policeman – the greatest loss of life in South Armagh on a single day until the Kingsmill massacre of January 1976 when the IRA shot 10 dead Protestant Workmen from Bessbrook. The carnage began with the ambush of a 14-strong B-Special patrol mounted from McGuill's public house at Drumintee, later site of the Three Steps Inn pub from which Grenadier Guards officer Captain Robert Nairac was abducted and later murdered in May 1977.[10] The Altnaveigh killings all took place after 2.30 AM and lasted about an hour. Republicans are quick to bleat about the taking of life by the Crown Forces, but they have never been particularly open about their own bloody ways.

As sand-filled coffins were being prepared for the five soldiers, local government elections were held in Northern Ireland against the backdrop of the continuing hunger

---

9   Beresford, *Ten Men Dead,* p.216.
10   See Wharton, *Wasted Years,* Vol 1.

strike. In the increased tension in the region, 'moderate' parties all suffered a decline in support. The DUP achieved 26.6 per cent of the vote compared to the 26.5 per cent recorded by the UUP, and the SDLP obtained 17.5 per cent of the first preference votes compared to 20.6 per cent in 1977. Sinn Féin, however, rode the massive public empathy and increased its vote Province-wide. PIRA 'thinkers' such as Danny Morrison would soon be advocating the 'Armalite and ballot box' strategy as the Republicans began to rebuild themselves as an electoral party.

While the families of those lost in the Altnaveigh tragedy faced up to their loss, two more of the hunger strikers died within hours of each other. PIRA gunman Raymond McCreesh (24) who had been charged with conspiracy to murder soldiers and INLA member Patsy O'Hara (24) were on their 61st day of refusing to take food. They had started on the same day – 22 March – and were the third and fourth of the hunger strikers to die. Catholic Primate of Ireland, Tomás Ó Fiaich criticised the British Government's attitude to the hunger strike. Dillon writes that following the fourth death, the essentially Catholic dimension of the Provisionals meant that: "the cult of the martyr was present in a real and almost virulent form".[11]

On the 22nd, two more Catholic civilians died after being hit by baton rounds fired by soldiers; the third to die in this bloody month of May. Carol Anne Kelly (12), a Catholic girl, was shot on the 19th and died three days after being hit by a plastic bullet by the British Army as she walked along Cherry Park in the Twinbrook area of Belfast. She had been sent to the shops to buy milk and was able to purchase the last pint available. As she walked home, she was hit by a stray round and fatally injured. This author regrets the loss of this little girl and extends his deepest and genuine sympathy to her family. My words are no less genuine than those I send to the family of Julie Livingstone. In the early hours of that fateful day, following intense rioting in the Bogside area of Londonderry, Henry Duffy (44), father of seven children, was mortally injured after being hit in the head by another baton round. The Royal Anglians were attempting to control the rioting and three of their men had been seriously injured by a blast bomb containing nails. Baton rounds had been fired at the rioting mob and Mr Duffy who was not involved but had been caught up was then injured. He died several hours later in the Altnagelvin Hospital.

The day after the regrettable deaths from baton rounds, PIRA man Kieran Doherty became the sixth Republican to join the hunger strike. He joined *na Fianna* Éireann in 1971 and was interned in February 1973. In August 1976, he was on a bombing mission when the RUC, suspicious of the number men in the car in which he was travelling, gave chase. During the chase Doherty managed to temporarily escape and hijacked a car but was then recaptured by an RUC patrol. He was tried, convicted and sentenced to 18 years for possession of firearms and explosives. He was also involved in the incident at an RUCR officer's home when PIRA man Sean McDermott was shot dead 5 April, 1976[12]. The following day, INLA gunman Kevin Lynch also stopped taking food and became hunger striker number seven. He was from Dungiven in Co Londonderry. After joining IRSP/INLA, he was arrested in 1977 and sentenced to ten years for stealing shotguns,

---

11   Dillon, *God and the Gun,* p.91.
12   See Wharton, *Wasted Years,* Vol 1.

taking part in punishment shootings and conspiring to take arms from the security forces. He was sent to the Maze Prison in December of the same year.

On the day after the INLA man 'threw his hat into the ring', there was another vehicular death when Joseph Lynch (no relation) was killed by an RUC Land Rover in North Belfast. During heavy rioting and violent disturbances in the Nationalist Bone district, Joseph Lynch (33) was fatally injured in the incident, at the junction of Oldpark Road and Gracehill Street. Nationalist eyewitnesses claimed that the police mounted the kerb and deliberately drove at the man who was apparently drunk. The RUC driver gave a different version of events and stated that the man had run into the road and he swerved to miss him but that he then placed himself into the path of the Land Rover and a collision was unavoidable. Later that day and not far away in the Shankill Road district, the RUC carried out a raid on the headquarters of the UDA in and discovered a number of illegal weapons. At this time the UDA, although a Loyalist paramilitary group, was still a legal organisation and was not 'proscribed' until 10 August 1992.

On the 25th, an IRA ambush in Co Londonderry left a part-time soldier in the UDR dead. A two-vehicle patrol from 5UDR was driving along Gulladuff Road close to Bellaghy, when two gunmen stepped out from behind a hedge and opened fire from the rear with automatic weapons. Private Thomas Alan Ritchie (28) from the Magherafelt area was hit several times in his back and died before he could receive medical help. He had been a full-time soldier but had changed his role to part-time in order that he could help his widowed mother on the family farm.

On the 28th, a PIRA ASU which included Charles 'Pop' Maguire (21) and George McBrearty (23), father of three and two other 'Volunteers' were on a 'scout' along Lone Moor Road in the city's Brandywell area. They noticed a car in the area which aroused their curiosity and began trailing it; they suspected – correctly as it transpired – that it may contain an undercover British soldier. They followed the car to the bottom of Southway on the Creggan Estate. They forced the car to stop and Óglach (Volunteer) Maguire and Óglach McBrearty demanded that the man identify himself. Unfortunately for them, the soldier was from Det 14, and he opened fire and killed both the PIRA men and shot and wounded a third as he raced back to his car. The driver managed to reverse away at high speed with their tails between their legs and reach safety. They had picked on the wrong man and in this incident there were shades of the death of Colm McNutt of INLA who was also killed by undercover soldiers when he tried to hijack their car in the same city on 12 December 1977.[13] Naturally the Provisionals had to put a heroic 'spin' on the whole debacle and a spokesman claimed that the PIRA men had been ambushed by 'carloads of SAS troops' as it was clearly too painful to admit that a lone undercover soldier had single-handedly almost wiped out a PIRA ASU. Many people thought that the undercover soldier was Sergeant Oram who was later killed himself on 21 February 1984 and was awarded the MM. However, the author understands from an impeccable and trusted source that it was not Sergeant Oram, but an unnamed officer. A journalist may have started the rumours by publishing erroneous details.

As an aside on Sergeant Oram, the author was given the following information by the same source:

---

13   See Wharton, *Wasted Years*, Vol 1.

He was awarded his MM for an incident that took place at Leafair Park in the Shantallow area of Londonderry on 2 February 1983. He had already been awarded an MiD as a Corporal in 1981 for a previous tour with the Det. (*London Gazette*, October 1981) On the night in question, he was tasked to do a 'walk past' of a house where it was suspected that an INLA meeting was to take place. Not happy with the first attempt, he was ordered by the Det commander on the spot to do it again. This time he was dicked and attacked by two men, one armed with a rifle. As he was pushed over, Dougie managed to draw his Browning and shot both terrorists; killing one, Eugene McMonagle who was a well-known player, and wounded the other.

McBrearty was identified as one of the terrorists involved in the murder of Gunner Mark Ashford on 17 Jan 1976. He was 18 at the time and was arrested about a week later; despite being grilled for seven days, he refused to speak and the RUC were forced to release him. He then went on to be one of the most prolific terrorists in the city and was responsible for several murders. A Sinn Féin obituary to his comrade read: "Charles Maguire has shown to us the courage that is needed in our fight for freedom; it is with great respect we look back and remember his name both in story and in song."

During that day, Martin Hurson, a PIRA prisoner in the Maze Prison, joined the hunger strike to replace Brendan McLaughlin who had been taken off the strike on two days earlier. He was from Cappagh, near Dungannon in Co Tyrone and joined the Provisionals in 1974. He was convicted of involvement in three PIRA landmine attacks in Co Tyrone – at Cappagh, Galbally and at Reclain near Donaghmore between 1975 and 1976. In the last incident, in February 1976 several members of the RUC and UDR narrowly escaped being killed. He received concurrent sentences of 20, 15 and five years for attempted murder. He was hunger striker number eight, but would die much earlier into his strike than the others.

Shortly before midnight, as the 28th slipped away into history, the Provisionals shot an off-duty policeman as he unwound after a day of violence and mayhem in the wake of the latest hunger striker deaths. Constable Mervyn Robinson (47), father of three, had just left a pub in Whitecross, Co Armagh and was about to drive the few hundred yards to his house, when he was attacked by waiting gunmen. The pub was not one of his regular end of work habits and it is likely that he was dicked upon entering and gunmen were sent for. He was shot several times from point-blank range and died at the scene.

Margaret Thatcher paid a most unexpected visit to Northern Ireland to visit the Northern Ireland Office among other places. She made a statement to the effect that she was not prepared to negotiate with terrorists, but if they called off the strike, she and her government would consider some of the five issues. She added that it was her belief that the hunger strike was the 'last card' of the IRA. The following day, the names of four prisoners on hunger strike together with five other Republican prisoners were put forward as candidates in the forthcoming general election in the Republic of Ireland. Sinn Féin/IRA was clearly now trying to exploit the Nationalist wave of emotion over the deaths of Sands, Hughes, McCreesh and O'Hara and convert it into electoral support.

On the 30th, somewhat lost amidst the violence, terror and murder of the hunger strike aftermath, Sergeant Samuel Cameron McClean (52) of the Royal Artillery died. His cause of death is listed by the MOD as unknown; the author has no further details.

While the IRA and Sinn Féin and their apologists and supporters made political capital about the deaths of the hunger strikers and liken the 'H' Blocks of the Maze to 'concentration camps' it is worth having a look at the pre-war Irish Republic. Despite springing from the bosom of Irish Republicanism, President Eamon De Valera was no friend of the IRA. He interned and emasculated the organisation between 1939 and 1945 as he had no wish to breach the terms of Ireland's neutrality by allowing the IRA a free rein. There were many formal links between the Nazis and the terror group, and especially between the Nazi Abwehr (Intelligence) of Admiral Canaris and the IRA. Arms and agents were smuggled into the country from German U-boats and they acted out the role of fifth columnists to the extent that both British and Irish Governments saw the need for action.

The Curragh camp – which apparently resembled the later Maze – was specially constructed and reinforced in order to hold interned IRA men. Border crossers were often caught and interned by the Irish Army, and Ireland was not the safe haven for terrorists it was to become. How nice it would have been to have seen this spirit of co-operation exist during 1979–97 and thus reduce the Provisionals' capacity to 'shoot and run.' 'Dev' as he was known to his former IRA comrades even had to contend with hunger strikers in this period – it is an age-old Irish Republican tactic – but he stood firm against them and refused them the status of POWs which PIRA was demanding before and after the 1981 hunger strike.

There were two final deaths as May ended and both were men from the Security Forces. Sergeant Major Michael O'Neill (35), father of two, was an ATO in the Royal Army Ordinance Corps, or 'blanket stackers' as they are fondly known to soldiers from other regiments. Early in the morning, his ATO team were called out to examine a suspicious car which had been left at Drumalane Road in Newry. He had approached the car himself as the 'wheelbarrow' robot was not working and he was leaning into the back seats of the car, having examined it at least half a dozen times and was on the point of declaring it safe when a device in the rear exploded and he was killed instantly. He became the 26th ROAC soldier to die in the Troubles, and the 17th ATO to die while attempting to defuse a device.

Colin Dunlop (30), father of four, was a Mormon who lived in the Tullycarnet Estate in East Belfast. He was a full-time clerical worker but more importantly, he was a part-time policeman. As a member of the RUCR, he was detailed to guard a wounded patient in the RVH and was guarding the door to the man's Intensive Care Unit. As he was doing so, he noticed a woman walking towards him, with two men slightly behind, whom presumably he took to be visitors. Suddenly the woman stepped aside to reveal that the two men had guns. They shot him dead, leaving him in a crumpled heap on the floor of the corridor. He held the rank of Reserve Constable.

May was finally over and 27 people lay dead; it was the worst month for a year. A total of eight soldiers and four policemen had been killed as well as seven civilians. Five Catholics and two Protestants had died and one of the deaths was overtly sectarian. Republican paramilitaries lost eight; five were PIRA and three were INLA. During this month, Republican terrorists killed 11 and the Army/RUC killed six.

18

June

In absolute contrast to the previous month which witnessed almost a death a day, fatalities were reduced in June to just four; a soldier, two policemen and a civilian. The civilian was 'executed' by the IRA's 'nutting squad' or ISU, allegedly named by Peter Valente under torture. No further hunger strikers died this month, although four new strikers began to refuse food.

On the 3rd of the month, there was another example of the irresponsibility of the IRA and their complete disregard for the lives and safety of 'their' community. So great was their obsession with a 32 County Ireland, and so great was their blood lust, that they fired on an Army foot patrol despite the proximity of civilians. The soldiers were on the Creggan Estate in Londonderry and were between Bligh's Lane and Central Drive when gunmen began shooting. The shots were hopelessly wide and missed but one round mortally wounded Joseph Lynn (60) who lived in the Creggan. Although he was rushed by the Army to Altnagelvin Hospital he was dead on arrival. The two-faced side of the Provisionals was displayed for the entire world to see, when their apologists held a press conference and issued an utter untruth; they claimed that Mr Lynn had been killed by a soldier. The weapon which killed him was later recovered, and shown to be an IRA weapon which had been used before in other shootings. No apology either at the time or retrospectively has ever been issued by the IRA for the death of Joseph Lynn.

There was an unmistakable feeling of déjà vous about this incident. Seven and a half years earlier, the IRA's Brandywell Unit shot and killed a local girl – Kathleen Feeney who was only 13 – and blamed the Army for shooting her. Thirty two years after the IRA had claimed that the British Army shot her, it finally came clean and made a grovelling apology, and admitted that it had been an IRA bullet which had killed her. They acknowledged that in statements at the time it had "carried out an operation against the British Army in retaliation for the death of Kathleen Feeney."[1]

Also on the 3rd, the Irish Commission for Justice and Peace (ICJP) issued a statement on the hunger strike at the Maze Prison. The ICJP, which had been established by the Catholics Bishops' Conference, came out against political status but did support improvements in conditions in the prison. This would have effectively met three of the prisoners' demands: free association; no prison work; and civilian clothing. The ICJP's initiative was one of a number of attempts to resolve the hunger strike. It later ended most acrimoniously with the ICJP accusing the Northern Ireland Office (NIO) of going back on offers made in relation to the five prisoners' demands. At the same time, the

---

1   See Wharton, Ken, *Sir, They're Taking the Kids Indoors* (Solihull: Helion, 2011).

Loyalist paramilitary group the UDA announced that it was forming a new political party: it was initially called Ulster Loyalist Democratic Party (ULDP), but later the name was changed to the Ulster Democratic Party (UDP).

Many families in Northern Ireland lost loved ones, whether from their own nuclear family or from their extended families, what sociologists would refer to as 'the kinship network'. The Graham family of Co Fermanagh were more unlucky than most, as Mr and Mrs Graham lost three sons all at the hands of Republican terrorists. On the 5th of the month, terrorists, having observed Thomas 'Ronnie' Graham (39) both in uniform and in his civilian job, shot and killed him. Lance Corporal Graham, a father of three had been dicked by a 13-year-old boy who was a member of *an Fianna* Éireann who had also acted as a courier for the weapons used for the attack. In addition to being a part-time soldier, he was also a coal delivery man. On the day in question, he was delivering coal in the small town of Lisnaskea and had just reached a house near the Derrylin Road. He was confronted by masked gunmen who shot him in the head several times and then raced away in his delivery vehicle, leaving the part-time soldier dying and three more children fatherless.

Soldiers and RUC officers were immediately drafted into the area in an effort to trap his murderers. Official Unionist Ken McGinnis, in an angry statement to the press, said: "I am just sick at heart at the cowardly murder of another brave Loyalist. I sincerely appeal to the leadership of the Roman Catholic church to commit itself to take decisive action to prevent such violence." One of Ronnie's brothers – Cecil – was shot and fatally wounded on 9 November this year, dying two days later and another brother – James was shot and killed on 1 February, 1985 All three brothers were murdered by the Provisional IRA.

On Monday 8th, Thomas McElwee, PIRA prisoner, in the Maze became the 10th man to join the hunger strike. Brendan McLaughlin had been taken off the strike 13 days previously following a serious illness; McElwee died in August and was the ninth of the 10 men who died. In December 1976, McElwee was arrested for a firebomb attack in the town of Ballymena in which he was badly injured and nearly blinded. Just after he and others in the ASU arrived at a car park in the town, one of their bombs exploded inside the car; it was a classic 'own goal' explosion. Of the ASU, Colm Skullion lost two toes, Sean McPeake lost his leg, which was amputated above the knee, Benedict – McElwee's brother – was deafened, and McElwee himself was blinded in one eye. After his recovery he was charged with murder for the death of Yvonne Dunlop a 26-year-oldwoman, who was killed when one of the fire bombs they had planted destroyed her shop, the Alley Katz Boutique.[2] On conviction for her murder, McElwee was sentenced to life imprisonment in September 1977.

On the 10th, eight PIRA prisoners escaped from Crumlin Road Gaol; the eight included the killer of SAS Captain Herbert Westmacott, Joe Doherty. On the 10 June 1981, eight Republican prisoners on remand in Belfast's Crumlin Road gaol shot their way to freedom from one of the most heavily guarded prisons in Europe, in one of the most daring IRA escapes ever. The men came out the way they went in – through the front gate. The prison had been the scene of several protests regarding strip-searching

---

2   See Wharton, Ken M., *Wasted Years, Wasted Lives* (Solihull: Helion, 2013), Vol 1.

shortly beforehand, but the rules had been relaxed. On 'A' and 'C' Wings the remand prisoners had been taken outside in the yard for exercise. Several men were called for visits and they were escorted by prison officers to see family, friends or, in some cases, solicitors. An area of the prison was set aside to allow legal teams and the accused a place to discuss their business in private. However, when POs came to bring back one set of prisoners to their wing, the escape began.

One of the Óglach (Volunteers) produced a pistol and forced the POs to release other prisoners before locking some of the staff in a cell. Following that, they bluffed their way into another part of the gaol and seized more staff along with other visitors and legal teams. One brave officer tied to resist but he was assaulted by a prisoner and knocked to the ground. The escapees then stole PO uniforms and civilian clothing from the other hostages and walked to the gate and threatened gate staff with pistols and then dashed across the Crumlin Road to a clinic car park which was diagonally opposite. At this stage, three RUC officers who were waiting for a colleague in the gaol realised what was happening and gave chase. The escapees then opened fire and a minor fire fight broke out, before the eight raced off in stolen cars.

The men headed towards the loyalist Shankill area where they commandeered cars to help their getaway. All of the men were charged with crimes of violence – Doherty with killing an SAS officer – and one of them – Peter Ryan from Ardboe, Co Tyrone was charged with killing an RUCR officer and a UDR soldier.

Saoirse 32, an extremist Republican organisation, laughingly tried to romanticise the escape and claimed: "British army sentries poured a hail of automatic fire at the prisoners from a watch tower before they could reach the front gate. Undeterred, the prisoners dashed through the bullets, weaving from side to side to throw off their attackers." When I did the research for this particular section of the book, I had to glance at the front to ensure that I had not accidentally picked up Paul Brickhill's superb account of the 'Great Escape' which detailed the mass breakout from a German POW camp: Stalag Luft III at Sagan in 1943.[3]

On the 11th, there was a general election in the Irish Republic, during which two Maze prisoners were elected to the *Dáil* (Irish Parliament). The results were inconclusive, and a minority government was formed between a coalition of *Fine Gael* and Labour. On 30 June 1981 Garret FitzGerald replaced Charles Haughey as Taoiseach. The day following the Irish Election, The British Government published proposals to change the Representation of the People Act making it impossible for prisoners to stand as candidates for election to parliament. The move was partly to stop the Republicans from gaining propaganda value from the election of a convicted terrorist and partly to ensure that constituents had a Parliamentary representative whom they could actually take their problems to.

On the 12th, a PIRA mortar team set up a mortar base in a back garden in a house in the Ballymurphy Estate, putting at risk the lives of residents and civilians in the 'flight path' of the missiles. 'Fort Whiterock' (sometimes known as 'Pegasus') was the main target and several mortars landed in the base. However, other than cuts and bruises, there were no injuries, civilian or military.

---

3   Brickhill, Paul, *The Great Escape* (London: Faver & Faber, 1951, reprinted by Cox & Wyman, 2002).

Lord Gardiner was a Labour politician who served as Lord High Chancellor of Great Britain from 1964 to 1970. He was also a leading proponent of the concept of declaring what Republicans saw as 'political' crimes as criminal. On the 13th, he survived a failed assassination attempt when a bomb containing 3 lb (1.4 kgs) of explosive was attached to his car by the IRA during a visit to Belfast. The device fell off the car and failed to explode and was later found near the junction of University Road and Elmwood Avenue, Belfast, and defused by ATO. The IRA released a statement saying: "We meant to kill Gardiner, the political architect of the criminalisation policy and the H-blocks."

On the 15th, Sinn Féin announced new changes to the hunger strike. Their spokesman declared that a Republican prisoner would join the hunger strike every week. By this stage, four hunger strikers had died, five were on strike, with Paddy Quinn due to start refusing food that very day, and one had been taken off due to illness; 12 more would subsequently join the strike. Quinn would be taken off by his family after refusing food for 47 days. However, within a fortnight, Margaret Thatcher would again reiterate her resolution when a government spokesman issued a statement on prison policy in Northern Ireland. He announced that the government would not grant special category status and would retain control of the prisons.

Quinn was an IRA member who had been behind bars for almost four years when he became one of the hunger strikers. On 25 June 1976, Quinn, his brother Séamus, Danny McGuinness and Raymond McCreesh prepared an ambush on an Army patrol at the Mountain House Inn on the Newry-Newtownhamilton road. They hijacked a car from a farm in Sturgan but were observed by undercover soldiers as they set up firing points. They prematurely opened fire on soldiers as they investigated and their getaway driver panicked and drove off, abandoning his fellow terrorists. The remainder of the gang attempted to hide in a nearby farmhouse but were surrounded by soldiers. A brief fire fight broke out, but being outnumbered, they surrendered to a local priest who led them outside where they surrendered.

On the 17th, RUCR officer Christopher Kyle (25) was shot by the IRA close to his home near Carrickmore, Co Tyrone. The young officer was a part-time policeman and a full-time mechanic. During the late afternoon of the 17th, he was driving home from work and was very close to his home at Beragh when he was ambushed by IRA gunmen. The men opened fire on his car and he was fatally wounded in a hail of bullets. Leaving him dying, the murderers drove off in their stolen car and abandoned it in a Nationalist area in nearby Carrickmore. Constable Kyle's father went out to investigate and found his son, mortally wounded. He was rushed to Tyrone County hospital but he died of his wounds shortly afterwards.

Just three days later another policeman was murdered by the Provisionals, this time a full-time officer. Neal Quinn (53), father of three grown-up children, had been in the RUC for almost 30 years. The Newry man was off-duty and at around midday, he was in a pub in the town in civilian clothes enjoying a quiet drink. He was dicked by IRA sympathisers, and acting on the information received, gunmen were sent to the 'Bridge Bar' in North Street, close to Sugar Island in the centre of the mainly Nationalist town. Two men wearing motorcycle helmets walked into the bar which is close to the canal, and walked towards him. He realised the gravity of the situation and raced out of the back door to try and escape, but the gunmen followed him and shot him nine times in the head and chest; he died almost immediately. He was a Catholic and became the 100th RUC officer to be killed since the present Troubles began.

On the 22nd, INLA member Michael Devine became the 12th Maze prisoner to join the hunger strike. In the early 1970s, he joined the Northern Ireland Labour Party and Young Socialists, before becoming a founding member of IRSP/INLA in 1975. In 1976, after an arms raid in Co Donegal, in the Republic, he was arrested in the North and sentenced to 12 years. Known in Irish as *Arm Saoirse Náisiúnta na hÉireann,* it was founded by people such as Seamus Costello, Bernadette McAliskey, Gerard Steenson and others such as Devine who left the OIRA in the wake of what they considered its revolutionary and military inertia.

On the 26th, as the British summer kicked in, the fallout over the 'execution' of Peter Valente and what he may have said or not said, continued. The ISU were again action, and Vincent Robinson from the mainly Nationalist Suffolk area of Belfast was abducted and taken to an IRA safe house in the Divis Street area. There he was interrogated and tortured over information which led to the finding of an unprimed bomb in Andersonstown. The device was designed to kill troops in the Andersonstown/Falls Road area and the Security Forces found it following a tip-off from an informer. Mr Robinson (29), father of two, was accused, found guilty and executed for the 'capital' crime of touting. He was shot on one of the upper floors of St Jude's in the Divis area and his lifeless body was dumped in a rubbish chute. Dungannon priest, Father Faul, taking time off from his role as a mediator over the hunger strike, dismissed the IRA claims as false and was most condemnatory of their actions. The ISU or 'nutting squad' was composed of men who enjoyed inflicting violence upon those who had transgressed the rules of the IRA's 'Green Book' and who had no qualms about inflicting sadistic torture or death upon those who were unfortunate enough to fall into their hands. Marty McGartland, in his gripping book, speaks of how he drove members of the ISU around Belfast and how they boasted of beatings.[4] It was considered funny that in certain cases, innocent Óglach – in the sense that they hadn't touted – had often incurred the wrath of another fellow IRA man and would be beaten just on the grounds of personal dislike. There was talk of an IRA man who had designs on another man's wife and the ISU were ordered to teach him a lesson.

Finally, on the 29th, IRA prisoner Laurence McKeown became the 13th man to begin a hunger strike; he was to last a staggering 70 days. Only two men lasted longer – and both died – before his family insisted on taking him off. He joined the IRA when he was only 17 and, and he was arrested in August 1976 and charged with causing explosions and the attempted murder of a police officer. In April 1977, he was found guilty and sentenced to life imprisonment and was sent to the Maze.

As the second month of the strike ended, four were dead, eight were still refusing food, and one man – Brendan McLaughlin – had already been taken off the strike. The following month would see two more deaths, but 13 more Troubles-related killings as the violence rumbled on.

In June, five people had died; one soldier and two policemen had been killed by the IRA, a Catholic civilian had been shot by the same Republican terror group in crossfire and a suspected informer had been executed by them. All five deaths this month were the bloody handiwork of the Provisional IRA.

---

4   McGartland, Martin, *Fifty Dead Men Walking* (London: John Blake Publishing, 1997).

19

July

There would be 13 Troubles-related deaths this month, as two more soldiers would die and two of the hunger strikers would die also. A former police officer was killed because of his past associations and baton rounds would again raise their ugly heads. Paddy Quinn's family removed him from the hunger strike; the second striker to end their fasts.

On the 1st of the month, a man was abducted by the IRA in the Irish Republic and was never seen alive again. The man – Danny McIlhone (age unknown) has become one of the 'Disappeared.' He was abducted around May 12, 1981, from the Nationalist Pearse Tower in Ballymun, close to Dublin Airport, where he was staying at the time. McIlhone was shot a number of times before being buried in a secret grave on a remote mountainside, an inquest held in October 2009 revealed. A PIRA 'nutting squad' lifted him and interrogated him over an alleged theft from one of their arms caches. Geoff Knupfer, an investigative scientist who is leading the search for the bodies of the 'Disappeared,' told the inquest that the IRA had admitted details of the shooting to the Independent Commission for the Location of Victims Remains. He was quoted in the *Belfast Telegraph* as saying: "I'm absolutely satisfied from information we received from direct sources in the Republican movement that he was shot." The partial remains of Mr McIlhone were uncovered in November 2013 in lonely bogland at Ballynultagh, near the village of Lacken in the Wicklow Mountains, in the Republic.

The Provisionals admitted in 1999 that it murdered and buried at secret locations nine of the 'Disappeared.' These included Eamon Molloy in 1975, Brian McKinney in 1978 and the most famous of all, Jean McConville. The widowed mother of 10 was killed in 1972 and her body was discovered in 2003. [1] The bodies of six of the disappeared have now been found, but the Provisionals have refused to reveal details of a further seven bodies, including that of British Army officer, Captain Robert Nairac.

Cardinal Ó'Fiaich served as the Roman Catholic Archbishop of Armagh and Primate of All Ireland from 1977 until his death; he was created a Cardinal in 1979. During the 1981 hunger strike, he worked tirelessly in an attempt to halt the deaths, not just inside the Maze Prison hospital but also on the streets of the island of Ireland. He paid a visit to 10 Downing Street, in order to plead with the Prime Minister to compromise over the prisoners' demands. She was determined not to compromise and proved as intransigent to the Cardinal as she had done to many others before him. Reading through David Beresford's account of the meeting, she comes across as pushing her steadfastness

---

1 See Wharton, Ken, *The Bloodiest Year: Northern Ireland 1972* (Stroud: The History Press, 2011), for more details about Mrs McConville.

almost to the point of being glib. In response to one of his questions, Thatcher replies: "Why can't the Irish be friendly? We fought against the French; we fought against the Germans, and they are friends; why must the Irish be exceptions?" The Cardinal did however manage an admittedly superb point with his riposte: "Because you're no longer in occupation of the Ruhr!"[2]

On the 2nd, Northern Ireland Secretary, Humphrey Atkins, suggested the setting up of an advisory council to help govern Northern Ireland. It was envisaged that the council would be comprised of 50 elected representatives. It was one of many pipe dreams and airy fairy ideas produced by government 'think tanks' and it received very little political support and was later dropped. Across the Atlantic, a US Federal court ruled that NORAID would have to register as an agent of the Irish Republican Army; this was somewhat of a belated effort on the part of the Americans and too little, too late.

On US 'Independence Day' during secret negotiations between the NIO and the Provisionals, it appeared – one writes with the benefit of hindsight, of course – that the government was making some concessions. It seemed that the issue of prisoners wearing their own clothing was about to be conceded and also the issue of visitation rights was also to be agreed. The government was keen to be seen to be reasonable but at the same time, no capitulating to the demands of convicted terrorists. However, it would not budge on three of the issues and the prisoners obviously felt that they were negotiating from a position of moral strength and were not prepared to compromise. History – particularly that seen from the narrow, insular and bigoted Irish-American perspective – would judge Thatcher as the intransigent one, but the Republicans inside the Maze were equally so. The government, however, was prepared to talk but insisted that if news of their willingness to talk to the Republicans were made public, the negotiations would cease immediately.

On that same day, the Royal Corps of Signals lost one of their men – Signalman Brian Richard Cross (26) – in an RTA; the author cannot confirm anything further than this, but his death is officially listed as such and there is a possibility that the accident may have been duty-related. I have been unable to clarify any details with the MOD. From Paul Drummond – to whom I am most grateful – I discovered that the accident happened on Rock Road, in the HQNI town of Lisburn, Co Antrim. Signalman Cross was apparently en-route to the RUC Centre at Castlereagh and had been visiting a friend in a Nationalist area.

Ian McKay

I was Brian's Detachment Commander; his nickname was 'Aussie' and he died as a result of car accident on his way back to the Det at RUC Castlereagh. He was a member of the CIST Det based there. If my memory serves me right he had been visiting a girlfriend but had previously been warned to stay away. He received a military funeral and was buried in Ashton under Lyme; myself and members of 39 Brigade Signal Squadron were the funeral detail.

---

2   Beresford, David, *Ten Men Dead* (London: Harper Collins, 1994), p.276.

On the 8th, the fifth hunger striker died. After 61 days of refusing food, Joe McDonnell (30) passed away; he had gone on strike to replace Bobby Sands. The Irish Commission for Justice and Peace (ICJP), which had been established by the Catholics Bishops Conference, accused the Northern Ireland Office of retreating from earlier offers made to the ICJP on the hunger strikers' five demands.

Just a few hours after McDonnell's death, Mrs Nora McCabe (33), mother of three small children was on a shopping errand and was walking along Linden Street, close to Dunville Park in the Lower Falls. Linden Street where she was killed, once stood between Clonard Street and Waterford Street; it is no longer there and the blackened terraces have been replaced by more modern semis and rows of neat town houses. It is, however, debatable whether the old attitudes and hatreds have also been replaced. Mrs McCabe was returning from the shops when an RUC officer in a mobile patrol unit fired a single baton round at two petrol bombers he had seen. The projectile hit the woman and fatally injured her. She was taken to the RVH which was less than 100 yards away; sadly, she died of her injuries on the morning of the 9th. The then Attorney-General, Sir Michael Havers Q,C refused a request to have the case re-opened in 1984, some three years after the IRA's London Department had tried to blow him up in his own house.[3]

On the same day that Mrs McCabe was fatally injured, a gang of youths, some of whom were members of *an Fianna* Éireann, hijacked a van during rioting in the Falls Road area and headed towards the bus depot close to Andersonstown RUC station and Milltown Cemetery, close to Divis Drive. The gang smashed their way into the depot with the stolen van and jumped, several of them with unlit petrol bombs in their hands. Unfortunately for them, a unit of eight soldiers was inside the depot, in order to guard both the premises and the garaged buses. The soldiers warned the youths to halt; some did, but several turned around and tried to escape. John Dempsey (16) was one who tried to escape, and after being warned three times, under the 'yellow card' rules, with him still refusing to stop, a single round from an SLR was fired and he was hit in the chest. He died at the scene and several days later, having had his obituary printed in both the *Irish News* and *An Phoblacht* [Republican News], was given a full IRA 'military' funeral.

Shortly after Mrs McCabe had died from her injuries, Daniel Barrett (15) was shot by a soldier outside his home in the Ardoyne. He had spent the evening with friends at a local disco and had returned to his home in Havana Court. This was a small square of recently-built, red-brick terrace houses with small gardens surrounded by two-foot high brick walls. An Army OP was located on a part of Flax Street Mill which overlooked the Barrett house, giving the soldiers inside the post a clear view of the entire length of the small street and the section of Flax Street that backed on to it. Major disturbances were going on in that area of the Ardoyne and an RUC Land Rover came under fire from PIRA gunmen located near to Havana Court. Young Barrett was sitting on his garden wall when soldiers in the OP returned fire; one shot struck the boy and he died almost immediately. Later in Court, the soldier who fired the shot was assaulted by a relative of the dead boy after he had explained why he had fired. It emerged that a local had begged the PIRA ASU not to open fire as there were too many civilians in the area. The plea

---

3   See Chapter 23.

was ignored by the OC of the Ardoyne IRA and his refusal led indirectly to the death of young Daniel.

On 10 July, hunger striker Joe McDonnell was buried in the Republican plot in Milltown Cemetery; shots were fired over his grave by masked gunmen wearing the 'uniform' of the IRA: black berets, masks, combat jackets and black gloves. Circling above was an Army Gazelle helicopter on surveillance duties and using telephoto lens. The soldiers on board managed to track the firing party to a house in Andersonstown Road and radioed their location to an Army mobile unit. The soldiers converged on the house which was identified as being on St Agnes Drive, just over half a mile as the crow flies from Milltown Cemetery. The soldiers confronted two men in the street carrying rifles and a brief exchange of fire saw both men stumble after being hit. But they escaped, and an extremely hostile crowd of mourners-cum-rioters turned on the small unit of soldiers. A hail of rocks and other objects rained down on the troops and they were forced to retreat and await reinforcements; when they did arrive, the wounded firing party had been spirited away. Meanwhile two soldiers had burst into the house and another member of the firing party had shot at a soldier who returned fire and the IRA man slumped to the floor wounded. The IRA man was none other than Patrick Adams, younger brother of Sinn Féin President – and the man who never ordered the 'Bloody Friday' bombing or was an IRA commander in the Ballymurphy – Gerry Adams. Patrick was named in honour of their uncle who was in the IRA and was interned during the Second World War. He was taken to hospital and later charged with terrorist offences.

The funeral was over and the following day, the *Daily Mail* referred to it as "another well-managed melodrama, another notch on the gun barrel in their propaganda war," and continued:

> The Republicans have long had their martyrs and whether or not they have voluntarily starved themselves to death, been shot by the RUC or by British soldiers or blown themselves up with their own bombs, their names and memories are forever preserved in their own folklore. First come the open coffin wakes in the front rooms of their homes, then the hearse drives off, followed by a multitude of mourners, many bearing the Irish Tricolour, bears down upon their local cemetery. Speeches, masquerading as eulogies, which are generally no more than Brit-hating propaganda and rhetoric are read out, and conveyed by loudspeaker to the gathered thousands. Then several masked men in the 'uniform' of the IRA step out and fire several volleys of shots over the coffin and then they melt back into the crowd. Masks, berets and gloves are stuffed into pockets, Armalite rifles are disassembled and dozens of people walk away with just one part each, hidden inside jackets or even babies' nappies. Afterwards it is the responsibility of the song-writers to immortalise a dead terrorist's name in a song which by nightfall will be on the lips of their supporters; within a day or two, it will have crossed the Atlantic and will be tunelessly rendered in a dozen or more Irish-American bars on the Eastern Seaboard.

On the aforementioned Eastern Seaboard, staff at both the British Consulate in New York City and at the main Embassy in Washington DC, were constantly under attack, either physically or more often, verbally by both Irish-Americans, generally from five generations back or from gullible Americans with a generally irrational hatred of the English. In several offices, the Union Flag had been taken down so as not to antagonise the locals. When it comes to propaganda exercises, the Irish abroad have no peers; they love the international stage and where better than the USA?

On the day of the funeral, Hugh O'Neill (21) was accidentally shot and killed by his best friend at a house in the Ballymurphy Road. An INLA handgun had been discarded in a garden, no doubt thrown there during pursuit by the Security Forces and not retrieved. The two friends were messing about with it and it discharged a round which mortally wounded Mr O'Neill. His friend was later given a suspended sentence for manslaughter and the dead man's family stated that they bore no animosity for the accidental loss of their son.

BRAVE LOCAL
Marcus Townley, Welsh Guards

About three-quarters of the way through our tour, the platoon found itself on 'mill clearance' which was town patrols. This particular day, we were tasked with doing multiple VCPs. My four-man brick took our turn doing stop and search; anyway, we pulled one particular car up, and the driver looked rather nervous and kept looking over his shoulder, which made us jumpy. As I made my way over to the car, the driver whispered to me that he'd seen two men digging by the side of the road a few miles back. Anyway, I called my brick commander over and explained what this gentleman had just told me. So as not to raise suspicion, we made the chap get out of his car in order to give the impression to any dickers watching that the Brit Bastards were hassling some 'poor wee guy.' The road was deserted, but we took no chances, and just kept up the charade. He gave us the location and he even gave us a grid ref!

We noted the information while maintaining the impression that we were doing a 'P-check' before thanking the brave gentleman and sending him on his way. He seemed a bit bemused and replied: 'No; thank YOU, soldiers!' We gave the info to the INTCELL, which they duly noted, and a fortnight later, a road side bomb was discovered and ATO sent for in order to defuse it. This was all down to one brave local man, whom I believe was pissed off by the antics of the so called freedom fighters.

Thirty-three years have now passed since those events, and I have often wondered what became of this gentleman whose action saved lives of not only soldiers and police but probably also of civilians. I think that all he wanted was some sort of normality in his country. I often think about him and just hope that he lived to enjoy the sights and sounds of his grandchildren; I surely do.

On the 12th, the ugly head of sectarianism was raised once again when a Republican gang cornered a Protestant as he walked home in the Ballygomartin area which has both Catholic as well as Protestant enclaves. At its northern end are the Loyalist Woodvale and Crumlin Road and at its southern or western end is the Nationalist New Barnsley. George Hall (28) was walking home late on the Saturday night or in the *'wee hors'* of Sunday morning after drinking with friends. He was seized and stabbed to death by a gang of Republicans, presumably seeking revenge for the latest hunger striker death. His killers were never found. Just 72 hours later and in very much the same area, another Protestant was murdered in what can only be viewed as an overtly sectarian attack.

On the day afterwards, another hunger striker – the sixth – died in the Maze Hospital. Martin Hurson (29) died after 46 days on hunger strike, having been imprisoned for attempted murder, involvement in explosions and IRA membership. At this stage, there were still seven men refusing food and the following day, IRA prisoner Patrick McGeown became the eighth. In November 1975, he had been arrested and charged with possession of explosives, taking part in the bombing of Belfast's Europa Hotel and IRA membership. He was convicted and received a five-year sentence plus two concurrent fifteen-year sentences for the bombing and possession of explosives. In March 1978 he attempted to escape along with Brendan 'Bic' McFarlane and Larry Marley. The three had wire cutters and wore stolen PO uniforms, and carried replica wooden pistols. The attempt was unsuccessful. McGeown was also named as one of the PIRA gunmen who murdered Catholic mother, Jean McConville in December, 1972.[4]

Phillip Bradfield, writing in the *Belfast Newsletter*, said:

> The man who allegedly shot Belfast mother-of-10 Jean McConville was yesterday named as former Sinn Féin councillor and Belfast IRA commander Pat McGeown. It was claimed yesterday that he also shot dead 'Good Samaritan' Protestant workman Sammy Llewellyn when he went to help Catholics on the Falls Road board up windows after an IRA bomb in 1975. "I was recently approached by grassroots Republicans who were sympathetic to the McConville family," Jean McConville's son Jim said yesterday in a Sunday paper. "I was given some details of what happened and only two weeks ago I gave Pat McGeown's name to my solicitor."

The paper claimed that McGeown was only 17 when he shot Mrs McConville in the back of the head, and that he later rose to become a close political confidant of Sinn Féin president Gerry Adams. The *Newsletter* understands McGeown's name had been widely linked to Mrs McConville's murder before he died in 1996. Gerry Kelly MLA said at McGeown's funeral that he had been a prisoner in Cage 11 of the Maze with Gerry Adams. Adams officially launched the Pat McGeown Community Endeavour Award at Belfast's Upper Springfield Development Trust in 1998. He described McGeown as "a modest man with a quiet, but total dedication to equality and raising the standard of life for all the people of the city," adding that McGeown "would have been one of the last people to expect an award to be given in his name, and yet few others could have deserved the honour more."[5]

On the 14th, Matthew 'Matt' Devlin of the IRA became the nineth prisoner to join the hunger strike. He was born in Ardboe, Co Tyrone and joined the IRA in the mid-1970s. He was arrested in 1977, and charged with the attempted murder of RUC officers; he received a seven-year sentence. On the same day, the government of the Irish Republic turned to its traditional allies in the USA and asked the US government to use its influence with Britain to put pressure on Margaret Thatcher on the issue of the hunger strike.

---

4   See previous books by Ken Wharton.
5   Source: http://www.newsletter.co.uk/news/regional/jean-mcconville-killer-is-named-1-5670723

The day after, Humphrey Atkins announced that representatives of the International Committee of the Red Cross had been invited to carry out an investigation of prison conditions in Northern Ireland.

On the 15th a Republican gang – possibly the same one which had stabbed George Hall to death three days earlier – attacked a lone Protestant as he walked to his home in Forthriver Drive in the early hours of the morning. Forthriver Drive is located off the Ballygomartin Road and as stated earlier, is close enough to both Loyalist and Nationalist areas to attract roving elements from both communities. Robert Campbell (40) and a father of five, was walking home from the Shankill Road area where he had been drinking with friends. He had walked along the Ballygomartin Road and was about to turn into his street, when he was seized by thugs who dragged him off the road and punched and kicked him before fatally stabbing him several times. As they proceeded to attack him like a pack of wild animals, neighbours, alerted by the screams chased off the gang who jumped into their car and raced off. He left a pregnant daughter, who poignantly told *The Belfast Telegraph* that he was looking forward to welcoming his first grandchild into the world. The second sectarian murder took place only three days and 300 yards apart. No one was ever convicted of either murder.

On the 16th, Representatives of the International Committee of the Red Cross paid a visit to the Maze Prison and met with Republican prisoners. Those Republican prisoners taking part in the hunger strike rejected attempts by the International Committee of the Red Cross to act as mediators with the British. Indeed, over the course of the next eight days the delegation met with both sides to the dispute but announced later – on the 23rd – that they were unable to help resolve the hunger strike. Back in mainland Britain, it was announced that a planned visit to the USA by the Queen's sister, Princess Margaret had been cancelled on security grounds. It is thought that it was the first time in recorded history that such a Royal visit had been called off, but clearly the anti-British feelings in the USA, whipped up skilfully by both Sinn Féin and their sycophantic supporters on the other side of the Atlantic made the trip unwise. One Irish-American supporter positively drooled with an almost sexual pleasure, when he excitedly told journalists: "It's the first time a member of the Royal Family has been afraid to visit a foreign country."

On the day that the 'great and the good' of the International Red Cross were trying to help resolve the grave situation inside the Maze, what one Green Jacket described as a *'cluster fuck'* was taking place at Glassdrummond, South Armagh, close to the border with the Irish Republic. Under the watching eyes of the Provisionals, a four-man unit from the Royal Green Jackets was being inserted into what was supposed to be a secret observation post. As the unit was being inserted into a scrapyard and a nearby field, a firing position was being set up over the border and a heavy machine gun – an M60 – plus other lighter automatic weapons was being put in place by a PIRA ASU. The two soldiers who were wounded in the subsequent attack – one of them mortally – were Rifleman John Moore and Lance Corporal Gavin Dean (21); the latter was from Rainham in Kent. Rifleman Moore is now confined to a wheelchair.

GLASSDRUMMOND AMBUSH
Rifleman John Moore, Royal Green Jackets

With only a couple of weeks before our four month tour was due to end, our platoon was given one big final operation. Intelligence suggested that IRA units were mounting illegal vehicle checkpoints along the border – we were to stop them. We were transported from Bessbrook in 'Q' vans to a spot south of XMG near the border and from there we patrolled to our various given locations in the dark to setup covert OPs. Our brick chose a derelict van in a scrap yard about 150 metres from the border to watch and listen for IRA activity. Conditions in the van were cramped – during the day we sweltered and at night it got pretty chilly.

On the 16 July on the third night of our mission as dusk approached I took the stag position. Moments later our hide was raked by heavy automatic gunfire from across the Irish border. Terrorists had discovered our patrol and used an M60 and Armalite rifles to counter ambush us, the IRA unit were later thought to be about 6–8 strong. My brick commander, Lance Corporal Gavin 'Deano' Dean was immediately struck by two bullets. I returned fire using two weapons. During the short but intense fire fight I was hit in the upper spine by a high-velocity bullet instantly paralysing me from the chest down. The other member of our brick was slightly injured but managed to walk out of the yard and was flown by chopper to Musgrave Park Hospital, Belfast, along with 'Deano' and me both on stretchers. The contact occurred only ten days before we were to be reunited with our families at home.

As we reached hospital 'Deano' died, aged just 21. I was very seriously ill and the next day my parents were taken to Belfast to see me. I was then flown to London to begin a lengthy period of recovery in QEMH, Woolwich. During the first few days on Intensive Care, as I was upside down on a special bed, I was told that 'Deano' – my friend – had died; the news hit me hard.

Lance Corporal Gavin Thomas Dean (21) died of his wounds in a Belfast hospital the day after being wounded; he had turned 21 only nine days earlier. He was the 23rd Green Jacket to be killed in or as a consequence of the Troubles; 26 more would die before the Troubles ended.

On Saturday the 18th, there were serious clashes between Republican demonstrators and Gardaí following a demonstration outside the British embassy in Dublin; over 200 people were hurt during the clashes, as feelings of anger were whipped up against Thatcher's stance. However, as the 'Iron Lady' herself said: "Crime is crime is crime; it is not political."

On the afternoon of the 21st, a PIRA ASU drove up to a damaged shop near the centre of Maghera, Co Londonderry where a building crew was renovating. One of the workers was a part-time UDR soldier and the others were innocent Protestant civilians. One of the civvies was John Hazlet (43), father of two, and he had his back to the men as they walked towards where he was working. The gunmen shot him several time in the back of the head and he died at the scene. When it was announced that they had killed an innocent man, an apologist 'apologised' for mistaken identity and said that they regretted the death. Several days later as he was buried in Maghera, the shooting was denounced as shameful and senseless. As a Minister said when referring to the IRA's admission that it had made a mistake, "some mistakes are so permanent, and so final, that they cannot be rectified. Apologies cannot exchange a coffin for a chair.

They cannot give sparkle to a tear-dimmed eye, nor bring joy to a desolate and broken-hearted family."[6]

On the 24th, in what may well have been a tragic error by a Royal Marine, Peter Doherty (33) was fatally injured by a baton round. He lived in the Divis Street Flats and had been watching marines giving protection to an Army bulldozer which was clearing barricades. A marine stated that he had seen petrol bombs being thrown from a window in the flats and fired back. Sadly for Mr Doherty, he had just gone to close the window – the author is not claiming that he was the one who threw a petrol bomb – when a baton round hit him in the head. He died in hospital a week later on the 31st.

On the 29th, as the month drew to a close, representatives from Sinn Féin and the Irish Republican Socialist Party (IRSP) visited those taking part in the hunger strike, coordinated inside the Maze by Brendan 'Bic' MacFarlane. It is claimed – largely for propaganda purposes – that both Sinn Féin and the IRSP suggested that the strike be suspended for three months to allow time to monitor prison reforms. This suggestion was rejected by the hunger strikers and Republican prisoners.

On the very last day of the month, Republican paramilitaries targeted a former member of the RUC in Strabane, Co Tyrone. Thomas Harpur (31) had been a policeman, but had resigned three years previously on the grounds of ill-health. He was visiting a friend on the Nationalist Ballycolman, the same estate where Heather Pollack had been shot and fatally wounded the previous December.[7] It would seem that he was recognised as gunmen were quickly on the scene and they shot him at point blank range just as summer dusk was falling. The killing was claimed by the INLA, but it was later attributed to the Provisionals. Whoever did it, it was a senseless and vindictive killing – murder by association.

On that last day of July, the family of Paddy Quinn, then on day 47 of his hunger strike, intervened and asked for medical treatment to save his life. This series of events was to be repeated a number of times, especially in August and September, towards the end of the hunger strike as more and more families intervened to save their menfolk.

Another month of the hunger strikes had ended with no end in sight to the deaths inside the Maze and the consequent deaths in the streets and fields outside. Six hunger strikers were dead – three more would die over the next eight days – and eight others were still refusing food and awaiting death for their five demands. During July, 14 people had died; two soldiers and one former RUC officer had lost their lives. A total of eight civilians – five Catholics and three Protestants – had also been killed, two of the deaths were overtly sectarian in nature. Three Republican paramilitaries had died, two of whom were hunger strikers. The IRA was responsible for six of the deaths and the Army for four.

---

6   Thornton, David, Seamus Kelters, Brian Feeney and David McKittrick. *Lost Lives: The Stories of the Men, Women and Children who Died as a Result of the Northern Ireland Troubles.* (Edinburgh: Mainstream, 1999, revised ed. 2007), p. 873.

7   See Chapter 12.

20

August

August would prove to be another bloody month and, while it would pale alongside some of the violent months of the early to mid-1970s, measured by the standards of the previous year it was a terrible time for Northern Ireland. Sixteen people would die, including six soldiers, two policemen and four more hunger strikers.

On the first day of August, INLA prisoner Kevin Lynch (25) died following a period of 71 days on hunger strike; he was the seventh to die. A former member of *an Fianna Éireann*, he joined the OIRA before the split and then joined IRSP/INLA.

Retaliation was swift and it was a case of gross hypocrisy that the Provisionals justified the murder of two RUC officers by claiming that it was revenge for the death of Lynch; this killing would have happened anyway. On the 2nd, after investigating a suspicious blaze near Omagh, Co Tyrone, Constables John Smyth (34), father of three and Acting Constable Andrew Woods (50), RUCR and the father of six children, were part of a two-vehicle mobile patrol returning to Omagh. When their vehicle reached passed over a culvert just outside of the village of Loughmacrory, a PIRA bombing team, hiding close to a quarry, triggered a 600 lb (273 kgs) device by command wire. Both officers were killed instantly; a massive crater, pieces of body parts and wreckage were all that was left. Officers in the following vehicle opened fire on the PIRA men who were running away, but unfortunately missed their targets. The border was 10 miles south of them and there were enough back roads on which they could quickly reach the sanctuary of the Irish Republic in stolen vehicles.

Later that day, another hunger striker died – the eighth – and this left five more prisoners still refusing food. Kieran 'Doc' Doherty (25), an IRA prisoner and also an elected member of the Irish Parliament (the Dáil), died on the 73rd day of his strike. His Mother had famously raged at Sinn Féin leaders during a meeting in West Belfast when she cried out: "I don't think decisions are being made in the prison. I think decisions are being made by people inside the room." Cracks were beginning to appear, and for all the unity of the hunger strikers, it is this author's firm belief that much pressure, subtle or otherwise, was being placed by the leadership of the Provisionals. As dedicated as many of the strikers undoubtedly were, they felt that they would be letting down the movement if they ended it.

On the 3rd, INLA prisoner Liam McCloskey became the 16th man to join the hunger strike. He was a friend of Kevin Lynch and they joined the IRSP/INLA at around the same time. His family said they would intervene if he became unconscious as was to prove the case the following month.

At this fairly late stage of the hunger strike, as more and more pressure was being applied from all around the world, especially from the USA, where the arch-enemy of

Britain – Senator Edward Kennedy – was busy sending telegrams to Margaret Thatcher, it became increasingly clear that she had support at home. She had the backing of her entire cabinet, the Leader of HM's Loyal Opposition, Michael Foot, British SDLP leader, Roy Jenkins, and the Liberal Leader, David Steel. As David Beresford points out, Roy Jenkins as Home Secretary in the last Labour Government – under James Callaghan – had shown no mercy or qualms when IRA hunger striker, Frank Stagg starved himself to death in Wakefield Gaol on 12 February, 1976.[1] She was also – somewhat surprisingly – supported by US Presidents Carter and his successor Reagan, as well as some EU leaders.

On the 5th, the Provisionals carried out a series of car bomb and incendiary attacks in seven areas of Northern Ireland including Belfast, Londonderry and Lisburn. The attacks caused serious damage to property and minor injuries to a many people.

On the 9th, Thomas McElwee (23), one of the Ballymena bombers responsible for the death of Yvonne Dunlop, died after 62 days on hunger strike. This weekend marked the tenth Anniversary of the introduction of Internment and there were widespread riots in Republican areas. Three people were killed during disturbances over the weekend. One of the deaths was a sectarian killings, by Republicans, one was another baton round death, and the third was committed by a member of the UDR who, for no apparent reason, killed an innocent young man. He was denounced as having brought shame on the Regiment by the Court.

On Monday 10th, Patrick 'Pat' Sheehan, IRA prisoner, joined the hunger strike. Pat Sheehan was born in 1958. At the age of 19, he had been sentenced to 15 years in gaol for IRA activity and had entered the Maze. He is a now a Sinn Féin politician in Northern Ireland. In December 2010, he succeeded Gerry Adams as MLA for Belfast West, Adams having resigned in order to contest the Irish general election, 2011. Sheehan retained the seat for Sinn Féin at the 2011 Assembly election. He provoked anger and controversy by describing the Troubles as "probably quite civilised" and claimed that the IRA "could have left a 1,000 lb car bomb on the Shankill if it wanted to kill Protestants!"

Nationalist areas in Belfast, Londonderry, Strabane, Newry and a whole host of other towns exploded with anger after the latest hunger striker death and, taking advantage of this, a renegade member of the UDR who was off-duty at the time shot and killed a lone Catholic boy as he walked home in the very early hours of the morning, with his girlfriend along Alliance Avenue in the Ardoyne. The off-duty UDR soldier – Brian Roberts who was 34 at the time – who had only been in the regiment for some seven months, was hiding in a derelict building on Etna Drive, when Liam Arthur Canning (19) walked by. Using his service issue personal protection weapon, the soldier shot Mr Canning twice; once in the back and once in the head; he died in hospital a few hours later. He was caught and convicted and sentenced to life imprisonment for the murder and also for three other sectarian shootings which he admitted to in Court. He brought shame to the good name and reputation of the UDR. It is considered highly likely that he was also a member of the UDA/UFF.

Shortly before the murder of Mr Canning, a PIRA ASU took over a house near St Anne's Cathedral in the centre of Belfast. They held the family hostage while they waited for their victim to arrive. Charles Johnston (45), father of two was an executive in the

1   Beresford, David, *Ten Men Dead* (London: Harper Collins, 1994).

travel industry and his office was close by the house chosen by the IRA. Shortly after 0700 hours, Mr Johnston arrived at car park close to Exchange Street and Talbot Street where today the posh St Anne's Apartments are located. It is thought that the gang was under the impression that he was a former police officer, but the man they were after was Mr Johnston's brother. Two gunmen walked up to him and shot him in the head and chest at point-blank range; he died almost immediately.

There was a third person who died that day. During heavy rioting that evening along the Shore Road in North Belfast, Loyalist extremists took advantage of the mayhem and began intimidating Catholic families who lived on the fringes of a Protestant area, at Greencastle, forcing them to leave. One man – Peter McGuinness (41), father of five – was imploring rioters to leave his Bawnmore house alone, when soldiers arrived and mistook him for a rioter. He was hit in the chest by a baton round and died shortly afterwards. This author is convinced that he was an innocent victim of the Troubles and was playing no part in the rioting.

BACK IN BELFAST FOR THE TRIAL
William Clive Hawkins, Royal Regiment of Wales

The term 'stitched up' went round and round in my head; I then realised why not a single person had discussed the matter in all the months since Belfast. I had a heavy sense of betrayal; so much for loyalty and comradeship, the whole platoon must have known what was going on, and decisions that had been changed and made that I was going to get it. Yet no one, not one single person spoke with me; was I alright, did I know what had happened, why I had got the blame, what support was available? Nothing at all was said to me.

I don't remember being informed about the court, the details, day, date, travel arrangements. I just remember boarding a plane at Cardiff Airport accompanied by a very young officer; he stood out a mile because he was over 6ft 2in, fresh faced having never shaved in his life, and looking every bit a 'fresh out of Sandhurst Rupert.' I remember thinking to myself that I would be better off on my own travelling across Belfast, because this guy might as well have been a Martian. As we got off the plane at Belfast Aldergrove airport, I thought to myself that it couldn't possibly get any worse.

Just then, our 'escort' introduced himself and I realised that it could! He was an RMP Corporal, but in the Red Caps all that being a Corporal means is that you completed training and nothing more. He looked about 12; he was armed with a Browning 9-mm and 14 rounds. I really wanted to take his weapon off him; I didn't feel safe at all. He couldn't protect himself let alone three of us. I asked where our car was and it transpired that we had no bulletproof vehicle, just a handpainted bus which appeared to have been 'undercover' in Belfast since 1969! It must have been on the streets so much, that even the IRA's spottiest kid must have known it. I don't remember the journey, just stared at the RMP and resisting the urge to relieve him of his Browning. If I am now a marked man, and remember that two of the dead girl's brothers are in the Maze for murdering a soldier and her father is PIRA, you can appreciate why I felt really deficient in the resource department, to put it fucking politely.

Anyway at some point – I don't remember when or where – Corporal 'RMP Browning pistol' parted company with us. I had grown to hate and despise the back of his head but, my only flimsy link to life had gone. We arrived at the court too early, and the doors were locked, with a huge crowd outside. The tall Rupert looked like a flag in the 18th hole, and anyone anticipating my arrival now knew that I was here. I was convinced he would say that we had a private room through a side entrance; just follow me! But no, this was bad news from start to finish! We stood there for an eternity with our backs to the court door on a one-foot deep step, with the crowd in front of us. Then a woman who was a 'Bet Lynch' looka-like with a bleach blonde beehive hairstyle walked out of the crowd and stood next to me. I waited, hardly able to breathe; for a bullet, a camera flash or for the crowd do go berserk; those minutes on that step took years off my life.

At long last the doors slowly opened, and we all shuffled inside; there was a large foyer with rooms leading off, and it became apparent that the case was being heard in the first room on the right. I was getting more and more anxious and the minutes dragged as a crowd was growing to the right of the courtroom door. They all looked like car salesmen and 60s prostitutes, and then a guy with greasy black hair fixed eyes with me, every time I looked in their direction he was staring. I told the Rupert that if the guy kept staring at me I was going over there to give him a piece of my mind! Rupert promptly replied: "I wouldn't go doing that; it's her father and the family!" I just thought: "You prick; are you trying to get me killed." So I said: "What are we doing stood here then?" He just shrugged and told me that there was nowhere else to go.

Finally, in desperation I stopped an usher and asked for an anteroom, or a side chamber, and with great relief we were ushered off. Twenty minutes or so later another usher came into our room and said to me: "You can go now". So I asked him what had happened and he explained that the Court had decided that it was "justifiable homicide" and that compensation was being discussed. The sacrificial lamb lived another day. I don't remember leaving that court or getting home, I haven't got a clue, in fact I don't remember the journey all the way to the court either. Needless to say, on my return I was posted to another company without explanation. I was just told that I was going to the MT. No good-byes, no farewell do; nothing.

The actual damages awarded to Julie Livingstone's family were £18,500, a substantial increase on the £1,500 which the British Government initially offered. It was never shown exactly who fired the fateful round – Army or RUC – although the debate obscures the death of a young girl who was caught up in the rioting. That the rioting over the death of the hunger striker Francis Hughes was PIRA-inspired and PIRA orchestrated there is no doubt, and they too must bear some of the responsibility for the death. Time and time again, the IRA Army Council sanctioned the turning of residential areas into battlegrounds in order to get at the 'Polis' or the equally hated Brits. The 'Godfathers' of Republicanism must accept some of the blame for the peril under which they placed their communities in general and for the tragic death of Julie Livingstone in particular.

On the 16th, a South Armagh man became one of the 'Disappeared.' Charles Armstrong (54), father of five, left his home in Crossmaglen in order to attend Sunday morning mass. However, he never arrived and the following day, his car was found abandoned in Dundalk across the Irish border. Despite extensive searches by both the RUC and Gardaí, no trace was ever found and repeated appeals to his likely killers, the Provisional IRA, fell on deaf ears. Informed speculation says that the IRA suspected him of being an informer and he was abducted and interrogated before being handed over to the ISU or 'nutting squad.' The IRA may well have realised their mistake shortly afterwards and so as to not alienate their supporter, have always strenuously denied killing Mr Armstrong. But then, as the reader is aware, the Provisional IRA never told lies! His family wrote the following poignant note:

> Charlie was medium in height and roughly 5' 4". He was 54 years old when he disappeared and he had receding brown hair. Charlie was a very pleasant, outgoing man. He was a very talkative person who loved a bit of *craic* with other people and he could be very funny. His hobbies were mainly around animals. He loved horse racing and backing horses; he also loved dogs and caged birds. He was a football fan and enjoyed gardening, decorating and fishing. Charlie's friends would describe him as being very obliging, always willing to help neighbours. Nothing was too much for him to do for other people.

On 30 October, 2010, his body was found buried in a shallow grave in a remote rural area of Co Monaghan in the Irish Republic; he had been shot in the head.[2] To this day, the President of Sinn Féin, Mr Gerry Adams, continues to deny all knowledge of the 'Disappeared' or that he was in any way involved, but anecdotal evidence from the late Brendan Hughes[3] and the late Dolours Price contradict this statement. In February 2010, it was reported by *The Irish News* that Price had offered help to the Independent Commission for the Location of Victims' Remains (ICLVR) in locating graves of three men: Joe Lynskey, Seamus Wright and Kevin McKee, who were allegedly killed by the Provisionals and whose bodies have not been found. She also claimed that Adams had been her OC when she was in the IRA. He has never admitted to being a member of that group, and has of course, denied the allegation. Ms Price admitted to driving the kidnapped Jean McConville, accused by the IRA of being an informer, to the place where she was killed in 1972. She claimed the killing of McConville, a mother of 10, was ordered by Adams. On 24 January 2013, Dolours Price was found dead at her home, but the cause of death is not being investigated by the Gardaí Síochána. She was buried in Milltown Cemetery four days later.

On the 17th, IRA prisoner Jackie McMullan became the 18th man to join the hunger strike. In 1973, aged 17, McMullan joined the IRA's Belfast Brigade where, two years later, he acquired the nickname 'Teapot' after the top of his ear was sheared off when he was shot by soldiers following a PIRA attack on an Army foot patrol. He was arrested in 1976 in possession of a revolver following a gun attack on a RUC base, and remanded to Crumlin Road Gaol charged with attempting to murder police officers. He was sentenced to life in prison in the Maze.

---

2   Sources: http://cain.ulst.ac.uk/issues/violence/disappeared.htm and http://thedisappearedni.co.uk/charlie-armstrong/

3   Moloney, Ed, *Voices from Beyond the Grave: Two Men's War in Ireland* (London: Faber & Faber, 2010).

On the 20th, INLA man Michael Devine (27) died after 60 days on hunger strike; he was serving a long sentence for possession of firearms and attacks on the Security Forces. At that stage, the hunger strike still had 44 days to run but no further hunger strikers would die. There was a further blow for the Provisionals when, on the same day the family of Patrick McGeown, who had been on hunger strike for 42 days, agreed to medical intervention to save his life. At this stage, 10 hunger strikers were dead, three had resumed eating food again and five were still on hunger strike; a further five prisoners would shortly join them.

A by-election was held in Fermanagh / South Tyrone to elect a Member of Parliament to Westminster to the seat that became vacant on the death of Bobby Sands. Owen Carron, who had been Sands' campaign manager, was proposed by Sinn Féin. Carron won the by-election with an increased number of votes over the total achieved by Sands. The SDLP had again decided not to contest the election. Shortly afterwards, having won the Fermanagh / South Tyrone seat for the second time Sinn Féin announced that in future it would contest all Northern Ireland elections.

On the same day as the last hunger striker died, UDR soldier Private David Samuel Whiteside (19) died in an RTA somewhere in the province. The author regretfully has no further details. Over the course of the next nine days, five more soldiers died; one in another RTA, and the others in 'accidental shootings' or in 'circumstances unknown.'

On the 22nd, Sergeant Major Emanuel Mariotti (34) from the Royal Engineers died on duty; the author has no further details, other than to record that he was from Stockport, Cheshire. The following day, Sergeant William Corbett from the Royal Marines (34) was accidentally shot dead at the military wing of the Musgrave Park Hospital. He was from Dundee and was cremated at Dundee Crematorium The author has full details of the death, but has been asked not to make them public; I absolutely respect this and will make no further comment. On the 24th, Lance Corporal Robert Pringle (25) from the RAOC died at his base in Kinnegar, Co Antrim. His death is listed as 'Violent or unnatural causes.' He had celebrated his 25th birthday only 16 days previously. He was from Kirkcaldy in Fife, East Scotland. On the 26th, Private Stephen Humble (19) of the Royal Pioneer Corps was shot in what was thought to be a negligent discharge; no further details of the circumstances have been made public. He was a Sunderland boy and his funeral was held at Bishops Wearmouth Crematorium, in his hometown. Finally the toll of dead soldiers – to circumstances other than terrorism – reached six in nine days, when Private Kevin Andrew Brewer (18) of the Royal Anglian Regiment died in an RTA on the Glenshane Pass, Co Londonderry.

On the 24th, IRA prisoner Bernard Fox, joined the five other hunger strikers in the Maze. He was serving a twelve-year sentence in the Maze Prison for possession of explosives and bombing a hotel. He was from the Falls Road area and joined the IRA in 1969 aged 18. As a result of his IRA activities, Fox was imprisoned on four occasions and spent over 20 years in prison, before being released in 1998 under the terms of the Good Friday Agreement.

On the last day of the month IRA man Hugh Carville also joined the hunger strike. This meant that there were six now on strike and 10 had already died and three had come off. Carville was therefore, the 19th prisoner to begin refusing food.

August had ended and 16 people had died; six of them were soldiers, although none had perished at the hands of a terrorist bullet or bomb, and two policemen had been murdered. Four civilians – three Catholics and one Protestant – had died and two of these deaths were sectarian in nature. Finally four IRA/INLA hunger strikers had died at their own hands. Republicans were responsible for eight of the deaths this month. One must suppose that the Republican paramilitaries assumed that the average Protestant watching the killings would have simply dismissed the carnage by thinking: "Well, it will all be OK, once Ireland is reunited and these people responsible for the killings will became nice politicians!"

21

September

Seonable eptember would see the Provisionals resort to the 'honey trap' again and kill an off-duty soldier. Four soldiers and a staggering five policemen would die during the month. There was another sectarian killing and the IRA's 'nutting squad' was again in action.

On the 1st, a great but short-lived initiative to break down sectarian barriers was introduced to Northern Ireland. The country's first religiously integrated secondary school, Lagan College, opened. The integrated school movement was mainly driven by the desire of parents to have schools which would provide the opportunity for greater cross-community contact among young people.

DUP leader and firebrand preacher Ian Paisley was again in the news when he called for the establishment of a 'third force' along the lines of the disbanded Ulster Special Constabulary (USC) and 'B-Specials.' He envisaged a legal Loyalist paramilitary group which would be used to counter both wings of the IRA as well as splinter groups such as the INLA. To many Loyalists, it seemed a simple solution, but he was trying to turn the clock back 12 years to the days of civil unrest from the Troubles were spawned.

On Friday 4th, the family of Matt Devlin, then on day 52 of his hunger strike, intervened and asked for medical treatment to save his life. A mere two days later, the family of IRA prisoner Laurence McKeown, then on day 70 of his hunger strike, also intervened and asked for medical treatment to save his life. The INLA issued a statement saying that it would not replace men on hunger strike at the same rate as before. At this stage the INLA had only 28 prisoners in the Maze Prison compared to the 380 IRA men inside the Maze. They had previously been contributing one INLA prisoner for every three Provisionals on the hunger strike. A spokesman told South Carolina's *Spartanburg Heralds-Journal*: "We have only 28 protesting prisoners and if we continue to maintain this ratio all our prisoners will be dead within six months." The newspaper's article which had a predictably anti-British stance also quoted Sinn Féin spokesman Richard McAuley as saying: "INLA's decision to scale down its participation was expected and we understand it." There were more voices of dissension, when Cahal Daly, Catholic Bishop of Down and Connor, called on Republican prisoners to end the hunger strike.

On the day that Devlin ended his fast, a soldier from the Royal Irish Rangers was killed in strange circumstances. Ranger Sean Fearon Reilly (19) was from Newtownabbey, Co Antrim; he was home on leave with Fellow Ranger Stephen McCord, in Rathcoole. They apparently found a shotgun close to the Diamond in Rathcoole and were examining it when Stephen McCord pulled the trigger, killing Ranger Fearon.

On the next day – a Saturday – Private Sohan Singh Virdee (20) who was a Sikh, along with another colleague from the Royal Pioneer Corps – Private John Lunt – stationed in the HQNI town of Lisburn were having a night out together. They were approached in the Robin's Nest Bar by two women who told them that they were Protestants and that they were quite safe with them. The women were in fact members of the *Cumann na mBan* – the women's' IRA – and had been instructed to persuade the soldiers to come with them to a party in an area of South Belfast. The journey from Lisburn to Stranmillis is about nine miles, and the four arrived at a flat which the Provisionals had rented some four weeks earlier. En-route, their car – a mini – stalled and one of the girls and Private Virdee walked to the nearby house. Private Lunt stayed with the car but he and the other girl followed shortly afterwards. As the second group entered the house, waiting gunmen opened fire on them from very close range, mortally wounding Private Virdee and seriously injuring the Pioneer. Private Lunt, who was 23 at the time, survived his wounds but Sohan Virdee died at the scene. At the later court trial, as reported in *The Belfast Telegraph*, John Lunt said:

> I walked in and sat down next to Virdee. We were sitting on the settee a matter of seconds when the door in front of us burst open and two figures came in with handguns and started shooting. They held the guns in a two-handed grip. I put my hands up and felt slight pains. They ran out of the door and another man came in and fired a few more shots. I think I was hit once or twice and fell back on the floor.

The soldier then told the court hearing that he spent seven days in the Intensive care Unit of the RVH. He was able to give the RUC a detailed description one of the women and picked her out at an identification parade in May of the following year.

Two Belfast women – Alice Martha Taylor who was 22 and Maureen Teresa O'Neill from the Falls and New Lodge areas respectively – were tried for murder under the 'Thompson Rule'. This was applied to those conspiring or actually committing a terrorist murder in Ulster during the Troubles. If the accused had carried the weapons, disposed of them afterwards, provided a stolen car or conspired in any way, they were as guilty as the actual gunman or bomber. This was the third time which the Provisionals had success-fully used the 'honey trap' and Private Virdee was the seventh fatality of such a tactic.

The 7th of the month fell on a Monday. On this day, two more RUC officers were killed by Republican terrorists. A two-vehicle RUC patrol from Pomeroy was dispatched to investigate another suspicious fire, this time in a forest near Cappagh, Co Tyrone, approximately 10 miles north of the Irish border. In the leading vehicle as they returned to Ballygawley were two very young constables, Mark Evans (20) and Stuart Montgomery (18). Approximately two miles from Cappagh, and close to the home of dead hunger striker Martin Hurson, a watching PIRA bombing crew, hidden on the nearby hillside triggered a massive culvert bomb as the lead vehicle passed over it. The device obliterated the vehicle, killing both officers absolutely instantly. The explosion was so powerful, that it left a crater 50' wide and 5' deep. One of the shattered bodies was found over 100 yards away. The RUC Roll of Honour confirms that Constable Montgomery was the youngest policeman to die in the Troubles. He was on his first day of duty after finishing training. Two IRA members were arrested, but charges were withdrawn after two prosecution witnesses were threatened by the Provisionals.

Also on the 7th, IRA gunman and Maze prisoner, John Pickering joined the hunger strike. He was serving a 26-year sentence for the murder of an RUC officer in an ambush.

He was to last for 27 days; after he joined, only two more prisoners would follow him as the strike ended on 3 October.

On the 12th, the Provisionals targeted and killed an off-duty UDR soldier as he walked through the town centre of Maghera, Co Londonderry. Private Alan Clarke (20) who was a full-time soldier lived in Upperlands in the town. As he walked along Hall Street, he was being watched by two men in a parked car on the opposite side of the road. It pulled into the road and drew level with him; as it did so, a gunman fired three rounds from an American Armalite into his body from close range, mortally wounding him. The car raced off and passers-by rushed to the dying man's aid. He managed to gasp a few words before he lost consciousness and died. *Lost Lives* records that one of the pall-bearers at his funeral was RUCR Constable John Proctor, who himself was shot dead by the IRA on the same day as the funeral.[1]

On the 13th, Humphrey Atkins, stood down as Secretary of State for Northern Ireland, and was appointed as deputy Foreign Secretary. James 'Jim' Prior who had been Margaret Thatcher's Secretary of State for Employment from May 1979 to 14 September 1981 was appointed to replace him. Just three days later, he flew to Northern Ireland and went to the Maze Prison where he had a three-hour meeting with those on hunger strike. During his previous role at Employment, it is widely considered that he had angered the right wing of the Tories, as well as Thatcher herself, for not pressing far enough with anti-trade union legislation. He stayed at the NIO until September 1984.

On the 14th, a baby boy with the surname Proctor was born in the Mid-Ulster Hospital in Magherafelt, Co Londonderry; although his proud father visited him, he would never get to know his father, as cowards were waiting for him in the hospital car park and shot him from behind. RUCR officer John Proctor (25), father of two, had a day of mixed emotions. He had attended the funeral of his UDR friend, Alan Clarke who was murdered by the IRA two days earlier and then he had attended the maternity wing at the hospital, to see his wife and newborn son. As he arrived, he had clearly been dicked after a possible leak of information from an IRA sympathiser on the hospital staff. Before the author is accused of slander, there are documented cases of Republican sympathisers who conspired to cause deaths while employed at both the Royal Victoria Hospital and the Musgrave Park Hospital in Belfast. Constable Proctor was shot in the back of the head as he returned to his car in the hospital car park. Mrs Procter named her child after her dead husband and called his killers "filthy cowards." *Lost Lives* includes her full moving quotation which includes the following eloquent words: "They may think that they are heroes but every decent person knows them for what they really are. They shot him in the back without giving him a chance."[2] These moving words merely serve to reinforce this author's lack of sympathy for the 10 dead hunger strikers.

In 2013, a man was sentenced to at least 20 years for the RUCR man's killing. Seamus Martin Kearney, 57, of Gorteade Road, Maghera, denied murder and possessing an Armalite AR15 rifle. However, although convicted, under the terms

---

1   Thornton, David, Seamus Kelters, Brian Feeney and David McKittrick. *Lost Lives: The Stories of the Men, Women and Children who Died as a Result of the Northern Ireland Troubles.* (Edinburgh: Mainstream, 1999, revised ed. 2007).

2   *Lost Lives*, p.878.

of the Good Friday Agreement, Kearney will serve about two years. The murder was investigated following a review by the Historical Enquiries Team; Kearney was charged with murder.

Judge David McFarland told a court in Belfast: "This has to be one of the most appalling murders committed during that period in our history that has become known as the Troubles. The passage of 30 years has in no way diminished the brutality of this murder. That a man can be targeted when he is attending a hospital to visit his wife and newly born son continues to appal all right-minded members of society." Prior to publication of this book, Kearney failed to have the verdict overturned at the Court of Appeal.

On the 14th, Gerard Hodgkins became the 22nd – and penultimate – prisoner to join the hunger strike. He was a member of the IRA convicted of possessing a firearm and attempted robbery in 1976. He was arrested along with Eamon McConvey and both were sentenced to 12 years.

I do believe that Thatcher wanted the strike to end but she could not be seen to weaken in the face of Sinn Féin/PIRA pressure. The following statement from the British Government was made in order to try and persuade the hunger strikers to end their fasts:

When the hunger strike and the protest is brought to an end (and not before), the Government will:

I. Extend to all male prisoners in Northern Ireland the clothing regime at present available to female prisoners in Armagh Prison (i.e. subject to the prison governor's approval);

II. Make available to all prisoners in Northern Ireland the allowance of letters, parcels and visits at present available to conforming prisoners;

III. allow the restoration of forfeited remission at the discretion of the responsible disciplinary authority, as indicated in my statement of 30 June, which hitherto has meant the restoration of up to one-fifth of remission lost subject to a satisfactory period of good behaviour;

IV. ensure that a substantial part of the work will consist of domestic tasks inside and outside the wings necessary for servicing of the prison (such as cleaning and in the laundries and kitchens), constructive work, e.g. on building projects or making toys for charitable bodies, and study for Open University or other courses. The prison authorities will be responsible for supervision. The aim of the authorities will be that prisoners should do the kinds of work for which they are suited, but this will not always be possible and the authorities will retain responsibility for decisions about allocation.

3. Little advance is possible on association. It will be permitted within each wing, under supervision of the prison staff.

4. Protesting prisoners have been segregated from the rest. Other prisoners are not segregated by religious or any other affiliation. If there were no protest the only reason for segregating some prisoners from others would be the judgment of

the prison authorities, not the prisoners, that this was the best way to avoid trouble between groups.

5. This statement is not a negotiating position. But it is further evidence of the Government's desire to maintain and where possible to improve a humanitarian regime in the prisons. The Government earnestly hopes that the hunger strikers and the other protesters will cease their protest.

Many brave members of Ulster's divided society – Catholics as well as Protestants – wanted to give something back to their communities and joined the RUC Reserve (RUCR). Like those part-time members of the UDR, they had daytime jobs but gave up their spare time to help police the country. One such RUCR was Silas Lyttle. Through the day he worked as a shopkeeper in Ballygawley, Co Tyrone, but on an evening and a weekend, donned the bottle-green uniform of the RUC. On the evening of the 18th, he locked up his shop as usual and started to walk home, but as he entered his garden, masked gunmen, who had hidden behind a hedge, jumped out. They shot him several times, badly wounding him before running to their stolen car and driving off. He was rushed to hospital but died some seven weeks later on 17 November.[3]

On the 19th, a roving UVF murder gang cruised along the Nationalist area around Belfast's Ormeau Road looking for a known IRA member to kill. Thwarted by the presence of RUC patrols, they abandoned their objectives, and began to drive back towards the north of the city. However, just before midnight, they saw a lone man walking along the Ormeau Road and decided that 'any Taig will do.' They tried to persuade him to come over to their car where they intended to shoot him but the man was wise enough to run away. They drove on and saw another man, local Barber Eugene Mulholland (25) and the father of two very young children. This time they took no chances and as they pulled alongside him, a passenger shot him three times; he was mortally wounded and fell dying in the street. The cowards then drove off leaving him lying in a pool of blood. *Lost Lives* states that his UVF killers were also responsible for the later sectarian murders of Mary McKay (the following month), John O'Neill[4] and Joseph Donegan. [5]

On the 21st, James Devine, IRA prisoner, joined the hunger strike; he was the 23rd and final Maze prisoner to do so. He would last only 13 days, as the Provisionals called off the strike on the 3rd of October. Devine was Glasgow-born but his parents moved to Strabane when he was a child. He joined the IRA in 1976; in September 1978 he was arrested and charged with various gun and bomb attacks and held on remand for 16 months, and then in January 1979 he was sentenced to ten years' imprisonment. On the day that he joined the hunger strike, the Social Democratic and Labour Party (SDLP), hitherto a passive and non-critical supporter, made an announcement which was openly critical of the campaign.

On or about the 23rd, Catholic priest Father Denis Faul, publicly appealed to the loved ones of Liam McCloskey and Bernard Fox to intervene and save their lives. After visiting the hospital, he warned that not only Liam McCloskey, but Bernard Fox, was

---

3   See Chapter 23.
4   See Chapter 33.
5   See Chapter 34.

entering a critical phase. He said Liam McCloskey was going blind and that Bernard Fox was in danger of suffering kidney failure due to his inability to hold down sufficient water. Father Faul was tireless in his efforts to bring an end to the hunger strikes and – although he fundamentally disagreed with Cardinal Hulme's assertion[6] that the strikes were tantamount to suicide – he tried to bring them to an end. Martin Dillon, in his evocative book, speaks of Father Faul's efforts to talk to the strikers and persuade them that their sacrifice was enough. He writes: "The battle between Faul and the Provisionals was bitter. Every time the priest met a hunger striker to persuade him to cease, members of Sinn Féin were present who read letters of support from relatives. Faul reckons that many of these letters were forgeries 'written somewhere on the Falls Road.'"[7]

The next day, Bernard Fox, then on day 32 of his hunger strike, ended his fast, as his condition had deteriorated quickly and Sinn Féin panicked and announced that he was "dying too quickly". On the 26th, another hunger striker – INLA man Liam McCloskey, then on his 55th day – ended his fast. McCloskey's family had said that they would call for medical intervention to save his life if he became unconscious. Liam McCloskey was close to death in the Maze Hospital wing, when his mother came to him and said told him that he was wasting his life. So he took himself off the fast and was put on life support equipment. A few weeks later, as he was recovering, he was apparently reading a Bible in his cell and he reportedly said: "I've come to the conclusion, reading that Bible, that I either have to follow the IRA or I have to follow Jesus Christ." By all accounts, he became a born-again Christian.

With this action, it meant that there were just six hunger strikers continuing their protest. The men were: Patrick Sheehan, Jackie McMullan, Hugh Carville, John Pickering, Gerard Hodgkins and James Devine; all were members of the Provisional IRA.

The final five days of September witnessed a death-a-day as five more lives were ended prematurely. Late on the evening that the INLA prisoner, McCloskey ended his strike, Constable George Stewart (34) was enjoying a point at his girlfriend's pub in the small town of Killough, Co Down. The town is just 20 miles from the Irish border and sits in a small, picturesque harbour off the Irish Sea. At around 2230 hours, two IRA members entered the pub and walked over to where Constable Stewart – dressed in civilian clothing – was chatting at the bar; they pulled out pistols and shot him the head and back from extremely close range, killing him instantly. They ran out of the pub and jumped into a stolen car parked outside and drove off into the night. He was the fourth policeman to be killed that month.

That same evening and 70 miles to the north of Killough, an innocent Protestant died at the hands of the UVF. David Smyth (24), the father of a young child, was drinking with a friend who was a part-time soldier in the UDR at a UDA club in Greenisland, close to Belfast Lough. The UDR soldier was drunk and pulled out his personal protection handgun and discharged several rounds into the air. This was witnessed by some UVF members in the club and they attempted to take the weapon from him to add to their own armoury. They knocked the soldier unconscious with a hammer and grabbed

---

6   From 1979 Hume served also as President of the Catholic Bishops' Conference of England and Wales, and
     held these appointments until his death from cancer in 1999.
7   Dillon, Martin, *God and the Gun* (London: Orion Books, 1997), pp.91–2.

the gun; Mr Smyth attempted to prevent this and was stabbed to death by the UVF gang. On 6 October, the gang used the stolen gun in a robbery attempt but were caught at the scene by the RUC. The gun was then traced back to the murder of Mr Smyth and the gang were later convicted of his murder.

On the 27th, Anthony Braniff (27), father of three, went voluntarily to the IRA's ISU and was interrogated by them somewhere in the Falls Road area. He had been earlier arrested by RUC Special Branch and was taken to Castlereagh for questioning. It would appear that pressure was put on him to act as an informer, given his location in Etna Drive in the heart of the Nationalist Ardoyne area. He had apparently agreed to do so, in order to gain his release. When he returned home, he reported what had happened to the local PIRA commander and was charged with being an informer. Somewhat staggeringly, the 'kangaroo court' found him guilty and he was executed by a shot in the back of the head and his body was dumped in Odessa Street in the Clonards area just off the falls Road. The Braniff family, who also lost another member when David Braniff was murdered by the UVF eight years later, campaigned to prove that he wasn't an informer. Finally, on 23 September 2003, in a statement released through *An Phoblacht,* the Provisionals admitted that they were wrong and that Mr Braniff was not an informer. They said:

> Following requests from the family of Anthony Braniff, the IRA has conducted a lengthy investigation into the circumstances surrounding his death. On 27 September 1981, Anthony Braniff, a Volunteer in the IRA, was executed in Belfast. Our investigation has found no evidence to support the claims made at the time that Anthony Braniff was responsible for passing information concerning the location of arms dumps and the movement of Volunteers and that he met his Special Branch contacts regularly... while receiving, in return, sums of money. Our investigation has established the following: During a period of interrogation in Castlereagh, Anthony Braniff agreed to work for Special Branch. Upon release he reported what he had done to the IRA. He was charged with a breach of General Army Orders and court martialled. He pleaded guilty to the charge. He was sentenced to death. No appeal was lodged against the sentence. The IRA accepts that proper procedure was not adhered to in relation to the process of appeal.

There was a postscript to this when the Braniff family, again through that *esteemed organ* of the IRA (author's own italics) *An Phoblacht,* somewhat sickeningly announced: "On behalf of the entire Braniff family, we would like to express our sincere gratitude to the Republican Movement and the present day leadership."

On Sunday 27th, Garret FitzGerald, the new Taoiseach gave an interview on Irish State Television, RTE where he set out his vision for a new Republic of Ireland in what became known as his 'constitutional crusade'. The central core of his ideas was to make the Republic of Ireland a society where the majority ethos would be expressed in a way so as to not alienate Protestants living in Northern Ireland. In short, the Republic was weakening the dogmatic links with the past and not demanding that the North be returned to them. This has been the one thing which Republicans claimed 'legitimised' their violent campaign to reunite the island of Ireland.

The day after, the Provisionals killed another RUC officer, this time launching a Soviet-made and supplied RPG-7 in an attack in a residential area of West Belfast. The RPG-7 is a portable, unguided, shoulder-launched, anti-tank rocket-propelled grenade launcher; it has a muzzle velocity of 445' per second. Its effective range is 200 yards and it self detonates on impact. On the 28th, a mobile RUC patrol was driving along Glen Road in the Andersonstown area and had slowed down at the junction with Suffolk Road close to Donegal Celtic's football ground. As it did so, a PIRA Volunteer thought to have been located in or close to Hannahglen Heights, fired an RPG-7 at the vehicle. It detonated and Constable Alexander Beck (37), father of two was killed absolutely instantly and another colleague lost both legs. One of the men charged, but later released, in connection with the attack was Danny McCann who was killed by the SAS in Gibraltar on 6 March, 1988 along with Sean Savage and Mairead Farrell.

On the second day of the 1981 British Labour party's annual conference, a motion was passed committing the party to 'campaign actively' for a United Ireland by consent. This was the party of Michael Foot, defeated by Margaret Thatcher in 1979, and which was turning in on itself with internecine squabbles and recriminations. It had made a savage turn to the left and had alienated much of the moderate wing. Moderates such as former Home Secretary Roy Jenkins, former Foreign Secretary David Owen and Shirley Williams, formerly Secretary of State for Education, all of whom had served in the Callaghan Government of 1976–79, would shortly tear the party in two and defect to a new alliance. There was little wonder, that given the state of the Labour Party, that it would support the notion of a united Ireland. The author is a life-long supporter of the Labour Party but, given their childish arguments and the insensitivity of this motion in the light of the appalling attack at Glen Road only hours earlier, was disgusted and sickened by their actions.

September which had turned into a bloody month was not yet over, and on the 29th, INLA gunmen murdered a part-time soldier in the UDR at his place of work. Private Mark Stockman (20) worked at Mackies factory on the Springfield Road in Belfast and was enjoying lunch with his workmates. One of the gunmen was Gerard Steenson – who unfortunately still had over five years left to live and five years in which to demonstrate his psychopathic tendencies – and he and another gunmen opened fire on the group of workers. Mark Stockman was badly wounded and fell to the floor, while another man was wounded and he too slumped to the ground. Steenson then stood over the helpless body of the UDR man and shot him several more times at very close range; he died within seconds. Mark 'C', a fellow UDR soldier, pointed out in an interview with the author, that he and Mark Stockman went to the same secondary school as did another murdered UDR man, Colin Quinn.[8]

September ended with the deaths of 12 people; four soldiers and five police officers died during the month as well as three civilians. Of the civilians, two were Catholic and there was one Protestant. One of the killings was overtly sectarian. Republican terrorists were responsible for nine of the 12 deaths in September.

---

8   See Chapter 12.

22

October

This was the month in which the hunger strike came to an end; it was the month that 13 people died – three of them soldiers – and it was the month in which the Provisionals once again turned their attention to England and three people died in bombs in central London.

On Saturday 3th and Sunday 4th of October, the hunger strike ended. Ten had starved to death inside the Maze and over 60 people had been killed outside of those high, barbed-wire topped walls. Republican prisoners issued a statement blaming pressure on their families as the reason for the ending of the hunger strike. A Sinn Féin spokesman said: "Mounting pressure and cleric-inspired demoralisation led to family interventions and five strikers have been taken off their fast."

So that early October weekend saw the hunger strike finally came to an end; 10 men had lost their lives and upwards of 60 people, mostly civilians had died in the upsurge of violence and Nationalist anger which followed each striker's death, as surely as night follows day. Thirteen others had joined the strike between 14 May and 21 September, all prepared to die for their five demands. In the end, the demands were met either in part or totally; but gradually, bit by bit. Prime Minister Thatcher was seen as the victor in what many saw as a pyrrhic, or meaningless victory. From her perspective, she had not been seen to weaken, if anything her hand had been strengthened as she was seen as a powerful leader, resolute and courageous.

The Republicans had misjudged her and felt that she would cave in to their emotional blackmail, as well might a James Callaghan or a vacillating Harold Wilson. She was firm and laid out her stall and stuck to her guns. But she too, misjudged the Provisionals and the INLA; she didn't think for a second that they would allow 10 of their top men to die in a bid to gain all of their demands. She was also seen as uncaring, as intransigent and even criminally obstinate, although not by this author one hastens to add. In the end, once she had refused their demands and the strikers began to die, one by one and more were willing to take the places of the dead, she was backed into a corner. Even had any emotional instincts superseded her resoluteness, she was not quite able to back down; at first, nor would the Republicans; people were dying inside and outside the Maze as political impasse ensued. Thatcher's dilemma was that she wanted to be known, in the vernacular of the time, as a 'bad arse', but she was also not so stupid as to be unaware of what this intransigence was producing. It was producing another generation of Brit-haters among the children of the Nationalist ghettos as well as among even decent Irish men and women.

The crescendo of deaths which followed cannot be laid solely at the door of Thatcher and, in my opinion, the blame rests with both the evil men of PIRA who manipulated the hunger strikers and also with the British Prime Minister who failed to recognise that there would be a price to pay for her stance. I support her resolution and refusal to negotiate with terrorists but I do feel that a small compromise might have saved lives inside and outside the Maze. If PIRA had been serious about negotiating with Thatcher instead of trying to blackmail her, and if they had wished to save the lives of their men in the Maze, would they have continued to escalate their offensive on the streets of the Province? But as the death toll mounted, it became a case of which one would blink first. That person was never going to be Margaret Thatcher.

Stevie, UDR
She, or at least her back-room fixers, were working to get a deal of some sort out of the strike. She was a year or more off a general election and needed something to boost her chances; luckily the Falklands War came along and did that job for her.

The British press hailed the hunger strike as a triumph for the Prime Minister, with The Guardian newspaper stating that: "The Government had overcome the hunger strikes by a show of resolute determination not to be bullied." However, the hunger strike was a pyrrhic victory for Thatcher and she became a Republican hate figure. Danny Morrison described her as "the biggest bastard we have ever known!" There soon followed condemnation from some countries, especially the freedom-fighter-besotted USA, and the relationship between Britain and Ireland remained a strained one, certainly until the mid-1990s. Moreover, as with other seminal moments from the Troubles such as Internment, 'Bloody Sunday' et al., recruitment into PIRA and the INLA received a massive boost and even more Irish-Americans were willing to dig deeply into their pockets for the NORAID collection tins. US Customs officials were more willing to turn a blind eye to arms smuggling into Ireland. Like those two aforementioned seminal moments, there was an upsurge of violence after the comparatively quiet years of the late 1970s.

What of the 13 who survived – how did life treat them post-strike? Thirteen others began refusing food, but were taken off hunger strike, either due to medical reasons or after intervention by their families, or by the calling off of the protest. Many of them still suffer from the effects of the strike, with problems including digestive, visual, physical and neurological disabilities. Some are now in politics; others have left the movement, but all will remember the desperate days when their lives hung in the balance. Many now seem to revel in the 'heroic' sobriquet of 'former hunger striker' and it will always get them an additional cheer, when they turn up to make a speech or a wet eye or two, when they describe their time as a prisoner of the 'oppressive Brits'. Today, IRA 'veterans' of what they term the 'struggle', are unhappy with what they now see and hear from Gerry Adams and many of them now view Adams' machinations as 'betrayal'.

Mick 'Benny' Hill, Royal Anglians
On thinking more about the hunger strikes, the stance of the Roman Catholic Church was puzzling. Suicide is (supposedly) a mortal sin, which should result in excommunication, yet the Church at best condoned the strikes, and, at worst, was strictly ambivalent. That always was a puzzle to me. But then, what do I know? I was just your average, non-believing squaddie.

Several towns and cities in France subsequently named streets after Bobby Sands, including Paris and Le Mans, and the Iranian Government also named a street running alongside the British Embassy in Tehran after Bobby Sands, which was formerly called Winston Churchill Street. A memorial to the men who died in the Irish Rebellion of 1798, the Easter Rising and the hunger strike stands in Waverley Cemetery, Sydney, Australia. The British were seen as the oppressors, but those ignorant of world affairs and whose knowledge does not stretch beyond the coastlines of their own countries, can have little understanding of the war that was ongoing against terror in part of the UK at this time, or that Thatcher had to be a '*bastard*' in order to help combat that terror.

Interestingly, the writer Martin Dillon had this to say about the British Prime Minister, who died in April, 2013: "Lady Thatcher's personal crusade against terrorism obscured the problems within the security forces and tainted her political judgement. She did not defeat terrorism, despite all her promises, and left no meaningful political legacy for Northern Ireland."[1]

There have been, of late, revisionists who have taken a different stance on the hunger strikes, and in 2005, the role of Gerry Adams was questioned by former prisoner Richard O'Rawe, who was the public relations officer inside the Maze during the strike. O'Rawe states in his book *Blanketmen* that Adams prolonged the strike as it was of great political benefit to Sinn Féin.[2] Certainly, it kept funds coming in from the USA and other countries where there are large Irish émigré populations. I believe that the strings of the hunger strikers were pulled by the leaders of their movement and while people like 'Bic' MacFarlane were genuinely moved by each death, I believe that they, as an organisation became less moved by each subsequent death. The propaganda value around the world, particularly in their 'spiritual' home of the USA was tremendous, as witnessed by the public outcries in many other countries. The hunger strike proved useful to the IRA as it portrayed their convicted members who chose not to take food as POWs; further, it portrayed the Maze as a 'concentration camp'. It was good for their image both at home and abroad and it guaranteed that Irish-Americans, Irish-Canadians and Irish-Australians would weep into their pints of *Guinness* and force them to dig deeper into their pockets. It would guarantee that their tears would continue to flow as they belted out the words to '*The Men Behind the Wire*'. Sinn Féin is extremely skilful at playing the 'Irish sympathy card' and manipulating the international press, in order to whip up the frenzy of hatred for the British and support for their own movement.

Richard O'Rawe wrote tellingly:

And so I wrote my first book, *Blanketmen*, in which I said that the British Government had made an offer to end the hunger strike in the days before the fifth hunger striker, Joe McDonnell, died. (At the request of those involved in creating the archive I did not reveal Boston College's role in my journey to writing the book.) I added that the offer, communicated to Bik McFarlane during a prison visit, had been accepted by Bik and myself because it meant we could end the fast with honour. And I described how a committee, headed by Gerry Adams, had

---

1   Dillon, Martin, *25 Years of Terror: IRA's War Against the British* (London: Bantam Books, 1998), p.257.
2   O'Rawe, Richard, *Blanketmen: An Untold Story of the H-Block Hunger Strike* (Dublin: New Island Books, 2005).

rejected this offer, despite the prison leadership having endorsed it. The message came in a terse comm smuggled into the gaol which said that he was 'surprised' that we had accepted the offer and that it did not validate the loss of the first four hunger strikers' lives.

I can sum up in a single sentence the question my book posed to Gerry Adams and his colleagues on the committee: Why had they turned down a deal that we, the prisoners' leaders, had approved and which would have saved the lives of six of our comrades? The book's publication caused ructions, with defenders of the committee lining up in the media to attack me. Ed Moloney had advised me against publication, saying that I would be savaged those who supported the Gerry Adams/Sinn Féin leadership. He had been right. But I stood firm behind what I knew to be true. Simply put, I had nowhere else to go.

From the start, those shouting the loudest in defence of the committee, principally Bik and Danny Morrison, were in opposite corners. While Bik publicly said there had been no British offer 'whatsoever', Danny, a committee member, said there had been an offer and it 'was a better offer than that which the Irish Commission for Justice and Peace (a body which tried to mediate between the parties) believed they had secured.' These two positions are irreconcilable and indicative of the malaise that infected the committee's position. Of fundamental importance is Danny's contention that the prison leadership and the hunger strikers ran the fast, and not the committee.

The irony in this whole saga is that it is Maggie Thatcher, speaking from beyond the grave, who has now proved to be the decisive voice. Upon her death in April 2013, her private papers were published and they showed that the hunger strikers – by the force of their sheer courage – had broken her resolve. Amongst her documents is a copy of a letter that is also in the Brendan Duddy files (dated 11.30pm 6 July 1981) entitled HUNGER STRIKE: MESSAGE TO BE SENT THROUGH THE CHANNEL. The substance of the offer is outlined in this message. Notably, the message contains amendments to the offer in Margaret Thatcher's own hand-writing. Undoubtedly Thatcher's amendments would have been incorporated in the final text that was sent to the committee (minus her handwritten notes, of course). The question therefore arises: why would Thatcher bother to amend a text if she never intended it to be read by those with whom her government were negotiating?'[3]

The dissension continued when an unnamed former Maze prisoner made the following comments in the Derry Journal on 19 June 2009, dealing with an apparently secret offer made by the Government which promised to consider some of the issues relating to the five demands. The unnamed prisoner wrote:

I was in that wing with Bik and Richard at the time and I had previously shared a cell with Bobby Sands there. As anyone who was on the protest would know I also shared a cell in H4 with Tom McElwee and we remained close friends. Tom gave

---

3   Source: http://thebrokenelbow.com/2013/05/03/thatchers-archive-finally-settles-dispute-over-hunger-strike-deal-says-ira-prison-leader

me his rosary beads before he went on hunger strike and I still have them today. This leaves us with the question why weren't the hunger strikers themselves fully informed of these developments? In a comm to Gerry Adams dated 7.7.81 (which is reproduced in the book *Ten Men Dead*) 'Bic' (MacFarlane) said that he told the hunger strikers that parts of the offer were vague and the only concrete aspect seemed to be clothes and in no way was this good enough to satisfy us.

Surely four of the five demands amounted to a lot more than a vague offer and contained a lot more than just clothes? Not only that, the INLA members who were on hunger strike and their representatives stated they were never made aware of any offers from the British that contained what amounted to four demands. Gerard Hodgkins, who was also on hunger strike and a member of the IRA, also publicly stated this.

As well as all this Bik told the hunger strikers on Tuesday 28.7.81 that: "I could have accepted half measures before Joe died, but I didn't then and wouldn't now." What he failed to say was that these half measures contained four of the five demands as I've already pointed out.

The hunger strike eventually fell apart after the families started taking the men off the hunger strikes when they lapsed into unconsciousness. Yet three days after it ended, James Prior implemented four of the five demands.[4]

Indeed, Martin Dillon quotes a former Provisional whom he names as 'Sean' when he speaks of his disillusionment over Adams and Sinn Féin's role in the eventually abortive hunger strike: '*He* [Sean] *felt that the IRA could have called it off earlier, that the men had lost their lives in vain....the organisation had exploited the hunger strike for political gain.*'[5] The former terrorist stated that he felt that Sinn Féin/IRA were now turning their attention towards the political arena and that the way forward was through politics. The sacrifice of the 10 prisoners focused the world's attention nicely on the organisation's political credibility.

Stevie, UDR

It was a draw; neither gained much but both gained something, and it was the beginning of the politicisation of the struggle, something Adams and co were aiming toward. HMG made the valid point that they were willing to allow Nationalist young men to die for their cause if they wanted to, something their mothers were not keen on. It also established machinery for negotiations with Sinn Féin. For myself, I was down in the lower depths of Co Fermanagh at the time of Sands' death; it came over the net at about 0230-ish. We were literally right on the border, watching a part-time UDR man's farm and thought we were going to have the shit thrown at us; we could not have been more wrong. The border was dead; it was all going on in the cities.

The ten men who died were undoubtedly brave and it takes much courage to forcibly starve oneself to death; man's instinct is to eat, drink and be merry and to voluntarily

---

4   Source: http://www.derryjournal.com/news/letters/hunger-strike-we-need-closure-1-2138612
5   Dillon, *25 Years of Terror*, p.210.

refuse life's sustenance cannot be easy. The comradeship of the men's last days together in the Maze hospital wing cannot be underestimated, but let us not get too weepy-eyed about these men. Yes, let us remember their bravery but let us not forget one salient factor. These men were convicted terrorists; they were dedicated to removing Northern Ireland from the United Kingdom and they did not care how that was achieved. They were prepared to shoot and bomb their way to achieving this; they turned their communities into battlefields and a major proportion of the 1,781 people killed by the Provisional IRA between 1970 and 2004 were civilian. They killed at least 621 innocent civilians according to Cain, as well as executing between 60 and 100 of their own people. They orphaned well over 2,000 children and they spread terror through many communities by their ruthless choice of terror. Let us not forget that they murdered people in their own homes and beds, shot men down in front of their terrified wives and children and even murdered inside and outside churches. Let us not forget also that they murdered inside hospitals and even exploded a bomb in the Musgrave Park Hospital which involved a member of the hospital staff carrying a primed bomb through a children's ward.

One of the men who died on hunger strike was Francis Hughes who was suspected of killing upwards of a dozen members of the Security Forces; one of them, Kevin Lynch took part in 'punishment' shootings; another, Martin Hurson, tried on several occasions to kill soldiers. Remember also that Seamus McElwee planted an incendiary bomb in a boutique in Ballymena which burned a woman to death as her child listened outside to her screams of agony. Many PIRA apologists point to Bobby Sands and his 'innocence' and state that he never killed anyone and that all he did was to: 'cause an explosion and to be caught in possession of a pistol.' Do these apologists not realise that this 'angel-faced' terrorist would have had no compunction in using that pistol had he been forced to? Do they not realise that the bomb he helped place at Balmoral Furniture in Dunmurry could have killed innocent people, and that other bombs his comrades placed did? Whenever this author becomes teary-eyed at the sacrifice of the 10, all he needs do is turn to a certain photograph. That photograph shows the scene after a PIRA bombing outrage in Donegal Street in Belfast on 20 March 1972. A young Para – Lance Corporal Wayne Evans – is shown cradling a young woman who has been seriously injured by the PIRA bomb blast which killed six and injured over 100. He is covering her eyes, desperately trying to avoid her seeing that both of her legs have been blown off. This is why I personally will not shed a tear over the 10 who died on hunger strike. To all those 'plastic Paddies' who sing 'The Fields of Athenry' or 'The Wearing of the Green' in their Irish bars along the Eastern seaboard of the US or in pubs in Sydney and Melbourne and Brisbane, I want you to look carefully into Wayne Evans' eyes and tell me that you are comfortable singing about Bobby Sands; or are you so steeped in your hatred of the English that you can dismiss that look?

Low lie the Fields of Athenry
Where once we watched the small free birds fly.
Our love was on the wing we had dreams and songs to sing
It's so lonely 'round the Fields of Athenry.

Now go and sing that to the loved ones of the 306 RUC officers or 18 Prison Officers or 1,300 soldiers or to children of all those murdered by the Provisionals or by the OIRA or by the INLA. Go sing those words to the families of the women who were shopping in Belfast City Centre, or drinking coffee in the Abercorn restaurant when PIRA bombs exploded; sing the '*The Fields of Athenry*' to the families of those killed in the slaughter at Protestant bars such as the Bayardo or the Mountainview Tavern. To my critics, please do not lose sight of my equal detestation of the Loyalist paramilitaries who did the self-same thing to innocent Catholics. I do not reserve my opprobrium for Republican terrorists, and condemn equally the Loyalist psychopaths who revelled in the death of a man, woman or a child simply on the grounds that they were of the Catholic faith.

A former soldier told the author:
It was alright for those people in America, Canada, Australia, France etc where Brit-bashing is considered good sport; but they never suffered from IRA bombs or shootings. They never lived in fear of a bomb in their local railway station or in their local pub. It is easy to get all romantic about what they saw as 'urban guerrillas' and the like because they never had to endure it. I have seen the results of an IRA bomb in London, because I was at Hyde Park when an IRA car bomb blew up the soldiers from the Blues and Royals and their horses. I was in Belfast when they shot two UDR lads and I saw their lifeless bodies under bloodstained white sheets. I comforted a mate when he had his leg blown off and I saw how white his face was and how scared he looked. The Provisionals were terrorists, pure and simple and when I get told by Americans and some Aussies – usually because they are called O'Brien or some such shit – that they supported the IRA, I just think: what the fuck do you know?

I once got told by a loud-mouthed Aussie who had never left his sun-soaked country and was some sort of armchair expert on the world, that it was our fault because we 'invaded Ireland.' I told him about one of my tours of Londonderry and he interrupted me and told me that it wasn't called Londonderry; it was Derry! I lost two mates who were over there ensuring that the name of the city stayed as Londonderry. I read about French and German students chanting 'Victory to the IRA' and I just laughed and thought what the hell do they know? When the Muslims bombed New York on September 11, 2001, I grieved for the innocent dead but I felt deep down that they have supported terrorism for all of these years and now it has come back to bite them on the bum. Poetic justice? I'm not sure, but it might one day make them wake up from this dream world in which they seem to exist. I'm knocking on these days and my pension beckons me, but I know one thing: the IRA were fucking terrorists; they were murdering cowards and I will give anyone who tells me otherwise a bloody good debate.'

The contributor is known to me as both a friend and a comrade, and he requested anonymity because of his place in the public eye. I will defend his right to do so and am happy to honour his wishes.

HUNGER STRIKE POSTSCRIPT

In January, 2015, prior to publication of this book, the *Belfast Newsletter* ran an article which showed compelling evidence that the strike was in many ways unnecessary and took place because it suited the Provisional IRA and its leaders. It elevated their 'struggle' onto a world stage, and the 'oohs' and 'aaahs' from Americans, Australians, South Africans, Canadians, French etc., around the world, combined with venom from the same, ensured that the IRA's campaign was generally the only side of the story on the lips of the world. The following article is based on a Roman Catholic priest's opinion that the Thatcher Government was not the pantomime villain which Adams and the others made it out to be.

A Roman Catholic chaplain at the Maze Prison secretly told the Secretary of State that the IRA's main justification for its 1981 hunger strike was entirely wrong, a declassified government file has revealed. The IRA had called off a hunger strike in 1980, after the Government issued a 30-page document setting out an offer to the prisoners. But, just months later, the IRA claimed that the Government had gone back on its word and said that it would begin a second fast, in which 10 prisoners would starve themselves to death. However, that account is challenged by one of the few outside figures to have sustained contact with prisoners over the period. A stray document from 1981 included in a file which did not close until 1986 contains the clear and repeatedly stated view of Monsignor Tom Toner that the Government had not gone back on its word. The implication – though it is not spelt out in the document – is that the second hunger strike was begun on a false premise.

The comments came in a meeting between the Secretary of State, three senior NIO officials and three Catholic representatives – Cardinal Tomás Ó'Fiaich, Father Toner and Father Murphy – on 18 February (10 days before the hunger strike began) in Hillsborough Castle. A confidential note of the meeting said that prior to the meeting Cardinal Ó'Fiaich "emphasised ... that it was most important that the fact that the meeting was taking place should not be disclosed. At the beginning of the meeting he and the two chaplains emphasised this point, Father Toner commenting that it would adversely affect their relationship with the prisoners, who would even be annoyed that the prison chaplains had discussed the hunger strike with the Cardinal, let alone with the Secretary of State." Father Toner – who died in 2012 – told the Secretary of State that the atmosphere in the prison was "frightening". The minutes say: "There appeared to be a determination to have a 'sacrifice'."

The prisoner's (sic) attitude was that the Government did nothing following the end of the hunger strike, though Father Toner himself acknowledged that the Government had done what they had undertaken to do. "The attitude of the prisoners was more extreme than on the previous occasion. They did not really expect to succeed, although privately they probably had some faint hope that they might." The minutes continue: "The Cardinal explained that, in that context, he thought the intransigence of Sands as the leader of the hunger strike might not be typical of the rest. He therefore wondered whether the prisoners could be permitted to meet together to discuss what they were setting out on." The minutes also show that the Catholic chaplains openly disagreed with their Cardinal in the meeting, with Cardinal Ó'Fiaich suggesting that the prisoners be allowed to meet together to discuss what they were setting out on, but the priests saying they did not believe that could stop the impending action.

Later in the meeting, Father Toner again indicated his belief that the Government had acted appropriately. He said that from the prisoners' point of view, they needed some concession from the Government in order to call off their 'dirty protest' but the minutes add: "That was how the prisoners saw it;" he for his part acknowledged that the Government had complied with their undertakings, and had treated the prisoners reasonably. "It was noteworthy that the seven who had been on hunger strike had, in Father Toner's view, been affected by the humane and considerate treatment which they received while in the prison hospital." After the meeting, Fr Toner spoke privately to an NIO official and was "gloomy" about the future in the prison. "He believed that Sands had deliberately put himself in a position where he would be under maximum pressure to continue his fast to death, and he believed he would do so." Father Toner for his part recognised that the Government's position had been very clearly set out, and he quite understood why they could not shift from it.[6]

Hector Hall (22) joined the UDR briefly as a teenager but resigned after a short stay in the regiment and went to work in the Transport Department at Altnagelvin Hospital in Londonderry. His short time in the UDR was, however, sufficient for the IRA to mark him for death. One does not doubt their dedication or passion, but it is also a ruthless, obsessive and blinkered philosophy. In their eyes, the killing of a young man who was no longer a member of the Security Forces was an 'important' step in their bid to reunite Ireland. On the afternoon of the 5th, having finished work for the day, he walked into the Hospital car park and got into his car. As he did so, a stolen car containing PIRA gunmen pulled across him and two masked men got out and began firing at him. The former part-time soldier was shot twice in the head and despite the best efforts of the medical staff, he died.

This, as any student of the conflict which we refer to as the Troubles will know was, the catalyst for another revenge or tit for tat killing. Every drop of spilled Security Forces' or Protestant blood was generally visited back twofold on the Catholics, and PIRA not only calculated this but, indeed, thrived upon it. On virtually every occasion that an off-duty UDR or RUC officer was killed, after almost every bomb and gun attack in a Loyalist area, the Provisionals know that there will be a 'backlash.' Of course the same mindset applies to the Loyalist paramilitaries and they too, calculate the effects of their actions and the retaliation which they invite back into their own areas is equally calculated. Whenever an innocent Catholic was killed by Loyalist paramilitaries or was caught in the crossfire between Republicans and the Army or RUC, it was PIRA's opportunity to step in as 'defenders of the community.' It was an opportunity for the old IRA maxim of 'See, we told you so; the Brits and the Protestants are your real enemies; we will protect you!' to be rolled out.

Three days after the hunger strikers ended their fasts, the new Secretary of State for Northern Ireland, James Prior, announced a number of changes in prison policy. One of the changes was one which allowed prisoners to wear their civilian clothes at all times. This was one of the five key demands that had been made at the start of the

---

6   Source: http://www.newsletter.co.uk/news/regional/maze-hunger-strike-prison-chaplain-absolved-govern-ment-of-blame-1-6503221

hunger strike. He also announced other changes: free association would be allowed in neighbouring wings of each H-Block, in the exercise areas and in recreation rooms; an increase in the number of visits each prisoner was allowed; and up to 50 per cent of lost remission would be restored. The issue of prison work was not resolved at this stage but he indicated that this issue too would be addressed.

In relation to the murder of Hector Hall, it took only 72 hours, and the UFF made an incursion into Nationalist territory when they launched an attack using automatic weapons on the Shamrock Social Club in the Ardoyne. On the night of the 8th, the medical volunteers of the Knights of Malta – a volunteer medical force – were having a dinner and dance at the club which was located near Flax Street Mill. The club was always going to be a likely target for Loyalists as it was the regular meeting place for the PIRA-dominated Ardoyne Local Defence Co-ordinating Committee. It had previously witnessed a Loyalist bomb attack. Several stolen cars drove into the Ardoyne and armed men jumped out opposite the venue and immediately opened fire on a group of people standing outside. Two men were hit. One of these was hit by seven rounds, but recovered later in the nearby Mater Hospital. The other, however, a local Councillor, Lawrence Kennedy (35), was mortally wounded and despite also being rushed to the same hospital, was found to be dead on arrival.

The focus then switched to England and several cells already embedded there sprang into action. As eminent writers such as Martin Dillon contend, the British/English were prepared to tolerate a certain level of violence so long as it is confined to Northern Ireland, but a mainland bombing campaign concentrates the mind of the Government. Chelsea Barracks was located in the City of Westminster, London, on Chelsea Bridge Road. Originally built in the 1860s to house two battalions of troops, it was closed and sold off by the Government in 2007. However, in October 1981, the Irish Guards were in occupation and in their 81st year as a regiment. Formed on 1 April 1900 by order of Queen Victoria, in order to commemorate the Irish people who fought in the Second Boer War for the British Empire, their motto is 'Quis Separabit' [Who Shall Separate Us?]. Before the 10th of October was over, two civilians would be dead and a score or more Irish Guardsmen would be in hospital.

PIRA's England team had purchased a second-hand commercial van in London and placed a device containing over 1,000 six-inch nails and hundreds of nuts and bolts inside. The blast of the 30 lb (14 kgs) explosive device would shatter anyone nearby, but the c. 2,000 pieces of metal would fly out at in excess of 200 mph and cause terrible shrapnel injuries to anyone unfortunate enough to be in its path. The bomb was not simply designed to damage prestigious or even military targets without casualties; it was designed by the sickest minds with the Army Council as an anti-personnel bomb to cause maximum damage to fellow humans.

The van was left at Ebury Bridge Road and exploded at precisely noon. Mrs Nora Field (59) was hit in the chest by a 6-inch nail, travelling at approximately 200 miles an hour. The effects of a bomb blast can be viewed in Desmond Hammil's Pig in the Middle:

> A bomb blast in a confined space is devastating. First the shock wave spreads out, faster than the speed of sound. Some heavy objects deflect the waves, but other solid material is changed instantly into gas, creating an enormous increase in volume and pressure. People in the way can have their limbs torn off, and in the millisecond

which follows, the energy waves go into their mouths and upwards, taking off the tops of their skulls and other parts of the body so that sometimes all is left is the spine, held together by the vertebrae. The shock wave, travelling at 13,000 miles per hour pulverises the floor immediately below the explosion. It slows down quickly, but more damage is done by the blast wave which follows at half the speed. This has the pressure of pent-up gas behind it and it can also tear off limbs, perforate eardrums.[7]

Mrs Field's chest simply caved in and she was killed instantly. A young Irish boy – John Breslin (18) – who had gone to live in England, was sitting on a nearby wall when the blast hit him. It caused massive head injuries which removed his scalp, severely damaged his brain, fatally injuring him. He was rushed to hospital, but died three days later. His distraught father was interviewed by the Press and he said: "It's their own people they are killing. They are Irish; I am Irish and they killed my son." In total, 46 people were injured, including 40 soldiers from the Irish Guards; many of those injured suffered traumatic amputations. Of the six civilians injured, two were children. The soldiers were being transported back to Chelsea Barracks after performing ceremonial duties at Buckingham Palace. The bomb was detonated by command wire by a watching member of the bombing team, and fired just as the first of three coaches of soldiers arrived at the barracks. Had he waited a minute or two longer, a further two coaches arrived together, and the carnage would have been much worse. An apologist for the Provisionals claimed responsibility for the atrocity within three hours and regurgitated the usual clichéd nonsense about attacking the British for occupying part of Ireland and 'killing' Irish people. Given that the British Army killed some 400 people, mostly terrorists during the Troubles and the IRA killed over 1,800, just who did the spokesman think that he was fooling?

The *Sunday Express's* headline read: 'Guards Bomb: Start of New Terror?' The reporters continued:

The IRA struck in London yesterday, possibly announcing the start of a new terror campaign on the mainland. Their target was a coach load of Irish Guardsmen. A huge bomb was exploded as the coach was nearing Chelsea Barracks. Long sharp nails inflicted frightful injuries on soldiers and civilians. A woman died, it is believed from a heart attack [sic]. "These are some of the worst bomb injuries I have ever seen," said a surgeon at Westminster Hospital. "People arrived with long nails sticking out of their bodies. Some nails were six to nine inches."

The newspaper also quoted an unidentified Republican source as saying: "There is no way the IRA and the INLA are going to let the deaths of the hunger strikers remain unavenged."

On the 12th, the Daily Express led with 'Callous Brutes' and the front page showed Margaret Thatcher visiting a heavily bandaged soldier in hospital. Another headline

---

7   Hammil, Desmond, *Pig in the Middle* (London: Methuen, 1985).

under 'Maggie's Fury' screamed: "They are just killers with no regard for human life. They will never get special status." The writers continued:

A shocked Mrs Thatcher yesterday condemned the IRA nail bomb outrage as a "new depth in brutality." After comforting two child victims of the blast in hospital and holding the hand of an injured soldier, the Premier said: "This attack was about the most cold, callous, brutal and subhuman thing … these people are just murderers …" But at times, Mrs Thatcher seemed lost for words after seeing the heavily bandaged victims of London's latest bomb horror.

News of the outrage occupied the first three pages and more information was given under the sub-headline of 'The Wire That Led To Murder.' Reporters Sydney Brennan and Ashley Walton wrote under the heading 'Peeping bomber watched his carnage.' The article read:

The callous IRA killer who triggered the London van bomb knew that inno-cent bystanders including women and children would be killed or maimed. He was peeping around a corner a very safe 100 yards away, picking his moment to unleash the carnage. The bomb with its shrapnel of bolts and bent nails was a 'command detonation' which went off when the terrorist pressed the button, a Scotland Yard chief explained yesterday. He added that earlier – at about 8:30AM – a man in green overalls was seen by eyewitnesses attaching a wire to scaffolding stretching in front of a block of flats. This was the detonation wire which was later attached to the bomb. The triggerman with his end of the wire probably attached to a battery detonator, waited until the coach was opposite the bomb … and pressed the button.

The author has seen a photograph of the Army coach, its white bodywork mangled and torn with hundreds of dents and indentations where the deadly shrapnel had pene-trated; every window has vanished. How scores of soldiers were not killed is beyond my comprehension. Christopher Long of the London Newspaper group wrote:

Guardsmen come from all over Ireland and from both Protestant and Roman Catholic communities in Liverpool and Birmingham. Only half an hour before the explosion occurred, officers of the Guards had been saying at Buckingham Palace that the battalion represented the sort of peaceful existence and harmony that most people would wish to see in Ireland itself.

Ten minutes later the previous night's guardsmen were on their way back to Chelsea Barracks from Buckingham Palace in two buses. The deafening explosion was clearly heard by Guards officers and off-duty journalist Christopher Long as they made their way from Buckingham Palace to the Officers' Mess at St James's Palace. Within minutes news of the disaster reached senior officers and police and security teams who cordoned off the area fearing that a second bomb would be detonated later. Twenty-two of the twenty-three guardsmen in the bus were injured as Pimlico resident Mrs Nora Fields lay dead in the road and a total of 40 were ferried to Westminster Hospital for treatment.[8]

As Martin Dillon comments in several of his excellent Troubles-related books, a by-product of any mainland bomb is the vilification of all Irish people living or working in England. Abuse, insults in the streets and pubs and ostracising in the work place or neighbourhood are all consequences of IRA activity. Mass suspicion and fear of anyone with an Irish accent, even someone who has lived as a friend or neighbour for many years, all occur as the PIRA Army Council know they will. This shunning suits the purposes of the IRA Godfathers as it builds their support in England; it shows that even to those Irish who have been in England for many years that the English are the real enemy of Ireland.

As many of the injured guardsmen lay on their hospital beds and surgeons, doctors and nurses devoted their energies to reducing the men's pain and poor young John Breslin fought for his life, the UFF were already in the process of carrying out the first of their revenge attacks. Deerpark Road is situated in North Belfast, and is sandwiched between Ballysillan and Cliftonville Road. It is a small Catholic enclave surrounded by larger Protestant areas. That evening, the Ewing family were watching the TV news which covered the funeral of Lawrence Kennedy who had been murdered by the UFF four days earlier. As Robert 'Bobby' Ewing (34), father of three, watched the latest sad procession which epitomised Northern Ireland in those violent days, UFF gunmen – possibly the same murder gang who attacked the Shamrock Social club – burst into the house and immediately opened fire on Mr Ewing. He died almost at once and, like the murder of Mr Kennedy in the Ardoyne, it was a blatant sectarian killing. Loyalists had now killed twice in four days and would strike again twice more before the month of October was up.

On the 13th, a young RAF Technician was killed in an RTA, in the Ballykelly, Co Londonderry area. Junior Tech David Just Gold Gilfillan (26) of RAF, Bishop's Court was a native of Scotland. He was buried at Cambusnethan Cemetery in Lanarkshire.

Loyalist paramilitaries struck again on the 15th when they murdered a Catholic woman at her home in the Nationalist Markets area of Belfast. The murder gang from the UVF had gone to an address in Stewart Street, which is close to the Lagan River and the main Belfast railway line. Ostensibly they were in the area to assassinate a known INLA player as part of their retaliation for the Chelsea bomb. Their Intelligence, like many other times was flawed, however, and they went to the wrong house. The men, having entered the house found Mrs Mary McKay (68) asleep in her bedroom and they opened fire, hitting her several times as she lay in her bed; she died almost immediately.

Less than 30 hours later, the Republicans struck; an INLA murder gang containing 'Dr Death' himself, Gerard Steenson, drove into the heart of Loyalist territory in the Shankill in order to assassinate a top UDA man. William 'Billy' McCullough (32), father of six, lived in Denmark Street, a thoroughfare which connects the Crumlin and Shankill Roads. He was a leading member of the UDA's West Belfast Brigade, holding the rank of Lieutenant-Colonel. As he prepared to drive one of his daughters to school,

---

8   Source: http://www.christopherlong.co.uk/pri/chelseabomb.html

a motorcycle drove up, and the pillion passenger opened fire just as McCullough was getting into his car. He was shot twelve times and despite prompt medical attention died a few minutes later. The dead man was living only a few doors away from West Belfast Brigadier Tommy Lyttle at the time, and it was thought that INLA's target that day was Lyttle. However, McCullough appears to have been a 'target of opportunity.' An INLA man who turned Queen's Evidence later and testified against his former terrorist colleagues stated that Steenson was not involved and that the shooter had been a man he would only name as 'Bronco.'

On Saturday the 17th, Lieutenant-General Sir Steuart Robert Pringle, then Commandant-General of the Royal Marines, was badly injured when the IRA struck again and exploded a bomb under his car. A PIRA bombing team had attached a device to his red Volkswagen car outside his home in Dulwich, South London. It exploded as he went to take his Labrador, Bella to the park for a run. One of the first questions he asked was about his dog. The dog was uninjured, but the senior Royal Marine lost a leg in the incident. The following day, the Sunday Express headline reflected the fear which gripped many Londoners: 'Bomb Blast General Loses A Leg.' Their reporters continued:

> The IRA struck in London for the second week running, when a car bomb exploded, seriously injuring Lt-General Sir Steuart Pringle. The bomb went off as General Pringle was driving away from his Dulwich home, one week almost to the minute since the bomb which killed two near Chelsea barracks. Doctors at King's College Hospital…were forced to amputate [his] right leg below the knee. The general also suffered extensive injuries to his left leg – but this was saved. He drove off but within a few yards, the car exploded. "Suddenly there was a big flash and I saw the bonnet of the car fly up over a house," said eyewitness Mike Mullins. I rushed to the car and I could see the driver who was still conscious but his legs were badly smashed and he was bleeding from the head. I tried to calm him down, but all he could say was: "What about my dog?"

Stephen Hamilton (24) was a convicted Loyalist paramilitary and a member of the UFF. On the 18th, he had secured an early release from prison after serving just over half of a nine-year sentence for armed robbery and possession of a firearm. He had gone with fellow UDA/UFF members for celebratory drinks in the Woodvale/Shankill area and, during the course of the evening, he and friends had stolen a taxi. As the men drove through Woodvale, they were called to stop at a VCP manned by RUC officers. The officers had been told to look out for the stolen vehicle and warned that there were armed men inside it. As the taxi stopped, one of the policemen saw an arm come through a window and thought that he saw a gun; consequently, he fired one round and Hamilton was hit and mortally wounded, dying at the scene.

On the 21st, an IRA murder gang drove to Belfast Zoo on the Antrim Road to seek out one of the Zoo's employees who was also a part-time soldier in the UDR. The zoo is located at the top of Antrim Road in the northern suburbs of Belfast between Belfast Lough and Newtownabbey. Julian 'Ricky' Connolly (49), father of two, was a sergeant in the UDR but had worked as a gardener for some time. He answered a knock at the door and having checked that it was a man in GPO uniform opened it and was shot immediately. He slumped to the floor, badly wounded and the IRA gunman in a stolen postman's uniform shot him several more times as he lay helpless; he died at the scene and the IRA gunman escaped in a waiting stolen car. The IRA gunman was Charles McKiernan who lived in the Unity Flats in Belfast. He admitted under police questioning to also taking part in the murder of Prison Officer Albert Miles on 26 November 1978 when the Deputy Governor was killed by fellow terrorist Kevin Artt, one of the 1983 Maze escapers.[9] McKiernan also allegedly said to the RUC who questioned him at Castlereagh: "I wish that I could turn the clock back." The report in *The Belfast Telegraph* on the 31st day of his trial claimed that the PIRA murderer had started to cry when he admitted taking part in the two aforementioned murders.

Four days after the murder at the Zoo, the Royal Corps of Transport (RCT) lost one of its soldiers in circumstances unknown. Driver Paul Johns (18) was from South Wales; the author has no further information as to his death, but through a trusted NIVA contact, the following was learned. Driver Johns was cremated on 2 November at Glyn-taf near Pontypridd and his ashes were scattered on Lawn Number Two. He has a stained glass window in his memory in the chapel. A good friend of the author has promised to lay some flowers there in the soldier's memory.

On the 26th, the IRA's England team struck again; the third such attack in a little over a fortnight and again it was in London. At precisely 1451, a man with a Northern Irish accent contacted Reuters News Agency in London and warned that there were three bombs. One was in Bourne and Hollingsworth in Oxford Street and another was in a Wimpy Bar in the same location. The caller was not clear about the ones in the Department store but was precise about where the bomb in the Wimpy Bar had been placed. The caller then added that there was also one in a Debenhams but failed to state which one. Scotland Yard's Anti-Terrorist branch swung immediately into action; it was a well-oiled machine, because after all they had been dealing with IRA terrorists for over 10 years. One of the first one the scene was Kenneth Howarth (49) who was a former ATO in the RAOC. He had spent 23 years in the Army and had reached the rank of Sergeant Major, leaving in 1973. The expert, who was married with two children, was trying to defuse the device, which had been planted in the basement toilet, when it exploded killing him instantly. In 1983, he was posthumously awarded the George Medal for bravery. In 1985, IRA bombers Paul Kavanagh and Thomas Quigley, both from Belfast, were convicted of his murder, as well as other attacks including the Chelsea Barracks nail bomb. They were each handed five life sentences with a minimum tariff of 35 years. They were released in 1999 under the terms of the Good Friday Agreement.

The following day's *Daily Express* led with 'The Moment a Brave Man Died' and their front page photograph captures the scene in Oxford Street – seen a hundred or more times in Belfast – of a huge cloud of smoke billowing from the front of what we know is a Wimpy Bar; it is so obscured that it is difficult to say with any accuracy what the building is. The reporter wrote: "This is the moment a brave bomb expert was murdered by the IRA. Shoppers and police look on helplessly as a blast rocks the Wimpy Bar in Oxford Street, minutes after father-of-two Kenneth Howarth had entered to defuse a deadly device." The reporter mentioned Mr Howarth's service in Northern Ireland and quoted a neighbour from Bracknell as saying: "He never showed that he was

---

9   See Wharton, Ken M., *Wasted Years, Wasted Lives* (Solihull: Helion, 2013), Vol 1, Chapter 47.

frightened about what he did. He was very close with his family and they were always ready to help others."

The newspaper continued, under a smaller headline of 'Another Day, Another Job', to continue how a smiling Mr Howarth arrived in a police Range Rover, gathered his equipment and then before disappearing inside the building, cracked a joke with other officers. Apparently, when he arrived with colleagues he was given a choice of which bomb to defuse and he opted for what, in 1981 passed as a 'fast food' outlet. Two minutes after he entered the building, the device exploded and he would have stood no chance. A medical acquaintance told the author: "His eyes and brain might have registered a flash of whiteness, but that would have been all. We can only conjecture about what bomb victims experience, because so few who are that close have ever survived. It would have been mercifully quick."

The month was completed by the murder of a suspected informer and Republican paramilitaries – the INLA – employed their versions of PIRA's ISU. On the evening of the 27th, an INLA team picked up fellow member Edward Brogan (28) in his hometown of Strabane and drove him to a safe house in Londonderry, possibly on the Shantallow Estate, some 17 or 18 miles away. He had recently been arrested on petrol bombing charges and had been interrogated by the RUC. After several hours of grilling by his INLA 'superiors' he was judged guilty and shot in the head. His lifeless body was taken by car and dumped on a rubbish tip close to the Carnhill Estate. Just over a week later, the UFF proved that they could be as ruthless with their own people as they were with innocent Catholics and carried out their own execution.

A NORMAL NIGHT IN THE SHANTALLOW
William 'Jock' Young, Royal Artillery

We were on our usual night patrol; two Land Rovers with two gunners on the tail-gate, each facing in opposite directions. We had RAF-type flight helmets, which we did not like as you couldn't hear properly with them on, plus our SLRs and we were wearing US Military flak jackets. The evening was slow and on an earlier drive down Racecourse Road, a vehicle sped up behind us and turned his headlights on. I cocked my weapon and took aim at the driver, and he sensibly slowed down and turned his headlights off; it's unlikely I would have shot him, but we had to show we were serious. On our second drive down Racecourse Road there was the usual group of teenagers, lobbing rocks and bottles at us from outside a small newsagents, which we all knew and expected and it was a nightly ritual.

On one side of Racecourse Road there were a few houses and just behind them were a block of flats. These flats used to make us nervous as they were excellent cover for IRA snipers, and we had quite a few pot-shots at us from there. The opposite side of the road was farm fields and there was a small, but very thick hedge along the street; similar to a French bocage-type hedge. On turning into the aforementioned road, we all put 'one up the spout' in our weapons and got ready for the nightly routine of bottles, bricks, etc. I noticed a man, mid-20s and he was walking with an unusual limp. He was walking with his right leg in sync with his right arm. As I watched him (about 30 yards away), he swung his arm up and produced a very recognizable Armalite semi-automatic rifle. The Armalite has a distinctive profile with the sights and carry handle in a unique shape on the weapon.

The bullets started coming very fast from his weapon, and I seemed to be the only one who saw the man. My fellow Gunner standing next to me opened up on the teenagers outside the supermarket; fortunately he never hit any of them and all the youngsters, having grown up in those times had all hit the ground, and I glanced at all of them, crawling behind the store. The bullets from the man's rifle were hitting my vehicle, which strangely didn't scare me and my only emotion was that I was a little pissed at the man. I remember the sound of the rounds as they passed by us and fortunately the gunman was firing wildly. I raised my rifle and aimed at him as he was moving. He ran down the street holding the rifle at waist level. The man then did something I couldn't understand. He stopped under a streetlamp, turned and then continued to fire on us with his weapon at waist level. I still have a mental picture of his silhouette as he was firing.

I was looking at him from over my sights and then, looking through my sights decided to shoot him. Time seemed to stand still and I wasn't too happy about having to shoot someone, but I had no choice. Before I could squeeze off a round, hand grenades started landing. There was someone from behind the hedge on Racecourse Road throwing hand grenades at us while the gunman was firing. I leapt off the vehicle and tried to decide who to go after first (gunman or mad bomber!). I took cover behind a telegraph pole until I realised that bullets will pass through these things very easily. Our Bombardier called out: "We have casualties," and my first concern was for who had been hit. One of our drivers had been deafened by a hand grenade and that was our only casualty. I took a last look back at the Armalite-carrying gunman and caught a glimpse of him disappearing behind the flats. I immediately regretted not bringing him down and that he got away.

Back-up arrived and we then spent a couple of hours picking up cartridge cases, looking for any evidence. The gunman and the weapon were in the flats but we couldn't kick in every door to find it. Racecourse Road became 'Indian Country' after that and we would batten down our hatches and cruise very smartly down the road. Over the years I have relived that particular night, even though getting ambushed and sniped at became a routine event. I have mixed feelings over whether I should have ignored the grenades and just taken the man out. Did he go onto to better things? Did he ever kill anyone? How old was he? And could I have saved someone's life by shooting him?

These obviously are questions that will never be answered. Over the years I have had the opportunity to return to Northern Ireland, but I have no desire to ever go back there. I hope you can edit my experiences and perhaps include them in your book. I am now retired US Navy and live in the US.

I am indeed indebted to William for his account of a night in Londonderry into this particular account of the Troubles. Racecourse Road starts in the Maybrook Park area and terminates in the Nationalist Shantallow Estate. Shantallow, affectionately known as 'Shanty', was the first major housing estate built in the townland in the mid-1960s. It is where PIRA proxy bomb victim Patsy Gillespie lived before he was forced to drive his own car, packed with explosives to a VCP at Coshquin while his wife Kathleen and children were held at gunpoint by gunmen. He drove to the PVCP on the border crossing where he tried to save the lives of five young soldiers of the King's Regiment. Sadly he was killed along with all five of the Kingos on the night of 24 October, 1990. Gunner Kerry Venn of the Royal Artillery was killed there by the IRA on 28 April, 1973. Second Lieutenant Michael Simpson of the Staffordshires was killed there in the same year, also by an IRA gunman.[10]

On the last day of the month, Sinn Féin held its *Ard Fheis* (annual conference) in Dublin. Danny Morrison, then editor of *An Phoblacht*, gave a speech in which he addressed the issue of the party taking part in future elections. He asked the assembled supporters and membership: "Who here really believes we can win the war through the ballot box? But will anyone here object if, with a ballot paper in one hand and the Armalite in the other, we take power in Ireland?" This statement is often misquoted as: "the Armalite in one hand and the Ballot box in the other".

The month of October ended with 13 deaths; four soldiers and one officer serving with the Metropolitan Police were killed. A total of five civilians died – four Catholics and a Protestant – of whom three were overtly sectarian. Republican paramilitaries lost one member and the Loyalists lost two. Six of the dead were killed by Republicans and three were killed by Loyalists.

---

10   See Wharton, Ken, *Sir, They're Taking the Kids Indoors* (Solihull: Helion, 2011).

23

November

This month would witness 14 deaths. Five of these would be deaths of soldiers or former soldiers, all of whom would be UDR as the Republicans targeted them at home and work. Three police officers would be killed and, in targeting a fourth, the Provisionals killed an RUC officer's son as he learned to drive.

On the 4th, the UDA/UFF's own version of PIRA's 'nutting squad' was in action in the Loyalist heartland of the Shankill Road. Silvio Street is located between the Crumlin and the Shankill Roads and was the home of Arthur Bettice (35) who was a senior member of the UDA/UFF. He had recently been arrested on arms charges but had been released earlier than expected after questioning. This put the hint of suspicion into the minds of other top UDA men and the order was sent to their 'military wing' the UFF to kill him. During the evening, gunmen burst into his house and shot him several times as he relaxed in his lounge. It was said that he had close ties with Jim Craig, at that time the top man in the organisation.

On Friday 6th, Irish Taoiseach, Garret FitzGerald held talks with his British counterpart Margaret Thatcher in London. As a result of the meeting it was decided to establish the Anglo-Irish Inter-Governmental Council which would act as forum for meetings between the two Governments. It further served to heighten Loyalist fears of a 'sell-out' by the Government and it was putting them on what they perceived as the inexorable road to unity with the Republic. This, however, was allayed in part just 96 hours later, when Margaret Thatcher told the House of Commons: "Northern Ireland is part of the United Kingdom – as much as my constituency is." This statement was subsequently often misquoted as: "Northern Ireland is as British as Finchley."

On the 8th, a PIRA bombing team attempted to kill an off-duty UDR soldier at his home in Ballymoran, Co Armagh; they failed but killed instead his teenage son Trevor Foster (17). The boy's father was a part-time soldier in the UDR and as such, was targeted by the South Armagh PIRA. He was learning to drive and practised as often as possible, and one of his tasks was to put the car in the garage. He got into his father's car, but a PIRA bombing team had planted a UVBT and it exploded, killing him instantly. His distraught father told the media: "Trevor said he would garage the car. The next thing I heard was a huge bang and the windows of the house shattered. I dashed out and found him lying on the path next to the car." Meanwhile, the teenager's death was clearly helping to *progress* the IRA's desire for a united Ireland. [Author's own use of italics.]

As a writer, I find it next to impossible to remain dispassionate about the subject matter in hand, especially as, unlike some other authors, I cannot find a single thing about the terrorists which is to be admired. However, sometimes one must attempt to present the bare facts without expressing one's opinion, but without coming across as cold. The following piece from the son of an RUC officer describes the emotion and shock of being involved in a terrorist incident. I am indebted to the contributor and honoured to have his words in this book.

THE DAY THEY TRIED TO KILL MY DAD
Robert Stewart

My Dad was an RUC officer and if he were alive he would have been a difficult man to talk to or to interview; getting him in right form would have been critical, he told things once and that was it; if you missed it the moment was lost. I remember him telling me of being on one of the Royal Navy MTBs sent out sink the Nazi's Brest Squadron when they forced the Channel in 1942, and how his MTB was one of those tasked with taking Howard's Paras off from Bruneval; for him it was all water under the bridge, which was sad.

The morning he was almost killed is really burnt into my memory, from my mother screaming, to getting out of bed (usual teenager who tried to get the last minute in bed before school). Then the bang, instantly awake; that frantic run downstairs, out across a lawn still wet with dew thinking that is wet. Hitting tarmac which was superheated from the energy of the bomb; kneeling beside him asking if he was alive; glancing to my left seeing a neighbour looking on. I remember glancing at the garage; the small crater; smoke still rising from it. The blood sprayed in an arc from the point of injury like a glass of wine tossed against the garage door; seeing something bloody in the garage. I remember the boot of the car blown open, some holes punched in it; small but you say to yourself that should not be like this, and this is not really happening yet your feet tell you that the tar should not be burning and almost as quickly you feel it cooling.

Then he began to talk: 'Take that dog away!' Our dog had come over and he was licking blood which, when I glanced back, was running down from my Dad in small streams of bright red. The sound of that small bomb, the dull thud, the screams of my mother, the wet grass, heat of the tarmac – nearly 40 years ago but so much like it was only yesterday.

Later, it turned out that I could recall seeing them (PIRA) scout the place out; my brother Donald, who was also RUC, disturbed them when they tried to kill the dog by poisoning it. We had a large stone which was set against the back gate – to alert us if anyone went around the back of the house. They heard Donald coming out and high tailed it, because he went out armed, but when Dad came home, he told him he was imagining it; don't worry was his view. When they were lifted some months later, they got several hundred years gaol, turned out my father knew them all, some even greeting him when he met them in town, calling out things like: 'How you doing Bob?'

On the 9th, another part-time soldier in the Regiment was singled out as he carried out his full-time job as a painter. He was tasked to paint a wall on premises in the centre of Londonderry. He was standing at the top of a ladder, when masked gunmen approached him and shot him six times; seriously wounding him. He later recovered in Altnagelvin Hospital. Later that day, another UDR soldier was shot while off-duty and fatally injured. Private Cecil Graham (32) and his wife had recently had a baby son who was born with a heart murmur; it was thought better that mother and child stay with her parents in the Nationalist area of Donagh, Co Fermanagh. As he arrived he was dicked by PIRA sympathisers, and gunmen were sent for. As he left and walked towards his car, waiting gunmen shot him six times with American Armalites; desperately injured, he attempted to crawl back to his in-laws' house, but one of the gunmen stood over his help-less body and fired 10 more times into him. He was rushed to hospital, but died on the 11th. It was stated by his father-in-law that all of his fellow Catholic neighbours refused to help and never offered any sympathy for their loss. Private Graham was the second of three brothers who were killed by the Provisionals.[1]

The day after, Charles Neville (56), father of six, who was a former soldier in the UDR, was murdered by the IRA because of his past associations. He had resigned in the autumn of the previous year and was employed at Armagh Technical College. On the afternoon of the 10th, he was driving out of the premises on the Loughall Road, when masked men threw a home-made hand grenade at his car, the explosion causing him to crash. The men then opened fire and he was hit multiple times. The men escaped in a stolen car, leaving the former UDR man dying. He was rushed to hospital, but died en-route. On that same day, in another attack in Co Fermanagh, an off-duty UDR soldier had a lucky escape when he was ambushed on a country lane as he drove to his farm. Waiting gunmen who had been hiding behind a hedge opened fire with automatic weapons hitting him several times. He drove on, but his injuries caused him to crash. Undaunted, he walked and crawled for over a mile across farmland until he reached a neighbour's house. He recovered in hospital.

Friday the 13th is unlucky for some but in a perverse sort of way, for the British Attorney-General, Sir Michael Havers, it was not. The IRA's England team planted a large device at his London home. Although there was a tremendous explosion, the house was empty at the time. Because of his high-profile position in the British judicial system and for his part in sentencing IRA terrorists, Sir Michael's Wimbledon home had 24-hour police guard. When the device – which had been smuggled onto the premises by an IRA bombing team – exploded, three police officers were hospitalised with cuts and bruises and a female officer was treated for shock. A neighbour – Anne Dennistoun-Sword – said: "There was the most enormous explosion; it was absolutely frightening. We were sitting in our drawing room just thinking about going to bed. Suddenly I was thinking that we were in another war."[2]

On the same day, a spokesman for the INLA issued a statement indicating that on 1 December 1981, their prisoners would end their protest over the issue of prison work. There was an inevitability over the whole issue and one was left wondering just how badly damaged both the Provisionals and Sinn Féin were. Thatcher's resolve – some might say intransigence – was unshakeable and 10 prisoners had starved themselves to death and more 60 other people had been killed for virtually no concessions.

Up to this point in the Troubles – over 13 years since the onset – MPs and para-military leaders had been untouched, certainly in Northern Ireland. On the mainland, Airey Neave MP had been murdered in 1979 and Ian Gow, MP would be murdered in 1990 – both by the IRA. However, the day after the Wimbledon bomb, UUP MP

---

1   See Chapter 18.
2   *Spartanburg Herald-Journal*, South Carolina, USA (14 November 1981).

the Reverend Robert Bradford (40), was shot and killed, along with a civilian worker, in South Belfast by the Provisionals. His murder sparked off a flurry of three sectarian murders by the UVF in the space of nine days. As this author has previously written, the retaliations were confidently expected by PIRA's Army Council who authorised the killings. There is no better evidence of the pathological and cunning mindset of the Republican paramilitaries.

The Reverend Robert Bradford, MP (40) was conducting his normal Constituency 'surgery' in a community centre in Benmore Drive, Finaghy. The Loyalist Finaghy area is south of Nationalist areas such as Lenadoon and Andersonstown and as such was only a short drive for the IRA assassins. As he began preparing for his surgery, two men wearing paint-covered overalls, purporting to be decorating the centre walked in and the first one pushed the MP's RUC bodyguard to the ground and covered him at gun point. The second man fired a single shot at one of the centre's employees – Ken Campbell (29) and mortally wounded him. The gunman then walked towards the MP and shot him three times in the head and neck, killing him instantly. The two men fled to a waiting car and the RUC bodyguard fired three shots at them, unfortunately missing his target. Mr Campbell died shortly afterwards. An apologist for the IRA felt able to somehow justify the killings by describing the dead MP as: "one of the key people responsible for winding up the Loyalist paramilitary sectarian machine."[3]

The author John Potter in his excellent account of the UDR,[4] describes the murdered MP as 'immoderate' and further states that he was asked not speak at the funeral of a murdered UDR soldier, killed with two others in a PIRA landmine at Castlewellan.[5] Loyalists were predictably angry, and the Reverend Ian Paisley verbally attacked Jim Prior when the Northern Ireland Secretary attended the dead MP's funeral on the 17th. There were also angry scenes as 'mourners' jostled and threatened Mr Prior. The RUC announced that it was cancelling all holiday leave for its officers.

Irish Taoiseach, Garret Fitzgerald was quick to condemn the killers and to praise the Unionist MP:

> The killing of an elected representative of the people calls for particular condemna-
> tion in the strongest possible terms and serves to remind us of the real objectives of
> the organisation responsible. The IRA has once again shown its utter contempt for
> human life and for the democratic process which it has recently sought to distort
> for its own ends. Its true attitude to democracy and freedom was summed up in
> a recent statement of an IRA spokesman who, when asked by an interviewer for
> a foreign newspaper about the wishes of the people in this part of the country
> concerning an aspect of reunification, replied, "We call the shots. We don't really
> give a damn what they want!"

3   Thornton, David, Seamus Kelters, Brian Feeney and David McKittrick. *Lost Lives: The Stories of the Men, Women and Children who Died as a Result of the Northern Ireland Troubles.* (Edinburgh: Mainstream, 1999, revised ed. 2007), p.886.

4   Potter, John, *A Testimony to Courage*, (Barnsley: Pen & Sword, 2001).

5   For further details of the explosion, see Chapter 1 of this book.

THE SHOOTING OF REVEREND BRADFORD AND KENNETH CAMPBELL
Mark 'C', RA and UDR

On the 24th Nov 1981, I was back home living in the Finaghy area, serving full-time with 10 UDR after five years as a Gunner. On this day Reverend Robert Bradford, Unionist MP for South Belfast, was brutally murdered by PIRA gunmen, alongside a friend Kenneth Campbell in the Community Centre in Finaghy Estate; he was the first MP to be killed by terrorists since the start of the Northern Irish war/conflict.

Growing up in the Finaghy area I knew Kenneth Campbell very well. As well as being one of my best friend's neighbours, he was also the caretaker of the local community centre where, as young teens, we would go for the youth club and weekend discos. I also knew the Rev Bradford from my school, before he got into politics full time; he taught RE at my school in Suffolk in the early 1970s. I remember him being a very tough teacher who took no nonsense and would often throw the odd duster at your head if you were talking or not paying attention. I suppose in a way he was the same in politics, taking a very hard line with terrorists and being very uncompromising on the Union.

Kenneth and Robert were very well liked in the Finaghy area and I attended Kenneth's funeral later that week. The people were very angry at the lack of action against the Provos, something we would get used to over the years, but you never forget people like this.

Retaliation was both swift and bloody and over the course of the next nine days, three more Catholic families would be grieving the loss of their loved ones. The murder gangs of the UVF pulled the triggers, but the PIRA murder gang who shot the two men at Finaghy community centre, metaphorically loaded the guns! The very next day, indeed, in the very early hours of the next day, on his way to his home in Madrid Street, in the Nationalist Short Strand, Thomas McNulty (18) was shot dead by the UVF. Two UVF members on a stolen motorbike were driving around the nationalist area when they saw a lone man. The young man saw them and tried to escape; attempting to enter the house of a relative, but it was locked. They shot and wounded him in an initial burst of gunfire, but he ran into another street, before collapsing; the gunmen followed and shot him several times in the head as he lay helpless in the street. This is precisely what the Provisionals expected and indeed, needed in order to continue to intimidate both the Catholics and the Protestants.

Also on the 14th, Stephen Murphy was shot by a UVF murder gang, while answering a knock at the front door of his home late in the evening. He had been living in England and had only returned home to Belfast several weeks earlier. He was rushed to hospital, but died 10 days later.

On the 16th, there was a Loyalist 'Third Force' rally in Enniskillen, Co Fermanagh. Which was addressed by Ian Paisley; in his provocative speech, he threatened that Unionists would make Northern Ireland 'ungovernable.' A series of rallies were held in Protestant areas of Northern Ireland and a number of businesses closed. The DUP and the UUP held separate rallies at Belfast City Hall. The 'Third Force' held a rally in Newtownards, County Down, which was attended by an estimated 15,000 men. On the same day, three DUP MPs were suspended from the House of Commons when they protested about the British Government's policy on security in Northern Ireland.

The next day, the UVF shot two Catholic men who were chatting in a car close to Lurgan, Co Armagh. Another car drew alongside where Peadar Fagan (20) and his friend were chatting and two men inside opened fire killing Mr Fagan and badly wounding his friend. The gang then drove off, leaving one man dying and the other, wounded and distraught at the shock of seeing his friend cut down. The UVF leader Billy 'King Rat' Wright was arrested for the murder but the case against him collapsed when the main witness withdrew his evidence. Wright was later killed inside the Maze, when INLA gunmen shot him in 1997 as he made his way to the visiting area.

On the same day, RUCR officer Silas Lyttle (59) died from the injuries which he had received, after being shot by the Provisionals.[6] Before the 17th was over, another UDR soldier was dead as the IRA's Fermanagh Brigade targeted an off-duty NCO. Corporal Albert Beacom (42), a father of five, was a member of the Lisnaskea Company. In addition to being a soldier, like many others, he was also a farmer, operating land in remote Maguiresbridge. He had just returned from an errand to drop off two of his sons in Brookeborough, had parked his car and was walking towards the house. As he did so, PIRA gunmen stepped out from behind a building and shot him several times, before running off. His wife was feeding their baby daughter and dashed outside after she heard the shots. She found her husband dying on the ground and desperately cradled him in her arms. An ambulance was summoned, and he was rushed to Erne Hospital but died en-route.

The Provisionals had been targeting an RUCR man for some time and succeeded in planting a device underneath his car. When the part-time policeman returned to his vehicle, it exploded as he got into it. He was appallingly injured, and was rushed to hospital; he suffered traumatic amputation of both legs. Less than two months later, his nephew was killed by another IRA booby-trap.[7]

The following day, it was again 'guilty by association' as another former member of the UDR was murdered by the Provisionals. Mr James McClintock (57) had been a Corporal in 5 UDR but had resigned in May and was working as a driver. An armed PIRA gang had stolen a van in a Nationalist area of Londonderry and had driven to Foyle Crescent in the Newbuildings area of Co Londonderry, which is located on the eastern bank of the River Foyle, some three miles south of the city. Mr McClintock had been dicked on several occasions and gunmen lay in wait close to a bend at which point, drivers had to slow down in order to negotiate safely. As he slowed down, the gunmen opened fire with automatic weapons, hitting him several times and killing him almost immediately. They escaped in the stolen van and abandoned it in the Nationalist Shantallow area. A local churchman described the killing as both "horrible and brutal" and stated that it was "deliberately designed to incite and provoke retaliation." The following day, his cousin-in-law, a part-time UDR soldier was also murdered by the IRA.

Ian Paisley's 'Ulster's Third Force' were in action on the following day, and their less than professional newsletter screamed: 'The Crisis of Our Generation Now Upon Us!' It announced another day of action and catalogued the RUC and UDR personnel who had been killed and injured during the past week. It declared that there would be a 'day of action' and called upon all Loyalists to strike in order to demand action

---

6   For a fuller account see Chapter 21.
7   See incident on January 1 in Chapter 25.

to halt Republican attacks. This apparently, however, did not apply to the UVF. The 'Third Force' planned a huge cavalcade of vehicles to converge on the major roads and cause traffic chaos and congestion. The 'Third Force' paraded at New Buildings in Co Londonderry where James McClintock was murdered the following day. Masked men then produced guns in a show of bravado for the assembled press photographers and fired several volleys of shots into the air.

Mr McClintock's cousin-in-law was Lance Corporal John McKeegan (40) father of three, who was a soldier in 6 UDR. His regular job was delivering wood from a carpenter's around the Strabane area. Earlier, a woman had booked a delivery to the Ballycolman Estate in Strabane and an armed IRA gang had taken over the intended delivery address the night before, holding the family at gunpoint. The Ballycolman Estate is, or was, a hard-line Nationalist area and support for the IRA is strong. The part-time soldier and his workmate arrived at the house in Olympic Drive, and as he turned to collect his delivery, armed men came out of the house and shot him from close range in the back. He fell dying as his shocked colleague could only look on in horror. The murderers escaped in a stolen car which was parked nearby.

Strabane was affected by countless violent episodes between 1970 and the late 1990s. These incidents included gun battles, car bombings, incendiary devices exploding in commercial premises, sustained rioting, hoax bomb alerts and pipe bomb attacks. Particularly in the early to mid-1970s, such incidents occurred on a daily basis and mostly in the Ballycolman and Head of the Town areas. Strabane was a stronghold of the Provisional IRA and, to a lesser extent, the INLA.

BEATING AN AMBUSH
Ken Pettengale, Royal Green Jackets

One Saturday in late November 1981, my section was on 10-minute standby at North Howard Street Mill.[8] As the RMP were doing their rounds delivering cash to the post offices, I was tasked to do random mobile patrols in the area of the Falls and Springfield Road areas to give them some cover. After being out for around ten or so minutes, we started getting bored; we drove up toward the Falls. As we drove past the top of Leeson Street, I noticed that something wasn't 'right', so I got my driver, Mick Connolly to go around again. This time the penny dropped! There was not a single person in the street; no kids, no women and only a single vehicle facing away from us. I got both of my vehicles to straddle either side of the road and well out of view as I assumed it was a bomb. A quick plate check returned it as stolen. At this point I asked for the immediate bricks to come on foot (not a great distance from the Mill) across the waste ground toward the Plevna gap, and to keep talking to me.

A couple of minutes later, the immediate commander – Corporal John Hammond – reported that he had seen a rifle being thrown from an upstairs window of one of the houses, and he was making as best speed as he could. I now realised that this was an ambush! I got John to count the chimneys down for me from the back, and I followed them down the road, till I got to the house; the

---

one with the car outside! I became 'John Wayne' and 'he' took over and I kicked the front door in and was immediately in the front room. Two women, 'done up to the nines' (Belfast style) were sitting on a settee with two kids and a baby in a pram. Neither of them said a word to me; not a single solitary word, so I knew there was something up! At this point a bloke came from upstairs, again saying nothing, so I told him to adopt the position against the stairs. As he did this, John Hammond came over the radio and told me he was in the back yard and had found an M14 with a broken butt lying on the ground. Also at this point, an RUC Sergeant and Inspector, plus my RSM and one of the CO's Rover group came through the front door. Without any preamble, I was physically grabbed by the RUC Sergeant and pulled outside. Right there, in the middle of a rapidly filling Leeson Street, I was bollocked about following the rules' of hot-pursuit!

At around this moment, an ice-cream van came into the street and pulled up just beyond the stolen car, and, as I was being chastised, the guy from the house came out with the two kids – holding each of them by the hand. My 2/ IC Si Coe (real name!) pointed this out and I told the RSM and coppers that the guy was getting away. Unbelievably they STILL carried on trying to explain why I shouldn't have gone in! I tuned them out as best I could and watched as the guy got to the ice-cream van, he looked over his shoulder, left the kids and carried on walking. I had had enough by now, so I shoved the copper to one side and ran after the guy, shouting: 'Army! Stop or I will fire!' However, as I pulled my rifle up to the shoulder, still running, I hit a speed bump, lost my balance, dropped my rifle (which was attached to my wrist!) and fell over! I scrambled to my feet, flew after him and rugby tackled him to the ground, desperately trying to get my rifle up.

It turned out that this scrote – Paul Kelly from Crocus Street and an INLA member – had set up, in conjunction with French TV, an ambush intending to kill one of us on foot patrol, and this was being filmed from the upstairs of the Sinn Féin offices! I was lucky to have been where I was when I was and feel that I really did do my bit on that day.

On the 24th, the death toll of innocent Catholics continued, when Stephen Murphy (19) from the Oldpark area, died after being shot and fatally wounded by the UVF at his home on the 14th. He had fought for his life for the past 10 days. When he was shot, it was only a few hours after the Provisionals had killed two men at Finaghy, one of whom was an MP. At the inquest, he was described by the Belfast Coroner as: "a poor unfortunate boy, chosen out of spite and at random; a perfectly innocent victim." One of the killers was also a member of the Shankill Butchers' gang and was later convicted of his part in the murder of Joseph Donegan in October, the following year.[9]

On the 24th, the INLA proved whatever the Provisionals' European team could achieve, so could they. First of all, an INLA bombing team planted a device outside the British Consulate in Harvestehuder Weg. A 20 lb (9 kgs) device inside a gas bottle was left on the steps of the building but it failed to detonate properly and caused only minor structural damage. The device, left inside a travelling bag was designed to kill or

---

9 See Chapter 34.

maim consular staff which included, at the time, Sir Jock and Lady Taylor, the British Ambassador to West Germany and his wife, plus some other personnel. The attack was aimed at the Ambassador as it was known that he had travelled from Bonn to Hamburg in order to give a speech. At first it was thought that the device had been planted by Baader-Meinhof, but the INLA claimed responsibility.[10] Thwarted this time, the bombing team moved on to attack a BAOR base in Herford, approximately 100 miles further south. Herford is located in the lowlands between the hill chains of the Wiehen and the Teutoburg Forest and was the HQ for the British 1st Armoured Division. Within the garrison, there were three main barracks, all formerly used by the German Wehrmacht during the last war: Wentworth, Hammersmith, and Harewood Barracks. The INLA bomb was designed to kill and maim sleeping soldiers, but fortunately, there was only one injury; a guard received cuts and bruises.

On the 28th of the month, the IRA killed a policeman in the vicinity of the Nationalist Unity Flats in North Belfast. The flats were a hodgepodge of four-storey homes – maisonettes was the posh word for them – complete with aerial walkways, arranged in blocks and faintly resembling Alcatraz Prison. They were designed as over-spill housing for Catholic families from the Belfast slum clearances of the 50s and 60s and were soulless and uninspiring. Quite what the architect or Belfast Housing Executive had in mind when they built the flats just off the Shankill Road is anybody's guess. It was then, and still is, a Loyalist/Protestant heartland. Families whose flats faced the Shankill Road/Peter's Hill and along parts of Carrick Hill had to permanently board up their windows and live in an almost surreal, perpetual artificial light, in order to prevent bullets and rocks from entering their dwelling places. To the west of the flats was the Shankill Estate, and all that kept the warring factions apart was a rusting, disused railway line, which was later dug up. The city's A12 Westlink now runs along the course of the old railway tracks.

The Provisionals had watched police patterns and were aware of the handover routines and locations. An explosive device had been planted near one of the possible locations, but an RUC informer inside the New Lodge IRA had warned his handlers of this. It would appear that this warning was not conveyed to officers. Back on that late November evening in 1982, as such an on-site RUC shift change took place, Constable William Coulter (23) was about to drive off in a Land Rover at the junction of North Street and Peter's Hill when the device, placed behind a fence exploded. He was killed instantly, leaving a heavily pregnant widow. His was the last death in November.

The month had claimed 14 lives, five of them soldiers or former soldiers, and two policemen had been killed. A total of six civilians died: three Protestant and three Catholic. Three of these killings were overtly sectarian. One Loyalist had died in an internal 'execution.' This month, 10 of the dead were all killed by the provisional IRA.

10   *Glasgow Herald* (25 November, 1981).

24

December

There were only three deaths this month, the second lowest for the years which the author has covered from 1972 to 1982. One death was probably the result of terrorist activity and the other two – of military personnel – were Troubles-related but not the handiwork of paramilitaries. The one death where suspicion falls upon the Provisionals has always been denied by them; but it could probably be a case of "well they would, wouldn't they?"

On the 3rd, Ian Paisley, claimed that the 'Third Force' had between 15,000 and 20,000 members. Secretary of State for Northern Ireland, James Prior said, in response, that private armies would not be tolerated. Quite what he thought that the paramilitary forces of both the Republicans and Loyalists were, is not recorded!

The 'Disappeared' is a term which this author has discussed *passim*, and relates to the c. 18 people who have been murdered by the Provisional IRA and their bodies either have never been found, or were not found for a number of years afterwards. The esteemed publication *Lost Lives* speculates that there may have been a 19th; Sean Murphy (25) who disappeared from the Crossmaglen area on or around 4 December, 1981.[1] The IRA has never admitted that they killed him nor have they admitted that they were behind his disappearance. Sean Murphy was an arsonist – and as such would have been considered to be an 'anti-social' element by the pious Republican terror group. He was en-route to see his girlfriend and both he and his car vanished. However, in the summer of 1986, his badly decomposed body and damaged and rusted car were found in Dundalk Bay in the Irish Republic. He is considered a victim of the Troubles, but one cannot attribute his death to any paramilitary group with any certainty. Those still missing, as of the date of publication, according to the group *'Forget Me Not'* are: Kevin McKee (IRA); Robert Nairac (British Army); Seamus Wright (IRA); Seamus Ruddy (INLA); Lisa Dorrian (Catholic civilian); Joe Lynskey (Catholic civilian) and Columba McVeigh (Catholic civilian). In September 2014, human remains thought to be those of Brendan Megraw were found in a bog in Co Meath. All of the disappeared, with the exception of Lisa Dorrian are either known or believed to be victims of Republican paramilitaries; Ms Dorrian was a victim of Loyalists.

On the 21st, the US Department of State announced that it had revoked Ian Paisley's visa to visit the USA. The firebrand preacher and leader of the DUP had made some inflammatory statements over the 'Third Force' and other comments he made

---

1   Thornton, David, Seamus Kelters, Brian Feeney and David McKittrick. *Lost Lives: The Stories of the Men, Women and Children who Died as a Result of the Northern Ireland Troubles.* (Edinburgh: Mainstream, 1999, revised ed. 2007).

in Northern Ireland. Over 100 US Congressmen had lobbied the State Department to revoke the visa. These presumably were the same ones who supported the IRA as 'rebels' and 'revolutionaries' and the same ones who would lobby on behalf of convicted murderer Joe Doherty. To this author's previous criticisms of American naivety, please add 'hypocrisy.'

On Christmas Day, two soldiers died in the Province; one from the Coldstream Guards and one from the Parachute Regiment. On a day which loved ones wanted to celebrate Christmas with a wish that their son or husband or father was safe, CVOs were dispatched to two households in England. Corporal John George Spensley (26) of the Coldstream Guards died in an RTA; the author has no further details. On the same day, Lance Corporal Peter Hampson (25) of the Parachute Regiment died as a result of 'violent or unnatural causes.'

Earlier in this book, we looked at negligent discharges, and subsequently, I interviewed several other former soldiers for their experience in relation to the seemingly ubiquitous NDs and to that all-embracing term 'death by violent or unnatural causes'.

Steve 'T', Royal Artillery
One of the most disturbing things I saw among our own troops was, I'm sure, down to stress but it could have turned out very nasty. We had just come back into the mill after a patrol one afternoon; when we finally got to our room, a violent argument broke out between two of the lads. This was because one of them had put something on the other's bunk. It led to one of them loading a full mag onto his SLR, cocking it and pointing it from a distance of six inches right between the other guy's eyes! You can imagine the room went deathly silent for a few seconds; fortunately he saw sense and lowered the rifle and gave it to me. I immediately unloaded it and made it safe. I suppose my point is did anyone else experience shit like this between our own? I will never forget that awful feeling, thinking 'Fucking hell he's gonna do it!' That day was fucking horrible.

Jock 2413, Royal Artillery
Had a 'base rat' Signaller at our location in Londonderry who got a 'Dear John' from his bird. He didn't handle it well and somehow got hold of a bottle of whiskey and got pissed. He was blubbing so much about life not worth living without her that one of the lads said: 'Why don't you give us all a break and top yourself?' The lad grabbed a rifle and stuck a mag on it. Someone had the sense to grab a baton gun and it was quietly loaded with a 25 grain and if he had cocked the rifle, he would have copped one. Happily, commonsense prevailed and he handed over the rifle. As was normal in those days, it was all kept 'in house'. Just as well, as our CO at that time was a right bastard, and would have had no hesitation in gaoling him, and would probably have tried to do the same to the anonymous lad who loaded the baton gun.

CARELESS DEATHS
Former Subaltern, Infantry Regiment
I served in Northern Ireland during the years of your research and witnessed some incredibly stupid incidents involving firearms and was also privy to some

confidential reports concerning avoidable deaths. One will not divulge names or places and one trusts that one's words will be taken at face value. In one incident while based in a 'hard Green' area of Belfast, I was called in to interview eyewitnesses to a barrack room shooting which involved two young soldiers who were playing 'quick draw' with Browning 9-mms. Unknown to the participants in a re-creation of the 'Wild West' one of the Browning pistols was cocked and the safety catch was off. Apparently one of the young men was playing the 'baddie' and the other was in the role of gunslinger 'Wild Bill Hickock'. It was the sort of scene which is recreated every day as children, having just seen the latest Western film, decide to re-enact the scenes which had just thrilled them.

The scene was, somewhat incredibly, witnessed by a Junior NCO who did nothing to stop the horseplay and indeed, according to some accounts, actually encouraged it. It transpired that both had won one quick draw each and the game was to be decided by the next draw. As one might imagine, this was a tragic accident just waiting to happen and, sure enough, 'Wild Bill's' pistol discharged a round and tore through the top part of the Baddie's right shoulder making quite a mess. By the time I arrived, the wounded man had been taken away to hospital and his 'opponent' was already under close arrest.

When I walked into the room in the company of the Colour (Colour Sergeant) the men jumped to attention and one swears that every man there had white faces. The Baddie's blood lay in a congealing puddle on the floor next to one of the bunk beds and there were bloodstains on one of the top blankets. Naturally everyone there was interviewed and, while many were reluctant to 'shop' their mates, enough evidence was produced to show definitively what had taken place. What had scared a couple of the men was the fact that both were standing behind the wounded man and could easily have become victims themselves. I left it to the Colour Sergeant to give a group rollicking and one will never forget his words: "You fucking stupid set of idiots; you fucking shower! Isn't it enough that the bleeding IRA are trying to kill you all without doing it to yourselves?"

I am also aware that in another regiment there was an 'eternal triangle' killing at a base in North Belfast. One man had been seeing the wife of another and had become more than intimate with this lady who was contemplating leaving her husband for her 'paramour'. Apparently the cuckolded soldier's pleas for an end to the affair had fallen on deaf ears and in time-honoured fashion, the wronged man took his revenge – bloodily. As a patrol including said man returned to base, they made their weapons safe. For the uninitiated, this involves removing the magazine from their weapon, rapidly cocking the weapon three times, then, pointing it at sandbags or sandpit squeezing the trigger. On this occasion, the aggrieved soldier walked past the 'make safe' area and on seeing his love rival, pointed his SLR at him and fired one round. The 7.62mm hit him square in the chest and he was dead within seconds. Both myself and the author are aware of the identity of the dead soldier and both of us are committed to never disclosing it.

As my old Colour said, it was dangerous enough on the streets of Northern Ireland without our men killing and wounding each other.

Nigel Ward, Queen's Lancashire Regiment

There were many times on our tour in 1980–81 that I was tempted to put a round through my own skull! If it hadn't have been for my brick commander I feel I would have done it. I was sat in my billet in XMG one Sunday night and Cyril came in to see me. He found me with the barrel of my SLR in my mouth and for over an hour, he sat and talked to me and eventually persuaded me to put my weapon down and give it to him. I suppose it was the stress we were put under, but I will never know if I would have pulled the trigger if Cyril had not walked in. Sadly I am still living that tour to this very day.

December ended with a civilian death and two military deaths; it was the quietest month for over a year, but the terrorists on both sides of the sectarian divide were plotting and counter-plotting, and the New Year was just around the corner.

AWARDS FROM THE 1981 TOUR
Carl Ball, Royal Welch Fusiliers

At the end of the tour the 1st Battalion was complimented on its performance by Commander Land Forces Ireland, who wrote that all members of the battalion have distinguished themselves in the most difficult and dangerous of situations. Colonel PH Reece was awarded the DSO, and other decorations to the battalion including an MBE for Gallantry an MC, a DCM, an MM, six mention in dispatches and 9 GOC's commendations. The number and value of these awards to a single battalion during a six-month tour is unprecedented and demonstrates their contribution

1981 had ended and fatalities were well up compared to the previous year; much of the increase was down to the hunger strikes and its aftermath.

The figures were as follows:

Total	136	(110)
Army	46	(46)
Police	23	(13)
Prison officers		(2)
Civilians	45	(40)
Catholics	31	(25)
Protestants	14	(13)
Republicans	18	(7)
Loyalists	3	(2)

Of these, 14 could be said to be sectarian murders, over double the 1980 total.

Part Three

1982

This was a year in which the death toll again reached over the 100 mark, and it would see the deaths of 46 soldiers or former soldiers. It would also witness the deaths of 12 policemen. It was a year made infamous for cowardly attacks by the IRA, and one which would see the word 'outrage' appear often in the British press: outrages such as Hyde Park and Regents Park in London, and the Droppin' Well disco in Ballykelly.

25

January

In this month, a leading UDA official was assassinated and the Kincora School abuse scandal hit the headlines again. Eight people were killed in January.

The New Year was just 23 hours old when the Provisionals struck, this time in a car park at Newcastle, Co Down. A UDR soldier had been dicked as he went for a night out with his friend at the coastal resort. Newcastle is a seaside town and lies on the Irish Sea coast at the base of Slieve Donard, one of the Mourne Mountains. While the two men were drinking, a PIRA bombing team planted an explosive device underneath the car which was owned by the UDR soldier. The car started and began to move forward when the bomb exploded. Samuel Pollack (19) was mortally wounded, dying very shortly afterwards. The soldier, who was a member of 3 UDR, lost part of his leg. Two months earlier, one of Mr Pollack's relatives, a policeman, was appallingly injured by a PIRA UVBT.[1]

Ian Paisley was quick to blame the British Government in general and Secretary of State for Northern Ireland, Jim Prior, in particular. He accused the Thatcher Administration of not tightening up security and for allowing known players to be still walking the streets. Measures were put into place by the UDR's Security Section to survey their soldiers' homes and provide advice on locks, external lighting and security blinds so that would-be killers could not see inside. These measures, though well-meaning, could have done nothing for another UDR soldier who would be shot dead at work just seven days later. During this year, 14 UDR soldiers would be killed, six of whom would be murdered at home or at work or travelling between the two places.

On the 4th, PIRA's ISU were in action again when they stormed into a house at Horn Drive, just north of Andersonstown Road on the Nationalist Lenadoon. Their target was an alleged informer, John Torbett (29), father of four whom they suspected of 'touting' for the RUC. The ISU had 'investigated' a claim that, after his arrest by the RUC, he had agreed to be a paid informer. In this instance, he was given 72 days to leave Northern Ireland, and when he refused, they shot him in his own living room. He was fatally wounded in the attack and died 15 days later in hospital, on the 19th.

The ISU had unlimited access to IRA members, apparatus, and resources in carrying out its duties. Its remit could not be countermanded except by order of the Army Council. It had five major duties: Security and character vetting of new recruits to the IRA; collecting and collating material on failed and compromised IRA operations; collecting and collating material on suspect or compromised individuals (informers); interrogation

---

1   See Chapter 23.

and debriefing of suspects and compromised individuals, and finally, carrying out executions of those judged guilty by IRA courts martial. As Marty McGartland said, they were a group within the Provisionals which no one wanted to meet on a 'professional' basis.

On the 8th, armed PIRA gunmen walked into St Paul's Church which is located at the junction of Cavendish Street and the Falls Road, close to Springfield Road RUC station. A family of churchgoers was held at gunpoint after being forced out of their home near Glen Road and taken to the church. While they were inside St Paul's, other PIRA men took their car and drove across North Belfast to a petrol station on the Antrim Road. Part-time UDR soldier Private Steven Carelton (24), father of a small child, worked there when not on duty with the regiment. The gunmen went inside the station where he was working and shot him in the head and chest several times, mortally wounding him. He died very shortly afterwards.

On the 13th, Lord Gowrie, from the NIO made a statement which would not have pleased Loyalists but at the same time, given that Gowrie was a 'posh Tory type' would have left them sceptical anyway. The NIO Minister, said that Direct Rule was "very un-British" and indicated that he personally preferred a form dual citizenship, with Britain and the Republic of Ireland being responsible for the administration of those who considered themselves to be Irish. The Loyalists would have seen this as 'reunification by the back door' and it would have merely served to inflame their fears about being handed back to the Republic.

Two days later, Lord Gowrie's boss – Jim Prior – was in the news again when he announced the setting up of a Committee of Inquiry into the sexual abuse of children who lived in the Kincora Boys' Home in Belfast. The scandal first broke on 3 April 1980 when three staff members of the Kincora Boys' Home, Belfast were charged with acts of gross indecency and sexual abuse of the boys in their care. Allegations continued to be made that civil servants and a number of Loyalists had been involved in the abuse of young boys at Kincora. Among those later convicted was William McGrath, leader of Loyalist group Tara. The Kincora Boys' Home was a children's home in Belfast, pre-troubles; three members of staff at the home, William McGrath, Raymond Semple and Joseph Mains, were charged with a number of offences relating to the systematic sexual abuse of children in their care over a number of years. All three were later convicted and gaoled; Mains, the former warden, received a term of six years, Semple, a former assistant warden, five years and McGrath was gaoled for four years. John McKeague, who was killed by the INLA later in the month, was said to have strong links with the paedophile ring at the Kincora. Tara was an extreme Loyalist movement which preached a brand of evangelical Protestantism. Tara enjoyed some influence in the late 1960s before declining and being overtaken by other groups such as the UDA.

Ian Paisley was accused of failing to report the fact of McGrath's suspect sexual practices to the relevant authorities, although he initially denied ever being advised by a fellow church member – Valerie Shaw, – that McGrath worked in a boys' home. Unsubstantiated allegations were later made that senior RUC officers had also been informed of the abuse at the home for years previously, but had not moved to prevent it. The paedophile McGrath was released from prison in December 1983 after serving two years of his four-year sentence, later moving to Ballyhalbert, Co Down. He attempted to regain his membership of the Orange Order but was vetoed consistently in his attempt. He died in the early 90s.

On the 19th, an INLA member proved that negligent discharges (ND) were not the exclusive property of the British Army. Deborah Rowe (17) was shot dead by her INLA boyfriend when he accidentally fired a round into her chest while cleaning what later turned out to be a faulty handgun. She was from the Creggan Estate in Londonderry and was at her boyfriend's house in nearby Rosemount Gardens when the accident occurred. Miss Rowe died at the scene and her boyfriend was convicted and sent to prison. On the same day, John Torbett who had been fatally wounded by the IRA's ISU died from his wounds; see earlier in this chapter for further details.

BELFAST BAPTISM
William Clive Hawkins, Royal Regiment of Wales

We arrived at Moscow Barracks, Belfast Docks, just before dark. We kitted up, got on our vehicles and within an hour were sent to Moy Yard SF base. We had to drive from Moscow Barracks between three and five miles along an unlit road with forestry either side, in two 'locked down' Saracen armoured cars. To the uninitiated, that means that there was no visibility except for the driver and commander.

Within 100 metres of leaving the barracks, there was a shout of: 'Contact front!' This indicated that we were being shot at from the front, so both vehicles stopped immediately and we deployed into a ditch on our right hand side. We watched the 'bullet strikes' hitting both vehicles near their tops of them. We were waiting for a command to open fire, when someone announced: 'Stand down', as it was all clear. It transpired that the driver of the front vehicle had lost control of his vehicle and hit a telegraph pole which was carrying un-insulated power lines; in turn these power lines bounced on the tops of both vehicles, throwing flashes, sparks and flames all over the place, which were mistaken for gunfire. This was my initiation into Northern Ireland as it was my first tour, so it was back onto the vehicles and on to Moy Yard.

We got to Moy Yard some time later, to be briefed that we would be acting as a QRF (Quick Reaction Force), being deployed as and when required anywhere in Belfast. We were told that we would be relieving worn out troops who hadn't slept for three or more days, bolstering their numbers at operations where they are in danger of being overwhelmed, and sharing their camp duties. We had been there for some three hours when a disturbance broke out at 'Kelly's Corner' which was three hundred yards to the right of the camp. There was gunfire and petrol bombs were aimed at a two-vehicle Saracen Patrol and IRA men were trying to roll aluminium beer kegs under the front of the Saracens in order to lift the wheels off the floor and strand them. This was so that they could attack them at leisure.

All of a sudden there was a huge crashing sound; someone from outside had stolen a lorry and driven it into our perimeter fence (16-foot corrugated iron sheeting) and dragged it off down the street! I felt terrified and naked; we were open to the world and I was absolutely stranded in a sangar. How would I be able to tell who was coming up the stairs? It was pitch dark, and there was a heavy steel hatch in the floor that I would have to lift to let anyone in; if it was IRA it would already be too late, as they would shoot through the floor.

The camp was only the size of a football pitch, yet it seemed like miles to the accommodation which was just Portacabins. It seemed like ages before any of our lads emerged to form a base line to secure the camp. We were extremely vulnerable, even if they only threw house-bricks they would probably go straight over our heads and out the other side of our tiny defenceless camp, and we still had to go and bail out the lads in the Saracens at 'Kelly's Corner' yet. So half the base contingent was sent down there while the rest of us secured the camp and waited for the engineers to come and re-instate our perimeter fence. I didn't sleep well, having had such an eventful first three hours and seeing how vulnerable we really were.

A number of Republicans were able to enter the US illegally during the late 70s and early 80s. Canadian sympathisers organised what they called an 'underground railway' through which members of Sinn Féin and the IRA would be provided with forged documents and escorted across the US border. Some participated in clandestine fundraising and weapons procurement ventures while others simply tried to blend into society and avoid federal agents. US immigration officers began investigating this Canadian pipeline and conducted surveillance of suspects under 'Operation Shamrock.' Information from this investigation led to the apprehension of Owen Carron and Danny Morrison on 21 January 1982. Shortly afterward, agents captured Edward Howell and Desmond Ellis as they were trying to enter the United States illegally at the Whirlpool Bridge near Niagara Falls. The authorities described both men as key IRA explosives experts. The pair had entered Canada and were trying to reach New York in order to discuss the purchase of arms with NORAID. The four men were later deported back to Canada, as the US showed a little backbone in dealing with Irish terrorists. Later both men were convicted on a charge of making false statements to American immigration officials. Morrison was director of publicity for Sinn Féin from 1979 until 1990. He was then charged with falsely imprisoning a suspected informer – Sandy Lynch – and conspiracy to murder him. He was sentenced to eight years in prison and was released in 1995.

Carron's path to 'respectable' politics was almost equally coloured. In 1986, an AK47 rifle was found in a car in which he was a passenger and, though charged, he was released in order to stand as a Sinn Féin candidate to fight a by-election in Co Fermanagh! He lost, but jumped bail, crossed the border and went to live in Co Leitrim. He was arrested in 1988 in the Republic and held in custody for two and a half years while the British Government tried to have him extradited. The Irish Supreme Court, like their supine and pusillanimous colleagues in the USA, fought tooth and nail to prevent him being sent to stand trial. They ruled in the end, that possession of an automatic weapon was a 'political' offence and he could not be extradited!

On Friday 22nd and Saturday 23rd, Loyalist killed Loyalist as even their hatred for their own equalled that of their hatred for the Republicans. The UVF considered Robert Mitchell (45) a leading figure in the UDA, to be an RUC informer. His son, Robert Mitchell (25) was, judging by his inclusion on a UDA/UFF 'roll of honour,' also a member. In the very early hours of the Saturday morning, both were at home in Roseberry Gardens in South-East Belfast near the Ormeau Embankment. As they prepared for bed, UVF gunmen burst in and shot both men, who died almost immediately. For good measure, they shot the family dog, but ignored a younger son who was also in the house.

TOO TIRED TO EAT
Dave Judge, Royal Green Jackets

A little one here; remember how tired you could sometimes get when you were on the streets of Northern Ireland? We were in Londonderry early '80s and were always on the streets, facing many thousands (not hundreds) of rioters and these riots were marathons! They went on so long that the CQMS would sometimes have to do water replens and also brought out tea bombs, even though we may be no more than 500 metres from an SF base. Well, my good friend Paddy Sexton could sleep – boy, could he sleep! We were at the Little Diamond on one occasion and the shields we had were the 6-foot Makralon ones and there was a mountain of rubble piled up at the front of them. Paddy was holding his shield with his head resting on His arm that was through the arm handles and he was fast asleep while standing! On another occasion, he was asleep in the gutter and it was raining; the water was running down the gutter and going into the neck of his combat jacket and seeping out of his trousers by his boots! They are two vivid memories of Paddy Sexton. The man who truly could sleep on a washing line!

On the 24th, a UDR foot patrol chanced upon two men who were attempting to break into a shop in Armagh City. What followed next is open to conjecture as the family and friends of Anthony Harker (21) have one version, and the part-time soldiers who shot him state the opposite. The two men were challenged and one of them – Mr Harker – refused to stop and was shot as the soldier feared that he was armed. In such fraught circumstances, with over 2,600 people, many of them soldiers already dead, it was apparent that the UDR couldn't take a chance. The family and friends, and in particular Sinn Féin, state that he was not challenged and simply shot out of hand. Although he was a thief or would-be thief, the man had a history of pro-Republican activity and had been arrested and gaoled several times. Sinn Féin was able to point to this as a reason why he was killed. As in all of these incidents, it is a matter of who does one believe; this author's instinct is to back the soldiers at the scene.

Three days later, in the Irish Republic, the Coalition Government of Fine Gael and the Irish Labour Party collapsed when independent Teachta Dála (TDs) voted against proposed tax increases on items such as petrol, alcohol, and tobacco. It did little to encourage the British Government that the strong, leadership which was required in the South in order to stand firm against the IRA, would happen.

On the 29th, John Dunlop McKeague (29), the founder of the Red Hand Commando (RHC), extreme Loyalist and a man with links to the Kincora scandal was shot dead. Among many allegations levelled against him were claims that he was homosexual, and a paedophile who abused young boys in Kincora Boys' Home. Conspiracists also claim that he was also an agent working for the British Government. He owned a hardware shop in Albertbridge Road on the southern border of the Nationalist Short Strand, in East Belfast. As he prepared to lock up for the night, two masked men from the INLA burst into the shop and shot him in the head from point-blank range. They ignored his assistant and walked outside to a waiting car and disappeared in the direction of the Short Strand.

Some 11 years earlier, McKeague's reputation for promiscuous sexual relationships with young male recruits into the UDA, and a tendency to make public his extremist views about Catholics, had upset senior figures in the Loyalist movement. This had provoked a fire-bomb attack on his shop in 1971, which killed his elderly mother – Isabella McKeague – who lived on the premises. Four years afterwards, the Provisionals then bombed the shop and a Catholic, Alice McGuinness, was injured and died three days later. She was buried in the rubble and seriously injured; she died that same evening. She had no known paramilitary associations and was merely making a purchase; her death left eight children without a mother. McKeague's sister was badly injured in the attack.[2]

Earlier in the month, John McKeague was called in by the RUC and questioned further by detectives investigating Kincora and his involvement in the paedophile ring. It is alleged that he had intimated that he would name others, hitherto not mentioned, who were also involved in the scandal, in order to avoid being charged himself. Some writers allege that he was involved with Military Intelligence and that his energies and 'talents' and prominent position in Loyalist circles made him useful. Further, it is alleged, but totally unsubstantiated, that some senior military figures were also involved in Kincora. For that reason, the conspiracy theorists maintained that British Army Intelligence was behind the killing of McKeague. This author will keep an open mind, but instinctively believes that he was, and had been for some time, a target for Republican paramilitaries and that his death was at the hands of the INLA.

By the end of the first month of the New Year, eight people were dead; one soldier had been killed as well as four civilians. Three Catholics were killed as well as one Protestant. Three Loyalist paramilitaries had been killed; two as a result of internecine fighting one at the hands of the INLA. Republicans had killed five and Loyalists were responsible for the deaths of two.

---

2   See Wharton, Ken M., *Wasted Years, Wasted Lives* (Solihull: Helion, 2013), Vol 1, Chapter 10.

26

February

J ust three people died this month, a soldier, an Irish policeman and a civilian. It was almost as though both sides of the paramilitary struggle had tired of the bombings and shootings, and had paused in order to draw breath. Only a fool would have been lulled into a sense of security over this; July and the Royal Parks would soon be in the news.

On the 1st, Representatives of the UUP held a meeting with Secretary of State for Northern Ireland, James Prior. They told him that they were opposed to his policy of 'rolling devolution'. Since the imposition of 'direct rule' some years previously, the Loyalists had become both increasingly suspicious and increasingly pessimistic about the prospect of being sold out to the Republic. Indeed, they looked for support from Michael Foot, then leader of the Labour Party, who had just started a three day visit to Northern Ireland.

The author has previously written about the dangers of joy-riding, especially in such a volatile period as the Troubles. Four joy-riders had been killed by the Security Forces in the last two years, as a consequence of failing to stop at a VCP. On the 5th, there was another such incident, when a stolen car containing Martin Kyles (19) and Gerard Logue crashed through an Army VCP in the grounds of the RVH. The soldiers were forced to scatter, one of whom was badly injured, but fired at the vehicle as it roared past them. Kyles was fatally wounded and died in the same hospital some 48 hours later. Incredibly, it emerged that he had been shot and wounded by a soldier in exactly the same situation four years earlier. One of the survivors – the aforementioned Gerard Logue – was killed nearly three years later when he tried to outrun the RUC at a VCP in West Belfast. He was the second joy-rider to die in the space of a few days in January 1985.

Between the 12th and 18th of the month, the scandal of Kincora Boys' Home was again in the news with recriminations ringing out like church bells. Allegations were later made that the RUC had been informed of the abuse at the home for years previously, but had done nothing to prevent it or arrest the perpetrators. In this context, three of the five members of the Committee of Inquiry set up to investigate the scandal resigned, also accusing the RUC of deliberate inaction. The committee had been set up under the Commissioner of Complaints, Stephen McGonagle, to deal with a growing catalogue of allegations. It was almost as though the police attitude had been one of *laissez faire*. On the 18th, prodded into action by the growing controversy, James Prior announced that a full public inquiry would take place into the matters surrounding the events at Kincora. The recent murder of an alleged member of the paedophile ring, John McKeague, had sent shock waves around those with things to hide and there were accusations of cover ups at the highest levels.

On the 16th, an officer in the Royal Marines, attached to HQNI was killed in an RTA, while on duty. Major John Richard Cooper died in the accident, but the author unfortunately has no further information.

On the 18th, there was another General Election in the Irish Republic as the Coalition Government of Fine Gael and the Irish Labour Party sought a working majority. However, their hopes were dashed and Taoiseach Garret FitzGerald lost the election; a minority Fianna Fáil Government under the former Taoiseach Charles Haughey was elected instead. Encouraged by their electoral successes during and after the hunger strikes, an increasingly politicised Sinn Féin stood in seven constituencies, but lost in each one.

The following day – Friday 19th – Garda Patrick Reynolds (23) was on night duty. It had been a hectic week for him and his Gardaí colleagues, as they had policed the General Election the previous day, and he was excited about a home nations Rugby Union match between Ireland and Scotland the following day. He was intending to attend this game with his brother and sister. In the early hours, an emergency call had been received at his station, reporting 'suspicious activity' at a block of flats in Tallaght. Five officers, including Reynolds were dispatched to investigate to an address in Avonbeg Gardens. When they arrived, two of them forced their way inside, where they found a number of armed men counting the proceeds of a bank robbery. There was a tussle and two of the robbers escaped, but a third man, armed with a revolver, chased after an unarmed Gardaí Reynolds and shot him in the back, mortally wounding him. The man, believed to be INLA gunman Sean 'Bap' Hughes, escaped from the building and fled the country to France. The Gardaí Síochána tracked him down and he was arrested by French police and held on an extradition warrant.

Extradition proceedings dragged on for a number of years, with the delay resulting in the extradition being refused by the French courts in 1987. In this instance, the French Courts proved as pusillanimous as their counterparts in both the USA and the Republic of Ireland. 'Bap' served some time in a French gaol on false passport charges, but was then deported and disappeared again. In 1997, he surfaced in Ireland again and was arrested in Foxford, Co Mayo, after robbing a bank there. He was tried for the murder of Garda Reynolds in March 2000, but was acquitted of the murder. It is widely believed that he also spent time in the terrorist haven we know as the USA and was also involved in smuggling arms for the INLA in Europe. Of course these allegations are not as yet proven.

The Provisionals had declared very early on the campaign that their intention was to cause disruption of British maritime traffic out in and around the Port of Londonderry. Their actions forced both British and Irish authorities to deploy security guards in order to protect merchant ships. It was clear that they regarded British shipping as legitimate targets in their so-called 'commercial war.' Indeed, in February, 1981, they had attacked and sank the British ship 'Nellie M' while it was at anchor in the Lough Foyle inlet, barely 300 yards from the Republic's shoreline.[1]

On the 23rd, British ship St Bedan was at anchor in the same location, awaiting the tide to proceed upstream. An IRA boarding party, composed of 12 members seized

---

1   See Chapter 14.

a pilot boat at Moville, and boarded the ship and forced the crew at gunpoint into lifeboats. Explosive devices were planted and the ship abandoned. All of the explosives detonated and the cargo vessel sank on her starboard side in about 50 feet of water. The wreck was raised and scrapped some nine months later

Both the Royal Navy and the RAF were forced to increase their patrols in Northern Ireland waters following the attacks, and warships were often shot at by the IRA, especially from Carlingford Lough. One vessel was actually attacked by an IRA unit firing armour-piercing rounds in one incident. In 1990, the Royal Fleet Auxiliary 'Fort Victoria' was boarded by an IRA team while moored off Belfast. Two devices were planted in the engine room, one of which caused considerable damage; ATO defused the other.

February ended with only three deaths; a soldier, a policeman and a Catholic civilian. It was a quiet month, but there were still three funerals to be arranged and attended, and three sets of loved ones to grieve their losses.

27

March

Nine people died this month, including six soldiers or former soldiers, one policeman, a Loyalist paramilitary and a Republican paramilitary; in the latter two cases, both as a result of either feuding or at the hands of the 'nutting squad.'

On the first Tuesday of the month, Lord Lowry, then Northern Ireland Lord Chief Justice was attacked by the Provisionals, as he paid a visit to Queen's University Belfast. Gunmen fired several shots at Lowry who was not injured but a lecturer at the university who was standing close by was wounded by the gunfire.

Following the killing of the MP Robert Bradford on 14 November the previous year,[1] there was a by-election in the constituency of South Belfast on the 4th to fill the vacant Westminster seat. Martin Smyth, then head of the Orange Order, won the election as a UUP candidate. The election campaign witnessed much antagonism and unpleasantness between the rival Unionist parties, Ian Paisley's DUP and the winning party, the UUP.

Gerard Tuite, formerly a member of the IRA, was arrested in the Republic of Ireland following a period 'on the run'. He became the first person to be charged in the Republic for offences committed in Britain, and had escaped from Brixton Prison on 16 December 1980 where he had been serving a sentence for bombing offences in London. After his escape, he returned to the Irish Republic and continued his terrorist activities. On 4 March 1982, he was finally discovered, during a Special Branch raid on a flat in Drogheda. He was held on remand, then taken before the Irish Special Criminal Court which sentenced him to 10 years imprisonment in July 1982. Tuite is today a businessman in the south Cavan and North Meath region.

Sometime on Friday 5 March, Seamus Morgan (24), father of four, who was a member of the Provisionals' Co Tyrone Brigade was picked up for questioning by the ISU. He was tried before a kangaroo court and judged guilty of betraying the location of an IRA arms dump which was empty at the time to the RUC. It is stated by Moloney in his very biased account of the Provisionals[2] that the ISU were particularly cruel with him. He writes: "his hands tied behind his back and white tape wrapped tightly over his eyes." He was shot in the back of the head and his body was dumped by a roadside outside Forkhill, Co Armagh. It is further claimed that his captors poured whisky and vodka down his throat and that he "cried over photos of his children before his life was abruptly ended." It is thought likely, that he was killed in the early hours of the 6th.

---

1   See Chapter 23.
2   Moloney, Ed, *A Secret History of the IRA* (Harmondsworth: Penguin Books, 2002).

There is a suggestion also that the alleged British double agent Freddie Scappaticci was involved in his death, as part of the 'nutting squad.'

With exquisite timing, the cynical PIRA Army Council announced an amnesty on 26 March. Via their Sinn Féin apologists, they stated that the 'amnesty' would be granted to: "any informers who retracted evidence given to the security forces." With the four Morgan children – all under five – now fatherless, the irony of their timing was not lost on observers, nor was their cynicism. Clearly their age-old paranoia about 'touts' was in the ascendancy. Just one year after the hunger strike, the Provisionals had become more 'popular', yet conversely, less secure about informants within its ranks. The talk of the proposed amnesty offer to informers led to a self-confessed Informer appearing on TV and, while he remained anonymous, told of being turned by the RUC and of begging the IRA for forgiveness via a local Catholic priest.

Five days later, they went back to their tactic of targeting what they considered as 'easy kills', the type where the victim is off-duty and relaxed and generally with his or her back to them. Norman Hanna (28) had served in the UDR for three years, while aged 18 to 21, and resigned in 1975. He lived in Carnbane Gardens, in the northern outskirts of Newry and worked at a vehicle test centre at Rathfriland Road, some three miles to the east of the Co Down town. He had parked outside the test centre, leaving his wife, Sandra and young child in the car, an orange Sunbeam Talbot which they were going to take while he worked, when a motorcycle pulled alongside. He was half in, half out of the car, when the pillion passenger pulled out a pistol and shot him several times; he fell back inside the car and died at the scene. His wife ran screaming to his side and other members of staff alerted by the shooting dashed outside and helped carry his life-less body into the building. As a poignant reminder of the tragedy, his lunch box was left lying outside on the road where it had fallen as he was shot. A colleague said of him: "We are all terribly distressed at what has happened. He was very well liked and a splendid clerical officer."

It is alleged that the PIRA 'supergrass' Eamon Collins had selected Mr Hanna as a target based on flawed information provided to him by a former IRP member who is not named for legal reasons.[3] Collins states that the man who murdered Hanna shot him eight times and then was violently sick as he saw all of the blood and then apparently shot himself in the leg as he struggled to conceal the still-smoking weapon. Mrs Hanna could only look on in horror as her daughter screamed: "Daddy, Daddy, Daddy." The Provisionals stated somewhat piously that they should be 'kept informed' when a man leaves the UDR in order to remove him from the target list. In this instance, Collins and his 'former-IRP' informer were the ones responsible for the murder.

Collins, as a leading member of the Provisionals' Newry and South Down Brigade was partially responsible for the tragic events of the 15th. At around about 1730 hours, the traditional British (as well as Irish) tea-time, Alan McCrum (11) was standing in Bridge Street in the centre of Banbridge waiting for a lift home; although he didn't know it, he had left school for the last time. Without warning or preamble, in a street crowded with late afternoon shoppers and workers setting off home, a car exploded. People were blown off their feet; others were cut down by the blast or cut by a myriad of pieces of

3   Collins, Eamon, *Killing Rage* (London: Granta, 1997).

flying glass. Little Alan was caught by the full rage of the bomb and was killed instantly. The Ulster Bank, Bridge Café, Thompson's Dye Works, McAleenan's Hairdressers and a local butcher's shop bore the brunt of the deadly device and 34 people were injured, some seriously.

Collins himself had helped to 'scout' the bomb in and, while he was not responsible for the death and injuries directly, he is equally culpable as the bombing team who prepared the bomb and drove it and abandoned it on Bridge Street. Reaction around the world was swift and the condemnation by the *New York Times* rang extremely hollow as their initial reports inaccurately stated that a warning had been given. Reuters reported:

Car Bomb West of Belfast Kills Child and Injures 10

BELFAST, Northern Ireland, March 15 – A car bomb exploded today in Banbridge, killing a 9–year-old [sic] child and injuring 10 people [sic], five of them seriously, the police said. They said the bomb was detonated without warning on a crowded main street in Banbridge, 30 miles west of Belfast.

Banbridge is actually 30 miles south-west of Belfast.

The young boy's funeral was held three days later, and the TV crews were allowed to report from Alan's High School in Banbridge, and filmed the poignancy of his school assembly, followed by the funeral from Loughbrickland farm.

On the 17th, with the dust barely settled on the Banbridge outrage, Irish Taoiseach Charles Haughey, paid a visit to the United States, as part of St Patrick's Day celebrations. During the visit he called upon the Government of Ronald Reagan to put more pressure on Britain to consider the possibility of Irish unity. The Irish leader was fully aware of the goodwill which was extended towards his countrymen on this day and equally cogniscant of the enormous pressure which was being piled on by the powerful Irish-American lobby. It is not recorded whether he also visited Senator Kennedy and his cronies, but would seem plausible that he would indeed do so.

On the 20th, the UDR lost another of their soldiers in an unexplained shooting accident. His death has been attributed to a negligent discharge. Private Jonathan Gilbert Moorhead (24) of Bearbrook, Co Armagh was in the Bellinghome area of the city when he was shot. The author has no further information.

On the 25th of the month, a routine escort trip turned into an appalling tragedy for the Royal Green Jackets (RGJ). Formed in 1755 as the 62nd of Foot – the Royal Americans – it fought at Québec with Wolfe and all through the American War of Independence of 1775–83. Through various incarnations it fought alongside generals of the stature of Wellington and Sir John Moore against Napoleon and served through the 19th and 20th centuries. It was one of the first British Army units to wear green and break the static Redcoat 'Box' style of fighting and attack as skirmishers ('fire and move'). Its battle honours are proudly displayed on its cap badge and include Waterloo, Inkerman, Ladysmith, Ypres ('Wipers'), the Somme, El Alamein and Pegasus Bridge. The regiment's predecessors – the Ox & Bucks – landed on the Orne-Caen Canal and helped to liberate the first part of Nazi-occupied France; one of its officers, Lieutenant Den Brotheridge was the first British soldier to die on D-Day.

From the heights of Québec and the fields of Abraham to a sordid back street in West Belfast; that was the journey of this famous and notable regiment. A two-vehicle unit from 2RGJ was tasked to escort an RAF sergeant on the short, but potentially deadly journey to North Howard Street Mill (NHSM) from the fortified RUC base at Springfield Road. Today – and indeed before the Troubles – Violet Street is and was, a through road, but back in 1980 it was blocked off at the top where it meets Springfield Road for security reasons. At the bottom of the street, where it meets Cavendish Street, it is a one-way system and military traffic had to endure three right turns before it was able to enter Springfield Road.

Some 11 hours before this patrol set off, clearly waiting for a target of opportunity, a PIRA ASU had occupied a house on Cavendish Street where it meets Crocus Street. The family had been held under armed guard and an M60 machine-gun set up. At that point, their lookouts spotted two military vehicles turn into Cavendish Street and drive towards the turn-off into Crocus Street. As the first vehicle turned, the gun crew opened fire and both Rifleman Daniel Roy Holland (19) from South-East London and the un-named RAF Sergeant were hit in the head. Rifleman Holland was mortally wounded and his RAF colleague was critically wounded, although the RAF man later survived. The driver sped away to the top of Crocus Street but the second vehicle then came under fire. The driver of this vehicle stopped, and Rifleman Anthony Michael Rapley (22) from Oxford jumped out to return fire but was immediately hit in the head and slumped to the ground, mortally wounded. His comrade, Rifleman Nicholas Panyiotis Malakos (19) from Surrey and of Greek-Cypriot extraction was hit by a fresh burst and wounded in his face, neck and stomach; he too was mortally wounded.

Several other civilians and another soldier were also caught by the deadly fire of the M60, but a Corporal – later awarded the Military Medal – jumped out of the lead vehicle and ran back down the street, firing at the gunmen. At this, the gunmen fled through the back of the house and made good their pre-arranged escape. They had left a pressure-pad explosive device in the back yard in order to deter pursuers, or kill them but fortunately this was spotted and made safe.

There was now a scene of utter carnage in the street and back up troops were quickly there. One Jacket was dead, a second was either dead or about to die, but one man was still alive, if barely. A thoroughly reliable source from the Regiment told the author that as Rifleman Holland lay, barely conscious, a fellow Rifleman cradled him in his arms and whispered: "This is really going to fuck up your mum's weekend." The young soldier smiled and then lost consciousness and died a short time later on the operating table at the nearby RVH. This man has been criticised for his 'tactless' comments but this author believes that the young soldier went to his maker with a smile on his face; further, this author will not condemn the man who cradled a dying brother-in-arms.

The unit – 2RGJ – was in the last 48 hours of its tour of Northern Ireland and was due to return to Minden, West Germany on the 27th. Anthony Rapley's grieving mother said later that her son was depressed and 'down in the dumps.' She told a journalist that when her son left home for Belfast, she had a premonition that she would never see him alive again.

Rifleman Rapley's funeral was held at Oxford Crematorium; Rifleman Malakos's was held at Croydon Crematorium and Rifleman Holland was buried at Woolwich Cemetery.

CROCUS STREET MURDERS
Dave Judge, Royal Green Jackets

On 25th March 1982, the IRA killed three riflemen from 'C' Company, the 2nd Battalion Royal Green Jackets. They were: Riflemen Daniel Holland, Nicholas Malakos and Anthony Rapley. The three were part of a two-vehicle patrol which had just left Springfield Road police station taking an RAF Sergeant to North Howard Street Mill. The patrol left the base and drove down to the bottom of Violet Street into Cavendish Street and then turned right into Crocus Street as per routine. I was in North Howard Street Mill and had just entered the ops room and was speaking to an officer. Suddenly, there was a prolonged burst of machine gun fire which was obviously some distance from the mill. Almost immediately I heard Billy Lindfield send a contact report over the net! It went something along the lines of: "Contact wait out! Contact one minute ago; machine gun fire; three casualties; one almost definitely dead; two VSI (very seriously injured)."

That's about as much as I remember of the contact report itself. I was also just about to go out on the ground and was tasked to collect and take a dog (groundhog) to the scene, just after our Quick Reaction Force (QRF) had gone in. I can't remember where I got the dog team from or how long it took for me to arrive at the scene. By the time I got there,[4] all of the casualties had been taken to RVH (Royal Victoria Hospital). I delivered the dog to the firing point which was a house in Cavendish Street., where IRA gunmen had taken the occupants of the house hostage; an 81-year-old woman, her daughter and son-in law. I accompanied the dog and his handler into the house, and he nearly flipped when we found the house full of RUC officers smoking, and female officers wearing perfume; the place was full of perfume and dozens of different smells and the dog was unable to pick up any meaningful scents.

We went through the hall and into the kitchen and out of the rear door into the yard of the house. I remember the yard was full of the usual things you would find any back yard in Belfast. But what we did not know was that there was a black bin bag with a device inside it on a pressure release plate. This bag had been sprinkled with ash from the fire so as to appear old and look like it had been there for a long time. This I only found out at the end of the incident. The dog followed the route of the escape down the alleyway up until we think a car took those responsible away! I was now re-tasked and was not happy with this! I was told to go to the RVH and collect the flak jacket from one of the soldiers as the glacis plate was still on the secret list.

We were in two vehicles; the commander of the second Land Rover was Dave 'Barney' Barnfield, and together we entered the ER (emergency room) of the hospital and asked the nurses about the three soldiers who had recently been brought in. We already knew at this point that all three were dead and they told us that all of the soldiers' clothing had been returned. So we headed back to the Mill having informed the ops room about the clothing. Before I got to the mill the QM had told the ops officer that a flak jacket was still missing! We were again

---

4   Author's note: Crocus Street is approx. 400 yards from the site of the now demolished Mill.

tasked to return to the hospital. This time I spoke to the doctors! They again said no equipment was in the hospital, so Barney and I went outside and passed on the same information. But I was told in no uncertain terms that I was to locate it!

So in we went again and the doctor handed me a small brown envelope and this contained one of the dead soldier's rosary beads! I insisted that there was equipment in that bloody hospital and he told me I would have to go and check the bodies myself which were now in the mortuary. So off we went and we had to explain the whole thing over again to the mortuary assistant. Barney was still with me was with me and a driver had also come into the room with us. We all soon wished that he had not entered as we were shown the bodies of two of the lads. The nosey driver left and had thrown up outside. We only saw Tony Rapley and Nicky Malakos because Danny Holland had made it to the operating theatre but died before they could help him. We knew that he didn't have it as it would have been removed while they tried to save his life. We eventually found the offending item but it was pointed out to us that for forensic reasons, it had to remain on the poor lad's body. I have deliberately not gone into the condition of the lads as they lay in this awful cold dull room for the sake of any family member that may someday stumble on this book!

One of our Sergeants – Steve Wareing – and his platoon commander had to go to the morgue the next day to officially identify the bodies. I think I warned Steve what was awaiting them! This incident was just about the worst thing I ever got involved in not because of the casualties, because I had seen this sort of thing before, but I was infuriated at the amount of effort that was put into finding a flak jacket! I was extremely fucked off by this and still am to this day! The RAF Sergeant was wounded in the head and a few civilians were also wounded. This incident has remained clear in my mind as if it were yesterday!

Ken Pettengale, Royal Green Jackets

I echo the words of the previous contributor with whom I served; that day lives we me as one of the shockers. I was told to move my section up to give immediate assistance at this incident. So we went to give mobile cover in and around the area so that we would at least be on the ground. I remember getting very angry and frustrated because I couldn't get any real detail of what was going on or how bad the casualties were. I just knew that they were from my company. I really have a problem fixing this tragedy in my head. Most of what I remember of it comes from flashbacks and, to be honest, I can't remember what is real and what is not; so I keep it inside. The day was a physically and mentally draining one for all concerned; it was also numbing. This was not the end of the incident for me though. A couple of days later, I was told to take my guys down to Queen's Street RUC station to clean the vehicles for recovery as forensics had now finished with them.

When we arrived I was shown to the Landies, but my blokes refused point blank to do it. The vehicles were exactly as they had been after the ambush. I cleaned them on my own, and recovered other things into a small bag that I thought should not be washed away in a drain, and took them to the Police. They didn't want them, so I took them back to NHSM (North Howard Street Mill). I was told to chuck the bag away, but I couldn't, so I buried it. I am sitting here crying while I type this; all of the memories have just smacked me in the face again.

Those deaths were needless. They happened when they shouldn't have, and I hold ONE man responsible for them. RIP lads, never forgotten. *Celer e Audax*. By the way Dave, the rosary was Nicky Malakos's I think.

Dave Judge

I could not recall who the doctor said they belonged to! I found it a bit strange that this was the only personal item to be handed to me, but I suppose the initial group which took the lads to the hospital also took all of their gear and personal stuff. I remember you writing about cleaning the vehicles down. This should have been given a bit more thought and another Company should have been tasked to do it; *Celer et Audax*.

Tim Marsh

I got there just after it happened and saw Danny Holland as you describe, but I was ordered to clear the firing point area which I did. However, I saw that the ground had been disturbed at back of house and moved back. An RUC man said that we should wait for Felix to sort out the device, which was a good call! Major Hearne was in tears as he approached me, and I felt sick at our losses, but then he moved away to speak to RUC constable.

The previous 10 months had been very difficult for the Regiment losing eight of its 'chosen men' and much worse was to come in Regents' Park just five months in the future. By the end of July, the Jackets would have lost 15 of its soldiers in just 14 months.

Two days after the Crocus Street shooting, a dispute between a member of the UDA/UFF and its Loyalist rivals the UVF, led to the death of one member of the 'other' side. Stephen Boyd (24), a man who had been questioned by the RUC for several crimes, including attempted murder got himself involved in a dispute in the King Richard Tavern. The pub is located on the busy A23, a trunk road which links Ballygowan with East Belfast and tapers out close to the Nationalist Short Strand and merges into the equally busy A20. Boyd was involved in a savage argument and was shot dead by the UVF member whom he had accused of theft. The man who killed him was also later convicted of the death of another Protestant in a punishment attack in the following year.

The day after, a career policeman was shot dead by the Provisionals as he came out of a service at a church in Strand Road, Londonderry. Inspector Norman Duddy (45) joined the RUC in the more 'peaceful' times of 1960, just as the IRA's 'Border War' was limping to a close. He had policed before and during the Troubles and was known for his fair-mindedness and for the fact that he lived until recently in a Catholic/Nationalist area. As he walked outside the Strand Road Presbyterian Church, masked men who had driven there on a stolen motorbike were waiting for him. He was accompanied by his two sons but despite this, the gunman fired several rounds at him and he slumped to the ground, mortally wounded. He died en-route for the Altnagelvin Hospital. He was buried in the same church just two days later. Condemnation was swift, with Ian Paisley and another MP demanding the return of the death penalty for terrorist crimes. Michael

Canavan, the SDLP's Law and Order spokesman called the murder: "cruel, criminal and devoid of all consideration for humanity." Church Minister and friend Maurice Bolton said: "We are shocked that a man who contributed so much to the life of the church and had been singing in the choir...should be shot dead as he left with his sons after the service." One of his killers was eventually caught and was convicted on 11 April, 1984. *The Glasgow Herald* reported:

> An IRA man was given gaol sentences yesterday ranging from 10 to 16 years, to run concurrently, when he admitted involvement in the killing of two policemen. Adrian Kelly, 22 of Beechwood Avenue, Londonderry, admitted he drove a motorcycle which carried the gunman who murdered RUC Inspector Norman Duddy in March 1982 and admitted the manslaughter of another policeman three months later.[5]

Inspector Duddy was the 158th policeman killed since the start of the present troubles; the RUC's Roll of Honour was just over halfway complete.

Sadly for the RUC, their 159th victim was only a matter of weeks away. On the 30th, having carried out the same routine for weeks, possibly months and having been observed by PIRA dickers for much of that time, Constable David Brown began his final car drive. The officer who was based at new Barnsley RUC station made the same journey each morning over to Springfield Crescent in order to collect one of the station cleaners. From the RUC base to the woman's house is a short two-minute drive along the B38 Springfield Road. The trip involved a right turn into Springfield Crescent and then a U-turn at the bottom of the cul-de-sac and then back to the station. On this morning, IRA gunmen lay in wait for Acting Sergeant Brown and opened fire, hitting him three times. The woman who was waiting for a lift rushed to his aid, as did a passing Coldstream Guards foot patrol; both parties gave the badly wounded policeman rudimentary medical assistance. He was taken to hospital where he fought for his life for almost three weeks. He died in the RVH on 16 April.

Also on the 30th, REME lost Lance Corporal Philip Charles Harding (21), who was killed in circumstances unknown. The author has no further details as to how he died. He is thought to have come from Macclesfield, Cheshire and is buried at the Prestbury Road Cemetery in the town.

Ten people died during the month; six soldiers (including a former soldier) and one policeman. One Protestant civilian was killed in a PIRA bomb blast and paramilitaries on both sides of the sectarian divide lost one man each. Of the 10 deaths, the IRA was responsible for six this month.

---

5   See Chapter 30.

28

April

Deaths increased to 15 this month, including six soldiers and three police officers. A total of six civilians were killed but these included a former IRA member, executed by the 'nutting squad' and an ODC was killed by a punishment squad. On the first of the month, there was an incident which took place in the Bogside area of Londonderry, the consequences of which left two soldiers dead in circumstances which made an utter mockery of security. It also precipitated the dispatch of two CVOs to houses in Oxfordshire and London to deliver the news which two sets of loved ones simply did not wish to hear. The plain simple facts were that two men from the Royal Signals and REME, having arrived at Rosemount RUC station to do a maintenance job, were dicked on entering and an ambush prepared for them on leaving. If, by the 13th year of the conflict, of what the Provisionals called the 'long war', the Army or RUC were unaware of the concept – and indeed, efficacy – of dicking, then perhaps that was precisely the moment to pack up and go home. A PIRA ASU had entered the area the previous night, on the route which soldiers would take on leaving the RUC base. Rosemount RUC station was located on the northern periphery of the notorious Nationalist Creggan Estate and was constantly under observation by PIRA personnel. Its positioning was crucial to the Security Forces, not only for watching the Republican hotbed but for fast responses to terrorist incidents.

Jock 2413, Royal Artillery

As you go up Creggan Street, Brooke Park is on your right. Just as you pass Brooke Park there is a small cul-de-sac and that was the location of the RUC station. The building was dismantled and the land purchased by Derry Council in 2009 and brand new houses were built. The buildings are called Rosemount Cottages. The 'admin' route from Rosemount took you down Creggan Road, left into Infirmary Road, onto Northland then right into Asylum then on to the Strand. If they were returning to Ebrington Barracks, that would have been the normal route. It could be that as they slowed down to make the turning into Infirmary Road, that made them an easy slow moving target.

Shortly before 2100 hours on 31 March, the ASU had forcefully taken over a house lived in by theology students. The house was at the crossroads with Infirmary Road/ Creggan Road and Marlborough Terrace. They had set up weapons and planned to shoot at a 'target of opportunity' when it inevitably presented itself. In the late morning of the 1st, the two soldiers, dressed in civilian clothes and driving a nondescript grey-coloured Mini-van van drove out of the RUC station and began driving towards the centre of Londonderry in the direction of the Little Diamond. It seems highly likely that a dicker using a radio alerted the ASU to this fact. As the author's Royal Artillery source told him: "They were heading towards what might be considered a safer area." As their vehicle reached the crossroads at St Eugene's Cathedral, four gunmen, all armed with a variety of weapons, opened fire – hitting the van approximately 30 times and causing it to slew across the road. The men were dreadfully injured and both died at the scene within minutes. The terrorists made good their escape, and the hitherto captive theology students could only look on in shock.

The Bishop of Londonderry, Dr Daly, was one of the first to attend and the dying men were given the last rites. One of the priests said: "The passenger appeared to move and I believed that he was alive at the time. I gave him the last rites, but I think that he died a short while later." Dr Daly told the *Derry Journal*: "When I got outside, priests and some people had taken the men from the van. Both were very obviously seriously injured and there was a lot of people about who were hysterical and worried." He added that: "the shooting was too terrible for words." Schoolchildren in the nearby Francis Street Primary School were too frightened by the events to be allowed outside and the school sensibly asked all parents to call and take their children home. Councillor Joseph Fegan, the Lord Mayor of Londonderry condemned the murders without reservation. He said: "despite repeated condemnations by the public at large, it is appalling to think that this type of thing is still happening." Another eyewitness who had been in Marlborough Post Office told the same newspaper:

> I couldn't believe the number of shots. I saw the van coming down Creggan Road. The gunmen seemed to be firing from Marlborough terrace but I didn't see them. I hear at least one automatic weapon. Everything seemed to be in slow motion. The van continued across the Creggan Cross junction and crashed into the bakery. I ran to help. The van had been very badly shot up. Both men were very badly hurt.

He very naturally declined to be identified for fear of reprisals from the Creggan PIRA unit which was famed for its ruthlessness and brutality.

The soldiers were Sergeant Michael Burbridge (31) from REME and Royal Signals Corporal Michael Ward (29), father of one. The Ulster stone building from which the deadly assault was launched still stands on the crossroads; a silent witness to the savage murder of two young men who were sacrificed on the IRA's altar of a united Ireland. The author drove around the area in 2013 and he noted the tension and the most suspicious atmosphere. Just the simple act of driving through and around the Creggan attracted attention, as the latter day dickers clocked the strangers in their midst. One has to be most careful as the Creggan is still known as a hard-line dissident Republican area.

Jock 2413, Royal Artillery

In the '70s, the thinking behind the 'Admin' routes was that they were supposed to eliminate the chances of a 'blue on blue'. All troops on the ground knew about them so if by chance you stopped a vehicle at a snap VCP in, say, Infirmary Road and you spotted that the occupants were armed, there would be a 'pause for thought' before taking action, thereby giving the vehicle occupants a chance to identify themselves. The downside to this was that any 'Q' vehicle exiting a base such as Rosemount, Piggery Ridge or Bligh's Lane could be easily clocked by a dicker and, using a CB radio, could pass its details on to a waiting ASU. The junction of Creggan and Infirmary was like a meeting point from all three of those bases.

Near the end of 1973, an admin vehicle from 94 Locating Regiment RA heading towards its base in Bligh's Lane was ambushed at almost the same spot. Several shots were fired from an Armalite rifle, fortunately only wounding one of the Gunner occupants. If you read Raymond Gilmour's book *Dead Ground*,[1] he describes an IRA operation to ambush Security Forces vehicles in almost the same location by taking over a house. He managed to warn his handlers about it and all military and police vehicles were diverted. This happened a year before the events that you describe. So you have to ask the question, why did the Army still carry on using that route, knowing that the terrorists knew it was used regularly by Security Forces' admin vehicles? Words like slack security and carelessness doesn't cover it. Criminal negligence would be a more fitting description.

Scouse 'B', Royal Signals

The use of civilian vehicles was widespread throughout the Province, having the obvious advantages for covert ops by various agencies. One reason for their use by the Royal Signals, was a reduction in the manpower needed to perform duties such as periodic maintenance. To travel around in Land Rovers (Green) you would have to use at least four men and two Land Rovers, whereas to perform the same duty with civilian vehicles there would only be a need for two men and one vehicle. One such duty performed by this method was the Brigade Comms Standby Vehicle. This consisted of two Royal Signals radio operators in a civilian vehicle. They were on 20-minute standby, 24/7 for a one month rotation. Most combat roles could be as diverse as covering a manned hilltop site, Rover Group, Brigade Radio Room and Heli Tele to name but a few. They could be called upon to repair any number of radio faults, both secure and unsecure, anywhere within the Brigade area. Another use of civilian vehicles was the Brigade Commander's Rover Group. This would consist of two civilian vehicles; one for the Brigadier along with the bodyguard and driver and one escort vehicle with Royal Pioneer personnel as the Brigadier's personal escort. This civilian option was used when the Brigadier was engaged on official functions in Stormont or other such civilian led events. We also used this method when the Brigadier was traveling to and from the ferry or airport on leave. The Brigade Commander also had a dedicated (green) Rover Group this consisted of two Land Rovers, a Brigadier's Land Rover and an escort Land Rover. The fire power on the escort vehicle in the early 70s was the standard SLR for each man; however during the mid-70s this was increased to include smoke grenades and baton guns.

On the 3rd, Patrick Scott (27) was picked up by the West Belfast 'nutting squad' despite the fact that he was actually on his way to speak to them at the time. Rumours

---

1   Gilmour, Raymond, *Dead Ground: Infiltrating the IRA* (Bosston: Little, Brown & Co).

had been circulating in the Lower Falls area for some time that lapsed IRA member Scott had been touting. He informed his mother that he was going to see the leadership in order to 'sort things out.' However, he was taken to a safe house, close to Cairns Street, where he was bound hand and foot, and his eyes covered with plastic tape. After interrogation, he was carried outside to an alleyway between Cairns Street and Dunville Place before being shot in the back of the head and dumped. Dunville Place was close to Dunville Park and, like many of the other streets in the area, has been bulldozed to extinction in the massive post-Troubles improvements. Lincoln Street and Theodore Street have gone, so has the aforementioned Dunville Place; Spinner Street has been redeveloped into the more fashionable sounding Spinner Square. A Florida newspaper – the Daytona Beach Journal – for 5 April reported:

> The IRA said Sunday it had shot another informer and the Roman Catholic Bishop of Londonderry appealed for Catholics and Protestants alike to pass information about terrorist murders to police. An Irish Republican Army statement issued here claimed the group shot a man whose body was found Saturday in Catholic West Belfast because he was an informer who had helped the police and Army. But a spokesman at Belfast Police headquarters said the dead man, Patrick Scott was: "another innocent victim of Provisional IRA paranoia." He was not a police informer.

On the 5th, the British Government published its White Paper, 'Northern Ireland: A Framework for Devolution.' The paper set out proposals for the establishment of an elected 78-member Assembly at Stormont. The Assembly would then be asked to reach agreement on how any powers devolved to it from Westminster would be administered. The proposals indicated that it would need the agreement of 70 per cent of Assembly members before powers would be devolved. It was also envisaged that power would be passed to particular Northern Ireland Departments one at a time. Because of this the scheme became known as 'rolling devolution'. The ideas contained in the White Paper had been discussed for some time prior to its publication and most of the political parties had expressed opposition to it.

Two days later, REME lost one of their soldiers and this author has only the bare bones of information. Corporal Bernard McKenna (24) who was attached to the Army Air Corps died on duty. He was from Preston, Lancashire and is buried at St Maria Goretti's, Gamull Lane in the town. On the same day, a fellow Lancashire lad – Sapper Christopher John Beattie from the Royal Engineers – was killed in an accidental discharge at Forkhill RUC base. A comrade, Sapper Robert Adams of 8 Field Squadron, was later gaoled for six years for his manslaughter. Sapper Beattie (22) was from Rochdale and his funeral was held in the Crematorium on Bury Road in the town.

On the 14th, RUC officers carried out a raid on UDA headquarters in the Shankill Road, Belfast. The raid uncovered ammunition and gun parts; four leading members of the, as then, still legal (i.e. not proscribed) organisation were arrested. The UDA was not declared illegal until 10 August 1992. At the time, James Prior, in answer to a growing number of questions about the organisation and a growing disquiet about its actions, announced in the Commons that he had no plans to ban it.

On the 16th, there was a further tragedy involving the use of baton rounds, this time in Londonderry. Gangs of rioters were stoning soldiers in the Bogside area and petrol bombs were being thrown at troops on foot, and also at a Saracen crew. One of the soldiers identified a ringleader and fired a baton round in his direction. However, because of what later transpired to be faulty equipment, the round hit a small child. Stephen McConomy (11) was accidentally struck on the head and fatally injured. He was rushed to Altnagelvin Hospital where he fought for his life; sadly the child died on the 19th. This author regrets and will always regret the loss of any innocent and in particular a young boy whose life had barely started. At a later Inquest, the Coroner listened to forensic evidence which showed that the baton round gun was faulty and the aimed shot had not been intended to hit little Stephen. The author extends his heart-felt condolences to the family of this little boy. Approximately a month later, on 13 May 1982, following agitation from Irish MEPs (Member of the European Parliament) the European Parliament called on member states to voluntarily end the use of plastic bullets.

On the 17th, proving that mental exhaustion and stress is not the exclusive domain of the pressurised jobs in high finance etc. a soldier driving an armoured personnel carrier rammed the vehicle into the gable wall that formed 'Free Derry Corner'. The soldier was later taken into military custody, thought to be suffering a complete nervous breakdown. The white gable end, which still stands today, is all that is left from the redevelopment of the Bogside. Republicans consider it a symbolic reminder of their 'struggle' and it is a good focal point for 'Troubles tourists' as they are driven and escorted around the trouble spots of the North. It is a useful place for teary-eyed, camera-slung Yank tourists whose distant ancestors left Ireland for the Americas six generations back. They can renew their 'faith' and remember to dig even more deeply into their pockets the next time that the NORAID collection tins comes around their local Irish bar.

On the same day that the 'sacred cow' of Irish Republicanism was damaged, the IRA killed a Protestant farmer on his land at Kiltubrid, Middletown, Co Armagh. Middletown itself is the western part of the county and sits to the east of where a huge salient of the Irish Republic protrudes into the 'underbelly' of the North. It is rural and the remote farm in question is less than two miles from the border. William Morrison (42) was a Protestant and belonged to the local Orange Order, but had no connections with either the Security Forces, or with Loyalist paramilitaries. During the evening of the 17th, masked gunmen took over a farm building and held two brothers at gunpoint before they launched an attack close to the building in which Mr Morrison lived. He was hit and fatally wounded, but he tried to crawl away to safety. The gunmen stood over his helpless and bleeding body and fired at least eight more shots into him. He died almost immediately. The gunmen escaped over the nearby border where the provisional IRA were always sure of a traditional friendly Irish welcome.

Richard Newsone

After a border fire fight, in which we were involved, several 'players' were picked up by the Irish Army and Police on their side of the border. All we could do was watch the bastards get whisked away by the Police! Funny thing that I myself observed was that the IRA gunmen were all carrying their weapons as they were loaded onto Police Land Rovers; funny that!

On the 20th the IRA launched a massive bombing offensive throughout Northern Ireland as they demonstrated their ability for destruction. A total of eight cities were hit, all within minutes of each other. The results were two men dead and many injured, and over one million pounds worth of economic damage was caused. A branch of the Ulster Bank in Strabane was hit by a 900 lb (409 kgs) car bomb; a garage and car showroom in Armagh City was destroyed by three firebombs; a car bomb exploded at the Linen Hall in Ballymena; a 900 lbs car bomb exploded in the centre of Londonderry and a further huge device was detonated in Bessbrook followed by a smaller 40 lbs (18 kgs) device which also detonated in Bessbrook some hours later. However, it was the lack of adequate warning giving by the IRA in Magherafelt, Co Londonderry which caused the most human misery.

LARGE SCALE BORDER OPS 1982
Mark 'C', RA and UDR

During my time in 10 and 7/10 UDR, the full-time Companies took part in several very large scale operations to either rebuild or reinforce the RUC/SF Base at Crossmaglen or XMG at it was known to us. It was a constant target for PIRA and it is estimated that at least 180 soldiers and police were killed in and around that South Armagh area which also included, Newtownhamilton (NTH), Forkhill, Cullyhanna and Keady. We would either be flown direct to Bessbrook Mill or transported to Drummad in Armagh City or the NTH Base itself, to start the operations, one of which was called 'Op Congo Line'. At Bessbrook, I had never seen so many troops in place for one op outside the NATO exercises in Germany; there were hundreds, us, other infantry units, dog handlers, engineers; all ready to be transported out onto the ground by chopper from what was at that time the busiest heli-pad in Europe if not the world.

Because so many troops were taking part, we were all given stick numbers and times to report to the actual Pad, when it came for our time to go, I was really up for it and you knew you were taking part in something huge. There were lines and lines of soldiers, some with search dogs all waiting for their chopper to come in and whisk them out onto the ground; choppers were landing every few minutes, loading up, taking off, then others coming in to take their place and so it went on; it felt as if you were in a Vietnam War film or something.

The whole purpose was to take over and dig in on all the main high ground and road junctions in and around XMG, thus denying PIRA room to operate, so the Engineers could safely bring in all the building supplies by convoys, so part of our job was also to clear part of the route, something similar which the today's soldiers do in Afghanistan. By the time we got lifted and dropped into our initial positions it was getting near dusk, so it was decided to put sentries out and the rest to get a couple of hours kip and brew before we moved into our permanent sections positions in the morning. Most of us chose a quick shell scrape and a bit of a basha, but two others – a corporal and his sidekick both called Billy – decided to do the full fire trench job, well it was South Armagh I suppose! Anyway, Northern Ireland being Northern Ireland, the clouds came in and it began to pour. (Something similar happened me before in Newry.)[2] We and all our kit got

---

2   Mark 'C's experience in Newry is related in Wharton, Ken, *Bombs, Bullets and Cups of Tea* (Solihull: Helion, 2009).

absolutely drenched but the two Billys fared even worse. As most who served there know, South Armagh is very peaty and boggy, so their trench filled up with about two feet of water and their kit nearly floated away. Of course this was hilarious to the rest of the Platoon and set the tone for the rest of the four days. The boys used to sing "How deep's the water Billy?" when any one of them said anything.

But we finally got the proper op going early the next morning and patrolled to our various section positions were we set up a patrol base, with gun pits, tripwire flares etc. Our job was then to consolidate the high ground and to send patrols onto the road for snap VCPs and route clearances. Luckily for us the sun came out and we were able to get most of our kit dried out, and that was basically it for four days.

Another time we actually dug in on the side of crossroads on the outskirts of NTH and did the same type of operation, route clearance and denying the enemy (PIRA) the ground. Another time, we were dug in on top of a hill over-looking the same crossroads, but had a section on the ground at all times. My section had dug a fire trench overlooking the crossroads to cover the sections coming up and down the hill and we had built our bashas back from it on a small track. Two other sections were also dug in in a sort of triangle position with HQ in the middle near a disused cow barn, and one morning the farmer accidently or otherwise (the reader can make their own minds up) decided to herd all the cows up the lane to the barn, trampling all over our area. Of course a few words were exchanged and he buggered off.

This may all sound fun, but it was very hard work and serious and it was proven so when, during one of these ops, PIRA still had the balls to launch a mortar attack on Forkhill, despite the number of troops on the ground. On another occasion, during a two-week op at NTH, I was told by Intelligence that our patrols on the ground made PIRA call off an attack on our base because we were doing our job so professionally and they did not want to risk it. The threat was there and was very real; we did our job and XMG was able to be mortar-proofed which saved lives in later attacks.

Magherafelt (*Machaire Fíolta*, meaning plain of Fíolta) is a small town and civil parish in the southern part of Co Londonderry; it is a plantation town built around a central diamond, which forms the heart of the town. Lying three to four miles north west of Lough Neagh, Magherafelt sits astride the busy A31 – the road which takes traffic from Cookstown to Castledawson where it then becomes the A6 Antrim Road. It is the A6 that links the two major centres of population in the Province: Belfast and Londonderry. On 20 April, 1982, in conjunction with bombs being primed and placed in seven other locations, a PIRA bombing team drove into Magherafelt and parked their car – stolen, naturally – outside the Arches Hotel in the Diamond and abandoned it. They then walked over to a second stolen car which had followed them into the town, and probably without a backwards look, drove away to a place of safety. A warning was telephoned through but, as always with the IRA, it was either deliberately misleading or insufficient time was allowed. If the reader casts his or her mind back to the Claudy outrage in July when nine innocents were torn apart by three IRA car bombs in a sleepy little village,[3] their excuse for the inadequate warning was a series of damaged telephone boxes which delayed their call. One seems to remember that the Sinn Féin apologist omitted to acknowledge that that telephone had been damaged earlier by an IRA bomb!

Noel McCulloch (31) had stayed overnight at the Arches in the centre of the town and was waiting in the car park for a lift. He had just had dinner with his friend Wilbert Kennedy (37) who was about to load up his car when the alarm was raised. Mr Kennedy was in the process of moving his car when the car which had been abandoned minutes earlier by the PIRA bombing team exploded. Both men were killed instantly and a dozen more people were injured. The RUC accused the Provisionals of irresponsibility and of failing to give adequate warning. The Army Council metaphorically shrugged their shoulders and made a mental note to issue a hollow apology some 30 years in the future.

There was a further postscript to this attack in 1982; on 23 May 1993, a 500 lb (228 kgs) IRA car bomb caused extensive damage to the commercial centre of the town. The bomb was placed outside the Ulsterbus depot on Broad Street, a main thoroughfare of Magherafelt. The bus station was entirely demolished by the blast, along with extensive damage to the town's Ulster Bank branch.

On the 23rd, the pious Provisionals decided to rid the Ladybrook area of South West Belfast of some of its anti-social elements. Raymond Devlin (19) was, in the parlance of the day a 'hood.' He was infamous for his petty theft, graffiti, joy-riding and general vandalism. So much so, he was known as 'gangster' and had been previously kneecapped by the Provisionals. Ladybrook is a Nationalist area which sits to the south of 'hard green' areas such as Lenadoon and Andersonstown, and north of the more established Protestant areas such as Finaghy and the Upper Malone Road. Devlin was sitting on a low garden wall close to Finaghy Park Road North when he was shot several times at close range in his back by a PIRA gunman who had crawled up behind him. He died instantly, very close to his own house. There can be little doubt that Devlin was a young man with anti-social behavioural problems, but it was rich coming from the IRA that they had sought to rid the area of his sort. *Kettle, copper, black*; please rearrange this famous word or saying.

On the same day, the RUC lost three more officers when a tragic accident en-route to the scene of terrorist activity claimed their lives. Constable Gordon Arnott Anderson (21), Constable Denis Joseph Maguire (25) and Woman Reserve Constable Mabel Elizabeth Cheyne (29) were all killed when their vehicle was involved in a dreadful accident in Co Armagh. As they were answering an emergency call, their car crashed on a bend at Ballymoran between Armagh City and Newtownhamilton at approximately 2100 hours.

Four days afterwards, a part-time officer in the UDR was murdered in Londonderry by the IRA as he carried out his civilian job. Lieutenant Leslie James Hamilton (36), father of two, delivered bread products from a local bakery to supermarkets in the Waterside area. He had been very obviously dicked, and two masked gunmen lay in wait outside his regular morning delivery point. He was expected at around 0830 and he duly arrived with an assistant and they proceeded to unload their bakery produce at the goods-in bay. As they did so, the gunmen got up close behind the young officer and shot

---

3 See Wharton, Ken, *The Bloodiest Year: Northern Ireland 1972* (Stroud: The History Press, 2011).

him more than a dozen times at point-blank range. He died immediately; his colleague was untouched but deeply shocked. Lieutenant Hamilton was buried at Dunnalong Parish Church, Co Londonderry.

RELIGIOUS DIFFERENCES?
Derek O'Loughlin, Royal Artillery
Another time we were patrolling in the Loyalist Waterside area; there had been some shots in from the Bogside and it was pitch black as the street lights had been turned off. These two old ladies invited us in for tea, but I had to laugh; they were staunch Protestants and five of the six-man patrol were Catholics; 'Taigs' they would have called us! I was mentally thinking about religious bigotry when she got some photos out of her son, who had died in the Army in Hong Kong. To my surprise, it turned out that he was our Patrol leader's best friend when he was stationed out there. That was a revelation which I hadn't expected.

The Royal Hampshire Regiment was a British Army line infantry regiment from 1881 to 1992, and its lineage is continued today by the Princess of Wales's Royal Regiment. In World War I it took part in the Battle of Gallipoli in 1916, when it engaged in the fatal Landings at Cape Helles as part of the 29th (UK) Division. It had suffered during the Irish War in 1921 and engaged the IRA; in one incident, seven soldiers, all with the band of the 2nd Battalion Hampshire Regiment, were on their way to Youghal Co Cork when a road mine exploded under the truck they were travelling in. Three soldiers were killed outright with a further four being mortally wounded.

Sixty one years later, the Hampshire 'Tigers' were in action at Belleek, Co Fermanagh, just yards from the border with the Irish Republic. Belleek (Irish: *Béal Leice* meaning mouth of the flagstones) is a village in Co Fermanagh. While the greater part of the village lies within Fermanagh, part of it crosses the border into Co Donegal, a part of Ulster that effectively lies in the Republic of Ireland; this makes Belleek the western-most village in the United Kingdom. A patrol of the Hampshires was passing through remote countryside close to the border in the vicinity of Meenatulla when a PIRA bombing team detonated a huge roadside device. Several members of the patrol were injured, some badly, but Private Colin Phillip Clifford (21) was mortally injured by the blast of a 1,000 lbs (454 kgs) bomb which had been placed under a culvert; he died in hospital, shortly after arriving. He was from Jersey in the Channel Islands and is buried in the Rondel Family plot at St John's Parochial Cemetery. Sinn Féin mouthpiece and MP, Owen Carron, was reported as saying that any deaths were regretted, but whilst troops remained in Ireland such deaths would continue.

There is a simple brass plate memorial to the young Hants lad; it reads: "In memory of Private Colin Clifford. The Drums Platoon, 1st Battalion, The Royal Hampshire Regiment, Killed by Terrorist Action, Belleek, Northern Ireland, 30 April 1982."

Phil Newton, Royal Hampshire Regiment
On that fateful day in April 1982, I was a section commander on foot patrol south of Enniskillen; we heard the explosion and within 30 minutes we were airlifted to Belleek RUC station for the follow-up operation. I knew Cliff; tidy bloke. The ironic twist to the story is that I now live in Enniskillen and I know the location of where

Cliff was murdered as I laid a poppy wreath on the 20th anniversary, as I will do this month the 30th anniversary.

The Jersey News reported:

> The mother of a Jersey soldier, killed by the IRA in Northern Ireland, has been presented with an Elizabeth Cross medal. Colin Clifford was just 21 when he died in a bomb blast 28 years ago. His mother Dorothy Parette collected the award – granted to the next of kin of Armed Forces personnel killed in service or as a result of terrorism. Mrs Parette said: "It's a very proud day for me today. I'm highly honoured to be receiving it on behalf of my late son, but if it would been far better if it had been my son here today receiving it."
>
> Drummer Colin Clifford, from the First Battalion of the Royal Hampshire Regiment, died in 1982. He was on foot patrol when he was hit by an IED explosion. Despite first aid at the scene, he died in hospital. Mrs Parette said the grief she felt had never gone away, but that hard work had helped her through the nightmare.

The month of April was over and 15 people lay dead; six were soldiers, four of whom had died at the hands of the Provisionals and three were police officers. Six civilians were dead; three Catholics and three Protestants. One of the deaths was overtly sectarian in nature and for all the pathetic Irish-Americans who glibly followed the IRA's refrain of how British troops were murdering the Irish, their 'freedom fighters' killed nine people this month. The British Army was responsible for one death, tragic though that was.

29

May

Deaths were reduced to six this month, which included three soldiers or former soldiers and another policeman. The UVF committed two senseless sectarian killings this month and blamed their actions on the IRA's murder of a Protestant the previous month.

The month began with the death of a UDR soldier. This time the loss was to that seemingly ubiquitous cause: an RTA. Private Brian Walmsley (21) was from Lisnaskea in Co Fermanagh. He is buried at Holy Trinity Church in the small border town. Further, it was announced that by this, the 14th year of the conflict, the financial cost to the British Government – and hence to the taxpayer – was in excess of £11 billion!

On the 2nd of the month, with the battle to recapture the Falkland Islands from the invading Argentinians at full stretch, HMS Conqueror sank the Admiral Belgrano with the loss of 323 lives; for the men battling in the South Atlantic, it was at this moment that the war became very real. Condemnation from the USSR and its satellite nations, as well as from the South and Central American nations, was swift and vitriolic. This was entirely expected, but there were loud dissenting voices for Thatcher's decision much nearer home. Patrick 'Paddy' Power was, at the time an Irish politician. He was first elected to Dáil Éireann as a Fianna Fáil Teachta Dála (TD) for the Kildare constituency at the 1969 general election, and served as Minister for Fisheries and Forestry from 1979 to June 1981. However, it was in his role as Minister for Defence in the Irish Republic between March and December 1982, that Power told a Fianna Fáil meeting at Edenderry, Co Offaly: "Obviously Britain themselves are very much the aggressors now."

When Argentina invaded the Falklands, the Republic of Ireland originally sided with the international consensus in condemning their actions. However, the Fianna Fáil Government position changed sharply after the sinking of the Belgrano. Charles Haughey was never shy of Brit-bashing and the actions in the icy cold waters of the South Atlantic allowed the ineffectual Irishman to do some tub-thumping. Sabre rattling was perhaps too extreme, not to say misleading, a description.

On the 4th and approximately 8,000 miles further north, the IRA killed a young RUC officer who had only been a policeman for eight months. Constable Alan Victor Caskey (21) was from Desertmartin, Co Londonderry and been stationed in Londonderry only since early February. He was patrolling with a female colleague in the area between Ferryquay Street and Butcher Street, known as the Diamond. A baker's van pulled alongside the pair and they instinctively thought that the driver wanted directions. Unknown to them, armed PIRA men had hijacked the van and a gunman was crouched in the passenger footwell, out of sight of anyone outside the vehicle. As the van stopped level with the officers, the hidden gunman raised himself up and opened fire with a semi-automatic weapon and cut the officers down. Constable Caskey died almost immediately and his female colleague was badly wounded in her back and in her legs.

On the 5th, on the first anniversary of the death of Bobby Sands, a patrol from Support Company 2nd Battalion Coldstream Guards was involved in an incident in Durham Street, close to Grosvenor Road, Belfast. A 'Coldcreamer' takes up the story:

Tony Joynes, Coldstream Guards

One of our units was despatched to close the gate at Durham Street; it was a regular patrol and with the limited resources in the area, no sniffer dog was provided. The gate on Durham Street was a pole-type gate, which on this day had been filled with explosives by a PIRA bombing team. The task of closing the gate was given to Guardsman Wayne Goodram, who instead of lifting and walking the gate, shut simply swung it shut. This decision probably saved his life, as on moving the gate, it exploded. Wayne suffered severe leg injuries. I believe from the reports that he a severed his femoral artery, and the ceramic plate of the new NIBA vest stopped a piece of shrapnel the size of an orange from penetrating his chest. One of our NCOs – Lance Corporal Jones – was mentioned in despatches for retrieving Wayne to a safe place. He was taken to the nearby RVH by civilian ambulance where a large group of civilians were singing songs and cheering. I remember the Battalion holding its breath collectively, waiting for news but there was slight confusion, as he had borrowed some kit from Jim Cree and it had his ZAP number on. I am pleased to report that he recovered from this PIRA attempt on his life.

On the same day, the UVF staged a robbery at a post office in Killinchy, Co Down. The village is located on the western side of the Ards Peninsula close to the shores of Strangford Lough. It was a short journey for several members of a UVF gang from Belfast to make as they went there for the sole purpose of robbing the local post office. There were two main reasons why robberies were carried out by paramilitaries – of both sides; one was to add to their respective 'battle funds' and the other was for some 'spending money.' The motive of the robbery at Killinchy has never been made clear, but in the course of this particular theft, Maureen McCann (64) went to the aid of her brother with whom she worked and was stabbed to death by a masked UVF member. She died at the scene – a Protestant killed by a Loyalist terrorist. Two men were later gaoled for her murder but subsequently released on appeal after one of the, now famous, supergrass trial collapses.

On the 8th, Nicholas Budgen, then an Assistant Government Whip, resigned his post because of his opposition to the Northern Ireland Bill which would introduce a new Assembly. Two days later on the 10th, making no mention of Budgen's resignation, during a debate on the Northern Ireland Bill, James Prior set out proposals for a new Assembly at Stormont. He said: 'A policy of continuing with Direct Rule does not offer a long-term answer. We either move to a position of total integration, or we seek a gradual devolution of power.' Across the Irish Sea in the Dáil, partly for political expediency and to demonstrate their symbolic failure to recognise the 'border', Taoiseach Charles Haughey appointed Northern Ireland politician Seamus Mallon, then Deputy Leader of the SDLP, to the Irish Senate.

Four days later, it was guilt by association with the past as the Provisionals killed a former member of the UDR in Strabane. Thomas Cunningham (23) had joined the UDR as a part-time soldier in 1979, but had resigned after two years' service in July 1981, almost a year prior to his murder. He worked as a builder for Strabane Housing Executive and was employed on a property in Fountain Park in Strabane. It was a new development on the eastern outskirts of the town off the Spout Road. The houses on which he was working still stand, semis in regulation Council off-white with the street name in Gaelic; *Pairc an Gobair*; there are no references to his death.

As he carried building materials to help complete a roof on the small estate, a stolen car parked up on Spout Road and two men, one of them carrying a .45 Colt automatic pistol, walked over to the house where he was carrying tiles and, without a word, shot him four times. He died at the scene and the news was conveyed to his heavily pregnant widow. A spokesman for the Provisionals who had murdered him made the following wretched comment: "he would not have been at risk if we had been informed of his retirement from the UDR." A man was gaoled for life for the murder and the 'armourer', who was only 15, was imprisoned for five years.

Later that day, the UVF targeted a Catholic father of four young children as he worked in a shop on the Antrim Road in North Belfast. Francis Toner (26) lived on the Ballymurphy Estate and delivered fruit and veg throughout the city. He had just unloaded at the shop when masked UVF gunmen walked in and opened fire. The owner of the shop, who was a relative, a female shopper and an off-duty nurse were in the shop at the time and were forced to dive for cover. A female was hit in the face, but Mr Toner was mortally wounded in the neck and chest and died en-route to the Mater Hospital on the Crumlin Road. The off-duty nurse did her very best to save him but the wounds were too severe. The senseless sectarian murder left four children under six without a father. Mr Toner had no paramilitary connections and was murdered simply because he was a Catholic.

Given the tragic number of accidental deaths – particularly of young children – in the late 70s and early 80s in Northern Ireland, it was no surprise that Irish MEPs pushed the issue in Brussels. On the 13th, the European Parliament called on member states to ban the use of plastic bullets and prohibited plastic bullets throughout the European Union. The British Government however vetoed the move and chose to ignore the ban.

On the 24th, the Royal Anglians – 'Angle-Irons' as they are known to soldiers of other regiments – were called into action in order to quell rioting in the Butcher Gate area of Londonderry. The 3rd Battalion was instructed to deploy into the area in armoured vehicles and, as they arrived, one of the vehicles was hit by several petrol bombs. Their assailants were members of the unofficial grouping known as the DYH (Derry Young Hooligans), some of whom were as young as 13 and 14. One of the vehicles was set alight and the young soldiers leapt clear, but two of them – including Private Tony Anderson (22) – were set on fire. Together with another comrade whose clothes were also burning, they tried to beat out the flames. But in doing so, young Anderson fell under the heavy wheels and was crushed to death. He was from the Grimsby area. The 3rd Battalion was known as the '*Pompadours*' because of the purple facings of their former tunics.

On Saturday 29th, a United States Congress-sponsored organisation called 'Friends of Ireland' paid a fact-finding visit to Northern Ireland. It was founded in 1981 by Senator Edward Kennedy, Senator Daniel Moynihan and House Speaker Tip O'Neill to support initiatives for peace and reconciliation in Northern Ireland; three of Britain's enemies and three of the biggest Irish-American apologists for the provisional IRA. The visit passed largely unnoticed by the world's press, but the three Irish-Americans would no doubt have cast half an eye on the publicity and vote-garnering which it would have produced 'back home.' With no keen eye at all for irony, the late, unlamented Edward Kennedy said: 'The Friends of Ireland is a bipartisan group of Senators and Representatives opposed to violence and terrorism in Northern Ireland and dedicated to maintaining a United States policy that promotes a just, lasting, and peaceful settlement of the conflict that has cost more than 3,100 lives over the past quarter century.' One wonders at which point he actually stopped to consider that many of the bodies which were piling up were as a direct result of Irish-American money, US-led interference and their *laissez-faire* attitude to the harbouring of convicted terrorists within their shores.

Six people died in this month; three were soldiers or former soldiers and there was one policeman. In addition, two civilians died – one Catholic and one Protestant. The Catholic death was overtly sectarian in nature.

30

June

Deaths were reduced to just five this month, and the deceased included a soldier and a policeman. However, the IRA shot dead a former RUC officer, aged 60, in order to "hasten the British departure" from Northern Ireland. Clearly the Provisionals' seven-member Army Council, or GHQ, felt that killing a 60-year-old pensioner would help achieve their goal of a united Ireland.

On the 1st of the month, the British Army in Northern Ireland received a new General Officer Commanding (GOC) when Lieutenant-General Robert Richardson, succeeded Richard Lawson. General Richardson had previously commanded both an emergency tour as well as a resident brigade in Northern Ireland, giving him experience of the issues faced in the region. His tour as GOC was mainly marked by a gradual process of reducing the role of Army units in day-to-day security, and, in handing over control to the RUC, accelerating the process of 'Ulsterisation.'

Sometime in the early hours of the morning of 2 June, an INLA team stole a motor-cycle from a leisure centre in the Andersonstown area and placed explosives underneath the petrol tank, before abandoning it along a known Army/RUC foot patrol route at Rugby Road in the south of the city, close to Stranmillis Embankment. It was apparently ignored by a passing Security Forces patrol, but later in the morning, three friends from the Markets area chanced upon it and one of them took hold of the handlebars. Patrick Smith (16), a Catholic teenager who had just left school, was killed instantly and his friends injured in the blast. *Lost Lives*[1] claims that the bombing was ordered by INLA leader Jimmy Brown, himself killed some 10 years later. He was a member of the IRSP/INLA and later joined the IPLO, at the same time as Gerard Steenson. Brown was shot and killed in an internal IPLO feud in August 1992 as he sat in his car in Clonard Street in the Falls area.

A mere 48 hours later, the INLA was again involved, this time in re-opening the feud with the Official IRA (OIRA). Five years previously, James 'Jim' Flynn had shot dead Seamus Costello[2] during the early stages of the OIRA/INLA feud. During a hastily arranged truce, Costello was shot dead as he sat in his car on the North Strand Road in Dublin by Jim Flynn on 5 October 1977. It was stated at the time that it was an opportunist killing as Flynn chanced upon Costello outside a shop. Four and a half years later, Flynn was standing in the car park of Cusack's Pub just a few yards away from where he

---

1   Thornton, David, Seamus Kelters, Brian Feeney and David McKittrick. *Lost Lives: The Stories of the Men, Women and Children who Died as a Result of the Northern Ireland Troubles.* (Edinburgh: Mainstream, 1999, revised ed. 2007).
2   See Wharton, Ken M., *Wasted Years, Wasted Lives* (Solihull: Helion, 2013), Vol 1, Chapter 34.

allegedly killed Costello. An INLA gunman walked up to him and without a word, fired several shots into his body; Flynn died at the scene.

On the 11th, a policeman was killed by a booby-trapped device allegedly placed by Eamonn 'Bronco' Bradley, in the Shantallow area of Londonderry. Bradley was himself killed, on 25 August of this year.[3] What was interesting about the death of the IRA man was the sheer hypocrisy of the IRA and its sycophantic supporters who claimed that Bradley was 'executed.' This was rich coming from an organisation which specialised in cold-blooded executions. On the occasion of the policeman's death, an RUC team was searching a consignment of stolen electrical goods which had been found in a building in Shantallow. It is thought that the pile had been searched by Army sniffer dogs, but an explosive device had been missed. Detective Constable David Reeves (24) triggered the device and was killed instantly.

The Falklands War which had lasted 74 days ended with the Argentine surrender on 14 June, when British forces captured the capital Port Stanley with barely a shot fired on the day of surrender. It was a different story however, with savage, hand-to-hand fighting taking place at the mountains which defended the capital: Longdon, Tumbledown, Kent and Wireless Ridge. The Argentinian surrender returned the islands to British control. During the conflict, 649 Argentine military personnel, 255 British military personnel and three Falkland Islanders died. Thousands of miles to the north, for the Provisional IRA, however, it was business as usual.

As Britain celebrated victory and mourned her losses, Private Hugh Alexander Cummings (39), a part-time member of the UDR was murdered by PIRA gunmen while he was off duty. Private Cummings was also known as 'Lexi' due to there being an actress by the same name; he was a member of 'A' Company, 6 UDR. PIRA dickers had noted his regular habits and were aware that he drove home at lunchtime. On this occasion, a car containing two gunmen pulled alongside his car and opened fire at him; he died at the scene. There is a report in *Lost Lives* which states that a letter of sympathy, from Secretary of State Jim Prior to the family of Private Cummings, was rejected by them. The family felt that, given the circumstances of the lack of protection afforded to the part-time soldier, his death lay at the feet of the NIO. There was a demand that the security forces should be allowed to do their jobs and take on the killers of the Provisional IRA, many of whom were known to both the Army and the RUC.

On the same day as the murder of the UDR man, INLA made a statement about the recent killing of OIRA man Jim Flynn in *The Starry Plough*.[4] A spokesman for the IRSP/INLA said:

> First of all, let me make perfectly clear that the execution of Jim Flynn is not part of a feud between the Workers Party/Official IRA and the INLA. Our action against Flynn took place after we were informed by former members of the Officials that he had murdered Seamus Costello. The ex-Officials who passed on this information are basically Republicans, and they left the Workers Party at the time of the hunger strike because they realised that their party did not represent their own political beliefs. They were particularly disturbed about the murder of Costello both because

---

3   See Chapter 32.
4   Source: http://irsm.org/history/starryplough/inla_interview.html

of his impeccable anti-imperialist credentials and because of the circumstances surrounding his death.

We know that the Official IRA, which is well armed, would turn its guns against those of us who are fighting for a Socialist Republic. We have definite proof that the Officials, besides the Costello killing, were involved and are involved in providing intelligence to the loyalist death squads, and it was exactly such intelligence that was responsible for the deaths of Miriam Daly, Ronnie Bunting and Noel Little. Their decision to murder Costello, and to help in the murder of other leaders of the INLA and the IRSP, is definitely a political decision to try to wipe us out as a force for socialism. This will not happen.

Observers of the Troubles might well note the proliferation of acronyms and abbreviations as well as the factions and sub-factions, especially on the Republican paramilitary side. The original Irish Republican Army (IRA) split into two wings: Provisional (PIRA) and Official (OIRA). The OIRA then split with a faction forming the Irish Republican Socialist Party (IRSP) and its political wing the Irish National Liberation Army (INLA). From this came the Irish Peoples' Liberation Organisation (IPLO) which was formed in 1986 by disaffected and expelled members of the INLA. From all these sets of initials, the PIRA emerged triumphant in the 90s and gobbled them all up; almost literally. Were it not for the serious and murderous mayhem these Republican paramilitaries caused, one might almost find it comical. The reader might be reminded of the scene in Monty Python's 'Life of Brian' when there is a 'serious' discussion about elements of the resistance to the Roman occupation of Judea. In that discussion, the revolutionaries list the factions – such as the People's Front of Judea (PFJ); Judean People's Front (PJF); Judean People's Popular Front (JPPF) and Judean People's Liberation Front JPLF) and the People's Liberation Front of Judea (PLFJ) – all of whom are invariably denounced as 'splitters.' One wonders how many similar discussions were held amongst the protagonists of the Irish 'Revolution.'

On the 18th, a senior NIO official, who could have easily come from another Monty Python sketch – 'The Upper Class Twit of the Year' – made a statement which was guaranteed to increase Loyalist resentment and leave them under even more a 'siege' mentality. Lord Gowrie said: "Northern Ireland is extremely expensive on the British taxpayer … if the people of Northern Ireland wished to join with the South of Ireland, no British Government would resist it for 20 minutes."

Only, on that particular day, the humour was replaced by grief in the White household in Balmoral Park in Newry. Albert 'Bertie' White (60) had been a career RUC officer and had reached the rank of Detective Inspector with the Newry force before his retirement in 1974 at the age of 52, following injuries which he had received from the IRA. He had retained his links with the RUC and worked as a civvie in an administrative role. He posed no threat to the Provisional IRA who in their various terror forms had twice tried to kill him. They had tried as recently as 1973 and even earlier during the 1956–62 'Border Campaign.' On both occasions they had tried unsuccessfully to shoot him. Dickers had watched his movements and were aware that his wife collected him from the station by car every day. One of the dickers who helped set him up was Eamonn Collins.

A month or so prior to the attack, Collins had waited outside the church where the Whites worshipped and then followed them to their home in Dora Avenue, which is located in the north-eastern section of Newry, between Balmoral Avenue and Windsor Hill. He noted their car – a blue Saab – and memorised the number plate. As he wrote: "I thought: this is where we'll kill him … White was as good as dead."[5] Collins noted that Mrs White picked up her husband at different times and in different locations, and was forced to factor this unpredictability into the murder attempt. On the day of the murder a three-man team in a stolen car got themselves into position and the killers comprised 'Mickey' (Collins' cousin), 'Declan' and a man alleged to be Davy Hyland. The stolen car blocked the path of the Saab and one of the gunmen fired three shots through the windscreen, wounding Mr White who got out of the car and tried to defend himself with his umbrella. One of the gunmen then fired repeated shots into the defenceless man who died at the streets. The cowardly killers raced off with the words: "Bastards! Bastards! Bastards!" ringing in their ears as Mrs White cried out in desperation. By a touch of irony a member of the Collins' extended family network – the Reverend Raymond Collins – said the mass at Mr White's funeral.

Hyland appeared in court accused of killing former Royal Ulster Constabulary Inspector Albert White but the case collapsed after IRA man Eamon Collins withdrew statements made to police. Hyland now lives in Newry where he is a former chair of Newry and Mourne District Council and a former Assembly member for Newry and Armagh; he is a schoolteacher. Collins himself was murdered by the Provisionals in Newry on 27 January, 1999 with injuries so severe that the RUC thought that he was a victim of a car accident.

Throughout the 1980s, in what was seen as an unusual but no less welcome example of Anglo-American co-operation, FBI agents investigated a number of IRA gunrunning operations. One of these was an arms deal led by Gabriel Megahey and involving perhaps 11 Irish-American sympathisers. Megahey himself was born in Belfast and was involved with the Provisionals for some time. He worked in England for many years at the Southampton docks, but was expelled from the UK because of his involvement in a scheme to import explosives and weapons from New York. He then went to the US and worked as a bartender in New York City. He maintained his Republican connections and was considered to be amongst leading Provisionals in the country. He came to the attention of the FBI and then became the target of constant surveillance

On June 21, 1982, the FBI operation reached a climax in when Megahey and his co-conspirators tried to send a consignment of 51 rifles and remote-control devices to the Irish Republic. The weapons were packed into wooden cases marked 'roller skates' and 'comforters'. US agents working in close co-operation with their British and Irish counterparts seized the arms at Port Newark. Megahey and another IRA man Andrew Duggan were arrested at a construction site in Manhattan by FBI agents. They also apprehended two brothers from Northern Ireland – Colm and Eamonn Meehan – who were involved in the conspiracy. The four immediately received legal aid from Irish-American Republicans, and a panel of lawyers began investigating ways to thwart the prosecution. The two PIRA men had originally tried to buy surface-to-air missiles on

---

5   Collins, E. *Killing Rage* (London: Granta Books, 1997), p.123.

behalf of the IRA's Northern Command. It is also alleged that they approached Irish-Americans employed in the US arms industry and who had knowledge of electronic timing systems. The terrorists of Óglaigh na hÉireann were becoming more and more sophisticated in their methods of killing soldiers, policemen and innocent civilians.

Despite intercepting the arms shipment in Newark, the FBI permitted a small consignment to travel on to Limerick on board a cargo ship but alerted Gardaí Síochána who were waiting when the ship docked. Gardaí arrested IRA members Patrick McVeigh and John Moloney as they collected the arms. The men were later gaoled for seven and three years respectively for possession of an Armalite rifle and IRA membership.

June was over, but carnage in London's Royal Parks was just around the corner. In all, five people had died during the month: one soldier, one policeman and two civilians. One Catholic and one Protestant had died, both at the hands of Republicans. Additionally one Republican paramilitary was killed at the hands of a rival Republican group. All of the deaths this month were at the hands of those seeking to reunite Ireland.

31

July

This month was the month of slaughter in the Royal Parks; it would see deaths rise again, as 14 people died, 12 of whom were soldiers. The month was relatively quiet until the 17th and all 14 Troubles-related killings were squeezed into the last fortnight. Lenny Murphy was released from prison and killed again within 24 hours of freedom

The month began with a rare show of cooperation between the Gardaí Síochána and the RUC. Following tip offs from informers, a Gardaí search was made at Castlefin (also spelt Castlefinn) in Co Donegal. The small village is approximately one mile from the border with the North and there are good communications with Nationalist hotspots in Northern Ireland such as Sion Mills and West Londonderry. In caches around the market town, explosives, detonators and ready-to-be-primed bombs were found and seized. It is thought that they were to be transported into the Creggan Estate area before being planted in the city centre of Londonderry.

James Prior, Secretary of State for Northern Ireland, was in the news between the 14th and the 19th of the month. Firstly, he announced that elections to the new Assembly at Stormont would be held on 20 October 1982. This was greeted by indifference from the Nationalists and with suspicion by the Loyalists. Then, on the 19th, he paid a visit to the USA to explain his 'rolling devolution' plans; effectively to 'sell it' to the powerful Irish American lobby and win favour from President Reagan.

Colm Carey (28) joined the IRA via the usual route of rioting and being a member of the DYH, then afterwards, a keen civil rights activist and, as Hugh Jordan writes: "willingly joined the Provos," which gave him some standing among his impoverished local community. He then developed a skill for rudimentary bomb-making and was eventually arrested by the RUC. Having served a gaol term, he went straight back to his IRA comrades on release and again immersed himself in their activities. He came from a background of profound alcohol abuse and soon drifted into alcoholism. He was reduced to begging or even stealing communal wine as he descended into a semi-perma-nent alcoholic haze. On the morning he was killed – June 16 – he had been drinking with Kevin 'Biggsy' Johnston and they needed money to replenish their stocks, so Carey swaggered into an off licence in the Bogside and openly stole a bottle of whiskey. He did this in full view of the owner and a queue of shoppers; unfortunately for him, he did it in full view of a leading player.

The Provo immediately reported the incident to his OC and handguns were sent for, to carry out a punishment shooting which would teach Carey a lesson and demonstrate that the IRA did not tolerate such anti-social behaviour in 'their' community. Unfortunately, handguns could not be obtained, so rifles were sent instead. The punishment squad went directly to Carey's home in the Old Strabane Road in the Gobnascale Estate. They burst in and dragged Carey through the house and into the back yard, past his drunken father. He was shot in both legs, but such were the high-velocity shots that one leg was blown completely off and the other was hanging by tattered strips of muscle. An ambulance was called for but Carey died at his house; the Provisionals had ensured that 'justice' was done. For further information see the excellent *Milestones in Murder* by Hugh Jordan.[1]

On the 16th of the month Lenny Murphy, the leader of the Shankill Butchers (most of whom were now behind bars) and psychopathic Loyalist, was released from prison. 24 hours later, he 'celebrated' his freedom by killing again. Hugh Leonard Thompson Murphy was born on 2 March, 1952. He died in December of this year under review and we shall deal with his death in Chapter 36 of this book. Back in March 1976, Murphy shot and injured a young Catholic woman, and was arrested the next day while retrieving the gun used. He was charged with attempted murder and remanded in custody for a prolonged period. However, as a result of plea-bargaining – the RUC knew that he was a member of the 'Butchers' but were unable to prove it or find anyone brave enough to testify against him – Murphy was allowed to plead guilty to the lesser charge of firearms offences, and received 12 years' imprisonment on 11 October 1977. He was released four years and eight months later. He left the Maze on the Friday afternoon and headed straight for the Shankill Road area where he commenced drinking, fêted by his admiring Loyalist paramilitary cronies. He was to kill four more people, as far as it is known, and possibly more. It is thought that the 'romper rooms' where the Butchers tortured and humiliated their victims were invented by Murphy himself. However, research done by Jeanne Griffins indicates otherwise. Davy Payne, a former British paratrooper and a UDA man is credited with having invented them. He was a man with a fearsome reputation. Kevin Myers who was acquainted with him described Payne as "… one of the most ferocious savages in the history of Irish terror."

On the day after his release, Murphy drank heavily, partly to celebrate his release from the Maze and partly to drown his sorrow following the finalisation of his divorce. He was 'holding court' in Rumford Street Loyalist Club when he began picking on Norman Maxwell. Mr Maxwell (33) who was known to have learning difficulties apparently failed to show the psychopathic UVF leader sufficient respect, and he was taken outside into the pub's yard where he was beaten almost to death; immediately after this, a car was driven over his dying body several times. At later inquest found that the man's death was: "the most savage, barbaric and brutal assault one could imagine, quite ruthless and quite merciless". His body was transported over a mile away and dumped in an alleyway on Rocky Road, a sectarian interface, thus making the killing look as though it was sectarian and carried out by Nationalists.

Three days later, the IRA's reformed England team struck in London with a barbarity not entirely unexpected, especially in light of the recent bombing of Chelsea Barracks. However what happened on that summer's day was an outrage and can only have pleased Britain's enemies such as the Nationalist communities of Northern Ireland and of course the entire Irish-American community in the United States. By the end of the day, 10 soldiers would be dead, many others including civilians badly injured and one squaddie

---

1   Jordan, Hugh, *Milestones in Murder* (Edinburgh: Mainstream Publishing, 2002).

would be fighting for his life in hospital; he would die within 72 hours. Ceremonial horses would be dead and littered around Hyde Park, covered by bloodied tarpaulins and the name 'Sefton' would be on every animal-lover's lips. The Royal Parks outrage would be etched indelibly into the psyche of the British public. Secretary of State James Prior was still in the USA when news of the tragedy of Hyde Park began to filter through the world's press agencies, followed shortly afterwards by the events at Regent's Park. Without naming NORAID, he was quick to ask Americans not to give money to organisations which supported terror. Unfortunately Mr Prior's words mainly fell on deaf ears. Indeed, it would be not until after the World Trade Centre attacks on September 11, 2001, that the USA finally woke up to the fact that they had bankrolled terror for far too many years and NORAID was almost embarrassed into closure.

The first attack took place a little before 1100 and involved a large shrapnel bomb, placed in a blue Austin car parked on Hyde Park's South Carriage Drive, at Rotten Row. This was along the route used by the Queen's official bodyguard – the Household Cavalry during the Changing of the Guard – between Buckingham Palace and Knightsbridge. Two soldiers of the Blues and Royals were killed instantly, one died later that day and another died on 23 July from his injuries. The other soldiers in the procession were all badly wounded and shrapnel and nails sprayed into the crowd of tourists assembled to watch the parade, causing further injuries. Seven of the Regiment's horses were also killed or had to be put down because of their injuries. The bomb is believed to have been detonated by a member of the IRA who was watching from within Hyde Park. The bomb detonated just eight feet (less than three metres) from the horses and men as they rode past.

As the echoes of that terrible explosion were dying down, and while the pall of black smoke hung in the air over London, the bombers struck again, just over two hours later. A little over a mile away as the crow flies, a bomb hidden underneath the bandstand in Regent's Park exploded during a performance of the band of the Royal Green Jackets. Over 100 civilians were relaxing to a performance of 'Oliver.' The crowd was peppered by shrapnel from the iron bandstand, causing many injuries. The blast wounded the entire band and killed seven soldiers instantly. It was so powerful that body parts were hurled over 30 yards. The bomb was placed under the bandstand weeks in advance, with a timer set to the date and time of the advertised concert. Approximately two dozen civilians who had been listening to the performance were injured in the explosion.

The Blues and Royals soldiers killed at Hyde Park were: Trooper Simon Andrew Tipper (19), from Stourbridge, West Midlands; Lance Corporal Jeffrey Vernon Young (19), father of two very young children, from Tonyrefail, Mid Glamorgan and Lieutenant Denis Richard Anthony Daly (23) from Slough. A fourth soldier was hit in the head by a large piece of shrapnel and fatally injured; Corporal-Major (nominally Colour Sergeant) Roy John Bright (36) died of his wounds on the 23rd.

The Royal Green Jackets killed at Regent's Park were: Sergeant Major Graham Barker (36), father of two, from Salisbury, Wiltshire; Bandsman Laurence Kevin Smith (19) from Mortlake, Surrey; Bandsman Keith John Powell (24) from Rawmarsh, near Rotherham; Bandsman John Heritage (29) from Cardiff; Bandsman George James Mesure (19), from the Jackets' spiritual home of Winchester and Corporal Robert Alexander Livingstone (30), also from Winchester. Both of the Winchester boys were buried at Magdalene Hill Cemetery in Hampshire.

THE HYDE PARK BOMB

The following morning's *Daily Express* showed a scene of carnage in the Royal Park, with the bloodied bodies of the ceremonial horses scattered around, under a banner headline: "The Day Britain Bled Again." There could have been no more fitting headline! The following two pages covered the outrage in Regent's Park under smaller headlines: "When the Music Turned to Screams" and "A Callous Cowardly Crime Says Maggie." The report described how "IRA killers turned a happy, sunny, carefree morning in the park into a scene of appalling horror."

Because so much had occurred in those dreadful incidents, the *Daily Express*, like all of the British press, was at a loss as to where to place the information and the personal accounts and in what sequence and in what priority. Pages 4 and 5 declared: "All The Queen's Horses" and "Pride of the Cavalry. Bred in Ireland ... but the terror bombers are that country's shame".

The report read:

> The Street ran with the blood of men and horses. In one petrifying second, death and carnage struck at the heart of Royal London. It was a scene of grievous mutilation. Two [sic] Household Cavalrymen and seven of their horses died when an IRA nail bomb exploded in Hyde Park. Twenty three other people, some of them innocent bystanders were injured. One horse was left stumbling with blood pouring from its neck. It was shot by a police officer to put it out of its misery ... The 16 men of the Blues & Royals had been on their way to change the guard at Horseguards in Whitehall. The death toll would have been almost certainly higher if it had not been for the horses because they absorbed the impact of the explosion. Some of the cavalrymen fell to the ground under their dead horses....The remote control bomb was hidden inside a blue Austin parked...on South Carriage Road. Witnesses told how cavalrymen were thrown into the air by the blast and how their horses were torn to pieces. (An eyewitness said): "I was standing in Rotten Row when half of the roof of a car landed at my feet! A Cavalryman covered in blood staggered up to me and asked me to hold his horse which had a hole in its side. I saw one man lying on top of his horse which was still alive but half of its insides hanging out. It was so awful that I was sick. I turned away when I heard shots because they had started shooting the wounded horses."

The report continued to describe the scene of blood and mayhem on the South Carriage as many onlookers rushed to help the wounded men and tried to pull them clear of their stricken horses. Civilians in tee-shirts rushed to help other wounded civilians who moments earlier had been enjoying the traditional pageantry of ceremonial horse and soldiers in blue coats and brass breastplates and plumed helmets as they rode past – as indeed they had done for the past several hundred years.

The reporter described how an injured woman of about 45 was tended to by people who had hitherto been enjoying the spectacle:

> Her right leg was swaying. Part of the top of her head seemed to be torn off. Shop assistant Mr Bernard Bygraves said: "I saw horses all over the place kicking and struggling to get up. There was blood everywhere. You could hardly recognise

horses and men. One middle-aged woman pedestrian looked as if half her head was missing and she was screaming: 'Help me.'" Tourist David S…, 19, from California said: "As I rushed up, I saw blood all over the pavement and the Cavalry officers had blood up to their elbows. Some of the military men were trying to console those in tears and others were rushing about shooting the horses." An elderly woman who sells souvenirs nearby wept as she described the carnage. She said: "It was too awful to look at … How could anybody hurt those dear boys?" Businessman Mr John Marriott 35, who lives in nearby Wilton Place said: "I saw one trooper with his head blown off and two others lying on the ground covered in blood. The horses were making pitiful sounds."

In the USA, their July 20th edition of ABC News led with the atrocity. Their sombre-faced Anchor-man said: "Murder in the parks; two parks. Amongst the loveliest in London; but not today. Today London has been rocked by slaughter. Eight people killed and 50 people injured in separate terrorist attacks." Their on-the-spot reporter described how two of London's summer traditions were rocked by the bombs of the IRA. Harrowing footage in vivid colour brought back nightmarish memories to this author who was living in Leeds at the time, 200 miles away from the slaughter on the streets of the capital. ABC News interviewed one eyewitness who looked dazed and bedraggled. He said: "The soldiers were just wandering around shouting: Bastards! Bastards! Bastards!"

The ABC reporter went on to describe how the horses and men rode past every day at the same time and how crowds of Londoners and visiting tourists would stop to watch, as people had done for over a hundred years. Debris was hurled 500 yards and even striking hospital workers instantly abandoned their picket lines and rushed to help the grievously wounded soldiers and injured spectators. But two hours later, even as the smoke still clung to the air, over Hyde Park another explosion took place at Regent's Park. The sound of this second explosion would have been audible to the injured from the first outrage being ferried to hospitals, to the rescue workers in the park and to those attempting to make sense at the scene of carnage on the South Carriage Road.

A civilian wrote of that day:

It was a typical summer's day in London, and I was a young engineer who had spent six of the previous nine years working in offices where I could get a good view each morning of the Horse Guards trotting along Carriage Road on the south side of Hyde Park. I was just one of hundreds of office workers who would congregate around their park side windows to admire the daily spectacle of plumes on high helmets bobbing up and down in perfect unison. Mirror polished breastplates reflecting the sun in blinding flashes and black leather thigh boots, burnished to a patent gloss, atop perfect black mounts whose clinking harnesses provided a triangle-like backing to the rhythmic thudding of hooves on tarmac.

That July morning I was busy on a sales enquiry and could only glance across the six heavily trafficked lanes of Hyde Park Corner to see the Blues and Royals passing by. I saw the usual mixture of locals and tourists strolling along the pavement, cameras clicking, fingers pointing. As I lowered my head below the nondescript partitions of my cubicle I heard a sound like thunder, louder even than the intense concussion you get when lightning flashes directly overhead. The next sound was a crack and a glass window just a few yards from me split diagonally from top to bottom as it failed to resist the pressure wave of the explosion. I looked up again knowing that something was badly wrong, and saw a guardsman crawling along the road on all fours behind the remains of a car that was on fire. The previously animated spectators were now horizontal, scattered all over the pavement by the blast, and large dark shapes that were the dead or injured horse lay in the road. Two small family cars that had been parked one behind the other were now burned out shells, one shattered carcass on top of the other, perfectly placed as though they had been lifted into position by a crane following the instructions of a movie director making a war film. I spent much of the rest of that day wondering how those two cars could have ended up so perfectly placed by an IRA bomb. Two guardsmen killed, seven horses killed or destroyed, with 17 passers-by injured and there was I puzzling over those two cars – I've heard that shock can affect people in strange ways, and that was my reaction.

Then the screaming started; distant sounds of people hurt and panicked by an experience that hadn't been seen in London since 1944. From that point until the emergency services arrived it was total confusion, people running in every direction, some of them dashing across the still busy roadway braving the cars, trucks, buses and taxis to bring relief to whatever would greet them on the other side. I saw the owner of a neighbouring hairdresser dash out with his arms full of white towels.'[2]

THE REGENT'S PARK BOMB

At approximately 1300 hours, and a little under 120 minutes since the first explosion at Hyde Park, the band of the Royal Green Jackets (Regimental motto: *Celer et Audax*, 'Swift and Bold') was playing a well-publicised public concert from the park's bandstand. An appreciative audience of around 120 people were listening to music. At that moment, the world changed forever for the men of the Black Mafia and for those who were present as a large explosive device tore the band to pieces.

The *Daily Express* wrote:

Beside the lake in sunny Regent's Park, the band was playing a selection from 'Oliver' when the bomb went off. The musicians from the Royal Green Jackets were blasted from the grandstand into the audience of 200 sitting in canvas deckchairs on the grass. Six [sic] of the bandsmen were killed. Twenty were injured along with 10 spectators. The sheer horror of the carnage was described by Mr David McCulloch who had just left the scene to return to work on a nearby building site at the end of his lunch break. "The blast hit me in the back. I landed on my face. People were running round screaming and trying to get away … I ran over and tried to help. One soldier reached out his hands for help, but his body had been blown in half – he was completely cut in two but he was still alive. Another soldier had half his face blown away and another was completely paralysed and his face was all burned. There was nothing that I could do for him." The IRA's bomb was apparently planted under the floor of the bandstand. The explosion literally tore the band apart – bodies were thrown 50 yards – yet hardly affected the structure itself except for spilling bloodstains on the inside of the roof. This part of Regent's Park is a magical place in summer. Mothers take their young children to feed the ducks, older people go to admire the flowers, youngsters row by on the lake – and all love to listen to the band. Yesterday it was the turn of the Royal Green Jackets to play. Bandsmen, of course, are non-combatants – they become stretcher-bearers in war – but the fighting men of the Royal Green Jackets are presently on a tour of danger duty in Northern Ireland. That warring Province seemed far away from the peace of this London park.

The *Express* journalist had skilfully assembled and interviewed several of the eyewitnesses.

Mr John Kingaby

The band was playing rumpty-tump when there was a blinding flash followed by a terrible explosion. There was an eruption of debris followed by a ball of fire. Then the air was filled with dreadful screams and groans – and then a silence when you could suddenly hear the birds singing and the ducks clucking on the lake. It was horrific.

Iris Stringfellow

It was a massacre without warning. Children were splattered with bits of body from the bandsmen.

Frederick Douglas

It was an awful sight; Spectators were running in shock all over the place. I counted 16 soldiers lying on the ground. One soldier was lying there groaning, with his hands on his stomach and blood pouring through them. Another's head was a mass of blood – it looked as though the instrument he was playing had gone into his face with the blast.'

David Sherwood

The whole stand just erupted. A leg from a woman victim came flying past me. The injuries were horrendous.

Ronald Benjamin

I was just sitting in a deckchair when everything seemed to come up from the bottom of the bandstand and blow right into the air; the band, instruments, everything. There were mangled bodies all over the deckchairs.

Miriam Sheridan:
There were soldiers lying all over the grass, terribly injured. One had blood all over his face. I stroked his head to try and comfort him. Others looked beyond help. I was screaming. They were all lovely young chaps.

The journalist managed to find one Green Jacket who had survived the blast and he interviewed Corporal John Mitchell who said: "We were playing away and away – that was it. People were wounded. There were bodies everywhere. They were all my friends; I have been working with them for 10 years."

The reporter finished his piece with a description of the aftermath:

A kettledrum and a stand were blown 30 yards from the bandstand. A mangled French horn lay amid deckchairs 40 yards away. On the stand itself was a mass of wreckage – instruments, chairs, music stands. Serious casualties were taken to St Mary's in Paddington where health service workers immediately called off industrial action. One nurse said: "Everyone dropped their banners in the road and ran to the ambulances to help." University College Hospital treated eight victims of the blast. All but one were released after being interviewed by the police.

Later that day, regimental flags at Peninsula Barracks in Winchester, the spiritual home of the Green Jackets, flew at half-mast to mourn the loss of seven of its soldiers and the maiming of several others. The Depot Commander, Lieutenant-Colonel Richard Prideaux said: "We are very much a family regiment. We are extremely sad and outraged by what has happened." The Prime Minister Margaret Thatcher said: "These callous and cowardly crimes have been committed by evil and brutal men who know nothing of democracy. We shall not rest until they are brought to justice".

In the *Daily Express*, Andrew Taylor and Percy Hoskins wrote:

Meanwhile security chiefs have warned people to be on their guard against further attacks. For weeks they have been searching desperately for a small terrorist group known to be in London. British agents who have penetrated the IRA in Belfast warned that a tiny 'active service unit' of bombers was on the mainland with orders to stage a spectacular attack on a military target. But no one knew precisely where or when the attack would happen. With IRA man Gerard Tuite gaoled for 10 years last week and Ulster Secretary James Prior touring the US to sell investments in the Province, IRA chiefs clearly felt the time was ripe. They wanted to avenge Tuite and torpedo Mr Prior's bid to boost jobs in Northern Ireland.

Around the world, reaction was of predictable outrage; in Australia, the *Melbourne Times Age* led with: 'London Bombs Kill 9.' The article read:

Nine people were killed today when two huge IRA bombs hit Royal troops and tourists in the heart of London. The Irish Republican Army claimed responsibility for the first blast in Rotten Row 200 metres from the cavalry's Hyde Park Barracks. The band of the Royal Green Jackets was playing in Regent's Park when the bomb tore apart the bandstand.

The New York Times, with its large Irish readership wrote that the bombings were: "dastardly cowardice … a disgusting insult to the heritage of which millions of Irish-Americans are rightfully proud."

US *Time Magazine* contributed:

> The bright morning sun sparkled off the plumed metal helmets of the Blues and Royals troopers of the Queen's Household Cavalry as they left their barracks for the daily mounting of the guard at Whitehall. Resplendent in blue tunics, white buckskin breeches and silver-coloured breastplates, the tips of their unsheathed swords jauntily resting on their right shoulders, the colourful 16-man troop trotted along Hyde Park's South Carriage Drive while admiring tourists lolled in the grass and snapped pictures. The cavalrymen never reached their destination.[3]

In the Republic of Ireland, papers released in 2012, under the Eire Government's 30 year rule showed many Irish people were revolted by the actions of Irishmen that day. Numerous letters were received by the Taoiseach, Charles Haughey, the majority of which called on the Irish Government to do more to stamp out the IRA. They came from Ireland and elsewhere, penned by Irish and non-Irish alike. The day after the bombing, the Department of the Taoiseach received a letter from Templeogue, in Dublin, in which the 'totally revolted' author urged him to "use the powers you have under the various Anti-Terrorists acts to intern known IRA members immediately." In the response, dated 13 August, the suggestion was noted. While the correspondence reassured the original author that Haughey "shares the revulsion felt by you and all decent people at the London bombings", it further stated that interning members of the IRA wasn't felt to be "an effective or appropriate measure at this time."

LONDON: THE END OF THE DAY

By the end of that bloody day – the worst in London since the last German air raids in 1944 – 10 British soldiers were dead, a dozen or more were injured, and one – Corporal-Major Bright of the Blues and Royals – was fighting a desperate struggle to stay alive; he lost that battle on the 23rd.

The outrage was well planned, well executed and ruthless in the extreme. It calculated that civilian casualties would also occur – as had had happened in the Chelsea Barracks bombing – but, as the intention was to sicken the British public, the IRA didn't care. In both outrages, civilian slaughter was avoided, but this was more a result of good luck than good judgement. Back in Northern Ireland and in the Republic, senior PIRA men – the Army Council – were rubbing their hands with glee at the carnage, bloodshed and misery which they had caused at the very heart of the 'enemy'. It wouldn't take many more days, many more spectaculars, many more atrocities of this kind in order to force the British to pressurise their Government into withdrawal from Ireland. However, what it failed to take into consideration was the famous, yet oft-derided 'spirit of the blitz' for which London and Londoners are rightly known. It calculated that there would be a

---

3   Source: http://www.time.com/time/magazine/article/0,9171,925586,00.html#ixzz2SgKWRzpl

wave of revulsion, but they didn't consider that this 'wave' would spur them on to resist what Thatcher aptly called the 'men of evil'. The sight of one of the bloodied horses, in great pain and trying to escape from the carnage and its later recovery – the animal was named 'Sefton' – was also an inspiration for decent people and not just animal lovers or those who adored the brave horse on TV programmes such as 'Blue Peter'. On that fateful day, 'Sefton' suffered 34 serious wounds but miraculously survived.

The wartime graffiti daubed on many shattered walls and ruined houses during the German bombing in the last War was never more appropriate. 'Mister Hitler; you can break our walls, but you will never break our hearts,' could so easily read: 'Mr Adams and Mr McGuinness, you can break our walls …'

THAT DAY
Michael Sangster, Royal Artillery
Although I didn't witness any of the bombs up close, I was in a security van in Knightsbridge when the bandstand bomb went off. Even inside an armoured vehicle, I heard the explosion then witnessed the panic as people ran out of the park exits. It was only when we got back to our base in Shoreditch did I find out there had been two bombs, their targets and the number of fatalities. A large number of the lads I worked with were ex-forces, and the anger we all felt was there to be seen. In hindsight, I suppose the question must be asked. With a two hour gap between the bombs, why wasn't a specialist dog tasked to go over any open, unguarded places that soldiers congregate – like the bandstand?

Only one man was ever convicted for his part in the two bombings in London on 20 July, 1982. Danny McNamee who was found guilty of the Hyde Park bombing later appealed and won his appeal against his conviction. However, Appeal Court judges did not entirely exonerate McNamee. At the time, prosecutors relied heavily on traces of Mr McNamee's fingerprints found on remnants of the bomb and two other arms caches to convict him in 1987. But three Court of Appeal judges accepted that it might have made a difference had jurors known that many more prints from a known IRA bomb-maker were also on the bomb remains. The Appeal Court judges said their decision that although the conviction was unsafe did not mean that he was innocent of the charge. Lord Justice Swinton Thomas said a strong case had been made at his 1987 trial that Mr McNamee was guilty of conspiracy to cause explosions.

McNamee (38), from Crossmaglen, South Armagh, was sentenced to 25 years in gaol for his alleged part in the bombing. He was released in 1999 from the Maze Prison in Northern Ireland after serving 12 years under the Good Friday Agreement on the political future of Northern Ireland. McNamee claimed that one of the three prints claimed to be his on tape connected with the bomb-making equipment was not his. At his trial he said his prints had got onto the equipment innocently because had had used the tape working at an electrical repair shop. His case was referred back to the Court of Appeal by the Criminal Cases Review Commission after inquiries into a number of issues, including disclosure of more fingerprint evidence at the time of his trial.

There was another sad postscript to the Hyde Park bomb and it involved Household Cavalryman Michael Pedersen who rode 'Sefton' during the attack. On 1 October 2012, after a blazing row with his estranged wife, he took his children out for a visit. After arriving at a beauty spot in Hampshire, he killed them both and then himself. Pedersen was riding Sefton when the IRA nail bomb exploded in Hyde Park killing four of his colleagues and seven horses. His horse 'Sefton' became a national hero when he returned to active service briefly before retiring. Pedersen, a Corporal of Horse who performed ceremonial duties at Buckingham Palace and Windsor Castle, was uninjured in the blast, but badly shocked.

At the time of publication of this book, a man was arrested for the Hyde Park bomb, some 31 years after the outrage. A man charged with the murder of four British soldiers in the 1982 Hyde Park IRA bomb blast has been granted conditional bail at the Old Bailey. John Downey, 61, of Co Donegal, in the Irish Republic was arrested at Gatwick Airport in May, 2013. He was accused of being responsible for a car bomb left in South Carriage Drive which killed the soldiers as they rode through the park to the changing of the guard. Downey was charged with murdering Roy Bright, Dennis Daly, Simon Tipper and Geoffrey Young, and with intending to cause an explosion likely to endanger life. At the time of writing, he had been due to stand trial at the central London court in 2014.

However, on 25 February, 2014, the BBC reported as follows:

A man accused of killing four soldiers in the 1982 IRA Hyde Park bombing will not be prosecuted because he was given a guarantee he would not face trial. It follows a judge's ruling that an official assurance given in error meant John Downey – who had denied murder – could not be prosecuted. It may affect 186 people wanted for terror-related offences in the Troubles who received similar assurances. Victims' families said they felt "devastatingly let down." Police Service of Northern Ireland Chief Constable Matt Baggott said the PSNI accepted the court's decision and full responsibility for the failures which resulted in this outcome. He said the matter would be referred to the Police Ombudsman for Northern Ireland. "I wish to apologise to the families of the victims and survivors of the Hyde Park atrocity," he said. "I deeply regret these failings which should not have happened. We are currently carrying out a check of these cases to ensure the accuracy of information processed by the PSNI."

The Independent Newspaper provided more detail about the alleged Hyde Park bomber, writing of Sean O'Callaghan's *The Informer*. O'Callaghan named Downey as a member of the England group involved in bombings on the mainland, and wrote that Downey had been active periodically in England:

He first came to the notice of the authorities in 1971 as a member of the Provisional IRA in Donegal. He also appears in a file in relation to the murders of two members of the Ulster Defence regiment, Alfred Johnston and James Eames, killed by an IRA remote-controlled bomb hidden in an abandoned car and detonated when their patrol approached at Cherrymount, near Enniskillen in 1972.

The following is taken from the author's *The Bloodiest Year*:

The UDR was the next regiment to suffer when it lost two its soldiers while checking a suspiciously abandoned car at Cherrymount close to Enniskillen. The car which had been stolen had been booby-trapped by the IRA and it exploded in what the dead men's comrades described as a "blinding yellow flash" (*Lost Lives*, p.255). All the men in the patrol were injured, but Jimmy Eames (33), a father of three and Alfie Johnston (32) and also a father of four were both killed instantly by the 150 lb device. The explosion also rocked a passing mobile patrol of the Royal Artillery.[4]

Alfie Johnston's daughter – Donna Johnston –made it her lifelong goal that the man who robbed her of her father will be eventually brought to justice for this and other terrorist crimes. Donna was only three months old at the time and has vowed to fight for justice for her lost dad. So far, Downey has only served a short sentence – for IRA membership – at Portlaoise Prison in Ireland; one hopes that in a future book, this author may supply further information.

In March, 2014, it emerged that whilst Downey will not face charges relating to the Hyde Park bomb, two score or more former Paratroopers who were on duty in Londonderry's Bogside on 'Bloody Sunday' would be investigated. A soldier facing questioning in the new Bloody Sunday investigation has spoken of his fury after suspected IRA bomber John Downey was given a police guarantee he would not face trial. Breaking his silence after 42 years, a former paratrooper told the *Daily Mail* that it was appalling that Downey had escaped prosecution for the 1982 Hyde Park terror blast, which left four soldiers and seven horses dead, when he received a letter from the same force warning his identity may now be exposed because of a fresh inquiry into the Londonderry massacre. Condemning what he called 'double standards', the ex-soldier said: "So much for British justice. Being named could end my life." He was interviewed by the newspaper in early March (2014) and said:

> Downey receives a letter promising him he will not have to face justice and I am warned I face another investigation. Why don't they just throw the Bloody Sunday paratroopers to the IRA wolves and be done with it? I've had Bloody Sunday hanging over me for more than 40 years, even though I didn't even fire a shot on the day. This has been a lifetime of suspicion and fear that our anonymity will be lifted. Who cares about us? Everything has swung the terrorists' way.

A mere 24 hours after the explosion at Hyde Park, the Cavalry were back entertaining the crowds; those watching from alongside the park side showing the same defiance to the IRA as those men marching in place of their fallen and wounded comrades. The *Daily Express* of 22 July headlined with 'Soldiering On' and Michael O'Flaherty wrote:

> Life even after death must go on. And this was how the Household Cavalry defiantly proved the point yesterday. Only 24 hours after the IRA bomb outrage which killed three of their comrades and seven of their horses, the cavalrymen rode past the scene of the slaughter in London's Hyde Park. An eerie quiet hung over the park as the 16 men of the Life Guards lowered their swords in memory of their fallen

---

4   Wharton, Ken, *The Bloodiest Year: Northern Ireland 1972* (Stroud: The History Press, 2011).

colleagues from the Blues & Royals. The men had been three minutes late leaving Knightsbridge Barracks after Prince Philip paid the Household Cavalry a surprise visit. A few people applauded the Life Guards as they passed by but mostly the tributes were silent. A few minutes later the men changed the guard at Horseguards in Whitehall, relieving troopers who had been on duty 48 hours because of the tragedy. Commanding Officer Andrew Parker Bowles summed up his men's feelings: "It will take more than a cowardly attack like yesterday to stop us doing our duty," he said. As the old guard returned home, they too dipped their swords at the place of death. And under a tree someone had left their tribute – a bunch of pink carnations bearing the message "In loving memory. Father forgive."

In the same edition there was predictable and justifiable anger from the newspaper's Patrick Cosgrave who called for *'Action Not Words.'* He wrote: "It was quite understandable that on Tuesday afternoon, after the bomb outrages in London, the prevailing mood in the House of Commons should have been one of shock. The bereaved mood – not only of the house but of the country too – should perhaps excuse our political leaders from answering the demand for specific proposals for measures against the IRA."Mr Cosgrave went on to say: "Not a single specific proposal emerged from Tuesday's Parliamentary exchanges – at least from the two front benches." Mr Cosgrave set out some draconian but justifiable measures to thwart the threat of the Irish terrorists. He proposed that the border with the Irish Republic be sealed and to hell with upsetting the Irish. He called for vigorous checks on all Irish passengers at sea and air travel points. He demanded that visitors from other countries with known links to the IRA be stopped from entering. Further those holders of Irish passports be treated as aliens and not given easy access to the UK. He also added: "Take the gloves off the Army in Northern Ireland. Most soldiers I have known who have served there complain bitterly that any spontaneous reaction to a terrorist incident or the threat of one might well involve a regimental enquiry, the casting of doubt over a career possibly even a lengthy ... prosecution." He finished his angry article with demands for the re-institution of the death penalty and the return of Internment in Northern Ireland.

On the 23rd, on the day that the last victim of Hyde Park lost his fight for life, *An Phoblacht* (Republican News) stated that "One bomb in London is worth a hundred in Belfast ... It is obvious that the IRA has overcome the extremely difficult logistical processes of carrying out operations in England. By Britain's own yardstick, such actions are the only thing it will listen to." In the USA, the US mouthpiece of the Provisional IRA, NORAID was quick to voice its opinions. Martin Galvin, head of the fund-raising organisation predictably refused to condemn what Phillip Finn (*Daily Express*) called: "the IRA thugs who bombed London." Galvin was an Assistant District Attorney in New York who conducted a war against murderers, rapists and thugs in his home state, but turned a blind eye to what 'the boys back home' were doing in the name of the Irish. Mr Finn wrote that the NORAID man:

in his spare time ... is a chief spokesman for the Irish Northern Aid Committee which is a principal fund-raiser for the IRA. Mr Galvin yesterday watched the TV pictures of men and horses dying in London Parks and then shrugged off the outrage. He said: 'We of course regret loss of life but the attacks were aimed at

British soldiers. The Royal Green Jackets regiment is notorious in Northern Ireland. The Household Cavalry is part of the same British Army which occupies part of Ireland. It is legitimate for the Irish people to fight against them.'

Galvin was close to Sinn Féin and PIRA for many years, but like NORAID's founders Michael Flannery and Pat O'Connell, he gradually drifted away from Sinn Féin following the end of the party's policy of abstention from the Irish and British parliaments. He resigned from his positions at NORAID and The Irish People following the Provisional IRA's declared ceasefire in August 1994. In 1998, Galvin aligned himself with the 32 County Sovereignty Committee, a splinter group made up of Sinn Féin members who opposed the Provisional IRA's second ceasefire in July 1997 and the negotiations leading up to the Good Friday Agreement. The '32 County Sovereignty Committee' is the political arm of the Real IRA. The two groups were reportedly led by Galvin's friends, Michael McKevitt, the Provisional IRA's former Quartermaster General, and Bernadette Sands McKevitt, the younger sister of IRA hunger striker Bobby Sands. When the Real IRA claimed responsibility for the Omagh bombing in August 1998, the worst single bombing of the 30 year conflict, Galvin refused to condemn the bombing which reportedly had been planned by McKevitt.

Finally, when making comparisons between the 2013 bombing of Boston, Mass, and the London Parks, a former EOD soldier had this to say:

Americans were perfectly OK with funding terrorism then. Now that they are the victims of bombings themselves they seem to have some sort of amnesia about their evil past and their role in terrorist financing, and are quite beside themselves that their country and so called freedoms are now being attacked. Americans are always harping on about democracy, but they seem to have overlooked that the vast majority of people in places Britain has staunchly defended, such as Northern Ireland and The Falklands, want to remain British.

Another staunch NORAID/PIRA supporter was the obnoxious US House of Representatives member Peter Thomas King. King began actively supporting the Irish Republican movement in the late 1970s. He frequently travelled to Northern Ireland to meet with senior members of the IRA, many of whom he counted as friends. He once laughingly compared the leader of Sinn Féin, Gerry Adams, to George Washington! He asserted that the British Government was a murder machine. Despite the fact that the Provisionals had murdered over 1,700 people, including over 600 civilians, King said: "If civilians are killed in an attack on a military installation, it is certainly regrettable, but I will not morally blame the IRA for it." He also called the PIRA "the legitimate voice of occupied Ireland." Speaking at a pro-PIRA rally in 1982 in New York, King pledged support to "those brave men and women who, this very moment, are carrying forth the struggle against British imperialism in the streets of Belfast and Derry." In 1985, the Irish Government boycotted New York's annual St Patrick's Day celebrations in protest at King serving as Grand Marshal of the event, at which he again offered words of support for the IRA. The Irish Government condemned him as an "avowed supporter of IRA terrorism."

On June 24, 2013, the author, paid a visit to the Hyde Park blast site and later to the site of the Regent's Park outrage.

Ken Wharton

As we arrived at the memorial close to Rotten Row and the south carriageway, a troop of Cavalry rode past and as they reached the memorial to their fallen men and horses, their NCO screamed out: "Eyes, left!" and as one, they turned their heads to pay their twice-daily tribute. We stood to attention to acknowledge this, and a tear fell onto my cheeks; and then another and another. What a moment to walk up to the site of the bomb-blast. The soldiers were clad in blue jackets, gleaming silver breastplates and helmets, snow-white gloves and red plumes; rather as they had been on that infamous day in 1982. Later we walked to Regent's Park and stood in silent tribute at the memorial to the Jackets who were butchered by the IRA that day. Several more tears streaked down my cheeks as we remembered that sunny day, almost 31 years to the day previously. A friend of the author was a nurse at a nearby hospital and remembers the day so well. The wooden bandstand is now gone and has been replaced with a solid concrete base for security. One imagined that day, in the moments before the bombers struck at the band, a crowd of people, revelling in the sunshine, trying to ignore the palls of black smoke which hung over Hyde park to the south, the wailing sirens of the ambulances to the south west of the park. Then that awful blast!

Six days after the Parks' blasts, Lance Corporal Michael Clive May (22) was killed in an RTA in the Province. He was from the Plymouth, Devon area of South-West England and his funeral was held in his home town. Nothing further is known.

On the 29th, Prime Minister Margaret Thatcher sent a conciliatory message to the Loyalist population of Northern Ireland, when she stated: "No commitment exists for Her Majesty's government to consult the Irish Government on matters affecting Northern Ireland." Whether or not she was believed by the Protestant populace is not entirely certain.

For the first half of the month, there had been no Troubles-related deaths, but after the 16th, 14 people were killed. Twelve soldiers were killed, 11 of who were at the hands of the IRA; additionally one innocent Protestant civilian was killed and the Provisionals killed one of their own.

32

August

During this month, it was as though the entire Province had taken a deep breath and tried to distance itself from the killing. While it was merely the lull before a further storm, 'only' three people were killed in Troubles-related incidents. An IRA man was killed by soldiers; a former UDR man was killed by the IRA because of his past association and a Loyalist murder gang carried out a pointless sectarian murder.

On Sunday 8 August, an Internment anniversary rally in west Belfast was addressed by representatives of NORAID on the same platform as the IPLO. It was rumoured that the chief-PIRA apologist – Martin Galvin – was due to address the anti-British rally alongside his comrades, but having been banned from the UK, on this occasion he was not present. Galvin portrayed himself as an Irish-American patriot with the best intentions of supporting the 'struggle.' In fact, Galvin, purely and simply was anti-British, anti-English and he was able to follow through his anti-Limey tendencies in leading NORAID. This author makes no apologies for his assessment of the man.

The first death of the month took place in Londonderry, when a PIRA man – Eamonn 'Bronco' Bradley (23) – was shot dead by soldiers. He became involved in Republicanism at a young age; at 16 he was appointed OC of *Na Fianna Éireann* in the Shantallow area and soon became the second-in-command of the Fianna in Derry. At 17 he moved from the Fianna to the IRA; he was known as a ruthless terrorist before being arrested in April 1976 and sent to the Maze. He was released in 1981 and straightaway reported back to active service with the IRA. On the 25th of the month, he was spotted by a foot patrol of the Royal Anglian Regiment and immediately recognised as he had been on the 'lift on sight' list for questioning. He was wanted in connection with two recent murders of Security Forces members, including PC David Reeves on the 11th of the previous June.[1] He had been drinking at a social club in the Racecourse Road area and was walking with a man named Paul McCool when soldiers from the Angle-Iron's 2nd Battalion challenged him.

At this point, there is a divergence between what the locals claimed and what the soldiers state actually happened. This author will criticise his former comrades where necessary, but on this occasion feel that the soldiers' version is far more credible. It was stated that Bradley was seized but ran off and in the confusion received a gunshot wound and then a second, fatal wound. Both arresting soldiers state that they felt that he was making a grab for a gun and considering their life in danger, opened fire under ROE. McCool states that he fell over the bonnet of a car and heard the shots but didn't

---

1   See Chapter 30.

see them fired. Several people ran out of the club, one of whom gave the dying man the last rites and an angry crowd gathered around Bradley's body. No trace of a weapon was traced, but it is not beyond the realms of possibility that one such weapon could have been spirited away by the crowd? One does not wish to make light of the grief of the IRA man's family, although following the actions of his comrades in the England team, sympathy for any Republican was not high on the agenda of the men in uniform. On countless occasions, forensics, actual weapons and sometimes dead or wounded terrorists were removed before the Security Forces could examine the scene, The removal of a gun would then leave a dead 'unarmed' paramilitary and 'reputable eyewitnesses' could swear blind that soldiers or RUC had 'executed' a Republican. This was grist for the mill for apologists such as Martin Galvin and Peter Thomas King, as well as for hundreds of sycophantic Irish-Americans.

Eyewitnesses said a soldier had shot Mr Bradley in the head as he lay wounded and helpless on the ground, but one thinks that they may be confusing their own side who developed the killing of helpless victims into an art form. People who were in the area at the time were adamant that no other shots were fired apart from those fired by the soldiers and the author does not dispute that this was the case. Speaking shortly after the shooting, Mr McCool described it as 'cold blooded murder.' Following the reported comments of NORAID leader Galvin and the myriad number of cold-blooded murders by PIRA over the long and bloody course of the Troubles, his author is not inclined nor prepared to take lessons in morality from either a militant Republican or an IRA supporter. The IRA were playing a big boys' game and had to abide by big boys' rules. Mr Bradley was unarmed but he was a known player and was wanted for murder; if the soldiers were not prepared to take any chances with a possible killer, who can blame them?

His sister – Catherine Bradley – added that her family and community deserved a fresh inquiry into the manner in which her brother was '...*slaughtered*...' as he walked home. She told *The Derry Journal*:

> We're looking for an inquiry now. We're all grown up now and we've all moved on but, at the end of the day, Eamonn was my brother and he did not deserve to die in the horrible way that he did. We want an inquiry into his death to get to the truth. If they wanted him so badly, they could have shot him in the leg. He was just in the pub playing pool with his friends. The soldiers were everywhere, they were trained marksmen. To shoot him the way they did was cruel, it was an execution, an assassination.

What did Ms Bradley think that her community's freedom fighters did to almost 2,000 people? Her other comment about shooting her brother in the leg brings to mind a question once asked of this author, whilst home on leave: "Why can't you shoot the guns out of their hands?" She failed to take heed of what being shot in the leg by a high-velocity rifle actually entails as was seen in the 'punishment' shooting of Colm Carey!

Bradley was buried with a full IRA paramilitary show of strength honours and thousands of people attended his funeral. Three masked IRA members fired a volley of shots over the coffin as the funeral cortege left the Bradley family's Carnhill home. *The Glasgow Herald* reported:

A police spokesman said "A full investigation is being carried out." A Sinn Féin spokesman said: "We challenge the RUC to deny that there is a summary policy of execution in force against Republicans." The shooting followed raids in the City on Tuesday when 32 people were taken away for questioning by detectives investigating a series of murders.

The two soldiers were later tried and found to be not guilty of murder and the judge – Mr Maurice Gibson – ordered their release. The Provisionals vowed their revenge and waited almost five years to obtain it. The Judge was killed by a PIRA bomb on 25 April, 1987.

The second killing of the month occurred the following day, this time in North Belfast. Francis McCluskey (46) was the father of eight children and his pregnant wife was expecting their ninth child. He worked in North Belfast and was en-route for work on the morning of the 26th. He had left his home in Greenhill Grove, Ligoniel and was walking across a grassy area in the direction of Mountainhill Road with a workmate. As he did so masked gunmen from the UFF who had been waiting in a stolen car ran towards him and fired several times. Mr McCluskey, attempted to run, but was hit in the head and chest, dying very shortly afterwards. The men who had hijacked a car earlier in the Manse Way district of Newtownabbey jumped back into the vehicle and raced away. The stolen car was later found abandoned in a Loyalist area. A few weeks later, Mrs McCluskey gave birth to a girl whom she named Francine. McKittrick and McVea include a most poignant quotation from his widow in their *Making Sense of The Troubles*:

> I remember him asking for a kiss but I laughed that he had already had his share of two that morning. Those were the last words he said. Francis went out full of fun. That night he came home in a coffin. Francine will know that her daddy loved us all very much. I hold no bitterness towards my husband's murderers. I can just feel sorry for them and their parents. The baby will grow up without any hatred or malice, but love for the father she never knew.[2]

It was another senseless sectarian slaying in a list of well over one thousand senseless sectarian slayings.

Near the end of the month, in a ratification of their policy of abstentionism, the Northern Ireland SDLP announced that although it would contest the forthcoming Northern Ireland Assembly elections, those elected would not take their seats. Following this decision Sinn Féin confirmed that it would oppose the SDLP in a number of constituencies. The Republicans made clear that its preference would have been to support a complete boycott of the poll by all shades of northern Nationalism; however it stated that under no circumstances would any of its successful candidates sit in the new assembly. Instead they stated that their tactics would give: "the nationalist electorate in Northern Ireland an opportunity to reject the uncontested monopoly in leadership which the SDLP has had." Sinn Féin later decided to field 12 candidates in six of the 12 Northern Ireland constituencies.

---

2   McKittrick, David and David McVea, *Making Sense of the Troubles: A History of the Northern Ireland Conflict* (Belfast: Blackstaff Press, 2002), pp.152–3.

On the 27th, it was once again a case of the IRA killing a man not because of who he was or what he represented, but rather a case of who he had once been. Wilfred McIlveen (37), father of four had once been a member of the UDR but left some time after his brother William who was a member of the RUCR was killed by the IRA in 1973. William McIlveen worked at a factory in Armagh City as a security guard. It was there that the IRA targeted him and he was lured over to a parked car containing an IRA murder gang and, as he approached, they shot him dead.[3] Wilfred, who was no longer connected with the UDR had been watching a football match at Killylea, Co Armagh and was driving away from the game. While he was preoccupied watching the football, a PIRA bombing unit had sneaked into the car park and had planted an explosive device under his car. The former UDR man returned to his car and set off; the device exploded as the car turned into the main road and he was killed instantly.

On the 28th, acting on a tip-off from an informant inside the IRA, the RUC found one and a half tons of commercial explosive hidden in a lorry near Banbridge, Co Down. It is unknown whether the same informant also tipped off police in the Irish Republic, because at the same time, the Gardaí Síochána found 10,000 rounds of ammunition and commercial explosives at Glencree, Co Wicklow, south of Dublin. Because of the distance between the two sites, the arms and explosives would belong to different cells and different brigades of the IRA.

After the slaughter in the parks of July, just three people had died in August; an innocent Catholic civilian, a former soldier and an IRA man. The appalling slaughter at the Droppin' Well, the worst mass killing since Warrenpoint in August 1979, was a mere four months away.

---

3   See Wharton, Ken, *Sir, They're Taking the Kids Indoors* (Solihull: Helion, 2011).

33

September

A total of 12 people were killed this month, including five soldiers and two young schoolboys who were killed by an INLA blast in the Divis Street Flats Complex. Lenny Murphy's Shankill Butchers *Mark II* killed twice, as the previous month's death toll was dwarfed.

On the 1st of the month, the INLA shot and wounded Billy Dickson, then a Democratic Unionist Party (DUP) member of Belfast City Council. Dickson who was seen by many as a hard-line Loyalist had attracted the attention of the INLA. Accordingly, seeing him as an enemy of Republicanism, the INLA set out to kill him. During the early evening, masked gunmen attacked the DUP Councillor at his home in North Belfast and shot him several times. He was badly injured, but survived the assassination attempt. He was one of three Protestants targeted by the psychopathic Republican group over the course of the next several months; in September, they shot and fatally wounded a Sunday school teacher, Karen McKeown and then shot and badly wounded a School Headmaster in front of his shocked pupils.[1]

On approximately the same day that the Republicans failed to kill their target, Lenny Murphy continued his rapid descent into hell and lured a fellow Protestant to his death. James Galway (34) was a part-time UDR soldier and barman from the Shankill Road area and, although he shared a name with the celebrity flutist, he shared none of the lifestyle. For reasons which Murphy and another UVF member who also belonged to the UDR never revealed, sometime between Sunday 29 August and Wednesday September 1, they killed Mr Galway. The UDR man who helped kill him was Cyril Rainey. Murphy, who had already killed once since his release from prison lured Mr Galway (33), who was alleged to have passed information to Ballymena UVF to the village of Broughshane. Murphy had decided to kill him and the three men went to a building site in the village which was near to Ballymena. Murphy shot Galway in the head and his body was buried in a deep pit. By the time it was found in November 1983, it was already badly decayed; he had not been seen since leaving for a short holiday at the end of August 1982, so the timing of his death was only approximate. The location of the body was only revealed when the third man was in custody and possibly trying to reduce his likely sentence. The UDR man received 12 years for aiding Murphy and was dismissed in disgrace from the Regiment. By the time that his body was found, Murphy the sadistic killer had already been dead himself for almost a year. Cyril Rainey, who was also OC of 'D' Company, UVF in Ballymena was gaoled

---

1   See Chapter 34.

for 12 years for his part in the murder. He was again gaoled in 2008 for the possession of an illegal firearm.

If one accepts that James Galway was killed on the 1st of the month, Murphy wasted almost no time before he killed again, shooting Brian Smyth (30) dead a mere 96 hours later. This meant that Murphy, in the 51 days since his release from the Maze had killed three men. This time, his motive was money as he had refused to pay Mr Smyth, who was a car dealer, money owed for the purchase of a car on the day of Murphy's release. Smyth made the mistake of demanding the money that he was owed and Murphy attempted to poison him in a Loyalist club on the Shankill Road. The car dealer probably realised that he was seriously ill and, being in some considerable pain allowed himself to be lured into the car of a friend of Murphy – a member of the Red Hand Commandos named Sam 'Mambo' Carroll – on the promise of being given a lift to the Mater Hospital on the Crumlin Road. Murphy followed the car on a stolen motorbike and when the car obligingly slowed down in Crimea Street, he pulled alongside and shot Smyth eight times, killing him instantly.

Five days later, an elderly female resident of Violet Street, Belfast, had a lucky escape when she walked out of her house and almost trod on a blast bomb left there by the Provisionals, possibly under cover of darkness. The woman aged 72 had the presence of mind to call a soldier over and the device was disposed of. Just 10 days later, she and some other equally elderly neighbours had a further escape when the same terror organisation fired an RPG-7 at the nearby police station; the blast killed a young soldier.

On the 16th, the INLA proved as irresponsible, as ruthless and as uncaring of their own community as did their 'big brothers' in the Provisional IRA. Their intention was to kill and maim soldiers from an anticipated foot patrol of the Worcestershire and Sherwood Foresters, or 'Woofers' as they are known to other regiments of the British Army. How they achieved that, they either didn't plan thoroughly enough, or possibly didn't even care. This was after all the organisation of mad dogs which boasted members of the psychopathic nature of Steenson and McGlinchey. The 'Woofers' were the 29th/45th of Foot and were formed in 1970, although they can trace their lineage back to around the time of the Indian Mutiny and boast the siege and capture of Kotah, 1857–1858 as a battle honour. Now amalgamated into the Mercian Regiment, their motto was 'Firm.'

INLA bombers placed an explosive device inside a drain pipe and ran a command wire to Cullingtree Walk which was part of the Divis Flats Complex known to soldiers as the 'Zanussi.' As the anticipated foot patrol began walking along a raised walkway, a bomber detonated the device, apparently on a signal from an observer that the soldiers were in the killing zone. The bomb detonated and in the blast Lance Bombardier Kevin Waller (20), who was attached to the WSF foot patrol, was fatally wounded, dying four days later. A number of other children in the flat nearest the seat of the explosion were also injured, some of them very seriously. However, Stephen Bennett (14) was killed instantly, and Kevin Valliday (11) was fatally injured and died the following day in hospital. One other soldier was grievously wounded and suffered traumatic amputations. There was deep anger that the INLA had placed a bomb on walkway in the heart of the densely populated Divis Flats Complex. This was home territory to the IRSP/INLA and was derisively known as the *'planet of the IRPS'* by their Republican rivals. Over 200 women from the 'Zanussi' and surrounding areas marched on the nearby IRSP offices expressing their fury at the callous irresponsibility of the 'freedom fighters.'

Irene Bennett, mother of one of the dead boys said:

I was down the town shopping that fateful day and I heard the blast but I never thought it had happened on my own doorstep. When I got home, I saw the way my neighbours went silent when they saw me and I knew Stephen had been hurt. We were on our way to the hospital when the priest came along in the car and told us he was already dead. It was like a nightmare. I've never got over it. Even 20 years on I still walk into a room and expect Stephen to be there.[2]

Lena Doherty (sister of Kevin Valliday) said:

I was seven months pregnant at the time and I was round visiting my mum. I sent him round to my house for a hammer. I've always felt so guilty. We heard the bomb go off and immediately I thought of Kevin. I knew he would be on his way back home with the hammer. We ran out in a panic and some of the neighbours said "What kind of runners is your Kevin wearing?" My mother described them and we decided it wasn't him but we soon found out it was.[3]

In 2002, some 20 years later, a spokesman for the INLA made the following hollow, PIRA-type apology: "We acknowledge and admit faults and grievous errors in our prosecution of the war. Innocent people were killed and injured and at times our actions as a liberation army fell far short of what they should have been. For this, we as Republicans, as socialists and as revolutionaries do offer a sincere, heartfelt and genuine apology."

In 2002, some 20 years later, a spokesman for the INLA made the following hollow, PIRA-type apology: 'We acknowledge and admit faults and grievous errors in our prosecution of the war. Innocent people were killed and injured and at times our actions as a liberation army fell far short of what they should have been. For this, we as Republicans, as socialists and as revolutionaries do offer a sincere, heartfelt and genuine apology."

The day after the INLA attack, Private Alan Bruce (21) of the Royal Scots was on duty in the Province when the vehicle in which he was travelling was involved in a serious RTA; he was killed. Sadly, other than his service number, the author has no further information.

On the 20th, as Lance Bombardier Waller was losing his fight for life, the 'Woofers' suffered another casualty and within a week, they would suffer another. The RUC station on the Springfield Road – intimately known to this author – was positioned some 80 yards from the strategic crossroads with the Falls Road and Grosvenor Road; it was in the buffer zone between the Loyalist Shankill Road and the Republican Falls Road and Divis Street. It was attacked on numerous occasions and was the scene of three fatal attacks on soldiers. On 25 May, 1971, Sergeant Martin Willetts GC was killed when an IRA bomb was thrown into the station; he was killed when he deliberately placed himself between the bomb and women and children in the station reception area. On 30 May 1972, Kingsman Marcus 'Jimmy' Doglay of the King's Regiment was killed by an IRA bomb which had been smuggled inside the soldiers' rest area of the station.

---

2   *Andersonstown News* (16 September 2002)
3   Ibid.

On 20 September, 1982, the IRA struck again. Private Martin Kane Jessop (19) from Derbyshire was manning the roof top sangar at the rear of the station which faced on to Violet Street. For security, Army Engineers had erected a huge metal screen which had turned the street into effectively a cul-de-sac and rear or side access was only possible from the bottom of Violet Street and Cavendish Street. An RPG-7 was fired from the bottom of the street and it penetrated the reinforced concrete sangar, killing Private Jessop instantly.

On the same day as the attack on Springfield Road RUC station, the INLA were also busy, this time south of the border when they blew up a radar station belonging to the Irish Army. The attack was on a station in Schull, Co Cork and was followed by an announcement that they had attacked an 'Imperialistic' target and that the Irish Government was technically assisting the British Government to remain on Irish soil!

On the 23rd, a UDR soldier – Private William 'Billy' Acheson (23) – died from what is euphemistically known as 'death by violent or unnatural causes.' The author has no further information on this soldier's death other than he is buried at Roselawn Cemetery in Belfast. On the same day, John Hermon, the Chief Constable of the RUC, stated that both the IRA and the INLA were 'reeling' from the evidence given by the so-called 'supergrass' informers and a series of arrests as a consequence. Sadly, many of these cases collapsed or convicted terrorists were subsequently released on appeal.

On the 25th, following a spate of shootings – by the UVF – in the Short Strand and another shooting in the Markets area, the INLA announced that they would retaliate. Still reeling from Nationalist criticism over the killing of two Catholic schoolboys in the Divis Flats Complex, they were desperate to show that once again they were the defenders of their communities. Quite why Karen McKeown was targeted is not known; she was aged 20 and a theological student, who also taught at Sunday school. As she left her church on Albertbridge Road in Belfast, she walked towards her car and paused to unlock the door; as she did so, a gunman from the INLA came up behind her and shot her in the back of the head, fatally wounding her. She was rushed to hospital but died the following month, just over three weeks after the shooting. An INLA apologist shamefacedly denied involvement in the fatal shooting, but the gun used was from their armoury and had been used in previous INLA shootings. One man of whom we shall hear more later – Billy Giles – was greatly influenced by the shooting of Miss McKeown and, on the day that she was shot, the countdown to the end of Michael Fay's life began.

Shortly afterwards, the same terror organisation shot a retired man – a Protestant – as he waked along Harland Walk, close to the Loyalist Newtownards Road. William Nixon (68) was an innocent man, with no British military background and no paramilitary links; he was simply a Protestant in a Protestant area and his murder was purely sectarian. Although the INLA again denied responsibility, forensic evidence linked the murder weapon to the INLA's armoury and previous killings.

This author has previously written about the 'Berlinisation' of Belfast describing how small walls which became large walls sprang up; seemingly overnight in order to keep the warring sectarian factions apart. Many of those mini Berlin Walls still exist today, over 40 years after their construction. West Belfast's Cupar Way, which divides the Shankill from Springfield Road and the Falls is now a mecca for the coachloads of tourists who visit only the 'sanitised' areas of the former urban conflict, is but one. They pose under the sectarian or paramilitary graffiti and have their photos taken to simply show their friends that they have 'braved' the Troubles.

One such wall or security gate was situated between the Loyalist Highfield Estate and the Nationalist Springfield Road. The estate is very close to the Nationalist 'Murph as well as the aforementioned Springfield Road. The gates were controlled by the Army/RUC and part of Security Forces duties involved locking and unlocking them. During the darkness of the 26/27th, an INLA unit had placed a booby trapped explosive device to the gates. In the morning, a unit from the 'Woofers' turned up to unlock the gates. Often they had to move gangs of children who gathered to taunt the children of the 'other side.' On this morning, there were no children around. As Nottingham boy Corporal Leon Bush (22) touched the gates, the device exploded and he was killed instantly; he was the third 'Woofer' or attached arms to die in the space of a week. He was from the Notts area, and is buried at Woodhouse cemetery in Mansfield.

Mallusk is a small suburb on the northern outskirts of Belfast and Newtownabbey, and today sits in the shadow of the busy M2 motorway as it snakes northwest in the direction of Randalstown where it becomes the A6 Antrim Road and continues towards Londonderry. In September 1982, it was the scene of an RUC stake out as police, acting on information received from informants, lay in wait for an armed robbery to take place. It has been alleged that UDA members had warned the police of the raid and that the motives were purely personal as one of the would-be robbers had earned the displeasure of the Loyalist paramilitary organisation. Armed officers were hiding in an adjoining room and burst out to arrest two men who had entered the post office with guns drawn. One of the robbers – Ronald Brennan (22) – is said to have pointed his pistol at an officer and was shot several times. The other robber immediately surrendered but Brennan staggered outside, mortally wounded and tried to get into the getaway car which was driving away. He eventually collapsed and died in a nearby garden. Both of his accomplices were arrested and received long gaol sentences. Brennan's mother Anne was fatally wounded by UFF thugs in September 1976 and died three weeks after the attack.[4]

On the final day of the month, Lenny Murphy's gang was again in the news as they murdered an innocent Catholic simply because of his religion. John O'Neill (28) worked in a petrol station on the Ormeau Road in Belfast and was cashing up for the night when several masked men burst in. Mr O'Neill thought that he was being robbed and grappled with the intruders who were members of the Butchers mark II. One of the men shot him several times and they ran out of the garage leaving him dying in a pool of his own blood. One of the killers was Noel Large, who had links with the Shankill Butchers; he was gaoled later for this murder and the murder of Eugene Mulholland on September 19, 1981, also on the Ormeau Road.[5]

The month was over and although Murphy was again involved in murder, his day was coming and one of the most evil men of the Troubles had less than two months to live. Twelve people died this month; five soldiers and seven civilians. Of the civilians, four were Catholic and three were Protestant; two of the killings were overtly sectarian. Republican terrorists killed six and Loyalist terror groups killed three; the INLA were responsible for five deaths with a sixth fatally wounded.

---

4   See Wharton, Ken M., *Wasted Years, Wasted Lives* (Solihull: Helion, 2013), Vol 1.
5   See Chapter 21.

34

October

A total of 12 people died in this month, including three soldiers and five policemen. Another prison officer was killed as the result of a car crash caused when PIRA shot an off-duty UDR man.

The month started with the murder of an off-duty RUCR officer as he drove to work. John Eagleson (49), father of three, was from Cookstown, Co Tyrone and worked for a local company as well as being a part-time policeman. He was known to habitually drive along the same stretch of road to work each morning and to ride his motorbike on an isolated road close to Drum Manor. On the morning of the 1st, he took the road as usual and paid for that decision with his life as IRA gunmen lay in wait for him and shot him dead. The part-time policeman who had also served in the UDR was found dead by a passing motorist. On the same day in an act of what many observers saw as an act of crass insensitivity, a motion was passed at the Labour Party conference which called for a ban on the use of plastic bullets in the whole of the UK.

Less than 96 hours later, the IRA killed another RUCR officer when they struck at Altnagelvin on the eastern outskirts of Londonderry. Charles Crothers (54), father of five, was a part-time policeman who also worked for Londonderry Environmental as a security guard. As he was unlocking the security gates, a car drove towards the entrance and a man jumped out and fired several shots, hitting Mr Crothers and knocking him to the ground. The gunman then calmly walked over to where he lay helpless and fired three more shots into his head; he died almost immediately. The gunmen escaped in the car which had been stolen in a Nationalist area and abandoned it a couple of miles away.

On Wednesday 6th, Des O'Malley, the Irish Minister for Trade, Commerce and Tourism, resigned from the Government in the Republic of Ireland. O'Malley resigned because of disagreements with Taoiseach Charles Haughey on matters related to Northern Ireland and the Republic's economy. O'Malley later formed a new political party in the Republic called the Progressive Democrats.

On the 7th, the INLA's South Armagh team were able to claim 'two for the price of one' when they killed a part-time UDR soldier and, in the process, also killed a female PO. Lance Corporal Frederick 'Fred' Williamson (33), father of three was driving to work near Moy in Co Armagh. INLA gunmen had set up an ambush and were waiting for him as he drove along the road. At least two gunmen firing automatic weapons sprayed the part-time soldier's car and, although he was not hit, he immediately lost control. His car careered across the road and into the path of an oncoming vehicle which contained WPO Elizabeth Chambers (28) who was en-route for work at Armagh Gaol. Both people were mortally injured from the high speed crash and died at the scene.

Lance Corporal Williamson's funeral was held at St Mark's Church in Armagh City, and Miss Chambers' was held at First Broughshane Presbyterian in Co Armagh.

On the 17th of the month, Karen McKeown (20), the student and Sunday School teacher who was fatally wounded the previous month, died of her injuries, following a brave fight for life. She was one of two innocent Protestants who had been shot and killed by the INLA in a tit for tat involving Loyalist murder gangs. Saddened and shocked by the death of the soft spoken and forgiving Miss McKeown, Billy Giles had vowed revenge on the Catholics. He had joined the UVF in 1975, left and re-joined in the wave of the 1981 Republican hunger strikes. It would be a month before he killed, but Giles was biding his time. On the same day as the student died, the INLA carried out a bomb attack on the headquarters of the Ulster Unionist Party (UUP) in Glengall Street, Belfast. The blast left the building badly damaged.

On the 18th, in what was seen as a further attempt by the INLA to disrupt the coming Assembly elections, there was a murder attempt on the life of one of the candidates. Mr David Wright, Headmaster of the Model School in Newry, Co Down, was teaching a class of 10 and 11-year-olds, when INLA gunmen burst into the classroom. The men had held the school caretaker at gunpoint and demanded to know his location. The frightened man directed them to a classroom where he was teaching religious education and shot him at point-blank range with a shotgun. Leaving him terribly wounded, and a score or more young children in a state of shock, the masked men escaped in a stolen car. The wounded Head later recovered from the blast. This cowardly and shameful attack followed a UVBT attack on the car of another candidate – Robert Overend – outside his farm at Bellaghy, Co Londonderry. The man's 24-year-old son, Andrew was driving and escaped with cuts, bruising and shock in the blast which left the car badly damaged.

On the 22nd, Sergeant Thomas Cochrane (54), a part-time soldier in the UDR was kidnapped by IRA gunmen en-route for work. Dickers were aware that he motorcycled to work from the Bessbrook area to a factory at Glenanne and were waiting for him on a quiet stretch of the road. Armed IRA men in a stolen car deliberately rammed his bike and forced him off the road before bundling him into the back of the car. He was taken to a secret location in the South Armagh countryside where he was kept, unseen by the dozens of soldiers and RUC officers, backed by helicopters that were desperately searching for him. It is thought very likely that, after a short period of torture, he was shot – although it was not until the 27th that his body was found hidden in a ditch. It is uncertain if there was an official announcement that the Sergeant was being held hostage but it is considered likely that the Provisionals kept the story alive, or failed to suppress it, in order to keep his family's hopes alive.

On the same day as the abduction of the UDR soldier, REME Sergeant Richard Terrance Gregory (39) collapsed and died while on duty, in, it is thought, Lisburn. The Shropshire man may have been taken ill while working and he died in hospital. His funeral was held at St Mary's Red Lake Church in Ketley, Shropshire.

Two days later, enter Mr Lenny Murphy and the remnants of the Shankill Butchers. In retaliation, they seized a Catholic man who was also a father of seven from outside the Pound Loney Social Club in the Falls Road area. The Pound Loney was a little lane (loney) which ran off Divis Street to Durham Street. The lane ended at the side of Barrack Street's old Belfast Animal Pound hence its name, a little stream called the Pound Burn ran along one side of the animal Pound. In later years, streets of working class two up and two down houses were built on the west side of the Pound stream which were bordered by Divis Street, Albert Street and Durham Street; this district became known as 'the Pound Loney' after the original old lane and stream. Murphy and his cohorts, including William 'Wingnut' Cowan, William Mahood and Noel Large had hijacked a taxi and then gone looking for 'fares' in the staunchly Nationalist area. Joseph Donegan (48), who had seven children, thought that the taxi was safe and willingly climbed inside. He was immediately subdued by members of the gang, but mainly by Murphy himself who was sitting in the back, and driven to 65, Brookmount Street to a house where Murphy had once lived.

In his excellent and certainly definitive account of the gang, Martin Dillon describes the scene in the back of the taxi as thus: "Donegan put up a fierce struggle and ... [the] rear windows were covered in blood."[1] Badly injured, the Catholic man was dragged into the empty house at Brookmount Street, close to the junction with Azamoor Street. North Howard Street Mill was only some 300 yards away and soldiers based there regularly patrolled the area. Murphy went for a spade and a pair of pliers while two of the gang continued to beat the injured man. While Cowan and the other man held Mr Donegan, who was barely conscious, Murphy pulled out all but three of the man's teeth and left them scattered around in bloody piles. This was an act of barbarity and torture which sickens this author to the stomach. Mr Donegan who must have been in terrible agony, was dragged into the back yard, where he was then beaten to death with the spade as he lay on the ground.

Murphy however was determined to keep up the illusion that the man was still alive and would be kept as a hostage and 'swapped' with the Provisionals for the abducted UDR man, Sergeant Cochrane. Both sides – and here PIRA can under no circumstances maintain the 'moral high ground' – kept the mockery going, falsely fuelling the hopes of the loved ones of both men. This illusion was maintained for several days and even involved churchmen from both sides of the religious divide. Eventually, both paramilitary extremes tired of the game and the dead men's bodies were discovered and two sets of families could begin the grieving process. Martin Dillon describes the scene at 65, Brookmount Street following the discovery of Mr Donegan's body in an alleyway. 'When police arrived at the scene they found Murphy's back door lying open and they proceeded to search the premises. Blood was spattered over the ceiling, walls and floor of the kitchen and teeth with their roots attached were lying on the floor. In a small room leading to the yard, they found more blood and teeth.'[2] Murphy was arrested and questioned but released through lack of evidence, but the depraved killer had fewer than 21 more days to live.

Martin Dillon examined the pathologist's report and wrote: "there were twenty lacerations to Donegan's head and body and bruising and abrasions to most of his limbs. He would have lost consciousness from severe internal bleeding ... there were only three teeth left in his mouth, numerous fractures of facial bones, ribs, skull and thyroid cartilage."[3] In other words, he had been subjected to a systematic, vicious and pathological assault before being murdered. As we will see later, the words 'Here Lies a Soldier'

---

1   Dillon, Martin, *The Shankill Butchers* (London: Arrow Books, 1990).
2   Ibid., pp.305–306.
3   Ibid., p.306.

are engraved upon his grave stone and there can be nothing further from the truth, for the epithet 'soldier' and Lenny Murphy have absolutely nothing in common.

During the maintenance of this joint illusion, the UVF targeted and killed a Sinn Féin worker who was involved in the election campaign for the British Government's latest 'white elephant' the Northern Ireland Assembly. He had been dicked by UVF members, and it was known that he left his house in the Loughall Road area of Armagh every Monday morning to walk to the Labour Exchange in Alexander Road. Peter Corrigan (47), father of 11, was born and raised in lower English Street in the city. He was educated in the Christian Brothers' School. After school he excelled in his chosen career and was widely known around the country for his craftsmanship in brick and stonework. After a time in England, where he met his wife Jean, they returned to Armagh and settled in Banbrook Hill, moving eventually to the then new housing estate of Drumbreada. He joined the IRA in 1969 and became very active, later being interned. He was released in 1972, but continued working for Sinn Féin; arrested again in 1973, he was finally released in 1975. On the 27th, as he walked along Alexander Road, two masked UVF men stepped out from a garden and shot him twice in the head and chest and he died at the scene. His killers, one of whom was also a UDR member, raced off in a waiting stolen car. The killing was later claimed by the Protestant Action Force, which was merely a cover name for the UVF. One of his killers – a UDR member who had experienced the deaths of his comrades at the hands of the IRA – was later gaoled for life. UDR man Geoffrey Edwards, was sentenced to life for this killing. He also was convicted of five other attempted murders, one of which was an attempt to kill INLA gunman Seamus Grew, who was later shot dead by the RUC in December of this year. Interestingly enough, although the cold-blooded murder of Mr Corrigan can in no way be justified, it is interesting nonetheless that here was a man, committed to the overthrow of the British, but equally at home accepting their financial hand-outs.

MY FIRST CORPSE
Dave Judge, Royal Green Jackets

I was on patrol with Joey Earwaker in Londonderry and we were near the docks; I think it may have been Shipquay Street. A drunken, smelly old man, obviously alcoholic and probably drinking meths and the like, approached our patrol and was slightly overcome with grief and shock! He blurted out 'they' had killed him; Who killed who we wanted to know? "My mate," he said, "he's dead; they killed him." He asked us to follow him which we did with some trepidation, as we had no idea if this was a 'come on' or not. We entered a sort of drinking den, come squat and sure enough there was a dead bloke on an arm chair curled up and looked as if he was fast asleep! However when we shook him he was as stiff as a board! Cold and very much dead! His mate was crying in that drunken blubbering way only a pisshead can do! We called it in to base and we left. The police must have dealt with it, and we continued with our patrol; the end! Well it was for that poor old bloke; it was quite sad really to die in your sleep on a chair in a squat. At least he had one friend in the world who cared for him!

Just 48 hours later, on Wednesday 27th, the IRA killed three RUC officers when they detonated a landmine as a patrol passed near Oxford Island, near Lurgan, Co Armagh.

A total of 18 police officers were killed during this year and to the ever growing roll of honour were added the names of Sergeant Sean Quinn (37), father of three; Constable Paul Hamilton (26) and Constable Alan McCloy (34), father of two. The three officers had been dispatched to Lurgan following reports of robberies from cars in the area. It was clearly a 'come on' and, via an informer, RUC INT were aware that the route which they would need to take was highly vulnerable to PIRA culvert bombs. Despite this, the information was not passed on and the three men driving an armoured Ford Cortina set off to investigate. As they drove through a roundabout at Oxford Island along the Kinnego Embankment, a watching bombing team detonated a massive bomb estimated at 1,000 lb (454 kgs) as the RUC vehicle passed a culvert. All three officers were killed absolutely instantly by the blast which left a crater over 15 feet deep and almost 40 feet in diameter.

Two of the IRA bombing team – Sean Burns and Eugene Toman – were shot dead the following month, at Tullygally East Road, near Lurgan while they were en-route to kill an off-duty man in Portadown. This incident will be dealt with in the following chapter. The RUC had set up a special anti-terrorist grouping – Headquarters Mobile Support Unit or HMSU – from within Special Branch to counter this type of situation. Twenty-four men per unit, in part, trained by the SAS, conditioned to work in covert roles along the border, they were to be renowned for aggression, something which had hitherto been missing in their previously reactive, rather than proactive role. On November 11, they would be witnessed in action.

So, October had ended and with it, the lives of 12 more people. Three soldiers had been killed and five policemen had lost their lives also. A PO was killed as were two civilians – both in overtly sectarian circumstances – and one Republican was killed. The Provisional IRA or INLA was responsible for nine of the 12 deaths in October.

35

November

During this month, a total of 14 more people would die, including just one soldier and one policeman. Additionally, the IRA would kill a former policeman and the RUC's HMSU would kill three Republican terrorists. More significantly, it would be the month that a man who more than many, typified the evils of the Troubles, would breathe his last; Lenny Murphy was killed.

On Tuesday 2nd, representatives of the SDLP held a meeting at the NIO with James Prior, then Secretary of State for Northern Ireland, and informed him that the party would not reconsider its planned boycott of the proposed Assembly. Prior realistically knew that they would maintain this stance, but privately he had hoped that they would have second thoughts. When the first sitting of the new Northern Ireland Assembly took place at Stormont, Belfast, neither the SDLP nor Sinn Féin took up the seats which they had won. Still on the subject of politics, south of the border the Irish Coalition Government was defeated in a vote of confidence in the Dáil. As a consequence, later in the month a new General Election was held in the Republic of Ireland, which returned a new Coalition Government of Fine Gael and the Irish Labour party; Garret FitzGerald became the new Taoiseach.

In the United States on the 5th, a court acquitted five men of charges of conspiring to ship arms to the IRA during 1981. Given the immense propaganda efforts of the Provisionals and their cronies inside the Irish-American lobby, this came as no major surprise. The accused men used the defence that the Central Intelligence Agency (CIA) had approved the shipment of arms, although this was denied.

On 8 November, during a planned operation by 5 UDR, PIRA gunmen opened fire on a patrol in rural Co Londonderry. Following a brief exchange of fire with terrorists, the patrol arrested Seamus Kearney, a gunman who was wanted for numerous offences. He allegedly shot Reserve Constable John Proctor who had just visited his wife June and their newborn baby son in the Mid-Ulster hospital in Magherafelt. Father-of-two Reserve Constable John Proctor, 25, was shot dead by an IRA gunman as he got into his car in the hospital car park in September 1981. Kearney was finally arrested in 2010 and charged with the historical murder.

On the 9th, a PIRA bombing team targeted an off-duty RUC officer after he parked his car outside a leisure centre in Enniskillen. Whilst the officer was inside the building, they planted an explosive device underneath the car. After he had finished an archery lesson, he drove away with a female colleague and was possibly too tired after a day's duty followed by the lesson to check for devices. As he reached Paget Street, close to the town centre, the device exploded. Detective Constable Garry Ewing (31), father of two, was killed instantly. His colleague Helen Woodhouse (29) was mortally wounded, dying en-route to hospital. With a poignant irony, her father was an ambulance driver at the same hospital. The Provisionals later issued one of their hollow and totally meaningless apologies stating that they regretted her death but warning civilians from accepting lifts from members of the 'Crown forces.'

The following day, a part-time UDR soldier was killed by the Provisionals at his place of work in Co Armagh. Corporal Charles 'Charlie' Spence (44), father of three worked for HM Customs at Monaghan Road between Middletown and Armagh City. PIRA INT had already established that he finished work at around 1800 hours and, during the late afternoon of the 10th, under cover of the late-autumn early winter darkness, had cut through the security wire of the Customs compound. Consequently they were in position with automatic weapons ready as the part-time soldier came out of his office. Corporal Spence got into his car and at that point the Republican terrorists opened fire on him, hitting him almost 20 times; he died within seconds of the assault. The masked gunmen escaped the way that they had entered and into a waiting car where they were ferried the two miles or so to the Irish border, or 'terrorist bolt-hole' as the Irish Republic is better known.

On the evening of 11 November, 1982, three IRA members — Eugene Toman (aged 21), Sean Burns (21) and Gervaise McKerr (31) — were shot dead at Tullygally East Road, near Lurgan. That night, acting on intelligence received, the RUC's HMSU were trailing the three men. A Special Branch informer had told them that they were en-route to kill a member of the Security Forces in Portadown. In addition, the RUC suspected Toman and Burns of having killed three officers in a landmine attack at Oxford Island, near Lurgan, on 27 October 1982. The HMSU set up a road block and the car containing the PIRA ASU broke through it, endangering the life of an RUC man. Consequently, the RUC officers opened fire. One bullet, they said, caused a flash when it struck the metal of the car, leading them to believe that they themselves were under fire, and naturally they continued firing until all three IRA men were dead.

The shooting of Toman and the others was therefore, in the opinion of this author justifiable; these were dangerous men on a murder mission; there was no time for niceties. At a subsequent inquest, as Deputy Chief Constable Michael McAtamney later testified, the officers were part of a unit given special training for undercover operations. As such, he stated, they worked on the principle that: "if you decide to fire, you shoot to take out your assailant; permanently." In the past, McAtamney elaborated: "RUC men had hesitated in such situations and suffered the consequences. No hesitation was possible." It would be unrealistic to ask the RUC to hesitate before firing at a dangerous suspect because they might face a possible murder charge. The HMSU officers were all charged with murder, but subsequently acquitted. There were similar incidents on 24 November and 12 December of this year. Eventually the British Government set up the Stalker inquiry – later taken over by Sampson – into the incidents.

This gave rise to the myth of 'shoot-to-kill.' One uses the word 'myth' advisedly because, irrespective of whether one believes that there was an actual 'policy' in place to kill rather than arrest, there is only one intention when shooting; that is to kill, or at the very least incapacitate your opponent so that he or she is no longer a viable threat. Hollywood may perpetuate the myth of shooting to wound or in the clichéd manner of the Westerns' movie-makers, shooting the weapon out of the baddie's hand, but in real life, it simply is not like that. All soldiers and police officers are trained to shoot for the biggest target – the chest – and most hits, especially with high-velocity rounds in that area are likely – not always, but likely – to be fatal. The standard issue British Army and NATO weapon used by the Security Forces in Northern Ireland during the Troubles was the Belgian FN or SLR 7.62 mm. It was a British Commonwealth derivative of the Belgian FN FAL battle rifle, produced under licence. It has seen use in the armies of Australia, Canada, Jamaica, Malaysia, New Zealand, Rhodesia, as well as by the British. It held a magazine of 20 rounds and was semi-automatic which meant that it didn't need to be cocked after every shot, but was designed to fire only a single round at a time. It had a muzzle velocity of 2,700 feet per second (823 m/s) with an effective range of 984 feet (300 m). On the streets of Northern Ireland, it was generally used at distances of less than 100 yards and as such, with the stated muzzle velocity, it caused major tissue damage to the human body when striking solid flesh and bone as the round accelerated to maximum velocity. The 7.62 mm round makes a small entry wound but can tumble on impact and pushes human tissue ahead of it, leading to an exit wound many times the size of the initial entry. As such, being hit in the chest is more often than not, fatal.

As a young soldier, the author, in common with all other recruits was taught to aim at the biggest body mass and not to even consider 'trick' shots. Even an impact on an arm or a leg would cause massive trauma which would probably also lead to death. In any case, in a life or death situation, the soldier or policeman wishes to preserve his own life, the lives of those comrades around him or the lives of the innocent public; the civil rights or human rights of the armed or potentially armed terrorist is never paramount in the minds of the lawfully armed man. During the Troubles, many a soldier or policeman died or was seriously injured when they hesitated in taking a shot; as the RUC officer said, there is no time for niceties and that split-second delay can be the difference in the member of the Security Forces being returned to their loved ones in a coffin or the terrorist being afforded the 'coveted' space in the Republican plot in Milltown cemetery. This author believes that 'shoot-to-kill' was not some political excuse to kill paramilitaries rather than arrest them, but rather a 'shoot-to-survive' policy.

Critics of both the Army and the RUC – almost exclusively Republican or their British mainland apologists on the Left – are very happy to overlook the shoot-to-kill policies of the IRA/INLA and their targeting of unarmed men and women. However, they are unforgiving about what they perceive as the self-same thing from the Security Forces. Northern Ireland was a war – make no mistake about that, whatever the British Government or the Press might claim – and it was a dirty war like all conflicts. There is no nobility in being gunned down in a filthy alley in the Shankill or Ardoyne or on a modern housing estate such as the Creggan or Ballymurphy. The war against paramilitaries – whether green or orange – was a war which needed to be won and this author believes that with a few exceptions, a few regrettable incidents, the Security Forces carried out the prosecution of that war in the way that was required and indeed expected of them.

On the 16th of November, two men by the name of Murphy were killed violently in Belfast; one would be mourned by his loved ones, the other's death would be cheered and the words 'may he rot in hell' would be mouthed by a myriad number of decent people. Patrick Murphy (64), father of six, was a shopkeeper who conducted his small business from a shop in South Belfast. Lenny Murphy (30) was a psychopathic mass murderer who killed mainly Catholics seemingly for a perverted pleasure. Both men were killed on the 16th, just hours apart, close to each other but poles apart.

Patrick Murphy ran a grocery shop in Mount Merrion Avenue, Belfast, close to the Cregagh Road and the RUC interrogation centre at Castlereagh. He had no known links to the Republicans, but for his UVF killers, the fact that he was a Catholic was reason enough to kill him and leave six people fatherless. A man, now known to be a member of the UVF and the man who would kill Mr Murphy, walked into the shop, looked around and then left. However, just minutes later, he returned and pulled out a handgun, shooting the shopkeeper three times and mortally wounding him. The man ran outside to a waiting motorcycle, and was whisked away by his accomplice. Mr Murphy, whose death was condemned by Unionist politicians as well as Protestant clergy, staggered into the back room where he collapsed and died in the arms of his daughter.

The scene of the killing then switched to Forthriver Park in North-West Belfast and involved the mass murderer Lenny Murphy, UVF killer and leader of the sectarian murder gang, the Shankill Butchers. Hugh Leonard Thompson Murphy, who commonly went by the name Lenny, was born on 2 March 1952. As mentioned times *passim* by this author, he had killed around 30 people, either individually, or as part of the aforementioned Butchers' murder gang. He was a Protestant, possessed with a fanatical hatred of Roman Catholics. He was released from prison on the 16th of July this year, and killed four people between that date and the date of his death on the 16th of November. The murders gave him an almost 'god-like' status in the hard-line Loyalist areas of the Shankill, Crumlin *et al.*, but the cruel, sadistic torturing and beating to death of Joseph Donegan on 24 October[1] left even some of the top Loyalist paramilitary leadership slightly disturbed by both his methods and his apparent blood lust. One such man was UDA leader James Craig and it is considered highly likely that he gave information to the IRA which led to Murphy's death.

James Pratt Craig served as a fund-raiser for the UDA and sat on its Inner Council. He also ran a large protection racket from west Belfast's Shankill Road area, where he lived. He was once described as 'Belfast's foremost paramilitary extortionist' due to the protection rackets which he controlled in the Loyalist areas. He also allegedly colluded with Republican organisations such as PIRA and INLA, providing them with information on key Loyalists, leading to their deaths. He was eventually killed by his fellow Loyalists in October 1988 and it is, as previously stated, considered highly likely that he informed PIRA leaders where Murphy was staying and when he would be at the address.

During the evening of the 16th, Murphy had just driven to a fish and chip shop in the Glencairn area of North Belfast and intended to drive to his girlfriend Hilary Thompson's house in Forthriver Park. As usual, he was driving his distinctive bright yellow Rover SD1 and as he drove along, munching his fish supper, he failed to notice a black or blue Morris Marina van which pulled out from a roadside parking space and began following him, albeit from a short distance. Murphy arrived at the house, on a small estate just a few hundred yards from the Crumlin Road and parked at the rear. He would have seen the van overtake him, and apparently continued eating; however the van stopped and its rear doors opened and two masked gunmen leaned out and

---

1   See Chapter 34.

immediately opened fire on him. The men fired a 9 mm SMG and a .38 pistol, hitting Murphy 22 times (some reports state 26) and killing him instantly; his blood splattered all over the newspaper which contained his fish and chips. He was hit in the head by seven rounds, as his PIRA assassins left no room for mistakes. The Beast of the Shankill was dead at last; killed by his hated enemy and likely delivered into their hands by a man he had crossed many times. Coincidentally, he was gunned down just around the corner from where the bodies of many of the Butchers' victims had been dumped.

Mark 'C' UDR and Royal Artillery

His very distinctive yellow car was brought into Hastings Street RUC station. The front seats were covered in Murphy's blood and his half eaten fish supper was still there, also covered in his blood. UDR Soldiers had to pass the car which was in a dimly lit garage to get to the sangar on Divis Street; of course squaddies being squaddies played many pranks on said soldiers; never seen so many roughy tuffy soldiers scream when one of their mates jumped out from behind Lenny's car.

The PIRA gang abandoned the van on waste ground in West Belfast and then set fire to it, thus destroying all forensic evidence. Later a spokesman stated that they had killed Murphy. He was given a large paramilitary funeral by the UVF with a guard of honour wearing UVF uniform and balaclavas. A volley of three shots was fired over his coffin as it was brought out of his house and a piper played 'Abide With Me'. He was buried in Carnmoney Cemetery in North Belfast; on his tombstone the following words were inscribed: 'Here Lies a Soldier'. In 1989, his gravestone was smashed by vandals, or was it perhaps by the loved ones of the 30 or so people he savagely butchered? Martin Dillon quotes an aunt of Murphy as saying: "Nothing could be more beautiful than the memories we have of you; to us you were very special and God must have thought so too."[2] As we say in my native Yorkshire: *'There's none so blind as them that can't see.'*

In 2013, the author in the company of Mark 'C', my cousin John Leighton and a UDR comrade whom we shall call 'BR' paid a visit to the cemetery in Carnmoney. As I took a photograph of his grave for this book, I felt a sudden chill, as though the evil which was buried there had stirred; perhaps it was my imagination? I visibly shivered in the heat of a 28°C Belfast afternoon, while all around me sweated in the heat. As I contemplated the monster buried beneath my feet, I thanked God that the nearest I would ever get to Murphy was just six feet. I muttered a few words of contempt and then gratefully strode away. Pausing to look back at his grave, I shuddered once more.

A former Royal Artillery soldier told the author:

I was at Carnmoney in 2013, also. I refused to soil my camera by photographing the gravestone. My daughter even refused to look at it even though she was not born when Murphy was active. Only a mother could say what Murphy's mother said. I saw photographs of his handiwork in 1976 so I'll say it as I saw it; he was a psychotic, murdering scumbag who got his just desserts.

---

2   Dillon, Martin, *The Shankill Butchers* (London: Arrow Books, 1990), p.318.

Jude Collins, an Irish writer added:
The people of the Shankill were not simply intimidated into silence. That's not to say they weren't intimidated. As May Blood pointed out, if you didn't want to set yourself up as the next victim, you closed your door and shut your mouth, which the people of the Shankill did. But the idea of a population who loathed the killers in their midst got shattered with the funeral accorded to at least one of them – Bobby 'Basher' Bates. Thousands of people lined the Shankill to pay their last respects to this shockingly cruel man.'

The last words will be left to his mother, who like all of our mothers can see no wrong in their sons: "I don't honestly believe he was a bad man."

On the same day, the INLA killed two more policemen, both members of the RUCR, in Markethill, Newry. At approximately 1730 hours, as two police officers stood at security gates in Markethill, a stolen car containing at least two INLA members – one of whom was believed to be Mary McGlinchey – drew up close to where the men were on duty and opened fire with automatic weapons from very close range. Between 40 and 50 rounds were fired at the two officers and both were mortally wounded. Leaving them lying in pools of their own blood, the killers jumped back into the car and raced away in the direction of the nearby border. The Nationalist Derrybeg Estate was closer, but the Security Forces was known to flood the area after attacks in Newry. An on-duty nurse and a doctor from a nearby surgery ran out to help, but both men died at the scene. They were Constable Snowden Corkey (40), father of three very young children, and Constable Ronnie Irwin (24). Constable Corkey who left it late in life to have children left a pregnant widow; four more children would grow up fatherless thanks to the ruthless Republican terrorists.

One of the suspected killers was Mary McGlinchey, wife of INLA gunman Dominic 'Mad Dog' McGlinchey. She was killed in her Dundalk home by gunmen who broke in while she was bathing her children on 31 January 1987; shot down as ruthlessly as she had shot down others. Dominic McGlinchey was unable to attend her funeral as he was still imprisoned in the Republic of Ireland; he was killed himself in Drogheda, Ireland in February of 1994.

Raymond Gilmour was a former INLA, as well as PIRA, volunteer who worked as an informer for the RUC from 1982 within those paramilitary organisations. He was forced to flee Northern Ireland in 1982 and agreed to become one of the first 'supergrasses' and aid in the conviction of dozens of terrorists. His testimony was one of the main elements of the supergrass policy, which hoped to convict large numbers of paramilitaries. On the 18th, the IRA kidnapped Patrick Gilmour, Raymond's father and smuggled him into a safe house as a hostage. The IRA later said that Mr Gilmour, senior would not be released until his son retracted his evidence.

On the 19th, in Newtownards, East Belfast UVF member Billy Giles abducted a Roman Catholic married man, Michael Fay (25), and shot him in the back of the head, killing him instantly. He then stuffed the body in the car's boot. Fay had been Giles' friend and workmate, and the killing was in retaliation for the fatal shooting of Karen McKeown, a young Protestant Sunday school teacher by the INLA some seven weeks earlier. Giles was arrested by the RUC and brought to the Castlereagh interrogation centre, where he confessed to the killing. He was found guilty of the murder and sentenced to life in the Maze Prison.

On Wednesday 24th, the RUC's HMSU was called into action again, but this time an innocent man was killed and another wounded, albeit through their own curiosity. From information received from a well-placed informant inside the Provisionals' Armagh Brigade, the RUC discovered an arms cache on farmland close between Derrymacash and Ballyneery in the Craigavon area. HMSU officers were instructed to carry out surveillance of the farm, although British Intelligence were already aware of the cache and had 'jarked' the weapons. 'Jarking' is a process in which arms are surreptitiously fitted with tracking devices, have the firing charges in the ammunition reduced to lessen the risk of death if they are fired or even have the firing mechanisms tampered with in order to cause a stoppage when fired. Two young local boys from the Ballyneery area were aware of the weapons and visited the shed where they were being stored, out of juvenile curiosity. When they entered and began to interfere with arms, HMSU officers opened fire and Michael Tighe (17) was shot several times and died almost immediately. His friend Martin McCauley was badly wounded although he later made a full recovery. Young Tighe had no paramilitary links and was an unfortunate victim of the violent times and the violent land in which he lived. This author regrets his death and the injuries sustained by his companion, McCauley.

On the 25th, full-time RUCR officer, Constable William Harrison Moffatt (32) died after his own car skidded on ice and hit a lamppost, while going on an emergency call. He was fatally injured in the accident at the Junction of North Road and Bangor Road, Belfast. When UDR soldier Charlie Spence was killed by the IRA on the 10th of this month, there was shock and sadness amongst his neighbours in his neighbourhood, particularly in Knockannell Drive in Armagh City where he lived. Amongst those shocked by the murder, just a few doors away, was the Martin family. Just 17 days later, there was further mourning in the same street when a former RUCR officer, now a petrol station employee, was also killed by the IRA; he had left the police in 1979. John Martin (34), father of two was cashing up for the night and his son aged 10 was also there for company. Just on closing time, a masked man walked in holding a handgun and Mr Martin selflessly pushed his son to the ground below the counter. The gunman fired four shots at him, hitting him in the head and chest and he slumped to the floor, dead. His son, despite the incredible shock, attempted to telephone for the police but his hands were shaking so much, that a passer-by, alerted by the sounds of the gun shots rushed in and dialled 999. An apologist for the Provisionals claimed that they knew that he was no longer a member of the RUCR but made an outrageous claim that he was working undercover for the UDR. It was a lie and confirmed the utter bankruptcy of their policies and tactics.

On Tuesday 30 November, James Prior, addressed the Northern Ireland Assembly and announced that the strength of the RUC and RUCR would be increased by 800. With the deaths of RUC officers now approached 200 and with injuries over 3,000, it was a welcome boost to both their numbers and their morale.

A momentous month had ended and it included – at long last – the final demise of Lenny Murphy. In all 14 people had been killed violently; one soldier and four policemen had died, including a former police officer. Five civilians had died – three Catholics and two Protestants – and two of these deaths were overtly sectarian. Four paramilitaries had died – three Republicans and one Loyalist. Republicans were responsible for seven of the deaths and Loyalists for two. Surprisingly, the RUC had killed four, and all four of the killings were at the hands of the HMSU.

36

December

D ecember was an incredibly violent month, with 22 people dying, although 17 of these deaths were in the INLA attack on the 'Droppin' Well' disco in Ballykelly. Eleven of the dead were soldiers including a former UDR soldier. The HMSU were again in action and two more PIRA terrorists were killed.

On the 2nd of the month, having ascertained the working habits of bus driver John Gibson (50), PIRA gunmen set up an ambush which left him dead and many school-children shocked by their callous actions. Mr Gibson, a father of seven, had served in the UDR but had resigned two years earlier and had narrowly escaped death when an IRA landmine wrecked his Land Rover some years before that. Although he was a Protestant, he was collecting Catholic schoolchildren on the afternoon that he was killed, in order to take them home from school. His movements had clearly been observed by the IRA because gunmen were waiting at Annaghmore where his bus stopped in order to allow children to get off. As Mr Gibson stopped, two masked men got on and in full view of the children, opened fire, hitting and mortally wounding the former soldier. Although dying, he tried to drive away but lost control and crashed into a ditch. The distraught children were forced to climb out of the rear emergency exit to safety.

Lost Lives quotes a passage from his funeral, where a churchman delivered his eulogy: "I leave you with this thought; he was helping Catholic schoolchildren to find their way home from school, on that cold December day. Let that be his epitaph."[1] The area lies to the west of Lough Neagh and east of Cookstown and Coagh, so the border is not readily accessible. This means that the escaping killers would have to find shelter in the outlying Nationalist areas.

Kevin O'Neill aged 21 from Aughamullen, a bricklayer and PIRA member, was found guilty of taking part in the murder and received a life sentence. Aughamullen, Co Monaghan is some five miles inside the Irish Republic. Lord Justice Kelly who sentenced O'Neill described the killing as a "cold blooded and ruthless execution." As he was led away, the IRA man cried "*Tiocfaidh* ár lá," a clichéd comment meaning 'our day will come.' His sister caused uproar as she tried to climb into the dock and had to be restrained. O'Neill did not fire any of the fateful shots but, as the Judge said: "He knew that someone was to be shot and he agreed to conceal the murder weapon after the shooting." It is also entirely possible that he also provided it before the killing, thus

---

1   Thornton, David, Seamus Kelters, Brian Feeney and David McKittrick. *Lost Lives: The Stories of the Men, Women and Children who Died as a Result of the Northern Ireland Troubles.* (Edinburgh: Mainstream, 1999, revised ed. 2007), p.927.

making him an accessory before, during and after the fact. He was captured hiding in a ditch after soldiers spotted him.

Alerted by radio, Lieutenant Jay Nethercott, commander of the operations platoon 8 UDR gave chase to the gunmen who had just murdered the former UDR soldier. He opened fire on the gunmen's car with his 9-mm pistol, and eventually forced them to abandon their vehicle and flee. Calling up one of his patrols in the area, he mounted an immediate search operation which resulted in the discovery of an Armalite rifle and the arrest of one of O'Neill's killers. Lieutenant Nethercott was awarded the Queen's Gallantry Medal for his action, although clearly the whole patrol acted in a brave and meritorious manner.

During the morning of Tuesday 7 December, the Irish Supreme Court made a ruling which opened up the possibility of extradition between the Republic and the UK. Somewhat surprisingly, in view of previous intransigence and indeed open hostility to Britain and her demands, the court rejected the claim that paramilitary offences were politically motivated. However, the news that day would be dominated by a more significant and tragic matter which took place in the far north of Northern Ireland.

There were many attrocities committed by both sets of paramilitaries during Ireland's bloody period known as the Troubles; too many to chronicle in this period of history which covers 1980–83. In strictly numerical rather than emotional terms, however, there are several which stand out: McGurk's bar in 1971 when 15 were killed by a UVF bomb; La Mon Restaurant in 1978 when a PIRA bomb killed 12; Warrenpoint in 1979 when PIRA bombs killed 18 soldiers and Omagh in 1998, when the so-called 'Real' IRA slaughtered 29 civilians in a no-warning bomb attack. To that list of shame, can also be added the name of the Droppin' Well public house in Ballykelly.

The name of Ballykelly is taken from the Irish: *Baile Uí Cheallaigh*, which means O'Kelly's Townland and is a village in Co Londonderry, Northern Ireland. It lies three miles west of Limavady on the main Londonderry to Limavady A2 road and is approximately 15 miles east of the city. RAF Ballykelly was a wartime base and, latterly, Shackletons were flown from there. Then came the Troubles and it became a British Army base from where many two-year residential postings were based.

On Monday 6 December 1982, the INLA exploded a bomb at the Droppin' Well Bar and Disco in Ballykelly, which killed 16 people and fatally wounded another who died ten days after the incident. The dead included 11 British soldiers and six civilians. Over 30 people were also injured in the blast, some of them seriously, including a soldier who was paralysed for life by his injuries. The bar/disco was a part of the Shoppin' Well centre was a regular social haunt for soldiers and, before them, RAF personnel. The resident battalion at the time was the Cheshire Regiment, or simply the 'Cheshires.' The regiment was created in 1881 by the linking of the 22nd (Cheshire) Regiment of Foot and the militia and rifle volunteers of Cheshire. Its motto is *'Ever Glorious'* and its lineage can be traced back to Louisburg, Martinique in 1762. Its battle honours include the Retreat from Mons, 1914, all four battles of 'Wipers' (Ypres), first Somme offensive, Dunkirk 1940 and the Normandy landings. Until the night of 7 December, 1982, it had lost only one soldier in the Troubles: Corporal David Smith, who died of his wounds after being shot by a PIRA sniper outside Kelly's Bar at the junction of the Whiterock Road and Springfield Road on 4 July, 1974. That was all to change as soldiers and civilians alike danced to the music of the Droppin' Well disco.

Over the period from October to late November, INLA dickers had regularly visited the pub and had assessed just how many soldiers used the bar on a regular basis and whether or not they could kill enough military personnel in order to make an attack 'viable.' They also had to assess the religion of the civilians who also attended and decided that as the majority were likely to be Protestants, an attack which killed large numbers of them was justified. They chose the 6th of December because a disco was scheduled and it was guaranteed that a large number of soldiers would be there. After the disco started, an INLA operative thought to have been a woman, left a bomb inside the pub. There were about 150 people inside. It was estimated that the bomb, small enough to fit into a woman's handbag, weighed around 10 lb (4.5kgs) and was composed of a commercial explosive known as Frangex. The bomb was left beside a support pillar and, when it exploded at 45 minutes before midnight, the blast brought down the roof. Many of those killed and injured were crushed by fallen masonry. Following the explosion, it took over four hours to pull survivors from the rubble, with the last survivor being freed at around 0400 hours. It was not until 1030 that the last of the bodies was recovered.

Of the 11 soldiers who were killed, eight were from the Cheshire Regiment, two from the Army Catering Corps and one from the Light Infantry. The Provisionals were immediately suspected, and they, as they had done many times before, denied any involvement. However, within 24 hours, the Army was blaming the INLA on the grounds that the IRA, in a mixed village, would have made greater efforts not to risk killing civilians. Sure enough, shortly afterwards, the INLA issued a statement of responsibility:

> We believe that it is only attacks of such a nature that bring it home to people in Britain and the British establishment. The shooting of an individual soldier, for the people of Britain, has very little effect in terms of the media or in terms of the British administration.

All of the dead civilians were Protestants and their collateral deaths were dismissed out of hand by the INLA as being 'consorts' of soldiers. In an interview after the bombing, INLA leader 'Mad Dog' McGlinchey said that the Droppin' Well's owner had been warned six times to stop offering entertainment to British soldiers. McGlinchey added that the owner, and those who socialised with the soldiers: "knew full well that the warnings had been given and that the place was going to be bombed at some stage."

Tomás Ó Fiaich, then Catholic Primate of Ireland, called the killings "gruesome slaughter," and Margaret Thatcher said: "This is one of the most horrifying crimes in Ulster's tragic history. The slaughter of innocent people is the product of evil and depraved minds, and the act of callous and brutal men."

The toll of the dead was as follows: Private Terence Adams (20); Private Paul Delaney (18); Lance Corporal Steven Bagshaw (21); Lance Corporal Clinton Collins (20); Private David Murray (18); Corporal David Salthouse (23); Private Steven Smith (24) and Lance Corporal Philip McDonough (26); all were from the Cheshire Regiment. Killed alongside them were Private Neil Williams (18) and Private Anthony S. Williamson (20) both from the Army Catering Corps and Light Infantry soldier Lance Corporal David Wilson-Stitt (27). The following Protestant civilians were killed: Alan Callaghan (17); Ruth Dixon (17); Angela Hoole (19); Valerie McIntyre (21) and Carol Watts (25). Patricia Cooke (21) was pulled alive from the wreckage and was rushed to hospital; sadly she died on the 16th. Angel Hoole was from Lytham St Anns in Lancashire and was only drinking in the Droppin' Well as she was visiting her sister who was married to a Cheshire soldier. The dead civilians were mainly from Ballykelly and Limavady.

The *Daily Express's* headline was to the point and most apt: 'Horror Without End.' The front page read:

> When the terrible wreckage of the Droppin' Well yielded its final bomb victim last night, it added up to the blackest day even Ulster has seen. Sixteen [sic] including 11 soldiers, 60 injured with 15 soldiers among the most serious cases. Ulster Secretary Mr James Prior went to Ballykelly and visited the injured at nearby Londonderry. (He said) "This dreadful outrage was committed against young people intent on enjoying an evening out.......it must rank amongst the most cold-blooded acts of savagery carried out in Northern Ireland throughout all the years of violence here. It was a massacre without mercy. Words are inadequate to express the sense of shock and horror and outrage felt throughout the community."

The inside pages of the same edition continued under a secondary headline of 'Massacre'. "If I could get my hands on my son's murderers, I'd tear them apart," said the mother of Lance Corporal Clinton Collins, Mrs Enid Mountford of Stockport. "What these people have done is an act of cowardice."

THE DROPPIN' WELL BOMB
Steve 'Taffy' Horvath, RAMC (attached Cheshire Regiment)
Prior to reading the following extracts, I wish to inform the reader that there are some awful recollections of the Droppin' Well Public House bombing at Ballykelly in Dec '82. Therefore, should the reader have any personal knowledge, be related to any victims, or know anyone from this incident then you may find this part of the book upsetting or traumatic, so please put the book down. It is not my intention to cause any pain or suffering to the reader in any way.

As I write this in 2013 I was in two minds as to whether I would be able to. This is only the second time I've ever been able to put pen to paper and tell my version of what little I can remember from that fateful night. As you, the reader, travel through my memories with me, there is so much pain in my eyes and heart. Not only for the loss of life during the night of 6th December onwards, but knowing how much suffering was inflicted on the families and friends of victims, but especially those that survived and have to spend the rest of their lives trying to come to terms with it.

Not far outside the main gates of Shackleton Barracks was a very nice village pub called the Droppin' Well, in squaddie lingo our 'local haunt'. The locals were a pleasant lot who welcomed us with open arms. Above the pub were a series of shops, my memory fails to recall what they were but I think one was a hair salon or a florists and the rest I cannot remember. From the time I arrived in Ballykelly the Droppin' Well had become our watering hole. On occasions we had our fair share of altercations with some of the Republican sympathisers who would travel up from Greysteel to give us some grief. On one particular night one of our lads took a serious kicking for no apparent reason outside the pub. Needless to say, the next night a huge number of us made a late night visit to Greysteel and executed our revenge on the local men with such aggression and violence that we made it clear: "Screw with one of us you screw with all of us."

We'd already had several bomb threats at the pub, and on these occasions the commanding officer would put the pub out of bounds until such time as the 'Int Sect' deemed it safe for us to venture back in. Naturally we were extremely suspicious and weary once we stepped outside the gates of camp, though somehow we were relaxed within the village of Ballykelly. After all, we weren't in central Belfast, Londonderry or 'Bandit Country' as South Armagh was known. To all intents and purposes we were in the middle of a quiet, non-hostile friendly community.

Much of what happened during the event of the night of 6th December '82 is still locked up in the dark recesses of my brain. Someday, maybe the memories will come to the fore and I will hopefully then be able to put them into perspective. The day was a typically nondescript day in Ballykelly with the normal routine activities happening during the day. The evening's activities had been focused on chilling out in the NAAFI and then over to the pub to celebrate one of the lad's promotion. The atmosphere within the Droppin' Well was one of a relaxed environment; both civilian and military alike enjoying each other's company. My memory of the few hours before the event, and much of the immediate aftermath, are very fragmented. My brain has, in its own self-protecting way, even 31 years after the event, refused to allow me to recall most of my memories from that night. I do however remember some of it, just enough enabling the darker psychological scars and injuries to the innermost part to surface. I remember getting a round of beers in for the boys, placing the tray of drinks on our table and heading through the toilet door for a piss. A couple of the boys I was celebrating with sadly lost their lives that fateful night.

I remember the shit-house door slamming behind me. The next thing I remember is all hell broke loose. Apparently, the explosives were placed in such a position that they blew away the concrete pillars of the disco room. As a direct consequence of this, the whole shopping precinct above the pub came crashing down on us. As I was in the bog, and close to the external walls of the pub, I was lucky to escape with minor cuts and bruises and able to get myself out of the rubble. What seemed to be hours passed by, in fact it was only a matter of seconds or minutes, before our lads from the camp started to arrive, along with the emergency services. For what appeared to be an eternity, I stared in total disbelief that this could happen to 'our pub'. Once our lads arrived from the med centre laden with emergency med kit we got to work. This is what all my military and medical training had been designed for; to get in and do the job, and get the lads and lasses out alive if we could. I remember scrambling over the piles of rubble, trying to shout for and find my girlfriend Avril, as she was likely trapped in the collapsed pub. I was scared shitless that she'd been hurt or killed.

Looking at the state of the place and the devastation around, it's a miracle that I wasn't crushed by the tons of rubble from the shops above, as I and many of the emergency services, crawled through the rubble to try to reach the injured. My paramedic instinct naturally tried to take over, but there was so much emotion, fear, anger and tears that my brain went into some sort of overload as I started trying to dig my way through the rubble. I remember one casualty whom our MO was having a crap time with, trying to get a drip into the man's arm. The MO shouted for me to get the 'cut-down' kit so that we could cut open his veins to get a drip in. As he shouted I noticed that the young lad was pissing blood from both his shattered legs like a fucking river, as he had a piece of steel 'Rebar' (The type used to reinforce concrete walls and pillars) through him. 'Fuck the cut-down kit', I told the MO, 'cut his fucking jeans off and get me more bags of Hartman's solution. I dropped like a fucking stone onto the lad's right thigh with my kneecap straight into the crease of his groin an attempt to stop the femoral artery pissing out more blood. At which point the screaming just went through the roof, so to speak. Almost simultaneously I had cut the end of the drip tube, ripped what was left of his clothes from his backside area and rammed the end of the drip tube some 5/6 inches up his arse. His screaming and fighting during this was making me feel as if I was going to puke, never mind the poor bugger's life I was trying to save. By pumping fluids up his arse, it would get into his system faster than if we had tried a cut-down as he would have bled out by the time we managed to get a drip in his arms. 'Get me more bags' I yelled to the doc, 'unless you want him to fucking die on me!'

All I do know is that my methods, which were not in any training manual or very orthodox, were an automatic reaction. As a result of my actions, my Medical Officer tried to get me court-martialled for my unorthodox method of getting fluids into the dying soldier and disobeying his orders. As it turned out the MO was bollocked and told not to be a c***!

In June 1986, four people received life sentences for the attack and a fifth person received a ten year sentence. Anna Moore, Eamon Moore, Helena Semple and Patrick Shotter all were sent to prison for life for the bombing; another woman – Jacqueline Ann Moore (19) – was given 10 years for manslaughter as the judge believed she had been coerced by family members; all of the INLA bombing team were from Londonderry.

In 2013, the author paid a visit to Ballykelly and Greysteel in order to take photographs for this and future books. The town/village is a quiet place close to the North Antrim Coast which picturesque cottages, green fields as well as the ubiquitous bland council housing scattered about. Our party took photographs of the Rising Sun Bar in Greysteel – the 'trick or treat' massacre which took place in 1993 will be dealt with in a later book – and then drove into Ballykelly on an exceptionally warm July day. The old 'Shoppin' Well' Centre which housed the bombed pub is no longer there; in its place is a petrol station and attached convenience store; what the Australians would call a 'Servo.' Under the banner 'Super Valu' [sic] it also hosts an off-licence. It sits alongside the busy A2 Clooney Road which becomes Main Street through the village and thereafter the Ballykelly Road. Posters adorn the lamp posts proclaiming 'On the banks of the Foyle.' The disused RAF base is less than 200 metres away and there is no air of menace in this place. How different the scene in 2013 to that night of carnage on the build-up to the 1982 Christmas season.

HUMAN KINDNESS AMIDST THE CARNAGE
Bob Horton, Cheshire Regiment

The day after the Droppin' Well bomb in '82, we were all anxious to phone home to tell our relatives we were ok, but the NAAFI only had two phones and all the BHQ phones were in use. An old lady from the bungalow across from the camp started shouting at us to come over. She very generously let everyone use her phone and refused any payment, but the poignant thing was, as we thanked her for her kindness she gave each one of us a hug and a grandmotherly peck on the cheek.

The next morning her front garden was filled with flowers and boxes of chocolate. On that dreadful morning she gained hundreds of surrogate grandsons.

On Wednesday 8th, British Home Secretary William Whitelaw imposed a banning order on Gerry Adams, then Vice-President of Sinn Féin, and Danny Morrison, a leading member of the same organisation. The order was imposed under the Prevention of Terrorism Act and meant that Adams and Morrison could not enter Britain. The two men had received an invitation from the leader of the Greater London Council (GLC) – IRA apologist Ken 'Red Ken' Livingstone – to go to London for a series of meetings. Livingstone, who was born in 1945, was a British Labour Party politician who twice held the leading political role in London Local Government, first as the Leader of the GLC from 1981 until the Council was abolished in 1986, and then as the first elected Mayor of London from the creation of the office in 2000 until 2008. He also served as the MP for Brent East from 1987 to 2001. He permitted Irish Republican protesters from the H-Block Committee to hold a 48-hour vigil and fast on the steps of County Hall throughout the 1981 Royal Wedding celebrations, during which they launched 100 black balloons over the city. Two days earlier, the *Daily Express* had opened its front page with the banner headlines: 'Keep Out!' with secondary headlines of 'Fury over Red Ken's invitation to the IRA's two henchman.' Its leader writer also proclaimed: '*They must be denied a platform to sustain their campaign of hate.*' Forty-eight hours later, in what was applauded by most right minded people as a victory, the same newspaper proclaimed: 'Banned' and 'Red Ken's 'guests' face five years in gaol if they deny order by Whitelaw.' *Express* Political Editor John Warden wrote:

> In swift action last night Home Secretary Mr William Whitelaw banned three Sinn Féin leaders from entering Britain. By police request he signed an Exclusion Order under the Prevention of Terrorism Act. Two of the men, Gerry Adams and Danny Morrison were invited to visit London last week by GLC leader Ken Livingstone. The third, Martin McGuinness, was added to the ban for good measure.

On the 12th, the HMSU were again in action and again, from the Republican point of view, it was another 'controversial' incident in which they were involved. Rodney Carroll (22) and Seamus Grew (31), both members of INLA, were shot dead by an undercover unit of the RUC at a VCP in Mullacreevie, Co Armagh. This became the third incident where allegations were made that the security forces were operating a 'shoot-to-kill' policy. Grew's brother was a PIRA gunman who was shot and killed on 9 October 1990; Dessie Grew was killed in a shoot-out with British soldiers in Co Armagh.

Prior to the deaths of the two INLA men, a former Sinn Féin worker who had turned informer for the RUC passed on details of the whereabouts of three INLA members in the Republic. An undercover member of the RUC's E4A team spotted the men – Grew, Carroll and Dominic McGlinchey – inside the Irish Republic and a decision was taken to tail them into the North and either arrest or eradicate them. The E4A was an anti-terrorist, intelligence-gathering unit of the RUC, established in 1978. It was primarily made up of police officers who conducted surveillance to be acted on by RUC Special Branch. At this stage of his terrorist 'career' McGlinchey had killed several members of the security forces and was responsible also for some civilian deaths including that of a helpless elderly lady. Bearing in mind his murderous activities and the danger he presented, it is thought likely that a decision was taken in order to 'take him out.'

In the event, McGlinchey did not cross into the North, and Seamus Grew and Rodney Carroll drove into Co Armagh on their own. An RUC VCP was set up at Killylea Road at a spot close to where Cortyman Road which leads directly from the Irish border joins it. The reliable source informed the RUC that McGlinchey was coming across the border that night in a car driven by Grew. The information was that all three men were likely to be armed and, in view of the long sentences they would face if caught, would resist arrest. The officers of the HMSU squad were probably nervous, but in anticipation of a shoot-out were not prepared to take any chances. When they stopped the suspect car and saw that two INLA men were inside, they opened fire and both Grew and Carroll were hit several times and killed instantly. Because they were both unarmed, Republican sources as well as left-wing apologists on the mainland immediately accused the RUC of shooting rather than arresting, as though the luxury of choice was actually available to the officers participating in the incident. Carroll had only recently been released from custody after an informer retracted evidence he had initially agreed to give against him. An RUC friend of the author who was a member of HMSU told me: "When a local Doctor examined the two dead INLA men, and pronounced life extinct, he told me later told me he'd never seen men so dead!"

The *Irish Times* felt that such a policy of 'shoot-to-kill' existed, but further commented:

> This ... illustrates again the depressing and demoralising nature of the British role in Northern Ireland. To stay is to connive at the erosion of supremely valuable prin-ciples, for no one can deny that British standards of law enforcement and adminis-tration of justice have both suffered severely from events in the province. To leave is to betray a majority of people who want us to remain and probably to precipitate a civil war.

On the 16th, Seamus Mallon, the Deputy Leader of the SDLP, was removed from his Northern Ireland Assembly seat by an Election Petition Court. The reason given was that Mallon was also a member of the Irish Senate at the time of the election. Shortly afterwards on the mainland, Parliament approved the increase in the number of MPs representing Northern Ireland at the House of Commons from 12 to 17; in 1997, this figure was increased to 18. Parliament also decided that the number of members of any future Northern Ireland Assembly would be increased from 78 to 85, which represented five members per constituency.

On the 19th, a carefully laid plan by the Provisionals led to the death of Corporal Austin Smith (44), father of three, as he returned home from work. In addition to being a part-time soldier, he also worked at a UDR-run social club and had clearly been dicked several times by IRA volunteers. He finished work close to midnight and as usual drove home to the Windmill Estate in Armagh City; as usual, he parked some distance from the house and walked towards the home which he shared with his family. The soldier who was a member of two UDR had gone only a few yards when gunmen who had been waiting patiently behind a garden wall stepped out and shot him several times at very close range. They ran off and Corporal Smith's family, alerted by the sound of gunshots ran to his side, but he died within seconds of them arriving. A local Unionist MP, Harold McCusker, spoke at his funeral, saying: "Austin Smith was by any standards a very brave man, in stark contrast to the cowards who killed him." His was the last military death of 1982; it would not, however, be very long into the New Year of 1983 before there was another.

With just 48 hours before Christmas, Prime Minister Margaret Thatcher paid a surprise and highly secret one day visit to Northern Ireland. She mainly spent the time visiting members of the security forces, naturally under heavy guard as the troops prepared for their 14th Christmas of the Troubles. It was a very cold day as the PM chatted to soldiers, no doubt glad to be off the streets of the Province for even a few minutes. Although overall deaths were down, still 53 of their comrades, in some cases former comrades, had died in or as a consequence of the Northern Ireland Troubles. However, at the end of the 23rd, Margaret Thatcher returned to the warmth of 10 Downing Street and the soldiers prepared for their next freezing-cold footsies on the streets and estates of the hard-line nationalist areas, because the gunmen and the bombers of the Provisionals and the INLA never slept.

1982 ended with the death of a petty thief – Patrick Pearse Elliott (19) – on the 27th, when soldiers surprised two men in the execution of a robbery. Elliott who lived close to the Broadway in West Belfast and a friend decided to rob a fish and chip shop in Andersonstown Road. They wore the terrorist 'accoutrement' of black balaclavas and as they left the shop with their meagre gains, they encountered a foot patrol from the Black Watch who immediately challenged the men to stop. One of the soldiers thought that Elliott was armed as he made an aggressive move. The soldier fired, striking and killing the teenager. It was a pitch-black night, with only the street lighting of Andersonstown Road to illuminate the scene and the Scottish soldier had only a split-second in which to evaluate the situation. At that stage of the Troubles – the 14th year of conflict – and with nigh on a thousand dead soldiers over that period of time, the Black Watch man did not have the luxury of an option. Too many policemen and soldiers who had hesitated now lay in a myriad number of graveyards throughout the United Kingdom.

The month had been particularly violent with 22 deaths. A total of 13 soldiers, including a former UDR man had been killed and seven civilians – six Protestants and a Catholic – had died also. Two Republican paramilitaries were killed during December. Of the 22 deaths, the INLA were responsible for 17 and the Provisionals for two; the RUC shot two Republicans and the Army shot a petty thief.

1982 had ended with 124 deaths in or as a consequence of the Troubles.

The breakdown was as follows:

Military	53
Police	16
Prison officers	1
Civilian	39*
Protestant	20
Catholic	19
Republican	10
Loyalist	5

* Of these civilian deaths, seven had been overtly sectarian in nature.

369/371, Antrim Road: Scene of May, 1980 killing of SAS Captain Herbert Westmacott.

Looking towards the junction between Antrim Road and Cavehill Road where their expected SF targets would stop at traffic lights.

Red Hand Commando mural: Shankill Road, Belfast.

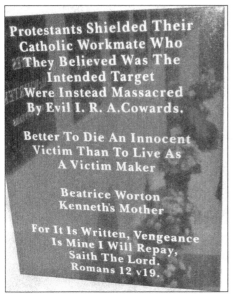

Plaque at site of 1976 Kingsmill Massacre where a PIRA murder gang shot down 11 Protestant workmen, 10 of whom died.

Site of the former RUC station, Andersonstown, Belfast; exact spot where Blues & Royals' soldiers Thornett and Dykes were killed by PIRA M60 gang in August, 1979.

Crumlin Road Courthouse, scene of many dozens of terror trials.

Bogside mural depicting the then Bernadette Devlin, the 'MP in blue jeans'

Loyalist heartland: Rathcoole, North Belfast.

UFF Mural, Rathcoole.

Lower Bogside in Londonderry; close to the PIRA haunt of the 'Bogside Inn.'

'Boundary Bar' Shore Road, North Belfast; interface between sectarian areas; scene of several killings, including sectarian murders.

Lenny Murphy.

The rebuilt La Mon House restaurant. PIRA napalm-bombed the crowded restaurant in February, 1978, killing 12 people.

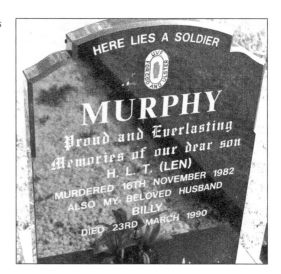

Warrenpoint:
Parachute Regiment
memorial to the
18 dead soldiers;
destroyed by
Republican thugs.

Part Four

1983

This was the year which saw the INLA plumb the very depths of depravity with the infamous attack on a church congregation at Darkley. It was the year where the press employed the term 'supergrass' at least once a day. It was the year of the so-called 'Great Escape' from HMP, Maze. It was also the year of the Harrods' bombing.

37

January

A total of nine people, including six members of the Security Forces died this month; PIRA killed a Catholic Judge and another robber was killed by the RUC. In the Irish Republic, the INLA after several bloody months was finally declared illegal.

The New Year was only a few days old before the Troubles began to claim lives afresh. On the 2nd and 3rd, two soldiers died; both in circumstances unknown, but it is widely thought that that both were accidental shootings inside Security Force bases. The Royal Regiment of Fusiliers lost Lance Corporal Wayne Thomas Makin (22) and the UDR lost Private Alan Darrel Maule (19); both were listed as 'death by violent or unnatural causes.'

On the 5th, the Irish Government, plagued by the curse of coalition rule and all that entails, frequent elections, unreasonable minority party demands and lack of political stability, finally made a decision about the INLA. It had been responsible for attrocities such as the Droppin' Well massacre and a spate of violent attacks and killings over the last few months. The Irish Government – Rialtas na hÉireann – declared the INLA an illegal organisation and membership of such was punishable by a prison sentence. The Taoiseach was acutely aware that his country was harbouring known INLA terrorists such as McGlinchey and Dessie Grew and acted at long last against them.

The RUC's HMSU lost their first officers when two were killed and a third seriously wounded while they were guarding a Post Office in Rostrevor, Co Down on the 6th. The circumstances of why the officers were in that location are unclear; they may have received information that an intended robbery was planned and were in-situ to thwart it and take the robbers out. Their positioning may also have been to simply guard a likely or possible target, but whatever the circumstances, they were alerted by the presence of a suspicious-looking car which had parked close to the post office. The three officers went out to investigate and inside the car were armed PIRA members who opened fire and shot all three officers down. Two died immediately upon arriving at Daisy Hill Hospital and a third was badly wounded but survived after receiving emergency medical treatment. The car drove away but the killers were not apprehended until 1985 when a Warrenpoint man was charged with the murders. The two dead RUC men were Sergeant Eric Brown (41), father of three from Moira, Co Down and Constable Brian Quinn (23) from Bangor, Co Down. Just as the reason behind the officer's deployment remains a mystery, so too does the reason behind the PIRA attack; were they there simply to carry out a raid and were startled by the presence of the RUC or did they have prior knowledge that the police were there and had gone there in order to carry out a mass killing?

Two days later, a leading Loyalist paramilitary – Tommy Edgar (28) – was killed in an internal Loyalist feud in the Woodvale area of North Belfast. He was also the leader of the Woodvale Defence Association (WDA) and a friend of John McKeague, who had been killed almost a year to the day earlier. On the 8th, Edgar was found dead with a gunshot wound behind the ear – the hallmark of a professional kill. An RUC spokesman stated that the killing was not sectarian and the UDA denied it was connected to an internal feud. Edgar's body was found in a flat just 200 yards from his home in Glenwood Street, close to the Shankill Road. UDA man Samuel Murphy got life for the murder of his friend Tommy Edgar. He was not one of the gunmen, but he ordered the killing because Edgar refused to hand over five guns be was keeping for the WDA; the actual gunmen were never convicted.

On the 10th, the Royal Irish Rangers lost one of their soldiers when Ranger David Malvern Lanham (26) was killed in a car crash whilst on duty. The author has ascertained that he was buried at the Church of the Holy Ascension in Upton, Cheshire. It is thought that Ranger Lanham was English born and bred.

On Sunday 16th, William Doyle (56), a leading Northern Ireland Judge was shot dead and an elderly companion seriously wounded by the IRA. The Judge had sentenced scores of convicted terrorists to gaol during the four years he sat on trouble-related cases in Belfast. He had just come out of a Catholic church – St Bridget's at Derryvolgie Avenue in South Belfast – and was assisting a 77-year-old companion into her car. As he did so, two masked PIRA gunman walked up to the pair and fired at least six shots, five of which hit Judge Doyle and he died shortly afterwards. His companion was rushed to hospital where she later recovered. A priest who had just carried out Mass gave the last rites to Mr Doyle. The Provisionals claimed responsibility and attempted to justify their cowardly actions in a prepared statement:

> His religion to us is irrelevant. That he was prepared to accept this post, knowing full well the political connotations, demonstrates all too clearly his willingness to support fully the British and Loyalist establishments and the oppression they create in order to survive and prosper. We regard all such persons as legitimate targets.[1]

The same newspaper's headlines that day read: 'Belfast Judge Gunned Down by IRA as He Leaves Church.' Although he was clearly murdered by Republicans, Mr Doyle had also angered the Loyalist UDA when, two years previously, he had labelled them as 'sinister' and criticised the sway that they held over Protestant areas. At the time of his death, he was in the process of listening to evidence in the trial of several UDA paramilitaries.

UNITY FLATS SHOOTING
Mark 'C', UDR and Royal Artillery
By the early 1980s, the UDR had taken over the security of Belfast City Centre; this included mobile and foot patrols as well as manning the remaining segment gates. Most of these had been removed or had turnstiles for entry, with only four

---

1   *Schenectady Gazette*, 17 January, 1983.

remaining which were still manned. These were X17 at Castle Street which was manned from 0600 – 1800; X23, Royal Avenue and X24 Donegal Place: manned from 1800–2359 and X21 at High Street which was manned from 1800–0600.

On one occasion, whilst on route from Girdwood, via the Shankill Road in a three-Land Rover convoy to man the gates, we unwittingly drove into a gun attack on a RUC Land Rover which was static at the junction of Peters Hill/Carrick Hill; the shots being fired from the nearby Unity Flats. At the moment the shots ripped out, we thought we were the target, so a contact report was radioed and we drove through the ambush and debussed at the corner of Upper North Street opposite the flats. We quickly got ourselves in order; weapons cocked and, under the command of a colour sergeant, decided to do a follow up into the flats. Even though we were not allowed into certain Republican areas, Unity being one, under the circumstances we thought we were justified.

Your training kicked in very quickly as we hard-targeted and covered each other into the side entrance of the flats. At one point a male appeared at the bottom of one of the stairways; I pointed my weapon at him and ordered him to halt and put his hands on his head as at that point I didn't know if he was a terrorist or not. He panicked and shouted: "Fuck's sake, mate; fuck's sake!" or something like that, but did as he was told. I ran over to him and realised he was more elderly that I thought and a bit drunk, so after a quick search told him to stand beside the wall and not move. Then about four of us went up the stairway towards the second floor, from where we thought the shots had come. We had to remain aware of the threat of booby-traps as we covered each corner onto this floor. However, before we could identify which door or house had been the firing point we were ordered out by our CO who had arrived on the scene very quickly.

There then followed a lot of "What the fuck's going on?" as we thought we had the terrorists possibly still holed up, but ordered out we were! Needless to say and to put it mildly, the boys were not well pleased, but this was another example of the politics we were up against. We were forced to fight this war with one hand behind our backs. The next day the RUC did find the firing point and apparently we had been on the right floor all along!

A similar incident took place a couple of years later when a PIRA team fired an RPG at a RUC Land Rover from the flats. One of the officers lost both arms in the attack and, like the above incident, a nearby UDR patrol went into the flats, but again were ordered out by the CO. Our soldiers could possibly have captured the terrorists but because of politics, we were not allowed to do our job.

On the 18th, just as Peter Barry, then Irish Foreign Minister, began a fact-finding visit to Belfast, the Provisionals attacked and killed an off-duty RUCR officer at his shop in Londonderry. As the Irish politician was 'fact finding', a two-man team from the Gobnascale IRA barged into the post office, which was run by Constable John Olphert (39) when he was away from his RUC role. The shop was located in Nelson Drive on the east bank of the Foyle and close to the Nationalist 'Gob.' John Olphert had decided to leave the police reserve and was in the final few days of his notice period. He saw the gunmen and attempted to escape through one of the internal doors, but the gunmen fired through the panelling, wounding him and knocking him to the ground. They pushed open the door and shot him several more times as he lay helpless on the floor; he died shortly afterwards. Earlier, the PIRA gang had stolen a car and held the owner and his family hostage at their house close to the Strabane Old Road. A Church of Ireland bishop said of the killers at the funeral: "If such people are the so-called liberators of the Irish people, then God help Ireland." The RUCR man's murder was condemned by the Catholic Church and one priest said: "People often seek to justify their evil deeds by attempting to portray their victims as enemies of some noble cause and, on that account, as somehow deserving of their fate."

The author interviewed Mark Olphert, the murdered policeman's son, in 2013; I am honoured that he chose to speak to me and honoured also to be able to print the following words which he wrote about his slain father.

Mark Olphert

My dad was 39 and died in my mother's arms after the fatal shots were fired. She was serving customers in the shop and witnessed the whole thing. My grandad, Andy, ex-RUC was also in the shop at the time. The murder of his son affected him terribly hard. The terrorists whooped and hollered as they left and fired a shot into the roof, as though in celebration. The killers used a red Ford Cortina as a getaway car which had been taken from a family in Robert Street at 1 pm, 20 minutes before the killing. The family were held at gunpoint until after the shooting when the car was found abandoned on Rossdowney Road.

No one was ever convicted of my dad's murder; no one has ever been charged. I know the identities of the men who killed my dad and I know the weapon used to kill him; it was a Browning 9-mm. It was recovered when the SAS eliminated PIRA Volunteers Fleming and Doherty en route to murder a part-time UDR soldier who was also nurse in Gransha hospital, Londonderry in December 1984. Even though there is not enough evidence to put anyone in the dock, in my eyes justice was served by that SAS team and rightly so. As a 12-year-old I answered the phone twice to hear a man sing: "We got him, we got him!" in the days after the murder. Also me and my brother attended Foyle and Londonderry College and on a wall on the Northland Road, on the bus route to school, someone had sprayed "John Olphert Ha-ha." The Provos took great pleasure in rubbing salt into our wounds and that is something I've never forgotten.

My brother, Peter, also joined the RUC and then the PSNI. While serving in RUC Peter was in L1 MSU Fermanagh and worked alongside the Army on the border for many years. He is still a police officer and is a trustee of the Police Memorial Fund. It's down to us still on earth to keep the memory of those killed alive. We cannot allow Sinn Féin/IRA to re-write history and make out that the Security Forces were to blame for everything. There is a concerted effort to vilify The Army and Police and glorify the terrorists; this is wrong and history must judge terrorists for what they were, not what they believe they were.

On the 19th, another robber or 'ordinary decent criminal' was killed by the RUC after a hold up at a petrol station in West Belfast. Francis McColgan (31) had launched a raid on a petrol station on Lisburn Road, South Belfast. Although armed with only a replica gun, the civilians in the station were not to know that it was a non-deadly weapon, and nor were the RUC officers who, alerted by the reckless driving of the getaway driver chased after it. The robbery was violent and at least one of the civilians was beaten. Eventually the robbers escaped and drove off at high speed down the Lisburn Road and their erratic driving brought it to the attention of a passing RUC patrol car. The chase continued down the Upper Lisburn Road and the thieves turned left on to Black's Road. At least one of the men came from the Turf Lodge area and the route they were taking would have taken them to the Stewartstown Road and Andersonstown and thence the Nationalist Turf Lodge. As they raced along Black's Road, the RUC car overtook the car driven by the robbers and forced it to a halt. The officers saw a handgun being pointed at them, and fired two shots at him, before being forced to leap out of the way as the car roared off again. Finally as they reached Oranmore Drive, less than 400 yards from Stewartstown Road, two of the three men jumped out and ran in different directions, leaving a badly wounded man still inside the car. McColgan died within a few seconds and a replica handgun was recovered. Naturally there were further, groundless accusations of 'shoot-to-kill' but in the circumstances, how could any of the RUC officers have known that the gun being pointed in their direction was a fake? They did what their training and instincts conditioned them to do: they shot to survive. One has to remember, that this was the 15th year of the Troubles and in the tense atmosphere which prevailed, waving anything which resembled a deadly weapon only invited death in return; big boys' rules.

That was the final death of the month and it had ended with nine people dead; three were soldiers and three were policemen. Additionally two Catholic civilians had died, one of whom was a judge. One Loyalist paramilitary was also killed; the Provisionals were responsible for four of the deaths this month.

38

February

O n Tuesday 1st, Peter Barry, Irish Foreign Minister, met with James Prior at the NIO in London to continue what many saw as pointless discussions. Barry expressed his view that the Northern Ireland Assembly would not prove successful, but many observers knew that the crux of the problem was the porous border and the perception that the Republic was just a bolt-hole for terrorists. Dundalk in Co Monaghan, for example, was full of PIRA and INLA men who were OTR (on the run) from the North and it had become a sort of Dodge City where lawless men congregated in the days of the American 'Wild West.'

MY BITTERNESS
Ron Francis, 1st Battalion, Royal Welsh Fusiliers

They called it a 'police action' but to us, it was a war, but a war with your hands tied behind your back. We patrolled and we did as we were told and that was to protect the same people who called us 'British bastards,' the same people who spat at us and gave us verbal abuse. But we did our jobs and we helped to protect them. We didn't care about the politics, we just knew that we were soldiers sent to do a job; we bled, we died, and those who survived cried for our mates. But we still did our jobs and for over 30 years, we kept on doing it.

Now it is over, but we live it over and over again every day; and we are forgotten but we are still the same band of brothers who boarded that ferry to Ireland which changed our lives forever. Do we regret it? No, we did our job but for what? We still do not know. Guilt and our ghosts still haunt our memory. Smells, sounds all haunt us and some have blamed soldiers for all of the political and sectarian problems; that was not of our doing.

We served, often bleeding, stuck in the middle like pawns in a game which no one cared about, but history will remember us for what? History will remember us as soldiers who were hated by both sides, and for doing our job; and we did our best in a situation we didn't understand and we did it because the politician who had no idea what it was like on the ground told us to! They sent us into situations which we as soldiers knew were mad, situations which we could not effectively control but we did as we were ordered.

There were days on patrol when you looked at people and they just blanked you as though you did not exist; we stood on street corners wondering why the hell we were doing this. We did our job and no one can take that away from any of us and we spent hours in the wet and cold, being abused, shot at, bricked and bombed; but we did our job.

The following day, a shooting on the Nationalist Shantallow estate in Londonderry would have possibly given both politicians food for thought. In what INLA's *Starry Plough* now termed 'shoot-on-suspicion', an undercover soldier killed one of their volunteers. The soldier, possibly from Det 14 was noticed by two INLA men in Leafair Park and they attempted to 'arrest' him. In what was widely seen as a third incident in the best way to remove oneself from the gene pool,[1] the undercover soldier produced a pistol and in fear of his own life, shot both men. Neil McMonagle (23) fell dead and his companion was badly injured and slumped to the ground. There is speculation that the soldier was Paul Oram MM, who was later killed by the IRA in February the following year. *The Starry Plough* eulogised the dead INLA man as follows:

> His short life was marked by an outstanding dedication to the land of his birth and the class of his origin. For him the struggle for international socialism began and ended on the streets of his own city.

The same publication somewhat laughingly continued:

> The Derry Brigade of the INLA deeply mourns the assassination of our comrade Neil McMonagle by the SAS on Wednesday. He was a fearless soldier who will not go unforgotten. His powers of leadership and his untiring devotion to the cause of Republican socialism made him a prime target for the emissaries of British imperialism who in the end took his young life.

McMonagle was shot near his home in the Shantallow district. His fellow terrorist Liam Duffy was shot several times and badly wounded and was rushed to Musgrave Park Hospital, over 90 miles from his home. His family, blind to their relative's paramilitary background, despite evidence available to the contrary, remain adamant that the shooting was 'premeditated cold blooded murder' and told pressmen of the death threats issued by the RUC against their brother after he was released from gaol, for insufficient evidence against him.

The Derry Journal wrote:

> Mrs Marian Robinson, the sister of the dead man, said that her brother had been baby-sitting in Mrs Helena Breslin's house at Leafair Park and had said that he had been expecting Liam Duffy to call and keep him company. She said that Mr Duffy had obviously called with him as there were cups and plates left sitting in the house, suggesting that the two youths had been eating together in the house before the shooting had occurred. The McMonagle falmily said they believed the two youths were decoyed out of the house: they said that their brother must have been lured out of the house otherwise he would not have left the Breslin children, aged one and two years unattended. It is still unclear how the two men came to leave the house and go to the area where the shooting occurred.

---

1   See the 1977 shooting of Colm McNutt in Wharton, Ken M., *Wasted Years, Wasted Lives* (Solihull: Helion, 2013), Vol 1, and the deaths of Charles 'Pop' Maguire and George McBrearty in Chapter 17 of this book.

An INLA/IRSP spokesman stated that their two members had seen a man behaving suspiciously in the area and had challenged him. Although they had claimed that the two men were unharmed, given their paramilitary training, the murderous attitude of the INLA and the fact that they would have felt threatened by the appearance of a 'stranger' in their area, it is highly unlikely that they would have confronted anyone without some form of weapon. It is also interesting to note that in the follow up, the Army recovered ammunition, explosives and other bomb-making paraphernalia from a nearby INLA cache.

On the 8th, another Royal Engineer was killed when Corporal Thomas Gourlay Cox Palmer, QGM, MM (32) from Falkirk, Stirlingshire lost his life in an RTA. The Corporal was awarded the Queen's Gallantry Medal as well as the Military Medal, and is laid to rest at St Martin's Cemetery in Hereford. He left a widow – Caroline – and two daughters. He was attached to the SAS and was on the M1 motorway near Lurgan, Co. Armagh. He joined the SAS in 1973 and was attached to D and B Squadrons, Training Wing and B Squadron.[2] He is believed to have been one of the SAS men who stormed the Iranian Embassy in London in May 1980 to end the siege by terrorists from Khūzestān Province.

On the 14th, the Women's Royal Army Corps (WRAC) also lost one of their female soldiers in an RTA in Northern Ireland. Woman Corporal Elaine Needham (28) was killed in the accident in the Lisburn area; she is buried at City Road Cemetery in Sheffield, South Yorkshire. She was attached to HQNI in Lisburn. Less than 100 yards away from her grave is the final resting place of Private Errol Pryce who was killed in action in January 1980.[3] The following day, an RTA claimed the life of a third soldier in a week, when the RAOC lost Private Ian Archibald (22). He was from Arbroath, Angus Scotland; his funeral was held at Perth Crematorium and his ashes were scattered near Crieff in Scotland. He was killed just a week before his 23rd birthday.

On the 17th, the British Labour Party – in what many saw as a further act of gross insensitivity – took the decision to oppose the Prevention of Terrorism Act in its existing form. The party had been devastated by the 1979 General Election defeat and then split asunder by the defection of much of the party's Centre and Right Wings to join a new party, the Social Democratic Party. After the resignation of labour leader James Callaghan, the Parliamentary Labour Party (PLP) had voted for a wonderful old Socialist, Michael Foot who was, as history has proven, unelectable. The Act needed to be renewed on an annual basis, and Labour leader Michael Foot's decision led to continuing friction between Labour and Thatcher's Conservative Government. The Prevention of Terrorism Act was actually a series of Acts passed by the British Parliament between 1974 and 1989. They conferred emergency powers upon police forces where they suspected terrorism. The first Act became law in 1974 following the IRA bombing campaigns of the early 1970s. It was introduced by Roy Jenkins, then Labour Home Secretary, as a severe and emergency reaction to the Birmingham pub bombings carried out by the IRA on 21 November 1974. Twenty-one people died and 184 were injured as a result of these

---

2   See http://www.specialforcesroh.com/roll-4950.html
3   See Chapter 1.

bombings.[4] There was a strong desire to respond to what was perceived as "the greatest threat to the country since the end of the Second World War."

Home Secretary Jenkins stated at the time: "The powers ... are Draconian. In combination, they are unprecedented in peacetime." Parliament was supportive and had passed the Bill by the 29th November, virtually without amendment or dissent. The Bill passed through the Commons on 28 and 29 November and passed through Lords on 29 November. In fact, much of the Bill had been drafted in secrecy during the previous year. It was rewritten in 1976, 1984 and again in 1989, but continued to stay as emergency 'temporary' powers, which had to be renewed each year. The first three Acts all contained final date clauses beyond the annual renewal; this provision was not included in the 1989 Act.

On the 19th, the agenda turned back to killing, as the IRA killed a postman who was deputising for a colleague who was also a member of the UDR. Allan Price (52), father of grown up children, was a postman in Co Fermanagh. On the day that he was murdered, he had been asked to stand in for the regular postman – a part-time UDR soldier – who was attending a funeral. Two days earlier, a member of the IRA had posted a letter to be delivered to a farmhouse in the remote rural area of Sessiagh. Early on the morning of the 19th, they held the family who lived there at gunpoint and waited for the UDR/postman to arrive. When Mr Price arrived instead, they came out of hiding and shot him at point-blank range with a shotgun. The innocent Protestant died almost immediately.

The same Republican terrorist group then killed two policemen in the space of 24 hours as they stepped up their efforts to sicken the British into withdrawing. On the 20th, an RUCR Constable walked out of Warrenpoint Police Station at lunchtime on a shopping errand and almost directly into a hail of bullets from a well-planned PIRA ambush. Within seconds of leaving the security gate, he was observed running back with armed men in pursuit. He was shot 13 times with automatic fire and even as other RUC officers grabbed for their weapons, one of the attackers threw a hand grenade into the station. There were no further injuries, but Constable William Magill (20) lay dying in the street, very close to the station. Arrests were made later based on the evidence of IRA 'supergrass' Eamon Collins, but charges were later dropped when he was intimidated into dropping his evidence.

Constable Magill's family ran the following obituary to him in the *Belfast Telegraph*:

Called Home February 20, 1983, (suddenly), whilst on duty at Warrenpoint, very much-loved youngest son of Eddie and the late Barbara and dearly-loved brother of Jim, Bobby, Valerie and Barbara Ann. For almost 21 years as a family we enjoyed great fellowship and many other memories we each have. Thank you Lord because of Calvary we shall be together again. Missed dearly by his dad Eddie, Belfast, Jim, Jacqui and family, Carrickfergus, Bobby, Ann and family, Coleraine, Valerie, Geoff and Emma, Ballymoney, Barbara Ann, Simon and Wee Max, Limavady. Till He comes or calls.

---

4   See Wharton, Ken, *Sir, They're Taking the Kids Indoors* (Solihull: Helion, 2011).

To the PIRA gunmen who no doubt toasted their 'success' in a Republican bar that night or the IRA's Army Council who chalked off another Crown Forces' enemy, Constable Magill was just another statistic. As the obituary shows, to the family of the dead policeman he was something much more.

Twenty-four hours later, the IRA struck again, this time in Co Armagh, and this time with a bomb. Constable William Brown (29), father of a baby girl, was due to celebrate his 30th birthday the next day – the 22nd – and was on patrol with RUC colleagues in Armagh City. Along with a colleague, he had gone into a fish and chip shop in Lower English Street, while other colleagues stood guard outside. The intention was to buy takeaway meals for all the members of the patrol. Earlier, although exactly how much earlier has never been ascertained, a PIRA bombing unit had placed a 50 lb (22 kgs) device in the ruins of the Albert Bar. It was detonated by remote control by a watching bomber just as the RUC was returning to the patrol car. The blast tore into him; he was killed instantly and several colleagues were injured. There can be no question of dicking, because a bombing unit would have been unable to plant and prime the device in the short time available while the officers made their purchases; it was thought possible that the device was planted days, possibly weeks earlier and then detonated when the right opportunity arose.

Four days later – on the 25th – another member of the UDR was killed when part-time soldier, Corporal Colin McNeill (22) was shot dead by the Provisionals in Ballygawley, Co Tyrone. The UDR man worked full-time at an engineering company in the Co Tyrone town through the day, but gave up his nights and his weekends in order to protect his part of the United Kingdom. Northern Ireland is part of the UK; 1,300 soldiers died to keep it that way and 66% of the population wish to stay British. McNeill had been very obviously dicked and the PIRA Intelligence had observed his regular habits: time of arrival, where he parked, time of departure etc. Just before 08:30 hours, he arrived for work and as he prepared to get out of the car, gunmen in a stolen car opened fire on him with automatic weapons, hitting him in the head and killing him instantly. His lifeless body was discovered by his father who also worked at the same company. He left a young fiancée to whom he had only been engaged a matter of weeks. The American-supplied Armalite which was used to kill him was traced to three other PIRA murders.

On Saturday 26th, controversial GLC leader Ken Livingstone, travelled to Belfast to begin a two-day visit at the invitation of Sinn Féin. The visit drew strong criticism both from Unionists and from Londoners who had suffered at the hands of the Provisionals' bombing campaign. The gross insensitivity displayed by this man clearly marked him out as a person who didn't care what anyone said or felt. An officer from the Royal Green Jackets told the author:

As you know, we had just returned from a particular horrid tour of Ulster where we had suffered casualties at the hands of the IRA. I had also had close relatives who had been either injured or shocked by explosions and of course, our regimental band had been almost wiped out by the Regent's Park bombing. So as you would imagine, one wasn't too enthralled by this odious little man cow-towing to the Provisional IRA. I can't find the words in my vocabulary to describe how I felt about this insensitive, uncaring, thoughtless and tactless little toad and what he did. Can you imagine had he been a politician during the London blitz, would he have invited Goering or Hitler across for 'exploratory talks' or perhaps he might have flown to Berlin for meetings with the heads of the Luftwaffe and praised them for their bombing accuracy? If I say more, Ken, you might be liable to be sued for libel. Suffice to say, Mr Livingstone was an unpleasant and insensitive oaf.

The officer concerned is a good friend of this author, and while I try to remain independent of the words and thoughts of my contributors, one finds it impossible not to identify with all his comments.

February ended with eight deaths; four soldiers and two policemen were killed. Additionally a Protestant civilian was killed by the IRA and one Republican terrorist was killed. The Provisionals were responsible for half of the deaths in February.

39

March

There were just six deaths this month, with both sets of paramilitaries losing one member each and, sadly, two more policemen died. The INLA shot a Protestant dead for purely sectarian reasons. The Provisionals shot and badly wounded an Irish prison officer – the only one to be killed by the IRA during the Troubles – although he did not die until late the following year.

Lindsay McCormack (50) was a career policeman; he would be described in some quarters as a 'community policeman' and in parts of the author's native Yorkshire, as a 'village bobby.' On 2 March he was on duty outside a school in Serpentine Road, Greencastle, North Belfast, very close to the Antrim Road and west of Belfast Lough. He was on lone duty when he was attacked by masked IRA gunmen; a struggle ensued as he may have tried to wrest the gun from one of his assailant's hands, but he was shot and slumped, badly wounded, to the ground. One of the attackers then stood over his helpless body and fired five further shots into his head from close range.

On the same day, the Northern Ireland Assembly passed a motion urging the British Government to do all in its power to stop the proposed inquiry into the Northern Ireland conflict by the Political Committee of the European Parliament. James Prior said that the British Government would not cooperate with the inquiry on the conflict.

On Wednesday 7th, James Prior announced a new anti-terrorism Bill which would have a five year life and be subject to annual review. Naturally Michael Foot's Labour Party criticised both the concept and the timing, but Prior, with the full support of Margaret Thatcher and a working majority in Parliament, saw off several half-hearted Labour challenges and won the day. Thatcher would win a landslide majority in June of this year, as buoyed by sizeable Opinion Poll leads and continued internecine struggle on the opposition benches, she went to the country 10 months early.

Two days later, UVF gunmen targeted a Republican in North Belfast, shooting and badly wounding him. He was rushed to hospital for emergency treatment, but as soon as the news of the attack reached the ears of the INLA, revenge was being planned. Just five hours later, in Armagh City, INLA gunmen walked into the car park of Armagh Housing Executive's Building department and secreted themselves behind a tree. As soon as they saw James Hogg, a 23-year-old Protestant, walk towards his car, they stepped out and shot him at very close range, mortally wounding him. They made good their escape, as the victim of the senseless tit for tat lay dying in a pool of blood. Despite the very prompt attentions of nurses from a nearby health centre, alerted by the shooting, Mr Hogg died in the car park, his box of tools lying nearby. He had no paramilitary links and was a victim of a sectarian murder gang.

On the 11th, Eamon 'Hatchet' Kerr (35), a well-known OIRA gunman was killed at his home in Cape Street off the Falls Road. Kerr was with his partner, when masked gunman burst into his bedroom, shouting out that they were members of the Provisional IRA, before shooting him at least five times. He died at the scene and the men escaped. The Provisionals have always denied that they were involved and no one has ever claimed responsibility. Suspects include his own comrades in the OIRA who may have killed him in an internal feud or organised criminals with whom he had crossed paths. Another theory was that members of the IPLO killed Kerr, and the late Brendan Hughes of the IRA made this claim to Ed Moloney whilst being interviewed for *Voices From the Grave*.[1] Given that some former members of PIRA, OIRA and INLA joined the IPLO – including Gerard Steenson – it is entirely plausible that the men who killed Kerr were former comrades and this was yet another internecine Republican death. Kerr was with fellow OIRA man, Sean Fox, when he was shot by INLA gunmen, outside Divis Street Flats Complex on 25 February, 1975.[2]

On the same day as the killing of the OIRA man, the Irish Government announced that it was establishing a forum which became known as the New Ireland Forum. It was proposed by the SDLP and it was thought by many that it was a response to the very real threat that was presented by Sinn Féin to the electoral position of the SDLP as the main Nationalist party in Northern Ireland. All the constitutional Nationalist parties in Ireland, with the exception of the aforementioned Republican Party, were invited to attend the Forum. Indeed, in a district council by-election in Omagh, Co Tyrone, a Sinn Féin candidate won the seat. This was the first local government election contested by Sinn Féin during the current conflict. On the 24th, the Ulster Unionist Party (UUP), the Democratic Unionist Party (DUP), and the Alliance Party of Northern Ireland (APNI), all refused invitations to take part in the New Ireland Forum. The first meeting of the Forum took place on 30 May 1983 and the final report was published on 2 May 1984.

On the 15th, the Provisionals shot and killed another RUCR officer, opting for the 'soft target' option of making an attack whil the subject was off-duty and carrying out his full-time job. Bessbrook Constable Frederick Thomas Morton (59), father of two grown up, children had been a member of the RUCR for many years and was close to retirement. His full-time job was delivering bread in the Co Down area. On the morning that he was killed, he was making his scheduled run at Lisdrumgullion close to the town of Newry. Just before 0700 hours, he was ambushed by IRA gunmen hiding in a field and his 'Mother's Pride' van was sprayed by automatic weapons. He was hit almost a dozen times in the head and upper body, dying instantly. As he slumped across the steering wheel, his out of control van crashed down a steep incline into the banks of the River Clantyre. Eamon Collins, the HM Customs Officer turned PIRA member, turned 'supergrass' was charged with his involvement in the killing; whereas it is likely that he dicked the RUCR man, it is unlikely that he participated in the actual ambush.

The following day, the UVF lost one of its paramilitaries, when William Miller (26) Loyalist gunman was shot dead and another of their gunmen badly wounded, by RUC officers in Belfast. On the night of the 16th, a three-man UVF murder gang was en-route to kill a leading INLA member in the Queen's University area of Belfast. Acting upon

---

1   Moloney, Ed, *Voices from Beyond the Grave: Two Men's War in Ireland* (London: Faber & Faber, 2010).
2   See Wharton, Ken M., *Wasted Years, Wasted Lives* (Solihull: Helion, 2013), Vol 1.

information received, a heavily armed RUC squad was in place to ambush the gang. The men were armed with a sub-machine gun and handgun, and Miller made the fatal mistake of pointing his weapon at police – a decision that cost him his life. The police officers fired upwards of 40 rounds, mortally wounding Miller and seriously injuring Bobby Morton who was shot five times. There was a third man in the car but he fled in the vehicle seconds before the officers opened fire. Morton was sentenced to 15 years in prison for his part in the attempted murder.

MY OWN GOAL IN THE NEW LODGE
Michael 'Spike' Lane, Royal Green Jackets

During 1981–1983, IRGJ were the resident Belfast Battalion; based at Girdwood Park. It was around the time of the August marching season, and 'B' Company were the duty company. We had had a good day's patrolling but, as we relaxed, we were informed that there might be some 'trouble' during the course of the early evening.

We had the usual briefings, and got ourselves kitted up ready for the call to go. In their infinite wisdom, whoever was in control of the rest area video recorders decided to whack on a tape of 'Tom & Jerry' cartoons, and we were all giggling like idiots before we were crashed out. We moved into the New Lodge area of the city, and were met with a gathering of locals getting quite vocal. Setting ourselves up across the road, we stood behind the shields and watched what was going on. The adrenaline was really pumping, as for the majority of us it was our first time actually in a hostile riot situation, although I must say, the NITAT training was excellent, and it basically went as they said it would. We waited for what seemed like hours before the first thing was thrown, and then it kicked off.

I was one of the baton gunners, and was frantically searching for a target, when I saw one of the snatch squads going out and tracked them, saw who they were after, took aim and fired. I was chuffed to hear the grunt as it hit. We were out for most of the night, and as we got back in the company commander walked past and asked me: 'Has the CSM had spoken to you yet?' I replied that he hadn't, and the OC smiled and just, nonchalantly walked away. Then, there in the breakfast queue, the CSM – Dave Bennyworth – came limping along, looking at the people in the queue, saw me and immediately launched into me. Apparently what had happened was when I fired, the baton round had shot off down the road and struck him, smack on the leg. I was lucky that he couldn't put his full weight on the injured leg, so it was a half-hearted beating, and the only one that I have laughed at while receiving!

On Thursday, 17th, President Reagan made an announcement which will have greatly displeased the Irish-American lobby when he said that those who supported terrorism were no friends of Ireland. Senator Edward Kennedy, the IRA's biggest apologist in the US, predictably proposed a Senate motion calling for a united Ireland. It was well known that British Prime Minister Margaret Thatcher and the American President were great friends as well as allies, back in 1983, when the USA and Britain were much more of an alliance than today. What was less well known was the pressure which the grocer's daughter from Grantham was putting on the Californian 'B' movie actor turned

President. This was particularly so over the efforts to extradite convicted PIRA killer Joe Doherty who had escaped from Crumlin Road Gaol while being tried for the murder of SAS Captain Herbert Westmacott.

On the 19th of the month, an RTA claimed the life of Private John Mayer (20) of the Army Catering Corps, or the Aldershot Cement Company as they are affectionately known by the rest of the Army. His funeral was held at Carmountside Crematorium in Stoke-on-Trent. As with the bulk of these op banner-related deaths, the author has no further information.

On the 21st, Margaret Thatcher held a brief meeting with Garret FitzGerald, then Taoiseach, at an European Economic Community (EEC) summit meeting. This was Thatcher's first meeting with a Taoiseach in over 15 months since the bitterness and fall-out over the 1981 hunger strikes.

On the 25th, the IRA shot a PO in the Republic of Ireland. Brian Stack had been crossing a busy Dublin street after leaving a boxing contest at the National Stadium when he was gunned down. Two armed PIRA members came up behind him and shot him twice in the back of the neck. He was the only prison officer murdered in the Republic during the Troubles. The PO worked at Portlaoise Prison and held a senior position there. Brian Stack was left paralysed and brain-damaged from the shooting and suffered for a further 18 months before dying from his injuries at the age of 47. His death will be covered in a future book by this author.

In 2013, some 30 years after the attack on Brian Stack, Sinn Féin leader Gerry Adams has expressed his 'regret' to the PO's family over the killing. The former officer's children, Austin and Oliver, held talks with Mr Adams and a former IRA as part of a long campaign to secure a confession. Mr Adams said he accompanied the two brothers to a meeting with an ex-Provo boss, who admitted the IRA shot their father. In yet another belated and begrudging apology, Adams said: "I want to pay tribute to the Stack family – to Sheila Stack and her sons, Austin, Kieran and Oliver. On behalf of Sinn Féin I extend my regret at the killing of Brian. I hope that these recent developments will help them achieve the closure they have sought for 30 years."

PIRA's hollow-sounding and insincere statement read:

> Prison officers were killed by the IRA in the north. These killings were sanctioned by the IRA leadership but none were sanctioned in the south and none was asked for in the case of your father. In Portlaoise a brutal prison regime saw prisoners and their families suffer greatly. This is the context in which IRA volunteers shot your father. This action was not authorised by the IRA leadership and for this reason the IRA denied any involvement. Some years later, when the Army Council discovered that its volunteers had shot Prison Officer Brian Stack, the volunteer responsible for the instruction was disciplined. This operation should not have taken place.

At no stage did the PIRA spokesman apologise for the 18 Northern Irish prison officers which it murdered, nor express regret to their loved ones; at no stage in its mean-ingless statement did it apologise to those POs whom they injured; at no stage did they apologise for their cowardly attacks.

On the 31st, Corporal Gerald Jeffrey was patrolling with his comrades of 1st Devon and Dorsets along the Falls Road. As they reached a two-storey derelict house, a bomb concealed earlier was detonated by remote control. The corporal, from Plymouth was at the front of the footsie and caught the full blast which involved explosives and nails. He was blown over but managed to regain his footing and staggered away from the building, before collapsing. A large nail was embedded in his skull and he was dreadfully injured, being rushed to the RVH for emergency treatment. The device was detonated by one of two PIRA men hiding in an alleyway and despite the close proximity of three children, they went ahead with the attempt to kill and maim soldiers. Two of the children were injured and were also taken to hospital, not that the Provisionals and their backers cared much about the 'collateral damage.' The soldier died just over a week later with his wife at his bedside.

Six people died during this month. The dead included one soldier, two RUC officers and an innocent Protestant whose death was overtly sectarian. A Republican paramilitary was killed as was a Loyalist.

40

April

In this month, 11 people lost their lives, including six soldiers, and the UVF were involved in three of the deaths. The Provisionals killed an innocent Protestant when they went to the house where a prison officer had once lived; they issued yet another, hollow, meaningless and pointless apology.

In what was seen as disgracing their uniform, two ex-members of the UDR and an RAF airman who was on the run from the service – all Protestants and Loyalists – beat to death an innocent Catholic close to the notorious Nationalist Kilwilkie in Armagh. John McConville (22) a man with no Republican or paramilitary ties was walking home to the notorious estate in the early hours of Sunday 3 April – Easter Sunday – when he was waylaid by the three men who were intent on sectarian murder. The three men had been drinking and deliberately set out to assault and possibly kill a Catholic. Mr McConville was walking towards his home and had just reached the Distillery Hill area and was walking along a narrow road called North Street. The three men pounced upon him and though he tried to fight back, he was pummelled to the ground and mortally injured; he died shortly afterwards. All three men were sent to prison and, during the court case, it was revealed that one of the former UDR men was dismissed from the service for striking an RUC officer.

Later that same day, a PIRA murder team, relying on flawed and out of date intelligence, killed an innocent Protestant at his home on the Kilcooley in Bangor, Co Down. The house which they targeted in Balligan Gardens was once the residence of a prison officer (PO), and they had gone there to murder the officer in question. The Kilcooley Estate is marked by a boundary which consists of the West Circular Road and the Belfast and Rathgael Roads in the south-west of the Co Down town. The estate is comprised of neat modern bungalows and semis and it was there on the night of 3 April, 1983 that the murder gang arrived in a stolen car. They arrived at the home of James McCormick (47), father of two, who was at home enjoying Easter Sunday and probably relishing the prospect of the following day's public holiday and a break from the local factory. As he relaxed, masked gunmen burst in, pushed past his wife and shot him a dozen times; he died on his own living room floor in front of his distraught family as his murderers rushed off, no doubt thinking *Tiocfaidh ár lá* (our day will come). Once they had realised the enormity of their mistake, their apologists issued a hollow and meaningless statement of regret. A churchman said: "No reason; no justification; no apology; no explanation can possibly affect the outcome."

One soldier, who did not wish to be named as he still lives in Northern Ireland, told the author:

I wish all those bastard Irish-Americans who cheered everything that the Provos did and threw money into the collecting tins in bars in Boston etc., could have been in that house and have seen those family members who were destroyed by evil cowards. They wouldn't be singing 'Wearing of the Green' and swilling down their pints of Guinness if they could see the results of what they had just paid for. Fucking idiots! I care not a jot for the people of Boston after their bombing this year; they brought that on themselves as far as I am concerned!

On the 7th, just over a week after being very seriously injured by a PIRA landmine, Corporal Gerald Jeffrey (28), father of two died from those wounds in the RVH. 1st Devon and Dorset was in residence at Abercorn Barracks, Ballykinler, between 1983 and 1985 and again from 2002 to 2004. Corporal Jeffery and Lance-Corporal Stephen Taverner were both killed by terrorist bombs in 1983.[1] A memorial bell dedicated to their memory stands outside the entrance to the Garrison Church of St Martin's in the Mournes and acts as the natural focus during services of remembrance. Memorials to all members of the regiment killed during the Troubles are concentrated together at Ballykinler. The D&Ds are affectionately known as the 'drunk and disorderlies.'

"An army marches on its stomach," so said Napoleon Bonaparte; this was never more so than in Northern Ireland, where the stalwart chefs of the Army Catering Corps (ACC) kept the soldiers of Op Banner marching along, with their ubiquitous 'egg banjos'. During the course of the Troubles, a total of nine members of the regiment died in Northern Ireland. The last soldier from the ACC to die was Private Richard Biddle (20) who was attached to 1st Battalion, the Queen's Regiment. He and another comrade were enjoying an off-duty drink in Omagh, Co Tyrone. He was the last member of the ACC to die in or as a result of Northern Ireland. Private Biddle, who was from the West Midlands, had been for a night out in Omagh with a colleague and had been drinking in the Royal Arms Hotel in High Street, close to Townhall Square in the northern part of the Town Centre. Unknown to the two soldiers, they had been observed entering the pub and during the course of the evening a UVBT was planted underneath Private Biddle's car. They emerged just after midnight and, as Private Biddle started the engine, with his friend outside directing the manoeuvre, the device, estimated at 10 lb (4.54 kgs) exploded. The car was thrown several feet in the air and the ACC man was thrown out of the car and down the street; he was killed instantly. The other soldier, thought to have also been ACC was horribly injured and suffered a traumatic amputation of the leg. A spokesman for the Provisionals said later: "We are giving a repeat warning to those who trade or entertain British Army personnel to cease this treacherous business or they will receive the same treatment as did last night's two soldiers. We are out to make the garrison town of Omagh completely unsafe for (them)."

The ACC (jokingly known as the 'Aldershot Cement Company') was merged with the RLC in on Monday, 5 April 1993, by the union of five British Army corps: Royal Corps of Transport, Royal Army Ordnance Corps, Royal Pioneer Corps, Royal Engineers Postal and Courier Service, and the aforementioned Army Catering Corps. The motto of the RLC is 'We sustain.'

---

1   See Chapter 47.

On the 10th of this month, there occurred a tragedy which became one of the most enduring, but certainly not the most endearing, mysteries of the Troubles. Rifleman David Anthony Grainger (21) of the Royal Green Jackets was shot dead in a base in Belleek, Co Fermanagh. Belleek (Irish: *Béal Leice* which means mouth of the flagstones) is a village in Co Fermanagh. Whereas the vast bulk of the village lies within the North, part of it crosses the border into Co Donegal; thus it is a part of Ulster that lies in the Republic of Ireland. This makes Belleek the western-most village in the UK. When the author began compiling his collection of books on the Troubles, he was told that the soldier had been killed inside the base by an IRA sniper operating externally; indeed this is the description which was entered on the Roll of Honour throughout his works.

Rifleman Grainger, who had just turned 21, had returned from a rural 'footsie' and had been called into the ops room to either make or receive a telephone call from his wife in England. A member of the unit was making his weapon safe when he accidentally discharged a round through the ops room window and it struck the young rifleman in the head. He died at the scene. This author is acutely aware of the dangers of NDs and understands better than most how easily they can occur; for that reason, he will neither name nor, more importantly, blame the soldier who fired the fatal round. A Green Jacket comrade of the man wrote:

> Words cannot describe how horrified XXX feels about what happened and has said to me in the past how suicidal he has been and will carry the guilt for the rest of his life. It is important to recognise there were two victims that day. Good luck with what you're doing and keep doing it. Swift and bold.

DAVE GRAINGER'S DEATH
Rifleman, Royal Green Jackets

I was a very young Rifleman when Dave was killed; I passed out with him in 1980 and we both went to the 1st Battalion in Hounslow. His father was in the 1st Battalion Green Jackets also, but was out by the time we got there. Dave was shot in the neck at close range by another Green Jacket; it was an ND from a 9 mm pistol. Dave was in the ops room of Belleek and the other guy whom I will not name – was the gate man. While Dave was apparently on the phone to his wife, the gate bell rang; the other guy was putting the 9 mm back together as was the procedure after a change around. He apparently put the mag on with the slide still back, released the slide and pulled the trigger, thus shooting Dave through the neck, severing both jugular veins and the bullet then passed into the CCTV monitor. The other guys tried to save his life but Dave lasted approximately 10–12 minutes and the chopper took about 14–15 to get to the helipad. A local doctor was asked for help but not sure if he did come. Dave is now at rest in the military cemetery in Folkestone. That's as much as I know mate. I wish to remain anonymous to avoid any further heartache.'

DAVE'S FUNERAL
Mick 'Doc' Hollowday, Royal Green Jackets

In 1983, I was serving as a Junior Leader at IJLB in Shorncliffe, Folkestone. As a Green Jacket I was with the rest of the Light Division lads in Corunna Company.

One morning, all of the Green Jackets were taken aside and told that we were going to a funeral. Our platoon Sergeant at the time was a 1LI bloke and we asked who the funeral was for. He told us that it was for a Rifleman David Grainger from 1RGJ who had been serving in Northern Ireland. A medic told us that Dave was on the phone to his wife when he was accidently shot by someone who had an ND in the same room. He then went on to lecture us on weapon handling and how important it was for us to be safe with our firearms.

We formed up outside Company lines on a chilly April morning and marched over to the Garrison church where we were asked to take the pews on both sides of the aisle. As the funeral began I looked over my shoulder to see the coffin draped in a Union flag and the thing which had a lasting effect on me, was the sight of his wife behind the coffin. She was in a terrible state and could not walk unaided. The veil could not hide the tearstained make up. I felt I shouldn't be there; I felt like I didn't belong and I felt that I was insulting RFN Grainger by being there. I felt like this because I didn't know him. I felt he should have had his mates there to see him off to the 'final RV', not ten spotty-faced kids in basic training. It was my first Regimental funeral and it is still clear in my mind to this day.

On Monday 11th, in a 'supergrass' trial in Belfast, 14 UVF members were gaoled for a total of 200 years, at the conclusion of a trial which was based on the evidence of Joseph Bennett. Bennett was granted immunity from prosecution for the crimes he committed, including involvement in killings, in return for his evidence. Their convictions were quashed on 24 December 1984. Joseph Bennett was a leading member of the UVF and after being arrested by the UVF took the decision to turn informant. Accordingly, he informed on 14 of his Loyalist comrades and this enabled the RUC to set up the arrests culminating in the trials in April, 1983.

On the 14th, the IRA killed another soldier – the fourth to die in just six days – when they killed TA Sergeant Trevor Alexander Elliott (38), father of five in Keady, Co Armagh. Sergeant Elliott was a member of the Royal Irish Regiment (V) and was off-duty, working in his shop at the time of his death. The weekend soldier or 'terrier' had walked from his shop to his car in order to make a grocery delivery. Unknown to him, masked PIRA gunmen were waiting close by the shop – W.K. Powell & Sons – which was located in Main Street, Keady. As he approached his vehicle, the Kildarton Temperance member was shot at point blank range by the gunmen and hit seven times. The murderers escaped over the nearby border into Co Monaghan. The TA soldier died at the scene. Several years later, UTV interviewed the twin sons of Mr Elliott. Paul Elliott, who was describing the funeral and how he walked behind his father's coffin, said: "I remember as wee boys walking behind Daddy's coffin; I remember it so well and the silence when we were walking. They talk about a 'glorious death' but there's no such thing as a glorious death, there's just a death." Despite being only 10 years of age, Paul who was the eldest had to immediately assume the mantle of 'man of the house' as a consequence of the cowardly and pointless murder of his father. He discussed the murder further when he said: "He was a member of the Orange Order; he was a member of the Royal Irish Rangers; he was a soft target. And … it was a statement from them [the IRA] that they would say this type of man is not acceptable in a town such as Keady." When the boys were taken to a neighbour's house after the shooting, they were told that their father had been shot. Paul recalls asking: "Is he dead" and the neighbour saying: "He is!" Gary asked: "Do you mean he's been killed" and they said "Yes, he's been killed." One wonders how the 'brave' beer-swilling patrons of numerous Paddy's bars in the Boston and New York and Philadelphia areas who would have cheered the death of the soldier 3,000 miles away might have reacted at the sight of these young children trying to comprehend the death of their dad at the hands of these 'Irish pay-tree-ots.'[2]

On the very same day, Loyalists proved themselves as repugnant as the Republicans when they murdered Paddy Barkey (36) one of 'life's social derelicts' simply because he was a Catholic. Three members of the Loyalist-associated 'NF Skinz' had taken exception to some of the things which Mr Barkey had been saying while he was intoxicated, and took it upon themselves to kick him to death. He was taken into a ruined house close to where the Crumlin Road meets Carlisle Circus and badly beaten before they delivered the coup-de-grace and dropped a heavy concrete block on his head as he lay defenceless. The three men were later convicted of his manslaughter. The skinheads, William Madine, Clifford Bickerstaff and Albert Martin were charged with murder. Madine and Bickerstaff pleaded guilty to manslaughter and got two years and 11 months at a young offenders centre. Martin was found guilty of GBH and got a 12-month suspended sentence. Press reports stated that the skinheads were provided with character references by some leading, but unidentified, Belfast Unionist politicians.

Between the 14th and the 16th, two UDR soldiers died. In the first incident Private Kenneth Kelly (47) was running to board a helicopter in order to fly to a remote rural area; as he ran, he collapsed and died shortly afterwards. He was from Richhill in Co Armagh and is buried in Kilmore cemetery. On the 16th, Private Leonard Greer (18) of the UDR was killed in an RTA while on duty in the Province. The author has no further information as to this soldier's death.

On the 20th, there was a Northern Ireland Assembly by-election in Co Armagh. The by-election occurred because Seamus Mallon, then Deputy Leader of the SDLP, had been removed from his seat because he had been a member of the Irish senate at the time of the election. The SDLP had called on voters to boycott the election and the turnout was 34.1 per cent. The Ulster Unionist Party (UUP) candidate, Jim Speers, won the by-election beating the only challenger, Tom French, of the Workers' Party AKA: Sinn Féin.

On the 23rd, the UVF struck again in two attempts at very obvious sectarian mass murder. Using their cover name of the 'Protestant Action Force' they firstly attacked a Catholic pub known as the 'Hole in the Wall' just off the Antrim Road in the nationalist Cliftonville area of North Belfast. PAF/UVF bombers threw a bomb inside the crowded bar and ran off, waiting for the devastation which would surely follow. It was only the bravery of doorman John Martin which prevented death and injury when he kicked the bomb outside the pub where it exploded, albeit causing some 19 injuries. An RUC spokesman said: "If it had not been for Martin's action, we would have been counting dead instead of wounded." A US newspaper's report read as follows:

---

2   The full interview can be viewed at http://www.youtube.com/watch?v=fMuGKCzWr5w

The Hole in the Wall was one of two bars bombed in Belfast during the night ... Police said Martin was apparently standing near the door way of the [bar] when the bomb bounced into the bar room. He immediately booted it back outside. John Donnelly who was walking nearby said the blast of the bomb knocked him across the street and shattered every window in the block. "When the smoke cleared, I could hear girls and men screaming inside the pub. There were at least two girls taken away from the club all covered in blood. They looked in a bad way."

The second attempt by the PAF/UVF was on Brennan's bar.

On the same night, the Provisionals attacked a front sangar at an Army base in the Bogside area of Londonderry and a young guardsman was seriously injured. Gelignite was stuffed inside a beer can and the device was thrown at the soldier's position. He attempted to hurl it away, but it exploded in his hands causing severe injury to Guardsman Michael Leary. He had part of his right hand amputated and he was left blinded in one eye. In Belfast, in a concerted operation by several Army units, scores of known players were lifted in several Republican drinking dens. All were taken to different Army bases for interrogation.

On the night of the 24th, there was a sectarian killing of a very different nature; the tragedy was of course in the death of Mervyn McEwan (32), a Protestant, but the twist was in the *whodunnit*! He was walking in the direction of a leisure centre in a solidly Loyalist area when he was abducted and beaten to death by a gang of undetermined sectarian grouping. It is not known if he was killed by Loyalists who thought that he was a Catholic, or by Republicans who correctly reasoned that he was a Protestant. Whichever scenario was correct, it was another pointless and outrageous sectarian murder. It was one which brings great shame on whoever murdered yet another innocent human being.

Finally, on the 30th, a Protestant was killed by fellow Protestants from the UVF as they attempted to steal a shotgun in Ravenhill, Belfast. David Galway (61) worked as a groundsman at Downey House Prep School and, on the night in question, both he and his wife were in bed when UVF gunmen broke into the school and entered their bedroom. Whether or not the intruders thought that the pair were resisting or stalling is not known; however, one of the men deliberately shot Mrs Galway in the spine and she collapsed, paralysed. Mr Galway bravely went to his stricken wife's rescue and attacked the man who had fired; immediately the cowardly Loyalist paramilitary retaliated and shot the groundsman, mortally wounding him; he died within a few minutes. As they fled, the gunmen fired a shot at a teenage son, narrowly missing him. Mrs Galway was left confined to a wheelchair as a consequence of the actions of the so-called Protestant Action Force. UVF members Edward Morton and William Morrison were found guilty of the shootings; they both were sentenced to life plus 10 years for UVF membership; both were from East Belfast.

By the month end, 11 people had been killed; six soldiers and five civilians. Of the five civilians, three were Protestant and two were Catholic; three of the killings were overtly sectarian. The provisional IRA were responsible for half of the deaths in April.

41

May

Seven people died during May, including two soldiers and a soldier's wife; two policemen were also killed, and 'Mad Dog' McGlinchey was involved in an INLA 'execution' as the Republicans realised that the PIRA curse of informants was not possibly restricted to their terrorist 'mentors.'

On 3 May, an INLA gang – which included Dominic McGlinchey – abducted one of their 'bit-players', Eric Dale (43) from his home on a farm in the Irish Republic. He was taken to a remote part of Co Clare where he was tortured and interrogated before being murdered and his body dumped inside the North. Dale was referred to as a 'minor figure' in the INLA by author Martin Dillon[1] who had been questioned by both the RUC and Gardaí Síochána about his involvement in terrorism. He had left the North and had set up home with a woman in Inniskeen, Co Monaghan. In the May of 1983, he had come under suspicion of being an informant for either – or both – of the Irish police forces and a decision was taken to lift him from his home. In particular, it was thought that he had passed on the information which led to the deaths of INLA gunmen Roderick 'Roddy' Carroll and Seamus Grew on 12 December of the previous year by the RUC's HMSU.[2] On the night of the 3rd, he answered a knock at his door and was confronted by armed and masked men, including McGlinchey, who forced their way indoors. He was taken outside and forced inside the boot of his own car which was then driven away by one of his INLA abductors. Four days later, his body, wrapped in plastic and showing signs of torture, was found dumped in a country lane at Killeen, Co Armagh just yards from the border. As Martin Dillon writes:

> A post-mortem revealed that he had been shot in the head, and his body bore signs of torture and severe beating. The discovery of the corpse was followed by a statement from the INLA that Eric Dale 'had admitted under interrogation' that he had supplied security forces with details of the movements of Seamus Grew and Roddy Carroll who had been shot dead by members of the RUC in December 1982. The INLA also claimed that he had provided information that led to a number of arrests and the seizure of weapons, ammunition and explosives … and that prior to his death, he had been making enquiries as to the whereabouts of Dominic McGlinchey.[3]

---

1   Dillon, Martin, *The Dirty War* (London: Arrow Books, 1999), p.216.
2   See Chapter 36 of this book.
3   *The Dirty War*, page 313.

The family of the dead man denied completely that Dale was an informer and it does not take a genius to realise that the barbaric torture employed by these 'freedom fighters' could extract any kind of information whatsoever from the person under torture.

So angry in fact was the daughter of Dale that she made the following statement to the press:

> There is not a shred of truth in what the INLA have alleged. My father was beaten and tortured by his murderers. They claimed he admitted giving information under interrogation but nobody could withstand the terrible torture inflicted on him. My father was a dedicated Republican who gave the last 11 years of his life to the Republican cause. These people who did the dastardly deed are worse than animals. They cannot call themselves Irishmen and are nothing but gangsters.

Dillon maintains, correctly in my opinion, that McGlinchey took a personal interest in the abduction, torture and murder of Dale as he had travelled in the car in which Grew and Carroll were ambushed and killed, but had changed travel plans at the last minute and delayed the 'executioner's axe'. For that reason he was highly involved and may have actually fired the death shot. Whether or not McGlinchey was a psychopath is, of course, a moot point, but listen to what one of his former supporters wrote on an INLA website:

> I think he was a psychopath, who if it hadn't been for the war in the north would have ended up as a serial killer anyway in a normal society. There were very few in his own organisation that weren't glad to see him arrested, as they lived in fear of him, and I think that is why he was killed in the end.

It emerged that Dale was one of a few INLA people to have been aware of the plans for the three terrorists to drive into the North, but that he wasn't the one who betrayed them. That role fell to a former Sinn Féin man who was working for the RUC; Dale's murder could not be justified by the terror group. That man was one George Poyntz, a Castleblaney man who had served at one time in the Irish Army. Poyntz was allegedly an informer of many years standing and was eventually smuggled out of Ulster after the fall-out from the Dale murder. I have no further information on the man other than to note that the various looney-Republican websites which prevail regard him as the anti-Christ, as they extol the virtues of 'soldiers' such as McGlinchey himself and other psychopaths such as Steenson.

On the 5th of the month, James Prior, then Secretary of State for Northern Ireland, travelled to Dublin for talks with the Irish Government. Prior, forever to be taunted by the epithet of '*Thatcher wet*' was desperate to make a success of the poisoned chalice of the NIO. It had defeated Whitelaw, Pym, Rees, Mason and Atkins; it would defeat the 'nice guy' Prior also. After he ended a thousand days in the hot seat in September 1984, it would go on to tax and defeat a further eight more Secretaries of State, before 'peace' arrived. Prior constantly had to fight the 'long game' of placating the Ulster Loyalists while not upsetting the moderate nationalists and, south of the border, he had to play a diplomatic game with the Irish Taoiseach at the same time as being firm about the cross-border activities of the Republican terror groups. The Republic of Ireland – like the USA – was viewed by many as simply being a bolt-holt for convicted terrorists or suspected murderers who wanted a 'breather' from the Troubles. There was no more galling sight for soldiers and policemen alike than to witness the death and maiming of their comrades and then watch their attackers thumbing their noses at them from a few fields away, albeit inside another country's boundaries. Prior, like all those who trod the corridors of the NIO before and after him, also had to deal with the constant and inherent suspicions of the Ulster Loyalists who saw the term 'sell out' in every action which the Northern Ireland Secretary took. Prior would no doubt have despaired a mere five days later, when the Northern Ireland Assembly began what was to become an all-night sitting to discuss devolution of powers from Westminster to the Assembly. Despite lengthy talks the parties were unable to agree a common approach.

On the 10th, the Londonderry IRA attempted to kill a soldier who had married a local girl and who was back in the city on a holiday; they failed in their mission, but almost as a 'consolation prize' killed the woman whom they considered a traitor. Alice Purvis (47) had met her husband, an RPC Sergeant in 1970 when he was 20 and she was 34. She had eventually married her soldier and moved away to England. In the May, after an absence of 11 years, she and her husband had returned to the Waterside area of the city to visit her elderly mother. PIRA dickers had noted their presence and a killing was set up with gunmen, likely from the Gobnascale area being sent for. As the couple relaxed at Mrs Purvis's mother's house, armed men burst in and ordered the soldier outside where presumably they were to shoot him. However, his wife and her sister bravely threw themselves in front of him and for their troubles, they were both shot and Mrs Purvis was mortally wounded. In the gunfire, her mother and husband were also hit before the PIRA men fled the scene. Mrs Purvis died very shortly afterwards. A Londonderry man was charged and later acquitted in connection with Mrs Purvis's killing.

A US newspaper – *The Observer-Reporter* – commented on 12 May:

Alice Purvis, 47, was shot in the back Tuesday night as she and a sister leaped to protect her husband Brian, 33, a Sergeant in the British Army, a police spokesman said. The soldier was hit in the chest and arm and his sister-in-law also wounded. "There is no doubt they (the guerrillas) opened fire knowing they would hit the two women who were shielding the man," said a police spokesman. An Irish Republican Army statement circulated to news agencies in Belfast, warned families that to conceal or defend British soldiers or allow their homes to be used by them "must accept consequences for their actions."

The IRA claimed that the shots which killed Mrs Purvis and wounded the others were 'accidentally' discharged. Just how many more 'accidental' discharges did they intend before even their most sycophantic Irish-American audience might begin to question their marksmanship?

On Monday 16th, the IRA killed a policeman as he arrived at his home close to the Upper Malone Road in Belfast. Constable Gerry Cathcart (49) lived in the safe, yet 'fashionable' part of South Belfast where many of the city's bourgeoisie had chosen to settle. However, acting upon intelligence received, possibly from a sympathiser in RUC Records department, a two-man PIRA murder team driving a stolen motorcycle arrived at the RUC officer's home in Linkview Park. They observed Constable Cathcart and his daughter unloading the family car and walked up to him and shot him four times from behind in the back of the head. He died instantly. The area is characterised by leafy suburbs and tree-lined lanes, with Queen's University playing field very close by. The killers abandoned their vehicle in nearby Finaghy before a waiting car whisked them into the Nationalist Andersonstown area. The Canadian newspaper –the Ottawa Citizen – in its 17 May issue noted: "Three years ago Cathcart foiled an attack on his life at the same spot when he discovered a bomb wired underneath his car." A friend of the family was also quoted as saying: "No better man ever walked; he was well-liked by all of us. He was a very respectable, clean-living person."

The name of Henry 'Harry' Kirkpatrick was on the lips of many Republicans during this month, as the INLA man turned informer against other members of the terror group. In February 1983, Kirkpatrick had been arrested on multiple charges including the murder of two policemen, two UDR soldiers, and Hugh McGinn, a Catholic member of the Territorial Army. On the 16th, the INLA kidnapped his wife Elizabeth, in order to expose a deal they believed he was making with the Special Branch. Then, in order to put further pressure on the 'supergrass' on 3 August, they kidnapped his sister and his stepfather, although all were released unharmed. INLA Chief of Staff Dominic McGlinchey carried out the execution of Kirkpatrick's lifelong friend Gerard 'Sparky' Barkley because it was believed that he may have revealed the whereabouts of the kidnapped Kirkpatrick family members to the police. Barkley's death is dealt with in Chapter 46 of this book.

Despite the pressure placed on him, Kirkpatrick continued with his evidence and, during this month, 10 INLA men were charged with various offences based his testimony. Those charged included IRSP vice-chairman Kevin McQuillan and former councillor Sean Flynn. IRSP chairman James Brown was charged with the murder of a police officer. Several others of those named managed to escape and fled the island of Ireland. Jim Barr, an IRSP member named by Kirkpatrick as part of the INLA, fled to the USA where, having spent 17 months in gaol, he won political asylum in 1993

On Tuesday 24th, the IRA planted a bomb, estimated at 1,000 lbs (454 kgs) outside the RUC station in Andersonstown opposite Milltown Cemetery. The base was devastated when the IRA detonated a massive van-bomb outside the front gate, having abandoned the vehicle, apparently under the noses of the guards. The bomb caused an estimated £1 million in damage. Although there were no fatalities, there were dozens of injuries both inside and outside the station. On the same day, Sergeant Leslie John McKenzie (30) became the victim of a road traffic accident in the Co Antrim area. Sadly, as in the majority of these instances, the author has no further information. As in all of these instances, I am indebted to the offices of Sergeant Albert Owens of the Palace Barracks Garden of Remembrance.[4]

On the 26th, a policeman was killed and a Catholic was murdered in another senseless sectarian attack. By the end of the day, six children were left fatherless, two more women were widowed, Northern Ireland was no nearer solving its myriad problems and the two respective paramilitary forces were no nearer achieving their respective

---

4   See http://www.palacebarracksmemorialgarden.co.uk/northern-ireland-rta-deaths-1969/

bloody objectives. Reserve Constable Colin Herbert Carson (31), father of two, was a Protestant; Trevor Close (33), father of four, was a Catholic. In all likelihood, they had ever met; equally, in all likelihood, they knew nothing of each other's thoughts, feelings and emotions. By the end of the 26th, the women to whom they were married and the children they had sired would all share one thing: loss.

RUCR Constable Carson was on duty at segment gates in the centre of Cookstown, Co Tyrone when a stolen commercial van drew alongside; unknown to him, mass murderer Dominic McGlinchey and his, apparently equally psychopathic wife, Mary and another INLA terrorist were in the vehicle. A door was slid open and one of the gang fired a burst of automatic fire from an Armalite at the RUCR man, cutting him down and mortally wounding him. More shots were then fired at the police observation post, forcing officers to keep their heads down. The gang escaped after firing 40+ rounds at the police, chased by an RUC vehicle which was abandoned and the terror group escaped across fields. Cookstown is a small town and sits some six to seven miles west of Lough Neagh; as such, it is quite some distance from the Irish border and it is highly likely that the INLA gang had another car waiting for them to aid their escape to a Nationalist area. Constable Carson died at the scene.

The Glasgow Herald reported the murder under a small headline: 'Policeman killed at Ulster Checkpoint':

> The spate of pre-election violence in Ulster continued with the murder of a 31-year-old police constable. The INLA has claimed responsibility for killing Constable Colin Carson at a checkpoint at Cookstown … He was about to check a van entering the town when a gunman, apparently lying in the rear of it, opened fire from close range with an automatic rifle.

Cookstown to Belfast is some 33 miles as the crow flies; of course, a crow can fly over Lough Neagh, for a car it is a different matter. To the north of the city lies the Cliftonville Road and various Nationalist areas sit astride this road. In one of these was a baker's shop where local milkman Trevor Close delivered milk throughout the week. At around 0700 that morning, as he chatted to another delivery man, he was approached by two UVF gunmen who deliberately targeted him because he was a Catholic and who because of the nature of his job, was guaranteed to be in a certain place at a certain time most days of the week. He was hit at least nine times and died in a pool of his own blood outside the bakers. His cowardly murderers fled the scene and abandoned their getaway car in Snugville Street which is less than a mile away. Mrs Carson and Mrs Close were united in grief; one wonders if the two widows were aware of each other and made contact.

On the 28th, another of those enduring stories of mysterious and unexplained deaths occurred at Camlough Lake, South Armagh when a young Royal Marine died from gunshot wounds. His name does not appear in *Lost Lives*, nor does it appear in the MOD's 'official' list of casualties of the Troubles. Marine Andrew Thomas Gibbons (20) of 40 Commando died in unknown circumstances from wounds received from unknown persons. He was from the county of Somerset and is buried at Milton Road Cemetery in Weston-Super-Mare; regrettably the author has no further information.

On Monday 30 May 1983, the first meeting of the New Ireland Forum took place in Dublin Castle, in the Republic. Sinn Féin was excluded because the renunciation of violence was made an essential prerequisite to joining the Forum. The UUP, the DUP, and the Alliance Party of Northern Ireland (APNI) all refused to attend. The Forum consisted of eight members of Fine Gael, nine members of Fianna Fáil, five members of Irish Labour and five members of the SDLP.

May had ended and the British summer now beckoned – the 15th of the Troubles – and seven more people had died. Two soldiers and two policemen lost their lives, as did two civilians. Both civilians were Catholic and one of the deaths was overtly sectarian; one Republican paramilitary died.

42

June

This month was very quiet; quiet that is, by the bloody standards of the Troubles, with only three deaths. Two soldiers were killed and the Provisionals indulged in a most obvious sectarian murder. Indeed, all three deaths this month were at the hands of the Provisional IRA. It was also a month during which Margaret Thatcher's Tory party stood for re-election and the electorate showed its gratitude for the Falklands' victory with a thumping majority for the Iron Lady.

On the 4th, the INLA, constantly thriving to match and even surpass the callous viciousness of the Provisionals, turned their attentions to the UDR and one of their bombing teams was in action in Tyrone. They were aware that an agricultural worker, employed on digging drainage ditches at the rural area of Boland was also a part-time soldier. Andrew Ferguson Stinson (35) from Eglish, Co Tyrone, was a Private in 8 UDR who also worked full-time driving earth-moving machinery. After he had finished work on the Tuesday or Wednesday evening, an INLA bombing team made their way under cover of darkness to Private Stinson's earth-mover which was parked by a farm in Caledon Road and planted a booby-trapped device weighing approximately 3 lb (1.5 kgs) inside the machine's cab. It is unknown whether he checked the equipment for explosives, but when he started the engine the concealed bomb exploded and he was killed absolutely instantly. He left three young children and a young widow. Based on the location of the earth-mover and its proximity, it is unlikely that the INLA discovered his identity other than through an act of betrayal; a neighbour or so-called friend informed the INLA that Mr Stinson was also a part-time soldier.

On 6 June, displaying an hitherto unseen 'pair of balls', the US State Department refused an application for a visitor's visa from Bernadette McAliskey, neè Devlin. The *New York Times* reported:

The State Department said today that a visa has been denied to Bernadette Devlin McAliskey, the Irish Nationalist, because of reports she intended to raise money in this country for a convicted member of the political wing of the Irish Nationalist Liberation Army. The group has taken responsibility for several terrorist bombings. Mrs. McAliskey, better known by her maiden name of Bernadette Devlin, had planned to speak in the New York area on behalf of Nicky Kelly, a member of the Irish Republican Socialist Party, who is imprisoned in Ireland for taking part in an attempted train robbery, State Department officials said. The department, however, linked its refusal to grant a visa to Mrs. McAliskey to the situation in Northern Ireland where the Irish Nationalist Liberation Army, a Marxist offshoot of the outlawed Irish Republican Army, has been active. It was responsible for the bombing in Ballykelly, Northern Ireland, last December in which 11 British soldiers and five civilians were killed in a disco-bar. It also took responsibility for bombings in two London parks last summer in which 11 soldiers were killed. U.S. Interests Cited: "Mrs. McAliskey's intention to participate in fund raising activities on this trip was considered contrary to the United States interest in seeing a peaceful settlement of the problems in Northern Ireland," the State Department said in a written statement. It said the Irish National Liberation Army "has claimed responsibility for numerous murders and bombings in the Republic of Ireland and in the United Kingdom.

The State Department added: "We are concerned that fund raising activities of this sort in the United States could benefit this organization." One wonders exactly where the Department's spokesman had been for much of the previous 13 years while NORAID had been raising funds in Irish bars in cities such as Boston, New York, Chicago, and Philadelphia *et al*. One also wonders had they chosen to overlook the NORAID collecting tins at St Patrick's Day parades in those same cities on days when the beer was dyed green and even some canals also ran green to remember the 'folks back home.' It is simply stretching the imagination too far for us to believe that it took the US State Department 13 years to wake up!

On Thursday 9 June, there was a General Election in UK and the Conservative Party was returned to power with an increased majority. In Northern Ireland the election was contested across the new 17 constituencies. The major event was the election of Gerry Adams, then Vice-President of Sinn Féin in the West Belfast constituency where he beat the sitting MP Gerry Fitt as well as Joe Hendron of the SDLP. The UUP won 11 seats (with 34% of the vote), the DUP won three seats (20.6%), Ulster Popular Unionist Party (UPUP) one seat, the SDLP one seat (17.9%), and Sinn Féin one seat (13.4%). Unionist candidates therefore took 15 of the 17 seats. Many commentators again speculated on the possibility of Sinn Féin replacing the SDLP as the main voice of Nationalism in Northern Ireland.

The Conservatives won 397 seats (+37), Labour was further reduced to 209 (-51) and the newly formed SDP lost 16 of the seats they had deserted when they broke away from Labour leaving them with just six. Labour leader Michael Foot, who had been at the helm since the resignation of James Callaghan (1976 to 1979) in late 1980, resigned soon after the election and was succeeded by Neil Kinnock. Although the election was one of the party's worst, there was some bright news as the new crop of MPs included two future Labour Prime Ministers, Tony Blair and Gordon Brown. There was one other significant result that night, as the election of Gerry Adams of Sinn Féin forced William Whitelaw, then British Home Secretary, to lift the ban on him entering Britain.

Thatcher's new Cabinet saw the reappointment of James Prior, as Secretary of State for Northern Ireland. A few days later, at the Northern Ireland Office (NIO), Lord Gowrie and John Patten were replaced by the Earl of Mansfield and Chris Patten respectively. The poisoned chalice was once more in the grasp of the 'Tory wet.' Prior would remain in the job until September 1984 before passing it on to Douglas Hurd – who would last 357 days.

On the day after the election, with some results – especially the rural Northern Ireland constituencies – still coming in, the Light Infantry lost one of their young soldiers to a lamp post-mounted IED, an historical equal to the perceived modern curse of IEDs that coalition soldiers encounter while fighting in the wastes of Afghanistan. A combined RUC/Light Infantry foot patrol was on the Ballymurphy Estate and had just reached Glenalina Park and Glenalina Road. They were close to the scene of the deaths of two King's Regiment soldiers in 1979 in Glenalina Crescent. On that day, Kingsman Christopher Shanley had been killed and Lance Corporal Stephen Rumble mortally wounded by an IRA sniper as they drove along in a Saracen with a faulty door.[1] Private Geoffrey Mark Curtis (20) a Grimsby lad was part of that patrol.

Private Curtis had stopped to chat to some children and then walked over to take cover behind a lamp post as the patrol went firm. Unknown to the Security Forces personnel, a PIRA bombing unit had placed an IED inside the metal inspection plate of the post and it was detonated by a member of the team who was watching from a nearby house. The young soldier took the full brunt of the 15 lb (7 kgs) device and was killed instantly; the blast also badly wounded two soldiers and two RUC officers. The explosion was triggered by watching men who were acutely aware of the presence of children nearby. The author has walked those streets, as a soldier and more recently as a 'tourist.' Where the blast occurred is all part of a built up residential area and leads directly to the hub of social life on the estate, the Bull Ring, which is only 30 yards away. Curtis was from Grimsby in South Humberside and is buried at Scartho Road Cemetery in the fishing town.

THE DEATH OF GEOFF CURTIS
Private Tim Castle, Light Infantry

I was on patrol on the day after the 1983 elections and the results were starting to come in on Breakfast TV. I was asleep and was shaken awake to run into the back of the PIG. Red 1 consisted of a PIG and Piglet (Armoured Land Rover). We crashed out of the gates to the Bull Ring, the notorious central area of the Ballymurphy Estate, and were briefed by 'G' on the way, "There has been an incident and Starlight has been called." Starlight, the unit medical officer, was based in our camp and went round in a six-wheeled Saracen. We had let him out of the gate in front of us!

We bumped around for about three minutes and piled out at the scene of a bombing just as the RMO was covering the body of Geoff Curtis with a blanket. Geoff had been third man in the 31L patrol call sign. The IRA were out to score a policeman or two on the day that Maggie won the election, a way of saying we haven't gone away and we haven't forgiven the Government for the hunger strikers' deaths. We must have been seconds behind the RMO yet there was nothing to be done. A few months earlier the INLA had tried to kill a policeman on patrol with a bomb, it went wrong and a local child was killed. The INLA were thrown out of the Divis Flats Complex where this occurred. The IRA didn't want the same thing to happen.

Geoff's patrol had two policemen at the front and Second Lieutenant Will Tricks behind; Geoff then crossed the Bull Ring and headed off up Glenalina

---

1   See Wharton, Ken M., *Wasted Years, Wasted Lives* (Solihull: Helion, 2014), Vol 2.

road. There was a lamp post behind a brick wall and a command detonated IED was hidden here with the lamp post as an aiming mark. Sadly for Geoff the two policemen decided to talk to a very young child, and the IRA must have seen this from their firing point and held off. One of them warned him to be careful. By the time it was safe for them to fire, the patrol had moved and Geoff was level with the bomb. He was killed instantly and two others were wounded, and his family and friends hurt beyond comprehension forever!

On Monday 27th, the IRA indulged in the loathsome practice of sectarianism, something which they had always – somewhat hollowly – denied they took part in. Malvern Moffitt (36), father of four, was a local businessman in the Omagh, Co Tyrone area. He contracted out his services as a hedge-cutter and was by all accounts very popular and successful. It was known that the Provisionals targeted both businessmen and their workforce if they were involved in any description of work for the Security Forces and many were assassinated in their places of work, usually on rebuilding bomb-damaged police stations. However, Mr Moffitt was not known to do any work for the Security Forces and why the IRA targeted him is unknown. He was driving his tractor along a country road at Striff, near Omagh. The father of four children under the age of 12 was shot in the back by a gunman using an American-supplied Armalite Rifle. His widow, Iris, pointed out that he worked as an agricultural contractor but had no connection with the Security Forces.

The RUC has always maintained that the IRA were responsible for Mr Moffitt's death and forensics and ballistics tests revealed the Armalite had been used previously in at least three other murders, including that of Constable Colin Carson the previous month. One theory is that Mr Moffitt may have unsuspectingly stumbled across an IRA arms cache while hedge-clearing, and they considered it necessary to silence him. Given the IRA's propensity for locating arms dumps in remote rural areas, especially under hedges, this is not beyond the bounds of possibility. Earlier in the day, in Co Fermanagh, PIRA gunmen had attempted to kill a Protestant workman as he worked on a Security Force base; he was wounded but later recovered. Both incidents demonstrated a most blatant sectarianism on the part of the 'non-sectarian' Provisionals.

Finally, on the 28th of the month, SDLP leader John Hume – known as 'Ireland's Peacemaker' – addressed the House of Commons in Westminster in his 'maiden speech,' following his election He spoke of Britain's 'psychological withdrawal' from Northern Ireland. Fifteen years later, he was awarded the Nobel Prize for Peace, following his efforts to bring about a measure of peace in his troubled country. As he accepted the award in Oslo, he said:

I want to see Ireland as an example to men and women everywhere of what can be achieved by living for ideals, rather than fighting for them, and by viewing each and every person as worthy of respect and honour. I want to see an Ireland of partnership where we wage war on want and poverty, where we reach out to the marginalised and dispossessed, where we build together a future that can be as great as our dreams allow.

The numbers of Troubles-related deaths in this month had reduced to just three; all three deaths were caused by the Provisional IRA and included two soldiers and one civilian. The death of a Protestant at their hands was overtly sectarian in nature.

43

July

Nine people died this month and this number included four UDR soldiers killed in one fell swoop in Co Tyrone and more murders involving Dominic 'Mad Dog' McGlinchey. It also featured a senseless sectarian beating which resulted in the death of an innocent Catholic.

On the first Sunday of the month, the West Belfast home of Gerry Fitt (formerly the MP for West Belfast) was set on fire by a Nationalist mob. The house was not occupied at the time and it was but one of many incidents where the house was attacked. Local thugs had often felt that Fitt – whose deciding vote had brought down the Callaghan Labour Government in 1979 – had showed a less than enthusiastic support for the Provisional IRA. Later in the month Fitt, was made a life peer.

On the 9th of the month, the Provisionals planted an explosive booby-trap at property belonging to a Private in the UDR. The soldier was away from home in Cookstown, Co Tyrone, and his house was being looked after by his sister, Mrs Lily McCollum. She would have been well aware of the dangers which her brother faced, as the Provisionals had twice tried to kill him; on one occasion, a UVBT attached to the underside of his car had actually fallen off without detonating as he was driving to work. On this particular day, however, she triggered off a large explosion and she was fatally injured in the blast. She lingered in hospital, fighting for her life but she died on 19 September.[1]

On the 12th, there was a lucky escape for several RUC officers in Downpatrick, Co Down. A local Provisional – Manchester born Barry Llewellan who was living with a local girl – worked his way close to the compound and hurled a Soviet-made (but no doubt Libyan-supplied) hand grenade into the station yard just as several officers returned for duty. Several were injured. Llewellan was also involved in the murder of a UDR soldier and Albert Miles, the Deputy Governor of Crumlin Road Prison. The incidents involving Llewellan are dealt with in other parts of this book.

In the early part of the month, there was debate at a high level into the question of the re-introduction of the death penalty for terrorist offences. After each PIRA atrocity, the question was inevitably raised again. At a convention of Catholic Bishops in Northern Ireland, the churchmen warned against the dangers of the reintroduction of the death penalty. They also called for a ban on the use of plastic bullets by members of the Security Forces. On the 8th, the Northern Ireland Assembly voted by 35 to 11 for the introduction of the death penalty for terrorist murders. However, less than 48 hours later, Secretary of State for Northern Ireland, James Prior, said that the reintroduction of

---

1   See Chapter 45.

the death penalty in Northern Ireland would lead to an increase in 'violent disorders' in the region. Days later, The House of Commons rejected a motion calling for the reintroduction of capital punishment in Northern Ireland.

The Murder (Abolition of Death Penalty) Act 1965 abolished the death penalty for murder in Great Britain, although the death penalty for murder survived in Northern Ireland until 1973. The Act replaced the penalty of death with a mandatory sentence of imprisonment for life. The Act was introduced to Parliament as a private member's bill by Sydney Silverman MP. The Act provides that charges of capital murder at the time it was passed were to be treated as charges of simple murder and all sentences of death were to be commuted to sentences of life imprisonment. The Act also contained a sunset clause, which stated that the Act would be repealed unless renewed by Parliament within five years. This was done in 1969 and the Act was made permanent, although the last executions in the UK were in 1964, for murder.

On 13 July, 1983 the worst atrocity in the history of the Ulster Defence Regiment to date took place in a remote area of Co Tyrone. A PIRA landmine which exploded on the Ballygawley Road, took the lives of four soldiers from 6 UDR. The area is very close to the border with the Irish Republic and as such, was of great strategic importance in the fight against cross-border incursions by Republican terror groups. It is equidistant between the town of Omagh and Ireland and sits in the rolling hills and woods of Lough Bradan and Carrickaholten Forest. On that fateful day, a convoy of military vehicles from 6 UDR was en-route from Omagh to Ballykinler for a day on the ranges. A UDR contact – Trevor Loughlin – informed me that the unit was due to travel to the ranges by bus from St Lucia camp, but the arrangements were changed to Land Rovers. The younger brother of one of the members of the convoy – Corporal Harron – who was in the same platoon was taken from the convoy and sent to a PVCP in the village of Clady on the border with Co Donegall. At approximately 07.45 hours, the convoy set off.

As John Potter writes in his excellent book:

> The soldiers were late and in a hurry to get away. There was a last minute problem with radios. There had to be one at each end of the convoy, but the rear vehicle had been issued without one. It was moved up to the middle of the convoy and Corporal Harron's Landrover took its place. In such circumstances are some men's fate sealed whilst others are spared … The convoy was about to begin the long descent of the hill down to Ballygawley when there was a massive explosion.[2]

The hill in question was Ballymacilroy Hill where a 600 lb (273 kgs) culvert bomb had been planted by a PIRA bomb team; it exploded underneath the last vehicle. The blast threw the vehicle 10 feet in the air and left a crater 15 foot deep and 40 foot wide; all four soldiers inside were killed absolutely instantly or mortally wounded. Two children were left fatherless and the lives of four sets of loved ones were left as shattered as the tangled wreckage of the UDR vehicle. The three killed instantly were: Corporal Thomas Harron (24), father of one from Sion Mills; Private Ronald 'Ronnie' Alexander (19) from Omagh and Private Oswald 'Ossie' Neely (20), father of one from Magheramason.

---

2   Potter, John, *A Testimony to Courage*, (Barnsley: Pen & Sword, 2001), p.255.

Private John Roxborough (19) from Drumquin had been standing up in the rear hatch and was blown from the car. A doctor was passing, en-route from the Republic, at the time and tried to treat the mortally injured soldier and fought to save the still conscious soldier. A helicopter landed nearby in order to airlift him to hospital but he died within minutes of it taking off.

Trevor Loughin, UDR

The contact point was some 200 yards east of the road; it was discovered on the follow up, in line of sight, on a small hump covered with scrubs with one lone tree which was used as the marker by the terrorist crew. When the contact happened, the soldiers moved up the high ground which was on the opposite side of the road, thinking that was where the firing point would be. One of the lads went over to Private John Roxborough who was lying about 100 metres away to see if he could help him, but as he lifted him, he could see his absolutely terrible injuries. The Colour Sergeant – Terry – got on the net and called out: 'Contact! We have been hit; for fuck's sake get somebody out here!' As there was no such thing as pin numbers then, the four soldier's names were sent over the net. When Tommy Harron's younger brother who had been taken off the convoy to go to the PVCP heard the contact, he went hysterical and had to be restrained and his weapon taken from him.

The area was no stranger to violence; on 26 August 1920, during the Irish War of Independence, the fledgling IRA attacked the Royal Irish Constabulary (RIC) barracks in Drumquin. In the ensuing fire fight, one RIC constable and one IRA volunteer were killed. On 27 March, 1973 a two armoured vehicle mobile patrol from the 16/5 Lancers headed towards Omagh. A 500 lb (227 kgs) device exploded and completely wrecked the leading armoured vehicle and Second Lieutenant Andrew Somerville was killed, instantly. With the hanging debate on-going, one of PIRA's motives for the bomb was to sway MPs into restoring capital punishment, as it believed cynically, that it would provide it with martyrs and thus swell its support amongst the Nationalist communities.

The blood-letting for the 13th was still not complete and, in South Armagh, Dominic McGlinchey was once more in murderous action. Again he was accompanied by his equally psychopathic wife Mary, who herself would be removed from the gene pool in January 1987. While Mr McGlinchey was in prison in January 1987, gunmen burst into the family home and killed Mary as she was bathing her children. They shot her nine times in the head; the bullets marking the form of a cross. Much mystery surrounds the murder of two Catholic men – Patrick Mackin (35), father of four and Eamonn McMahon (also 35) – who were murdered by the McGlincheys. Mackin lived at Glassdrummond, Crossmaglen and McMahon came from Cullaville; both deep in the heart of 'bandit country.' There are several theories as to the INLA man's motives, although given that he had personally killed upwards of 30 people, he was never short of a reason to murder, or indeed did not always need one. One is that he suspected the two men of being informants – although their families have denied that they were INLA members or part of an internal feud – or that they had 'embezzled' some of the proceeds of McGlinchey's cross-border smuggling racket. McMahon who may have had a tenuous link with the Republican terror group was known to be a friend of INLA man Eric Dale who had been shot by Dominic McGlinchey[3] on suspicion of betraying two INLA men who had been killed by the RUC in May. Both men were abducted by 'Mad Dog' himself and shot, before one of their bodies was stuffed into the boot of McMahon's car and the other dumped in the back and stripped naked, before being driven over the border and abandoned. Dominic McGlinchey was captured by Gardaí and later extradited to the North. He was released from gaol in 1993, and shot dead in an ambush in 1994.

On the 14th, there was a fortunate escape for a UDR soldier when a UVBT was found attached to his car which was parked close to the earlier bombing outrage. The soldier, who lived in Gortin, was about to go out to his car when a passing RUC patrol spotted the device and warned him while, at the same time, clearing the area. Police explosives experts made the device safe. Just hours earlier, a Catholic family in Dunnamanagh attempted to inflame local feelings, by flying an Irish tricolour outside their home. A mob of 150-plus angry Protestants stormed the house, and only repeated waves of charges and volley after volley of tear gas canisters and baton rounds by the RUC saved the provocative Catholic family.

On the 17th, it was revealed by former Secretary of State for Northern Ireland, Merlyn Rees that a Cabinet subcommittee had actually considered the possibility of withdrawal from Northern Ireland between 1974 and 1976 as the level of violence had reached both shocking and unacceptable levels. This came as absolutely no surprise to the Loyalist community who have long considered that successive British Governments have long since considered selling them out to their Republican 'enemies.'

On the 22nd, there was another senseless sectarian assault, this time on Shore Road in North Belfast which left a teenager, fatally wounded; he died on the last day of this month from the injuries received. Mark Kinghan, a Protestant from Newtownabbey, was involved in a fracas between rival sectarian gangs and, as his group tried to retreat, he was felled by a rock and then kicked repeatedly by a gang of Catholic thugs until he lost consciousness. The teenager was close to his home in the Graymounts when he was fatally injured. There are several Catholic enclaves to the west of the Shore Road and the confrontation took place near to the Gray's Lane/Shore Road interface. Mark Kinghan's life-support machine was switched off after a nine-day fight to save his life.

Three days later, there was further misery for Northern Ireland, this time on the economic front where, with a Troubles-worsened economy, more job losses were announced. The Goodyear tyre company announced that it was closing a plant in Craigavon, Co Armagh with the loss of 800 jobs. At approximately the same time, Peter Barry, then Irish Foreign Minister, travelled to London and told a group of Members of Parliament that democracy in Northern Ireland was being undermined by the increased vote for Sinn Féin. Gerry Adams, then Vice-President of Sinn Féin, was in London as a guest of GLC leader Ken Livingstone. Adams, newly admitted to the mainland as a consequence of being elected an MP, said that Britain had erected a 'wall of misinformation' around Northern Ireland. Although his audience that day would have been British, his remarks were doubtless aimed at representatives of a foreign power, many with Irish surnames, some 3,000 miles away across the Atlantic.

---

3   See Chapter 41.

REPUBLICAN BIAS
Mark 'C', Royal Artillery and UDR

I spoke earlier about an incident in 1980 and the second incident was in Castle Street a few years later. I remember the Hillsborough agreement meant it was the beginning of the time RUC had to accompany us on patrols. On this occasion but this time we were on our own and it involved a well-known Lawyer who would later be assassinated.

We had intelligence that a Republican meeting was taking place in the Bank Bar which had entrances on Castle Street as well as round the corner on Chapel Lane. We were ordered to go firm at the two entrances and to 'P' check anybody coming out, so I split my section in two; me and three soldiers in Castle Street, my section 2/IC and three soldiers in Chapel Lane. People started coming out of the pub, completely unaware we were there and quickly I had built up a suspect list of about seven men. There were a couple I recognised standing against the wall whilel awaited the 'P' check results and of course, we searched them. Then I heard shouting coming from a small crowd coming up towards me on Castle Street; one of them I recognised as Pat Finucane. He shouted: "Who's in charge here?" I informed him that I was and he demanded of me: "What's your name Corporal?" I responded: "None of your business!" Whereupon he shouted that he wanted all of the people released and curtly informed me that the RUC were on their way! I told him that there was no chance as I was awaiting information on their status. I had no fear that the RUC would back me up over this Republican mouthpiece.

How wrong I was? An RUC Sergeant arrived with a few others from nearby Queen Street RUC Station, I knew him slightly from being in there and doing the segment gates, anyway to my complete astonishment he said: "Right Corporal release all these men now and lift your position." I pulled him to the side and said something like: "What the fuck are you doing, do you not know there is a Republican meeting taken place in there and I'm under orders to 'P' check everyone and they're not going anywhere until I get the results back."

Honestly what he said next nearly flipped me over the edge and could not believe what I was hearing, he said: "Corporal release them all now and lift your patrol are I will arrest you!" I of course told him where to go and got unto my ops room explaining what had happened and what the RUC Sergeant had said, then my CO (Sunray) came on air and told me "lift the op and release everyone." Needless to say I and the men were severely pissed off and even though I had family still in the RUC at the time, my faith in them took a severe blow. I guess this was the start of the appeasement policy of Republicanism so that the Government could get them to the negotiating table, which they eventually did, but the reader must ask themselves at what cost to the trust of the Army. And to bring everyone up to date, the PSNI are carrying on this appeasement at the behest of the Government to ensure no bombs in England, in my opinion.

On the 26th, another 'ordinary decent criminal' (ODC) was involved in a robbery at a post office in Lurgan; for his troubles, he was shot dead by the RUC's robbery squad. An informant within the criminal fraternity had tipped off the RUC that a robbery was to take place. Accordingly, members of the force's HQMSU were lying in wait close to the shop in Monbrief Walk, between the Portadown Road and Tandragee Road in the town centre. Two men, including John O'Hare (25), robbed the Post office and then exited and split up. O'Hare was followed and challenged by RUC officers; he turned and opened fire and was shot dead. The other man was captured without shots being fired. The dead man was from the Nationalist Drumbeg Estate in Craigavon. The area was no stranger to trouble and, on 11 November 1982, PIRA members Eugene Toman, Sean Burns and Gervaise McKerr were shot dead by the HQMSU at a VCP, at Tullygally East Road, Craigavon. Over 100 rounds were fired at the car.[4] On 28 March 1991, Eileen Duffy, Katrina Rennie and Brian Frizzell (all Catholic civilians), who were working in a mobile shop in the Drumbeg estate, were shot and killed by the UVF using the cover name Protestant Action Force.

This author has consistently backed the under-resourced, under-estimated and heroic band of Ulster soldiers who made up the beleaguered and constantly under pressure UDR. That there were rogue elements, unsavoury elements and those who brought shame to their uniform cannot be questioned; there were some disreputable men who disgraced the cap badge, but these were largely in the minority. I have previously written of these people and the reader can refer back to incidents which I have refused to sweep under the carpet, so to speak. The vast, vast majority of what this force did was lawful and moral and, in view of the constant and extreme provocation, entirely justified. The SDLP described the UDR as "an armed wing of the British establishment designed to enable the unionist population to dominate the nationalists." Allegations such as this were addressed by UDR Brigadier Roger Preston in an interview with Irish State Television (RTE) in February 1985 when he stated that circa 32,000 people had served with the UDR, nine of whom had been convicted of murder, and six of manslaughter. There were those such as Boyle and Somerville who brought shame to the UDR through their participation in the Miami Showband massacre[5] in July 1975. The off-duty UDR killer of Liam Arthur Canning in August 1981[6] was another example of the rogue killers, but there were others which were less clear-cut.

One such example was the killing of Martin Malone (18) who was killed by a UDR soldier in an incident in Callan Crescent, Armagh City on 30 July. The bare facts are these: Martin Malone was with a group of friends when there was a confrontation with a UDR patrol. The soldiers demanded ID and in an apparent melée, some of the youths attempted to seize an SLR and Malone was shot and mortally wounded in the scuffle. The young man died en-route to hospital and there were, almost inevitably, Republican accusations that soldiers had delayed the ambulance which contributed to his death.

The soldier responsible – Corporal Baird – was tried for murder and acquitted the following year; his defence was that he had been punched and in the confusion had discharged a round. He stated that he felt in danger of his life and feared that the crowd would seize his SLR. He stated that he cocked the weapon and pointed it at the crowd but was certain that he had applied the safety catch. However, the rifle discharged and Malone was hit in the chest from a range of only a few feet. *An Phoblacht* naturally

---

4   See Chapter 35.
5   See Wharton, Ken M., *Wasted Years, Wasted Lives* (Solihull: Helion, 2013), Vol. 1.
6   See Chapter 20.

ran with claims of 'shoot-to-kill' and there were further outrageous comments, particularly from the Irish-Americans that the UDR was taking part in a modern day 'pogrom against Catholics.' This author will make no further comment on the regrettable death of Martin Malone, other than to say that this was only a short while after the deaths of the four UDR soldiers at Ballymacilroy Hill in a PIRA landmine. Feelings were bound to be running high and it was not exactly a rare occurrence that Republican thugs would confront soldiers with cries of '4–0' and the like. As I stated earlier, this was an incident which was less clear cut than others.

On the 31st, Mark Kinghan (19) died of the vicious beating which he had received at the hands of Republican thugs in North Belfast on the 22nd, covered earlier in this chapter. July was over and nine people had died; four soldiers were dead and five civilians. Of the civilians, four were Catholics and one was a Protestant; one of the deaths was sectarian in nature. Republican paramilitaries were responsible for six of the deaths this month.

44

August

A total of five people died this month, including one soldier. The Provisionals killed a Protestant in a blatant sectarian murder and two INLA terrorists were left dead after the terror group received a 'bloody nose' following an attack on the RUC in Dungannon, Co Tyrone. The popular all-girl group Banarama was in the news, but tragically for the wrong reasons.

On the first Friday of the month, a 'supergrass' trial which was being heard in Crumlin Road Courthouse came to an end after a period of almost four months. The 'supergrass' in question was Christopher Black, a member of the Provisional IRA. Black was arrested in 1981, and after securing assurances that he would have protection from prosecution, he made statements which led to the arrest of 38 PIRA members. On 5 August 1983, 22 of these men were sentenced to a total of more than 4,000 cumulative years in prison, based on Black's testimonies alone; four people were acquitted and others received suspended sentences. Almost four years later, 18 of these convictions were overturned on appeal.

After his arrest in November 1981, Black was taken to the RUC interrogation centre at Castlereagh, Co Antrim and questioned about his activities. He agreed to turn informer but was not prepared to go back to his PIRA unit and possibly fail the customary de-brief given to all those released from custody. The IRA's 'nutting squad' or Internal Security unit would exhaustively question any member who had been arrested and then released. Their motives were several-fold: to pick up intelligence on the latest RUC screening/interview techniques and to detect if a detainee had wavered or even passed on vital information; early detection of a 'tout' could save them manpower and weapon resources. For those reasons, Black refused to return to his unit and was held in protective custody while he named names and places, and arrests were made.

The RUC moved quickly to protect what they believed was a very important source of intelligence from within PIRA and quickly gathered up Black's wife, four children and mother-in-law from Belfast's Nationalist Oldpark area; all six people were helicoptered to a secret location in England. Over the course of the next several months, Black began naming names, operations, arms locations and the like and arrests began to be made in Nationalist areas of North and West Belfast. Almost certainly as a consequence of pressure from the local Provisional leadership, Black's extended family began to petition the courts for information about the rest of the family's whereabouts, especially those of his mother-in-law. The High Court ordered the then Chief Constable, Sir John Hermon, to appear in court in order to answer the family's demands. Black went straight to the top of PIRA's wanted list and they issued a statement claiming that he had toured RUC stations, under protection but in disguise, identifying men he had informed on. They also admitted that his information had led to the discovery of one of their arms caches on an island off the coast of Co Donegal in the Irish Republic. A family member was interviewed by the Irish media and she said: "We don't want an address; we just want to talk to her and see if she wants to come back." When pressed on the issue of their family member's safety, she replied that she would be safe and that no one would harm her. This belied the PIRA pressure on the family to get to Black and once his wife's mother was in their hands, they could pressurise Black into giving himself up to them and rescinding his evidence. One can only imagine the 'nutting squad' rubbing its collective hands in anticipation of that.

In 2010, Christopher Black appealed to be allowed to return to Northern Ireland, effectively seeking a truce with Republicans and seeking to have his 'sentence of death' removed. For people like Black – some say brave and principled, others label them traitors – there is little chance of going back. Those who betrayed the Republican movement, or are suspected of being agents still face extreme dangers. In an interview with the *Sunday Tribune* in 2009 the Real IRA named five men they wanted to kill; two of them were Christopher Black and Raymond Gilmour.

The *Chicago Tribune* of 6 June, 1985 spoke of the family of IRA member Gerald Loughlin who was gaoled on Black's evidence.

Chicago Tribune

Mrs Loughlin's 30–year-old husband, Gerald, is in the Maze Prison outside Belfast serving a life sentence for murder. He is one of more than 400 people who have been accused under the supergrass system, Britain's latest answer to terrorism in Northern Ireland.

Gerald Loughlin was arrested in November, 1981, and eventually was charged with being in the Irish Republican Army and with helping to plan the killing of a member of the Ulster Defence Regiment, a mainly part-time unit of the British Army. His accuser was Christopher Black, a member of the Provisional Irish Republican Army who agreed to testify against a number of alleged colleagues. Loughlin was held without bail until his conviction 21 months later. The trial lasted more than eight months.

Black's whereabouts are unknown. He is believed to be living a new life, under a new identity, in another country. The procedure that put Gerald Loughlin behind bars is a sharp departure from the norms of British justice. Trials are huge, involving as many as several dozen accused. The defendants spill out of the dock surrounded by scores of green-uniformed policemen and blue-uniformed prison guards. There are no juries. Virtually all of the evidence comes from the sole witness, the supergrass. The term derives from 'grass,' British underworld argot meaning to squeal or inform. The system has been aimed at Northern Ireland's paramilitary organisations: the Ulster Volunteer Force and, to a lesser extent, the Ulster Defence Association on the Protestant or Loyalist side; and the IRA and the Irish National Liberation Army on the mainly Catholic or Nationalist side.

Since Black agreed to testify, more than two dozen supergrasses have come forward. Their main motivation seems to have been to avoid serving long sentences. The system has had mixed results. Though more than 100 people have been convicted through the testimony of supergrasses, there have been some notable failures.

On the 9th, in the build-up to the anniversary of the introduction of Internment in 1971, there was rioting in Nationalist areas of Belfast. A young Catholic man was shot dead by a soldier following an altercation between local people and a foot patrol from the Light Infantry on the Whiterock Road, close to the Ballymurphy Estate. Thomas 'Kidso' Reilly (22) was a 'roadie' for the all-girl band, Bananarama (an English female group which was successful in the pop and dance charts from 1982). Reilly was involved in a verbal altercation with soldiers close to the Whiterock Road and the altercation led to blows; he ran off, but was shot by a soldier, later identified as Private Ian Thain. Reilly died instantly which led to massive rioting and the later arrest of Private Thain. He himself was later charged with and convicted of murder, receiving a life sentence. He appealed against the sentence and was later released and returned to the Army. A 'roadie' or road manager with a number of 1980s' pop groups, thousands attended Reilly's funeral including members of the female band with whom he had been working shortly before his death. Flowers and cards were also sent from several other pop stars including Paul Weller and Spandau Ballet. The female singers devoted their second album – simply called 'Bananarama' – to the memory of their dead friend. During the five-week trial Thain claimed he thought Mr Reilly was armed. However, this was rejected by the court after they heard that he had been wearing only a pair of shorts and had been searched prior to his murder.

During Private Thain's trial, Mr Justice Higgins rejected his defence, saying that it had obviously been 'concocted' during the soldier's time on remand in a military base in England. He said that Thain had been deliberately dishonest throughout. The soldier was sentenced to life but transferred to an English prison on the authorisation of the then Home Secretary Douglas Hurd before being released just over two years later

THOMAS 'KIDSO' REILLY
Pte Kev 'Errol' Flynn, 1st Light Infantry

I was out in Ulster with the Light Infantry on an op banner tour 1982/1983, and was nearby when a civilian by the name of Thomas Reilly was shot and killed by one of the lads in 1LI. Reilly was also the road manager for a well-known girl trio of the time. A couple of days later, these lovely girls decided to have a stroll around Springfield road etc., unbeknownst to myself, as I would certainly have asked for their autographs. While we were on the Springfield, they walked past my oppo' 'Spanner' Spence and poured out a whole load of foul-mouthed abuse at him etc., and finishing off with a projectile of phlegm right into his face. When he told us later in the patrol what had happened, we were in complete hysterics and full of mirth over the incident. Later that very same night, 'Spanner' was unluckily ordered out onto on the search team; he was called out in the very late hours, while the rest of the brick stayed in bed and had some well-earned zzzzzs.

The day after the shooting of Thomas Reilly, Fort Pegasus British Army base in Belfast came under heavy machine gun fire from a number of IRA units. On the Whiterock Road a British Army Land Rover came under attack from an IRA sniper, but there were no injuries. It is thought that the renewed activity in the area was a reaction to the shooting of the local 'roadie.'

On the 13th, the ranks of the INLA were thinned by two when four of their members attacked an RUC sangar in Dungannon and police officers returned fire. Brendan Convery (26) and Gerard Mallon (31) were killed during the attempted ambush at a security barrier in the Co Tyrone town. The two INLA members arrived at the RUC position in a stolen car along with two other members of the INLA. As they arrived, three of the terrorists leapt out of the car and opened fire, hitting and seriously wounding one police officer who had been observing traffic as it passed through the town centre. As the gun battle started, the arrival on the scene of undercover RUC officers took the four members of the terror group by surprise, and Convery and Mallon were hit as the officers returned fire. Although mortally wounded, Mallon was dragged into the car which roared off, leaving Convery dying at the scene. The getaway car crashed around a mile away from the incident with Mallon's lifeless body hanging out of the back; the other two gunmen escaped. It is believed that the leader of the attack was the INLA leader Dominic McGlinchey who was also believed responsible for another attack that day on the RUC in Co Armagh.

Convery was from Maghera, Co Londonderry and 1,500 people attended his funeral; Mallon, age 31, was from Madden, Co Armagh; 1,000 people were at his funeral. A memorial to Convery was unveiled in Maghera on 17 August 2003. As was usual for the 'romantic terrorists' a song was immediately produced and INLA supporters were able to sing the praises of the two dead men within a few days. That night, and the following day, Republican thugs rioted in Nationalist areas of Dungannon. Tyres were set on fire and petrol bombs were thrown at RUC officers; plastic bullets were fired back at the rioters. Property belonging to Ulsterbus, along with adjoining buildings were damaged by the out of control thugs.

There was a further blow for Republicans the very next day, when Security Forces in France uncovered a haul of weapons believed to be en route to the Provisionals on a ferry from Le Havre to Rosslare in the Republic of Ireland. Acting upon information received from British and Irish intelligence working in harmony with the French police, a 32-ton lorry was stopped and searched as it prepared to board the ferry. Hidden in a false tank were 28 pistols, 1,200 rounds of ammunition, hand grenades, detonators and other bomb-making equipment. PIRA member Michael Christopher MacDonald from Co Louth in the Irish Republic was arrested on the lorry along with two French accomplices and the three were taken to Rouen Prison. It was a major blow for PIRA but they were able to cheer themselves up later that day in Belfast when Gerry Adams made a rousing speech in tandem with NORAID leader Martin Galvin's stand-in. Rabble-rouser and PIRA apologist Galvin had been forced to remain behind in the USA. West Belfast MP – at the time – Adams said that the 'black flag' protest was to call attention to the shooting of Thomas 'Kidso' Reilly on the 9th. Adams called upon people to support the Provisionals as, he claimed, their campaign was '*just.*'

Ten days later, the Provisionals targeted and killed an off-duty UDR soldier, Corporal Ronnie Finlay as he finished work for the day and prepared to set off for home. Many part-time soldiers were attacked either as they left home for work, travelled to or from work or actually at their places of work as PIRA intelligence believed that that was the time that the victim would be concentrating on other matters. If he or she was focused on work or travel, they would be less likely to take out their service weapon – if indeed they had been issued with one – and use it on their assailants. In this particular attack, a family in Strabane had been held at gunpoint and their motorcycle stolen and driven off by two of the PIRA members.

On that afternoon – the 23rd – Corporal Finlay (32) father of three young children including a baby-in-arms was leaving his full-time job at a factory in Strabane, Co Tyrone. As the part-time soldier who had worked at the same place for 17 years was walking with a group of workmates, a gunman on a stolen motorcycle approached him from behind and opened fire. The Corporal was hit in the back and in the head and fell to the ground mortally wounded. His workmates were forced to dive for cover and the cowardly assassins roared off; the vehicle was abandoned and the PIRA gang escaped. Corporal Finlay was one of five brothers who had served in the UDR's Castlederg Company; two of whom were still serving at the time of the murder. The dead man's widow said: "I think the people who did this are a pack of cowards. Why can't they come out into the open to do their shooting instead of lying in wait for innocent men coming home from work? What sort of people would do a thing like this – leave a wife and three young children without a husband or father? They must be a bunch of cowards." The answer was simple: the cold-blooded assassins of the Provisional IRA and the Irish National Liberation Army were men who didn't care about the emotional consequences of their actions in their blood-lust to 'reunite' Ireland. They would strike when there was least risk to them and generally when it was an 'easy kill.' In their hapless and hopeless and impossible task to drive the British into the sea, it didn't matter to them whom they widowed or orphaned.

On the 24th, in what was described by Londonderry's businessmen as "a sinister development in a campaign to drive Protestant businessmen out of the city," the Provisionals killed William Young (52). The Republican terrorists – like their Loyalist paramilitary counterparts – were not renowned for having a great deal of either logic or pity, and would often act precipitously based on their own 'intelligence'. Analysis of their actions and attitudes over the past 30 years of the Troubles would show a ruthless, murderous streak but it would also show a characteristic which bordered on paranoia on two main themes: informants within their own ranks which was clearly justifiable, and a constant suspicion that undercover – in the main SAS – troops were around every corner. William Young was the owner of a carpet shop in the upper city centre in the 'city with two names.' Located on the western bank of the Foyle, it was close enough to trouble spots such as Leckie Road for the dangers of terrorism to be ever present.

The leadership of the Provisionals in the city had long suspected that the shop was being used as a covert OP by undercover soldiers and on the morning of the 24th, after Mr Young had left for a break, several PIRA members entered the shop. Had the shop been used for the 'nefarious' purposes which they supposed, they would have been cut down in a hail of bullets from undercover soldiers. Nothing was found, because their intelligence was wrong. However, Mr Young returned from his break and confronted the intruders. As was their way, one of the gunmen shot him in the chest and left him dying amongst the Axminsters and Wiltons. The RUC described the PIRA claim as a "total fabrication and just an excuse for the brutal murder of a totally innocent citizen."

The story relating to INLA informer Henry 'Harry' Kirkpatrick is dealt with in Chapter 41; that chapter also deals with the kidnapping of his wife, Elizabeth who has held by the INLA in order to pressurise him into rescinding his evidence. On Thursday 25 August, Elizabeth was released having been held captive by the INLA for over two months. Despite the kidnap, 10 INLA men were charged with various offences based on evidence from Kirkpatrick. Those charged included IRSP vice-chairman Kevin McQuillan and former councillor Sean Flynn. IRSP chairman James Brown was charged with the murder of a police officer. Several others escaped; Jim Barr, an IRSP member named by Kirkpatrick as part of the INLA, fled to the USA where, having spent 17 months in gaol, he won political asylum in 1993. This represented another triumph for the narrow-minded bigots in the Irish-American lobby.

Ken Livingstone, the then leader of London's GLC, made many outrageous statements in relation to his opinions on Ireland and the Troubles. This man who was described as 'odious' by a former officer in the author's Regiment seemed to delight in making remarks which were in appallingly bad taste. An example was his statement to the *London Evening Standard* on 21 July, 1981:

> The H-block protest is part of the struggle to bring about a free, united Ireland. They have my support, and they have the support of the majority of the Labour Party rank and file. I have been consistently in favour of withdrawal from Ireland and to get away from the idea that it is some sort of campaign against terrorism. It is in fact the last colonial war.

However, following a controversial meeting with Gerry Adams, his comments made on the 28 August were grotesquely outrageous and incredibly offensive. The comments were made during an interview with Irish State Radio; he stated: "Britain's treatment of the Irish over the past 800 years has been worse than Hitler's treatment of the Jews!"

August ended with five deaths; one soldier was killed by the IRA and two civilians – one Catholic and one Protestant also died. Two INLA members were killed by the RUC; there were no overtly sectarian murders this month.

45

September

Four people were killed during this month and, although a former soldier was murdered by the Provisionals, no serving member of HM Forces lost their life. The IRA also killed a policeman who, poignantly, was the second longest serving officer within the force and he was killed just a month before he was due to retire. It was, however, a month of grave embarrassment for the British Government and HMP, as no less than 38 convicted terrorists escaped from the Maze Prison.

On Wednesday 7 September, in what was a non-troubles related story, a referendum was held in the Republic of Ireland on whether or not to include an amendment to the Irish Constitution banning abortion. When the counting was completed, almost 67 per cent had voted in favour of the 'pro-life' amendment. A number of Unionists in Northern Ireland criticised the outcome as demonstrating the sectarian nature of life in the Republic. Many residents of the Republic may well have been major critics of the 'North' but these anti-partitionists would, somewhat hypocritically scuttle across the border to buy their birth control pills and condoms and occasionally a young unmarried mother-to-be would have her pregnancy terminated in a Northern Ireland clinic.

On the same day that such weighty matters were being expatiated and voted upon in the South, in the North, Constable John Wasson (61), father of five was shot dead by INLA terrorists outside his home in Armagh City. He had joined the RUC in 1942 and in the latter part of his career, had handled incoming 999 calls; he was just a month away from retirement. He worked in the comms room at the RUC base in Armagh and his routine was so regular that INLA dickers were able to supply their gunmen with accurate details of his movements. Shortly before he was due home from work, masked gunmen burst into a neighbour's house and held the family hostage. When Constable Wasson arrived home, the gunmen were waiting and shot him half a dozen times in the head and chest; he died instantly. The killers then roared off in a stolen car in the direction of a Nationalist area of the city. Constable Wasson was issued with a personal protection weapon, but steadfastly refused to carry it. Even by the cowardly and ruthless standards of the INLA, this killing was exceptional; the policeman was in his 60s; he was not an active anti-terrorist officer and he worked in the section of the police which dealt with emergencies.

His funeral was attended by representatives from both sides of the sectarian divide and he was honoured also by Catholics who recognised the 40 years of service to both communities. One of the INLA gunmen was later convicted of his murder and the murder of two other RUC officers. It was later revealed that some years previously, the murdered policeman had bravely dashed into a burning Catholic church and saved the lives of nuns and children. His death was a real 'tribute' to the INLA 'freedom-fighters.'

On the 13th, in the House of Commons, Secretary of State for Northern Ireland, James Prior, was forced to debate the issue of the current 'supergrass' trials which had attracted the opprobrium of both sets of paramilitaries and also the criticism of the Opposition Labour benches. Mr Prior defended the use of evidence supplied by 'supergrasses' and stated that their evidence was crucial in order to break down the 'wall of silence' in the Loyalist and Nationalist communities who were terrified to give evidence against the men of evil who terrorised entire sections of Northern Irish society.

Six days later, Mrs Lily McCollum (61) who had been fatally injured by a PIRA booby-trap in July died of her wounds. The incident is referred to in Chapter 43 of this book. Her brother had cheated death at the hands of the IRA twice before and the family was cursed by Republican terrorists, losing another two members at their bloody hands. Two further family members were killed in 1993 and 1994 respectively.

On the 20th, the Provisionals killed a former UDR officer in a 'guilt by association' attack and narrowly missed killing or maiming two small children who were very close by. John Truckle (61) had been an officer in the UDR but had resigned some years previously; that he had once served was sufficient for the Provisionals to pass a sentence of death on the Armagh clerical worker. He was an Englishman who had come to Northern Ireland with the Army in the pre-Troubles' days; he had married a local woman and became a respected member of the community in the town of Portadown. He was employed as a manager in the Wade Pottery in Portadown, but he served in The Royal Irish Fusiliers (TA) and on the formation of the UDR he volunteered for service in the new regiment. He lived at Woodside Hill, Portadown, and had walked the few yards from his door step and got into his car in order to take his grandchildren to school. Thankfully they were still close to the house as he turned the vehicle around which activated the UVBT; he was killed instantly. The children were blown off their feet but suffered only from shock. The trauma of losing a loved one would in all likelihood, never leave them.

On the 23rd, the Fair Employment Agency (FEA) said that it would monitor recruitment policy at Short Brothers aircraft factory in Belfast following allegations of an anti-Catholic bias in the organisation. The issue of using an applicant's religion in order to determine his worthiness for a job was something which had plagued the Northern Ireland State ever since the days of partition.

Two days later, on what would prove a colossal embarrassment to both the British Government and Her Majesty's Prison Service, and a source of invaluable propaganda to the Provisional IRA, no less than 38 convicted terrorists escaped from the Maze. On Sunday 25th, the 125 prisoners in 'H' Block, seven were engaged in their usual weekend leisure time pursuits while 'trustees' were cleaning. A total of 24 prison officers were on duty and most were counting down the minutes to Sunday evening meal which was about two hours away.

The Maze was considered one of the most escape-proof prisons in Europe. In addition to high fences, each H-Block was surrounded by a huge concrete wall topped with barbed wire; all gates on the complex were made of solid steel and electronically operated. The PIRA contingent had been planning to escape for some time and two of the organisers – Bobby Storey and Gerry Kelly – had tricked their way into trusted positions to enable them to make very detailed and well-prepared plans. Additionally, six revolvers had been smuggled into the prison. Some of the smaller working parts had found their way into the prison in a variety of visitors' anuses and vaginas. Earlier inspections using a mirror placed underneath the naked rears of visitors had been stopped because of complaints from human rights; apologists and Sinn Féin propagandists.

In addition to the aforementioned pair, the conspirators included Brendan 'Bic' McFarlane, Brendan Patrick Mead,[1] Dermot Finucane, Gerry Kelly, Kevin Artt, Pól Brennan, J. Burns, Seamus Campbell, James Pius Clarke, S.J. Clarke, High Corey, D. Cummings, J. Donnelly, Kieran Fleming, Gerard Fryers, W. Gorman, P. Hamilton, Paul Kane, A. Kelly, R. Kerr, Terrence Kirby, Tony McAllister, J. McCann, G. McDonnell, Seamus McElwaine, S. McGlinchey, Patrick McIntyre, Pádraig McKearney, Michael McManus, Dermot McNally, H. Murray. M. Murray, E. O'Connor, J. Roberts, Robert Russell, James Smyth and R. Storey. Smyth was arrested in California and, in October 1993, Bernadette McAliskey (née Devlin) gave evidence to a court in San Francisco on his behalf when he was fighting the British Government's attempts to extradite him. McElwaine was killed in a shoot-out with undercover soldiers in April 1986; Pádraig McKearney was also killed by the SAS at Loughall in 1988; Kieran Fleming drowned in the Bannagh River near Kesh in December 1984, while attempting to escape from a fire fight with British soldiers. Kevin Artt was involved in the murder of Deputy Governor Albert Miles' murder on 26 November 1978.[2]

Among the non-escaping conspirators was Laurence Marley, also known as Larry. He was a member of PIRA's Ardoyne unit, and was one of the masterminds behind the escape where he was imprisoned at the time, although he did not participate in the breakout. He came up with the idea with the aim of embarrassing Margaret Thatcher, as the Maze was considered to be one of the world's most secure prisons. He was described by British journalist Peter Taylor as having been a close friend of Sinn Féin president Gerry Adams. Marley was shot dead by a UVF unit two years after his release from the Maze. His shooting was in retaliation for the killing of leading UVF member 'John Bingham the previous September by the Ardoyne IRA. Marley was fatally shot shortly after 2100 hours on 2 April 1987 by a UVF unit that drove up to his Havana Gardens home in a Cortina. Two gunmen got out of the car; one was armed with a Browning pistol and his companion carried an automatic shotgun. The men knocked at the front door, and just as Marley arrived to open it, they began firing at him through the door. He was mortally wounded and died of his injuries shortly afterwards in hospital. This will be covered in a future book on the Troubles by this author.

Shortly after 1430 hours, prisoners seized control of the block, by simultaneously taking the prison officers hostage at gunpoint; one of the officers was stabbed with a Stanley knife. Other escapees forced the captive officers to strip and in turn they donned their uniforms and also took their car keys and forced the near-naked POs to reveal which cars they drove and where exactly they were parked. Some of the prisoners who were not intending to escape, stayed behind to intimidate and keep the other POs as hostages – a rearguard so to speak. Once they were certain that escape had been a success, they meekly returned to their cells to face retribution. Unknown to the remainder of the Maze, life and routine continued as normal and, when a Milk delivery lorry arrived

---

1   See Wharton, Ken M., *Wasted Years, Wasted Lives* (Solihull: Helion, 2014), Vol. 2, Chapter 54, where Patrick Mead is mentioned in connection with the murder of a UDR soldier killed in June 1979.

2   See *Wasted Years, Wasted Lives*, Vol. 1, Chapter 47.

outside the block, 'Bic' McFarlane seized the driver and his mate at gunpoint and the driver was instructed to drive out of the prison and in which direction to drive with his newly acquired 'passengers.' Storey, one of the ringleaders, successfully intimidated the man by saying: "This man," pointing at Gerry Kelly, "is doing 30 years and he will shoot you without hesitation if he has to; he has nothing to lose!"

Shortly before this, Brendan Mead, on the pretext of discussing a personal problem with a Senior PO and his assistant, was admitted to the office, thus distracting them from the on-going events. McFarlane approached another officer who was standing in the locked and gated lobby at the entrance to H7, and asked to be admitted in order to sweep the lobby. The gate was duly unlocked and the man who orchestrated the 1982 hunger strikes and who was known with PIRA circles as 'Bic' was admitted inside. Meanwhile Kelly had entered the block's communications room, where he could observe other officers and, almost simultaneously, Storey and McAllister entered the officers' tea room, where four members of the staff were relaxing. They then produced guns and subdued the four POs while Kelly, at the doorway of the communications room, pointed a gun through the locked grille and ordered that the door be unlocked. Another PO, part of the medical team, was also ordered to lie down and crawl across to where he was being covered by an armed escaper.

Other escapers then overpowered the remainder of the prison staff and two of them were attacked with a sharpened screwdriver and another Stanley knife. The final two members of staff had been in the toilets and, as each emerged, they too were subdued and held captive. Another PO who attempted to prevent the escape was shot in the head by Gerry Kelly, but miraculously survived; Kelly fired two shots at him, and he collapsed on the floor with a bullet through the head. Fortunately for the escapers, the sound of the shots did not carry through the closed doors of the block. It was then 1450 hours; the prisoners were in complete control of H7 and the alarm had still not been raised.

Just before 1600, less than 90 minutes after the start of the 'operation', all of the escapees left H7; the delivery driver and a prison orderly were taken back to the lorry, and the driver's foot tied to the clutch. Thirty seven prisoners climbed into the back of the lorry, while Gerry Kelly lay on the floor of the cab with a gun pointed at the driver. The lorry then drove towards the main gate of the prison, where the prisoners intended to take over the gatehouse. Ten prisoners dressed in guards' uniforms and armed with guns and chisels dismounted from the lorry and entered the gatehouse, where they took the gate staff hostage. However, the officers began to resist, and an alarm button was pressed. When other staff responded via an intercom, a PO with a gun at his head was forced to stammer that the alarm had been sounded accidentally. Then to complicate things further for the escapers, more staff began to arrive at the gate at the start of their shifts. As each entered, he was subdued and held at gunpoint.

PO James Ferris (43) chose that moment to arrive on the scene and, recognising a prisoner in the lorry, blocked the exit with his own car. The officer ran from the gatehouse towards the pedestrian gate attempting to raise the alarm, pursued by Dermot Finucane. Ferris had already been stabbed three times in the chest with a chisel, allegedly by Finucane, and he collapsed before he could raise the alarm. He died shortly afterwards from a heart attack, brought on it is considered, by the savage and cowardly attack. After several attempts the prisoners had opened the main gate, and were waiting for the prisoners still in the gatehouse to join them in the lorry. At this time two POs blocked the exit with their cars, forcing the prisoners to abandon the lorry and make their way to the outer fence which was 25 yards away. However, more escapers hijacked a car and crashed it through the gates, bursting it open. As the men ran off on foot, one of them was shot by a soldier and re-captured as was another armed prisoner, this time by an Army sniper in one of the camp watchtowers. A further escaper fell while being pursued on foot and was taken back into custody. All the other escapers scaled the fence and melted away into the Co Antrim countryside.

The Provisionals had planned a massive support operation, employing the services of over 100 armed members, but the escapers were too early for the rendezvous and were forced to continue their escape on foot, although some were able to hijack civilian cars. The Army and RUC immediately set contingency plans into motion and within 25 minutes of the alarm being raised, a cordon of vehicle checkpoints were in place around the prison, and others were later in place in strategic positions across Northern Ireland

In short, over 30 convicted terrorists were now free; one PO was dying, four POs had been stabbed, two shot and over a dozen kicked and beaten. More than 40 POs were forced to take sick leave with nervous disorders. The escape was the biggest in British history and the biggest in Europe since the 'Great Escape' from Stammlager Luft III in Lower Silesia during World War II.

A total of 15 escapees were captured on the first day, including four who were discovered hiding underwater in a river near the prison using reeds to breathe. Four more escapees were captured over the next two days, including Hugh Corey and Patrick McIntyre who were captured following a two-hour siege at a farmhouse and, of the remaining, 19 men were smuggled into South Armagh and then across the border into the Irish Republic. Their options were firstly to return to 'active service' or be smuggled into that other terrorist haven, the USA and given a false identity and support from the Irish-American community.

Kevin Barry Artt, Pól Brennan, James Smyth and Terrence Kirby were arrested in the USA between 1992 and 1994 and fought lengthy legal battles against extradition. Smyth was extradited back to Northern Ireland in 1996 and returned to prison, before being released in 1998 as part of the GFA. Tony Kelly was arrested in Letterkenny, Co Donegal, in October 1997 but fought successfully against extradition from the Irish Republic. Gerry Kelly and Brendan McFarlane were returned to prison in December 1986 after being extradited from Holland where they had been arrested in in the January of that year.

The firebrand Loyalist preacher, Ian Paisley called for the head of Nicholas Scott, the Parliamentary Under-secretary of State for Northern Ireland, and Margaret Thatcher was embarrassed by press questions while on a State visit to Canada. She was forced to make a statement in Ottawa saying: "It is the gravest (escape) in our present history, and there must be a very deep inquiry." The following day, James Prior announced an inquiry would be headed by the HMCIP James Hennessy; his report was published on 26 January 1984, placing most of the blame for the escape on prison staff, and made a series of recommendations to improve security at the prison. The Hennessy Report also placed blame on the designers of the prison, the Northern Ireland Office and successive prison governors who had failed to improve security.

On the 26th, Patrick Gilmour, the father of 'supergrass' informer Raymond Gilmour, was released by the Irish Republican Army (IRA) having been held for 10 months.

Gilmour junior had been a member of the Provisionals but had become an agent for the RUC. This author recommends his excellent autobiography and time inside the IRA.[3] On this same day, a group of representatives from the New Ireland Forum paid a visit to Londonderry. The New Ireland Forum was an organisation in which Irish nationalist political parties discussed potential political developments that might alleviate the Troubles in Northern Ireland. The Forum was established by Garret FitzGerald, then Taoiseach, under the influence of John Hume. It was initially dismissed by Unionists, Sinn Féin, and others, as a Nationalist talking-shop. The Forum's report, published on 2 May 1984, listed three possible alternative structures: a unitary state, a federal state, and joint British/Irish authority. The British Prime Minister, Margaret Thatcher, dismissed the three alternatives, one by one at a press conference, each time saying: "That is out." Journalists referred to her responses as the "Out, out, out speech." When members of the Forum arrived in Londonderry, they were attacked by a mob of DUP demonstrators in order to show Loyalist contempt for interference from the Irish Republic, or even from Nationalist residents of Northern Ireland.

September had ended with four deaths and a massive boost to IRA propaganda and recruitment as their escaped gunmen and bombers returned to the fold. The dead included a former soldier, a policeman, a PO and a Protestant civilian who died of her wounds following a PIRA bombing.

---

3   Gilmour, Raymond, *Dead Ground; Infiltrating the IRA* (Boston MA: Little, Brown & Co, 1998).

46

October

Ten people lost their lives during this month; the figure included three soldiers and three policemen and two more murders by Loyalist paramilitaries. It also included the murder of a fellow INLA terrorist, featuring a bizarre blood-letting by the Prince and Princess of Darkness: Mr and Mrs Dominic McGlinchey.

On the first day of the month, Private Brian Herbert George Kirkpatrick (24) of the UDR was killed in another of the seemingly ubiquitous and seemingly inevitable RTAs which took such a huge toll of UDR lives. There is no further public information relating to this death. This author has dealt with the phenomenon of RTA deaths in books *passim*, but it is perhaps worth another look at the subject. Although soldiers from virtually every Regiment or Corps which participated in Op Banner were affected, it was the UDR which bore the brunt of this type of death. Of the 300-plus deaths of UDR personnel, a minimum, and here I must stress that figures are just that – a minimum, 70 involved a death in an RTA. The proliferation of accidents can be attributed to just two main reasons: stress and fatigue. The majority of the regiment were part-timers and, as such, would often have a normal working day of eight to nine hours before embarking on night duties which would generally stretch in the *'wee hors,'* before returning home to grab some precious 'kip.' After a few hours on duty, the stressful trip home, watching for that telltale sign that you were being tailed by a PIRA dicker, there would be a few hours' snatched sleep. Then it was up again at some un-Godly hour and back to work in a factory or mill, or shop or office before starting the fatigue cycle all over again. Add to this the frequent weekend duties, and the stress and exhaustion became a seven-day a week slog. Small wonder that many of the 70 may have fatefully closed their eyes on the journey to or from the base.

One former UDR soldier who asked not to be named, told the author:

On the rural patrols, sitting in the back of a Landie on a long drive, and already shattered, it was difficult to stay awake; just staring at the endless white lines became quite hypnotic. One fellow I served with just got out of the back onto the tarmac before anyone could stop him. Fortunately, he did it (just) as we slowed to take a bend and he survived after minor breaks and severe bruising. When I asked him why, he explained that all the lines had merged into one and he thought that we had stopped!

Five days later, the Provisionals struck in Downpatrick, Co Down. The small town is 20 or so miles south of Belfast and north-east of Warrenpoint and the scene of the massacre of soldiers in 1979; its name is taken from the Irish for *Dún Pádraig*, meaning

Patrick's stronghold. The Meadowlands Estate is in the north-east of the town and sits close to the busy A7 which takes traffic north to Belfast. It is a Republican Estate and as such was being patrolled by the RUC; on this occasion, however, only two Community RUCR officers were on duty and patrolling through the houses. They had visited various shops and had engaged in conversation with several locals. Unknown to them, two armed PIRA men were hiding in trees and as the two officers drew level with them – there was a slight gap between the policemen – and opened fire immediately, using automatic weapons. Over a dozen rounds were fired into their upper bodies and, even as the two men were slumping to the ground mortally wounded, the killers sped away in a stolen car driven by a third PIRA member. Both officers died very shortly afterwards in hospital. They were RUCR Constable William 'Billy' Finlay (55), father of three, and RUCR Constable James 'Jimmy' Ferguson (53) and also a father of three. At William Finlay's funeral, the vicar said: "They were walking through the community on the beat. Doing their job, they were demonstrating that they are the men of principle who truly deserve to be called principled. Bill Finlay and his colleague died preserving and protecting a decent way of life for all the citizens of Downpatrick."

The following year, PIRA man, Manchester-born Barry Llewellan was gaoled for 14 years at Belfast Crown Court for his part in the murders; he was described by the judge as 'callous.' Llewellan was also described as 'determined' and it was stated that he had agreed to give evidence against seven Provisionals while he was being questioned at the RUC barracks in Armagh. He had taken the killers of the two RUC officers to a safe house where he disposed of their weapons and burned their clothes in order to destroy any forensic evidence. As the *Belfast Telegraph* reported:

The 14 year sentence was passed after Llewellan had been found guilty of throwing a Soviet grenade into the yard of Downpatrick police station on July 12 last year[1] as a large number of policemen returned from duty. He received other sentences for crimes ranging from conspiracy to murder, to possession of guns and explosives, false imprisonment and passing on information about security forces to the IRA.

An anonymous contributor from the South Armagh Anglican community wrote:

I was visiting in Meadowlands Estate Downpatrick when the two unarmed community policemen were shot. I followed the ambulance to the hospital where I was admitted to the Casualty Unit. Billy had already died from his wounds. As Jimmy had head injuries, I held his feet, while the staff worked desperately to save his life. The scenes in the casualty unit were described as emotional. The staff were in tears: "It's Jimmy and Billy." Both men were known to the nurses and doctors. The consultant was there in eight minutes from home six miles away, but it was too late. His three children were at church choir practice when the murder occurred. Councillor Edward McGrady SDLP (later MP) called at the home on the night of the murder to express his condolences. He was kept at the front door rather than being invited inside, an action which the widow later regretted.

---

1   See Chapter 43.

Just four days later, the Provisionals created yet another widow when they killed an entirely innocent Catholic civilian based on flawed intelligence and the utter incompetency of one of their ASUs. It was the colour of a man's hair which led to his death. Sean McShane (39) had red hair – a not altogether rare sight in both parts of the island of Ireland. A local police officer whom the IRA set out to kill also had red hair. Mr McShane walked into a Betting Shop on Monaghan Street, Newry in order to place a bet and inside were two armed men, one with a pistol and the other with a rifle, who were expecting a red-haired police officer of similar build to him. One walked up to the victim, and shot him in the head at point-blank range. As he fell to the floor, the other gunman fired above the heads of horrified staff and punters; they made their escape in the confusion.

The victim was a local businessman and a supporter of the GAA; described as a tireless worker for the community, charity worker and former Gaelic Rules Football player. The flawed intelligence was laid firmly at the door of Eamonn Collins, the IRA man who later turned informer, who had apparently set up the shooting. Right on cue, the Provisionals activated their 'Department for Shallow and Meaningless Apologies' and an apologist was forced to make a statement announcing:

> an urgent, internal inquiry into the circumstances surrounding the incident. While not attempting to minimise the tragedy, the nationalist community should bear in mind the circumstances under which we operate. While extreme caution is taken at all times in selecting and identifying targets, human error is unavoidable.

Displaying their usual sensitivity, a Sinn Féin Councillor claimed: "The vast majority of people will feel sorry for the man who pulled the trigger!" One can only imagine Sean McCane's widow's reaction to this not unexpected tactless and uncaring comment from a Republican politician! In response, an RUC spokesman denounced the comments and the murder as 'despicable'. The chairman of Newry and Mourne Council, Jim McCart stated: "The people of this district want no more killings, either planned or accidental. No excuse will bring Sean McShane back to life."

On the following day, Northern Ireland Secretary, James Prior, said that he would resign his post if the inquiry into the Maze Prison escape the previous month found that his policies had been responsible. The report of the inquiry was published the following January and will be covered in a future book by this author.

On the 15th of the month, the Creggan Provisionals proved that they were as prolific at killing soldiers as other PIRA units when they launched an attack close to the city cemetery. The author paid a visit to this cemetery in 2008 and, in addition to the graves of the Bloody Sunday dead which have their anti-Crown forces vitriol etched into the marble, there is a monument to the dead of the INLA. As a comrade remarked to me as we stood next to a statue if a masked terrorist gripping an Armalite: "Even their statues have to hide their faces!" Back in October 1983, on a cold autumn day, a 10 lb explosive device planted in a wall cavity exploded as a mobile patrol from the Queen's Regiment drove past. A command wire had been triggered by members of a PIRA unit over 100 yards away with a clear view of the two-vehicle patrol as it drove along Lone Moor Road.

Private Alan James Stock (22) was on top cover and was hit by hundreds of pieces of razor-sharp brick and stone from the shattered wall; he died almost immediately from the onslaught. Another soldier was injured. Shots were fired from an Armalite, possibly from the same position as the trigger point of the explosion in a high part of the cemetery. After that the terrorists would have melted away towards Iniscarn Road and into the rabbit warren that was the Creggan. Private Stock's funeral was held at South West Middlesex Crematorium in West London.

Tim Scott, Queen's Regiment

Alan Stock, from Hounslow in Middlesex aged 22 and married, was killed on a typically drizzly Derry Saturday night on 15 Oct 1983. Derek Kennedy was Stock's team commander, but was unable to take the patrol out that night due to a football injury. He later attended Stock's funeral and hosted his father's visit to Oakington. I heard the contact report on the radio: "Contact – Lone Moor Road," and we speed across the bridge arriving via the small road that linked from the Lecky Road near the Derry City football ground.

The patrol had limped back to Rosemount; there was debris all over the road, and a hole at the top of the stone wall by the cemetery. At this stage we weren't quite sure what had happened. I later heard at the scene via an RUC officer that Stock had been killed. A 10 lb bomb had been in a gas cylinder and placed against the grass where it met the top of the wall. A 300 foot command wire ran up into the cemetery and a click box was found at the firing point, behind a gravestone. There was also a gunman by the cottage near the cemetery gates.

As a result of this attack we went from both soldiers standing in the rear to one standing, one sitting. Stock had been standing in the back. His team commander Lance Corporal McGarry was wounded and taken to hospital. The Land Rover was patched up and later turned up when we were at Rosemount, much to the consternation of some of the lads!

Despite numerous attempts on off duty personnel and attacks on Army patrols throughout Ulster, there were no more deaths in the Province until the 24th, when the Provisionals targeted an off-duty UDR soldier in Co Tyrone. Private Cyrus Campbell (49) was ambushed on his farm where he lived with his elderly mother at Carricklongfield, near Aughnacloy, Co. Tyrone. In 1972, as a recent recruit to the UDR, he was commended for his reaction during an attack on his Land Rover by PIRA terrorists. During this attack, a comrade Lance Corporal Henry Gillespie was mortally wounded. As his mobile patrol neared the hamlet of Killyliss, IRA gunmen opened fire and he was hit, dying shortly afterwards.[2]

Private Campbell, who was reputed to drive extremely slowly, had left his home in Aughnacloy and was en-route to his farm. As he left his home, he may not have noticed a car parked at the side of the road which followed him and in view of his slow pace, quickly caught up with him and drew alongside. The windows of the overtaking car were down and two gunmen, armed with a shotgun and an American Armalite took aim. The gunman holding the shotgun may have recognised the off-duty soldier and declined to fire, but the Armalite-wielding assassin fired twice and hit Private Campbell in the head.

---

2   Wharton, Ken, *The Bloodiest Year: Northern Ireland 1972* (Stroud: The History Press, 2011), Chapter 5.

He died immediately and the car crashed into a ditch. He is buried in Brantry Parish Church of Ireland graveyard. A memorial plaque erected by his comrades in the UDR can be seen inside the Church.

As a postscript to the murder, the man who could not or would not fire the shotgun was later arrested and convicted of murder. The man who it is widely considered had fired the two fatal shots – Brian Campbell – was later shot and killed by undercover soldiers on 4 December 1983 at Coalisland. Also killed in that incident was fellow terrorist, Colm McGirr. The incident is dealt with later in this book.[3]

On the 26th, the ranks of INLA were reduced by one in an internal killing which involved, almost inevitably, Dominic McGlinchey. He and his wife Mary were known to some members of the Army and RUC as the 'Prince and Princess of Darkness' and this was an epithet well-earned by this evil duo. A friend of the author said that when he met her: "Her face was that of a hard woman; she looked pure evil to me and she showed it in her eyes." She was later killed in her Dundalk home by gunmen who broke in while she was bathing her children and shot her, on 31 January 1987. She was known to be involved in some bloody incidents with her husband. On one occasion when she was present, her husband and some fellow INLA members tortured another INLA man for hours. He was suspected of being an informer and, while the 'doting' wife watched on, they roasted him on an Aga cooker in their house.

McGlinchey, also known as 'Mad Dog' presided over the INLA at a time when it was riddled with dissension, internecine struggle and constantly on its guard against informants. Around this time – October of 1983 – tensions were running very high and McGlinchey was involved in the abortive plot to hold members of supergrass Harry Kirkpatrick's family.[4] He was convinced that one of his comrades – Gerard 'Sparky' Barkley – had tipped off the Gardaí and saw him not only as an informer, a tout, but also as a potential threat to his leadership. He was also suspected of carrying out 'unauthorised' robberies in the area for personal gain. Barkley (27) was lured by Mary McGlinchey to their family home in Co Louth on the pretext of a meeting. Barkley was greeted and given a drink and he settled to watch TV. As he did so, Dominic McGlinchey shot him through the back of the head, killing him, it is thought, instantly. They dragged him to the back yard, slit his throat and drained his body of blood to make it lighter to carry to his car; his lifeless body was then wrapped in plastic and McGlinchey and another INLA man, Paul McCann, drove off towards the border, under cover of darkness. The body, still wrapped in plastic was discovered at the side of a country road in Co Cavan.

Over 10 years later, on 10 February 1994, McGlinchey was making a call from a phone box in Drogheda in the Irish Republic, when two men got out of a vehicle and shot him 14 times. No one has ever been charged with his killing and it is not known who carried out the assassination.

Two days after the execution of Barkley, in an attack which had similarities with the murder of census worker Joanne Mathers on the Gobnascale in April 1981,[5] the IRA targeted a popular community policeman whom they knew refused to carry a firearm. Constable John Hallawell (35), father of three, was based in Londonderry and his 'patch'

---

3   See Chapter 48 of this book.
4   See Chapters 12 and 13.
5   See Chapter 16.

was the Nationalist Ballymagroarty Estate. He was renowned for refusing to carry a gun as he felt that both sides of the sectarian divide recognised him for his fairness and total lack of prejudice. On the night of the 28th, he had gone onto the estate in order to organise a holiday weekend designed at bringing together both Catholic and Protestant children in the hope of reducing sectarian hatred amongst the young. After chatting to locals in the area, he walked towards the quiet street where he had parked his car. Unknown to him, three PIRA members – two men and a woman, all armed – were lying in wait for him to return. As the RUC man started up his car, several gunmen fired at him, but the wounded policeman attempted to drive away before crashing. One of the attackers ran to the crashed car and fired another round into his head from point blank range as he lay there helpless.

The car containing the gunmen then drove off towards the Creggan Estate where it was later found abandoned. Like the killing of census worker Joanne Mathers, the attack was cynical and cowardly and served no purpose; the operation was put into effect because both victims were unarmed and therefore highly unlikely to present difficulties to the attackers. The murders were both cold-blooded and cowardly and demonstrated the sickness and bankruptcy of PIRA tactics. The killers of the policeman were described as 'a cancer in our midst' by a senior RUC commander. Earlier on that fateful day, the Provisionals had planted and detonated a car bomb in the centre of Armagh City, causing widespread panic. The area had been largely cleared at the time of the explosion but one policeman was injured as was a civilian. Several shops were set on fire by the blast as the Provisionals paralysed the town centre.

Also on the 28th, George Terry, a former Sussex Chief Constable, published a report on the scandal at the Kincora Boys' Home in Belfast. Terry said that he had found no evidence that civil servants, members of the RUC, or military intelligence, were involved in homosexual activities at the boys' home nor had anyone tried to suppress information about the events. In spite of a number of investigations into the events surrounding Kincora many people in Northern Ireland – this author included – remain convinced that some of the allegations were true.

The very next day saw two more murders, this time by the Loyalist terror group the UVF as they targeted a former OIRA man in Greencastle, North Belfast and then moved further south and killed a member or former member in what may be described as an 'in-house murder'. David Nocher (26), father of three, was a member of the Workers' Party but had served a conviction much earlier, for being an OIRA member. One of his children attended Stella Maris Secondary School in North Belfast. The school had an unenviable record of losing several pupils and parents during the Troubles. Twenty seven past pupils and parents are known to have lost their lives, 23 boys and three girls. Most were in their late teens or early twenties. One, John Rolston, was murdered within two days of leaving school. Three were killed by the Provisional IRA, another three accidentally when handling explosives; 20, including the three girls by Loyalist paramilitaries and one, Bobby Sands, died in prison on hunger strike shortly after he had been elected MP for Fermanagh and South Tyrone. Eight families who had one or other parent killed in those years also sent children to the school.

Of all those who lost their lives Bobby Sands is the best known. He attended Stella Maris from 1965 to 1969. Coming from a very supportive and close-knit family he was apparently well regarded by both staff and pupils. Shortly after he left school he was, as stated in the 1981 section of this book intimidated from his workplace and the family from their home in Rathcoole. The first deaths of past pupils occurred in 1972 and continued to 1994. Sharon McKenna was murdered in January 1993, the year the school closed.

On the 29th, David Nocher was cleaning shop windows at the Whitehouse Meat Centre on Mill Road where he was employed in the company of a teenage girl. As he continued his task, at least two masked gunmen belonging to the UVF walked up to him and opened fire from very close range. David Nocher was mortally wounded and died very soon afterwards; his teenage companion was wounded but recovered. The attack claimed by the UVF under their PAF pseudonym, claiming him as a 'legitimate target.' As a sickening postscript to the assassination, Loyalist song writers put together a tasteless ditty under the title of 'UVF Execute IRA Leader David Nocher.' Somewhat bizarrely, it is also available as a mobile phone ringtone.

Later that day, a UVF 'punishment squad' cornered George Taggart (26) in the Oakley Bar close to Castlereagh, South Belfast. The details of his misdemeanours are not known by the author, but it would appear that he was lulled – possibly by drink – and enticed into getting into a car driven by UVF members. The car apparently drove a short distance before stopping and the men, including Taggart got out to take a toilet break. Almost immediately, two shots were fired at him and he attempted to run off but was shot in the back of the head and mortally wounded. At this stage, one of the men bent down and cut the dying man's throat. Certainly, he was convicted of the murder and it was raised in court that he had another conviction, this time for manslaughter.

Back in 1973, the man who cut Taggart's throat was in a pub with a Loyalist friend, who admitted he was carrying a gun. When Taggart's killer asked to see it, his friend – Joseph Adair – obliged, but his 'friend' slipped while he was showing off, and Adair died.[6]

Although there is some question as to his membership of the Loyalist paramilitary organisation, Taggart's name is inscribed on a Red Hand Commando mural on Newtownards Road. The mural reads: 'Fallen Volunteers of 'C' Company, Red Hand Commando (Ulster Volunteer Force)' and names Taggart as one of the 'fallen'.

October had ended with the deaths of 10 people; three soldiers and three policemen died; five at the hands of the Provisionals. The same Republican terror group were responsible for the mistaken identity killing of an innocent Catholic. Paramilitaries from both side killed three fellow paramilitaries. Two Republicans and one Loyalist paramilitary member were killed. In all, Republicans killed seven and Loyalists killed two.

---

6   This episode is covered in Wharton, Ken, *Sir, They're Taking the Kids Indoors* (Solihull: Helion, 2011).

47

November

The month of November saw the return of the long winter nights and the mood of the country equally darkened with the deaths of 12 people; it included three soldiers and four more policemen. It also included an appalling sectarian massacre at place which would soon become synonymous with one of the vilest of acts by the Republicans: Mountain Lodge Pentecostal Church, Darkley in Co Armagh.

November is a cold, dark month and it began with an outrage perpetrated by Irish Republicans and ended in the same, vile manner. One major criticism levelled at me is my unswerving support for the Army in which I served and my detestation of paramilitaries from both sides of the sectarian divide. Until I draw my final breath that will never change. I am proud to have been a British soldier and remain steadfast in my support of the Army's role in Northern Ireland. It still angers me that many Brits have forgotten what happened on their own doorstep and those nations such as the USA – unless one is of the Irish-American persuasion – and Australia apparently have no clue that 30 years of violence ever occurred. One Aussie once asked me where I served and when I replied: "Northern Ireland" he responded with: "What happened on the North Island [of New Zealand]?" When the reader peruses the events of Jordanstown, Co Antrim and Darkley, Co Armagh, there will be no doubts, absolutely nothing unequivocal about my own personal feelings.

Jordanstown is the name of a small town within the urban area of the wider Newtownabbey Borough. The Ulster Polytechnic was located there, and on the 4th of the month, the RUC sent several officers to attend a Criminology lecture. Prior to the start of the lecture, officers had searched the room but nothing was found. However, at around midnight the previous night, PIRA operatives, almost certainly with the assistance of rogue members of the Polytechnic staff, had placed an explosive device in the lecture room's ceiling. Around 30 minutes before midday, with 30–40 people in the room, several of whom were RUC officers, the device exploded. A massive explosion which ripped out the side of the room killed two policemen and dreadfully injured a third who survived for almost a year before succumbing to his injuries; 20 other people were injured, amongst them civilian students, some of them seriously. The dead officers were Inspector John Martin (27), father of two, and Sergeant Stephen Fyffe (28), father of one child; their comrade Sergeant William McDonald died the following August. Nuala O'Loan, who was pregnant at the time, was attending in her capacity as a prison independent custody visitor and would become Northern Ireland's first Police Ombudsman some years later, was also injured in the attack. She lost the baby as a result of her terrible injuries.

The following day, the *Bangor Daily News* quoted RUC spokesman Dave Hanna's comments to the Press:

At least two of the wounded were in critical condition and 10 more were in serious condition. Hanna said that 20 policemen and women were attending the weekly class in the third-floor lecture room when the bomb exploded, blowing out the wall of an adjoining classroom and part of the floor of the room below. Hanna said the bomb was apparently hidden in the classroom earlier and timed to explode before noon. Police experts said it contained a 'substantial amount of explosives.' "This attack was insane. These people cold-bloodedly didn't give a damn who they killed," said Bill McAllister, Assistant Chief Constable. Gerard Shephard, president of the College's Student Union called the bombing: "The work of cowards and a deliberate attempt to promote strife."

The *Belfast Telegraph* described how a 'fleet of ambulances' was used to ferry the injured to the RVH and other hospitals. A photograph on their front page shows the third floor window, blown out and debris fluttering in the wind.

The newspaper quoted eyewitness statements as follows: "Some policemen lost limbs." "I am devastated by what has happened here; I can't describe my horror. What I saw was ghastly." The newspaper then described how even ambulance men, surely hardened and inure to the daily horrors on PIRA actions as being: "visibly shaken by the extent of the injuries inflicted on the victims." It stated: "One fireman was first on the scene said: 'All we could do was try to get the victims out as quickly as we could and get them away to hospitals'." Alliance Party spokesman Seamus Close was quoted as saying: "To strike at one of our centres of learning where there are so many young people demonstrates the depths to which some people will sink."

Several hours after the blast the Provisionals detonated a car bomb in the centre of Strabane in Co Tyrone. They chose their target wisely, because 'Jack's Bar' was known to be frequented by off-duty policemen. In an earlier book, the author gives more details about an attack at the Polytechnic in March 1977, when an IRA bomb wounded 14 people including a former senior member of the legal profession.[1]

The following day, the Provisionals struck again, this time targeting an off-duty RUCR officer as he returned home from work. Reserve Constable John McFadden (50) lived in Rasharkin in Co Antrim and the Provisionals had clearly done their intelligence homework. Like any cold-blooded killer or killers, they knew to bide their time and may well have followed the policeman home on a number of occasions, checking his routes, his timings and his habits. It is quite possible they intended to kill him earlier than they did but were thwarted. Another policeman in the vicinity, a passing Army foot patrol, even a neighbour being in a garden from where they had intended to hide before striking, might all have made a difference. On the evening of the 6th, however, John McFadden returned to him home in Bamford Park and, as he got out of his car to unlock his garage, masked gunmen who had been hiding leapt out and shot him several

---

1   See Wharton, Ken M., *Wasted Years, Wasted Lives* (Solihull: Helion, 2013), Vol 1.

times from very close range. He was mortally wounded and died shortly afterwards as his shocked family and neighbours tried to comfort him.

The day after the RUCR man's murder, Lance Corporal Stephen William Taverner (24) of the Devon and Dorsetshire Regiment died of his wounds following his fatal injury, 11 days previously. The incident is dealt with in the previous chapter. He was from Whipton in Devon.

On Monday 7th, Taoiseach Garret FitzGerald, travelled to England for a meeting at Chequers with Prime Minister Margaret Thatcher. Chequers is located near Ellesborough, to the south of Aylesbury in Buckinghamshire, England, at the foot of the Chiltern Hills. It has been the British PM's residence since 1921 and was built or added to between the 12th and 16th centuries. The meeting was seen as an opportunity for the two leaders to get to know each other and to discuss the burning issue of the day: the Troubles and Northern Ireland. For the hardliners on the Loyalist side, it was more ammunition to fuel their conspiracy theories that the UK was about to sell out the Protestant majority in the North and achieve direct rule from Dublin by stealth.

Even while the great and the good of British and Irish politics were meeting in a stately home in Bucks, surrounded by armed police and watched over by circling helicopters, the UVF were striking again, this time in Armagh City. To step back in time for a moment; Chapter 36 of this book covers the killing of INLA gunman Roderick Carroll, by the RUC's HMSSU, in some detail. On the 8th of November 1983, almost a full year later, Carroll's brother – Adrian (24) – was also murdered. His killers were the UVF and it is thought that because he was the brother of an INLA terrorist – albeit a deceased one – and was currently working for Sinn Féin that he was selected as a 'legitimate target' by the Loyalists. The case, however, involved several members of the UDR and led to much controversy over the next few years and indeed ill-feeling and accusations of collusion still lingers in the Carroll family and amongst Republicans.

Adrian Carroll was also employed by Armagh Council and was engaged in painting railings near Abbey Street in the centre of the city. Eyewitnesses – whose evidence was later discredited – stated that they saw a UDR Land Rover stop nearby and that one of the soldiers changed into civvies and was then marched away by two of his comrades, as though under arrest. The incident blurs at this stage, but a lone gunman – the killing was later claimed by the PAF, a cover-name for the UVF – walked up to Mr Carroll, shooting him several times. The Sinn Féin worker was mortally wounded and died in hospital a few hours later. It would appear that one of the UDR men who had donned civilian clothes – Neil Latimer – was dropped off close to where the killing would take place and then collected by the other three in the Land Rover. They would clearly have aware of what had happened especially as he then peeled off the civvie clothing and continued the patrol in his uniform.

Two and a half years later, all four of the UDR soldiers were tried and convicted of the murder and sent to prison for life. However, in the summer of 1990, the men who came to be known as the 'UDR Four' succeeded in taking the case to appeal. Three of the four were released but the fourth man – Latimer – had his sentence upheld and he went back to prison. The men who were cleared – Colin Worton, Noel Bell, and Winston Allen – did not return to the UDR. There were many accusations of collusion and bias and the fourth UDR soldier was clearly one of the rogue elements of whom this author has spoken times *passim*. I will not support those who used their military training to help the Loyalist paramilitaries. Further, I believe that although there were a few 'rotten apples' the overwhelming majority of the men and women who served in the Ulster Defence Regiment did so with honour, professionalism and bravery.

By way of a postscript, one of the 'UDR Four' Colin Worton from South Armagh who spent two and a half years in custody after being charged in connection with the 1983 murder attempted to gain compensation. He claimed that the police had obtained a confession from him under duress. However, in 2010, a judge found no evidence of police wrongdoing and upheld a decision not to compensate him. He spent 30 months in custody between 1983 and 1986, and later claimed that officers warned him he faced up to 20 years in prison unless he confessed to a role in events surround the killing. He also alleged police questioning him said he would be gaoled for just five years and get bail to marry his girlfriend if he made admissions.

This clearly is a story which will run and run and the August 13, 2013 issue of the *Belfast Telegraph* reported the following in relation to Neil Latimer:

> A specialist team of investigators has unearthed new evidence which could help mount a fresh legal challenge to the murder conviction of UDR 4 soldier Neil Latimer. *Belfast Daily* understands that part of the new evidence is a transcript of a conversation between a female witness, who allegedly saw Neil Latimer carry out the shooting, and a relative of one of his co-accused. James Hagan's father recorded the call from the female, known as 'Witness A', on his private home line after receiving notice that she was going to call him. 'Witness A' was unaware the call was being recorded.
>
> The phone call took place after the Court of Appeal quashed the murder convictions against Hagan, Noel Bell and Winston Allen in 1992. However, the Court of Appeal upheld the murder conviction of Neil Latimer for shooting dead Adrian Carroll in Armagh. Catholic Adrian Carroll was shot dead in 1983 and was the brother of the Sinn Féin councillor Tommy Carroll. Neil Latimer served a total of 15 years in prison, including three years on remand, before being released under the Good Friday Agreement. Campaigners say he still maintains his innocence and could have been freed earlier but refused to admit his involvement in a murder he says he never committed. During the phone call 'Witness A', whose testimony was crucial to prosecutors in securing Latimer's conviction, told James Hagan's dad that she was forced to give evidence by the RUC.

Two days later, the IRA carried out a carbon-copy of the murder of RUCR man John McFadden, when they murdered another part-time police officer, this time in Co Down. RUCR Constable William Fitzpatrick (47) was a rarity: he was a Roman Catholic in the RUC. There were few of this religion who served in the police force of Northern Ireland and all were targeted by the Provisional IRA. Whether or not William Fitzpatrick was targeted because he was a Catholic and, as such, was seen in the perverted logical of the Republicans as a 'traitor', or because he was another easy target is known only the Godfathers of the IRA who sanctioned the murder. The part-time policeman lived in the shadow of Ulster's beautiful and picturesque Mourne Mountains and worked at the Silent Valley Reservoir. It is located near Kilkeel, Co Down and supplies most of the water for the county's surrounding villages and most of Belfast. He lived close to the village of Annalong which is south of Newcastle and to the east of Warrenpoint, close to the Irish Sea. He had purchased a house in the area and was helping to refurbish in between working as a security guard and as a part-time policeman. A murder gang from the South Down PIRA brigade drove up to the remote house and a lone gunman walked into the garden. The gunman located Mr Fitzpatrick through a window and fired several shots hitting in the throat and the head; he died instantly, collapsing in a pool of blood on the floor of the house which he was so lovingly renovating. It was reported that he never considered it necessary to carry a gun and, therefore, was an easy target for the ruthless Republican terrorists.

On the 12th, in what was seen as a chilling dress rehearsal for the 1985 Newry mortar attack which killed nine officers, a PIRA mortar crew fired six explosive devices at the RUC base at Carrickmore, Co Tyrone. (The name 'Carrickmore' comes from the Irish: *An Charraig Mhor* which means the big rock.) Carrickmore is a small town which sits on a raised site known locally as 'the rock.' It is close to Cookstown, Dungannon and Omagh. The base was in the process of being renovated and fortified as it was sited in a largely Nationalist area. On the evening of Saturday 24th, November a large PIRA team consisting of 20-plus members set up a firing point on the back of a stolen lorry on the outskirts of the Nationalist area. A total of six mortar bombs were fired at the station passing over the houses of 'their' community and presumably over the sleeping heads of young children. Several fell short and landed in gardens, but one hit a hut in which several policemen were working. Constable Paul Clarke (29), father of three young children, was killed and five colleagues were badly injured; the base was badly damaged.

On the 14th, a freezing cold night and a desire to get home may have been the factors in a UDR man failing to check his car and dying in a PIRA UVBT blast which left eight children fatherless. Major Charles Armstrong (54) was also a local councillor, representing the Ulster Unionist Party on Armagh District Council. He had just left a meeting at Palace Demesne in the centre of Armagh City and had made his farewells to other members. As he got into his car the device, fitted by a PIRA bombing team while the meeting was taking place, exploded. *Lost Lives* reports that there had been angry scenes during the meeting when a placatory Major Armstrong called for a minutes silence for the death of a local Catholic – Adrian Carroll who had been murdered by UDR soldier Neil Latimer a few days earlier – and several Unionists refused.[2] Several of Charles Armstrong's fellow councillors, including those from rival parties, rushed to his aid – but he was already dead. Gerry Adams, who the day before had been elected President of Sinn Féin at the party's annual *Ard Fheis,* made a comment which unveiled his true colours. He described the killing of the part-time soldier as: '….perfectly legitimate in a state of war. Then the man who apparently was never in the IRA, who apparently was not behind the 'Bloody Friday' bombings of 1972 and apparently not behind the disappearance of Jean McConville said: "If my role lay within the IRA and within an armed struggle, I would have no compunction at all," when asked if he would kill soldiers or policemen. He replaced Ruairí Ó Brádaigh as President in a development that

---

2   Thornton, David, Seamus Kelters, Brian Feeney and David McKittrick. *Lost Lives: The Stories of the Men, Women and Children who Died as a Result of the Northern Ireland Troubles.* (Edinburgh: Mainstream, 1999, revised ed. 2007).

demonstrated the movement in political power from Republicans based in the south of Ireland to those in Northern Ireland.

Darkley is named from the Irish: *Dearclaigh*, which means a place of caves/hollows. It is a small village near Keady in Co Armagh, in the south west of Northern Ireland. In previous centuries, it was a mill village and produced linen. Prior to late November 1983, it had only been mentioned in passing in relation to the Troubles and that was back in February 1979.[3] On 24 February of that year, Martin McGuigan and James Keenan, both Catholic teenagers, were killed by a PIRA bomb hidden in a trailer and detonated when they walked past. It was parked on the roadside between Darkley and Keady on the Newtownhamilton road. They were mistaken for a British Army foot patrol. Three of their friends were also seriously injured in the bombing which left a five-foot crater in the road.

Perhaps the world had forgotten the name of this small village; perhaps it was only remembered by the loved ones of the dead teenagers and by the families of the boys who had been injured in that terrible blast. But on the evening of the 23rd of November, it would be on the lips of the civilised world; it would be a name forever associated with the black heart of Irish Republicanism and it would forever be associated with the evil essence of the INLA. It would be an act of terror which would even shame the 'Mad Dog' himself, Dominic McGlinchey into disassociating himself from the actions of his psychotic comrades.

During the research for this book, I visited the website of the Mountain Lodge Pentecostal Church and it gave the following message:

> We trust you will be blessed and refreshed as you peruse our site. At Mountain Lodge, we are committed to providing a place of worship that caters for all ages, with both traditional and contemporary songs and music as we praise the Lord.

Darkley is a predominantly Catholic village sandwiched between two lakes in the south western part of Co Armagh, a little over a mile away from the border with the Irish Republic. The actual church is situated in Mountain Lodge Road on a hill just two miles from the village centre and not far from the border with Monaghan. It is a place which preaches love and reconciliation. Indeed, the *Irish Times* reported in its issue the following day: "The Monaghan Border curves less than two miles away. With all its lights blazing, the little hall stood out on a hill, the easiest of easy targets."

Indeed, as the worshippers sat down to sing and pray on that cold November evening, that was precisely what was on their minds: to sing and pray. At a little after 1800 hours, INLA gunmen arrived, it is thought from across the border, just as David Wilson (44), Harold Brown (59), and Victor Cunningham (39), Protestant civilians and church elders, were standing in the entrance hall. A burst of automatic fire hit the three men and two of them crumpled to the floor, mortally injured from multiple gunshot wounds. Mr Wilson, despite the terrible wounds which would kill him within a few minutes, staggered into the church hall as he bravely tried to warn the congregation. He was observed to be bleeding heavily and trying to speak, but was in too much shock and pain to get his words out. Heavily bleeding, he fell, rather than walked down the length of the aisle before collapsing, dying shortly afterwards. The masked INLA men stepped over the dying men and burst into the hall where approximately 70 people, including 20 children were singing a favourite Protestant hymn: 'Are you Washed in the Blood of the Lamb?' The gunmen sprayed the assembled worshippers without discrimination, uncaring about the elderly and the infirm and the young children gathered there and now turning around with terror in their eyes. More than 40 shots were fired into the throng of people, hitting one woman five times in the stomach and chest, causing severe spinal injuries to another and shattering the elbow of the church organist. Even as they fled to a stolen car, outside waiting to rush them over into Co Monaghan, they again sprayed the outside of the hall several times more with automatic fire. Seconds after they fled, Mr Wilson died from his injuries and the place was in shocked chaos, the sobbing of the children, the soft groans of the wounded, the pools of blood, the gun smoke and the stench of cordite rendering a scene almost Dantè-esque.

Leaders of both the Roman Catholic Church as well as their Protestant counterparts were quick to condemn the murders of the worshippers on that Sunday evening, calling it: 'an act of sectarian slaughter on a worshipping community which goes beyond any previous deed of violence.' The following day, *The Irish Times* reported:

> William Brown and John Cunningham were standing at the church's back door discussing a friend who was in hospital. Their job was to welcome latecomers to the gospel service and find them a seat. The two men were gunned down immediately and died where they fell. Richard Wilson from Keady was standing a few yards away at the inner door. He staggered, wounded, through the double doors in an attempt to raise the alarm. He stumbled the full length of the aisle and died in a small room behind the platform.

FAIR (Fair Acting for Innocent Relatives) naturally condemned the murders and their spokesman said:

> Pandemonium followed instantly. The killers calmly stepped over the blood-stained helpless bodies already cut down and began firing at the congregation of mainly defenceless women and children. Fathers dived over their young children, and one man covered a seven-month-old baby, such was the indiscriminate nature of the attack. Children were screaming hysterically calling for their mothers and fathers who were lying among the upturned pews, prayer books and Bibles. All begged and pleaded for mercy as the gunmen stepped through the bodies and made their way outside. Such was their murderous intent that they reloaded their guns and sprayed the exterior of the wooden hall before cowardly disappearing into the rural landscape.

FAIR[4] is an organisation which carries out work for those left grieving for their loved ones through Republican terrorist actions. I support their aims as I support the aims

---

of any other organisation which carries out the same for those grieving after Loyalist terrorism also.

The minister who conducted the service said:

> It came just like a flash of lightning through the window to us. We didn't understand what was happening until it was half through. Somebody said: "Get down!" and everybody dived. The people reacted marvellously. The doctor said he never seen a place for such an atrocity to happen that the people were so calm. Nobody was screaming, nobody was screeching. There were 26 young children under their seats at the front, and except for them nobody cried.

He added: "The men that are dead are in Heaven. The men that did this terrible thing, if they do not repent they'll be suffering in Hell looking for a drop of cold of water."

In 2008, the *Belfast Newsletter* ran a memorial article to commemorate the massacre, 25 years later. It read:

> There can be few things more chilling than the sound of worshippers singing hymns of praise being perforated by the crack of gunfire and the shocked screams of children. But sound recordings of the service at Mountain Lodge Pentecostal Church outside the south Armagh village of Darkley played by the media 25 years ago convey just that, as the full horror of what happened on November 20, 1983, became clear to the people of Ulster.

One of the guns used in the massacre had been used before in INLA attacks; that is, in attacks for which INLA claimed responsibility. Dominic McGlinchey admitted that he had supplied one of the guns used but claimed he neither ordered the attack nor approved of it. Seven days later, the attack was claimed by the 'Catholic Reaction Force' (CRF) which was a cover name, a 'flag of convenience' used by the IRSP/INLA. Their spokesman fooled no one; the sickening murders were carried out by Dominic McGlinchey's INLA. McGlinchey's hands were clearly on the prepared statement from the CRF which read: "By this token retaliation – we could have easily taken the lives of at least 20 more innocent Protestants – were to serve notice to the PAF [Protestant Action Force] to call an immediate halt to their vicious indiscriminate campaign against innocent Catholics or we will make the Darkley killings look like a picnic." By way of a postscript, Tim Pat Coogan claims that the weapon used came from an INLA arms dump, but that the weapon had been given to the INLA member to assassinate a known loyalist and the attack on the church was not sanctioned.[5] The Provisionals and the INLA were two evil peas from the same pod. A final and even more poignant postscript was that seven children were left fatherless by the atrocity.

Seven days after the massacre, McGlinchey gave an interview to invited – and some might add, sycophantic – journalists at a cottage in Carrigtwohill in the Irish Republic. He admitted that one of the gunmen had been an INLA member and admitted

---

5   Coogan, Tim Pat, *The IRA*, revised edition. (London: HarperCollins, 2000).

supplying him with the gun, stating that member's brother had been killed by Loyalists paramilitaries. 'Mad Dog' explained that the INLA man asked him for a gun to shoot a known Loyalist sectarian killer. McGlinchey stated that the man was: "clearly deranged by the death of his brother ... and used it instead to attack the Darkley Gospel Hall." He added: "We are conducting an enquiry into the whole affair." *Belfast Telegraph* journalist Michael Devine, following on from an interview by Vincent Browne of the *Dublin Sunday Tribune,* later wrote:

> McGlinchey, self-styled chief of staff of the INLA, claimed to have personally killed about 30 members of the security forces, but denied taking part directly in the Darkley Gospel Hall shooting. He admitted supplying one of the weapons used in the Darkley killings to an INLA member and that he was involved in the Droppin' Well bombing in Ballykelly, in which 17 people died. He also said that the INLA was now better organised and better equipped to give the Brits a hard time in 1984.

Browne himself wrote: "[McGlinchey was] quiet spoken, relaxed and displaying a coldness which was chilling." Browne stated that the INLA leader failed to show any remorse for the killings and the suffering he had inflicted on the families. The *Tribune* Editor then asked McGlinchey about the Droppin' Well bombings[6] and asked if he could justify the killings. The Mad Dog then, somewhat deprecatingly and in a most self-serving manner, said: "The owner of that pub was warned six times about entertaining members of the security forces there. He knew full well, and girls that attended the disco knew full well, that the warnings had been given and the place was going to be bombed at some time or other." Displaying what this author believes is one of the hallmarks of the violent psychopath, he boasted to the Dublin journalist: "I like to get in close, to minimise the risk for myself. It's usually a matter of who gets in first and by getting in close you put your man down first. It has worked for me down the years." He was quizzed on his conscience and snapped back that he wouldn't be blackmailed by the talk of children being orphaned or left fatherless by his actions. Sadly for those he killed or maimed and for their families, it would be a further 11 years before he was cold-bloodedly shot dead in the same cold-blooded matter in which he went about his terrorist business. His wife had at this stage of the Troubles just over three years left to live.

Shortly after the interview, McGlinchey managed to escape a Gardaí cordon and went into hiding in the Republic. His escape from Irish Security Forces sorely embarrassed the Minister tasked with his arrest. Justice Minister Michael Noonan said that a warrant had been issued for the arrest of the man dubbed "the most wanted man in Ireland" and for his eventual extradition to the North. The South wanted rid of him in order that he could stand trial in Ulster for the murder of an elderly postmistress in Co Antrim.

The author has spoken to several former soldiers who met McGlinchey and his "cold-hearted, hard-faced bitch of a wife," (former UDR Soldier) and this is recorded elsewhere in this book. Never having had that dubious pleasure myself, one has be content with

---

6   Covered in Chapter 36 of this book.

archive photographs of the man. In one he is thinnish with longish hair but a rapidly receding hairline. He looks cold but strangely intellectual and he has the thin pencil moustache usually favoured by British Army captains and majors. On one photo which was taken when he was arrested by Gardaí, his hairline has almost vanished revealing a bald dome beneath; his moustache is bushier and he is wearing the sort of nondescript sweater which many British men would wear on a weekend while relaxing or about to play a round of golf. On a mural dedicated to his memory, he faces the viewer with an almost 'Chè Guevara' stare, complete with black beret, but this is more Frank Spencer than the Bolivian guerrilla leader; underneath are the words: "Proudly remembered by the INLA POWs Long Kesh." On an RUC 'Wanted' poster he is described as: "Medium build; black curly hair; receding; fleshy face, green eyes; tricolour tattoo on left arm." It added that he "maybe armed and should not be approached."

As stated earlier in this book, the Mad Dog himself was gunned down in February, 1994; hit four times by unknown gunmen as he made a telephone call in Drogheda, Co Louth, in the Republic. He was in the presence of his 16-year-old son – McGlinchey never had a single qualm about shooting down his victims in full view of their loved ones – when three men pulled up in a car and punched him to the ground. As he lay in a widening pool of his own blood, he called out: "Jesus, Mary help me." The monster who had shown no mercy in killing over 30 people and ordering the deaths and maiming of dozens more was calling out to God for help; it was a luxury which he himself had denied to his many victims. This author will not grieve his death. Martin McGuinness attended his funeral and the oration was read by Bernadette McAliskey née Devlin. Although not convicted, his son Declan has been arrested twice; once for possession of explosives in 2006 and the other time for the murder of PC Carroll in 2009.

Former Rifleman, Royal Green Jackets

Attacking a church full of innocent worshippers? You have to ask where the attackers' heads were at during this senseless slaughter and just what exactly they hoped to achieve by it. Because as far as any reasonable minded person can see the answer is absolutely nothing. When I learn of stuff like this it merely strengthens my conviction evermore that the majority of 'freedom fighters' were simply warped criminals and psychotics, hiding behind the convenience of a political cause, that in all honesty they weren't themselves too bothered about. In fact I'll bet that when the Troubles started to wind down these sorts were actually quite aggrieved and upset about it, because it deprived them of their 'respectable' identities and excuses for generally behaving like madmen.

Without doubt this man was a deeply sadistic psychopath. A heavy hint at this is his own desperate appeals to 'Jesus and Mary' to help him when he was struck down by assailants himself. During his own death he was understandably consumed with urgent concern at his own survival and profoundly felt himself an 'innocent victim'. Yet contrast this with his mocking hardness and casual callousness towards those genuinely innocent victims who fell beneath his bullets; well then he doesn't have a care in the world and is even defiantly proud of it. I'm no psychologist but clearly this man saw himself as some kind of superior being and everybody else as troublesome ants – in his way and unworthy of concern. In reading of your descriptions of him I found myself being uncomfortably grateful that he wasn't a bigger figure in a bigger war: imagine what this man could have done as a German army officer in WW2, massacring countless thousands and more with a grin and a shrug. We're lucky that this man's reign of terror was restricted to Northern Ireland – but that doesn't lessen the pain any for those who suffered and fell beneath him. He still had a huge and dreadful impact on the Emerald Isle, and the only consolation to be taken is that his victims numbered in the dozens and not, thank God, the thousands.

A former UDR soldier told the author: "I remember this very well; we were dispatched down to Newtownhamilton for two weeks just after this, to guard RC Churches in case of reprisal; it was snowing most of the time."

On the 24th, Don Tidey, an American supermarket executive, working for Associated British Foods was kidnapped by the Provisionals inside the Irish Republic. The kidnapping, which took place in Rathfarnham, Co Dublin, was designed to raise funds for the Republican terrorist group. Tidey was taking his 13-year-old daughter to school when he was stopped at what he believed to be a Gardaí VCP. The 'officers' however, were IRA volunteers, dressed in stolen police uniforms, or those donated by Gardaí with Republican sympathies of whom there were clearly many. Sean O'Callaghan claims that one of the men was Michael Burke who, in 2000, was a senior member of the 32 County Sovereignty Committee, the political wing of the 'Real IRA.' A gun was put to Tidey's head and he was bundled into a waiting car and driven off by masked men. A few days later his photograph was sent to his company and later a demand was telephoned through asking for IR£5 million in ransom money. Three weeks later, the Gardaí tracked Tidey and his kidnappers — four in all — to Derrada Wood in Ballinamore, Co Leitrim on 16 December. In the subsequent shoot-out, a trainee Gardaí and an Irish soldier – Gary Sheehan and Patrick Kelly – were killed. This incident will be dealt with in the next chapter. The kidnappers, one of whom was alleged to be 'Bic' McFarlane, all escaped in the confused aftermath.

On the same day that the supermarket chief was kidnapped, the RUC foiled a PIRA car bomb attack on Belfast City Centre. A bombing team from the West Belfast area was intercepted at a VCP on Andersonstown Road and, when their car was searched, over 100 lbs of high explosives, already primed were discovered, packed inside a beer keg. The snap VCP at the Busy Bee Shopping Centre was thought to have been sprung as the result of an informer inside the IRA's West Belfast unit. As the men were arrested, ATO was called in and disposal experts spent five hours rendering the device harmless using wheelbarrows. The nearby area was evacuated as the Provisionals demonstrated their absolute contempt for the safety of residents in 'their' community. Time after time, the Republican terrorist organisation treated the people of the Nationalist areas with utter contempt and lack of consideration as they turned the residential streets in battlegrounds. Often a spokesman would blatantly lie or colour the events in such a way as make the Security Forces responsible for their (IRA) irresponsibility. Even a belated apology would hardly ring with the truth and it would be left to their bearded spokesman – Gerry Adams – 30 years down the line to be publically wheeled out and issue a hollow, meaningless apology, through metaphorically gritted teeth!

This bloody month was not yet over and three more people were to die before the onset of December. After Darkley, the UVF were itching for a sectarian killing – not that this Loyalist paramilitary group ever needed a reason for such – and that came on the day after the Tidey kidnap when an innocent Catholic civilian was beaten to death. The UVF knew that the Republicans would retaliate and their move was seen as ruthless and calculated, aware that retribution was likely. Daniel Rouse (51), father of three, was by all accounts a harmless and friendly man "with a good word for everyone" who was targeted by a Loyalist murder gang because he was a hated 'Taig.' Some time in what Belfast people call the 'wee hors' of the 25th, he was attacked as he left the Stables Bar in Armagh. As he walked along the Old Portadown Road, close to Craigavon Lake, he was set up by Loyalist thugs belonging to the UVF who had been hiding in bushes. He was savagely attacked, beaten – it is thought – with metal bars and mortally injured. He was almost dead when a passing motorist spotted him and stopped to help; he died shortly afterwards.

On the 28th, in what Sinn Féin and other Republican apologists have described as 'controversial circumstances', there was a tragic death in Pomeroy, Co Tyrone. Pomeroy is approx 18 miles north of the Irish border, between Cookstown and Dungannon Brigid Foster (80) was collecting her pension from the main Post office there, when a raid by paramilitaries – none ever admitted responsibility but they were likely to have been either PIRA or INLA – began. Two gunmen burst in shouting "This is a raid!" and commanded everyone to get down on the floor. The postmaster John Grimes handed over the money in his till, just as the RUC arrived outside. It is thought that they had received a tip-off from an informant which would explain their speedy response. It is also thought likely that they had been consciously patrolling in the vicinity of banks and post offices in the run up to Christmas for obvious reasons. There was an exchange of shots between the two masked raiders and the police. In the confusion, the raiders escaped. Mrs Foster, a mother of five, was slightly disabled and unable to lie on the floor of the post office when the robbers demanded that everyone got down. Shots were fired and she was hit by one of five shots fired by the RUC and mortally wounded. She died shortly afterwards. She was a tragic victim of crossfire between armed robbers and the police. The *Glasgow Herald* of the 29th reported:

> She was killed during an exchange of shots between an RUC patrol and two masked men who managed to shoot their way out of trouble. A number of people accused the police of firing indiscriminately into the post office even after the raiders had fled ... John Grimes [postmaster] said: 'I was lying on the floor behind the counter when the shooting started. I did not see what happened." Mr Gregory Lagan who was in a shop across the street said: "There were 10 or 12 burst of gunfire, but it is hard to say who fired the first shots."

In September 2012, the case was raised again, when RUC officer Colin Keys sued the RUC/PSNI over a psychiatric disorder he says he suffered following exposure to the terrorist campaign in Northern Ireland. He claimed in court that police chiefs allegedly knew about an armed robbery which led to a pensioner being killed in 1983 but failed to give a proper warning in order to protect an informant, the High Court was told. It is thought that it referred to the murder of Mrs Foster. Mr Keys was one of 5,500 former and serving members of the RUC and PSNI who took a group action over post-traumatic stress suffered during exposure to the Troubles in Northern Ireland. The officers believed they secured victory five years ago when a judge ruled there had been systematic failures within the force. But any hopes of a multi-million pound compensation award were then dealt a crushing blow when 10 test cases were rejected.

Setting out the PSNI application, it was stated: "The essence of the issue is that the plaintiff wishes to include in this action a claim for negligence to the effect that on 28 November 1983 an armed robbery occurred at Pomeroy Post Office when the plaintiff was exposed to an exchange of gunfire with armed terrorists and during which an elderly woman was killed and others were injured." The allegation was that senior RUC officers knew about the armed robbery in advance and did not provide proper warning of the imminent attack to the officer involved in the shoot-out because of the need to protect the identity of a police informant. The case is apparently continuing and the outcome was not known at the time of publication.

The final death of the month was Lance Corporal Simon James Roberts (19) of the 5th Regiment Army Air Corps who was killed in an RTA in the Province on the same day as Mrs Foster's death. He was from Holywell in Flintshire and is buried at Gorsedd Church Cemetery in Wales.

November had ended with 13 deaths; three of those killed were soldiers and four were police officers. A total of six of the dead were civilians, three of whom were Catholics and three were Protestants. Five of the civilian deaths were overtly sectarian in nature. Nine of the deaths were at the hand of Republican paramilitaries and two were at the hands of Loyalists.

48

December

In the season of goodwill, the Provisional IRA showed none at all as they helped kill the majority of the 16 people to die in this month; it was the month of the Harrods' bomb in London's fashionable Knightsbridge which killed three members of the Metropolitan Police Force as well as an American tourist. Three Republican terrorists were killed and two members of the Irish security forces also died; an Irish soldier and a member of the Gardaí Síochána.

The SAS – or an undercover unit of the Army – were in action on the 4th day of November, when two Provisionals were shot dead at Clonoe Road/ Cloghodg Road in Coalisland, Co Tyrone. Acting upon information from an informant within the Tyrone and Fermanagh Brigade, an arms cache was under observation by several units of soldiers. By this stage of the conflict, the Provisionals were working on a tighter structure based on smaller cells and a strict 'need to know' basis. For this reason, one has to suspect that the informant was well-placed within the Brigade.

Colm McGirr (22) and Brian Campbell (19) were PIRA members and had gone to one of their arms caches in the Magheramulkenny area close to Coalisland. Campbell's brother Seamus was one of the prisoners who escaped from the Maze a few months previously and was very much a high profile player as a result. Soldiers were dug in around the cache following the tip off and, in the early hours of the morning, they observed a car pull up, containing three men. McGirr and Campbell went straight to a hedge where the weapons were hidden. McGirr unwrapped an American Armalite and passed it to the other volunteer and had just turned to return to the waiting car when they were challenged by soldiers. According to reports, McGirr – who had also collected a shotgun – turned towards the soldier who clearly felt threatened and under any interpretation of ROE was entitled to fire and indeed did so. McGirr was hit over a dozen times by automatic fire and died instantly. Campbell was hit twice and died at the scene. Two shots were also fired at the car in which the third terrorist was seeking to make a getaway and the driver was wounded but managed to escape. The car was later found abandoned with shattered windscreen and bloodstained seats. The Provisionals made a later statement, full of the usual hyperbole and accusations of 'cold-blooded executions' etc., and stated that the injured driver – a good, reliable and independent witness if there ever was one – had informed them that the shootings took place without warning or preamble before the two dead men had even collected the weapons. A tame Catholic priest was also wheeled out to claim that the bodies were found at the entrance to the field containing the cache, and that they were en-route to collect the weapons and were therefore defenceless.

McGirr was already dead, but Campbell was still breathing and the unit's medic tried to save his life; he dressed a wound in his shoulder and also inserted a breathing tube into his throat. However, the badly wounded man went into shock and died within five minutes as the soldier worked on him. Interestingly enough, this is ignored in subsequent – and coloured – Republican accounts of the incident. The author of *Blood and Rage* refers to the Armalite which both dead PIRA men had handled, which "had been used in 22 attacks on security forces since 1979 including four killings of off-duty policemen in and around Dungannon."[1]

There is much talk of 'shoot-to-kill' and 'cold-blooded executions' but these were difficult times. The men watching McGirr and Campbell were professional and superbly trained and were aware that the men at the arms cache were terrorists who would kill without hesitation if they had the edge; on this occasion, it was the undercover soldiers who had the edge. It is true that they could have had the men arrested later by the RUC but in exceptional, life-or-death situations such as these, they would have considered – correctly, in my opinion – their own safety to be paramount. Additionally, the end result was also two fewer terrorists to inflict pain and misery on the people of Northern Ireland. As Burleigh writes: "If it is true that the British Army ensured that the PIRA never achieved its basic fundamental objective, this was in no small part due to Special-Forces operations which made it very tricky for terrorists to operate."[2]

During the research process, one must trawl through site after site, especially on Republican websites and one does read the most inappropriate nonsense. The essence of some of the comments from supporters on PIRA and INLA sites, is that their 'Volunteer' was gunned down in 'cold blood' and despite being unarmed 'was given no chance to surrender.' Often there is the cry from a loved ones such as 'Why didn't they just arrest my boy?' These sites are both sycophantic and incredibly blinkered; they also ooze with hypocrisy. How many soldiers or policemen were given the opportunity to surrender? How many were unarmed when shot dead by Republican terrorists? The question is purely rhetorical because the answer is a deafening: none!

The following is an example of such terrorist rhetoric and is taken from *An Phoblacht* (Republican News):

> On 4 December 1983, at the height of the crown forces' shoot-to-kill policy, two unarmed IRA Volunteers were summarily executed by undercover British operatives. Nineteen-year-old Brian Campbell and 23–year-old Colm McGirr from Coalisland, County Tyrone, were gunned down in a hail of bullets on Sunday afternoon 4 December 1983 by an undercover SAS squad, seconds after they left their car to check an IRA arms dump off the Cloghodg Road. The fact that the SAS was in the immediate vicinity of the dump showed they had awaited the arrival of the Volunteers and executed them on the spot without any attempt to arrest or detain them.[3]

---

1   Burleigh, Michael, *Blood and Rage: A Cultural History of Terrorism* (London: HarperCollins, 2009), p.329.

2   *Blood and Rage.*

3   *Source:* http://www.anphoblacht.com/contents/14489

On 5 December, the UVF targeted and killed an INLA member and in the process, badly wounded his two brothers. That the Republican terrorist had just visited the Labour Exchange in order to draw his weekly dole money may appear somewhat of a surprise to some people, but to those who are cogniscant of the hypocrisy of the Republicans – bash the Brits but accept their welfare hand-outs – it is accepted and known. The incongruity of this is hard to swallow. The Unemployment Office is called the 'Buru' or 'Bru' (from Unemployment Bureau) in local slang, someone unemployed draws 'the Bru'. Joseph 'Joe' Craven (25) was an INLA gunman who might be said to have 'understandably' joined the ranks of the Republican paramilitaries. On 18 June, 1976, his father – Robert Craven– was killed in a UVF bomb blast at Conway's Bar, Shore Road, Belfast.[4]

As Craven and his brothers, John and Michael returned home to the Nationalist Bawnmore area, two UVF men on a stolen motor bike approached the three men and the pillion passenger opened fire with an automatic weapon. The burst of shots killed Craven and wounded his two brothers as they walked along the road in Newtownabbey, North Belfast. The UVF dumped the stolen motorbike in nearby Rathcoole, so one must assume that it was a Unit from this Loyalist area which carried out the attack.

Despite an IRSP promise not to turn the funeral into a paramilitary display, Craven's coffin was carried outside his Bawnmore home draped in the Starry Plough flag and the traditional black beret and gloves. Father Brendan McGee refused to accompany the coffin to Milltown and RUC officers naturally moved in, trying to prevent the para-military display. Consequently, clashes occurred between the mourners and the police. The coffin was eventually carried away by mourners with the beret, gloves, and Starry Plough flag on top. The author has seen a photograph of the dead PIRA man in his coffin, flanked by an 'honour guard' of two masked INLA terrorists. His face is adorned by rosary beads and the 'Starry Plough' and aforementioned gloves and beret rest on top. The killing was later claimed by the Protestant Action Force, which as most will under-stand was a flag of convenience for the UVF.

On the 7th, the Provisionals assassinated a leading Loyalist politician and sitting MP for Belfast South; Edgar Graham, MP (29) was shot dead outside Queen's University. During the morning, he was chatting to UUP party and Queen's colleague Dermot Nesbitt at the University Square side of the main campus library. As they conversed, he was approached by two men who had just got out of a parked car; without hesitation, they shot him twice in the head. He died almost instantly. The *Belfast Telegraph* published a photograph of the dead man on its front page; it shows a UDR soldier looking on and the MP's body covered in black plastic sheeting, his briefcase sitting almost forlornly alongside him. The newspaper poignantly reprinted a copy of Mr Graham's about-to-be posted Christmas cards on the same page. Three weeks earlier, the MP had addressed Stormont and told them that he had evidence that the Provisionals had liaised with Loyalist paramilitaries in a conspiracy to murder a leading Unionist; although he did not name himself as the target, it was generally accepted that it was himself to whom he referred. The newspaper reported that he had been offered personal protection, but that he had declined the offer.

---

4   See Wharton, Ken M., *Wasted Years, Wasted Lives* (Solihull: Helion, 2013), Vol 1. *The author erroneously refers to Robert Craven as Robert Conway on page 216, and sincerely apologises for this error.

An eyewitness told the newspaper about hearing shots and seeing the flash: "I looked across the street and saw a man curled up on the pavement. Another man was standing on the wall outside the students' library with a gun in his hand. I think there were two others behind him. They all ran off".

Two persons were later convicted of withholding evidence from the police, but no one was ever convicted for the MP's murder. The gunmen fled as Mr Graham lay in a fast-spreading pool of his own blood. A Sinn Féin/IRA statement that: "his killing should be a salutary lesson to those Loyalists who stand foursquare behind the laws and forces of oppression of the nationalist people." PIRA observers have speculated that his murder was because of aid and advice he had reportedly given to the Northern Ireland Prison Service.

Former IRA member turned police informer Sean O'Callaghan suggested that the IRA killed Mr Graham because he was "potentially the most effective political opponent facing Sinn Féin that the Ulster Unionists had yet produced,"[5] and a likely candidate for future leadership of the UUP party. There was much speculation that the Provisionals had many dickers within the Queen's University student population and it was further rumoured that they had a leading member actually working on the staff of the University.

Seanad Éireann is the upper house of the Oireachtas (the Irish Parliament), which also comprises the President of Ireland and Dáil Éireann (the Lower House). In the direct wake of Mr Graham's murder, a Senator made the following statement:

> I would like the Seanad to note with horror and dismay the death of the Assemblyman, Edgar Graham, who was murdered outside Queen's University, Belfast, this morning. It has been said by a noted writer that in the death of every man each of us dies a little. I think this is horribly true for us here in Ireland today that for every one of these victims of violence not only do we die a little but our hopes for our country die a little with every one of these outrages.

On the following day, the Fair Employment Agency (FEA) announced the startlingly unsurprising 'fact' that Roman Catholics were under-represented in the higher levels of the Northern Ireland Civil Service. That statement might well apply to the under representation of Catholics in most occupations, other those at the lower end of the occupational scale.

On the 10th, a bomb exploded at the Royal Artillery Barracks in London, injuring five people. The blast was claimed by the Scottish Liberation Army – and in their acronym SLA there was another set of initials to add the already bulging lexicon of the Troubles – but in reality, the blast was likely prepared, funded and planted by the IRA's England team. Just before dawn, the device exploded close to the Guardroom at the Royal Artillery Barracks in Woolwich, South East London. The explosion injured five people and caused minor damage to the building and left a crater 15 feet deep. A Christmas party was underway in the Sergeants' Mess, around 300 yards away, and most of those injured were taking part at the time. The SLA claimed responsibility for the bombing, with their spokesman warning that more attacks were likely against "the

---

5　O'Callaghan, Sean, *The Informer* (London: Corgi Books, 1999).

enemies of Scotland." Scotland Yard believed that the IRA was behind the attack, and the Republican terror group indeed later claimed responsibility. The SLA was a largely crank organisation consisting of a few drunken anarchists in a cellar somewhere in Edinburgh, adorned by posters of Chè Guevara.

Local pub owner John Clark who was amongst guests at the Sergeants' Mess party told the US Newspaper, the *Gainesville Sun*: "It was just a mass of glass and debris [after the blast]. There was a dull thump. I don't think that anyone realised that it was a bomb at first."

The SLA, or as it is sometimes known the SNLA and has been dubbed the 'Tartan Terrorists', was a militant group which aimed to bring about Scottish independence from the UK. The SLA/SNLA has been proscribed by the British Government. The group was founded by Adam Busby, a former soldier from Paisley after the 1979 devolution referendum, which the organisation claimed was fixed. Their statement read: "We warn the British that no mercy will be shown to the enemies of Scotland. The SNLA will carry out a full-scale bombing campaign in London and other major towns and cities." Despite the initial concern, some soldiers were able to find humour in the situation:

Andy Liptrot, Royal Artillery
I was in Woolwich barracks at the time, and if memory serves me right, it was placed by wall of the guardroom. All people in the barracks had to muster on the parade ground in whatever they were wearing at the time, and it was around about midnight. There were several Women's Royal Army Corps (WRAC) based on the barracks at the time, and they had to join us on a freezing night, still dressed in their nightwear. It was a sight I won't forget in a hurry, as there was plenty places to hang your hat on that parade ground that night.

The murder of a Protestant by members of a Protestant/Loyalist paramilitary group on the evening of the 12th in North-West Belfast was seen as score-settling rather than part of an internal struggle. John Molloy (21) lived in Tyndale Gardens, just off the Ballysillan Road in the Oldpark area; on the night that he was killed by UFF gunmen he was relaxing at home on what was his 21st and final birthday. It is thought that a family member had crossed the local UDA and several other family members had been intimidated out of the area by Loyalist bully-boys. Molloy obviously thought that the 'banning order' did not apply to him and refused to leave Oldpark. Gunmen burst into his house as he watched television and shot him dead in his own living room.

Earlier in the day of Mr Molloy's murder, the Political Committee of the European Parliament held the first of a series of meetings to consider its draft report on Northern Ireland. The Rapporteur was Mr N.J. Haagerup and the report called for power-sharing and the preparation of a plan by the, then, European Economic Community (EEC) to aid the economic development of Northern Ireland. The Committee had been asked to prepare the report on 23 February 1983. The report was passed by the European Parliament on 29 March 1984.

On the same evening, or in the early hours of the next day, there was an absolutely inexcusable shooting of a young Catholic by an apparently drunken and off-duty RUC officer. This author is well known for his support of the RUC but is unable to offer any support in the killing of Tony Dawson (18) in East Belfast. The teenager was standing outside a social club in Madrid Street chatting with with friends when a car pulled up alongside them and four shots were fired from the vehicle hitting him. The RUC man who carried out the shooting was later arrested, and when his gun was shown to be the one used in the killing he was charged with murder. He claimed at his trial he had been drunk and had a row with his wife and drove off in a bad temper. Driving through the nationalist Short Strand area he said he spotted a social club he knew from patrolling the area and turned his car around, and coming upon the group of youths he opened fire. Mountpottinger RUC is only minutes away and officers were quickly on the scene. The officer who had carried out the killing was quickly arrested and taken to Townhall Street RUC station to be charged. The trial of the RUC man – Constable Thomas Andrews – lasted only twelve minutes; he said he couldn't remember much about the incident. He was convicted for the killing. The disgraced police officer had earlier denied the killing, but as reported in the *Glasgow Herald*, he changed his plea in Court.

The newspaper reported:

> in a 12 minute hearing, it was stated that police forensic tests had matched the bullets used to kill the teenager with that from Andrews' police issue revolver. The Judge, Mr Justice Hutton said excessive drinking in various clubs had contributed to the crime. "It inflamed your mind and influenced you to commit this terrible crime," he told Andrews. The defendant's wife wept in the court room as sentence was passed and after hearing that her husband's drinking has also had a serious effect on their marriage.[6]

His wife had been in the car, but following a heated argument, she got out of the car and walked off. Andrews then drove around and found himself in Madrid Street outside the aforementioned social club. He was sentenced to life imprisonment. It is very easy to be sympathetic to the policeman, in that service fighting terrorism in Belfast may well have been a contributing factor in his excess drinking and that the row with his wife may well have tipped him, emotionally, over the edge. However, Anthony 'Tony' Dawson had a right to life and one cannot condone his murder.

The scene then switched to the Irish Republic as Gardaí and Irish Army closed in on the house where kidnapped US Executive Don Tidey was being held.[7] Irish Security Forces were deployed to Derrada Wood in Ballinamore, Co Leitrim, south-west of Co Cavan. Sean O'Callaghan claims that he was involved in the planning to the kidnap and tipped off his contact in Gardaí Special Branch as to the approximate location of the kidnap gang.[8] He further alleges that Gerry 'I was never in the IRA' Adams as then Chief of Staff, "must have known" about the kidnap. Something of this magnitude would have had to been approved by the leadership of the organisation. As Irish Security Forces moved in, there was a burst of gunfire and an Irish soldier – Private Patrick 'Paddy' Kelly was hit and mortally wounded. One of the soldiers involved in the attack – Corporal Patrick Shine – stated later that he heard a burst of gunfire and saw Private Kelly fall backwards against the trees and as his head went back he saw blood on his

---

6   *Glasgow Herald* (10 September 1985).
7   See Chapter 47.
8   In his book *The Informer*.

neck. He himself dived for cover, and he heard Private Kelly calling 'Paddy,' but there was then a loud explosion, which sounded like a hand grenade, and he put his hands over his head. A gunman then appeared with his rifle pointed at him and told him to drop his own rifle. "I thought the people were desperate enough to get out, that they would have shot me as well," he said. He later escaped from the gunman. Another burst of gunfire cut down a trainee Gardaí – Gary Sheehan (22) – who died almost immediately. One of the gang was confronted by a policeman and threatened to shoot Mr Tidey; the officer threw himself at the terrorist who then shot him in the leg, before abandoning the gang's victim and running off across fields. A further policeman was hit and wounded, before the PIRA kidnap gang raced off in a stolen car and escaped the tightening cordon. Mr Tidey was found in a dishevelled state – there are reports that a member of the gang had sliced off his ear – and was barely able to croak out the words: "Tidey; hostage." He was taken to the Gardaí station in nearby Ballyconnell before being taken under heavy police guard to hospital. Constable Gary Sheehan was single, but the Irish soldier killed with him was married and was the father of four children.

Margaret Thatcher congratulated the Taoiseach saying: "I am glad that the persistence and dedication shown by the Gardaí and the Irish Army during the search for Mr Tidey has been rewarded. I understand that great gallantry was displayed by those who released Mr Tidey. I offer my congratulations to all concerned."[9]

Maze escaper and one of the masterminds of the 1981 hunger strike, Brendan 'Bic' McFarlane was eventually tried for his part in the kidnapping and subsequent shoot-out in Ballinamore. The trial collapsed after incriminating statements he allegedly made following his arrest were ruled inadmissible. No one was ever convicted of the soldier's killing. Whilst the trial was in progress, Mr Tidey himself gave evidence. He graphically described the 'battleground' he found himself in when security forces rescued him from his kidnappers. Mr Tidey heard a burst of gunfire, followed by more gunfire and an explosion, after Gardaí and soldiers surrounded the hideout where he had been held captive for 23 days. The court also heard that Gardaí found three rifles, a Steyr submachine gun and parts of a Soviet-made fragmentation grenade in the woods, but never recovered the automatic weapons fired at Private Kelly and recruit Gardaí Gary Sheehan. O'Callaghan also claims that one of the kidnap gang was Francie McGirl who had been acquitted of the murder of Lord Mountbatten some four years earlier.[10]

On the day after the shoot-out, the *Belfast Telegraph* described how the freed hostage's happiness was tinged with sadness at the death of two members of the Security Forces who forced his release at the cost of their young lives. The Irish Taoiseach spent an hour with Mr Tidey and his family and was said to be pleased at the outcome. The supermarket man's family were reported as being 'delighted' to have him back safe and sound, although they too, expressed regret at the loss of the soldier and his police colleague. O'Callaghan claims that money was paid to the IRA by Tidey's company – possibly as 'insurance' against a future kidnapping, and that Southern Command seemed to be cash-rich very shortly afterwards.

During the 2010 Irish Presidential election, Private Kelly's eldest son, David, confronted Sinn Féin candidate and former IRA commander, Martin McGuinness.

9   Reported in the *Belfast Telegraph,* 17 December, 1983.
10   See *Wasted Years, Wasted Lives,* Vol 2.

The man once known as the 'Butcher of the Creggan' denied knowing the killers, and that he was a member of the IRA Council at the time. Kelly called him a liar, saying that before there could be any reconciliation, there had to be truth. He angrily declared: "I want truth today. Murder is murder." He went on to describe the former Creggan IRA commander's bid for the Irish Presidency as 'an obscenity.' He added: "I feel sympathy for all people who were killed by the Provisional IRA over the years – Detective Garda Jerry McCabe in Limerick and all the other people." Mr. McGuinness later responded to the incident, stating that: "As a Republican leader I have never and would never stand over attacks on the Garda Síochána or the Defence Forces." More significantly, however, he refused to condemn the killings of Kelly and Sheehan. After the murder of a Gardaí informer – Dean Corcoran on 23 March, 1985 – Sean O'Callaghan claims that McGuinness secretly congratulated him on the 'execution' thinking that he (O'Callaghan) was responsible.[11] In July 2012, Justice Minister Alan Shatter posthumously awarded the Military Star medal to the family of Private Paddy Kelly.

A tragedy on the mainland was simply waiting to happen and the wheels were already in motion for the Harrods' bombing on 17 December. Before that could happen, the Provisionals were busy in Co Londonderry. Lance Corporal Brown Vance McKeown (40), father of two was a part-time UDR soldier who lived in Maghera, Co Londonderry. Dickers already knew that he was a soldier and that he drove daily from his home in Hall Crescent near to Tobermore Road to a small supermarket on Coleraine Road, a drive of less than 300 yards in his Morris Mini, car. On the day of his death, he had allowed his 13-year-old to come with him to work in the pre-Christmas period in order to earn money for presents. At around 1800 hours on the 17th, armed PIRA men were waiting in the small car park attached to the supermarket and as the part-time soldier and his son got into the car in order to drive home, they sprayed the windscreen with automatic fire. Brown McKeown was killed almost immediately and by some miracle, his son suffered only glass cuts, but the psychological harm as will be shown in a moment was irreparable. The men raced off in a stolen car and later there were angry words from MP, William McCrea; he pointed the finger at the dickers who had done everything bar pull the triggers on the PIRA weapons. He said: "As far as I am concerned, 102,000 citizens of this Province have their hands and conscience stained with blood. It is a fact that the IRA could not survive without this active and passive support."

Those words were followed by even angrier ones – justifiably so – from Magherafelt Councillor Ivan Linton. He told the *Belfast Telegraph*:

> It is a real miracle that 13-year-old Darren McKeown escaped alive. I believe that every effort should be made by the security forces in this area to wipe out these known terrorists and round up the suspects. There is definitely someone living in Maghera who has to bear the responsibility for this because they set him up for someone else to do the dirty deed. I am disgusted and horrified.

The author understands that the soldier's son, who was 13 at the time of his father's murder, suffered grave emotional problems as a result of witnessing the attack. One can only imagine what this boy suffered, not only at the shock of having high-velocity rounds flying past his face, but also in seeing his father's bloodstained body and at seeing his life ebb away in seconds. It was stated back in 1992, some nine years after the attack, that it was unlikely that he would ever lead a normal life again.

THE HARRODS' BOMB

Harrods, as many British and indeed foreign readers will be aware is an upmarket department store located in Brompton Road in Knightsbridge. The store occupies a five-acre site and has over one million square feet of selling space in over 330 departments making it the biggest department store in Europe. As such, PIRA's England team saw it as a prime target for attack and chose Saturday December 17, the last weekend before Christmas, as they knew that the store and the area would be packed with Christmas shoppers. Around lunchtime, members of the bombing team drove a stolen Austin 1300 to Hans Crescent, primed the bomb and then walked off, their consciences presumably clear and uncaring of the carnage which was about to unfold. Hans Crescent is on the western side of the store where the side entrance is located; on this particular day, the main entrance would have been extremely busy. Not only this, but the PIRA 'sleepers' would have also been aware that Hans Crescent led into Sloane Street and would have been a popular cut-through for wealthy customers from Sloane Square, Belgravia Square, Cadogan Square and other nearby affluent areas. Killing ordinary Londoners would be good; killing a few 'blue bloods' would merely be a bonus.

Using accepted code words, an IRA member telephoned a warning through to Scotland Yard via the Samaritans; with the bomb due to explode in minutes, the timing was wholly inadequate and the caller was deliberately vague about the bomb's location. The 'warning' as such was designed to lure the police and shoppers towards the actual blast site and thus maximise the death and injuries. At approximately 1322 hours, the device in the car – 30 lb of explosives – detonated. One minute earlier, four police officers in a car, a dog handler, and an officer on foot approached the suspect vehicle when the bomb exploded. The police car absorbed much of the blast, probably reducing further casualties, but five people were killed more or less instantly and a sixth person was fatally wounded. The civilians killed were: Philip Geddes (24); Kenneth Salvesden (28) and Caroline Kennedy (25) mother of one. The Police officers were: Sergeant Noel Lane (28) and Woman Police Constable Jane Arbuthnot (22). Their colleague Inspector Stephen Dodd (34) was terribly injured and died a week later on Christmas Eve. Another Police Officer was caught in the blast but survived; Constable Jon Gordon was maimed in the explosion, losing both legs and part of a hand. Many more people were injured, some very badly. A total of nine children, including two sets of young siblings were badly hurt; out of a total of 92 casualties, 10 were very seriously hurt. Amongst the severely injured was an Irish-American: Mark McDonald from Michigan. He was later visited by Prince Charles and Princess Diana in hospital.

Britain's press reaction was justifiably predictable but the Monday morning edition of the Daily Express in true 'Spirit of the Blitz' mentality lead with: 'Business As Usual!'

There was a front-page interview with the mother of the dead policewoman. The article read:

> Dedicated WPC Jane Arbuthnot was the first police woman in Britain to be murdered by the IRA. Yesterday her grief-stricken mother vowed to visit Harrods where her 22-year-old daughter died. Her pilgrimage will back up her defiant message for the terrorists: "Nothing is going to stop us walking the streets of London," said 54-year-old Mrs Susan Arbuthnot. "My daughter has not been killed for people to stay away – that's important. The last thing we want is these IRA people bringing London to a halt. The Germans didn't manage it, neither will the Irish."

Included in the main article was an equally defiant comment:

> It will be business as usual throughout Britain today. The IRA bomb outrage which brought death and horror to London is not going to force any High Street store to put up the shutters. This was the message from all major stores last night – including Harrods of Knightsbridge. Less than 48 hours after the horrific blast which killed five people outside the store, the debris has been cleared up and Harrods too, will be back in business … Henry Sheppard said: "The only way that the terrorist will win is if people stay at home. I am sure that there will be millions in Oxford Street shopping this week, beginning tomorrow. We will all be open for them."

Michael Battye of Reuters wrote: "There was a colossal explosion, a huge ball of fire and then a pall of dirty smoke. Glass rained down like a hailstorm. People scattered in panic, screaming. There were hundreds and hundreds of people in the street." The *Belfast Telegraph* reported:

> The blast which was heard some miles away, is understood to have destroyed large areas from the ground to the fourth floor of the building and 24 cars in the street were said to be damaged. Some were on fire. The explosion left dozens of people scattered around with injuries. Ambulances were ferrying the injured to St Stephen's Hospital in Fulham and other London hospitals were standing by.

The newspaper interviewed Emma Lovell, a survivor of the blast, who said:

> I had just come out of the shop when it happened. There was an enormous explo-sion – the sound of breaking glass and people screaming. It hit the back of my head. I just went down to the pavement and stayed there trying to protect myself until the glass stopped flying around. I just thought: I must get out of here. I thought there might be another – that was the main thought in my mind. I just started running and ended up here.

('Here' was in the back of a police car where she was having wounds to the back of her head and to her knees dressed by police officers.)

It was also revealed that one of the dead – Philip Geddes – was a journalist for the *Daily Express* itself and that Kenneth Salvesden was an American who was living and working in London. The *Express* continued the story on several pages inside and under a headline of 'Debris of Death' journalists John McCormick and Alan Rees wrote:

> It was the day after an IRA car bomb had killed five people and terrorised hundreds of Christmas shoppers and the debris of death still littered nearby streets as Home Secretary Leon Brittan went personally to see the devastation. The day after and blood had mixed with rainwater in Hans Crescent where the bomb exploded. The wrecks of dozens of cars including three Rolls-Royces and Mercedes littered the area as silent symbols of the latest IRA outrage. The car in which the time bomb was planted, a modest Austin 1300, was unrecognisable, only its front wheels were intact. The rest, split into two halves six feet apart, might have been put through a crusher at a scrapyard.
>
> The blast was so severe that parts of the car were blown on to a 6th floor balcony of a building 60 yards away … on the other side of the road. The day after, slivers of glass and ripped up tarmac faced a team of clean-up workmen, with a seemingly endless task. Almost every pane of glass on the Hans Crescent side of Harrods had been shattered and eight of the store's green and gold canopies either hung in tatters or had been ripped off. In the middle of the road, lay a pile of heads, limbs and torsos from broken tailors' dummies – a grim reminder of the people who suffered a similar fate in the huge explosion.

The *Daily Express* then included eyewitness statements, all of which conveyed the true horror, the human story side of the outrage; a selection from their 19 December issue read as follows:

> Suddenly the whole place erupted. All the shop windows seemed to fall out. I seemed to be the only person standing. There were bodies everywhere. I saw a policewoman lying there. Two policemen were lying near her. There was blood all over the place. I saw a woman with her legs bright red. She had a huge lump of glass in her stomach. (Annie Eyston)
>
> I was blown in the air and smashed against a plate-glass window. A poor man selling chestnuts on the corner was in a terrible state – his legs were dangling off. (Godwin Miceli)
>
> There was a policeman sitting in the car; we could see him bending down. Suddenly there was a ball of flame and the whole of the car lifted up. (Gerald Westbury)

Nik Lawrence, another survivor, was in the Harrods store when the bomb went off:

> I had crossed the whole of London to get to Harrods after failing to get the book I wanted for my Dad for Christmas. I figured Harrods must have it. I had just walked past a first-floor window when the bomb went off in the street outside. It was literally a 'bang' sound, but furiously loud. The window blew in but the glass was caught by the special net curtains, weighted at the bottom. If it hadn't I would

have been cut to pieces. A mother clutched her two children in terror at the top of the stairs. I was strangely calm and tried to calm her but couldn't.

I knew a bomb had gone off but it still didn't register exactly what that meant. Then an employee arrived with customers in tow, he was leading us out. We came out the side entrance into the street which had the bomb, and that's when I realised what it meant. I glanced down the side street and saw cars were on fire with black smoke billowing. There were people sitting down being tended to by others. I couldn't imagine anything surviving that blizzard of glass shards. Sirens were wailing closer as I walked away. I got into the tube. Somebody said "they've bombed Harrods" and people started to talk about it but I didn't say anything.

An Associated Press report at the time stated that: "People were … running from the scene, their faces absolutely covered in blood; children, old people, men and women." (Jackie McPherson). "There was a tremendous explosion. There was blood everywhere. One policeman had an eye hanging from its socket. He was very brave. I can't describe the horror of it." (Michael Francis).

The newspaper then paid tribute to one of their young journalists who had been killed in the blast:

Daily Express reporter Philip Geddes died in the horror blast at Harrods while doing his job. Philip, 24, one of the William Hickey team, was shopping with his girlfriend Jane Beaton when he heard about a bomb warning and went to investigate. Minutes later he was caught in the carnage. Heartbroken Jane said: "He was always chasing stories; that was his life. He was dedicated. We had been shopping all morning in Harrods and I was to have lunch with my parents then we were going to meet again. My last words to him were 'I'll leave you to buy my present then'."

PIRA's Army Council made a statement within days admitting the bombing, but claiming that it had not been sanctioned and that the ASU had acted independently. The full statement read:

The Harrods operation was not authorised by the Irish Republican Army. We have taken immediate steps to ensure that there will be no repetition of this type of operation again. The volunteers involved gave a 40 minutes specific warning, which should have been adequate. But due to the inefficiency or failure of the Metropolitan Police, who boasted of foreknowledge of IRA activity, this warning did not result in an evacuation. We regret the civilian casualties, even though our expression of sympathy will be dismissed.

These were empty words from the Godfathers of a sick and ruthless terrorist organisation, and would have been received very badly by the loved ones of those injured and killed and treated with absolute cynicism by most of the population. Irish Republican terror at its most toxic had been revealed yet again. However, there is a very clear dissenting voice – from someone close the centre of power within the Provisionals – and Sean O'Callaghan rubbishes the claim that it was a 'maverick operation.' He writes:

Such was the shock and anger both in the United Kingdom and the Irish Republic that the IRA was reluctant to take responsibility: suggestions were leaked to the media that the bombing had not been authorised by the IRA leadership. These were untrue. The subsequent inquiry within the IRA – the results of which I heard from Doherty – found that specific permission had been given to bomb Harrods, which was seen as a symbol of the British establishment.[12]

O' Callaghan suggests that the high loss of civilian life did not accord with the IRA's plans and they would have been aware of the detrimental effect the carnage would have, particularly among their Irish-American supporters. The same author claims that Limerick Provisional Kieran Dwyer was unhappy about the operation, in that it had not caused sufficient casualties. It is suggested that Dwyer said that the IRA ASU should have driven a lorry packed with explosives to Harrods and issued no warnings. This would have killed a few hundred and "really given the Brits something to whine about."

In response to this statement, British Home Secretary Leon Brittan responded: "The nature of a terrorist organisation is that those in it are not under disciplined control!" Sir Kenneth Newman, then Metropolitan Police Commissioner, said: "The IRA statement of regret is contemptible … had they not maliciously misled by giving false locations five families would not now be tragically bereaved and 91 people would have not suffered injuries, scarring them for the rest of their lives. The IRA call to the Samaritans was not a warning; it was an invitation to death."

The following is taken from 'Hansard' (the Journal record of the House of Commons) and contains the bulk of the Home Secretary's statement:
With permission, Mr Speaker, I should like to make a statement about the bomb incident in Knightsbridge last Saturday afternoon.

At 12.41 PM on Saturday, 17 December, the central London Samaritans received a telephone message that the IRA had placed a car bomb outside Harrods and that there were two bombs inside Harrods, one in Oxford Street and another in Littlewoods store in Oxford Street. The telephone call was made by a man with an Irish accent, and a code word previously unknown to the police authorities was used to preface the message. As subsequent events showed, much of the message was false. In addition, the police had already received 22 other similar messages earlier that day about suspicious devices, all of which turned out to be false alarms.

The Samaritans passed on the message to New Scotland Yard at 12.44 PM. At 12.48 PM police units in the three divisions concerned were alerted. The stores were also alerted and put their own contingency procedures into operation. Police on ordinary and special security patrol and traffic duties instantly started a systematic search of the immediate vicinity for suspicious motor vehicles. Some roads were closed to the public and some premises were evacuated. Efforts were also made to establish the authenticity of the code word, but with no success. At Harrods police officers were stationed at each of the doors leading to Hans

12   *The Informer*, pp.236–7.

Crescent to prevent people leaving the store by that route, while the road outside was cleared and searched.

Nothing was found in Oxford Street; but at 1.21 PM a bomb estimated at some 25 lb exploded in a car parked in Hans Crescent. It killed five people: a policeman, a policewoman, a young mother, a reporter and an American citizen. In addition, 92 people were injured, of whom 20 are still in hospital, five of them seriously injured. Of the 92 civilians injured, several were children, of whom two are still in hospital. The bomb also caused extensive damage to property, including many homes in the area and cars parked in the street.

Subsequent investigations have established that the car used was a blue Austin 1300 GT, registration number KFP 252K, which the police are engaged in tracing. The bomb was detonated by a timing device similar to that used in other IRA attacks.

Secretary of State for Northern Ireland, James Prior, confirmed at the time that he had ordered his office to have no contact whatever with Gerry Adams, or any of his associates. Mr Adams steadfastly refused to condemn the bombing.

The men who planted this bomb, in a busy thoroughfare, at a busy time of the main shopping day, at the busiest shopping period of the year and outside an incredibly popular store can only have done so with but one intention: to kill and maim. It was yet another sick attempt by the Provisional IRA's England team to terrorise ordinary people into putting pressure on their Government to abandon Northern Ireland. A warning was telephoned through, but it was vague and deliberately misleading so as to give the police insufficient time to evacuate the people. Because the precise location was unknown, police were innocently herding the shoppers in the direction of the bomb. The Provisionals were old masters of this tactic and their intention was to cause mayhem. Their Irish-American apologists – if you were from Boston, Chicago, New York etc, you would demand the epithet 'supporters' – could then sickeningly claim that their 'Irish brothers' had tried to prevent slaughter by giving adequate warnings. The bombers knew that Irish-American support was crucial, through the NORAID dollars, and the IRA had to be seen to be the brave urban guerrillas that people such as Edward Kennedy, Governor Carey *et al.* portrayed them to be.

During the years covered by this work, the Provisional IRA attempted to bomb London into submission and the attacks on Chelsea Barracks, Hyde Park, Regent's Park and now Harrods – all contained within this book – are adequate and irrefutable evidence of this. This author is not ashamed, for the second time, to reiterate the words of the brave people of London during the Blitz: "Mr Hitler: you can break our walls, but you'll never break our hearts." For 'Mr Hitler' substitute 'Mr Adams' or 'Mr McGuinness.'

The police later disclosed that at the time of the explosion, a second warning call was made by the IRA. The caller stated that a bomb had been left in the C&A department store on the east side of Oxford Street. Police cleared the area and cordoned it off but this claim was found to be false.[13]

---

13 For further information on the outrage, the author recommends: http://www.youtube.com/watch?v=5G_-uQIFBkQ

HARRODS' POSTSCRIPT

Several days after the outrage, the *New York Times* ran the following:

LONDON, Dec. 21— Detectives made a series of dawn raids this morning, arresting four suspected sympathisers of the Irish Republican Army in connection with the explosion outside Harrods last Saturday. Comdr. William Hucklesby of the antiterrorist squad, who is heading the investigation, interviewed the four detainees, who were arrested under the Prevention of Terrorism Act. Under British law their names were not disclosed. Commander Hucklesby is also trying to trace the car, a blue Austin 1300, in which the bomb was planted. The four suspects, who can be detained for up to 48 hours without being formally charged, are being held at the top-security Paddington Green police station, which is ringed by electronic barriers. At least one of the four was reliably reported to be an Irishman.

In 1985, the newspaper *The Observer* published a picture of a prime suspect wanted in connection with the bombing. The report said that he and another suspect were still at large because they escaped last year after shaking off police surveillance. The weekly *Observer* newspaper said that escape had sparked a "furious row between the Scotland Yard department which mounted the surveillance and the anti-terrorist branch, which was unaware of it."

The picture showed the unidentified suspect emerging from a railway station in Northampton, 60 miles northwest of London, with two convicted IRA guerrillas, one of whom was gaoled in 1984 for a 1981 London bomb blitz that killed three people. *The Observer* said the picture was taken by a police undercover agent on 17 January 1984, and hours later, the three men, together with a fourth who was also a Harrods suspect and still at large, escaped after a high-speed car chase.

There it would appear that the trail ran cold and the author understands that no one has ever been charged or convicted with the bomb blast at Harrods on Saturday 17 December, 1983. The men and/or women responsible for one of the worst outrages visited upon London by Irish Republicans remain at large or were gaoled for other offences. Irish Republicanism remained as toxic as ever and their paramilitaries brought great shame to the Irish people. The refusal by politicians such as Gerry Adams to condemn the carnage and the support given by Irish-Americans is shameful. This author remains dumbfounded as to how an entire community in the USA could not recognise this toxic nature demonstrated by the Provisional IRA, fails to recognise how they were taken in so completely and fails to understand the incredible success which NORAID enjoyed in their fund-raising activities. The author's Australian friends cannot understand this author's enmity towards many things American, but especially Irish-American; perhaps perusal of this piece might help.

On the 21st, the UDR lost Private Robert Joseph (21) Alexander Irwin in an RTA in Co Tyrone. The young soldier was on duty when the accident happened. He was buried in his home town of Sixmilecross. The author regretfully has no further information.

On the 24th, Margaret Thatcher paid a six-hour visit to Northern Ireland. During the brief tour Thatcher met Christmas shoppers in Newtownards, Co Down, and visited members of the security forces in Co Armagh and Co Tyrone.She then flew back to England where she presumably spent a cosy Christmas with her family at Chequers, while soldiers and policemen shivered on the streets of Northern Ireland; their turkey and stuffing would have to wait.

With the death of Inspector Todd on Christmas Eve, the killing was over for the month and for the year of 1983. However, just nine days later, with the new Year's Eve hangovers still making their presence felt, a soldier was killed by the Provisional IRA; a familiar pattern.

December ended with 16 deaths; three soldiers died, including one Irish soldier. Four policemen lost their lives; three were mainland officers from the Metropolitan Police and the other was Gardaí Síochána. Six civilians died, including three in London in the Harrods' blast; two Protestants and one Catholic died in Ulster, one of which was overtly sectarian. Three Republican paramilitaries were killed in this month. The Provisional IRA killed 10 people and Loyalists killed two.

1983 DEATHS

British Army	32
Irish Army	1
RUC	17
Other police	4
Civilians	33
Protestant	14
Catholic	16
Republicans	10
Loyalists	3
Prison Officers	1
Total	101

*Of the civilian deaths, 13 could be said to be overtly sectarian.

British Army deaths include former soldiers – usually UDR – killed because of their association with the Security Forces.

Appendix I

Northern Ireland Roll of Honour (1,367 Military Names) 1969-98

N.B. Where the soldier was a member of the T.A. they are included in the roll for their parent Regiment with the TA initials annotated next to them; where known.

RTA: Road Traffic accident
DoW: Died of Wounds

9/12 Lancers

LT JOHN GARNER-RICHARDS	4/04/75:	RTA in Co Armagh in suspicious circumstances
TPR SEAN PRENDERGAST	5/04/77:	IRA landmine in Belleek, Co Fermanagh
SGT ROBERT MAUGHAN	8/05/79:	Shot on undercover duties by IRA, Lisnaskea
SGT PAUL ORAM, MM	21/02/84:	Shot dead on undercover duties by IRA, Co Antrim

13/18 Hussars

TROOPER ROBERT BARRACLOUGH	28/09/75:	RTA
TROOPER PAUL SHEPHERDSON	16/07/78:	RTA
TROOPER PHILIP SMITH	27/07/78:	RTA

14/20 Kings Hussars and 15/19 Kings Royal Hussars

SGT JOHN PLATT	3/02/71:	Killed in RTA following IRA ambush at Aldergrove
CPL IAN ARMSTRONG	29/08/71:	Ambushed at Crossmaglen by IRA
2ND LT ROBERT WILLIAMS-WYNN	13/07/72:	Shot by IRA sniper in West Belfast
TROOPER JOHN TYSON	28/02/74:	RTA
CPL MICHAEL COTTON	20/03/74:	Killed in friendly fire Co Armagh
CPL MICHAEL HERBERT	20/03/74:	Killed in same incident
TROOPER GARY LINES	28/05/79:	RTA

15/19 Hussars

TPR DAVID JOHNSON	18/10/71:	Accidental shooting
TPR JOHN MAJOR	29/11/74:	Death by violent or unnatural causes
SGT WILLIAM ROBSON	7/02/75:	DoW after being shot by IRA at Mullan, Fermanagh

17/ 21st Lancers

TROOPER JAMES DOYLE	24/11/70:	Cause of death unknown; died in Omagh
TROOPER ROBERT GADIE	17/02/71:	RTA at Ballygawley

CPL TERENCE WILLIAMS	5/05/73:	Booby Trap bomb Crossmaglen
TROOPER JOHN GIBBONS	5/05/73:	Killed in same incident
TROOPER KENEALY	14/09/73:	Killed in helicopter accident Gosford Castle

16/5th Lancers

CPL DAVID POWELL	28/10/71:	Bomb attack Kinawley, Co Fermanagh
2/LT ANDREW SOMERVILLE	27/03/73:	IRA landmine near Omagh

5 Regiment Army Air Corps

SGT I C REID	24/06/72:	IRA landmine, Glenshane Pass, Co Antrim
L/CPL D MOON	24/06/72:	Killed in same incident
C/SGT ARTHUR PLACE	18/05/73:	Booby trap bomb, Knock-na-Moe Hotel, Omagh
C.O.FH. BR COX	18/05/73:	Killed in the same incident
SGT DB READ	18/05/73:	Killed in the same incident
WO. D C ROWAT	12/04/74:	Killed in helicopter crash, Co Armagh
MAJOR. J D HICKS	18/12/75:	Aircraft accident
WO. B A JACKSON	7/01/76:	Aircraft accident
CAPTAIN MJ KETT	10/04/78:	Killed in helicopter accident
CAPTAIN. A J STIRLING	2/12/78:	Killed in helicopter accident
CPL. RAYMOND JACKSON	5/07/80:	RTA
CPL BERNARD McKENNA	6/04/82:	Died of natural causes on duty
L/CPL. SIMON J ROBERTS	28/11/83:	RTA
L/CPL. TONY ORANGE	20/10/87:	RTA
S/SGT. JEREMY CROFT	14/08/89:	Violent or unnatural causes

5th Royal Inniskilling Dragoon Guards

SGT FREDERICK WILLIAM DRAKE	3/06/73:	Died of wounds: bomb, Knock-na-Moe Hotel Omagh

Adjutant General's Corps

CPL GLEN A. SLAINE	3/11/95:	RTA
L/CPL PAUL MELLING	3/09/97:	Died whilst on duty

Air Cadet Force

CDT Leonard Cross	11/11/74:	Murdered by the IRA nr Creggan Estate, Londonderry
CPL EDWARD WILSON	26/01/75:	IRA booby trap, Cavehill Road, Belfast
MAJ WILLIAM MCALPINE	05/09/78:	Shot by IRA in Newry, Co Down

Argyll and Sutherland Highlanders

L/CPL DUNCAN MCPHEE	10/09/72:	IRA landmine Dungannon
PTE DOUGLAS RICHMOND	10/09/72:	Killed in same incident
L/CPL WILLIAM MCINTYRE	11/09/72:	DOW from same incident
2nd LT STEWART GARDINER	22/09/72:	Shot by IRA sniper Drumuckavall, Armagh
PTE DAVID HARPER	12/11/72:	Killed by passing train whilst on patrol
CAPT WILLIAM WATSON	20/11/72:	IRA booby trap Cullyhanna
C/SGT JAMES STRUTHERS	20/11/72:	Killed in the same incident
PTE JOHN McGARRY	28/11/72:	Friendly fire
PTE DOUGLAS MCKELVIE	20/08/79:	RTA
CPL OWEN MCQUADE	11/11/80:	Shot outside Altnagelvin hospital, Londonderry
CPL STEWART MARSHALL	20/08/98:	RTA
PTE WILLIAM BROWN	20/08/98:	RTA
PTE STEVEN CRAW.	20/08/98:	RTA

Army Catering Corps

PTE LEONARD THOMPSON	31/12/71:	RTA

PTE RODGER KEALEY	18/06/72:	Killed in Londonderry; death by violent or unnatural causes
SGT PETER GIRVAN	12/02/77:	RTA
L/CPL BARRY HYLTON	17/11/77:	Shot accidentally, Flax Street Mill
PTE GEOFFREY DAVIS	18/07/79:	Death by violent or unnatural
PTE TERENCE M. ADAM	6/12/82:	INLA bomb attack: Droppin' Well, Ballykelly
PTE PAUL JOSEPH DELANEY	6/12/82:	Killed in same incident
PTE JOHN MAYER	19/03/83:	RTA
PTE RICHARD R. BIDDLE	9/04/83:	IRA booby trapped car, Omagh

Army Cadet Force

| CAPTAIN PAUL ROGERS | 19/04/79: | Shot by IRA sniper near the Falls Road, Belfast |

Army Intelligence Corps

CORPORAL PAUL HARMAN ***	14/12/77:	Killed on covert op by IRA Monagh Road, Belfast
CORPORAL JOHN ROESER	31/08/78:	RTA
CORPORAL MICHAEL BLOOR	31/08/78:	Killed in same RTA
CPL MARCUS CHARLES-WILLIAMS	8/11/86:	Cause of death unknown
L/CPL BARRY JACKSON	16/02/88:	Cause of death unknown

Army Physical Training Corps

| WO2 DAVID BELLAMY | 28/10/79: | IRA ambush, Springfield Road, Belfast |

Army Staff

| Col Charles Eaton | 30/06/76: | Thought to have shot whilst off-duty by the IRA |

Black Watch

PTE DAVID STEIN	4/03/71:	Accidental Death
L/CPL EDWIN CHARNLEY	18/11/71:	Shot by sniper in East Belfast
PTE MARK D. CARNIE.	19/07/78:	IRA bomb Dungannon
PTE GEORGE IRELAND	21/06/95:	Death by violent or unnatural causes

Blues & Royals

TROOPER EDWARD MAGGS	25/02/79:	Death by violent or unnatural causes
STAFF CPL JOHN TUCKER	25/02/79:	Death by violent or unnatural causes
TROOPER ANTHONY DYKES	5/04/79:	Shot by IRA snipers, Andersonstown RUC station
TROOPER ANTHONY THORNETT	5/04/79:	Killed in same incident
LT DENIS DALY	20/07/82:	Killed in Hyde Park bomb outrage
TROOPER SIMON TIPPER	20/07/82:	Killed in same incident
L/CPL JEFFERY YOUNG	20/07/82:	Killed in same incident
SQMC R BRIGHT	23/07/82:	DoW from same incident

Cheshire Regiment

CPL DAVID SMITH	4/07/74:	DoW after being shot, Ballymurphy Estate, Belfast
PTE NEIL WILLIAMS	6/12/82:	IRA bomb Droppin' Well pub, Ballykelly
PTE ANTHONY WILLIAMSON	6/12/82:	Killed in same incident
L/CPL DAVID WILSON-STITT	6/12/82:	Killed in same incident
L/CPL STEVEN BAGSHAW	6/12/82:	Killed in same incident
L/CPL CLINTON COLLINS	6/12/82:	Killed in same incident
L/CPL PHILIP MCDONOUGH	6/12/82:	Killed in same incident
PTE DAVID MURREY	6/12/82:	Killed in same incident
PTE STEPHEN SMITH	6/12/82:	Killed in same incident

Coldstream Guards

SGT ANTHONY METCALF	27/08/72:	IRA sniper Creggan Heights, Londonderry
GUARDSMAN ROBERT PEARSON	20/02/73:	Killed by IRA snipers, Lower Falls, Belfast
GUARDSMAN MICHAEL SHAW	20/02/73:	Killed in same incident
GUARDSMAN MICHAEL DOYLE	21/02/73:	Killed by sniper, Fort Whiterock, Belfast
GUARDSMAN ANTON BROWN	6/03/73:	Killed by sniper, Ballymurphy Estate, Belfast
CAPTAIN ANTHONY POLLEN ***	14/04/74:	Shot on undercover mission, Bogside, Londonderry
GUARDSMAN PAUL SIMMONDS	12/01/76:	Accidentally shot, Springmartin RUC base, Belfast
CPL JOHN SPENSLEY	25/12/81:	RTA
CORPORAL TIMOTHY DREWETT*	15/06/84:	Death by violent or unnatural causes
GUARDSMAN STEVEN SHAW	21/01/89:	Shot accidentally
L/CPL SIMON WARE	17/08/91:	IRA landmine explosion, Cullyhanna, Armagh

Devon & Dorset Regiment

PTE CHARLES STENTIFORD	21/01/72:	IRA landmine, Keady, Co Armagh
PTE DAVID CHAMP	10/02/72:	IRA landmine, Cullyhanna, Co Armagh
SGT IAN HARRIS	10/02/72:	Killed in same incident
CPL STEVEN WINDSOR	6/11/74:	Killed by sniper, Crossmaglen
CPL GERALD JEFFERY	7/04/83:	DoW, IRA bomb, Falls Road, Belfast
L/CPL STEPHEN TAVERNER	5/11/83:	Dow, IRA bomb, Crossmaglen
L/Cpl Kenneth Paul DEARLOVE	22/0789:	Death by violent or unnatural causes

Duke of Edinburgh's Royal Regiment

CPL JOSEPH LEAHY	8/03/73:	DoW, booby trap, Forkhill, Co Armagh
S/SGT BARRINGTON FOSTER	23/03/73:	Murdered off-duty by the IRA
CAPTAIN NIGEL SUTTON	14/08/73:	Died in vehicle accident, Ballykinler
PTE MICHAEL SWANICK	28/10/74:	IRA van bomb attack, Ballykinler
PTE BRIAN ALLEN	6/11/74:	Killed by sniper, Crossmaglen
PTE JOHN RANDALL	26/06/93:	Killed by sniper, Newtownhamilton, Co Armagh
L/CPL KEVIN PULLIN	17/07/93:	Killed by sniper, Crossmaglen

Duke Of Wellington's Regiment

PTE GEORGE LEE	6/06/72:	IRA sniper, Ballymurphy Estate, Belfast
CPL TERRENCE GRAHAM	16/07/72:	Landmine attack, Crossmaglen
PTE JAMES LEE	16/07/72:	Killed in same incident
PTE BRIAN ORAM	7/04/73:	RTA
CPL DAVID TIMSON	7/04/73:	Killed in same incident
PTE JOSEPH MCGREGOR	24/05/73:	RTA
WOII PETER LINDSAY	28/08/73:	Unknown
2ND LT HOWARD FAWLEY	25/01/74:	Landmine attack, Ballyronan Co Londonderry
CPL MICHAEL RYAN	17/03/74:	IRA sniper at Brandywell, Londonderry
PTE LOUIS CARROLL	7/04/74:	RTA
CPL ERROL PRYCE	26/01/80:	IRA sniper, Ballymurphy Estate, Belfast
PTE JOHN CONNOR	24/02/88:	Shot by comrade, Palace Barracks, Belfast
PTE JAMES RIGG	25/11/88:	RTA
PTE JASON COST	25/05/95:	Accidentally shot

General Staff

Lt Gen VF Erskine-Crum	18/03/71:	Died on duty

Gloucestershire Regiment

PTE ANTHONY ASPINWALL	17/12/71:	DoW after gun battle in Lower falls area, Belfast
PTE KEITH BRYAN	5/01/72:	IRA sniper, Lower Falls area, Belfast
CPL IAN BRAMLEY	2/02/72:	IRA sniper Hastings Street RUC station, Belfast

PTE GEOFFREY BREAKWELL	17/07/73:	IRA booby trap, Divis St Flats, Belfast
PTE CHRISTOPHER BRADY	17/07/73:	Killed in same incident
L/CPL ANTHONY BENNETT	4/06/78:	Killed in vehicle accident, Limavady
PTE D.J. McCahill	17/08/78:	RTA

Gordon Highlanders

WO2 ARTHUR MCMILLAN	18/06/72:	Booby-trapped house in Lurgan, Co Down
SGT IAN MARK MUTCH	18/06/72:	Killed in same incident
L/CPL COLIN LESLIE	18/06/72:	Killed in same incident
L/CPL A.C. HARPER	8/08/72:	RTA
PTE MICHAEL GEORGE MARR	29/03/73:	Shot by sniper, Andersonstown, Belfast
CAPT RICHARD LAMB	17/05/77:	RTA
CPL ALEXANDER CRUICKSHANK	26/06/77:	Accidental drowning
L/CPL JACK MARSHALL	28/08/77:	Shot in gun battle Ardoyne, Belfast

Green Howards

PTE MALCOLM HATTON	9/08/71:	Shot by sniper, Brompton Park, Ardoyne
PTE JOHN ROBINSON	14/08/71:	Shot by sniper in Ardoyne, Belfast
PTE GEORGE CROZIER	23/08/71:	Shot by sniper Flax St Mill, Ardoyne
L/CPL PETER HERRINGTON	17/09/71:	Shot by sniper, Brompton Park, Ardoyne
PTE PETER SHARP	1/10/71:	Shot on Kerrara Street, Ardoyne
PTE RAYMOND HALL	5/03/73:	DoW: Sniper attack, Belfast
PTE FREDERICK DICKS	5/06/74:	IRA sniper, Dungannon
MAJOR PETER WILLIS	17/07/75:	IRA bomb, Ford's Cross, Armagh
CPL IAN METCALF	15/06/88:	IRA booby trapped lorry, Lisburn

Grenadier Guards

CAPTAIN ROBERT NAIRAC G.C.	14/05/77:	Murdered by IRA on undercover mission, Irish Republic
GUARDSMAN GRAHAM DUGGAN	21/12/78:	Killed in attack on Army patrol, Crossmaglen
GUARDSMAN KEVIN JOHNSON	21/12/78:	Killed in same incident
GUARDSMAN GLEN LING	21/12/78:	Killed in same incident
GUARDSMAN PAUL WEAVER	23/12/78:	Death by violent or unnatural causes
CPT HERBERT WESTMACOTT MC**	2/05/80:	Killed on SAS undercover mission in west Belfast
COL SGT JOHN WIGG	17/01/86:	Death by violent or unnatural causes
GUARDSMAN PAUL MACDONALD	5/03/86:	RTA on duty at Ballkelly
GUARDSMAN BRIAN HUGHES	11/03/86:	Killed in same RTA
LANCE CORPORAL GARY KITELEY	28/12/86:	Death by violent or unnatural causes
GUARDSMAN DANIEL BLINCO	30/12/93:	IRA sniper in South Armagh

Intelligence Corps

| CPT HENRIETTA STEEL-MORTIMER | 11/06/98: | RTA |

Irish Guards

| GUARDSMAN SAMUEL MURPHY | 14/11/77: | Murdered in front of his mother whilst on leave, Andersonstown, Belfast |

King's Own Royal Border Regiment

PRIVATE GEORGE P RIDDING	10/05/72:	Died of natural causes after being taken ill.
C/SERGEANT WILLIAM BOARDLEY	1/02/73:	Shot in Strabane by IRA gunman
CORPORAL JAMES BURNEY	20/12/78:	IRA sniper, Newington, Belfast
PTE OWEN PAVEY	11/03/80:	Accidental shooting, Crossmaglen
PTE JOHN B. BATEMAN	15/03/80:	IRA sniper, Crossmaglen
PTE SEAN G. WALKER	21/03/80:	DoW, car bomb, Crossmaglen
L/CORPORAL ANTHONY DACRE	27/03/85:	Bomb attack, Divis street flats, Belfast
PTE DAVID HATFIELD	24/02/92:	Vehicle accident, Londonderry

PTE MARTIN THOMAS	17/01/95:	Vehicle accident, Belfast
PTE DARREN MILRAY	21/02/95:	Road accident

King's Own Scottish Borderers

S/SGT PETER SINTON	28/07/70:	Violent or unnatural causes
L/CPL PETER DEACON SIME	7/04/72:	IRA sniper, Ballymurphy Est. Belfast
L/CPL BARRY GOLD	24/04/72:	DoW after gun battle at VCP in Belfast
C/SGT HENRY S. MIDDLEMASS	10/12/72:	IRA booby trap, Turf Lodge, Belfast
PTE JOHN GILLIES	6/10/76:	Cause of death known; will not be revealed
S/SGT H. SHINGLESTON,MM	25/11/76:	Accidentally shot.
PTE PAUL B. SCOTT	10/10/79:	RTA
PTE JAMES HOUSTON	13/12/89:	Killed at VCP in gun and grenade attack, Fermanagh
L/CPL MICHAEL JOHN PATERSON.	13/12/89:	Killed in same incident

Kings Regiment

CPL ALAN BUCKLEY	13/05/72:	Shot on Turf Lodge, Belfast
PTE EUSTACE HANLEY	23/05/72:	IRA sniper Ballymurphy Estate
PTE MARCEL DOGLAY	30/05/72:	IRA bomb, Springfield Road, Belfast
PTE JAMES JONES	18/07/72:	IRA sniper, New Barnsley, Belfast
PTE BRIAN THOMAS	24/07/72:	IRA sniper, New Barnsley, Belfast
PTE RENNIE LAYFIELD	18/08/72:	IRA sniper, Falls Road, Belfast
PTE ROY CHRISTOPHER	30/08/72:	DoW after bomb attack, Cupar St, Belfast
SGT DENNIS DOOLEY	15/03/75:	RTA Outside of Londonderry; died in hospital
PTE DAVID OWEN	14/10/75:	Died of natural causes
PTE PETER KAVANAGH	14/11/75:	Death by violent or unnatural causes
PTE CHRISTOPHER SHANLEY	11/04/79:	Ambushed and shot Ballymurphy Estate, Belfast
L/CPL STEPHEN RUMBLE	19/04/79:	DoW from same incident
L/CPL ANDREW WEBSTER	9/05/79:	Bomb attack, Turf Lodge, Belfast
PTE STEPHEN BEACHAM	24/10/90:	Killed by IRA 'proxy bomb' Coshquin, nr Londonderry. 5 soldiers killed
L/CPL STEPHEN BURROWS	24/10/90:	Killed in same incident
PTE VINCENT SCOTT	24/10/90:	Killed in same incident
PTE DAVID SWEENEY	24/10/90:	Killed in same incident
PTE PAUL WORRALL	24/10/90:	Killed in same incident

Life Guards

CPL of HORSE LEONARD DURBER	21/02/73:	DoW after riot in Belfast

Light Infantry
1st Battalion

PTE. RICHARD JONES	18/08/72:	Shot by sniper in West Belfast
PTE. R ROWE	28/08/72:	Shot accidentally in Ardoyne, Belfast
PTE. TA STOKER	19/09/72:	DoW after accidental shooting in Berwick Road, Ardoyne
PTE. T RUDMAN	30/09/72:	Shot in Ardoyne, Belfast (Brother killed in 1971 in Northern Ireland)
PTE. STEPHEN HALL	28/10/73:	Shot in Crossmaglen
PTE. G M CURTIS	10/06/83:	IRA bomb, Ballymurphy Estate, Belfast
PTE. NICHOLAS BLYTHE	12/11/87:	Killed in accident
PTE. J J WILLBY	6/02/88:	Violent or unnatural causes
PTE. B BISHOP	20/08/88:	Killed in Ballygawley coach bombing; one of 8 soldiers killed
PTE. P L BULLOCK	20/08/88:	Killed in same incident
PTE. J BURFITT	20/08/88:	Killed in same incident
PTE. R GREENER	20/08/88:	Killed in same incident

PTE. A S LEWIS	20/08/88:	Killed in same incident
PTE. M A NORWORTHY	20/08/88	Killed in same incident
PTE. S J WILKINSON	20/08/88:	Killed in same incident
PTE. J WINTER	20/08/88:	Killed in same incident
PTE. GRAHAME SMITH	3/12/88:	Violent or unnatural causes
PTE. A J RICHARDSON	12/03/97:	Killed in attempted ambush by IRA after ceasefire.

2nd Battalion

PTE. J R RUDMAN	14/10/71:	Shot in Coalisland area
SGT. ARTHUR WHITELOCK	24/08/72:	IRA sniper in Londonderry
CPL. T P TAYLOR	13/05/73:	Killed in bomb attack, Donegall Road
PTE. J GASKELL	14/05/73:	DoW from same incident
PTE. R B ROBERTS	1/07/73:	Shot by sniper in Ballymurphy Estate, Belfast
L/CPL TERENCE WILSON	1/07/78:	RTA
PTE KEVIN MCGOVERN	3/07/78:	RTA
PTE. R STAFFORD	20/07/79:	Killed in car accident
PTE. PAUL TURNER	28/08/92:	IRA sniper, Crossmaglen

3rd Battalion

PTE. P K EASTAUGH	23/03/71:	Shot accidentally in the Ardoyne area of Belfast
LCPL. A KENNINGTON	28/02/73:	IRA sniper, Ardoyne area of Belfast
LCPL. C R MILLER	18/09/73:	Shot in West Belfast
PTE. R D TURNBULL	29/06/77:	Ambushed and shot West Belfast
PTE. MICHAEL E HARRISON	29/06/77:	Killed in same incident
PTE. LEWIS J HARRISON	9/08/77:	IRA sniper, New Barnsley, Belfast
CPL. D P SALTHOUSE	7/12/82:	IRA bomb Droppin' Well pub, Ballykelly

Light Infantry (Bn unknown)

PTE GARY HARDY	16/08/78:	Death by violent or unnatural causes

North Irish Militia

RANGER SAMUEL M. GIBSON.	21/10/74:	Abducted and murdered off duty (TA)

Parachute Regiment

PTE PETER DOCHERTY	21/05/70:	Stabbed to death
PTE VICTOR CHAPMAN	24/06/70	Drowned
SGT. M WILLETTS GC.	25/05/71:	Killed saving civilians in IRA bomb blast, Springfield Road, Belfast
PTE. R A BARTON	14/07/71:	Shot protecting comrades, Andersonstown, Belfast
SGT GRAHAM COX	17/10/71:	Died of wounds after being shot by IRA in Oldpark area
FATHER GERRY WESTON, MBE	22/02/72:	Killed in IRA bomb outrage, Aldershot
PTE. Anthony KELLY	18/03/72:	Killed in accident, Holywood, Co Down
PTE. CHRISTOPHER STEPHENSON	24/06/72:	IRA landmine, Glenshane Pass, Londonderry
PTE. FRANK T BELL	20/09/72:	DoW after being shot on Ballymurphy Estate, Belfast
CPL. S N HARRISON	7/04/73:	IRA landmine, Tullyogallaghan
L/CPL. T D BROWN	7/04/73:	Killed in same incident
L/CPL. D A FORMAN	16/04/73:	Accidentally shot, Flax Street Mill, Ardoyne
WO2. W R VINES	5/05/73:	IRA landmine, Crossmaglen
A/SGT. J WALLACE	24/05/73:	IRA booby trap, Crossmaglen
PTE. R BEDFORD	16/03/74:	Shot in IRA ambush, Crossmaglen
PTE. P JAMES	16/03/74:	Killed in same incident
WO2 HERBERT COVEY	22/03/74:	Died on duty

PTE. WILLIAM SNOWDON	28/06/76:	IRA bomb, Crossmaglen
PTE. J BORUCKI	8/08/76:	IRA booby trap, Crossmaglen
L/CPL. D A JONES	17/03/78:	Shot in gun battle, Glenshane Pass, Londonderry
PTE. J FISHER	12/07/78:	IRA booby trap, Crossmaglen
CPL. R D ADCOCK	2/12/78:	Killed in helicopter accident
MAJ. P J FURSMAN	27/08/79:	Killed in IRA double bomb blast, Warrenpoint. One of 16 Paras and 2 other soldiers killed
WO2. W BEARD	27/08/79:	Killed in same incident
SGT. I A ROGERS	27/08/79:	Killed in same incident
CPL. N J ANDREWS	27/08/79:	Killed in same incident
CPL. J C GILES	27/08/79:	Killed in same incident
CPL. L JONES	27/08/79:	Killed in same incident
L/CPL. CG IRELAND	27/08/79:	Killed in same incident
PTE. G I BARNES	27/08/79:	Killed in same incident
PTE. D F BLAIR	27/08/79:	Killed in same incident
PTE. R DUNN	27/08/79:	Killed in same incident
PTE. R N ENGLAND	27/08/79:	Killed in same incident
PTE. R D U JONES	27/08/79:	Killed in same incident
PTE. T R VANCE	27/08/79:	Killed in same incident
PTE. J A VAUGHAN-JONES	27/08/79:	Killed in same incident
PTE. A G WOOD	27/08/79:	Killed in same incident
PTE. M WOODS	27/08/79:	Killed in same incident
PTE. P S GRUNDY	16/12/79:	IRA booby trap, Forkhill
LT. S G BATES	1/01/80:	Shot accidentally, at covert OP at Forkhill
PTE. G M R HARDY	1/01/80:	Killed in same incident
A/SGT. B M BROWN	9/08/80:	IRA booby trap, Forkhill
L/CPL. PETER HAMPSON	25/12/81:	Violent or unnatural causes
L/CPL. MICHAEL C MAY	26/07/82:	RTA
SGT. A I SLATER MM **	2/12/84:	Killed in anti-IRA operation, Fermanagh
SGT. MICHAEL MATTHEWS	29/07/88:	DoW, IRA landmine, Cullyhanna
PTE. ROBERT SPIKINS	25/03/89:	Hit by joyrider, Falls Road area, Belfast
L/CPL. STEPHEN WILSON	18/11/89:	IRA landmine, Mayobridge (3 soldiers killed)
PTE. DONALD MACAULAY	18/11/89:	Killed in same incident
PTE. MATTHEW MARSHALL	18/11/89:	Killed in same incident
PTE. ANTHONY HARRISON	19/06/91:	Murdered by IRA in fiancés' home, East Belfast
L/CPL. RICHARD COULSON	27/06/92:	Drowned crossing a river
L/CPL. PETER H SULLIVAN	27/06/92:	Drowned trying to rescue his friend
PTE. MICHAEL B LEE	20/08/92:	Violent or unnatural causes
PTE. P F J GROSS	13/05/93:	Accidental death at Holywood
PTE. CHRISTIAN D KING.	4/12/94:	Death by violent or unnatural causes
PTE. MARC RAMSEY	21/08/97:	Accidental death

Prince Of Wales Own Regiment of Yorkshire

PTE JAMES LEADBEATER	11/02/73:	Unknown Cause of death
PTE DAVID WRAY	10/10/75:	DoW after being shot Creggan area, Londonderry
L/CPL GRAHAM BIRDSALL	23/08/86:	Died on duty
PTE WILLIAM CARNE	20/07/96:	Cause of death unknown

Princess Of Wales Royal Regiment

MAJOR JOHN BARR	26/11/92:	Helicopter crash, Bessbrook Mill
L/CPL PAUL PARKIN	8/10/95:	Death by violent or unnatural causes

Queen Alexandra's Royal Army Nursing Corps

CAPT LYNDA SMITH	22/04/81:	Death by violent or unnatural causes

Queens Lancashire Regiment

SGT JAMES SINGLETON	23/06/70:	Died on duty
PTE STEPHEN KEATING	3/03/72:	IRA sniper, Manor Street, West Belfast
PTE MICHAEL MURTAGH	6/02/73:	Killed in rocket attack Lower Falls area, Belfast
PTE EDWIN WESTON	14/02/73:	IRA sniper Divis Street area, Belfast
PTE GARY BARLOW	4/03/73:	Disarmed and murdered by IRA, Lower Falls area, Belfast
PTE JOHN GREEN	8/03/73:	Shot whilst guarding school in Lower Falls area, Belfast
L/CPL WILLIAM RIDDELL	6/01/76:	RTA
PTE IAN O'CONNER	3/03/87:	Grenade attack, Divis Street flats, Belfast
PTE JOSEPH LEACH	4/06/87:	IRA sniper, Andersonstown, Belfast

Queens Own Highlanders

PTE JAMES HESKETH	10/12/73:	Shot dead on Lower Falls, Belfast
PTE ALAN JOHN MCMILLAN	8/07/79:	Remote-controlled bomb in Crossmaglen
L/CPL D. LANG	24/08/79:	Killed in helicopter crash with another soldier
L/CPL D.A. WARES	24/08/79:	Killed in same accident
LT/COL DAVID BLAIR	27/08/79:	Killed in IRA double bomb blast, Warrenpoint (one of 18 soldiers killed in same incident)
L/CPL VICTOR MACLEOD	27/08/79:	Killed in same incident
CPL RICHARD TURNER.	27/02/90:	Accidentally shot

Queens Regiment

PTE DAVID PITCHFORD	27/06/70:	RTA
PTE PAUL CARTER	15/09/71:	DoW after being shot at Royal Victoria Hospital, Belfast
PTE ROBERT BENNER	29/11/71:	Abducted & murdered by IRA off duty at Crossmaglen
PTE RICHARD SINCLAIR	31/10/72:	IRA sniper New Lodge, Belfast
PTE STANLEY EVANS	14/11/72:	IRA sniper Unity Flats complex, West Belfast
PTE PETER WOOLMORE	19/03/79:	Mortar bomb attack, Newtownhamilton, Co Armagh
PTE ALAN STOCK	15/10/83:	Remote-controlled bomb, Creggan, Londonderry
PTE NEIL CLARKE	24/04/84:	IRA sniper, Bishop Street, Londonderry
PTE STEPHEN RANDALL	23/05/84:	Death by violent or unnatural causes
WOI JEFFERY BUDGEN	31/10/84:	Accidental death
CPL ALEC BANNISTER	8/08/88:	IRA sniper, New Barnsley, Belfast
SGT CHARLES CHAPMAN	16/05/90:	IRA booby trap, Army recruiting office, Wembley, London

Queen's Royal Irish Hussars

TROOPER HUGH MCCABE	15/08/69	Killed by friendly fire, Divis Street, Belfast

Royal Air Force

FLT SGT JOHN WILLOUGHBY	7/12/69:	Natural Causes
LAC ROBERT CALDERBANK	10/07/71:	RTA
LAC JACK HAWKINS	28/08/79:	RTA
SGT ERIC SIMPSON	6/10/79:	Cause of death unknown
SAC STEPHEN HENSELER	12/03/80:	RTA
JNR TECH DAVID GILFILLAN	13/10/81:	RTA
SGT DAVID RIGBY	25/10/85:	Killed in Helicopter crash at Forkhill
CPL ISLANIA MAHESHKUMAR	26/10/89:	Shot by IRA in Wildenrath, West Germany and killed alongside baby daughter, Nivruti (6 months old)
F/SGT MALCOM WARNECK	10/08/92:	Died on duty, RAF, Aldergrove

SQN LDR ROBERT BURGE	16/10/92:	RTA
SQN LDR MICHAEL HAVERSON	26/10/92:	Helicopter crash, Bessbrook Mill base, Armagh
FLT LT SIMON S.M.J. ROBERTS	26/10/92:	Killed in same accident
FLT SGT JAN PEWTRESS	26/10/92:	Killed in same accident
SAC Gordon Charles Baird	8/04/95:	Death by violent or unnatural causes

RAF Regiment

AIRMAN IAN SHINNER	1/05/88:	Killed by IRA gunmen in Roermond, Holland
AIRMAN JOHN BAXTER	1/05/88:	Killed by IRA bomb, Nieuw-Bergen, Holland
AIRMAN JOHN MILLER REID	1/05/88:	Killed with his friend in the same incident
A/CPL JULIAN HART	29/06/89:	Death by violent or unnatural causes
SAC IAIN LEARMONTH	30/08/89:	Unlawfully killed at VCP, RAF, Aldergrove
CPL DAVID THOMAS	29/09/96:	Death by violent or unnatural causes

Royal Anglian Regiment

MAJOR PETER TAUNTON	26/10/70:	Death by violent or unnatural causes
PTE BRIAN SHERIDAN	20/11/70:	RTA
PTE ROGER WILKINS	11/10/71:	DoW after being shot on Letterkenny Rd, Londonderry
L/CPL IAN CURTIS	9/11/71:	IRA sniper Foyle Road, Londonderry
2/LT NICHOLAS HULL	16/04/72:	IRA sniper Divis Street flats, Belfast
PTE JOHN BALLARD	11/05/72:	IRA sniper, Sultan St. Lower Falls, Belfast
L/CPL MARTIN ROONEY	12/07/72:	IRA sniper Clonnard St., Lower Falls, Belfast
CPL KENNETH MOGG	13/07/72:	IRA sniper Dunville Park, Belfast
L/CPL JOHN BODDY	17/08/72:	IRA sniper, Grosvenor Road area of Belfast
CPL JOHN BARRY	25/09/72:	DoW after gun battle Lower Falls, Belfast
PTE IAN BURT	29/09/72:	IRA sniper Albert Street, Lower Falls, Belfast
PTE ROBERT MASON	24/10/72:	IRA sniper Naples St, Grosvenor Rd area, Belfast
PTE ANTHONY GOODFELLOW	27/04/73:	Shot manning VCP Creggan Estate, Londonderry
PTE N MARWICK	12/09/73:	Shot accidentally, Creggan, Londonderry
L/CPL ROY GRANT	2/11/73:	Death by violent or unnatural causes
PTE PARRY HOLLIS	13/11/74:	Died of natural causes during his tour
PTE STEPHEN FOSTER	13/11/78:	Accidental death
PTE PAUL WRIGHT	8/10/79:	Killed on covert operation, Falls Road area
PTE KEVIN BREWER	29/08/81:	RTA
PTE ANTHONY ANDERSON	24/05/82:	Killed by vehicle in confusion after petrol bomb attack Butcher Street, Londonderry
PTE MARTIN PATTEN	22/09/85:	Murdered off duty Limavady Rd Waterside, Londonderry
MAJOR ANDREW FRENCH	22/05/86:	Killed by remote-controlled bomb, Crossmaglen
PTE MITCHELL BERTRAM	9/07/86:	Remote-controlled bomb Glassdrumman, Crossmaglen
PTE CARL DAVIES	9/07/86:	Killed in the same incident
PTE DAVID J. KNIGHT	26/07/86:	RTA
PTE NICHOLAS PEACOCK	31/01/89:	Remote-controlled bomb Falls Road area, Belfast

Royal Army Dental Corps

SGT RICHARD MULDOON	23/03/73:	Murdered by the IRA whilst off duty.

Royal Army Education Corps

MAJOR RHODRI HOWELL	19/07/79:	RTA

Royal Army Medical Corps

PTE DENNIS 'TAFFY' PORTER	24/04/72:	Violent or unnatural causes
CAPTAIN HARRY MURPHY	15/03/73:	Violent or unnatural causes

CAPTAIN JANIS CANT	8/11/84:	Died on duty
PTE BRIAN ARMSTRONG (TA)	25/08/85:	RTA
WOII PHILLIP CROSS	2/11/91:	IRA bomb planted at Musgrave Park Hospital (killed with one other soldier)
CPL JOHN NEILL	13/04/92:	Death by violent or unnatural causes

Royal Army Pay Corps

PTE MICHAEL PRIME	16/02/72:	Shot in ambush at Moira roundabout near Lisburn
WOII GEORGE JOHNSON	16/03/76:	Died on duty
L/CPL ANDREW SNELL	19/03/80:	Shot accidentally, McCrory Park, Belfast
PTE M A MCLEOD	15/12/93:	Cause of death unknown
L/CPL HENRY M. MCGIVERN		RTA

Royal Army Ordinance Corps

CAPTAIN D A STEWARDSON	9/09/71:	Defusing IRA bomb Castlerobin, Antrim
WO2. C J L DAVIES	24/11/71:	Killed by IRA bomb in Lurgan
PTE T F McCANN	14/02/72:	Abducted and murdered by the IRA, Newtownbutler
SSGT. C R CRACKNELL	15/03/72:	IRA booby trap, Grosvenor Road, Belfast
SSGT. A S BUTCHER	15/03/72:	Killed in same incident
MAJOR B C CALLADENE	29/03/72:	IRA car bomb outside Belfast City Hall
CAPTAIN J H YOUNG	15/07/72:	Defusing IRA bomb, Silverbridge near Forkhill
WO2. WJ CLARK	3/08/72:	Defusing IRA bomb at Strabane
SGT. R E HILLS	5/12/72:	Attempting to make live shell safe Kitchen Hill
CAPTAIN B S GRITTEN	21/06/73:	Killed inspecting explosives, Lecky Road, Londonderry
SSGT. R F BECKETT	30/08/73:	Killed pulling bomb out of a post office Tullyhommon
CAPTAIN RONALD WILKINSON:	23/09/73:	Defusing IRA bomb, Edgbaston, Birmingham
2ND LT L. HAMILTON DOBBIE	3/10/73:	IRA bomb, Bligh's Lane post, Londonderry
SSGT. A N BRAMMAH	18/02/74:	Examining IRA road side bomb, Crossmaglen
CPL GEOFFREY HALL	20/09/74:	Cause of death unknown
SSGT. V I ROSE	7/11/74:	IRA landmine, Stewartstown, Tyrone
WO2. J A MADDOCKS	2/12/74:	Examining milk churn bomb Gortmullen
WO2. E GARSIDE	17/07/75:	Killed with 3 other soldiers IRA bomb nr Forkhill
CPL. C W BROWN	17/07/75:	Killed in same incident
CAPTAIN ROGER GOAD	29/08/75:	Killed defusing IRA bomb, Kensington, London
CPL DOUGLAS WHITFIELD	13/03/76:	RTA
SGT MICHAEL G. PEACOCK	13/03/76:	Killed in same incident
SGT. M E WALSH	9/01/77:	Killed dismantling IRA bomb Newtownbutler
L/CPL MICHAEL DEARNEY	31/05/77:	RTA
SIG. P J REECE	2/08/79:	IRA landmine near Armagh
WO2. M O'NEIL	31/05/81:	Examining IRA bomb near Newry
L/CPL ROBERT PRINGLE	24/08/81:	Death by violent or unnatural causes
PTE IAN ARCHIBALD	15/02/83:	RTA
L/CORPORAL DEREK W GREEN	15/06/88:	One of 6 soldiers killed by IRA booby trap, Lisburn
WO2. JOHN HOWARD	8/07/88:	IRA booby trap, Falls Road, Belfast
L/CPL ANDREW DOWELL	17/08/92:	Death by violent or unnatural causes

Royal Army Veterinary Corps

CPL BRIAN CRIDDLE, BEM	22/07/73:	DoW; was wounded whilst defusing IRA bomb
CPL. TERENCE O'NEIL	25/05/91:	Killed by hand grenade, North Howard St, Belfast

Royal Artillery

GUNNER ROBERT CURTIS	6/02/71:	Shot by IRA gunmen, New Lodge area, Belfast
L/BOMB JOHN LAURIE	15/02/71:	DoW after being shot on Crumlin Road, Belfast
GNR CLIFFORD LORING	31/08/71:	DoW after being shot at VCP, Belfast
SGT MARTIN CARROLL	14/09/71:	IRA sniper Creggan, Londonderry
GNR ANGUS STEVENS	27/10/71:	IRA bomb attack, Rosemount RUC station, Belfast
L/BOMB DAVID TILBURY	27/10/71:	Killed in same incident
GNR IAN DOCHERTY	31/10/71:	DoW after being shot in Stockmans Lane, Belfast
GNR RICHARD HAM	29/12/71:	Shot dead in the Brandywell area of Londonderry
L/BOMB ERIC BLACKBURN	10/04/72:	Killed in bomb attack, Rosemount Avenue,
L/BOMB BRIAN THOMASSON	10/04/72:	Killed In same incident
GNR VICTOR HUSBAND	2/06/72:	IRA landmine, Rosslea, Co Fermanagh
GNR BRIAN ROBERTSON	2/06/72:	Killed in the same incident
SGT CHARLES COLEMAN	7/06/72:	IRA sniper, Andersonstown, Belfast
GUNNER WILLIAM RAISTRICK	11/06/72:	IRA sniper Brooke Park, Londonderry
BOMBARDIER TERRENCE JONES	11/07/72	Shot in the back by IRA, Londonderry
GNR LEROY GORDON	7/08/72:	IRA landmine, Lisnaskea, Co Fermanagh
L/BOMB DAVID WYNNE	7/08/72:	Killed in same incident
MAJOR DAVID STORRY	14/08/72:	Booby trap, Casement Park base, Andersonstown
GUNNER ROBERT CUTTING	03/09/72:	friendly fire incident, New Lodge (ATT: Royal Marines)
S/SGT JOHN GARDNER CRAIG	15/09/72:	RTA
GNR PAUL JACKSON	28/11/72:	Hit by bomb shrapnel, Strand Road, Londonderry
GUNNER IVOR SWAIN	23/03/73:	RTA: North Belfast (ATT: Royal Marines)
GNR IDWAL EVANS	11/04/73:	IRA sniper Bogside area of Londonderry
GNR KERRY VENN	28/04/73:	IRA sniper Shantallow Estate, Londonderry
SGT THOMAS CRUMP	3/05/73:	DoW after being shot in Londonderry
GNR JOSEPH BROOKES	25/11/73:	Shot in IRA ambush in Bogside area of Londonderry
BOMBARDIER HEINZ PISAREK	25/11/73:	Killed in same incident
SGT JOHN HAUGHEY	21/01/74:	Remote-controlled bomb, Bogside, Londonderry
GNR LEONARD GODDEN	4/02/74:	Killed by IRA bomb on M62 in Yorkshire
BDR TERENCE GRIFFIN	4/02.74:	Killed in same incident
LT/COL JOHN STEVENSON	8/04/74:	Murdered by IRA gunmen at his home in Northumberland
GNR KIM MACCUNN	22/06/74:	IRA sniper New Lodge, Belfast
SGT BERNARD FEARNS	30/07/74:	IRA sniper New Lodge area of Belfast
GNR KEITH BATES	4/11/74:	RTA: Central Belfast
GNR RICHARD DUNNE	8/11/74:	IRA bomb in Woolwich, London pub bombings
GNR GEOFFREY B. JONES	9/06/75:	RTA
GUNNER ANTHONY JEAL	11/07/75:	Accidentally shot
GNR CYRIL MACDONALD	18/12/75:	IRA bomb attack at Guildhall Square, Londonderry
GNR MARK ASHFORD	17/01/76:	Shot at checkpoint, Great James Street, Londonderry
GNR JAMES REYNOLDS	13/03/76:	RTA
GNR WILLIAM MILLER (TA)	3/07/76:	IRA sniper at checkpoint Butcher Street, Londonderry
GNR ANTHONY ABBOT	24/10/76:	Ambushed and killed by IRA, Ardoyne, Belfast
GNR STEPHEN NICHOLSON	5/11/76:	Died on duty
GNR MAURICE MURPHY	22/11/76:	DoW from same incident as Gunner Abbot
GNR EDMUND MULLER	11/01/77:	IRA sniper at VCP in Old Park area of Belfast
GNR GEORGE MUNCASTER	23/01/77:	IRA sniper Markets area, Belfast
GNR PAUL SHEPPARD	1/03/78:	Shot in gun battle Clifton Park Avenue, Belfast

MAJOR GEORGE MILBURN	16/03/78:	Died on duty
GNR ROGER EDWARDS	2/07/78:	Accidentally shot at Musgrave Park Hospital
GNR RICHARD FURMINGER	02/08/79:	Killed in IRA landmine attack with RAOC comrade Cathedral Road, Armagh
GNR ALAN AYRTON	16/12/79:	Killed with 3 others in landmine explosion, Dungannon
GNR WILLIAM BECK	16/12/79:	Killed in same incident
GNR SIMON EVANS	16/12/79:	Killed in same incident
GNR KEITH RICHARDS	16/12/79:	Killed in same incident
GNR PETER A. CLARK	9/08/80	Killed accidentally whilst clearing barricades, Ligoniel
SGT SAMUEL MCCLEAN	30/05/81:	Accidental death
L/BOMB KEVIN WALLER	20/09/82:	Remote-controlled INLA bomb Divis St flats, Belfast
BDR PAUL CREE	5/02/88:	Cause of death unknown
GNR LYNDON MORGAN	26/04/88:	IRA booby trap Carrickmore
GNR MILES AMOS	8/03/89:	IRA landmine, Buncrana Road, Londonderry
L/BOMB STEPHEN CUMMINS	8/03/89:	Killed in same incident
L/BOMB DAVID SHEPPARD	18/03/89:	Death by violent or unnatural causes
MAJOR MICHAEL DILLON-LEE	2/06/90:	Murdered outside his quarters in Dortmund, Germany
GUNNER DARREN OLDFIELD	1/06/92:	Death by Violent or Unnatural Causes
CAPTAIN NIGEL FRENCH	12/03/92:	Died on duty
L/BOMB PAUL GARRETT	2/12/93:	IRA sniper Keady, Co Armagh
2 LT JAMES C. FOX	21/01/95:	Violent or unnatural causes
GNR PAUL KEARNEY	11/11/96:	Died on duty
GNR JON COOPER	22/02/97:	Violent or unnatural causes

Royal Horse Artillery

BOMBARDIER PAUL CHALLENOR	10/08/71:	IRA sniper, Bligh's Lane post, Londonderry
GNR DAVID FARRINGTON	13/03/74:	Shot by IRA gunmen at Chapel Lane Belfast city centre
GUNNER TIMOTHY UTTERIDGE	19/10/84:	Shot by IRA, Turf Lodge, Belfast, att 3RGJ
L/BOMB STEPHEN RESTORICK	12/02/97:	IRA sniper at VCP at Bessbrook Mill Army base

Royal Corps Signals

L/CPL MICHAEL SPURWAY	13/09/69:	Accidentally shot, Gosford Castle
Signalman PAUL GENGE	7/11/71:	Shot by IRA whilst off-duty in Lurgan
Sgt DAVID MCELVIE	14/03/73:	Died on duty
CPL JOHN AIKMAN	6/11/73:	Shot by IRA gunmen Newtownhamilton
Signalman MICHAEL E. WAUGH	4/02/74:	Killed by IRA bomb, M62, Yorkshire
Signalman LESLIE DAVID WALSH	4/02/74:	Killed in same incident
Signalman PAUL ANTHONY REID	4/02/74:	Killed in same incident
SGT DEREK BASSFORD	24/10/75:	Died on duty, Girdwood Barracks, Belfast
Signalman DAVID ROBERTS	13/03/76:	RTA
CPL ARTHUR FORD	7/01/76:	Aircraft accident
L/CPL RICHARD DAVIES	25/02/79:	RTA
Signalman PAUL J REECE	2/08/79:	IRA landmine, Armagh
L/CPL ROBIN LISTER	18/02/80:	Helicopter crash near Lisburn
L/CPL PAUL HOLT	3/11/80:	Death by violent or unnatural causes
Signalman BRIAN RICHARD CROSS	4/07/81:	Killed in road traffic accident, Lisburn, en-route to Castlereagh
CPL MICHAEL WARD	1/04/82:	Shot with REME soldier by IRA in Bogside, Londonderry
SGT LESLIE MCKENZIE	24/05/83:	RTA
Signalman KENNETH ROYAL	28/03/85:	RTA

CPL DEREK T WOOD	19/03/88:	Beaten by mob, shot by IRA, Penny Lane, Belfast
CPL DAVID HOWES	19/03/88:	Killed in same incident
L/CPL GRAHAM P LAMBIE	15/06/88:	Killed by IRA bomb, Lisburn (1 of 6 soldiers killed)
SGT MICHAEL JAMES WINKLER	15/06/88:	Killed in same incident
Signalman MARK CLAVEY	15/06/88:	Killed in same incident
CPL WILLIAM J PATERSON	15/06/88:	Killed in same incident
S/SGT KEVIN A FROGGETT	16/09/89:	Shot by IRA repairing radio mast Coalisland RUC station
SGT WILLIAM J JOHNSON	6/06/90:	Death by violent or unnatural causes
Signalman WILLIAM DRYDEN	7/08/91:	Shot by a comrade in negligent discharge
SGT MICHAEL NEWMAN	14/04/92:	Shot by INLA at Army Recruiting office, Derby, England
Signalman JONATHAN EDMONDS	27/05/92:	Died on duty
CPL PAUL SMITH	22/09/94:	RTA
SGT JOHN LIVINGSTONE	21/04/98:	Cause of death unknown

Royal Corps Transport

MAJOR PHILIP COWLEY	13/01/70:	Died on duty
CPL CHRISTOPHER YOUNG (TA)	29/07/71:	RTA
DRIVER STEPHEN BEEDIE	26/03/72:	RTA
DRIVER LAURENCE JUBB	26/04/72:	Killed in vehicle crash after mob attack, Armagh
L/CPL MICHAEL BRUCE	31/05/72:	IRA sniper Andersonstown, Belfast
S/SGT JOSEPH FLEMING (TA)	9/07/72:	Shot dead by IRA in Grosvenor Road area of Belfast
DRIVER PETER HEPPENSTALL	14/07/72:	IRA sniper Ardoyne area of Belfast
DRIVER STEPHEN COOPER	21/07/72:	IRA car bomb on 'Bloody Friday' Belfast bus depot
DRIVER RONALD KITCHEN	10/11/72:	IRA sniper at VCP in Old Park Road, Belfast
DRIVER MICHAEL GAY	17/03/73:	IRA landmine, Dungannon
SGT THOMAS PENROSE	24/03/73:	Murdered off-duty with 2 others, Antrim road, Belfast
CPL ANDREW GILMOUR	29/08/73:	RTA
L/CPL EDMOND CROSBIE	23/11/73:	RTA
DRIVER NORMAN MCKENZIE	11/04/74:	IRA landmine, Lisnaskea, Co Fermanagh
DRIVER HAROLD J. KING	19/04/75:	RTA
DRIVER WILLIAM KNIGHT	17/05/76:	RTA
SGT WILLIAM EDGAR	15/04/77:	Abducted and murdered by IRA whilst on leave in Londonderry
LT NIGEL BREWER	31/05/79:	RTA
DRIVER JOHN DORRITY	30/09/79:	Accidental death
DRIVER STEVEN ATKINS	29/11/80:	RTA
DRIVER IAN MACDONALD	8/03/81:	Drowned
DRIVER PAUL BULMAN	19/05/81:	Killed in IRA landmine attack along with 4 RGJs at Altnaveigh, South Armagh
DRIVER PAUL JOHNS	25/10/81:	Cause of death unknown
CAPT JOHN MEADOWS	8/08/84:	Accidentally shot at HQNI, Lisburn
L/CPL NORMAN DUNCAN	22/02/89:	Shot by IRA waterside area of Londonderry
THOMAS GIBSON (TA)	9/10/89:	Murdered by IRA as he waited for lift in Kilrea
DVR C PANTRY	2/11/91:	Killed by IRA bomb at Musgrave Park hospital, Belfast
PTE MAURICE CARSON (TA)	13/06/81:	RTA

Royal Dragoon Guards

TROOPER GEOFFREY KNIPE	7/08/72:	Armoured vehicle crashed after mob attack, Armagh

Royal Electrical & Mechanical Engineers

CFN CHRISTOPHER EDGAR	13/09/69:	Violent or unnatural causes
CFN ANDREW PATON	26/05/71:	Accidentally drowned at Bangor
SGT STUART C REID	24/06/72:	IRA milk churn bombs at Glenshane Pass, Londonderry
L/CPL D MOON	24/06/72:	Killed in same incident
CFN BRIAN HOPE	14/08/72:	IRA booby trap Casement Park, Andersonstown, Belfast
L/CPL COLIN HARKER	24/12/72:	DoW after being shot by IRA sniper Lecky Road, Londonderry
CPL DAVID JOHN BROWN	17/03/73:	Died on duty, Thiepval Barracks, Lisburn
SGT MALCOLM SELDON	30/06/74:	Shot in an incident inside his base; manslaughter by a comrade
L/CPL ALISTER STEWART	9/10/74:	RTA
L/CPL DEREK NORWOOD	5/03/75:	Cause of death unknown
CFN COLIN MCINNES	18/12/75:	IRA bomb attack on Army base in Londonderry
CPL ROBERT MOORE	15/09/79:	RTA
CPL PETER BAILEY	5/04/80:	RTA
CFN ALAN COOMBE	16/02/81:	RTA
L/CPL PHILIP HARDING	30/03/82:	Death by violent or unnatural causes
SGT MICHAEL BURBRIDGE	1/04/82:	IRA sniper Rosemount barracks, Londonderry
SGT RICHARD GREGORY	22/10/82:	Died of natural causes on duty
CFN WILLIAM PARR	6/07/90:	Death by violent or unnatural causes
L/CPL CM MONTEITH	5/08/91:	RTA
CPL MD IONNOU	15/04/95:	RTA
S/SGT SJ THOMPSON	30/06/95:	Died of natural causes whilst on duty
WO1 (ASM) JAMES BRADWELL	11/10/96:	DoW after car bomb attack by IRA on Army base Lisburn

Royal Engineers

SAPPER JOHN CONNACHAN	27/06/71:	Accidental death
SAPPER DEREK AMOS	28/12/71:	RTA
SAPPER RONALD HURST	17/05/72:	IRA sniper whilst working on base in Crossmaglen
S/SGT MALCOLM BANKS	28/06/72:	Shot by IRA Short Strand area of Belfast
SAPPER EDWARD STUART	2/10/72:	Shot whilst working undercover Dunmurry, Belfast
WO2 IAN DONALD	24/05/73:	IRA bomb, Cullaville, Co Armagh
MAJOR RICHARD JARMAN	20/07/73:	IRA booby trap Middletown, Co Armagh
SAPPER MALCOLM ORTON	17/09/73:	Accidental shooting: HMP Maze
S/SGT JAMES LUND	19/01/74:	Accident
L/CPL IAN NICHOLL	15/05/74:	RTA
SAPPER JOHN WALTON	2/07/74:	IRA booby trap Newtownhamilton
WO1 JOHN NEWTON	24/06/75:	Died on duty
SERGEANT ROBERT MCCARTER	17/07/75:	IRA bomb, Forkhill
SGT DAVID EVANS	21/07/76:	IRA booby trap Army base, Waterside, Londonderry
SAPPER GARETH GRIFFITHS	6/11/76:	Cause of death unknown
SAPPER HOWARD EDWARDS	11/12/76:	IRA sniper, Bogside area of Londonderry
SAPPER DAVIS THOMPSON	13/01/77:	Cause of death unknown
SAPPER MICHAEL LARKIN	10/02/77:	Cause of death unknown
CPL JOHN HAYNES	28/07/77:	Cause of death unknown
SAPPER STEPHEN WORTH	1/08/77:	Death by violent or unnatural causes
SAPPER JAMES VANCE	14/11/77:	RTA
CPL JAMES ANDREWS	4/09/78:	Cause of death unknown
SAPPER FRASER JONES	3/02/80:	Accidental death whilst on duty

COLONEL MARK COE	16/02/80:	Murdered by IRA gunmen at Army home in Bielefeld Germany
SGT KENNETH ROBSON	18/02/80:	Helicopter crash near Lisburn
WOII EMANUEL MARIOTTI	22/08/81:	Died on duty, Thiepval Bks, Lisburn
SAPPER CHRISTOPHER BEATTIE	6/04/82:	Unlawfully killed inside barracks
CPL JAMES ANDREW	4/09/82:	Thought to be in an RTA
CPL THOMAS PALMER QGM**	8/02/83:	RTA
L/CPL DAVID HURST	6/10/86:	RTA
L/CPL MICHAEL ROBBINS	1/08/88:	Killed by IRA bomb at Mill Hill Army camp, London
L/CPL PAUL CASSIDY	15/03/88:	RTA
S/SGT DAVID HULL	22/08/89:	RTA
S/SGT JAMES H. HARDY	12/06/90:	RTA
SGT MICHAEL CASHMORE	1/07/90:	Died at Lisburn HQNI
SPR DEAN PITTS	3/08/91:	Death by violent or unnatural causes
PTE JOHN WILLIAM ROBINSON	21/04/96:	Accidentally shot Ballykinler Army Base

Royal Green Jackets

L/CPL MICHAEL PEARCE	24/09/69:	Violent or unnatural causes
RFN MICHAEL BOSWELL	25/10/69:	RTA near Omagh
RFN JOHN KEENEY	25/10/69:	Died in same incident
CPL ROBERT BANKIER	22/05/71:	IRA sniper Markets area of Belfast
RFN DAVID WALKER	12/07/71:	IRA sniper, North Howard Street Mill, Belfast
RFN JOSEPH HILL	16/10/71:	Shot by gunman during riots in Bogside, Londonderry
MAJOR ROBIN ALERS-HANKEY	30/01/72:	DoW after being shot in Bogside area of Londonderry
RFN JOHN TAYLOR	20/03/72:	IRA sniper, William Street, Londonderry
RFN JAMES MEREDITH	26/06/72:	Shot in Abercorn Road, Londonderry
L/CPL DAVID CARD	4/08/72:	Killed by IRA gunman in Andersonstown, Belfast
CPL IAN MORRILL	28/08/72:	IRA sniper in Beechmount Avenue, Belfast
RFN DAVID GRIFFITHS	30/08/72:	IRA sniper, Clonnard Street, Lower Falls, Belfast
L/CPL IAN GEORGE	10/09/72:	Shot by an IRA sniper, Belfast
RFN RAYMOND JOESBURY	8/12/72:	DoW after being shot whilst in Whiterock area of Belfast
RFN NICOLAS ALLEN	26/11/73:	Death by violent or unnatural causes
RFN MICHAEL GIBSON	29/12/74:	Shot along with RUC constable at Forkhill on joint patrol
CPL WILLIAM SMITH	31/08/77:	IRA sniper, Girdwood Park Army base, Belfast
LT/COL IAN CORDEN-LLOYD	17/02/78:	Helicopter crash near Bessbrook
RFN NICHOLAS SMITH	4/03/78:	IRA booby trap Crossmaglen
MAJOR THOMAS FOWLEY	24/04/78:	Died of natural causes whilst on duty
RFN CHRISTOPHER WATSON	19/07/80:	Shot and killed off-duty in Rosemount, Londonderry
RFN MICHAEL BAGSHAW	19/05/81:	Killed along with 4 others IRA landmine at Altnaveigh
RFN ANDREW GAVIN	19/05/81:	Killed in same incident
RFN JOHN KING	19/05/81:	Killed in same incident
L/CPL GRENVILLE WINSTONE	19/05/81:	Killed in same incident
L/CPL GAVIN DEAN	16/07/81:	IRA sniper near Crossmaglen
RFN DANIEL HOLLAND	25/03/82:	Killed with 2 others in gun attack in Crocus Street, Belfast
RFN NICHOLAS MALAKOS	25/03/82:	Killed in same incident
RFN ANTHONY RAPLEY	25/03/82:	Killed in same incident

WO2 GRAHAM BARKER	20/07/82:	Killed in IRA bomb outrage, Regents Park, London
BANDSMAN JOHN HERITAGE	20/07/82:	Killed in same incident
CPL ROBERT LIVINGSTONE	20/07/82:	Killed in same incident
CPL JOHN MCKNIGHT	20/07/82:	Killed in same incident
BANDSMAN GEORGE MEASURE	20/07/82:	Killed in same incident
BANDSMAN KEITH POWELL	20/07/82:	Killed in same incident
BANDSMAN LAURENCE SMITH	20/07/82:	Killed in same incident
RFN DAVID GRAINGER	10/04/83:	Accidentally shot in barracks at Belleek
RFN DAVID MULLEY	18/03/86:	IRA bomb, Castlewellan, Co Down
L/CPL THOMAS HEWITT	19/07/87:	IRA sniper, Belleek, Co Fermanagh
CPL EDWARD JEDRUCH	31/07/87:	Killed in helicopter accident in South Armagh
SGT THOMAS ROSS	18/09/91:	RTA
L/CPL WAYNE HARRIS	8/11/91:	RTA. Hit a bridge in Armagh
RFN CHRISTOPHER WILLIAMS	8/11/91:	Killed in same incident
CPL MATTHEW MADDOCKS	14/11/91:	Helicopter crash, Gortin Glen, Omagh
CPL LARRY WALL	12/12/91:	Death by violent or unnatural causes
RFN JAMIE SMITH	10/08/92:	RTA
RFN RICHARD DAVEY	29/10/92:	Death by violent or unnatural causes
RFN DAVID FENLEY	17/02/93:	Accidentally shot in barracks at Strabane
WO2 KEITH THEOBOLD	2/10/95:	Death by violent or unnatural causes

Royal Hampshire Regiment

PTE JOHN KING	13/03/73:	IRA booby trap, Crossmaglen
PTE ALAN WATKINS	3/08/76:	INLA sniper, Dungiven, Co Londonderry
DRUMMER FRANK FALLOWS	10/11/76:	Died in accidental shooting, Magaheralin, Co Armagh
SGT MICHAEL P. UNSWORTH	2/01/77:	Drowned after helicopter accident River Bann
PTE COLIN CLIFFORD	30/04/82:	IRA landmine Belleek, Co Fermanagh
PTE ANDREW COCKWILL	17/05/89:	Cause of death not to be revealed at family's wishes

Royal Highland Fusiliers

FUSILIER JOHN B. MCCAIG	10/03/71:	Abducted and murdered by the IRA at Ligoniel, Belfast
FUSILIER JOSEPH MCCAIG	10/03/71:	Murdered in the same incident
FUS. DOUGALD P. MCCAUGHE	10/03/71:	Murdered in the same incident
L/CPL DAVID HIND	2/01/77:	Shot by IRA, Crossmaglen
CPL ROBERT M THOMPSON	20/07/80:	IRA car bomb, Moy Bridge, Aughnacloy

Royal Hussars

| S/SGT CHARLES SIMPSON | 7/11/74: | IRA booby trap, Stewartstown, Co Tyrone |
| LT ROBERT GLAZEBROOK | 14/11/76: | RTA |

Royal Horse Guards

| L/COH KEITH CHILLINGWORTH | 14/06/72: | RTA |

Royal Irish Rangers

SGT THOMAS MCGAHON	19/01/71:	RTA
CPL JAMES SINGLETON	19/01/71:	Killed in same incident
RANGER WILLIAM J. BEST	21/05/72:	Abducted and murdered when on home leave
RANGER THOMAS MCGANN	26/05/72:	RTA
L/CPL MICHAEL NORRIS	27/07/74:	Cause of death Unknown
RANGER H THOMPSON	6/12/77:	RTA
RANGER ROBERT QUAIL	5/07/79:	Cause of death unknown
RANGER SEAN REILLY	4/09/81:	Shot accidentally

RANGER DAVID LANHAM	10/01/83:	RTA
RANGER WALTER LLEWELLYN	22/05/86:	Accidentally shot
SGT JOHN PEDEN	7/10/86:	Drowned whilst training TA recruits
RANGER CYRIL J. SMITH QGM.	24/10/90:	Killed saving colleagues during bomb attack at Newry

Royal Irish Regiment

L/CPL MICHAEL W.A. PATTERSON	6/09/92:	RTA (HOME SERVICE FORCE)
SGT ROBERT IRVINE	20/10/92:	Shot by IRA in his sister's home, Rasharkin
PTE BRIAN MARTIN	20/10/92:	RTA (HOME SERVICE FORCE)
L/CPL IAN WARNOCK	19/11/92:	Shot by IRA as he met his wife in Portadown
PTE STEPHEN WALLER	30/12/92:	Shot by IRA when on home leave, Belfast
L/CPL MERVYN JOHNSTON	15/02/93:	Shot by IRA at his in-laws house West Belfast
PTE WILLIAM HARKNESS	27/03/93:	RTA
PTE ROBERT GARDNER	28/03/93:	RTA
CPL ROBERT NEWELL	5/03/93:	Death by violent or unnatural causes
PTE CHRIS WREN	31/05/93:	Killed by IRA bomb under his car in Moneymore
PTE MORRIS IRVINE	2/06/93:	Death by violent or unnatural causes
CPL ROBERT ARMSTRONG	21/11/93:	RTA
PTE SEAN MAIR	17/04/94:	RTA
PTE WILLIAM SALTERS	30/04/94:	Died in a fire at RUC station
PTE WILLIAM TOSH	30/04/94:	Killed in same incident
PTE ADRIAN ROGERS	15/05/94:	Died of injuries after fire
PTE REGGIE MCCOLLUM	21/05/94:	Abducted and murdered by the IRA whilst off-duty
CPL WILLIAM WOLFF	25/05/94:	Death by violent or unnatural causes
PTE SIMON LECKY	31/07/94:	RTA
CPL TRELFORD T. WITHERS	8/08/94:	Shot in his shop, Downpatrick Street, Crossgar
CPL RONALD JACKSON	10/10/95:	RTA
PTE WILLIAM MCCREA	10/10/95:	RTA
PTE PAUL KILPATRICK	13/12/95:	Death by violent or unnatural causes
CPL ROBERT ANDERSON	19/05/96:	Death by violent or unnatural causes
PTE ALAN MCCORMICK	1/06/96	RTA
L/CPL STEVE RANKIN	23/09/96:	Death by violent or unnatural causes
PTE JAMIE CATER	25/10/96:	Death by violent or unnatural causes
L/CPL THOMAS MCDONNELL	8/06/97:	Death by violent or unnatural causes
PTE WILLIAM WOODS	3/09/97:	Violent or unnatural causes
WOII ROBERT BELL	9/01/98:	Died on duty
PTE MATTHEW FRANCE	1/05/98:	Violent or unnatural causes
PTE RONALD MCCONVILLE	30/06/98:	Died on duty
CPL JACKY IRELAND	13/07/98:	RTA
PTE JOHN MURRAY	28/08/98:	RTA
L/CPL STUART ANDREWS	16/09/98:	Died on duty
CPL GERALD BLAIR	21/10/98:	Died on duty

Royal Irish Regiment (V)

WO2 HUGH MCGINN	28/12/80:	Killed by INLA in his own home in Armagh
SGT TREVOR A. ELLIOT	13/04/83:	Killed by IRA at his shop in Keady
CPL TREVOR MAY	9/04/84:	IRA bomb under his car in Newry outside his work

Royal Logistic Corps

CPL TERENCE HEFFY	7/12/93:	Killed in train accident
PTE MATTHEW EDWARDS	29/12/93:	Accidental shooting

L/CPL DAVID WILSON	14/05/94:	Killed by bomb attack at VCP at Keady, Co Armagh
L/CPL MARK TREHERNE	29/07/94:	Death by violent or unnatural causes; killed at Whiterock, Belfast
PTE PAUL SHEPHERD	25/12/95:	Death by violent or unnatural causes
L/CPL RICHARD FORD	30/10/98:	Died whilst on duty

Royal Marines

BAND CPL DEAN PAVEY	22/09/89:	Killed in IRA bomb outrage Marine Barracks, Deal
BAND CPL TREVOR DAVIS	22/09/89:	Killed in same incident
BAND CPL DAVE McMILLAN	22/09/89:	Killed in same incident
MUSICIAN RICHARD FICE	22/09/89:	Killed in same incident
MUSICIAN BOB SIMMONDS	22/09/89:	Killed in same incident
MUSICIAN MICK BALL	22/09/89:	Killed in same incident
MUSICIAN RICHARD JONES	22/09/89:	Killed in same incident
MUSICIAN TIM REEVES	22/09/89:	Killed in same incident
MUSICIAN MARK PETCH	22/09/89:	Killed in same incident
MUSICIAN ANDY CLEATHEROE	22/09/89:	Killed in same incident
MUSICIAN CHRIS NOLAN.	18/10/89:	DoW from same incident

Royal Marine Commandos
40 Cdo

MARINE LEONARD ALLEN	26/07/72:	Shot by IRA, Unity Flats, Belfast
MARINE ANTHONY DAVID	17/10/72:	DoW after being shot by IRA on Falls Road
MARINE JOHN SHAW	26/07/73:	RTA in highly controversial circumstances[1]
MARINE ANDREW GIBBONS	28/05/83:	Died Camlough Lake, Co Armagh from gunshot wounds

42 Cdo

MARINE GRAHAM COX	29/04/73:	IRA sniper, New Lodge, Belfast
MARINE JOHN MACKLIN	28/03/74:	DoW after being shot in the Antrim Rd, Belfast
CPL ROBERT MILLER	17/08/78:	IRA bomb attack, Forkhill
MARINE GARY WHEDDON	12/11/78:	DoW after bomb attack, Crossmaglen
MARINE ADAM GILBERT	15/06/89:	Shot in friendly fire incident, New Lodge Road

45 Cdo

CPL DENNIS LEACH	13/08/74:	IRA bomb, Crossmaglen
MARINE MICHAEL SOUTHERN	13/08/74:	Killed in same incident
MARINE NEIL BEWLEY	21/08/77:	IRA sniper Turf Lodge, Belfast
SGT WILLIAM CORBETT	23/08/81:	Accidentally shot, Musgrave Park Hospital, Belfast

Royal Marines (HQNI)

| MAJ John Richard Cooper | 16/02/82: | RTA |
| CPL Mark Harry Lazenby | 21/02/95: | RTA |

Royal Military Police

L/CPL WILLIAM G. JOLLIFFE	1/03/71:	Killed in crash in Londonderry after petrol bombing
CPL ALAN HOLMAN	11/02/73:	Accidentally shot
CPL RODERICK LANE	20/05/73:	RTA

---

1   Marine John Shaw's death is recorded by the Royal Marines as 'killed in action'

SGT SHERIDAN YOUNG	18/05/73:	Killed in IRA atrocity at Knock Na Moe Hotel
CPL RICHARD ROBERTS	30/05/73:	RTA
CPL STUART MILNE	20/02/74:	RTA
L/CPL PAUL MUNDY	20/02/74:	Killed in same incident
CPL THOMAS F. LEA	21/01/75:	DOW 8 months after IRA bomb attack, Belfast
CPL JOHN BOOTH	29/01/75:	Shot accidentally at Aldergrove Base
CPL MICHAEL HARDS	17/04/76:	Death by violent or unnatural causes
CPL WILLIAM SNAITH	25/01/79:	Death by violent or unnatural causes
CPL GEORGE MIDDLEMAS	8/11/77:	RTA
SGT DAVID ROSS	27/03/84:	Killed in Londonderry after explosion
L/CPL DUNCAN CHAPPELL	19/09/91:	Shot accidentally in 'friendly fire' incident
CORPORAL MICHAEL HEIGHTON	9/10/91:	Died on duty

Royal Navy

NA (AH) DAVID SHIPLEY	11/01/87:	RTA
AB MARK CARTWRIGHT	11/01/87:	Killed in same incident
Mem ALAN BALMER	29/07/88:	RTA
LT. A. R. SHIELDS.	22/08/88:	IRA bomb in Belfast; was Naval recruiter
LT CDR JOHN MCMASTER	18/07/91:	Shot off duty by IRA, Church Lane, Belfast
CK1 THOMAS GILLEN		RTA
L/SMN GAVIN STEWART		RTA
STWD ROBERT STEWART		RTA
L/WREN ANNIE BYRNE		RTA
MEM ALAN BALMER		RTA

Royal Pioneer Corps

PTE IRWIN BOWEN	2/08/72:	RTA
SGT JAMES ROBINSON	8/02/73:	Died of natural causes whilst on duty
PTE PHILIP DRAKE	26/08/74:	IRA sniper, Craigavon, Co Armagh
PTE GRAHAM HAYES	2/05/75:	Accidentally shot
PTE DAVID P. BONSALL	29/03/75:	RTA
PTE L. ROTHWELL	25/10/76:	Cause of Death unknown
L/CPL GRAHAM LEE	22/08/80:	RTA
PTE SOHAN VIRDEE	5/09/81:	Murdered by the IRA whilst off duty, Antrim Rd., Belfast
PTE S HUMBLE	26/08/81:	Killed in shooting accident: negligent discharge
CPL DEREK HAYES	21/05/88:	IRA booby trap, Crossmaglen

Royal Regiment Fusiliers
1st Battalion

FUSILIER. ANTHONY SIMMONS	15/11/74:	Shot by IRA at Strabane
CPL. PHILLIP BARKER	25/01/81:	Shot at VCP in Belfast
CPL. T H AGAR	18/05/84:	Killed by IRA bomb under car at Enniskillen
L/CPL. R V HUGGINS	18/05/84:	Killed in same incident
L/CPL. P W GALLIMORE	18/10/84:	Died of heart attack after bomb attack, Enniskillen

2nd Battalion

MAJOR. J J E SNOW	8/12/71:	DoW after being shot by IRA in New Lodge area
L/CPL JAMES J MCSHANE	4/02/74:	Killed in IRA bomb outrage, M62, Yorkshire
FUSILIER JACK HYNES	4/02.74:	Killed in same outrage
CPL CLIFFORD HAUGHTON	4/02/74:	Killed in same outrage
FUSILIER STEPHEN WHALLEY	7/02/74:	DoW: from same outrage
FUSILIER. K CANHAM	14/07/72:	IRA sniper in Lenadoon
FUSILIER. ALAN P TINGEY	23/08/72:	IRA sniper, West Belfast
CPL. D NAPIER	9/03/73:	RTA

FUSILIER. GEORGE FOXALL	16/06/80:	Accidentally shot: Magillan training camp
FUS THOMAS FOXALL	19/06/80:	RTA
FUSILIER. ANDREW GRUNDY	1/05/92:	IRA bomb at VCP at Killeen
L/CPL. MICHAEL J BESWICK	9/02/93:	DoW after IRA bomb in Armagh

3rd Battalion

CPL. JOHN L DAVIS	15/09/72:	Shot by IRA in Bogside, Londonderry
FUSILIER. CHARLES J MARCHANT	9/04/73:	DoW after being shot in ambush at Lurgan
CPL. DAVID LLEWELLYN	28/09/75:	RTA
CPL. E GLEESON	9/10/75:	IRA landmine, Lurgancullenboy
SGT. S J FRANCIS	21/11/75:	IRA booby trap, Forkhill
FUSILIER. M J SAMPSON	22/11/75:	Killed in major gun battle with IRA at Drumuckaval
FUSILIER. J D DUNCAN	22/11/75:	Killed in same incident
FUSILIER. P L McDONALD	22/11/75:	Killed in same incident
CPL. DONALD TRAYNOR	30/03/76:	IRA booby trap, Ballygallan
L/CPL. WAYNE MAKIN	3/01/83:	Violent or unnatural causes

BN Unknown

FUS TERRY THOMAS	25/01/72:	Death by violent or unnatural causes

Royal Regiment of Wales

PTE ALAN ROY ROGERS	13/03/71:	RTA at VCP
L/CPL JOHN HILLMAN	18/05/72:	IRA sniper Flex Street Mill, Ardoyne, Belfast
L/CPL ALAN GILES	12/06/72:	Shot in gun battle with IRA, Ardoyne, Belfast
PTE BRIAN SODEN	19/06/72:	IRA sniper in Ardoyne, Belfast
PTE DAVID MEEK	13/07/72:	IRA sniper, Hooker Street, Ardoyne, Belfast
PTE JOHN WILLIAMS	14/07/72:	Killed in gun battle with IRA, Hooker St., Ardoyne
PTE GARY CHANNING	21/11/86:	Accidental death at VCP in Omagh
PTE GEOFFREY JONES	5/01/87:	Death by violent or unnatural causes
WO1 (RSM) MIKE HEAKIN	12/08/88:	Murdered at traffic lights by IRA, Ostende, Belgium
PTE WILLIAM DAVIS	1/06/90:	Murdered in Litchfield railway station by IRA

Royal Scots

PTE RODERICK D W C. BANNON	31/03/76:	IRA landmine explosion, Co Armagh
PTE DAVID FERGUSON	31/03/76:	Killed in same incident
PTE JOHN PEARSON	31/03/76:	Killed in same incident
COL SGT NORMAN REDPATH	2/02/81:	Died of heart attack whilst on duty
PTE PATRICK J MCKENNA	15/03/81:	Accidentally shot
PTE ALAN BRUCE	17/09/82:	RTA
L/CPL LAWRENCE DICKSON.	17/03/93:	IRA sniper at Forkhill

Royal Scots Dragoon Guards

TROOPER IAN CAIE	24/08/72:	IRA landmine attack at Crossmaglen
TROOPER DONALD ROY DAVIES	18/11/74:	Cause of Death unknown

Royal Tank Regiment

L/CPL JOHN WARNOCK	4/09/71:	IRA landmine attack, Derrybeg Park, Newry
TROOPER JAMES NOWOSAD	3/03/78:	Shot by gunmen in 'Rag Day' killing, Belfast city Centre; also killed was a civilian searcher.
TROOPER JULIAN MILLS	18/09/77:	Drowned whilst on duty.
L/CPL NICHOLAS BUSHWELL	2/10/80:	RTA
CPL STEVEN SMITH	2/07/89:	IRA bomb under his car, Hanover, Germany

Royal Welsh Fusiliers

CPL GERALD BRISTOW	16/04/72:	IRA sniper Bishops Street, Londonderry
FUSILIER KERRY MCCARTHY	21/06/72:	IRA sniper Victoria RUC station, Londonderry
CPL DAVID SMITH	21/06/73:	IRA booby trap, Strabane
CPL ALAN COUGHLAN	28/10/74:	Van bomb attack at Ballykinler Army camp
FUSILIER ANDREW CROCKER	24/11/76:	Killed by IRA at Post Office robbery, Turf Lodge
LIEUTENANT STEVEN KIRBY	14/02/79:	IRA sniper Abercorn Road, Londonderry
CORPORAL DAVID WRIGHT	16/12/93:	RTA whilst on duty

Scots Dragoon Guards

TROOPER ANTHONY SUTTON	6/12/77:	Accidental death whilst on top cover in armoured vehicle
TROOPER DONALD DAVIES	17/11/74:	Cause of death unknown

Scots Guards

GUARDSMAN JOHN EDMUNDS	16/03/70:	Drowned
GUARDSMAN BRIAN HALL	4/10/71:	IRA sniper, Cupar Street, Falls are of Belfast
GUARDSMAN GEORGE HAMILTON	17/10/71:	Ambushed and killed by IRA, Cupar Street, Lower Falls
GUARDSMAN NORMAN BOOTH	30/10/71:	Killed in same incident
GUARDSMAN STEPHEN MCGUIRE	4/11/71:	IRA sniper Henry Taggart base, West Belfast
GUARDSMAN PAUL NICHOLS	27/11/71:	IRA sniper, St James Crescent, Falls Road, Belfast
GUARDSMAN JOHN VAN-BECK	18/09/72:	DoW after being shot by IRA, Lecky Road, Londonderry
GUARDSMAN GEORGE LOCKHART	26/09/72:	DoW after being shot by IRA, Bogside, Londonderry
L/SGT THOMAS MCKAY	28/10/72:	IRA sniper, Bishop Street, Londonderry
GUARDSMAN ALAN DAUGHTERY	31/12/73:	IRA sniper, Beechmount Avenue, Falls Road, Belfast
GUARDSMAN WILLIAM FORSYTH	5/10/74:	Killed in IRA bomb outrage, Guildford (with 4 others)
GUARDSMAN JOHN HUNTER	5/10/74:	Killed in same outrage
COL/SGT DAVID NADEN **	7/06/78:	RTA
L/CPL ALAN SWIFT ***	11/08/78:	Killed on covert ops, Letterkenny Rd, Londonderry
COL/SGT EDWIN MURRISON	9/04/80:	Killed on covert ops in a car chase
GUARDSMAN GARY CONNELL	12/10/80:	Death by drowning at end of tour
L/SGT IAIN HANNA	20/10/80:	Death by violent or unnatural causes
MAJ DONALD NICOL/ ARDMONACH	21/10/86:	Died of natural causes whilst on duty
L/SGT GRAHAM STEWART	5/05/90:	Killed on covert ops, Cullyhanna, Co Armagh
GUARDSMAN PAUL BROWN	2/08/90:	RTA
GUARDSMAN ALEX IRELAND	11/09/90:	Death by violent or unnatural causes
GUARDSMAN DAMIAN SHACKLETON	3/08/92:	IRA sniper, New Lodge, Belfast
GUARDSMAN ANDREW WASON	3/09/92:	Death by violent or unnatural causes

Staffordshire Regiment

S/SGT JOHN MORRELL	24/10/72:	DoW after IRA booby trap, Drumargh, Armagh
2ND LT MICHAEL SIMPSON	23/10/74:	DoW after being shot by IRA sniper, Londonderry
PTE CHRISTOPHER SHENTON	20/01/81:	IRA sniper whilst in OP Bogside, Londonderry
L/CPL STEPHEN ANDERSON	29/05/84:	IRA landmine, Crossmaglen
PTE MARK MASON	15/08/89:	Death by violent or unnatural causes
SGT DEAN OLIVER	9/05/92:	Death by violent or unnatural causes
PTE WAYNE G. SMITH	1/07/95:	RTA

The Highlanders

HIGHLANDER SCOTT HARRINGTON	9/07/95:	Death by violent or unnatural causes

The Royal Gloucestshire, Berkshire and Wiltshire Regiment

CPL GARY LLEWELLYN FENTON	22/06/98:	Run down and killed by lorry at VCP, Crossmaglen Posthumous Mention in Dispatches

Ulster Defence Regiment
2nd Battalion

SERGEANT HARRY D. DICKSON	27/02/72:	Murdered by the IRA at his home
PTE SIDNEY W. WATT	20/07/73:	Ambushed by the IRA at a friend's house
PTE KENNETH HILL	28/08/73:	Shot in Armagh City whilst attending an incident
CORPORAL JAMES A. FRAZER	30/08/75:	Killed by IRA at a friend's farm
L/CORPORAL JOE REID	31/08/75:	Murdered at home by IRA
L/CORPORAL D. JOHN BELL	6/11/75:	Killed by IRA as he returned from work
C/SERGEANT JOE NESBITT	10/11/75:	Shot by the IRA on his way to work
PTE JOSEPH A McCULLOUGH	25/02/76:	Stabbed to death by IRA
CORPORAL ROBERT McCONNELl	5/04/76:	Murdered at his home in Tullyvallen, Newtownhamilton
L/CORPORAL JEAN LEGGETT	6/04/76:	Ambushed and shot by IRA on patrol in Armagh
Lt JOE WILSON	26/10/76:	Killed at work by the IRA
PTE MARGARET A. HEARST	8/10/77:	Murdered at home by IRA near Middletown
CAPTAIN CHARLIE HENNING	6/10/78:	Shot by IRA whilst at work
L/CPL THOMAS ARMSTRONG	13/04/79:	Ambushed and killed by IRA on his way home
PTE JAMES PORTER	24/06/79:	Murdered at home by IRA
PTE JAMES H. HEWITT	10/10/80:	Killed by bomb under his car
PTE EDDIE COOKE	9/10/81:	Death by violent or unnatural causes
L/CPL FREDDIE A. WILLIAMSON	7/10/82:	Killed with a women prison officer in INLA-caused crash
SGT THOMAS G. COCHRANE	22/10/82:	Abducted and murdered by IRA
CPL CHARLIE H. SPENCE	10/11/82:	Shot by IRA as he left work in Armagh
CPL AUSTIN SMITH	19/12/82:	Shot by IRA after parking his car near home
MAJOR CHARLIE ARMSTRONG	14/11/83:	Killed by IRA bomb in Armagh City
PTE STEPHEN MCKINNEY	25/09/88:	Murdered by IRA as he arrived home after quitting UDR
L/CPL DAVY HALLIGAN	17/11/89:	Shot by IRA as he drove home
PTE ALEXANDER PHOENIX	16/03/90:	Killed at a VCP, Summerisland Rd. Loughall
PTE ROBERT DAY	25/09/90:	Death by violent or unnatural causes
PTE PAUL D SUTCLIFFE	1/03/91:	DoW after IRA mortar attack in Armagh
PTE ROGER J. LOVE	1/03/91:	DoW from same incident
PTE PAUL R. BLAKELY	31/05/91:	Killed in IRA bomb at the Glenane base with 2 others
PTE SIDNEY HAMILTON	31/05/91:	Killed in same incident
L/CPL ROBERT W. CROZIER	31/05/91:	Killed in same incident

3rd Battalion

L/CPL JOE JARDINE	8/03/72:	Shot by IRA whilst working
CPL JIM D. ELLIOTT	19/04/72:	Abducted and murdered by IRA; body then booby Trapped by his killers
C/SGT JOHN RUDDY	10/10/72:	Shot by IRA on his way to work
PTE THOMAS MCCREADY	17/11/74:	Shot by the IRA IN Newry
CPL CECIL GRILLS	12/01/78:	Shot by IRA as he drove home from work
PTE JIM COCHRANE	6/01/80:	Killed by IRA bomb at Castlewellen. One of 3 killed
PTE RICHARD SMITH	6/01/80:	Killed in same incident

PTE RICKY WILSON	6/01/80:	Killed in same incident
PTE COLIN H. QUINN	10/12/80:	Shot by INLA as he left work
MAJOR W.E. IVAN TOOMBS	16/01/81:	Shot by IRA in Warrenpoint where he worked
L/CPL RICHARD W.J. MCKEE	24/04/81:	Shot by IRA at Kilcoo whilst on duty
S/SGT WILLIAM A. MCATEE	12/06/82:	Death by violent or unnatural causes
PTE THOMAS WATTERSON	7/11/82:	Death by violent or unnatural causes
CAPTAIN GORDON HANNA	29/11/85:	Killed when IRA bomb exploded under his car at home
CPL D. BRIAN BROWN	28/05/86:	Killed by IRA bomb when searching after a warning
PTE ROBERT W HILL	1/07/86:	Killed when IRA bomb exploded under his car at home
CPL ALAN. T. JOHNSTON	15/02/88:	Shot by the IRA as he arrived for work
PTE W. JOHN MORELAND	16/12/88:	Shot in his coal lorry at Downpatrick
PTE MICHAEL D. ADAMS	9/04/90:	Killed by IRA landmine with 3 others at Downpatrick
L/CPL J (BRAD) BRADLEY	9/04/90:	Killed in same incident
PTE JOHN BIRCH	9/04/90:	Killed in same incident
PTE STEVEN SMART	9/04/90:	Killed in same incident

4th Battalion

PTE FRANK VEITCH	3/09/71:	Shot by IRA at Kinawley RUC station
PTE JOHNNY FLETCHER	1/03/72:	Abducted and murdered by IRA in front of his wife
L/CPL W. HARRY CREIGHTON	7/08/72:	Murdered by IRA at his house near Monaghan
PTE JIMMY. E. EAMES	25/08/72:	IRA booby trapped car at Enniskillen
L/CPL ALFIE JOHNSTON	25/08/72:	Killed in same incident
PTE TOMMY. R. BULLOCK	21/09/72:	Murdered along with his wife at their home
PTE J. ROBIN BELL	22/10/72:	Shot by IRA whilst with his father
PTE MATT LILLY	7/09/73:	Shot by the IRA on his milk round
PTE ALAN .R. FERGUSON	25/06/78:	Killed in IRA landmine and gun attack
2 BERNARD ADAMSON	31/05/72	Accidentally shot, Co Fermanagh
CPL HERBIE. G. KERNAGHAN	15/10/79:	Shot by the IRA as he delivered to his school; Witnessed by dozens of children
CPL AUBREY ABERCROMBIE	5/02/80:	Murdered by the IRA on his farm
PTE W. RITCHIE LATIMER	7/06/80:	Shot by the IRA at his hardware store
PTE NORMAN. H. DONALDSON	25/11/80:	Shot by IRA as he collected charity money at RUC Station whilst off-duty
PTE NICHOLAS LESTER	7/03/81:	Accidentally killed whilst on duty
L/CPL RONNIE GRAHAM	5/06/81:	Shot by IRA as he delivered coal; one of three brothers murdered by IRA
PTE CECIL GRAHAM	11/11/81:	DoW after being shot by IRA at his wife's house
CPL ALBERT BEACOM	17/11/81:	Murdered by IRA at his home
PTE JIMMY GRAHAM. BEM	1/02/85:	Shot in front of school children by IRA
PTE JOHN. F. EARLY	3/02/86:	IRA landmine
CPL JIMMY OLDMAN	3/04/87:	Shot by IRA gunmen as he arrived where he worked
CPL WILLIE BURLEIGH	6/04/88:	Killed by IRA bomb under his car

5th Battalion

CAPTAIN MARCUS MCCAUSLAND	4/03/71:	Abducted and murdered by the IRA
PTE THOMAS CALLAGHAN	16/02/72:	Abducted and murdered in the Creggan, Londonderry
PTE SAMUEL PORTER	22/11/72:	Shot and killed by the IRA as he walked home
PTE GEORGE E. HAMILTON	20/12/72:	Shot by the IRA as he worked on repairs at a reservoir

CAPTAIN JAMES HOOD	4/01/73:	Murdered by the IRA at home
SGT DAVID C.DEACON	3/03/73:	Abducted and murdered by the IRA
CPL JOHN CONLEY	23/07/74:	IRA car bomb in Bridge Street, Garvagh
PTE ROBERT STOTT	25/11/75:	Shot by the IRA on the way home from work
PTE JOHN ARRELL	22/01/76:	Shot on board his firm's mini bus by IRA
PTE JACK MCCUTCHEON	1/04/76:	Shot at work by the IRA
S/SGT BOBBY H.LENNOX	2/04/76:	Postman – lured to an isolated farm and shot
CAPTAIN W. RONNIE BOND	7/11/76:	Shot outside his home in Londonderry as he got home
L/CPL JIMMY SPEERS	9/11/76:	Shot by the IRA at his garage in Desertmartin
L/CPL WINSTON C. MCCAUGHEY	11/11/76:	Shot by the IRA as he stood outside his house in Kilrea
MAJOR J. PETER HILL	23/02/77:	Shot by IRA as he got home from work, Londonderry
PTE DAVID MCQUILLAN	15/03/77:	Shot by IRA as he waited for a lift to work, Bellaghy
L/CPL GERALD C. CLOETE	6/04/77:	Shot by the IRA as he drove to work in Londonderry
LT WALTER KERR	2/11/77:	DoW after IRA bomb under his car
CPL WILLIAM J. GORDON	8/02/78:	Killed along with daughter (10) after IRA bomb exploded under their car
L/CPL SAMUEL D. MONTGOMERY	10/02/81:	Shot by the IRA as he left work
PTE T. ALAN RITCHIE	25/05/81:	Killed in IRA ambush at Gulladuff near Bellaghy
PTE ALLEN CLARKE	12/09/81:	Shot by IRA as he walked through Maghera
L/CPL BERNIE V. MCKEOWN	17/12/83:	Murdered by the IRA in front of his 13 year old Son in their car
PTE JAMES MCSHANE	22/01/84:	Death by violent or unnatural causes
SGT BOBBY F. BOYD	18/11/85:	Murdered by the IRA at his front door
PTE CHARLES EDWIN MOORE	21/08/87:	Death by violent or unnatural causes
SGT TOMMY A. JAMISON	8/03/90:	Ambushed and killed by the IRA at work
PTE MICKEY BOXALL	6/11/91:	Killed in IRA mortar attack at Bellaghy

6th Battalion

PTE WINSTON DONNELL	9/08/71:	Killed by the IRA; manning VCP, Clady, Tyrone
SGT KENNETH SMYTH	10/12/71:	Shot whilst off duty by the IRA
CPL SYDNEY HUSSEY	20/05/72:	Died whilst preparing for foot patrol
PTE TED MEGAHEY	9/06/72:	DoW after IRA shooting
PTE WILLIAM J. BOGLE	5/12/72:	Murdered in his car as he sat with his children
PTE ROBERT N. JAMESON	17/01/74:	Shot by IRA as he got off a bus at Trillick
PTE EVA MARTIN	3/05/74:	Killed by IRA in rocket and gun attack at Clogher
CPL W. DEREK KIDD	18/11/76:	Shot and killed at work
CPL WILLIAM J. MCKEE	14/04/78:	Shot and killed by gunmen as he drove a school bus
PTE JOHN GRAHAM	25/04/79:	Shot by the IRA as he collected milk from farms
PTE JOHN A. HANNIGAN	19/06/79:	Shot by IRA as he came out of a shop in Omagh
PTE JAMES A. ROBINSON	19/10/79:	Shot and killed on his milk round
PTE WILLIE J. CLARKE	3/08/80:	Shot in the Republic visiting relatives
L/CPL JOHNNY MCKEEGAN	19/11/81:	Lured to a house in Strabane and shot by IRA
LT J. LESLIE HAMILTON	27/04/82:	Shot whilst delivering to a Londonderry supermarket
PTE H. A. (LEXI) CUMMINGS	15/06/82:	Shot by IRA as he prepared to drive home from work
PTE RONNIE ALEXANDER	13/07/83:	One of 4 men killed by IRA landmine at Drumquin
PTE OSSIE NEELY	13/07/83:	Killed in same incident

PTE JOHN ROXBOROUGH	13/07/83:	Killed in same incident
CPL THOMAS HARRON	13/07/83:	Killed in same incident
CPL RONNIE D. FINDLAY	23/08/83:	Shot by IRA as he left work
PTE GREG ELLIOTT	2/01/84:	Shot as he got into his van at Castlederg
L/CPL THOMAS A. LOUGHLIN	2/03/84:	Killed by IRA bomb planted underneath his works van
C/SGT IVAN E. HILLEN	12/05/84:	Shot and killed at his farm in Augher by IRA
CPL HEATHER.C. J. KERRIGAN	14/07/84:	One of 2 UDR killed in IRA landmine, Castlederg
PTE NORMAN J. MCKINLEY	14/07/84:	Killed in same incident
PTE W. VICTOR FOSTER	15/01/86	IRA bomb planted under his car at Castlederg
PTE THOMAS J. IRWIN	26/03/86:	Shot and killed by IRA at his work in Omagh
PTE WILLIAM C. POLLOCK	8/04/86:	Killed by IRA booby trap at home in Castlederg
CAPT IVAN R.K. ANDERSON	21/05/87:	Shot by IRA as he drove home from his school
L/CPL MICHAEL DARCY	4/06/88:	Murdered at home by IRA in Castlederg
CAPT TIM D ARMSTRONG	16/01/88:	Murdered by the UVF (Falklands veteran)
PTE JOHN STEWART	16/01/88:	DoW after being shot by IRA at his home in Coalisland
PTE SAMUEL H CAIRNS	25/01/88:	Cause of death unknown
PTE OLVEN L. KILPATRICK	9/01/90:	Shot by IRA at his shoe shop in Castlederg

7th Battalion

PTE JOHN B. HOUSTON	29/11/75:	Shot at work by the IRA
PTE PETER MCLELLAND	04/09/79:	Killed at VCP
PTE JOHN D. SMITH	27/03/81:	Shot by IRA as he walked to work in Belfast
L/CPL DAVID WHEELER	11/08/91:	Death by violent or unnatural causes

8th Battalion

PTE W. DENNIS WILSON	7/12/71:	Murdered at home in Curlough
L/CPL HENRY GILLESPIE	20/05/72:	Shot by IRA patrolling near Dungannon
PTE FRED D. GREEVES	15/12/72:	Shot by IRA as he left work in Armagh
CPL FRANK CADDOO	10/05/73:	Shot by IRA at his farm in Rehagey
CAPTAIN CORMAC MCCABE	19/01/74:	Abducted and murdered by IRA in Irish Republic
CPL ROY T. MOFFETT	3/03/74:	IRA landmine on Cookstown to Omagh road
WO2 DAVID SINNAMON	11/04/74:	IRA bomb in house in Dungannon
PTE EDMUND R. L. STEWART	29/04/76:	Lured to relatives house and shot by IRA
L/CPL STANLEY D. ADAMS	28/10/76:	Lured to remote farmhouse as mailman and shot by IRA
PTE JOHN REID	9/03/77:	Ambushed and shot by IRA as he fed his cattle
CPL DAVY GRAHAM	25/03/77:	DoW after being shot at work by IRA, Gortonis
CAPTAIN W. ERIC SHIELDS	29/04/77:	Shot by IRA outside his home in Dungannon
2ND/LT ROBIN SMYRL	13/09/77:	Shot by IRA as he drove to work at Plumbridge
PTE BOB J. BLOOMER	24/09/77:	DoW after being shot at home by IRA in Eglish
SGT JOCK B EAGLESHAM (MID)	7/02/78:	A postman, he was shot by IRA on his rounds
PTE G. SAMMY GIBSON	29/04/79:	Shot by IRA as he cycled to work in Tyrone
CPL FRED H. IRWIN	30/10/79:	Shot by IRA driving to work in Dungannon
PTE W. JACK DONNELLY	16/04/81:	Shot by INLA at his local pub in Moy
L/CPL CECIL W. MCNEILL	25/02/83:	Shot by IRA at his work in Tullyvannon
PTE ANDY F. STINSON	4/06/83:	Killed by INLA booby trap on his digger at work
PTE CYRUS CAMPBELL	24/10/83:	Shot by IRA at Carnteel as he drove to farm
PTE N. JIMMY JOHNSTON	8/05/84:	Shot by IRA disguised as ambulance men at his hospital
PTE ROBERT BENNETT	7/09/84:	Shot by IRA at his work in Pomeroy
PTE TREVOR W. HARKNESS	28/02/85:	Killed by IRA bomb at Pomeroy on foot patrol
PTE MARTIN A. J. BLANEY	6/10/86:	Shot by IRA as he drove home in Eglish

MAJOR GEORGE SHAW	26/01/87:	Murdered by IRA at his home in Dungannon
PTE WILLIE T. GRAHAM	25/04/87:	Shot by IRA at his farm in Pomeroy
CAPT TIM D ARRMSTRONG	16/01/88:	Murdered by unknown gunmen (Falklands veteran)
PTE JOHN STEWART	16/01/88:	DoW after being shot by IRA at his home in Coalisland
PTE NED GIBSON	26/04/88:	Shot by IRA as he worked on dustbins in Ardboe
PTE RAYMOND A. MCNICOL	3/08/88:	Shot by IRA as he drove to work in Desertcreat
PTE JOHN HARDY	14/03/89:	Shot by IRA as he drove his lorry to Granville
WO2 ALBERT D COOPER	2/11/90:	IRA bomb planted in car left at his garage in Cookstown

9th Battalion

SGT MAYNARD CRAWFORD	13/01/72:	Shot as he waited in a car at Newtownabbey
CPL ROY STANTON	9/06/72:	Shot by IRA as he drove home
PTE HENRY J. RUSSELL	13/07/72:	Abducted, tortured and shot by the IRA, Carrickfergus
CPL DAVID W. BINGHAM	16/01/73:	Abducted and killed by the IRA
PTE THOMAS J FORSYTHE	16/10/73:	Killed in a shooting accident; man charged with manslaughter
PTE STEVEN CARLETON	8/01/82:	Shot by the IRA at petrol station in Belfast
PTE LINDEN COLIN HOUSTON	20/01/84:	Murdered by the IRA at his home in Dunmurry

10th Battalion

PTE SEAN RUSSELL	8/12/71:	Murdered by IRA at his home, New Barnsley, Belfast
PTE SAMUEL TRAINOR	20/03/72:	IRA bomb, Belfast city centre
PTE ROBERT MCCOMB	23/07/72:	Abducted and murdered by IRA in Belfast
PTE TERENCE MAGUIRE	14/10/72:	Abducted and murdered in Belfast
PTE WILLIAM L. KENNY	16/03/73:	Abducted and murdered on way to UDR barracks
PTE KEVIN LIVINGSTONE	3/07/75:	Death by violent by unnatural causes
CPL JOHN GEDDIS	10/05/77:	Killed by UVF in explosion in Crumlin Road, Belfast
L/CPL GERALD W. D. TUCKER	8/06/77:	Shot by IRA as he left work at Royal Victoria Hospital
CPL JAMES MCFALL	27/07/77:	Murdered by IRA at his home in Belfast
CPL HUGH A. ROGERS	8/09/77:	Shot by IRA as he left for work in Dunmurry
PTE ROBERT REID	14/02/78:	Accidentally shot
SGT ROBERT L. BATCHELOR	27/11/78:	Shot by IRA as he left work in Belfast
PTE ALEXANDER GORE	6/06/79:	Shot by IRA at UDR base, Malone Road, Belfast
PTE MARK A. STOCKMAN	29/09/81:	Shot by INLA at work in Belfast
SGT RICKY CONNELLY	21/10/81:	Murdered at his home by IRA, Belfast
PTE BILLY ACHESON	4/09/82:	Death by violent or unnatural causes
PTE ALEX YOUNG	1/10/84:	Death by violent or unnatural causes
PTE FRED GALLAGHER	3/10/84:	Death by violent or unnatural causes
LT DUNCAN CARSON	6/04/85:	Death by violent or unnatural causes

11th Battalion

L/CPL VICTOR SMYTH	6/09/72:	IRA bomb underneath his car, in Portadown
2ND/LT R. IRWIN LONG	8/11/72:	Shot by IRA in Lurgan driving to collect his daughter
SGT ALFIE DOYLE	3/06/75:	He and two friends shot dead by IRA as they returned from a meeting in Irish Republic
PTE GEORGE LUTTON	15/11/76:	Shot by IRA on duty in Edward Street, Lurgan
PTE ROBERT J. MCNALLY	13/03/79:	Killed by INLA bomb under his car, Portadown

PTE S. DAVID MONTGOMERY	8/03/84:	Shot by IRA at his works, Moira on the Airport Road
PTE DAVID CHAMBERS	4/06/84:	Shot by IRA as he arrived for work, Dollingstown
PTE WILLIE R. MEGRATH	23/07/87:	Killed by IRA as he drove home to Lisburn
PTE STEPHEN MCMILLAN	19/11/89:	Death by violent or unnatural causes
PTE COLIN J. MCCULLOUGH	23/09/90:	Shot by IRA as he sat in his car with fiancé, Lurgan

4-6th Battalion

L/CPL KENNY A. NEWELL	27/11/91:	Abducted and murdered by IRA at Crossmaglen

7-10th Battalion

S/SGT ROBERT GALLOWAY	9/01/78:	Accidentally shot
PTE JAMES HUNTER	4/03/79:	Death by violent or unnatural causes
SGT DENIS TAGGART	4/08/86:	Shot dead outside his home by IRA in Belfast
PTE JOE MCILLWAINE	12/06/87:	Shot by IRA at his work in Dunmurry
PTE G. JOHN TRACEY	26/06/87:	Shot by IRA at his work in Belfast
PTE STEVEN W MEGRATH	17/09/87:	Shot by IRA at his relatives' house
PTE JAMES CUMMINGS	24/02/88:	Killed by IRA bomb in Belfast city centre
PTE FREDERICK STARRETT	24/02/88:	Killed in same incident
L/CPL ROY W BUTLER	2/08/88:	Shot dead by IRA in front of his family in West Belfast shopping centre
PTE BRIAN M LAWRENCE	17/06/91:	Shot by IRA as he arrived for work, Belfast

UDR (Battalion Unknown)

PTE THOMAS WILTON	22/10/70:	Died on duty
PTE JOHN PROCTOR	24/10/70:	RTA
S/SGT GEORGE GILKESON	11/10/71:	RTA
CPL THOMAS ADDIS	4/12/71:	Unknown
PTE EDWARD BROWN	13/12/71:	Unknown
L/CPL PHILIP THOMPSON	31/12/71:	RTA
PTE THOMAS MOFFETT	26/02/72:	Cause of death Unknown
PTE GEORGE CURRAN	12/03/72:	Cause of death Unknown
PTE DONALD KANE	4/04/72:	Cause of death Unknown
CPL BRIAN HERON	18/05/72:	Death by violent or unnatural causes
CPL SIDNEY HUSSEY	20/05/72:	Cause of death Unknown
SGT WILLIAM REID	28/05/72:	Death by violent or unnatural causes
PTE WILLIAM WILKINSON	12/07/72:	Cause of death Unknown
MAJOR ERIC BEAUMONT	25/07/72:	Cause of death Unknown
CPL ALBERT JOHNSTON	1/08/72:	Death by violent or unnatural causes
PTE ANDREW SIMPSON	18/09/72:	RTA
PTE THOMAS OLPHERT	6/10/72:	Death by violent or unnatural causes
PTE EDMUND SIMPSON	10/10/72:	Killed in an accident
PTE ROBERT MCKEOWN	13/10/72:	RTA
SGT WILLIAM CALDERWOOD	15/10/72:	Cause of death unknown
MAJ JOHN MUNNIS	16/10/72:	RTA
PTE THOMAS BOYD	28/12/72:	Death by violent or unnatural causes
PTE JOHNSTONE BRADLEY	23/01/73:	Died on duty
CPL PATRICK DAVIDSON	17/03/73:	Died on duty
PTE ALEXANDER MCCONAGHY	10/04/73:	Accidentally shot
PTE SAMUEL BEATTIE	14/04/73:	Accidentally shot
L/CPL HUGH WATTON	24/05/73:	Unknown
PTE COLIN MCKEOWN	17/10/73:	RTA
PTE WILLIAM MAGILL	19/10/73:	Accidentally shot in his home
L/CPL THOMAS BEATTY	4/11/73:	Unknown

CPL WILLIAM MARTIN	20/11/73:	RTA
PTE DAVID SPENCE	20/11/73:	RTA
PTE EDWARD GIBSON	30/05/74:	RTA
PTE NOEL SEELEY	26/06/74:	Unknown
PTE ROBERT RAINEY	27/07/74:	RTA
PTE SAMUEL WORKMAN	25/08/74:	RTA
PTE WILLIAM BELL	21/10/74:	Unknown
PTE ROBERT ALLEN	25/10/74:	Unknown
PTE JOHN S. MARTIN	18/11/74:	RTA
PTE JOHN TAYLOR	30/11/74:	RTA
PTE DAVID ARMSTRONG	28/01/75:	Accidentally shot
PTE DAVID WEIR MCDOWELL	26/01/75:	Shot accidentally by a soldier in Co Armagh
S/SGT IVAN NIXON	31/03/75:	RTA
SGT WILLIAM MILLAR	19/09/75:	RTA
PTE WILLIAM KEITH DONNELL	13/11/75:	RTA
PTE DAVID MOSGROVE	21/11/75:	RTA
L/CPL JOHN NIBLOCK	20/12/75:	RTA
PTE WILLIAM OVENS	27/03/76:	RTA
CAPTAIN GEORGE CHAMBERS	14/04/76:	Cause of death unknown
L/CPL ROBERT MCCREEDY	24/04/76:	RTA
PTE ISAAC STEWART	6/05/76:	RTA
PTE JOHN SCOTT	30/07/76:	Killed by PIRA bomb, Druminard, Co Londonderry
LT JOHN HIGGINS	8/08/76:	RTA
W/PTE ANN GAYNOR	9/08/76:	RTA
CAPT ERIC SCOTT	28/08/76:	RTA
CPL WILLIAM DUNN	27/11/76:	RTA
SGT FREDERICK PULFORD	18/02/77:	RTA
PTE ROBERT PURDY	29/05/77:	RTA
PTE SAMUEL GREER	30/06/77:	Cause of death unknown
PTE RAYMOND MCFARLAND	31/08/77:	RTA
PTE ALAN MCFARLAND	31/08/77:	RTA
PTE WILSON PENNEY	21/09/77:	RTA
CPL JOHN HILLIS	13/02/78:	Cause of death unknown
PPTE GEORGE FLEMING	23/02/78:	Accidental death
L/CPL WILLIAM CRAWFORD	15/03/78:	Cause of death unknown
PTE NOEL PATTERSON	2/09/78:	Cause of death unknown
CPL ALISTAIR COOKE	19/09/78:	RTA
PTE TREVOR HERRON	4/12/78:	RTA
PTE ARTHUR LANGLEY	5/12/78:	Cause of death unknown
L/CPL THOMAS FORDE	9/01/79:	Cause of death unknown
PTE JOSEPH HOGG	1/03/79:	Cause of death unknown
SGT PATRICK MCMULKIN	9/03/79:	Cause of death unknown
SGT THOMAS DOAK	13/03/79:	Died on duty
PTE VICTOR WILSON	30/03/79:	Cause of death unknown
PTE WILLIAM MORTON	29/04/79:	RTA
L/CPL IVAN MCCORKELL	8/06/79:	RTA
PTE NORMAN WYSNER	01/08/79:	Cause of death unknown
PTE ALAN MCCELLAND	4/09/79:	RTA
SGT JOSEPH AGNEW	15/09/79:	Cause of death unknown
WO2 JAMES WARNOCK	15/09/79:	Cause of death unknown
CPL ERNEST ATKINSON	23/09/79:	Died on duty
CPL CECIL ROLESTON	26/09/79:	Cause of death unknown
CPL WILLIAM MCCROSSAN	29/10/79:	Cause of death unknown
PTE MERVYN DOHERTY	14/10/79:	Accidentally shot
PTE HILARY GRAHAM	15/11/79:	RTA-caused injuries

PTE ALEXANDER ROWE	12/12/79:	RTA
SGT THOMAS MCCULLOCH	21/12/79:	Death by violent or unnatural causes
PTE GEORGE BROWN	27/12/79:	RTA
PTE ROBERT DAVISON	29/12/79:	Died on duty
L/CPL SAMUEL KELLY	5/02/80:	Death by violent or unnatural causes
W/PTE MARY COCHRANE	28/02/80:	RTA
PTE MALCOLM ODGERS	10/03/80:	Death by violent or unnatural causes
PTE CONSTANCE BEATTIE	25/09/80:	Cause of death unknown
LT DAVID PATTERSON	24/04/81:	RTA
PTE WILLIAM JACKSON	9/07/81:	Death by violent or unnatural causes
PTE SAMUEL WHITESIDE	20/08/81:	RTA
L/CPL BRENDEN MCKEOWN	26/03/82:	RTA
PTE JONATHAN MOORHEAD	22/02/82:	Shot accidentally with own pistol
PTE BRIAN WALMSLEY	1/05/82:	RTA
PTE ALAN D MAULE	2/01/83:	Death by violent or unnatural causes
PTE KENNETH KELLY	14/04/83:	Died accidentally whilst boarding an helicopter
PTE LEONARD GREER	16/04/83:	RTA
PTE BRIAN KIRKPATRICK	1/10/83:	RTA
PTE ROBERT ALEXANDER IRWIN	21/12/83:	RTA
PTE FRAZER BROWN	22/01/84:	RTA
PTE ROBERT KILPATRICK	3/09/84:	Death by violent or unnatural causes
PTE SAMUEL JOSEPH BRADFORD	21/12/84:	RTA
PTE ALBERT BROWN	21/04/85:	RTA
PTE SAMUEL HUNTER	29/05/85:	Death by violent or unnatural causes
PTE MERVYN SALMON	28/01/86:	RTA
PTE BRIAN NICHOLL	28/03/86:	RTA
PTE ALFRED ROY ALLEN	28/06/86:	RTA
PTE ANDREW MONTGOMERY	30/06/86:	RTA
W/CPL CIARA OUSBY	20/07/86:	RTA
LT PAUL MAXWELL	4/08/86:	RTA
PTE JOHN MCKERAGHAN	14/03/87:	RTA
CPL JAMES ANDERSON	25/04/87:	RTA
PTE PETER AC CLARKE	0/08/87:	Death by violent or unnatural causes
PTE THOMAS AICKEN	11/08/87:	RTA
PTE CARL PEARCE	11/08/87:	RTA
PTE GARY MOORE	19/08/87:	Cause of death unknown
L/CPL ROBERT J WHITE	29/08/87:	Cause of death unknown
PTE CLIVE CRAIG	5/11/87:	Death by violent or unnatural causes
PTE WILLIAM REILLY	8/11/87:	RTA
PTE ROBERT MCBURNEY	3/12/87:	Accidental death
PTE RONALD KELLY	31/12/87:	Accidental death
PTE FRANCIS GIBSON	26/04/88:	RTA
L/CPL THOMAS BAILIE	9/01/89:	Died on duty
COL SGT WILLIAM PAGE	13/02/89:	Cause of death unknown
PTE THOMAS JONSTON	8/05/89:	RTA
STAFF SGT RIBERT MCKIMM	22/07/89:	Died on duty
PTE JOHN GUNNING	5/09/89:	Cause of death unknown
PTE MATTHEW CHRISTIE	11/09/89:	RTA
PTE JOHN CRAIG JENNINGS	25/09/89:	RTA
PTE BRIAN CORDNER	4/11/90:	RTA
PTE DAVID WILLIAMSON	15/11/90:	RTA
PTE ALAN C. MCCONNELL	9/09/91:	RTA
SGT GEORGE ROLLINS	27/09/91:	RTA
W/PTE ELIZABETH SLOAN	13/04/92:	RTA in Ballymena area.
PTE STEPHEN SCANLON	11/05/92:	RTA

The following UDR Soldiers were killed in accidents; places unknown

WOPTE GEORGE ELLIOTT	26/06/72	
PTE WILLIAM HAMILTON	4/08/72	RTA
PTE KENNETH TWADDELL	5/08/72	RTA
PTE THOMAS I. MCCLELLAND	26/04/87	
L/CPL DAVID GASS	16/06/88:	Accidental Death
PTE WILLIAM CHERRY	28/08/88:	Died of natural causes whilst on duty
PTE THOMAS D LAMBE	27/09/88:	Accidental death
LT JOSEPH FORSYTHE	30/11/88:	Accidental death
PTE KEVIN HUTCHINGS	12/07/89	

Ex Ulster Defence Regiment Soldiers Killed in Northern Ireland

MR D.J. MCCORMICK	10/12/71:	Shot by IRA on way to work
MR ISAAC SCOTT	10/07/73:	Shot by IRA in Belleek, Co Armagh
MR IVAN VENNARD	3/10/73:	Shot dead by IRA on his postal round, Lurgan
MR GEORGE SAUNDERSON	10/04/74:	Shot by IRA at his school in Co Fermanagh
MR WILLIAM HUTCHINSON	24/08/74:	Shot by IRA at work
MR GEORGE MCCALL	2/08/75:	Shot by IRA in Moy, Co Tyrone
MR KENNETH WORTON	5/01/76:	1 of 10 men murdered in Kingsmill Massacre
MR NICOLAS WHITE	13/03/76:	Shot at youth club, Ardoyne, Belfast
MR SIDNEY MCAVOY	12/06/76:	Shot at his shop in Dunmurry
MR JOHN FREEBURN	28/06/76:	Shot in Lurgan
MR NORMAN CAMPBELL	15/12/76:	Joined RUC and shot in Portadown
MR ROBERT HARRISON	5/02/77:	RUCR: shot by IRA Gilford, Co Down
MR JOHN LEE	27/02/77:	Shot by IRA in club in Ardoyne, Belfast
MR JAMES GREEN	5/05/77:	Shot by IRA whilst working as Taxi driver, Belfast
MR GILBERT JOHNSTON	19/08/78:	Shot by IRA at his shop in Keady, Co Armagh
MR MICHAEL RILEY	19/08/78:	Shot at his home by IRA in Shankhill Rd Belfast
MR ROBERT LOCKHART	17/04/79:	RUCR: killed by IRA bomb at Camlough
MR JACK MCCLENAGHAN	19/05/79:	Shot by the IRA whilst delivering bread in Fermanagh
MR DAVID STANLEY WRAY	20/05/79:	Shot by IRA on his way to church in Claremont
MR DAVID ALAN DUNNE	2/06/79:	RUCR: shot by INLA in Armagh
MR GEORGE HAWTHORNE	5/10/79:	Shot by IRA in Newry
MR JAMES FOWLER	16/12/79:	Shot by IRA as he drove his fish van in Omagh
MR CLIFFORD LUNDY	2/01/80:	Shot at work by IRA near Bessbrook, Co Armagh
MR HENRY LIVINGSTONE	6/03/80:	Shot by IRA at his farm at Tynan, Co Armagh
MR VICTOR MORROW	17/04/80:	Shot by IRA at Newtownbutler, Co Fermanagh
MR WILLIAM ELLIOT	28/06/80:	Shot by IRA at cattle market in Ballybay, Co Monaghan
MR JOHN ROBINSON	23/04/81:	Shot by IRA driving works van in Armagh
MR PTE JOHN PROCTOR	14/09/81:	Shot by IRA at hospital after visiting his wife and newborn baby at Magherafelt
MR HECTOR HALL	5/10/81:	Shot by IRA outside Altnagelvin hospital
MR CHARLES NEVILLE	10/11/81:	Shot by IRA at work in Co Armagh
MR JAMES MCCLINTOCK	18/11/81:	Shot by IRA on his way home from work, Londonderry
MR NORMAN HANNA	11/03/82:	Shot by IRA at his works in Newry
MR THOMAS CUNNINGHAM	12/05/82:	Shot by IRA whilst working in Strabane
MR WILFRED MCILVEEN	27/08/82:	IRA bomb underneath his car in Armagh
MR CHARLES CROTHERS	5/10/82:	Shot by IRA at Altnagelvin
MR JAMES GIBSON	2/12/82:	Shot by IRA driving school bus at Coalisland
MR JOHN TRUCKLE	20/09/83:	IRA bomb underneath his car in Portadown
MR RONALD FUNSTON	13/03/84:	Shot by IRA on his farm at Pettigoe, Co Fermanagh

MR HUGH GALLAGHER	3/06/84:	Taxi driver; he was lured by IRA to Omagh and shot
MR MELVIN SIMPSON	8/10/84:	Shot by IRA at work in Dungannon
MR DOUGLAS MCELHINNEY	24/02/85:	Shot by INLA at friend's house in Londonderry
MR GEOFFREY CAMPBELL	25/02/85:	RUCR. One of nine killed IRA mortar attack, Newry
MR HERBET MCCONVILLE	15/05/86:	Shot dead by IRA whilst delivering in Newry
MR HARRY HENRY	21/04/87:	Murdered by IRA at his home in Magherafelt
MR CHARLES WATSON	22/05/87:	Murdered by the IRA at his home, Clough, Co Down
MR NATHANIEL CUSH	15/06/87:	IRA bomb underneath his car in Belfast
MR JOHN GRIFFITHS	4/05/89:	IRA bomb underneath his car
MR ROBERT J GLOVER	15/11/89:	IRA bomb underneath his car near Dungannon
Mr DAVID STERRITT	24/07/90:	RUCR: killed with 4 others by IRA landmine, Armagh
MR DAVID POLLOCK	20/10/90:	Shot by an IRA sniper in Strabane
MR NORMAN KENDALL	10/11/90:	Murdered with 3 others by IRA, Castor Bay, Lurgan
MR HUBERT GILMORE	1/12/90:	Shot by IRA Kilrea, Co Londonderry
MR ERIC BOYD	5/08/91:	Shot by IRA as he left work Cappagh, Co Tyrone
MR RONALD FINLAY	15/08/91:	Shot at work by the IRA, Co Tyrone
MR DAVID MARTIN	25/04/93:	IRA bomb underneath his car, Kildress, Co Tyrone
MR JOHN LYNESS	24/06/93:	Shot by IRA at his home in Lurgan
MR JOHN ALEXANDER BURNS	30/10/93:	Shot by UFF at Eglington
MR ALAN SMYTH	25/04/94:	Shot by IRA in Garvagh
MR ERIC SMYTH	28/04/94:	Shot by IRA at his home in Co Armagh
MR DAVID CALDWELL[2]	1/08/02:	Working on Army camp in Londonderry; killed by 'Real' IRA booby trap

Welsh Guards

SGT PHILIP PRICE	21/07/72:	IRA car bomb on 'Bloody Friday' Belfast bus depot
GUARDSMAN DAVID ROBERTS	24/11/73:	Killed by IRA bomb, South Armagh
GUARDSMAN PAUL FRYER	13/11/79:	IRA bomb, Fords Cross, South Armagh
L/CPL MARK HOWELLS	12/07/92	RTA

Worcester & Sherwood Foresters

PTE MARTIN ROBINSON	16/04/72:	Killed in gun battle at Brandywell base, Londonderry
PTE MARTIN JESSOP	20/09/82:	Killed in rocket attack, Springfield Road RUC station
CPL LEON BUSH	27/09/82:	IRA booby trap, West Circular Road, Belfast
CPL STEPHEN MCGONIGLE	4/05/89:	IRA landmine, Crossmaglen
L/CPL STEPHEN KENT	2/02/90:	RTA
CPL GARY KIRBY	2/02/90:	Killed in same accident
PTE DAVID PEAT	24/07/94:	Death by violent or unnatural causes

Women's Royal Army Corps

W/PTE ANN HAMILTON	5/10/74:	Killed with 4 others in IRA bomb outrage, Guildford
W/PTE CAROLINE SLATER	5/10/74:	Killed in same outrage

---

2   David Cadwell's name, although outside the dates parameter, is included, because it is believed that he was targeted by the 'Real' IRA because of his former UDR involvement.

L/CPL ROBERTA THAIN	25/03/75:	Accidentally shot dead in Shipquay Street, Londonderry
W/SGT ALISON STRYKER	4/06/76:	RTA
W/PTE KATHRYN WATERLAND	16/08/79:	RTA
W/CPL ELAINE NEEDHAM	14/02/83:	RTA
W/PTE MARIA HORNSBY	11/12/84:	RTA
W/PTE KAREN R. COWAN	10/11/85:	RTA
*		Att Intelligence Corps
**		Members of the SAS
***		Members of 14 Int.

Security Services (Date and cause of death withheld by MOD)

CHARLES APCAR	12/08/74:	Death by violent or unnatural causes

Although on the ROH, the following people are not included in the Total number of Military Deaths

Civilian Searchers

Norma Spence	3/03/78:	Shot by IRA in Belfast City centre by IRA
Brian Russell	28/09/78:	Shot by IRA waterloo Place, Londonderry

The following Army Women and Children were also killed as a result of terrorism

MRS EMILY BULLOCK	21/09/72:	Murdered by IRA, Aghalane
MRS LINDA HAUGHTON	4/02/74:	M62 Coach Bomb outrage
MASTER LEE HAUGHTON	4/02/74:	Killed in same outrage
MASTER ROBERT HAUGHTON	4/02/74:	Killed in same outrage
MR GORDON CATHERWOOD	30/10/74:	Killed by IRA sniper aiming at his UDR son and wife, North Belfast.
MR KIERAN MCCANN	22/01/75:	Shot by IRA gunmen in Eglish, Co Tyrone
TREVOR FOSTER	8/11/81:	Killed by IRA bomb meant for his UDR father
MISS LESLEY GORDON	8/02/78:	Murdered with her Daddy, by IRA, Maghera
MRS IRIS FARLEY	7/02/87:	UDR mother; killed by INLA, Markethill, Armagh
HEIDI HAZELL	7/09/89:	Murdered by IRA, Unna-Messen, Germany.
NIVRUTI MAHESKKUMAR	26/10/89:	Murdered with her Daddy, Wildenrath, Germany

Army Civilian Personnel Killed in Aldershot IRA bomb outrage 22/02/72

THELMA BOSLEY
JOAN LUNN
MARGARET GRANT
JILL MANSFIELD
JOHN HASLAR
CHERIE MUNTON

Army Civilian Workers Murdered in Terrorist Incidents

Noor Baz Khan	26/06/73:	Murdered by the IRA in Londonderry
John Dunn	11/01/74:	Murdered by the IRA, Waterside, Londonderry
Cecilia Byrne	11/01/74:	Murdered in the same incident
Donald Farrell	23/03/74:	Army Careers Officer; shot by IRA
Mohammed Abdul Khalid	22/04/74:	Murdered by the IRA at Crossmaglen
Hugh Slater	11/11/74:	Murdered by the IRA, Londonderry
Leonard Cross	11/11/74:	Murdered in same incident****
Patsie Gillespie:	24/10/90:	Killed by IRA at Coshquin in 'Proxy' Bomb
Brendan McWilliams	18/04/92:	Killed at home by IRA

**** Leonard Cross was a member of the Army Cadet Force and is also commemorated as such.

Former Army Personnel Killed as a Direct Consequence of the Troubles

Alfred Shotter (ex RN) Murdered by IRA, Londonderry: 1/05/74

Brian Shaw (ex-RGJ) Murdered by IRA in Lower Falls area: 21/07/74

Nicholas White (ex-Queens) Murdered by IRA in Ardoyne: 13/03/76

Victor Dormer (ex-RCT) Murdered by IRA   1/10/76

John Lee (ex-Parachute Regt) Murdered by IRA in Ardoyne: 27/02/77

Mr James Green (ex-Royal Irish Regiment) Shot by IRA whilst working as Taxi driver, 5/05/77:

Nigel Smyth (ex-Royal Artillery) Shot by IRA, Central Belfast   23/05/94

Petty Officer Frederick MacLaughlin George Medal. He was severely wounded during the vicious rioting in the Crumlin/Ardoyne in June 1970. A gunshot wound injured his spine. Died as a direct result of a gunshot wound he received whilst driving an ambulance during severe rioting in North Belfast on 27 June 1970. He refused medical treatment until he had completed the evacuation of another gunshot victim. He was awarded the George Medal for his bravery that day. Frederick died on 27 June 1993, aged 61, exactly 23 years to the day he was shot.

Other soldiers, military families and Civilian workers were killed or died during their time in Northern Ireland and the Author invites anyone with further knowledge of these people with Regiments, dates, or causes of death, to contact him on: ken_wharton@hotmail.co.uk. I apologise for any erroneous information, for missing names or for misspelled names.

I gratefully and wholeheartedly acknowledge the incredible services of Emma Beaumont without whom, the compiling of this comprehensive Roll of Honour could never have happened. Great assistance by individual Regimental Associations was also given and I would like to mention Mike Sangster, Royal Artillery, Mark Campbell, Royal Artillery and UDR, Norman Brown of the Royal Pioneer Corps, Kevin Gorman of the Scots Guards, Kevin Stevens, Royal Green Jackets, the late Pete Whittall, Staffords, Richard Nettleton, Grenadier Guards and Robert Osborne, QLR. I gratefully acknowledge the Armed Forces Memorial Roll of Honour and the Northern Ireland Veterans' Association for the ability to cross-reference between these two excellent sites.

RUC Roll of Honour 1969–98

Surname	Forename	Rank	Killed	By	How Killed
Arbuckle	Victor	Constable	11-Oct-1969	Loyalists	Shot dead during riot on Shankill Road
Donaldson	Sam	Constable	12-Aug-1970	IRA	Killed by booby-trap car bomb in Culloville, Crossmaglen
Millar	Robert	Constable	12-Aug-1970	IRA	Killed by booby-trap car bomb in Culloville, Crossmaglen
Buckley	Robert	Constable	28-Feb-1971	IRA	Shot dead during riots at Alliance Avenue, North Belfast
Patterson	Cecil	D/Inspector	28-Feb-1971	IRA	Shot dead during riots at Alliance Avenue, North Belfast
Leslie	Robert	Constable	18-Sep-1971	IRA	Shot and fatally wounded in Castle Place, Strabane
Cunningham	Cecil	Constable	15-Oct-1971	IRA	Shot dead in Ardoyne, Belfast
Haslett	John	Constable	15-Oct-1971	IRA	Shot dead in Ardoyne, Belfast
Dodd	Ronald	Sergeant	27-Oct-1971	IRA	Shot and fatally wounded at Gallagh, Toomebridge
Devlin	Alfred	Inspector	29-Oct-1971	IRA	Killed in bomb at Chichester Road RUC Station, Belfast
Corry	Stanley	D/Constable	1-Nov-1971	IRA	Shot dead in Andersonstown, Belfast
Russell	William	D/Constable	1-Nov-1971	IRA	Shot dead in Andersonstown, Belfast
Hurley	Dermot	Sergeant	11-Nov-1971	IRA	Fatally injured in gun attack on Oldpark Road, Belfast
Moore	Walter	Constable	11-Nov-1971	IRA	Fatally injured in gun attack on Oldpark Road, Belfast
Denham	Raymond	R/Constable	12-Jan-1972	IRA	Shot dead at his civilian employment in factory at Waterford Street, Belfast
Gilgunn	Peter	Sergeant	27-Jan-1972	IRA	Fatally wounded in gun attack at junction of Creggan Hill/Helen Street, Londonderry
Montgomery	David	Constable	27-Jan-1972	IRA	Fatally wounded in gun attack at junction of Creggan Hill/Helen Street, Londonderry
Carroll	Raymond	Constable	28-Jan-1972	IRA	Shot dead as he repaired his car in a garage on Oldpark Road, Belfast
Morrow	Thomas	Sergeant	2-Mar-1972	IRA	Died from gunshot wounds following gun attack in Newry Road, Camlough, County Armagh

Surname	Forename	Rank	Killed	By	How Killed
Logan	William	Constable	15-Mar-1972	IRA	Died from gunshot wounds following attack in Coalisland, Co Tyrone
McAllister	Ernest	Constable	20-Mar-1972	IRA	Killed by car bomb as they helped clear civilians from Donegal Street, Belfast
O'Neill	Bernard	Constable	20-Mar-1972	IRA	Killed by car bomb as they helped clear civilians from Donegal Street, Belfast
Houston	David	Constable	26-Jun-1972	IRA	Shot and fatally wounded in Newry. He was posthumously awarded the Queen's Police Medal
Laverty	Robert	Constable	16-Jul-1972	IRA	Fatally wounded during gun attack on Antrim Road, Belfast
Gibson	Robert	R/Constable	21-Jul-1972	IRA	Killed by car bomb at Oxford Street Bus Station
Harron	Gordon	Constable	21-Oct-1972	Loyalists	Died from gunshot wounds in attack at Shore Road Belfast. He was posthumously awarded the Queen's Police Medal
Calvin	Joseph	R/Constable	16-Nov-1972	IRA	Killed by booby-trap car bomb in Enniskillen
Keys	Robert	Constable	28-Nov-1972	IRA	Killed during rocket attack on Belleek RUC Station
Nixon	James	Constable	13-Dec-1972	IRA	Shot dead off duty as he left Antrim Road
Chambers	George	Constable	15-Dec-1972	Official IRA	Fatally injured in gun attack in Kilwilkie Estate, Lurgan, Co Armagh
Dorset	David	Sergeant	14-Jan-1973	IRA	Killed in booby-trap car bomb in Harbour Square, Londonderry
Sandford	Henry	R/Constable	14-Jan-1973	IRA	Fatally injured in a landmine explosion on Ballygawley/ Cappagh Road, Co Tyrone
Wilson	Mervyn	Constable	14-Jan-1973	IRA	Killed in booby-trap car bomb in Harbour Square, Londonderry
Morrison	Charles	Constable	8-Feb-1973	IRA	Shot dead in gun attack, Donaghmore, Dungannon, Co Tyrone
Wylie	Raymond	Constable	27-Feb-1973	IRA	Fatally wounded in gun attack at Aghagallon, Aghalee, Co Antrim. He was posthumously awarded Queen's Police Medal
McCauley	Robert	Constable	25-Mar-1973	IRA	Fatally wounded in gun attack at Aghagallon, Aghalee, Co Antrim. He was posthumously awarded Queen's Police Medal
Purvis	David	Constable	5-Jun-1973	IRA	Fatally wounded in gun attack in Enniskillen

Surname	Forename	Rank	Killed	By	How Killed
McElveen	William	R/Constable	13-Aug-1973	IRA	Fatally wounded in gun attack in Cathedral Road, Armagh
Campbell	William	R/Constable	16-Oct-1973	IRA	Fatally wounded in gun attack on Antrim Road, Belfast
Doherty	John	D/Constable	28-Oct-1973	IRA	Shot dead in gun ambush as he visited his mother's home at Ballindrait, Lifford, Co Donegal
Megaw	Robert	Constable	1-Dec-1973	IRA	Shot dead in gun attack at junction of Sloan Street/Edward Street, Lurgan
Rolston	Maurice	Constable	11-Dec-1973	IRA	Killed in booby-trap car bomb outside his home in Newcastle Co Down
Logue	Michael	Constable	29-Dec-1973	UDA	Fatally wounded in gun attack Forthriver Road, Belfast
Rogers	John	R/Constable	26-Jan-1974	IRA	Fatally wounded in gun attack in Glengormley, Co Antrim
Baggley	William	R/Constable	29-Jan-1974		Fatally wounded in gun attack in Dungiven Road, Londonderry
McClinton	Thomas	Constable	2-Mar-1974	IRA	Shot dead at point-blank range in Upper Donegal Street, Belfast
Wilson	Cyril	Constable	17-Mar-1974	Loyalists	Fatally wounded in gun attack at junction of Tullygally Road, Ardowne Roundabout, Craigavon, Co Armagh
Robinson	Frederick	Sergeant	19-Mar-1974		Killed by booby-trap car bomb at his home in Greenisland, Co Antrim
McCall	Thomas	Constable	16-Apr-1974	IRA	Fatally wounded in gun attack in Newtownhamilton, Co Armagh
Bell	Brian	Constable	10-May-1974	IRA	Fatally wounded in gun attack at Finaghy Cross Roads
Ross	John	Constable	10-May-1974	IRA	Fatally wounded in gun attack at Finaghy Cross Roads
Forsythe	John	Constable	18-Jun-1974	IRA	Killed by bomb in car of Market Street, Lurgan
O'Connor	Daniel	Sergeant	22-Jun-1974	IRA	Fatally wounded in gun attack in Crumlin Road, Belfast
Flanagan	Peter	D/Inspector	23-Aug-1974	IRA	Fatally wounded by gunmen who singled him out in premises in George's Street, Omagh
Elliott	William	Inspector	6-Sep-1974	IRA	Fatally wounded as he challenged armed raiders at bank in Rathcoole, Newtownabbey, Co Antrim. He was posthumously awarded the Queen's Police Medal
Henderson	Arthur	R/Constable	8-Oct-1974	IRA	Killed by booby-trap car bomb in Stewartstown, Co. Tyrone
Forde	Robert	Constable	20-Nov-1974	IRA	Killed by booby-trap car bomb in Rathmore, Craigavon, Co. Armagh

Surname	Forename	Rank	Killed	By	How Killed
McNeice	David	Constable	14-Dec-1974	IRA	Shot dead in gun attack at Killeavey, Co.Armagh
Coulter	George	Sergeant	31-Jan-1975	IRA	Shot dead in gun attacked at junction of Dungannon/Donaghmore Road, Co Tyrone
Harrison	Mildred	R/Constable	16-Mar-1975	UVF	Killed by bomb as she and a colleague performed beat duty in Bangor, Co Down
Gray	Paul	Constable	10-May-1975	IRA	Fatally wounded in gun attack on Derry's Wall, Londonderry
Davis	Noel	Constable	24-May-1975	INLA	Killed by booby-trap bomb in stolen vehicle at Ballinahone Road, Maghera, Co Londonderry
Johnston	Andrew	D/Constable	7-Jul-1975	IRA	Killed by booby-trap bomb as he examined the scene of a burglary at a school in Sloan Street, Lurgan
McPherson	Robert	Constable	26-Jul-1975	INLA	Fatally wounded in gun attack in Dungiven, Co Londonderry. He was posthumously awarded a Queen's Commendation for Bravery
Love	David	D/Constable	6-Oct-1975	IRA	Killed by booby-trap bomb at Terrydromond, Limavady, Co Londonderry
Baird	Andrew	R/Constable	14-Oct-1975	IRA	Fatally wounded by bomb placed at security hut at Church Street, Portadown
Clements	Joseph	R/Constable	16-Nov-1975	IRA	Fatally wounded in landmine explosion near Cloghfin, Sixmilecross, Co Tyrone
Clarke	Samuel	R/Constable	25-Nov-1975	IRA	Fatally wounded in gun attack at Clonavaddy, Dungannon, Co Tyrone
Maxwell	Patrick	Sergeant	25-Nov-1975	IRA	Fatally wounded in gun attack at Clonavaddy, Dungannon, Co Tyrone
Evans	Clifford	R/Constable	5-Jan-1976	IRA	Fatally wounded in gun attack between Toomebridge/Castledawson, Co Londonderry
Bell	George	Inspector	22-Jan-1976	Unknown	Killed by a booby-trap bomb at Donegal Pass RUC Station, Belfast
Cummings	Neville	Constable	22-Jan-1976	Unknown	Killed by a booby-trap bomb at Donegal Pass RUC Station, Belfast
Blakely	James	Sergeant	6-Feb-1976	IRA	Fatally injured in gun attack near Clifionville Circus, Belfast
Murtagh	William	Inspector	7-Feb-1976	IRA	Fatally injured in gun attack near Clifionville Circus, Belfast
Hamer	William	R/Constable	12-Feb-1976	IRA	Fatally wounded in gun attack in Claudy, Co Londonderry

Surname	Forename	Rank	Killed	By	How Killed
Crooks	William	R/Constable	23-Apr-1976	IRA	Fatally wounded in gun attack at Dernagh Crossroads, Coalisland, Co Tyrone
Evans	Thomas	R/Constable	15-May-1976	IRA	Fatally wounded when a booby-trap bomb exploded near Belcoo RUC Station, Co Fermanagh
Hunter	James	Sergeant	15-May-1976	IRA	Fatally wounded in gun attack near Warrenpoint, Co Down
Kettles	Francis	R/Constable	15-May-1976	IRA	Fatally wounded when a booby-trap bomb exploded near Belcoo RUC Station, Co Fermanagh
Keys	Harry	Sergeant	15-May-1976	IRA	Fatally wounded when a booby-trap bomb exploded near Belcoo RUC Station, Co Fermanagh
Nelson	Kenneth	R/Constable	16-May-1976	IRA	Shot dead as he let his dog out at his home at Dungannon, Co Tyrone
McCambridge	John	Constable	22-May-1976	IRA	Off duty, he was ambushed and shot dead as he stepped out of his car at Corrainey, Dungannon
Baggley	Linda	R/Constable	2-Jun-1976	IRA	Fatally injured in a gun attack in Chapel Road, Londonderry. Her father, who was also in the RUC, was killed in 1974
McAdam	Ronald	D/Constable	2-Jun-1976	IRA	Off duty, he was shot dead as he collected friends outside the Royal Victoria Hospital, Belfast
Cush	Thomas	Constable	31-Jul-1976	IRA	Shot dead at security barrier at Church Place, Lurgan
Heaney	James	Constable	26-Aug-1976		Off duty, he was working at his car at his mother's house in Andersonstown when he was fatally wounded in gun attack
Craig	Albert	Sergeant	18-Sep-1976	IRA	Fatally wounded in gun attack at Shamrock Park, Portadown
McKay	Arthur	R/Constable	8-Oct-1976	IRA	Killed in booby-trap bomb at Drumsaragh Road, Kilrea, Co Londonderry
McCabe	Noel	D/Constable	2-Nov-1976	IRA	Fatally wounded in gun attack at junction of Clonard Street/Falls Road, Belfast
Scott	Joseph	R/Constable	3-Dec-1976	IRA	Engaged in his civilian employment as traffic warden, he was shot dead at the junction of Circular Road/Killyman Road, Dungannon, Co Tyrone
Campbell	Norman	Constable	15-Dec-1976	IRA	Fatally wounded in gun attack at High Street, Portadown
Armour	Samuel	R/Constable	22-Dec-1976	IRA	Killed when booby-trap bomb exploded underneath his car at Maghera, Co Londonderry

Surname	Forename	Rank	Killed	By	How Killed
Greer	James	R/Constable	14-Jan-1977	IRA	Killed by booby-trap car bomb at his home at Portglenone, Co Antrim
McNulty	Patrick	D/Constable	27-Jan-1977	IRA	Shot dead as he left his car for service at garage in Strand Road, Londonderry
Harrison	Robert	R/Constable	5-Feb-1977	IRA	Fatally wounded in gun attack in Gilford, Co Down
McKane	Samuel	R/Constable	17-Feb-1977	IRA	Fatally wounded in gun attack at his home at Cloughmills, Co Antrim
Cobb	Harold	Inspector	24-Feb-1977	IRA	Fatally wounded in gun attack at Church Place, Lurgan, Co Armagh
Campbell	Joseph	Sergeant	25-Feb-1977	Unknown	Shot dead as he closed the gates to Cushendall RUC Station, Co Antrim
Brown	William	Constable	13-Mar-1977	IRA	Fatally wounded in gun attack between Ballagh Crossroads and Lisnaskea, Co Fermanagh
McCracken	John	Constable	8-Apr-1977	IRA	Fatally wounded in gun attack on the Moneymore Road, Magherafelt, Co Londonderry
Sheehan	Kenneth	Constable	8-Apr-1977	IRA	Fatally wounded in gun attack on the Moneymore Road, Magherafelt, Co Londonderry
North	Robert	R/Constable	20-May-1977	IRA	Was engaged in his civilian employment as bus driver when he was fatally injured in gun attack at Drumderg, Benburb, Co Tyrone
Davison	Samuel	Constable	2-Jun-1977	IRA	Fatally wounded in gun attack at Ardboe, Co Tyrone
Lynch	Norman	Constable	2-Jun-1977	IRA	Fatally wounded in gun attack at Ardboe, Co Tyrone
Martin	Hugh	R/Constable	2-Jun-1977	IRA	Fatally wounded in gun attack at Ardboe, Co Tyrone
Morrow	David	R/Constable	6-Jul-1977	IRA	Fatally wounded in gun attack at Aughnacloy, Co Tyrone
Crothers	Gordon	R/Constable	17-Feb-1978	IRA	One of 12 people killed in blaze which followed a bomb explosion at the La Mon House, Castlereagh, Co Down
Simpson	Charles	Constable	28-Feb-1978	IRA	Fatally wounded in gun attack at Clarendon Street, Londonderry
Moore	John	R/Constable	15-Apr-1978	IRA	Killed by landmine under his car at his home near Armoy, Co Antrim
McAllister	Millar	Constable	22-Apr-1978	IRA	Shot dead at his home in Lisburn, Co Antrim
Struthers	Robert	R/Constable	16-Jun-1978	IRA	Shot dead at his civilian employment in shop at Lorne Street, Londonderry
McConnell	Hugh	Constable	17-Jun-1978	IRA	Fatally wounded during gun attack on Camlough/Crossmaglen Road

Surname	Forename	Rank	Killed	By	How Killed
Turbitt	William	A/Constable	17-Jun-1978	IRA	Abducted after gun attack on Camlough/Crossmaglen Road. His body was recovered three weeks later at Cullyhanna
Rankin	Jacob	R/Constable	4-Jul-1978	IRA	Fatally wounded in gun attack outside Castlederg RUC Station
Lamont	John	R/Constable	2-Aug-1978	IRA	Fatally wounded in gun attack in George Street, Ballymena
Donaghy	Howard	R/Constable	11-Sep-1978	IRA	Off duty, he was fatally wounded as he worked at his house at Loughmacroary, Omagh
Baird	Richard	Constable	17-Apr-1979	IRA	Killed in a booby-trap van bomb at Millvale Road, between Bessbrook and Newry
Gray	Paul	Constable	17-Apr-1979	IRA	Killed in a booby-trap van bomb at Millvale Road, between Bessbrook and Newry
Lockhart	Robert	R/Constable	17-Apr-1979	IRA	Killed in a booby-trap van bomb at Millvale Road, between Bessbrook and Newry
Webb	Noel	Constable	17-Apr-1979	IRA	Killed in a booby-trap van bomb at Millvale Road, between Bessbrook and Newry
Prue	Norman	D/Constable	6-May-1979	IRA	Shot dead outside Holy Cross Chapel, Chapel Brae, Lisnaskea
Wray	Stanley	R/Constable	20-May-1979	IRA	Fatally wounded in gun attack as he and his family arrived to attend morning service at Claremont Presbyterian Church, Londonderry
Dunne	Alan	R/Constable	2-Jun-1979	INLA	Fatally wounded in gun attack outside his home in Armagh
Hanna	Stanley	Superintendent	3-Jun-1979	IRA	Killed by bomb near community centre, Clonalig, Crossmaglen
Thompson	Keith	Constable	3-Jun-1979	IRA	Killed by bomb near community centre, Clonalig, Crossmaglen
Scott	John	R/Constable	22-Jun-1979	IRA	Engaged in his civilian employment, he was fatally wounded in gun attack at Ardboe, Coagh
Walsh	George	Constable	31-Jul-1979	INLA	Fatally wounded in gun attack outside Armagh Courthouse
Davidson	Derek	Constable	2-Aug-1979	IRA	Fatally wounded in gun attack at Clondara Street, Falls Road, Belfast
Davidson	Gerry	Constable	18-Nov-1979	IRA	Fatally wounded in gun attack at Springfield Road RUC Station, Belfast
Hazelton	Stanley	R/Constable	22-Dec-1979	IRA	Off duty, he was fatally wounded in gun ambush at Glasslough, Co Monaghan
Crilly	Robert	R/Constable	3-Jan-1980	IRA	Fatally wounded in gun attack in Newtownbutler, Co Fermanagh

Surname	Forename	Rank	Killed	By	How Killed
Purse	David	R/Constable	12-Jan-1980	IRA	Fatally wounded in gun attack at Seaview Football Club, Shore Road, Belfast
Howe	Winston	Constable	11-Feb-1980	IRA	Killed in landmine explosion, Lisnaskea
Rose	Joseph	Constable	11-Feb-1980	IRA	Killed in landmine explosion, Lisnaskea
Montgomery	Bernard	R/Constable	4-Apr-1980	IRA	Fatally wounded in gun attack at Ligoniel, Belfast
Magill	Stephen	Constable	9-Apr-1980	IRA	Fatally wounded in gun attack at Stewartstown Road, Belfast
Wilson	Fred	R/Constable	11-Apr-1980	IRA	Shot dead as he arrived at his civilian employment in Franklyn Street, Belfast
Allen	Wallace	R/Constable	1-Sep-1980	IRA	Ambushed and abducted as he drove his milk lorry in Newtownhamilton area. His body was recovered 12 days later
Johnston	Ernest	R/Constable	22-Sep-1980	IRA	Fatally wounded in gun attack outside his home at Lisrace, Magheraveely, Co Fermanagh
McDougall	Lindsay	R/Constable	14-Jan-1981	INLA	Fatally wounded in gun attack in Great Victoria Street, Belfast
Stronge	James	R/Constable	21-Jan-1981	IRA	Fatally wounded in gun attack at his home, Tynan Abbey, Co Armagh
Lewis	Charles	R/Constable	6-Feb-1981	IRA	Fatally wounded in gun attack at Balmoral Avenue, Belfast
Scott	Alexander	R/Constable	8-Feb-1981	IRA	Fatally wounded in gun attack outside his wife's shop at My Lady's Road, Belfast
Acheson	Kenneth	Constable	2-Apr-1981	IRA	Fatally wounded in booby-trap car bomb at Berrywilligan Road, Bessbrook
Martin	Gary	Constable	27-Apr-1981	INLA	Killed in booby-trap bomb at Shaw's Road, Belfast
Ellis	Philip	Constable	6-May-1981	IRA	Fatally wounded in gun attack at Edlingham Street/Duncairn Gardens, Belfast
Vallely	Samuel	Constable	14-May-1981	IRA	Fatally wounded in rocket grenade attack at Upper Springfield Road, Belfast
Robinson	Mervyn	Constable	28-May-1981	IRA	Off duty, he was shot dead at Whitecross, Co Armagh
Dunlop	Colin	R/Constable	31-May-1981	IRA	Shot dead while he was on security duty at intensive care unit, Royal Victoria Hospital
Kyle	Christopher	R/Constable	17-Jun-1981	IRA	Off duty, he was fatally wounded in gun attack at his home near Omagh
Quinn	Neal	Constable	20-Jun-1981	IRA	Off duty, he was fatally wounded in gun attack in North Street, Newry

Surname	Forename	Rank	Killed	By	How Killed
Smyth	John	Constable	2-Aug-1981	IRA	Killed when a landmine exploded near Loughmacrory, Omagh
Woods	Andrew	Constable	2-Aug-1981	IRA	Killed when a landmine exploded near Loughmacrory, Omagh
Evans	Mark	Constable	7-Sep-1981	IRA	Killed in landmine explosion near Pomeroy
Montgomery	John	Constable	7-Sep-1981	IRA	Killed in landmine explosion near Pomeroy
Proctor	John	R/Constable	14-Sep-1981	IRA	Off duty, he was visiting his wife who had just given birth in the Mid Ulster Hospital, Magherafelt when he was shot dead
Stewart	George	Constable	26-Sep-1981	IRA	Off duty, he was fatally wounded in a gun attack at Main Street, Killough, Co Down
Beck	Alexander	Constable	28-Sep-1981	IRA	Fatally wounded when his Land Rover was hit by a rocket at Suffolk Road, Belfast
Lyttle	Silas	R/Constable	17-Nov-1981	IRA	Off duty, he was fatally wounded in gun attack outside his home at Grange, Ballygawley
Coulter	William	Constable	28-Nov-1981	IRA	Fatally wounded by booby-trap bomb at Unity Flats, Belfast
Duddy	Norman	Inspector	28-Mar-1982	IRA	Fatally wounded in gun attack as he and his sons left Strand Road Presbyterian Church, Londonderry
Brown	David	Sergeant	16-Apr-1982	IRA	Fatally wounded in gun attack at Springfield Crescent, Belfast
Caskey	Samuel	Constable	4-May-1982	IRA	Fatally wounded in gun attack at the Diamond, Londonderry
Reeves	David	D/Constable	11-Jun-1982	IRA	Killed by booby-trap bomb at Shantallow, Londonderry
Eagleson	John	R/Constable	1-Oct-1982	IRA	Fatally wounded in gun attack on way to his civilian employment in Upper Kildress Road, Cookstown
Crothers	Charles	R/Constable	5-Oct-1982	IRA	Fatally wounded in gun attack at his civilian employment at Altnagelvin, Londonderry
Hamilton	Paul	Constable	27-Oct-1982	IRA	Killed by bomb at Kinnego Embankment, Lurgan
McCloy	Allan	Constable	27-Oct-1982	IRA	Killed by bomb at Kinnego Embankment, Lurgan
Quinn	John	Sergeant	27-Oct-1982	IRA	Killed by bomb at Kinnego Embankment, Lurgan
Ewing	Gary	Constable	9-Nov-1982	IRA	Off duty, he was fatally wounded when a booby-trap bomb exploded under his car near the Lakeland Forum, Enniskillen
Corkey	Snowdon	R/Constable	16-Nov-1982	INLA	Fatally wounded in gun attack in Newry Street, Markethill

Surname	Forename	Rank	Killed	By	How Killed
Irwin	Ronald	R/Constable	16-Nov-1982	INLA	Fatally wounded in gun attack in Newry Street, Markethill
Brown	Eric	Sergeant	6-Jan-1983	IRA	Fatally wounded in gun attack at the Square, Rostrevor
Quinn	Brian	R/Constable	6-Jan-1983	IRA	Fatally wounded in gun attack at the Square, Rostrevor
Olphert	John	R/Constable	18-Jan-1983	IRA	Was serving customers in his shop at Sperrin Park, Londonderry when he was shot dead by gunmen
Magill	Edward	R/Constable	20-Feb-1983	IRA	Fatally wounded in gun attack at Warrenpoint RUC Station
Wilson	Gordon	Sergeant	21-Feb-1983	IRA	Fatally injured by booby-trap bomb at Lower English Street, Armagh
McCormack	Lindsay	Constable	2-Mar-1983	IRA	Fatally wounded in gun attack at Serpentine Road, Belfast
Morton	Frederick	R/Constable	15-Mar-1983	IRA	Was driving his bread van at Portadown Road, Newry when he was fatally wounded in gun attack
Cathcart	Gerald	Constable	16-May-1983	IRA	Fatally wounded in gun attack at Linkview Park, Belfast
Carson	Colin	R/Constable	26-May-1983	INLA	Fatally wounded in gun attack at Molesworth Estate, Cookstown
Wasson	John	Constable	7-Sep-1983	INLA	Fatally wounded in gun attack outside his home at Cathedral Road, Armagh
Ferguson	James	R/Constable	6-Oct-1983	IRA	Fatally wounded in gun attack at Meadowlands Estate, Downpatrick
Finlay	William	R/Constable	6-Oct-1983	IRA	Fatally wounded in gun attack at Meadowlands Estate, Downpatrick
Hallawell	John	Constable	28-Oct-1983	IRA	Fatally wounded in gun attack at Sheelin Park, Shantallow, Londonderry
Clarke	Paul	Constable	1-Nov-1983	IRA	Fatally injured in mortar attack at Carrickmore RUC Station
Fyfe	Stephen	Sergeant	4-Nov-1983	IRA	Fatally wounded by a bomb as he attended a lecture at the Ulster Polytechnic, Jordonstown
Martin	John	Inspector	4-Nov-1983	IRA	Fatally wounded by a bomb as he attended a lecture at the Ulster Polytechnic, Jordonstown
McFadden	John	R/Constable	5-Nov-1983	IRA	Fatally wounded in gun attack outside his home in Rasharkin
Fitzpatrick	William	R/Constable	10-Nov-1983	IRA	Fatally wounded in gun attack at his home near Kilkeel
Fullerton	William	R/Constable	10-Jan-1984	IRA	Fatally wounded in gun attack at Greenbank Roundabout outside Newry
Bingham	Thomas	Constable	31-Jan-1984	IRA	Killed by a landmine on the Newry/ Forkhill Road

Surname	Forename	Rank	Killed	By	How Killed
Savage	William	Sergeant	31-Jan-1984	IRA	Killed by a landmine on the Newry/ Forkhill Road
Dawson	Michael	Constable	12-Apr-1984	Loyalists	Killed by booby-trap bomb at University Street, Belfast
Elliott	Trevor	R/Constable	18-May-1984	IRA	Fatally injured in landmine explosion on the Camlough/ Crossmaglen Road
Gray	Neville	Constable	18-May-1984	IRA	Fatally injured in landmine explosion on the Camlough/ Crossmaglen Road
Todd	Michael	Constable	15-Jun-1984	INLA	Fatally wounded in gun attack at Lenadoon Avenue, Belfast
White	Malcolm	Sergeant	12-Aug-1984	IRA	Fatally injured by landmine on Gortin/Greencastle Road
McDonald	William	Sergeant	4-Nov-1984	IRA	Died as a result of injuries sustained in bomb attack at the Ulster Polytechnic, 1983
Campbell	Geoffrey	R/Constable	28-Feb-1985	IRA	Fatally wounded in mortar attack on Newry RUC Station
Donaldson	Alexander	C/Inspector	28-Feb-1985	IRA	Fatally wounded in mortar attack on Newry RUC Station
Dowd	John	Sergeant	28-Feb-1985	IRA	Fatally wounded in mortar attack on Newry RUC Station
Kelly	Ivy	Constable	28-Feb-1985	IRA	Fatally wounded in mortar attack on Newry RUC Station
McFerran	Paul	R/Constable	28-Feb-1985	IRA	Fatally wounded in mortar attack on Newry RUC Station
McGookin	Rosemary	Constable	28-Feb-1985	IRA	Fatally wounded in mortar attack on Newry RUC Station
McHenry	Sean	R/Constable	28-Feb-1985	IRA	Fatally wounded in mortar attack on Newry RUC Station
Price	Denis	R/Constable	28-Feb-1985	IRA	Fatally wounded in mortar attack on Newry RUC Station
Topping	David	Constable	28-Feb-1985	IRA	Fatally wounded in mortar attack on Newry RUC Station
McCormac	Hugh	Sergeant	3-Mar-1985	IRA	Fatally wounded in gun attack as he and his family attended Mass in Enniskillen
Bell	John	R/Constable	29-Mar-1985	IRA	Fatally wounded in gun attack at Rathfriland
Kay	Michael	R/Constable	3-Apr-1985	IRA	Killed by booby-trap outside Newry Courthouse
Baird	David	Constable	20-May-1985	IRA	Killed by bomb at Killeen Customs post
Doak	Tracey	Constable	20-May-1985	IRA	Killed by bomb at Killeen Customs post
Rodgers	Steven	R/Constable	20-May-1985	IRA	Killed by bomb at Killeen Customs post

Surname	Forename	Rank	Killed	By	How Killed
Wilson	William	Inspector	20-May-1985	IRA	Killed by bomb at Killeen Customs post
Murphy	Francis	Sergeant	21-May-1985	IRA	Fatally wounded in gun attack as he dropped schoolchildren at Drumsallon Primary School
Agnew	William	R/Constable	16-Jun-1985	IRA	Off duty, he was fatally wounded in gun attack as he sat in his car with his fiancée in Kilrea, Co Londonderry
Gilliland	William	Constable	18-Jun-1985	IRA	Fatally wounded by bomb at Kinawley Road, Co Fermanagh
Vance	Martin	Inspector	31-Aug-1985	IRA	Off duty, he was fatally wounded in gun attack at Crossgar, Co Down
Hanson	David	Constable	15-Nov-1985	IRA	Killed by landmine explosion at Castleblaney Road, Crossmaglen
Clements	William	R/Constable	7-Dec-1985	IRA	Fatally wounded in gun attack on Ballygawley RUC Station
Gilliland	George	Constable	7-Dec-1985	IRA	Fatally wounded in gun attack on Ballygawley RUC Station
McCandless	James	Constable	1-Jan-1986	IRA	Killed by bomb at Ogle Street, Armagh
Williams	Michael	R/Constable	1-Jan-1986	IRA	Killed by bomb at Ogle Street, Armagh
Breen	Derek	D/Constable	11-Feb-1986	IRA	Fatally wounded in gun attack in Maguirebridge, Co Fermanagh
Hazlett	James	Inspector	23-Apr-1986	IRA	Fatally wounded in gun attack outside his home in Newcastle, Co Down
McBride	David	Constable	22-May-1986	IRA	Killed by a bomb at Larkin's Road, Crossmaglen
Smyth	William	Constable	22-May-1986	IRA	Killed by a bomb at Larkin's Road, Crossmaglen
McVitty	John	A/Constable	8-Jul-1986	IRA	Fatally injured in gun attack as he cut rushes on his farm at Drumady, Rosslea, Co Fermanagh
Allen	Charles	Constable	26-Jul-1986	IRA	Fatally injured in gun attack in Market Square, Newry
Blackbourne	Karl	Constable	26-Jul-1986	IRA	Fatally injured in gun attack in Market Square, Newry
Kilpatrick	Peter	Sergeant	26-Jul-1986	IRA	Fatally injured in gun attack in Market Square, Newry
Dobbin	Desmond	R/Constable	12-Oct-1986	IRA	Fatally injured in mortar attack on New Barnsley RUC Station
Patterson	Derek	Constable	10-Nov-1986	IPLO	Fatally wounded in gun attack at Fitzroy Avenue, Belfast
Crawford	Ivan	R/Constable	9-Jan-1987	IRA	Fatally wounded in bomb explosion in centre of Enniskillen
Nesbitt	Peter	R/Constable	10-Mar-1987	IRA	Fatally wounded in bomb explosion at Ardoyne, Belfast

Surname	Forename	Rank	Killed	By	How Killed
Bennison	John	D/Sergeant	23-Mar-1987	IRA	Killed in booby-trap explosion at Magee College, Londonderry
Wilson	Austin	D/Inspector	23-Mar-1987	IRA	Killed in booby-trap explosion at Magee College, Londonderry
Shaw	George	R/Constable	3-Apr-1987	IRA	Fatally wounded in gun attack on Ballynahinch RUC Station
Armstrong	Frederick	R/Constable	11-Apr-1987	IRA	Fatally wounded in gun attack at Portrush
McLean	Robert	R/Constable	11-Apr-1987	IRA	Fatally wounded in gun attack at Portrush
Ead	David	Inspector	20-Apr-1987	IRA	Fatally injured in gun attack outside Newcastle RUC Station
Cooke	Thomas	Sergeant	23-Apr-1987	IRA	Fatally wounded in gun attack as he left his golf club in Londonderry
McClean	Sam	Constable	2-Jun-1987	IRA	Fatally wounded in gun attack as he worked on the farm of his elderly parents at Drumbreen, Co Donegal
Guthrie	Robert	Sergeant	23-Jun-1987	IRA	Fatally wounded in gun attack outside Antrim Road RUC Station
Kennedy	Norman	Constable	26-Jul-1987	IRA	Shot dead in his Ballymena home as he watched television with his wife
Carson	Ernest	D/Constable	26-Aug-1987	IRA	Fatally wounded in gun attack in docks area of Belfast
Malone	Michael	D/Constable	26-Aug-1987	IRA	Fatally wounded in gun attack in docks area of Belfast
Finlay	Winston	R/Constable	30-Aug-1987	IRA	Was getting out of his car - driven by his wife - outside his home near Magherafelt when he was shot dead by gunmen
Armstrong	Edward	R/Constable	8-Nov-1987	IRA	Killed in the Enniskillen Poppy Day bomb
Gilmore	Colin	R/Constable	25-Jan-1988	IRA	Fatally wounded in drogue bomb attack at Falls Road, Belfast
Graham	Clive	Constable	21-Mar-1988	IRA	Fatally wounded in gun attack in Creggan, Londonderry
Warnock	John	D/Constable	2-Aug-1988	IRA	Killed by booby-trap bomb near Lisburn RUC Station
Larmour	John	Constable	11-Oct-1988	IRA	Shot dead as he worked in his brother's ice cream shop on the Lisburn Road, Belfast
McCrone	Hugh	R/Constable	26-Oct-1988	IRA	Fatally wounded in gun attack near Kinawley, Co Fermanagh
Monteith	William	R/Constable	21-Nov-1988	IRA	Fatally wounded in gun attack at town barrier in Castlederg
Montgomery	Stephen	Constable	28-Jan-1989	IRA	Fatally wounded in drogue bomb attack at Melmont Road, Sion Mills
Breen	Harry	C/Superintendent	20-Mar-1989	IRA	Fatally wounded in gun attack at Jonesborough as he returned from Dundalk Garda Station

Surname	Forename	Rank	Killed	By	How Killed
Buchanan	Robert	Superintendent	20-Mar-1989	IRA	Fatally wounded in gun attack at Jonesborough as he returned from Dundalk Garda Station
Black	David	R/Constable	27-Jun-1989	IRA	Fatally wounded by booby-trap bomb under his car in Londonderry
Annett	Norman	Constable	1-Jul-1989	IRA	Fatally injured in gun attack on his mother's home in Garvagh
Bell	Alexander	R/Constable	24-Jul-1989	IRA	Fatally injured in bomb attack between Waterfoot and Cushendall
Harris	Alwyn	Superintendent	8-Oct-1989	IRA	Fatally injured by booby-trap bomb under his car as he and his wife travelled to church
Marshall	Michael	Constable	20-Oct-1989	IRA	Fatally wounded in gun attack in Belleek
Monteith	Derek	Inspector	22-Jan-1990	IRA	Fatally wounded in gun attack on his home in Armagh
Starrett	George	R/Constable	28-Mar-1990	IRA	Fatally wounded in gun attack on his home in Armagh
Beckett	Harry	Constable	30-Jun-1990	IRA	Fatally wounded in gun attack in Queen Street/ Castle Street, Belfast
Meyer	Gary	Constable	30-Jun-1990	IRA	Fatally wounded in gun attack in Queen Street/ Castle Street, Belfast
Hanson	William	Constable	24-Jul-1990	IRA	Killed in landmine explosion between Armagh and Caledon, Co Armagh
Sterritt	David	R/Constable	24-Jul-1990	IRA	Killed in landmine explosion between Armagh and Caledon, Co Armagh
Willis	Cyril	R/Constable	24-Jul-1990	IRA	Killed in landmine explosion between Armagh and Caledon, Co Armagh
Robinson	Louis	D/Constable	16-Sep-1990	IRA	Abducted as he travelled back across the border after a fishing trip to the south. His body was found two days later near Killeen, Co Armagh
Todd	Samuel	Constable	15-Oct-1990	IRA	Fatally wounded in gun attack in High Street, Belfast
Murphy	David	D/Inspector	10-Nov-1990	IRA	Fatally wounded in a gun attack on the shore of Lough Neagh
Taylor	Thomas	R/Constable	10-Nov-1990	IRA	Fatally wounded in a gun attack on the shore of Lough Neagh
Wethers	Wilfred	R/Constable	20-Dec-1990	IRA	Fatally wounded in gun attack at Banbridge Road, Lurgan
Mcgarry	Spence	D/Constable	6-Apr-1991	IRA	Killed by booby-trap bomb under his car in Ballycastle, Co Antrim
McCrum	Samuel	Sergeant	13-Apr-1991	IRA	Fatally wounded in gun attack in Lisburn, Co Antrim
Gillespie	Stephen	Sergeant	2-May-1991	IRA	Fatally wounded in gun and rocket attack in West Belfast

Surname	Forename	Rank	Killed	By	How Killed
Carrothers	Douglas	R/Constable	17-May-1991	IRA	Killed by booby-trap bomb under his car at driveway of his home in Lisbellaw, Co Fermanagh
Spence	Edward	Constable	26-May-1991	IRA	Fatally wounded in gun attack at Lower Crescent, Belfast
Clarke	Erik	Constable	17-Sep-1991	IRA	Fatally wounded in rocket attack in Swatragh, Co Londonderry
McMurray	Colleen	Constable	28-Mar-1992	IRA	Fatally wounded in mortar attack on Newry
Douglas	James	Constable	10-Oct-1992	IRA	Off duty, he was shot dead in gun attack in Belfast City Centre
Corbett	Alan	R/Constable	15-Nov-1992	IRA	Fatally wounded in gun attack in Main Street, Belcoo
Ferguson	Michael	Constable	23-Jan-1993	IRA	Fatally wounded in gun attack at Richmond Centre, Londonderry
Williamson	Reginald	Constable	24-Feb-1993	IRA	Killed by booby-trap bomb under his car near Moy, Co Tyrone
Reid	Jonathan	Constable	25-Mar-1993	IRA	Shot dead by sniper in Crossmaglen, Co Armagh
Woods	Brian	R/Constable	2-Nov-1993	IRA	Shot dead by sniper near Newry RUC Station
Beacom	William	Constable	12-Dec-1993	IRA	Fatally wounded in gun attack in Fivemiletown, Co Fermanagh
Smyth	Ernest	R/Constable	12-Dec-1993	IRA	Fatally wounded in gun attack in Fivemiletown, Co Fermanagh
Beacom	Johnston	Constable	17-Feb-1994	IRA	Killed in rocket attack in Markets area of Belfast
Haggan	Jackie	Constable	12-Mar-1994	IRA	Shot dead while having a drink with his wife at Dunmore Greyhound Stadium
Pollock	Gregory	Constable	20-Apr-1994	IRA	Killed in mortar attack in Spencer Road, Londonderry
Seymour	Jim	Constable	2-Mar-1995	IRA	Died having been in a coma for 22 years following a gun attack on Coalisland RUC Station on 4 May 1973
Bradshaw	Darren	Constable	9-May-1997	IRA	Off duty, he was shot dead in a city centre bar in Belfast
Taylor	Greg	Constable	1-Jun-1997	Loyalists	Beaten to death outside bar in Ballymoney
Graham	John	Constable	16-Jun-1997	IRA	Shot dead while on patrol in Lurgan Town Centre
Johnston	David	R/Constable	16-Jun-1997	IRA	Shot dead while on patrol in Lurgan Town Centre
O'Reilly	Frank	Constable	6-Oct-1998	Loyalists	Fatally injured in blast bomb attack in Corcrain Estate, Portadown

Select Bibliography

Barzilay, David, *The British Army in Ulster* (London: Century, 1973), Vol 1.

Beresford, David, *Ten Men Dead* (London: Harper Collins, 1994).

Brickhill, Paul, *The Great Escape* (London: Faber & Faber, 1951, reprinted by Cox & Wyman, 2002).

Burleigh, Michael, *Blood and Rage: A Cultural History of Terrorism* (London: HarperCollins, 2009).

Clarke, A.F.N., *Contact* (London: Secker & Warburg, 2009).

Clarke, George, *Border Crossing* (Dublin: Gill & Macmillan, 1983).

Collins, Eamon, *Killing Rage* (London: Granta Books, 1997).

Coogan, Tim Pat, *The IRA,* revised ed. (London: Harper Collins, 2000).

Cusack, Jim and Henry McDonald, *UVA: The Endgame*). (Dublin: Poolbeg Press, 2008).

Dillon, Martin, *Political Murder in Northern Ireland* (Harmondsworth: Penguin Books, 1973).

Dillon, Martin, *Killer in Clowntown* (London: Arrow Books, 1992).

Dillon, Martin, *Stone Cold* (London: Arrow Books, 1992).

Dillon, Martin, *The Shankill Butchers* (London: Hutchinson, 1992).

Dillon, Martin, *25 Years of Terror: IRA's War Against the British* (London: Bantam Books, 1998).

Dillon, Martin, *God and the Gun* (London: Routledge, 1999).

Dillon, Martin, *The Dirty War* (London: Arrow Books, 1999).

Dillon, Martin, *The Trigger Men* (Edinburgh: Mainstream, 2003).

Doherty, Richard, *The Thin Green Line: A History of the RUC* (Barnsley: Pen & Sword, 2004).

Feeney, Brian and Gerry Bradley, *Insider: Gerry Bradley's Life in the IRA* (Dublin: O'Brien, 2009).

Gilmour, Raymond, *Dead Ground: Infiltrating the IRA* (Boston: Little, Brown & Co, 1998).

Gilmour, Raymond, *What Price Truth* (Create Space Independent Publishing Platform, 2015).

Hammil, Desmond, *Pig in the Middle* (London: Methuen, 1985).

Harndon, Toby, *Bandit Country* (London: Hodder & Stoughton, 1999).

Holland, Jack and Susan Phoenix, *Phoenix: Policing the Shadows* (London: Hodder & Stoughton, 1996).

Jordan, Hugh, *Milestones in Murder* (Edinburgh: Mainstream Publishing, 2002).

Latham, Richard, *Deadly Beat* (Edinburgh: Mainstream Publishing, 2001).

McDonald, Henry and Jack Holland, *INLA: Deadly Divisions* (Dublin: Poolbeg Press, 2010).

McGartland, Martin, *Fifty Dead Men Walking* (London: John Blake Publishing, 1997).

McKittrick, David and David McVea, *Making Sense of the Troubles: A History of the Northern Ireland Conflict* (Belfast: Blackstaff Press, 2002), pp.152–3.

Moloney, Ed, *Voices from Beyond the Grave: Two Men's War in Ireland* (London: Faber & Faber, 2010).

Myers, Kevin, *Watching the Door: Cheating Death in 1970s Belfast* (London: Atlantic Books, 2008).

O'Callaghan, Sean, *The Informer* (London: Corgi Books, 1999).

O'Rawe, Richard, *Blanketmen: An Untold Story of the H-Block Hunger Strike* (Dublin: New Island Books, 2005).

Parker, John, *Secret Hero* (London: Blake Publishing, 2004).

Potter, John, *A Testimony to Courage* (Barnsley: Pen & Sword, 2001).

Simpson, Alan, *Murder Madness* (Beverley Hills, CA: GM Books, 1997).

Stone, Michael, *None Shall Divide Us* (London: John Blake Publishing, 2003).

Thornton, David, Seamus Kelters, Brian Feeney and David McKittrick. *Lost Lives: The Stories of the Men, Women and Children who Died as a Result of the Northern Ireland Troubles* (Edinburgh: Mainstream, 1999, revised ed. 2007).

Urban, Mark, *Big Boys' Rules* (London: Faber & Faber, 1993).

Van der Bilj, Nick, *Operation Banner* (Barnsley: Pen & Sword, 2009).

Wharton, Ken, *A Long, Long War: Voices from the British Army in Northern Ireland, 1969–1998* (Solihull: Helion, 2008).

Wharton, Ken, *Bullets, Bombs and Cups of Tea* (Solihull: Helion, 2009).

Wharton, Ken, *Bloody Belfast: An Oral History of the British Army's War Against the IRA* (Stroud: The History Press, 2010).

Wharton, Ken, *The Bloodiest Year: Northern Ireland 1972* (Stroud: The History Press, 2011).

Wharton, Ken, *Sir, They're Taking the Kids Indoors* (Solihull: Helion, 2011).

Wharton, Ken M., *Wasted Years, Wasted Lives* (Solihull: Helion, 2013), Vol 1.

Wharton, Ken M., *Wasted Years, Wasted Lives* (Solihull: Helion, 2014), Vol 2.

Index

Abercrombie, Aubrey, UDR 45, 46

Acheson, Kenneth, RUC 162

Adams, Gerry, Sinn Fein 33-4, 154-5, 168, 184, 187, 203, 205, 210, 213, 225-8, 306, 335, 361, 376, 383, 390, 392, 395, 410, 416, 432-3

Allen, Wallace, RUCR 111

Altnagelvin Hospital 89, 125, 130, 153, 166-7, 191, 195, 232, 243, 272, 278

Andersonstown, Belfast 29, 33, 46, 49, 60, 73, 77, 98, 103, 108, 123, 128, 154, 171, 175, 182, 199, 202-203, 223, 245, 257, 281, 288, 337, 340, 351, 372, 416

Antrim Road, Belfast 80-1, 148, 165, 184, 237, 258, 280, 286, 316, 339, 358, 367

Ardoyne, Belfast 35, 38, 109, 118, 126, 150, 160, 189, 202, 203, 210, 222, 233, 236, 324, 395

Armagh City 132, 170, 261, 279, 281, 311, 318, 323, 328, 337, 356, 358, 385, 393, 404, 408, 410

Atkins, Humphrey, NIO 37, 53, 76, 130, 153, 157, 172, 201, 206, 218

Atkins, Steven Nicholas, RCT 129

ATO 35, 44, 46, 71, 77, 85, 87, 93, 96, 101, 104-6, 113, 115, 116, 128, 194, 198, 204, 238, 265, 416

Aughnacloy 105, 402

Bagshaw, Michael RGJ 189

Bailey, Peter Lyle, REME 71

Ball, Carl, Royal Welch Fusiliers 85, 159, 188, 254

Ballycolman Estate, Strabane 130, 248

Ballykinlar 36, 175-6

Ballymurphy Estate, Belfast 43, 48, 85, 100, 188, 197, 286, 377, 389

Banarama pop group 387

BAOR 49, 250

Barkley, Gerard 'Sparky', INLA 131, 147, 372, 403

Bates, 'Basher', Shankill Butchers 327

Bates, Simon, Parachute Regiment 29

Beattie, Constance Evelyn, RUC 115

Belfast Telegraph 34, 47, 74, 178, 182, 200, 206, 217, 238, 355, 400, 407, 409, 414, 421, 425-6, 428

Belleek 282, 365

Bessbrook Mill 29, 279

Bligh's Lane, Londonderry 195, 276

Blues and Royals 25, 230, 295, 297, 301

Bogside, Londonderry 70, 164, 167, 191, 274, 278, 293, 304, 340-1, 368

Brown, Brian Michael, Parachute Regiment 108

Bulman, Paul, RCT 189

Burns, William, Prison Officer 133

Bushwell, Nicolas Paul, Royal Tank Regiment 118

Byrne, Henry Gardaí Siochana 101-2

Campbell, Nat, Royal Engineers 107

Campbell, Robert, IRA 80, 206

Cappagh, Co Tyrone 77, 193, 217

Carr, Robert, IRA 58, 69

Castle, Private Tim, Light Infantry 377

Castlewellan 36, 171, 245

Cheshire Regiment 330-2, 335

Clark, Peter Arthur, Royal Artillery 107

Clarke, William 'Willie' UDR 106

Cochrane, Jim, UDR 36

Cochrane, Mary Elizabeth Karen, UDR 51

Coe, Colonel Mark, Royal Engineers 49

Coldstream Guards 175, 252, 273, 285

Collins, Eamonn, IRA 290, 401

Connell, Gary, Scots Guards 119

Cookstown 109, 113, 165, 280, 317, 329, 373, 380, 410, 417

Cox, Graham, Prison Officer 41

Creggan Estate, Londonderry 102, 150, 153, 166-7, 192, 195, 259, 274, 293, 404

Crilly, Robert, RUCR 35

Crocus Street shooting 272

Crossmaglen 35, 54-6, 85, 87, 89, 92-3, 102

Crowe, Sylvia 48

Crumlin Road, Belfast 38, 82, 109, 189, 197, 204, 286, 313, 325, 340, 361, 367

Crumlin Road Jail/Gaol 82-4, 109, 133, 196, 213, 361, 380, 387

Daily Mail 203, 304

Daly, Miriam, INLA/IRSP 91, 98, 149, 290

Delaney, Kevin, IRA 40

Derry Journal 93, 227, 275, 309, 353

Derrybeg Estate 121, 327

Det 14, 192, 353

Dillon, Martin, author 33, 69, 83-4, 126, 159, 221, 226, 228, 233, 236, 319, 326, 369

Divis Street flats 123, 208, 312, 359
Doherty, Joe, IRA 80, 82-3, 97, 196, 252, 361
Doherty, Mary, killed by British Army ND 76
Donaldson, Dennis 154
Donaldson, Norman Henry, UDR 129
Downey, John, IRA 303-4
'Droppin Well' bombing 329
Dungannon 96, 105, 113, 149, 171, 193, 199, 387, 390, 410, 417, 420
Durrant, Dougie, ADU 38, 42, 79, 94

Éireann, Fianna 109, 160, 182, 191, 196, 202, 209, 308
Elliott, William, former UDR 98
Enniskillen 47, 123-4, 246, 282, 303, 322

FAIR (Fair Acting for Innocent Relatives) 412
Falls Road, Belfast 30, 42-3, 59, 74, 108, 116, 175, 182, 184, 199, 202, 205, 214, 221-2, 258, 314, 318, 359, 361
Federal Bureau of Investigation (FBI) 74, 291-2
Flax Street Mill 43, 118, 127, 202, 233
Flynn, Pte Kev 'Errol', 1st Light Infantry 389
Forkhill 39, 108, 266, 277, 279, 280
Fort Whiterock base 48, 159, 197
Foxall, George Wilfred, RRF 95
Foxall, Thomas 95
Francis, Ron, Royal Welsh Fusiliers 352
Fulton, Kevin 154
Fusco, Angelo, IRA 80, 82

Galvin, Martin, NORAID 305, 308-9, 390
Gardaí Siochana 38, 100, 105,119, 213, 264, 292-3, 311, 369, 419, 434
Gavin, Rifleman Andrew, RGJ 189
Gilmour, Raymond 154, 163-4, 276, 327, 388, 397
Glosters 92
Grand Central Hotel, Belfast 118, 134
Greenfinch (female UDR soldier) 47, 51, 112, 115, 124
Grenadier Guards 81, 151, 190
Griffin Jeanne 84, 294

Hanna, Iain, Scots Guards 119
Hardy, Gerald, Parachute regiment 29
Harman, John, RUC employee 86
Harrods' bombing 345, 426
Haughey, Charles, Irish Taoiseach 86, 94, 130, 153, 197, 264, 268, 284-5, 301, 317
Hawkins, William Clive, Royal Regiment of Wales 185, 211, 259
Hearst, Ross 112
Hewitt, Marcus James, UDR 119
Hill, Mick 'Benny', Royal Anglians 96, 225
HMP, Maze 184, 345, 393

HMSU (RUC squad) 321-3, 328-9, 335-6, 347, 369
'Honey Trap' attacks 145, 216-7
Horton, Bob, Cheshire Regiment 335
Horvath, Steve 'Taffy', RAMC 332
Howe, Winston, RUC 47, 115
Hughes, Francis, IRA 158-9, 168, 185-7, 212, 229
Hulme, John, SDLP 189
Hunger Strike, 1981 58, 78, 83, 85, 98, 115, 118, 124, 129-132, 145, 152, 157-160, 162-175, 182-7, 190-1, 193-6, 198-200, 202-6, 208-210, 212-221, 224-229, 231-241, 254, 264, 267, 289, 306, 318, 361, 377, 396, 404, 425
Hyde Park Bombing 302-3

IRSP 98, 110, 122-4, 129, 149, 160, 191, 199

Jackson, Raymond Joseph, Army Air Corps 101
Johnston, Ernest, RUCR 48, 114
Jones, Fraser, Royal Engineers 45
Joynes, Tony, Coldstream Guards 285
Judge, Dave, Royal Green Jackets 70, 261, 270, 272, 320

Kelly, Gerry, Sinn Fein 78, 205, 394-7
Kennedy, Sen Edward 83, 96-7, 170, 210, 286-7, 360, 432
Kincora Boys' Home scandal 69
King's Own Royal Border Regiment (KORBR) 54-6, 58, 87, 89, 92

Lambert, John, Royal Scots 175
Lane, Michael 'Spike', Royal Green Jackets 360
Latimer, Richard, UDR 92
Leach, Stewart, RMP 53
Lee, Graham, Royal Pioneer Corps 110
Light Infantry 55, 331, 376-7, 389
Liptrot, Andy, Royal Artillery 423
Lisnaskea 45, 47, 76, 104, 114, 127, 196, 247, 284
Lister, Robin, Royal Engineers 51
Little, Noel, IRSP 123, 290
Livingstone, Henry, former UDR 53
Livingstone, Ken 'Red Ken' 335-6, 383, 392
Livingstone, William, UFF 76
Lundy, Samuel, UDR 35
Lynch, Kevin, INLA 84, 191, 209, 229
Lynford, Errol, Duke of Wellington's Regiment, 43
Lister, Robin, Royal Engineers 51
Lyttleton, Donal Gardaí Siochana 120

Macdonald, Andrew, KORBR 56, 92
Magee, Paul 'Dingle', IRA 80
Magill, William, RUC 73, 80, 355

Maguire, Anne 29, 42
Maguire, Charles 'Pop', IRA 192-3
Mains, Joseph, Kincora 69, 258
Mallon, Seamus, SDLP 111, 285, 336, 367
Manning Brophy, Edward, IRA 42
Markethill, Co Armagh 95, 327
Marsh, Tim, RGJ 272
Mathers, Joanne, census worker murdered by
    IRA 162-3, 165, 403-4
Maze, 'Great escape' 197, 345
McAlinden, David, RUC 102
McAliskey, Bernadette (formally Devlin) 148,
    151, 158, 199, 375, 395, 415
McBrearty, George, IRA 192
McCreesh, Raymond, IRA 83, 160, 191, 198
McDonnell, Joe, IRA 158, 184, 202-3, 226
McElwaine, Seamus, IRA 115, 395
McFarlane, 'Bic', IRA 190, 205, 395, 396, 416,
    425
McGartland, Marty 154, 199, 258
McGinn, Hugh, TA 132, 147, 372
McGlinchey, Dominic, INLA 131, 147, 158,
    327, 336, 369, 372-3, 382-3, 390, 399, 403,
    411, 413
McGlinchey, Mary 327, 403
McGrath, William, Kincora 69, 258
McGuinness, Doreen, Joyriding death 30, 53, 60
McGuinness, Martin 163-4, 187, 335, 415, 425
McLaughlin, Brendan, IRA 51, 187, 193, 196,
    199
McNamee Thompson, Robert 'Bob', Queen's
    Regiment 105
McQuade, Owen, Argyle and Sutherland
    Highlanders 125
Meehan, Martin, IRA 126
Moan, Paul, joyriding 60
Moore, John, Royal Green Jackets 206, 268
Morley, John, Gardaí Siochana 101-2
Morrison, Superintendent Charles, RUC 82
Morrow, Victor, former UDR 76
Moynihan Senator Daniel Patrick 83, 97
Murphy, Lenny, Shankill Butchers 25, 182,
    293-4, 312, 316, 318, 320, 322, 324, 325,
    328, 342-3

Negligent Discharges 54-5, 252, 259
New Lodge, Belfast 38-9, 42, 46, 81, 165, 177,
    182, 184, 217, 250, 360
Newry 32, 36, 44, 46, 56, 58, 69, 83, 100-1,
    107, 116, 120-1, 126, 149, 160, 162, 190,
    194, 198, 210, 267, 279, 290-1, 318, 327, 359,
    401, 410
Newton, Phil, Royal Hampshire Regiment 282
Newtownhamilton 111, 113, 148, 198, 279,
    281, 411, 416
Niedermayer, Thomas, German industrialist 55

NORAID 50-1, 74, 83, 85, 98, 174-5, 201, 225,
    260, 278, 295, 305-6, 308-9, 376, 390, 432-3
North Howard Street Mill 127, 248, 269-271,
    319
'Nutting Squad' IRA 33, 86, 87, 126, 129, 131,
    150, 152, 154, 195, 199, 200, 216, 242, 274,
    276, 387, 388

Ó Fiaich, Tomás, Catholic Priest 53, 132, 159,
    191, 331
O'Loughlin, Derek, Royal Artillery 282
O'Callaghan, Sean, author of 'The Informant' 80,
    82, 154, 303, 416, 422, 424, 426, 430
O'Hara, Patsy, INLA 160, 191
O'Hare, Dessie 'The Border Fox' 112
O'Neill, Terence 'Teddy' IRA 100
O'Neill, Tip 83, 85, 286
Olphert, Mark 350

Paisley, Rev Ian 48, 70, 122, 130, 152-3, 166,
    175, 216, 245-7, 251, 257-8, 266, 272, 397
Parachute Regiment 27, 29-30, 55, 89, 98, 108,
    189, 252
Parsons, Bill, Royal Artillery 108
Pavey, Owen Christopher, KORBR 55
Peace People's Movement 29
Pettengale, Ken, Royal Green Jackets 32, 74,
    248, 271
Piwinski, Claire 108
Power, James, INLA 153, 183
Price, Dolours 78, 168, 213
Price, Marion 78
Prior, James, NIO 228, 232, 251, 263, 277,
    285, 293, 295, 300, 322, 328, 332, 352, 358,
    370, 376, 380, 394, 397, 401, 432
Purse, David, RUCR 38

Quaid, Seamus, Gardaí Siochana 120
Quinn, Hartley Colin, UDR 131

Reagan, Ronald, US President 172, 268
Rees, Merlyn, MP 190, 383
Regent's Park bombing 255, 272
REME 71, 129, 154, 273-5, 277, 318
RMP (Royal Military Police) 49, 53, 116,
    211-2, 248
Robson, Kenneth, Royal Engineers 51
Rogers, Peter, IRA 119-120
Rose, Joseph, RUC 47, 115
Rosslea 114
Royal Artillery 49, 59, 97, 104, 108, 114, 126,
    132, 138, 147, 163-4, 183, 189, 193, 239, 241,
    252, 274-5, 282, 302, 304, 326, 348, 384,
    422, 423
Royal Corps of Transport (RCT) 129, 158, 175,
    189-190, 238, 364,

Royal Engineers 45, 48-9, 51, 54, 58, 104, 107, 113-6, 118, 126, 214, 277, 364

Royal Green Jackets 30-2, 70, 74, 102-3, 126, 129, 145, 168, 173, 176, 178, 189, 206, 248, 261, 268, 270-1, 295, 298-300, 306, 320, 356, 360, 365, 415

Royal Hampshire Regiment 121, 282-3

Royal Highland Fusiliers 96, 105, 113

Royal Inniskilling Dragoon Guards 101

Royal Pioneer Corps 110, 214, 216, 364

Royal Regiment of Fusiliers (RRF) 46, 85, 91, 95, 119, 122, 151, 347,

Royal Victoria Hospital (RVH) 30, 100, 116, 151, 160, 166, 175, 185, 194, 202, 217-8, 263, 269, 270, 273, 285, 362, 364, 407

Sands, Bobby, IRA 85, 129, 132, 157-8, 160, 162, 165, 167-9, 171-6, 182-4, 202, 214, 226-7, 229, 285, 306, 404

Sangster, Michael, Royal Artillery 302

SAS (Special Air Service) 32, 57, 79-82, 115, 123, 158, 192, 196-7, 223, 321, 350, 353-4, 361, 391, 395, 419-420

Scappaticci, Freddie ('Stake knife') 155, 267

Scots Guards 71, 118-9, 165

Scott, Tim, Queen's Regiment 402

Semple, Raymond, Kincora 69, 258

Shankill Butchers 25, 84, 249, 294, 312, 316, 318, 325-6,

Shankill Road, Belfast 35, 58, 77, 160, 192, 206, 236, 242, 250, 277, 294, 312-4, 325, 339, 348-9

Shaw, Mark, ADU 46

Shields, Robin, Royal Navy 116, 160

Silverbridge 113, 115

Smyth, Robert, UDR 36

Snell, Andrew, RAPC 58

Springfield Road 69, 85-6, 123, 127, 188, 223, 248, 258, 269, 270, 273, 314-6, 330, 389

Staffordshire Regiment 40, 46, 150

Steenson, Gerard 'Dr Death', INLA 131-2

Strabane 40, 76, 124, 130, 208, 210, 220, 239, 248, 279, 286, 294, 350, 391, 407

Suicides in the UDR 114

Thatcher, Margaret, PM 48, 58, 82, 86, 122, 124, 129-130, 132, 153, 158-160, 167, 185, 193, 198, 205, 210, 218, 223, 225, 227, 234, 242, 300, 307, 331, 337, 358, 360-1, 375, 395, 397-8, 408, 425, 433

Tidey, Don kidnap 416, 424

Townley, Marcus, Welsh Guards 29, 50, 204

Tuite, Gerard, IRA 131, 266, 300

Turf Lodge, Belfast 30, 43, 85, 159, 351

Turnley, John, former British soldier 91, 149

'Ulsterisation' process 5, 113, 126, 136, 139, 140, 168-170,173, 176, 178, 181-2, 212, 251, 279, 302, 382

Unity Flats 126, 137, 238, 250, 348, 349

VCPs 30-1, 50, 60, 73, 105, 118, 127, 204, 280

Walker, Sean, KORBR 54

Ward, Nigel, Queen's Lancashire Regiment 254

Watson, John, Royal Green Jackets 102

Wells, Martin, Royal Green Jackets 168, 173, 176, 178

Westmacott, Captain Herbert, SAS 79, 196, 339, 361

Whitelaw, William 335, 376

Wilson, Frederick, RUC 74

Wilson, Richard 'Rickie', UDR 36, 412

Winston, Grenville RGJ 189

Women's Royal Army Corps (WRAC) 32, 116, 151, 354, 426

Wright, Michael UFF 94

Young, Dave, Ammunition Technical Officer 71, 88, 106, 127

Young, William 'Jock', Royal Artillery 239

Young, William, Royal Artillery 97, 391